Library of
Davidson College

THE CHRISTIAN TRINITY IN HISTORY

Studies in Historical Theology

Vol. 1 *The Christian Trinity in History*, Bertrand de Margerie.
Vol. 2 *The Invisible Father*, Louis Bouyer. *In preparation.*
Vol. 3 *The Paraclete*, Louis Bouyer. *In preparation.*

Studies in Historical Theology
Volume I

The Christian Trinity in History

Bertrand de Margerie, S.J.

Translated by
Edmund J. Fortman, S.J.

ST. BEDE'S PUBLICATIONS
Still River, Massachusetts

Originally published in France under the title *La Trinité Chrétienne dans l'Histoire*, © 1975, Editions Beauchesne. All questions concerning the rights of translation, reproduction, adaptation, in any language or in any manner other than what appears in this volume, must be addressed to the editor of the original French edition.

This translation has been read and approved by the author.

Copyright © 1982 St. Bede's Publications

All Rights Reserved

PRINTED IN THE UNITED STATES OF AMERICA

Imprimi Potest	Rev. Richard Lawlor, S.J.
Nihil obstat	Rev. John J. Bagley
Imprimatur	+Bernard J. Flanagan Bishop of Worcester

January 20, 1981

The *Nihil obstat* and *Imprimatur* are official declarations that a book or pamphlet is free of doctrinal and moral error. No implication is contained therein that those granting the *Nihil obstat* and *Imprimatur* agree with the content, opinions or statements expressed.

LIBRARY OF CONGRESS CATALOGING IN PUBLICATION DATA

Margerie, Bertrand de.
  The Christian Trinity in history.

  Translation of La Trinité chrétienne dans l'histoire.
  Bibliography: p.
  Includes index.
  1. Trinity—History of doctrines.   I. Title.
  BT109.M3513   231'.044   81-8735
  ISBN 0-932506-14-3   AACR2

CONTENTS

Foreword   xi
Abbreviations   xvi
Introduction   xvii

PART ONE
ANALYTICAL AND HISTORICAL STUDY OF THE DEVELOPMENT OF TRINITARIAN DOGMA

Chapter One   From Yahweh to God the Father, Son and Holy Spirit   3
   I. Preparation of the Trinitarian Revelation in the Old Testament   3
   II. Preparation of the Trinitarian Revelation in Pre-Christian religions   5
   III. Yahweh reveals himself as the Father of an only Son   7
   IV. The other Paraclete, Holy Breath of the Father and of the Son, the Third Person, called a) Holy Spirit, b) another Paraclete   17
   Appendix I The kerygmatic proclamation of the Three, constitutive of the community of Jerusalem   39
   V. The divine and redemptive Three: Father, Son and Spirit in the New Testament   42
   VI. The Father, the Son and the Holy Spirit in the cult of the New Testament   50

Chapter Two   Toward the Clear Affirmation of the Equality and the Consubstantiality of the Father, the Son and the Holy Spirit   57
   I. Is the Symbol of the Apostles Christological or Trinitarian?   57
     1. Evolution and Trinitarian structure of the Symbol   57
     2. Theological-pastoral significance of this evolution   59
   II. Trinitarian doctrines of Judeo-Christianity and of Gnosticism: reaction of Irenaeus   63
   III. The Trinitarian heresies of the third century: Modalism and Subordinationism   72
   IV. Tertullian, "creator" of the Trinitarian language of the Church   78

V. A remarkable declaration of Pope St. Dionysius of Rome in 262 — 85
VI. Arius, conscious denier of the equality between Son and Father — 87
VII. Response of Nicaea and clear affirmation of the equality between the Son and the Father — 90
VIII. Confrontation of Marxism and psychoanalysis with the dogmatic and critical realism of Nicaea — 92
IX. Macedonius, Basil, Constantinople I and the cult of the Holy Spirit — 100
  1. Statement of the question: conditions of the possibility of Semi-Arianism — 100
  2. Variety of opinions in the Church of the fourth century about the Holy Spirit — 101
  3. Reaction of Athanasius, Basil and Gregory of Nazianzus — 102
  4. Definitive solution: Constantinople I: the Holy Spirit co-glorified with the Father and the Son — 105
  5. The implicit affirmation of the consubstantiality of the Spirit with the Father and the Son in the New Testament — 109
X. The doctrine of St. Augustine on the Holy Spirit as communion and source of communion — 110
  1. The Neo-Platonic influence — 112
  2. The Spirit, communion of love between the Father and the Son — 114
  3. The Holy Spirit, the bond and principle of intra-ecclesial communion and of the communion of Christians with the Father and with the Son — 116

Chapter Three One Single Divine Nature in Three Distinct Persons: Constantinople II and Lateran IV — 122
I. Numerical or specific unity of the Divine Nature? — 122
II. From God the Father, Son and Holy Spirit to God in Three divine Persons or Hypostases — 126
  1. Vocabulary — 128
  2. History — 128
  3. The term of evolution: Constantinople II: three consubstantial subsistences in a single Divinity or Divine Substance — 130
  4. The meaning of this evolution to the eyes of faith — 132
III. Personal properties of the Three and their distinction by relations — 132
  1. Personal properties — 133
  2. Distinction through relations — 133

3. Relation and Revelation	137
4. Lateran IV: 1215: identity between relations on the one hand and essence on the other	138
5. Florence introduces relation into the dogmatic language of the Church	139
IV. Complementary reflections on the notion of Person in God	140
Appendix II Reply to a difficulty	145
Appendix III Lateran IV and Lyons II (1215 and 1274)	146

Chapter Four Relations of Origin, "Processions in God" — 147

I. Theology of God, the Father, Principle of the Divinity	148
II. Theology of the eternal Son: contemporary exegesis and mystery of the generation of the Only-Begotten	153
1. Does the New Testament teach the eternal generation of the Son?	153
2. St. Hilary, theologian of the eternal generation of the Son	156
3. Catholic doctrine concerning the eternal Son and the psychological analogy	158
III. Theology of the Spirit of the Son: the *Filioque* (Lyons and Florence)	160
1. Conditions of the possibility of the controversy: the diversity of theological schemas	161
2. Brief historical sketch of the introduction of the *Filioque* into the Symbol	165
3. Biblical foundation and profound meaning of the *Filioque*	168
4. Present state of the controversy	174
5. Theological-pastoral sense of the doctrinal evolution that led to the *Filioque* and prospects for the future	175
IV. Circuminsession or mutual indwelling or "inexistence" of the Three	178
V. Creation and Trinity	186
VI. The appropriation to each of the Three of their common works brings out their personal properties	193
1. Historical and pastoral introduction	193
2. Nature, foundation and importance of the appropriations	195
Appendix IV The doctrinal value of the Latin councils of the Middle Ages	198

Chapter Five Trinity, Ecumenism, Catholic Church — 199

I. Luther. The Holy Spirit, mediator of the real presence of Christ in the faith	199
II. Protestant and Catholic Pentecostalism and mystery of Pentecost. The charism of glossolalia	204

III. The problem of Trinitarian language in the modern age	212
1. Barth: do not speak of Persons but of Three Modes of divine Being	213
2. Rahner: do not speak immediately nor solely of Persons in God	216
IV. The Trinitarian "basis" of the World Council of Churches (1961)	221

Chapter Six   The Trinitarian Doctrine of Vatican II   223

I. Trinitarian ecclesiology of Vatican II	224
1. The Trinitarian mystery, origin and cause of the Church	227
2. The unity of the Trinity, supreme model of the unity between Christians in the unity of the Church	227
3. The vision of the Trinity, the end toward which the Church advances in its pilgrimage toward it	228
II. The ecclesiological pneumatology of Vatican II	229
1. The Holy Spirit fills and governs the whole Church, acting through the charismatic hierarchy	229
2. The Holy Spirit renews the whole Church by the simple and extraordinary charisms given to the laity	232
III. The Trinitarian doctrine of Paul VI and the Dutch catechism	235

PART TWO
SYSTEMATIC VISION: OMNIA PER MODUM UNIUS

Chapter Seven   The False Trinitarian Systematizations, Their Presuppositions and Their Consequences   249

I. Trinitarian mystery and medieval mysticism	249
1. Pantheist affinities of Eckhart	249
2. Does Ruysbroeck sufficiently salvage the eternity of the Trinity?	252
II. The pantheist savor of modern Trinitarian evolutionism	257
1. Is Hegel a theologian of the Trinity	257
2. Feuerbach, the Trinitarian mystery and the unity of the human race	262
III. The anti-Trinitarian evolutionism of spiritism	264
IV. The tritheist and rationalist tendencies of Günther	265
V. The Trinity, whose non-irrationality is demonstrable, is a mystery that is indemonstrable by reason: Vatican I	268
VI. The immutability of the divine Processions	270

Contents

Chapter Eight Family, Church, Human Soul,—Imperfect, Complementary and Revealed Analogies of the Divine Trinity ... 274
I. Familial intersubjectivity and friendship, first revealed analogy of the Trinity ... 274
  1. Gregory of Nazianzus ... 274
  2. Augustine ... 276
  3. Thomas Aquinas ... 278
  4. Scheeben ... 280
  5. Heribert Mühlen ... 280
  6. Conclusions and reflections ... 286
II. The ecclesial intersubjectivity, second revealed analogy of the Trinity ... 292
  1. The universal Church, icon of the triune God ... 292
  2. The universal Church, icon of the processions of the Word and Spirit ... 293
  3. The reciprocal immanence of Christians who are equal among themselves is the analogical image of the circuminsession of the divine Persons ... 295
III. Personal intrasubjectivity, an implicitly revealed analogy of the Trinity ... 297
  1. Trinity and unity of the human spirit in Augustine ... 297
  2. Thomist deepening and modifications of the Augustinian doctrine ... 305
  3. The psycho-social analogy of B. Lonergan: ... 311
  4. Conclusion about the "psychological analogy" and the created analogies of the Trinity ... 313
IV. The Spirit of the Father and of the Son, personal bond of the mutual love between Them ... 315
  1. Historical resume ... 315
  2. Toward a solution: Anselm, Thomas Aquinas, John of St. Thomas ... 317
  3. The distinctive property of the Spirit is to be the personal bond of love between the Father and the Son ... 319
V. Revelation affirms that there are only three persons in God ... 322
Appendix V The anthropological analogy (Intellect-Word-Breath in St. John Damascene ... 323

Chapter Nine The Active Presence of the Father, of the Son and Their Spirit in the World of Men ... 325
I. The Missions of the Word and of the Spirit, the bond between the Father and the world ... 325
  1. Structure of the Mission of a divine Person ... 326

    2. Visible and invisible missions of the divine Persons   329
    3. The mission of the Church, the historical unfolding of the
       historical missions of the coeternal Word and Spirit   333
  II. The Trinity redeeming the world in and by the Eucharist   337
    1. Trinitarian revelation, Paschal revelation   338
    2. Mass and Trinity: the twofold Trinitarian structure of
       the Mass   339
    3. The Eucharistic Heart of Jesus, symbol of the redemptive
       Trinity   346

Conclusion: The redemptive Trinity, Salvation and Beatitude
    of men   350

Indexes   355

  1. Names of Authors   357
  2. Biblical Citations   363
  3. Councils   372
  4. Texts of St. Thomas Aquinas   374
  5. Texts of St. Augustine   378
  6. Analytical Index   380

Bibliography   383

Foreword

It is a pleasure to be able to welcome the translation into English of Père de Margerie's remarkable book on the doctrine of the Trinity, for it can render a service in English that no other book on the subject is quite able to provide.

Although his concentration on the earlier history of the doctrine (and perhaps his ecumenical generosity) may be responsible for his having said very little about the problem, the career of the doctrine of the Trinity in the Protestant theology of the nineteenth and twentieth centuries was one of rather serious neglect. As Professor Welch has indicated, a variety of factors—including, for example, the decline in the standing of the Gospel of John as a "historical" source—contributed to this neglect.[1] It is only a modest exaggeration to suggest, for example, that the most influential Continental Protestant theologian between the sixteenth century and the twentieth, Schleiermacher, relegated the dogma of the Trinity to an appendix in his systematic theology, since his was a theology, to use Karl Barth's phrase, that "did not quite know what to make of the concept of the Trinity."[2] The widely influential interpretation of the history of the dogma of the Trinity by Adolf von Harnack, to whom the author refers more often than he does to Schleiermacher, both expressed and confirmed the hostility of many Protestants in the past two centuries, especially because Harnack presented the dissolution of the authority of dogma as a consequence and a continuation of Luther and the Reformation.[3] It was only during the middle third of the twentieth century, and that thanks in great measure to the theology of Karl Barth, that Trinitarian doctrine was restored to its place of honor within Protestant dogmatics. This suggests, in turn, that Father de Margerie's account should be able to find a broader response than it might

[1] Claude Welch, *In This Name.* (New York, 1952).
[2] Karl Barth, *Die protestantische Theologie im 19. Jahrhundert.* (Zurich, 1947), p. 410.
[3] Jaroslav Pelikan, "Adolf von Harnack on Luther," *Interpreters of Luther: Essays in Honor of Wilhelm Pauck,* edited by Jaroslav Pelikan. (Philadelphia, 1968), pp. 253-74.

have even two or three decades ago. If it does, its contribution to present discussion will be manifold and varied. Let me mention only a few aspects of that contribution.

Anyone who takes the time to study these chapters carefully will be impressed again with the emphatically soteriological accent of the patristic doctrine of the Trinity. The Greek and Latin fathers were as exercised as they were about this dogma because they were convinced that with it the very salvation of the human race would stand or fall: either the One who had achieved redemption was equal in nature to the Creator of heaven and earth, or there was no real salvation. In none of the fathers is this soteriological accent more explicit than in Athanasius, who seemingly never tires of insisting that the dogma affirmed at Nicaea protected the integrity of salvation from human corruption and shielded the worship of Christians from idolatry. Far from being a bit of alien metaphysics parading in Christian guise, therefore, the dogma of Nicaea was a direct corollary, and hence a necessary presupposition, of the Gospel message itself. As the author suggests, on the basis of a brilliant essay by Bernard Lonergan, Nicaea represented the transition from an uncritical dogmatic realism to a realism that was both dogmatic and critical.[4] As such, it became, for the centuries that followed, the central teaching of the Christian faith—not as a substitute for the doctrine of salvation, but as the only way for that doctrine to prevail.

Therefore the dogma of the Trinity, which is of course a doctrine about God, is nevertheless a doctrine about man as well. In the history of Western theology especially, this anthropological content of the dogma has undergone a truly distinctive development, thanks to what Schmaus calls "the psychological doctrine of the Trinity of St. Augustine."[5] In an all but unique insight (for which the parallel with John of Damascus, suggested by Father de Margerie, provides more contrast than analogy[6]), Augustine took the words of the creation story in the Book of Genesis, "Let us make man in our image," as proof not only that the Creator was the Trinity, but that the image itself was a Trinitarian one. Augustine's exploration, in the second half of his most profound work, the *De Trinitate*, of "vestiges of the Trinity" went on shaping the Western doctrine of man for more than a millennium. Charles Trinkaus has recently traced the continuing influence of the Augustinian speculations upon the anthropology of the Italian humanists.[7]

[4]See p. 94 below.
[5]Michael Schmaus, *Die psychologische Trinitätslehre des heiligen Augustinus*. (Münster, 1927).
[6]See p. 323 below.
[7]Cf. Charles Trinkaus, "Humanism and the Intellectual Traditions: the Pursuit of Christian Selfhood from St. Augustine to the Renaissance," *In Our Image and Likeness*. (2 vols.; Chicago, 1970), I, 18-28.

That influence went on even beyond the Renaissance. Indeed, without an understanding of what the Trinity meant for the evolution of such notions as reason (Logos), intellect, and memory, it is difficult to make sense of German Idealism or of the philosophy of Hegel. (For my part, I might wish that Père de Margerie had devoted at least a few paragraphs to the Trinitarian metaphysics and the Trinitarian anthropology of Nicholas of Cusa, but one cannot do everything in one book.)

Mentioning Cusanus leads naturally to the question of the Trinity as a speculative doctrine. For even though it may not be a speculative product in the first place, it certainly provided speculative thinkers with an exciting arena. Here I am thinking, of course, of Augustine, but even more of the Cappadocians, above all of Gregory of Nyssa, to whom Father de Margerie—following the lead of Cardinal Daniélou, as all of us must—has devoted some of his most trenchant comments. When the author speaks about an "audacious thought" of Hans Urs von Balthasar,[8] he suggests that for such contemporaries as Balthasar and Lonergan the dogma of the Trinity has continued to serve as a provocative starting point of speculation. Of course, one by-product of Trinitarian speculation has had fateful ecumenical consequences. The Augustinian doctrine of *Filioque*, whose connections with the Greek fathers the author probes with sensitivity and skill,[9] has had the rather ironic history of symbolizing the division of Christendom even as it was intended to symbolize the unity of the Godhead. The thoughtful effort to state the *Filioque* in a form that may be ecumenically acceptable, which I find admirable even though I do not find it convincing, is an example of how the author is able to put his historical erudition into the service of his deepest commitments. And that ecumenical commitment makes it all the more fitting that this English translation should appear at this time. It deserves to be read widely.

Jaroslav Pelikan,
Sterling Professor of History,
Yale University

The 1600th Anniversary of the
First Council of Constantinople

July 30, 1981

---

[8]See p. 192 below.
[9]See pp. 160-178 below.

THE CHRISTIAN TRINITY IN HISTORY

INITIALS OF THE REVIEWS AND LARGE COLLECTIONS UTILIZED IN THIS WORK

AAS	*Acta Apostolicae Sedis,* Rome, 1909—
DB	Denzinger-Bannwarth, *Enchiridion Symbolorum,* Fribourg.
DS	Denzinger-Schönmetzer, *Enchiridion Symbolorum,* Fribourg, 1963.
LG	Dogmatic Constitution *Lumen Gentium* of Vatican II on the Church.
DV	Dogmatic Constitution *Dei Verbum* of Vatican II on Divine Revelation.
GS	Pastoral Constitution *Gaudium et Spes* of Vatican II (1965) on the Church in the Modern World.
PO	Decree *Presbyterorum Ordinis* of Vatican II on the Ministry and Life of Priests.
AG	Decree *Ad Gentes* of Vatican II on the Church's Missionary Activity.
UR	Decree *Unitatis Redintegratio* of Vatican II on Ecumenism
DBS	*Dictionnaire de la Bible,* Supplement, Paris, 1928—
DC	*Documentation catholique,* Paris.
DSAM	*Dictionnaire de Spiritualité ascétique et mystique,* Paris, 1932—
DTC	*Dictionnaire de Théologie catholique,* Paris, 1903—
Nouv. Rev. Théol.	*Nouvelle Revue Théologique,* Louvain, 1879—
PL or ML	*Patrologia Latina* (J.P. Migne), Paris, 1878-1890.
PG or MG	*Patrologia Graeca* (J.P. Migne), Paris, 1857-1866.
SC	*Sources chrétiennes,* Paris, 1942.
RJ	Rouet de Journel, M.J., S.J., *Enchiridion Patristicum,* Rome, 1966—
RAM or R.A.M.	*Revue d'Ascétique et de Mystique,* Paris-Toulouse, 1920—
RSPT	*Revue des Sciences Philosophiques et Théologiques,* Paris, 1916—
BAC	*Biblioteca de Antores cristianos,* Madrid, 1942—
EF	*Encyclopédie de la Foi,* Cerf, Paris, 1967, 4 vol.
DHGE	*Dictionnaire d'Histoire et de Géographie ecclésiastique,* Paris, 1942—
MS	*Mysterium Salutis,* Cologne, 1967.
RB	*Revue Biblique,* Paris, 1894—
VD	*Verbum Domini,* Rome, 1921—

Introduction

In the dialogue which he takes up and ceaselessly renews with the world, the Christian must bear in mind himself and help others and the Church to bear in mind the fundamental affirmation: truth is the Trinity.

"A massive, enormous, paradoxical affirmation! When we affirm this in the presence of an atheist of today, his first reaction is legitimately to say to us: By what right are you to impose on me the duty of believing in the Trinity?" But J. Daniélou goes on, "this is precisely what I maintain. I maintain that I have the right to demand of any atheist today not only that he believe in man, not only that he believe in God, but that he believe in the Trinity, because the Trinity is the truth.... It is the Trinity that is the absolute itself, the abyss of being, the ultimate ground, which is revealed to us in Jesus Christ, so that on the day when opacities are dispelled, the opacities that go with this present existence, all without exception, the Mohammeds, the Confuciuses, the Karl Marxes, all whoever they may be, will be confronted ultimately with the Trinity.... The condition of a sincere dialogue with a non-Christian is to begin by saying to him: 'I must warn you that one day you will be confronted by the Trinity.' "[1]

If we truly believe that "the ground of reality is not the nuclear composition of matter but the Trinity,"[2] not the division of the infinitely small but distinction at the heart of the infinitely great, we cannot but dedicate all the resources of our logic, all the energies of our mind, all the fire of our heart to the loving study of the Father, his Word and their Spirit.

Today we are witnessing a very beautiful renewal of Trinitarian theology and spirituality in the bosom of the Church and of the Churches. As evidence of this let us just mention in addition to J. Daniélou[3] the names of a Sister Elizabeth of the Trinity, a Barth, a Hodgson, a Karl Rahner, a Bernard Lonergan.[4]

---

[1] J. Daniélou, S.J., *Mythes païens, mystère chrétien.* Paris, 1966, ch. VII: La Sainte Trinité, pp. 88-89.
[2] *Ibid.,* p. 89.
[3] J. Daniélou, *La Trinité et le mystère de l'existence.* Bruges, 1968.
[4] See the bibliography.

Could we however say today what St. Gregory of Nyssa wrote in the fourth century: "It is not possible to exchange money, to buy bread or to go to the baths without getting involved in discussions on the problem of whether one can or cannot speak of generation in the Trinity"?[5]

To posit the question is already to have answered it. Would the life of many Christians or even of a goodly number of preachers be turned upside down if, by an absolutely impossible hypothesis, the Church were to announce that there are two or four persons in God or no person at all, or that we must give the persons other names than those which Jesus saw fit to give us? Can we truly say that for the average Christian or even priest of our times the mystery of the Trinity is subjectively recognized and "lived" as the secret spring of their own salvation in time and in eternity?

Whatever the case may be, for the Christian the Trinity is the object par excellence of a reflection that puts all the resources of an historical and rational investigation at the service of faith and Revelation.

The work that we are offering along this line is entitled: "The Trinity in history." And it envisions not only a presence of the indivisible Trinity in the totality of human history, but also an analysis of the manifestation of the Trinity to the Church in the course of its history and to the world through the history of the Church. Such a manifestation continues today and will always continue in the future until its perfect revelation at the time of the Parousia.

The Trinity in history: this does not mean that either of the two parts of our work, analytic and synthetic, claims to exhaust its object. The author knows he is historically situated, conditioned, limited; he is not ignorant of the necessarily and inevitably limited and incomplete character of the inventory of the revealed deposit drawn up by positive theology, which he prefers to call analytic.[6] Our aim here, moreover, is to establish only a partial inventory; if we aimed at more it would be an unrealistic pretention. For an inventory of the inexhaustible Revelation is conditioned by the historical situation and by the problematic of the one who undertakes it.

But in reality the exploration and the inventory of the revealed data

---

[5] St. Gregory of Nyssa, MG 46, 557 B.

[6] On positive or analytic theology see P. Adnès, S.J., *La théologie catholique*. Paris, 1967, pp. 43-62; a work that was reviewed in *Science et Esprit*, 1968, by B. de Margerie, S.J.; note also Y.-M.-J. Congar, O.P.'s reflection in asking to what extent this applies to the Rahnerian treatise on the Trinity (*MS*, v. II): "Another type of theology appears in the wake of K. Rahner and his disciples. It does not follow the plan of a succession of an 'intellectus fidei' to an 'auditus fidei' it does not seek first to find for itself a wide knowledge of the data of Tradition in order to draw from these some elements of a response to eventually new problems. It is rather a sort of philosophical reflection on the relation which the matter of faith taken globally has with man.... There is question of a veritable theology that is less historical, more critico-reflective" (*Situation et tâches présentes de la théologie*. Paris, 1967, p. 20).

already suppose that one has a certain understanding of it in faith. This double process is inseparable from an effort of speculation and systematization already inherent in it, which we prefer to call: synthesis. The directive idea of the synthesis is already present in the analysis. Systematic and speculative theology, or as we prefer to call it, synthetic theology, is already the soul of analytic or positive theology.

The directive idea, underlying our Trinitarian analysis and synthesis is this: in the created world the total, though not adequate nor still less exhaustive, image of the Trinitarian mystery is man, personal and familial, in the bosom of the mystery of the Church, of the pilgrim Church that comes from God Father, Son and Spirit, shelters this God within it and sets out to encounter him by means of a language that in its letter and sense always maintains an identity but at the same time is always renewed.

We are faced with the necessity of choosing at the heart of the revealed data the elements that will allow us to achieve a better understanding of our leading idea. (We must not forget that dogma itself, as the Church's response to Revelation, the Church's word that answers to the divine word without ever exhausting it, is itself a choice, but a choice which unlike a heretical choice neither eliminates nor contradicts any revealed truth.) Our choice has been to study more deeply the doctrine of the Holy Spirit.

It would not be wrong then to say that our work presents itself as a pneumatology, although a very incomplete one. The opinion of St. Augustine expressed in 393 before an assembly of the bishops of Latin Africa, though somewhat attenuated by his own effort and that of later authors, still contains a certain amount of truth today: "About the Father and the Son many are the books that have been written by wise and spiritual doctors.... But the Holy Spirit on the contrary has not been studied so abundantly and carefully by the great and learned commentators of divine Scripture as to make it easy to grasp his proper character with equal clarity. As a result we can call him neither Father nor Son but only Holy Spirit."[7] Such a pneumatological orientation then seems to us an excellent way of achieving fruits of light and love for the restoration of visible unity among all Christians and among all the Churches in the bosom of the one and universal Church. If we have ears, should we not hear what the common Spirit of the Father and the Son is saying to the many Churches, about himself first of all (cf. Apoc. 2:11, 17, 29; 3:6, 13, 22), since he never ceases[8]

---

[7] St. Augustine, *De fide et symbolo,* IX, 18, 19; ML 40, 191.

[8] Cf. *DV* 8. 3: "God, who spoke of old, does not cease to converse with the Spouse of his well-beloved Son." To know whether one can say that the Holy Spirit speaks to the universal Church through the Churches partially separated from it, raises some delicate problems, which Vatican II partially considered in modifying the original text proposed for *UR* 21. 2; but it does not seem impossible to affirm that the Holy Spirit speaks through that which the

speaking to them? And should we not also, speaking of the Holy Spirit, investigate to what extent the Churches, that are in partial communion with the Roman Church, have "in part" not only conserved but even developed certain aspects of the deposit of Revelation[9] as a result of charisms of the same Spirit (cf. 2 Tm. 1:14)? If the Spirit is himself the "consubstantial and coeternal communion" of the Father and the Son, to use a formulation of Augustinian inspiration, is it not possible that, by scrutinizing—in and thanks to him—his own mysterious depths (cf. 1 Cor. 2:10), we might more easily succeed in establishing perfect hierarchical communion among the sister Churches[10] communion with that Church which is at the same time their mother and their sister?

Our work then aims at being such an investigation. It views itself as being like all Christian life an imitation of the pre-paschal[11] Trinitarian life of Jesus. For he, impelled by the Spirit, went into the desert to dialogue with his Father. And of what was he speaking with the Father if not of this Church whose raison d'être, like that of Jesus himself,[12] is to announce the Three, to become steeped in the Three, to consecrate the ensemble of men and of human relations to the Three and to their mutual relations?

In underlining this truth we show the insufficiency of some current and one-sided views of the economic Trinity. One is not really interested in the mystery of God if he sets out to consider only the love of God for men, while consciously abstracting from the intimate relations that unite the divine Persons among themselves, just as one could scarcely claim to know a friend while deliberately ignoring his whole family. Rahner was right in underscoring the identity between the economic and immanent Trinity. But as P. Gutwenger has noted (*Zeitschrift für Kath. Theologie*, 90, 1968, 325-328) this outlook has nothing especially original about it; it is that of the whole Augustinian and Thomist tradition that stresses the partial

---

separated Churches, insofar as they are still in partial communion with the universal Church, say that is true and even original; cf. Paul VI and his opening discourse at the re-assembled Vatican II, which is cited in the following note.

[9]Paul VI, *AAS* 55 (1963), 854: "reverentia religiosam hereditatem prosequimur antiquitus acceptam omnibusque communem, quam Fratres sejuncti servaverunt et ex parte etiam bene excoluerunt...germanos veritatis thesauros." One does not see how the separated brethren could have developed a true doctrine issuing from Revelation without some at least transitory charisms of the Spirit of Truth, whose existence does not exclude some errors collectively professed and transmitted in other areas.

[10]An expression used by Paul VI at Constantinople in July 1967, to define the relations between the Catholic Church and the Orthodox Churches.

[11]Cf. J. Guillet, S.J., "Baptême et S. Trinité," *Christus*, 6 (1959), 296-308; L. Hodgson, *The doctrine of the Trinity*. London, 1964, pp. 41ff. (The author is an Anglican.)

[12]Cf. Jn. 17:2, 3, 21, 11, 22: eternal life "consists in knowing the Father and him whom he has sent, the one in the other, in the most unbreakable unity" (F.-M. Braun, O.P., *Jean le Théologien*. Paris, 1966, v. III, p. 114).

identity between mission and procession, between temporal mission and eternal procession of the Word on one hand and that of the Spirit on the other. It must even be said (and this seems to have escaped Rahner) that St. Augustine had enunciated a principle, all of whose consequences are far from having been deduced; a principle which could constitute the fundamental axis of a new synthesis between the external manifestations and the internal life of the indivisible Trinity: "for the Son, to be sent is to be known in his origin from the Father... for the Holy Spirit, to be sent is to be known in his procession from the Father" (*De Trinitate*, IV. 20. 29; we will comment on this text in our chapters IV note 47 and IX notes 11 and 48). In other words, the raison d'être and the end of the mission is to manifest the eternal procession with which it is identified and which it prolongs in history. The Son sent is the Son begotten, given to reveal his eternal generation; the Spirit is sent by the Father and the Son in order to reveal that he is eternally their bond and their mutual love. The relations of the divine Persons with the human persons, relations of reason, have for their end to manifest the divine to the human so that the latter may participate in the former. The Absolute, eternally relative to itself, renders the internal relations that constitute it present to its relations with human persons, and at the same time makes use of human relations (paternity and filiation) to reveal those absolute relations, those pure relations that are identical with the absolute of its essence. The object is to make use of all human relations divinized by these eternal relations in order to lead to their unending contemplation. Is it not charity toward the neighbor that merits the loving vision of the Three?

So too the work offered to the reader would have been impossible without these "human relations," without utilizing the reflection of so many other theologians, and very especially the unpublished courses of R. P. Tillard, O.P., professor of the Dominican faculty of Ottawa and Rev. F. Crowe, S.J. (see below), professor of the Jesuit faculty of Willowdale near Toronto. We offer them our warm gratitude, and also Bernard Lonergan, the author of the most recent and original manual of Trinitarian theology. We also thank Rev. F. Laufer, S.J. and Rev. B. Kipper, librarians of the Faculty of Theology of Christ the King at St. Leopold, Brazil, where in 1968 we taught a course that was the origin of this work.

At the outset of this work, I should like to appropriate from St. Augustine the reflections found at the beginning of his *De Trinitate*.

> May my reader, if he shares fully my certitude, walk with me; if he shares all my doubts, may he search with me; if he finds the error is his, may he come to me; if he catches me in error, may he correct me. In this way we will advance together on the road of charity, toward him of whom it is written: "Seek his face untiringly" (Ps. 104 [105]:4). That is the prayer, strong and sincere, which I would like to apply to all my readers

and apropos of all my writings, but especially of those which treat of the unity of the Trinity, Father, Son and Holy Spirit. There is in fact no subject where error is more dangerous, investigation more laborious, discovery more fruitful.[13]

And here we might transmit to our reader as a last appeal this plea of Mgr. Charles Gay, a French spiritual writer and theologian of the nineteenth century:

> Do not fail to apply your faith very often and very energetically to this mystery which, because it is the most profound of all, contains the most perfect and most powerful notion of God: I mean the mystery of the holy Trinity.
>
> Then without much trouble you will grasp the inestimable lights and ravishing certitudes it offers us, which touch on the absolute perfection, sovereign independence, interior plenitude, essential harmony, glory, fecundity and beatitude of our lovable and adorable God: for there you will grasp what is incomparably most important and most savory to know.
>
> Advance in this endeavor as far as the power of your baptism will allow and develop it by means of both knowledge and prayer. Subject your whole being to your Christian understanding and apply this understanding to the three divine Persons, contemplating each one separately with his proper beauties and his distinctive perfections, so that you may then better contemplate them in their admirable relations and in their very unique unity. Advance steadily beyond each of your successive conceptions. As these reach higher levels, make of each a new stepping stone for your faith which, by its very nature, always ought to go beyond these: for when your understanding is beginning to fade faith still has fresh forces, and it alone definitively possesses here below the power to perceive the unknown God and to embrace his incomprehensible essence.[14]

---

[13]St. Augustine, *De Trinitate*, I, III, 5.
[14]C. Gay, *De la vie et des vertus chrétiennes*. Tours, 1874, v. I, pp. 162-163 (19th edition).
*A final remark: we have drawn inspiration here from certain reflections contained in the unpublished course of F. E. Crowe, S.J., *The Doctrine of the Most Holy Trinity*. Willowdale: Regis College, 1965-1966 (in manuscript form), pp. 8-10, 27-35, 35-40, 78-79 and 91-93: see our book ch. I, §1; §5 and 6; ch. II, §3 and 6; ch. III, §3.

Part I

Analytical and Historical Study of the Development of the Trinitarian Dogma

I
From Yahweh to God the Father, Son and Holy Spirit

The Old Testament spoke to the Jews and it still speaks to us today, of Yahweh. The New Testament speaks to us sometimes of God, sometimes of God the Father, sometimes of the only-begotten Son of God, or of God the only-begotten Son, sometimes of the Spirit of the Father or the Spirit of the Son.[1] How did the transition from the language of Old Testament theology to that of the New Testament writings take place?

That is the essential question to which this chapter will try to reply.

I. THE PREPARATION OF THE TRINITARIAN REVELATION IN THE OLD TESTAMENT

In spite of a certain number of apparently contrary patristic affirmations,[2] contemporary exegetes affirm unanimously that the Old Testament did not bring to the Jewish people a clear and distinct Revelation of the existence of a plurality of persons in God. In this they agree with the clear and frequent affirmation of Fathers such as Irenaeus, Hilary and Gregory of Nazianzus:[3] that the doctrine of the Trinity is revealed only in the New Testament.

It is however clear that even if God did not reveal himself as triune in the Old Testament, he did prepare his people for the reception of such a revelation. Did not St. Augustine say in one of those almost untranslatable formulas whose secret was all his own: *in Vetere Testamento novum latet et in novo vetus patet?*[4] Latent in the Old Testament is the New, patent in the New Testament is the Old. But how is the New Testament hidden in the Old? Can we recognize there some hints of the Trinity?

We reserve treatment of the Trinitarian preparations implied in the

---

[1] Jn. 1:1; Gal. 1:1; Jn. 3:16; Jn. 1:18; Jn. 15:26; 16:7.

[2] Cf. St. Gregory of Nazianzus: "The Old Testament clearly manifested the Father." *Or. theologica* 5, 26: PG 36, 161.

[3] Cf. P. Galtier, S.J., *De S. Trinitate in se et in nobis*. Paris, 1933, §20. In the text cited in the preceding note, St. Gregory of Nazianzus wrote: "It would have been perilous, when the divinity of the Father was by no means recognized, to preach the Son openly"...a statement that does not necessarily contradict the first part of the paragraph: for a manifested reality is not necessarily recognized.

[4] St. Augustine, *Quaest. in Heptat.*, 2, 73; PL 34, 632.

notions of word, wisdom, breath, for later sections. Here, we will consider only, and very briefly, the "divine plurals" of Genesis and Isaiah.[5]

Here are the four texts:

> "Let us make man in our own image, in the likeness of ourselves" (Gn. 1:26);
> "See, the man has become like one of us" (Gn. 3:22);
> "Come, let us go down and confuse their language" (Gn. 11:7);
> "Whom shall I send? Who will be our messenger?" (Is. 6:8).

Does this Divine "we" evoke a polytheist age anterior to the Bible? Or a deliberation of God with his angelic court? Or does it not rather indicate the interior richness of the divinity? How does it happen that only in these four passages the plural form of the name "Elohim" (used here) has influenced the verb, which is plural only here? And what is still more extraordinary is that these plural forms are introduced by formulas in the singular: "Elohim says" or "Yahweh says" (Gn. 1:26; 3:22; 11:6).

What is more, it is difficult to deny the exceptional character of these four passages with regard to humanity's relations with the Trinity: creation of man to the image of God, who is in fact triune, and then, after man's sin, his exclusion from the Trinitarian life, the failure of the first totalitarian attempt of humanity to build itself up independently of the Spirit of God, and, finally, the intimate relation between the mission of Isaiah and the divine decision relative to the mission of the only Son. Have we not here four key moments in the history of humanity?

A clearly pluri-personal interpretation of these texts was impossible before Christ. But do not these texts supply hints destined by God to suggest to people of good will a certain plenitude of his Being such that he is able to deliberate in himself as several persons deliberate among themselves?[6] To be sure, however, they by no means suggest the Trinity as such.

It must be noted further that the Old Testament did not yet have at its disposal a clear and distinct concept of human personality nor of person in general.[7] For the Hebrews, personality is a vital power which in a vague way extends beyond the limits of the body by way of the activities and even the instruments utilized by a man; thus the word of God, the name of God, even the things that belong to God, like the Ark of the Covenant, are a kind of extension of God, as it were identified with him.

---

[5]Here we have drawn inspiration from J. Isaac, O.P., *La Révélation progressive des Personnes divines*. Paris, 1960, pp. 12-17 (an excellent treatment of the subject).

[6]Cf. St. Ignatius of Loyola, *Spiritual Exercises*, §102 (the meditation on the Incarnation).

[7]Cf. A. R. Johnson, *The One and the Many in the Israelite Conception of God*, 1942; R. S. Franks, *The Doctrine of the Trinity*. London, 1953, p. 20: "the margin between what we distinguish as personal and impersonal was indistinct."

I
From Yahweh to God the Father, Son and Holy Spirit

The Old Testament spoke to the Jews and it still speaks to us today, of Yahweh. The New Testament speaks to us sometimes of God, sometimes of God the Father, sometimes of the only-begotten Son of God, or of God the only-begotten Son, sometimes of the Spirit of the Father or the Spirit of the Son.[1] How did the transition from the language of Old Testament theology to that of the New Testament writings take place?

That is the essential question to which this chapter will try to reply.

I. THE PREPARATION OF THE TRINITARIAN REVELATION IN THE OLD TESTAMENT

In spite of a certain number of apparently contrary patristic affirmations,[2] contemporary exegetes affirm unanimously that the Old Testament did not bring to the Jewish people a clear and distinct Revelation of the existence of a plurality of persons in God. In this they agree with the clear and frequent affirmation of Fathers such as Irenaeus, Hilary and Gregory of Nazianzus:[3] that the doctrine of the Trinity is revealed only in the New Testament.

It is however clear that even if God did not reveal himself as triune in the Old Testament, he did prepare his people for the reception of such a revelation. Did not St. Augustine say in one of those almost untranslatable formulas whose secret was all his own: *in Vetere Testamento novum latet et in novo vetus patet?*[4] Latent in the Old Testament is the New, patent in the New Testament is the Old. But how is the New Testament hidden in the Old? Can we recognize there some hints of the Trinity?

We reserve treatment of the Trinitarian preparations implied in the

---

[1] Jn. 1:1; Gal. 1:1; Jn. 3:16; Jn. 1:18; Jn. 15:26; 16:7.

[2] Cf. St. Gregory of Nazianzus: "The Old Testament clearly manifested the Father." *Or. theologica* 5, 26: PG 36, 161.

[3] Cf. P. Galtier, S.J., *De S. Trinitate in se et in nobis*. Paris, 1933, §20. In the text cited in the preceding note, St. Gregory of Nazianzus wrote: "It would have been perilous, when the divinity of the Father was by no means recognized, to preach the Son openly"...a statement that does not necessarily contradict the first part of the paragraph: for a manifested reality is not necessarily recognized.

[4] St. Augustine, *Quaest. in Heptat.*, 2, 73; PL 34, 632.

notions of word, wisdom, breath, for later sections. Here, we will consider only, and very briefly, the "divine plurals" of Genesis and Isaiah.[5]

Here are the four texts:

> "Let us make man in our own image, in the likeness of ourselves" (Gn. 1:26);
> "See, the man has become like one of us" (Gn. 3:22);
> "Come, let us go down and confuse their language" (Gn. 11:7);
> "Whom shall I send? Who will be our messenger?" (Is. 6:8).

Does this Divine "we" evoke a polytheist age anterior to the Bible? Or a deliberation of God with his angelic court? Or does it not rather indicate the interior richness of the divinity? How does it happen that only in these four passages the plural form of the name "Elohim" (used here) has influenced the verb, which is plural only here? And what is still more extraordinary is that these plural forms are introduced by formulas in the singular: "Elohim says" or "Yahweh says" (Gn. 1:26; 3:22; 11:6).

What is more, it is difficult to deny the exceptional character of these four passages with regard to humanity's relations with the Trinity: creation of man to the image of God, who is in fact triune, and then, after man's sin, his exclusion from the Trinitarian life, the failure of the first totalitarian attempt of humanity to build itself up independently of the Spirit of God, and, finally, the intimate relation between the mission of Isaiah and the divine decision relative to the mission of the only Son. Have we not here four key moments in the history of humanity?

A clearly pluri-personal interpretation of these texts was impossible before Christ. But do not these texts supply hints destined by God to suggest to people of good will a certain plenitude of his Being such that he is able to deliberate in himself as several persons deliberate among themselves?[6] To be sure, however, they by no means suggest the Trinity as such.

It must be noted further that the Old Testament did not yet have at its disposal a clear and distinct concept of human personality nor of person in general.[7] For the Hebrews, personality is a vital power which in a vague way extends beyond the limits of the body by way of the activities and even the instruments utilized by a man; thus the word of God, the name of God, even the things that belong to God, like the Ark of the Covenant, are a kind of extension of God, as it were identified with him.

---

[5]Here we have drawn inspiration from J. Isaac, O.P., *La Révélation progressive des Personnes divines*. Paris, 1960, pp. 12-17 (an excellent treatment of the subject).

[6]Cf. St. Ignatius of Loyola, *Spiritual Exercises*, §102 (the meditation on the Incarnation).

[7]Cf. A. R. Johnson, *The One and the Many in the Israelite Conception of God*, 1942; R. S. Franks, *The Doctrine of the Trinity*. London, 1953, p. 20: "the margin between what we distinguish as personal and impersonal was indistinct."

ever new angles of the inexhaustible Trinitarian Revelation contained in Scripture and Tradition. It contributes powerfully to the perpetual renewal of Trinitarian theology.

III. YAHWEH REVEALS HIMSELF AS THE FATHER OF AN ONLY SON

Our aim here is not to study in depth the self-revelation of Christ as only Son, but rather the revelation of God the Father in the New Testament. How has God prepared his people for this revelation: is he Father not only by creation or by moral adoption but also naturally and intimately?

1. In the Old Testament God successively presents himself as the Father of the chosen people, the Father of the just, the Father of the Messiah. But the expression (Father) is rarely employed in reference to God (at least in comparison with the New Testament) and is used only fourteen times.[13] From the beginning of its history the chosen people had a consciousness of being son of God (cf. Ex. 4:22-23). On the occasion of its exile the people of Israel came to understand more clearly that God is the Father of the world,[14] the Creator, and at the same time that its own privileged sonship did not exclude its being an ungrateful, unfaithful, disobedient son (Jer. 3:19-22; Is. 1:2-4; Osee 11:1-4). It was precisely the infidelity of one part of the people that led to the distinction between the just and the unjust. The "unjust" no longer belong to God, no longer can call him "Father." This distinction came rather late in the sapiential books: Wis. 2:13-20; 5:4-5. It led up to the beautiful prayer of the just man who is afraid of becoming unjust:

> Who will set a guard on my mouth
>   and a seal of prudence on my lips,
> to keep me from falling,
>   and my tongue from causing my ruin?
> Lord, father and master of my life,
>   do not abandon me to their whims,
>   do not let me fall because of them.
> Who will lay whips to my thoughts,
>   and the discipline of wisdom to my heart,
> to be unmerciful to my errors,
>   and let none of my sins go unchecked
> in case my errors multiply,
>   and my sins increase in number,

---

[13]Cf. J. Jeremias, *El Mensaje central tel N.T.* Salamanca, 1966, p. 18; H. Lesêtre, *Dictionnaire de la Bible*, v. I (1912), col. 130-131, art. "Père."

[14]Cf. Mal. 2:10; it is true besides that in this text there is question only of the Jews and of the Israelites (Juda and Israel); but the reasoning is implicitly valid for all men.

> and I fall before my adversaries,
> and my enemy gloats over me?
> Lord, father and God of my life,
> do not give me proud eyes,
> turn lust away from me,
> do not let lechery and lust grip me,
> do not give me over to shameless desire.

So Ecclesiasticus spoke (22:27-23:6). The notion of a special paternity of God with regard to the just includes and comprehends creative paternity without eliminating a more particular affective paternity for Israel taken as a whole. It offers a sketch of the notion of a paternity of divinizing grace and its correlative term: the filiation of grace proper to certain members of the people with regard to the heavenly Father.

If the exile occasioned a broadening of the notion of divine paternity, earlier the monarchy had favored its narrowing and its concentration in a special paternity with regard to the King-Messiah (2 Sam. 7; Ps. 2 and 89). This was an exceptional paternity transcending that of Yahweh with regard to the people and even with regard to the just. The divinity of the Messiah was thus hinted at: Is. 7:14; 8:8-10; 9:5: he is Emmanuel, the mighty God.

This was the culminating point of Old Testament preparation for the Revelation proper to the New Covenant: God in a unique way is the Father of an only Son and in him the Father of a multitude of sons.

2. As early as the Sermon on the Mount, Jesus begins to prepare his disciples, more even than the rest of the Jewish people, for the revelation of the Trinity.

How? By insisting on the Providence of the heavenly Father with regard to his hearers.[15] "Your Father," "thy Father," are expressions that recur fifteen times in the three chapters of the Matthean recension of the Sermon.

However, more careful examination shows that on the lips of Jesus, the formula "your Father" tends to refer only to the just: Jesus takes up the Revelation at the point where the last writings of the Old Testament had left it, reserving the divine paternity to the just, in exclusion of the other (unjust) members of the people.

In Mt. 5:43-48 God is not called Father of the wicked, on whom he makes his rain fall and his sun shine, but Father of the just who imitate this beneficence: thus love of enemies reveals not only the holiness of man, but through this the Paternity of God with regard to those who practice it.

Consequently, even in this passage and everywhere else in the gospel of

---

[15] We are here following very closely J. Isaac, *op. cit.*, pp. 29-33.

St. Matthew, the expression "your Father" always refers to the just and to the disciples of Christ ("the small remnant"). Jesus wishes to inculcate in them the conviction of a divine Paternity with regard to the just: here we have from the point of view of the Trinitarian mystery the central idea of the first preaching in Galilee.

Must one not live out in oneself these relations of the just soul with his heavenly Father in order to have access to the revelation of God's Fatherhood with regard to his Only Son? It is not a question merely of a moral condition required by God for the revelation of his secrets, but rather of a deeper psychological condition, of an interior experience that is indispensable for grasping the mystery of the eternal and intra-divine Paternity with regard to an only Son.[16]

In fact the formula "your Father" or "thy Father" encountered fifteen times in the Sermon on the Mount, is found only five times in the rest of the Matthean gospel, while conversely the formula "my Father" found only once (7:21) at the end of this sermon, reappears nineteen times under three different forms (my Father, the Father, Father) in Matthew.

We witness, then, a progressive transition from "your Father" to "my Father," from God the Father of the just to the Father of Christ.

Doubtless it would not be wrong to see in "the hymn of jubilation" (Mt. 11:25-27) a partial synthesis of these two modes of expression: the paternity of the Father with regard to the "little ones" flows from his single paternity with regard to the only Son, and it is by him and by him alone that he reveals it. Parallels to this point of view we shall shortly encounter again in the Gospel according to St. John.

3. *God, the Father of Jesus in agony, in the Gospel of Mark*

Was it not intentional that Mark placed the name of the Father in the form of address on the lips of Jesus only at the time of the Passion: "Father, all things are possible to thee: remove this cup from me; yet not what I will, but what thou wilt" (14:36)?

Since the Baptism, the Father would call Jesus "his well-beloved Son," but it is only at the hour of the agony that Jesus replies, like Isaac (Gn. 22:7) by means of an expression unknown in the Old Testament as an address to God, "Abba, Father."

God the Father appears to us principally as Father when he delivers his well-beloved Son to death. In saying "Father" Jesus reminds the Father that he has received life from him. How could it happen that the one who had given life to the well-beloved Son was now about to deliver him to death?

God reveals his unique Paternity with regard to Jesus precisely through

---

[16]You will find an analogous reasoning in J. Lebreton, S.J., *Histoire du dogme de la Trinité*. Paris, 1928, v. I, pp. 259-261; the author—and this distinguishes him from J. Isaac—stresses that in the New Testament the Father remains Father in a sense, with regard to sinners.

his decision to take back life from this Son for the salvation of the adoptive sons.[17]

4. *God, the Father of the Son and of the sons, in the Gospel of John*

Unlike the Synoptics, St. John never speaks of the heavenly Father, of the Father who is in heaven. But he speaks 123 times of the Father, ordinarily in the terms "Father" or "my Father"; only once does he place on the lips of Jesus the expression "your Father."

When Jesus says: "my Father" it is usually in the context of a polemic with "the Jews,"[18] who boasted that they had God as Father, father of their people (2:16; 5:17; 6:32; 8:41). Thus Jesus wanted to stress the transcendence of the divine paternity of which he was the object in contrast to the paternity which had for its term the whole people.

The expression, "your Father," is often on Jesus' lips during the Sermon on the Mount, but in John it is unique in 20:17, in contrast to 8:42: "If God were your father you would love me, for it is from God that I came forth.... Do not hold me, for I have not yet ascended to the Father. But go to my brethren and say to them: I am ascending to my Father and your Father, to my God and your God."

Mgr. F.-M. Catherinet has given a remarkable interpretation of this verse (Jn. 20:17). In it Jesus takes up as a song of triumph Ps. 21 (v.23) from which he had appropriated to himself on the Cross verse 1 (my God, my God, why have you abandoned me); an interpretation confirmed in the light of Heb. 2:12. The term "brethren" used by Jesus is not an *obiter dictum*. It expresses a real and new relation of the Savior with his apostles, a relation resulting from the redemptive work on which the entry of Jesus into the glory of his resurrection sets the seal. Now that he has redeemed and won them, he can "without blushing" not disdain to call them "his brothers," for that they have become. They were already his brothers according to the flesh, they have now become his brothers according to the Spirit. They were his brothers as sons of Adam, they have become his brothers in God the Father. In the light of the literary and doctrinal context, proximate and remote, Catherinet, pursuing the course already suggested by Dom Calmet[19] in the eighteenth century, reconstructs the sense of Jn. 20:17:

> It remains for me to ascend to my Father, who has now become your Father by a new title, to my God who, thanks to my redemptive work, has

---

[17]W. Marchel, *Dieu Père*. Paris, 1966, ch. 4, pp. 39-54, explains in a suggestive manner this passage of the Gospel according to Mark.

[18]St. John in using these words often alludes to the Pharisees, cf. Gregory Baum, O.S.A., *Is the New Testament Anti-Semitic?* Glen Rock, NJ: Paulist Press, 1965, pp. 138-144.

[19]Dom Calmet, *Epîtres de saint Paul*. Paris, 1746, v. IV, p. 450; Id., *Ev. de saint Jean*. Paris, 1722, p. 872.

truly become your God. Far from disassociating Jesus and the Apostles in the relation that unites them to God the Father, this text, if understood in this way, rather, and even primarily, expresses the idea of an association, a participation in the filiation of the only Son.[20]

Because of the Paschal mystery the disciples are really brothers of Jesus in the Spirit and brothers of one another according to this same Spirit. The only Son has made of slaves his brothers, freed from the slavery of sin (cf. Jn. 8:34-37).

We are thus led to ascertain the complex sense of the expression "the Father" in John. Harnack was not entirely wrong in saying that the essence of Christianity is the universal paternity of God. But he did not distinguish between the three forms of divine paternity: creative, divinizing, and natural.

In John the expression "the Father" signifies in the first place "Father of an only Son," the transcendent intra-divine paternity, but it also refers to the Father of all those who, through the mediation of the only Son, have received divine life (cf. Jn. 1:12-13).

"The Father" thus becomes a specifically Christian title, transcending the plane of simple creative Providence. That is why Jesus never uses it in John's gospel with regard to his disciples until he has realized the Paschal mystery, and he never says to them, "your Father" until after his resurrection. We call God "Father" not only because we are created and governed by him, but in addition because we are members of the Son: to the extent that we dwell[21] in the only Son we may speak of his Father as being our Father.

Under the same word "Father" St. John designates at once the paternity of God with respect to his adoptive sons and his unique paternity with respect to his pre-existent and only Son. The paternity of God with respect to men is viewed by John in the light of his paternity with respect to Jesus (cf. Jn. 11:52; 1:12; 1:18). John highlights the transcendence of the first and only-begotten Son with respect to his younger brothers by never using for them the expression *huios* which he reserves for Jesus alone and by employing the word *tekna*[22] instead to designate them.

The Father thus includes: "my Father" and "your Father." He is the supreme source of all authority and of all love.

We are at a high point in the New Testament: the only Son and we, his disciples, now have, though in a different manner, the same Father. This is

---

[20]F.-M. Catherinet, "Note sur un verset de l'Evangile de saint Jean," XX, 17, in the *Mémorial J. Chaine*. Lyons, 1950, pp. 56-58.

[21]Cf. Jn. 15:4-10.

[22]Jn. 1:12; 11:52; 1 Jn. 3:1-2; 3:10; 5:2; Paul on the contrary calls the Christian "huios" (Gal. 3:26 e.g.).

the central revelation of the New Testament in contrast to the Old. The universal paternity of God is concentrated in the only Son, only to pour itself out into all humanity.[23] In order that the Father could reveal himself as only Father of an only Son, this only Son had to have brothers. If the Trinity as such does not presuppose creation and supernatural elevation, the revelation of the Trinity does.

5. St. John, however, meant to present Jesus to us not only as the only Son but also as the Word, as the Logos. But what does this mysterious expression mean? We can distinguish three meanings, one derived from the Biblical context, one from the rabbinic context and one from the context of Greek philosophy.

In the *total Biblical context* of the Old Testament, the word of God is divine action and intervention in history, a call addressed to men so that they will collaborate with him in history (cf. Is. 55:10). It is not only salvation but judgment: Is. 11:4; Wis. 18:14-19; 16:12-26. The Word of God is the divine Wisdom which the Old Testament shows us as anterior to creation, associated with the creative work and sent on earth to reside in the midst of the Jewish people to enrich all men with its benefits (Wis. 7 and 9; Prov. 8; Sir.1 and 24).[24] In himself as the Word who is with the Father (Jn. 1:1) Jesus synthesizes all these meanings: he is Savior and Judge (Jn. 12:47-49), the God who creates and maintains in existence all of nature and history. The world owes its origin to the word of God (cf. Gn. 1, which repeats seven times "God said"... before coming to the eighth divine word that is creative of man): the Word is the creative utterance and at the same time the Thought that precedes every creative utterance.[25] We can thus understand the luminous commentary of St. Hilary who so admirably associates the different senses of Gn. 1:1 in a christologically oriented synthesis: "*Beresith* is a Hebrew word which has three meanings: in the beginning, in the head, in the Son (*in principio, in capite, in filio*)."[26] St. John certainly meant to allude to this interpretation which was already known to the rabbis.

In the *rabbinic context* St. John employs the expression *Logos* precisely to suggest the superiority of Christ over the law of the Old Covenant. The rabbis identified the law pure and simple with Wisdom (cf. Prov. 8; Sir. 24:32-35); for them the law existed before creation, of which it was the instrument; it pre-existed in the bosom of God as light and source of life; all this St. John affirms of Christ Jesus, master of the law.[27]

---

[23]We are thinking of the Son as incarnate; one could not say the same thing of the divine Person of the Word setting aside the Incarnation.
[24]Cf. M.-J. Le Guillou, O.P., *Le Christ et l'Eglise.* Paris, 1963, p. 26.
[25]Cf. our forthcoming notes 32 to 38 relative to functional theology.
[26]Cf. M.-J. Le Guillou, *op. cit.,* pp. 42-43.
[27]Cf. J. Lecuyer, C.S.Sp., *Le sacrifice de la Nouvelle Alliance.* Lyons, 1962, p. 119; F. M. Braun,

In the *context of Greek philosophy*, the Johannine Logos is a conscious and intentional allusion to Stoicism, to the thought of Plato and to Philo (who is a bridge between Judaism and Hellenism).

For the Stoics the Logos is universal reason, the universal soul of which all individual souls are a part. In their pantheistic system, Reason, or Logos, is the directive life principle or soul of the world. The point of view is cosmic.

For Plato, the Logos is the meeting point of the divine archetypes, the divine ideas of terrestrial and visible realities. It is the universal idea of the Good in which all the ideas of God are brought together. Material things offer an atrophied, disfigured and diminished representation of their exemplar which is contained in the Logos. The point of view is at once cosmic and religious.

For Philo the Logos is a Divine model. It is the idea of the world, the instrument and the first-born of creation.[28]

What use did John make of the Logos in terms of the Greek context? For we think it was not fortuitous but deliberate that St. John, the Semite, chose to speak about Jesus of Nazareth to the Greeks in categories that are both Greek and Biblical.[29]

John makes use of Philo's meaning but the inspired thought of the disciple whom Jesus loved goes beyond Philo's speculations. The Incarnate Word is God and man, Creator and creature, Mediator who unites these in

O.P., *Jean le Théologien*. Paris, 1964, v. II, pp. 142f.; J. Starcky, *DBS*, v. V. Paris, 1957, art. "Logos," col. 457-465 and 495.

[28]*Ibid.*, 473-475; F. Prat, S.J., *Dict. de la Bible*, art. "Logos," v. IV (1908), col. 325-328; C. Kannengiesser, S.J., in the collective volume on *Philon d'Alexandrie*. Paris, 1967, p. 294: "divine and creative thought... the Logos, immutable in itself, assures a necessary mediation between God and that which is not God, without however interposing itself between the Creator and his creatures." In the light of the remarkable work of C. Kannengiesser, entitled "Philon et les Pères sur la double création de l'homme," we can think that if St. John knew Philo's work he may have been much more inspired by it than we have hitherto judged possible, only the non-distinction between the Logos and the Person of the Father making him modify the Philonian views. We say this with reservations, given the complexity of the problem. It should be noted, in particular, that according to H. A. Wolfson (*Philo*, Cambridge, Mass., 1947, v. I, pp. 264-270) Philo called the Logos an instrument in only one sense—and that clearly acceptable to Christians: "the visible world was created thanks to the model supplied by the intelligible world itself identical with the Logos"; the Logos would thus not be exterior to the divine thought. See also R. S. Franks, *op. cit.*, pp. 19-23, on the Logos of Philo.

[29]*Ibid.*, pp. 48-49; 4: against Cullmann, Franks shows that it is arbitrary to deny the influence of Greek culture on the New Testament; but it should be added in the light of the Dead Sea documents that the influence of Hellenism had already profoundly penetrated pre-Christian Judaism. These same documents show us however that the sources of the New Testament and its spiritual climate are, first and foremost, directly and immediately Jewish: cf. W. F. Albright and his article on "L'archéologie du Nouveau Testament: son passé, son avenir," in *Bible et vie chrétienne*, no. 79 (1968) pp. 75-90.

himself, personally distinct from God the Father and yet Creator, immediate Creator. The divine paternity does not, in a sense, belong to the cosmological or anthropological order. It is natural and supernatural.

St. John rejects Stoic pantheism: the Word is "the life of every being" but it is not every being (cf. Jn. 1:4). John retains from Stoicism the idea of Christ (the Logos) as the "bond" of creation, but unlike Wis. 1:7 and Col. 1:17, he does not say this explicitly. For John the Incarnate Word is a synthesis of thought and action, who insures the logic of history, the rationality of existence. To say that Christ is the Logos, is to imply that the entire plan of God, recapitulated in Christ, is "logic," even if this transcendent intelligibility escapes or surpasses us.

The Logos proposed by St. John is the Platonic idea which has entered into history: the Word was made flesh (Jn. 1:14). He is not a myth, like the *logoi* invented by men. John invites his correspondents and auditors to abandon these false *logoi*, false doctrines and to take refuge in the "true light" of the Word (Jn. 1:9; the opposition of the First Letter of John to the "lies of the antichrists" 1 Jn. 2:18-23; 4:1-6). It is as if he were saying to them: "I have experienced what you feel and think when you speak of the Logos, but I have experienced this in the Incarnate Word, in a way that surpasses all the meanings you might give to the Logos. The *logoi* that you know owe their origin to human speculations on the meaning of the world; they are human creations; in contrast, the Logos of whom I am the witness is an historical reality, whose origin is in God."[30] Without ceasing to be inserted into our history he is nevertheless above history, an eternal reality.

John is the author of a Gospel whose primary purpose is to render testimony to the divinity of Jesus (20:31). He intended to show, by his use of the term Logos or Word with regard to the Son of God, that there are images more expressive of his eternal generation than those of Wis. 7:25-26 (pure emanation of the glory of the Almighty, a reflection of the eternal light) or of Heb. 1:3 (perfect copy of his substance): these images, though beautiful, are dead. He replaces them by an idea in order to exclude every purely material concept, every coarse representation of this divine generation. He thus replies in advance to an objection that even today haunts millions of Moslems. John was living in the midst of pagan polytheism. He set out to show that the Son of a purely spiritual Being is his Thought, his Word, distinct from him and yet present in him.[31]

John, in proclaiming that the Son of God is the Word, the Logos, was thinking of a newly discovered reality, the Man Jesus, and in a threefold relationship:

---

[30]Here we draw inspiration from M. Schmaus (*Teologia dogmatica*, I, La Trinidad de Dios. Madrid, 1960, § 44.3a).

[31]Cf. the reflections of M.-J. Lagrange, O.P., *Evangile selon saint Jean*. Paris, 1936, p. CLXXXIff.

—confronting Hebrew and Old Testament thought, he proclaimed that the Wisdom of the Old Testament is a person distinct from the Father who generates him;

—confronting the rabbinic position, he taught that Christ and not the law of Moses is the plenitude of life, pre-existent to the world;

—confronting the diverse aspects of Greek thought, John showed how Christ satisfied its aspirations. The Logos of whom St. John speaks directs the universe like the Logos of the Stoics; he is the archetype of visible realities like that of Plato; he is Priest like that of Philo. In the Johannine Logos we perceive the cosmic scope of Trinitarian doctrine.

Is this doctrine in the New Testament so bound up with affirmations about creation and revelation made to men that we can say the New Testament, and in particular St. John's prologue, do not intend to speak to us of the interior being of God but only of his relations with the world? Is the Johannine Logos exclusively God as turned to the world, God who reveals himself and brings about the history of salvation?[32]

If this were so, the Trinitarian mystery would be no more. There would not be in God any irreducible and eternal distinction of Persons. There would be, and this according to St. John, only one Person in God, eternally. The Trinity in God would be totally and uniquely constituted in function of creation and revelation. There would be a functional Trinity, corresponding to a purely functional Logos. The Trinity would be neither eternal nor even really creative.

L. Malevez has answered this question very well:

> The Son has received the power to create, since all things were made by him.[33] He has received this power, and this circumstance distinguishes him from the Father, but he truly possesses it, and it is as universal and as free as it is in the paternal fontal principle.
>
> Let us suppose that the power of creation in the Son no longer had the same sovereign independence with regard to its objects. In this case what acceptable meaning could be given to the Son's divine rank or divinity that we elsewhere acknowledge in him?
>
> The Son then does not owe his meaning and his *raison d'être* to the revelation of God *ad extra* alone: his being is not constituted by his creative function. The liberty of the nature with regard to the function constitutes the certain background of his (John's) theology of the Word.... In

---

[32]In this way L. Malevez, S.J., sums up the thoughts of O. Cullmann (*Rech. Sc. Rel.*, 48, 1960, 264-265: Nouveau Testament et théologie fonctionnelle). Later, Cullmann, in a letter published by the review *Choisir*, I, 1960, nos. 9-10 of Geneva, gave a quite different interpretation of his own thought. Cf. O. Cullmann, *Vorträge und Aufsätze*, 1925-1926. Zurich, 1966, pp. 591-600.

[33]Cf. Jn. 1:3, 10.

what sense could the Son still be proclaimed God if he possessed intelligibility only in his work *ad extra*?³⁴

John's Christology is at most affirmatively but not exclusively functional. Christ is called Word inasmuch as he is Revealer, but not exclusively for this reason. A solely functional Christology would lead logically to professing the disappearance of the Logos once the revelation is terminated: for he would have no further *raison d'être*!³⁵

But we think that the Johannine Christology, in what concerns the expression Logos (though evidently not under other aspects!), is not even affirmatively functional except secondarily. First and foremost St. John has designated Jesus as Word by reason of his relation to the Father, and only subsequently by reason of his role in creation³⁶ or in revelation. This is the unanswerable conclusion of the beautiful study of I. de La Potterie, S.J.³⁷ The preposition *pros* (Jn. 1:1-2; 1:18 [inclusion]; 1 Jn. 1:2) seems to indicate in John the direction, the orientation of the Word to the Father: "The Logos was turned toward God." This is exactly the opposite of what L. Malevez presented in summing up the functional theology of O. Cullmann: "The Logos is God turned toward the world." And numerous other exegetes understand the Johannine prologue in the same way as I. de La Potterie.³⁸ According to this same author, and for reasons that appear compelling to us,³⁹ 1 Jn. 1:2 should be translated thus: "We announce to you this eternal Life which, by its very nature, was turned toward the Father." We can then understand the conclusion of I. de La Potterie's study on this point: "It should be noted against those who hold to a purely functional interpretation of the prologue, that Johannine theology does not only describe for us the mission of the incarnate Logos in the world: it also shows us the Word, before the creation of the world, *in his relations with God*."⁴⁰

We make this conclusion our own.

---

³⁴L. Malevez, S.J., "Nouveau Testament et théologie fonctionnelle," *Rech. Sc. Rel.*, 48 (1960), pp. 289-290.

³⁵This position, which seemed to be that of O. Cullmann before the letter to *Choisir*, would be a return to that of Marcellus of Ancyra: cf. G. Bardy, *DTC* XV, 2 (1950), col. 1658-1659: art. "Trinité." It is possible that Marcellus' tendencies are at the origin of the insertion into the Creed of the words: "cujus regni non erit finis."

³⁶Cf. note 33.

³⁷I. de La Potterie, S.J., "L'emploi dynamique de 'eis' dans saint Jean et ses incidences théologiques," *Biblica* 43 (1962), 366-387.

³⁸With him we could cite (*Ibid.*, 380-381, notes 2 and 3), Cajetan, E. A. Abbott, E. F. Scott, C. Spicq, M. Zerwick, H.-M. Feret, J. Isaac.

³⁹*Ibid.*, p. 382: an indeterminate relative pronoun, *hetis*, brings out the dynamic sense of *pros ton theon*.

⁴⁰*Ibid.*, p. 381. It is the author who underscores this.

IV. THE OTHER PARACLETE, HOLY BREATH OF THE FATHER AND OF THE SON

Jesus revealed that he was the only Son of God in manifesting his unique relation to Yahweh his Father. At the moment of accomplishing his Paschal sacrifice and in order to reveal more fully the efficacy of his redemptive work, the only Son divulged to his apostles the existence of a third one between his Father and himself. He did this by declaring more clearly than ever before the personal and distinct character of this Third One, the Holy Breath, the other Paraclete (Jn. 14:16; 14:26).

It was clearly by design that the Incarnate Logos chose this double denomination to designate this divine Third One. What were his reasons? In order to understand this better, it is necessary to situate these two expressions in the context of the history of salvation revealed in the Bible. But it must be noted first of all that these two expressions have as point of departure a human experience that conditions them. On the one hand, the breath of the living being that man is, his respiration, his "spirit," his animal and affective life; on the other, the juridical relations within human society that lead to the establishment of lawyers, defenders and promoters of people's rights. It is against this background that we can understand the meaning Jesus wished to give to the expressions "holy Spirit or Breath" and "Paraclete," and why he chose them.

1. *This divine Third One is named Holy Spirit*

If, as it seems, Jesus revealed to the world at large with sufficient, though still veiled, clarity his own divine personality only about a year before his death,[41] we can better understand why he waited till the days immediately preceding his sacrifice to teach that his Spirit was irreducibly distinct from himself and from his Father. For the revelation of the person of the Holy Spirit was associated by Jesus with the revelation of the mission of this same Spirit, a visible mission posterior to and bound up with this sacrifice.

What is more, it was fitting that there be a time lag between the self-revelation of the Only Son and his proclamation of the Holy Spirit, his envoy. The Giver ought to reveal himself before revealing the Gift.

Moreover, faced with the "discursivity" of the human mind, the discourse of the Revelation ought to unfold itself in time. The disciples, whose minds were already sluggish in comprehending Jesus himself (Mk. 8:17; Jn. 14:9; 16:30), could not have borne everything at the same time (cf. Jn. 16:12).

---

[41]Cf. the interpretation of Jn. 8:58, given by J. Isaac, *op. cit.*, pp. 43-48; see a more nuanced explanation in A. Feuillet, P.S.S., "Les ego eimi christologiques," *Rech. Sc. Rel.* 54 (1966), 235-236.

In the light of the Johannine Christ's teaching[42] we must even go further: it was only after Pentecost and the visible gift of the Spirit that they adequately grasped the teaching of the pre-Paschal Jesus (Jn. 14-16) about the distinct personality of this Spirit who had given himself to them. Is it not striking to note that all the questions put to Jesus by the apostles during the discourse after the Supper concerned him or his relations with his Father ("Lord, show us the Father," Jn. 14:8) while not one question concerned this Holy Spirit whom Jesus was announcing to them as distinct, and about whom at the moment they showed no curiosity at all? It is only when Jesus has surrendered his last human created breath and after he has taken it up again that Jesus would be able through that breath to surrender and fully reveal his eternal divine and uncreated Breath (cf. Lk. 23:46; Jn. 10:18; 19:30; 20:22-23).

In saying that Jesus "committed, gave up his spirit" (Jn. 19:30) did not John intend, through a formula with a double meaning (a favorite device of his), to recall and complete the sense of Jesus' declaration in Lk. 23:46: "Father, into thy hands I commit my spirit"?[43] Did he not wish to show that the Son gave up his human soul, his created spirit to the Father only in order to fill humanity with his holy and uncreated Breath? Did not the last human breath of the dying Jesus prepare for and indeed merit the human insufflation by which the Risen One will breathe from his victorious mouth his divine Breath on the disciples whom he will charge to bathe all men therein?

It is certain that we must start from this highly significant gesture of the risen Jesus in order to understand all his teaching about the Holy Spirit, as Scheeben, following St. Cyril of Alexandria, saw so clearly.

In its application to the third person of the divinity, the word "spirit" really derives from the breath of man, this Cologne theologian noted;[44] we could even say from the breath and the breathing of the Man Jesus, who is the Man *par excellence*.

Cyril of Alexandria clearly orients us toward this interpretation: "Christ breathed the Spirit in a bodily fashion thus showing that as from the mouth of man comes the corporeal breath, so from the divine substance in a way that befits it, comes the breath that proceeds from it."[45]

On this subject Scheeben says: "The Fathers find that this is the case especially in the Savior's action of breathing upon the apostles: our Lord

---

[42]Jn. 14:26: it is precisely the mission of the Spirit "to recall all that I have said to you" (cf. Jn. 2:22; 12:16; 7; 20:9), and especially Jesus' teaching about the Holy Spirit himself.

[43]The Greek text says *to pneuma mou* and adds that in saying this Jesus expired: *exepneusen*, a composite of the word *pneuma*. You might read about this verse the interesting and suggestive development of J. Guillet, S.J., *Thèmes bibliques*. Paris, 1951, p. 227.

[44]M.-J. Scheeben, *The Mysteries of Christianity*. St. Louis, MO, 1946, pp. 97-98 (§17).

[45]St. Cyril of Alexandria, *in Jo.* 14:16: tr. IX, *MG* 74. 258.

intended to symbolize not only the external procession, but also the internal procession of the Third Person from the Son and the Father."⁴⁶ With the help of this affirmation, it is not difficult to show that it is in the light of the breathing action of the Risen One that we must understand Jesus' choice of the expression "holy Breath" or "Holy Spirit" to designate not only the third Person Himself, but also the purpose of his visible mission and the nature of his invisible procession.

   a) *Jesus names the divine Third One holy Breath in order to signify the effects of his visible mission*
   It is clear that in the thought and in the teaching of Jesus (Mk. 3:11 and 22 clarified by 3:28-30), the Holy Spirit is opposed and opposes himself to unclean spirits, the good Spirit⁴⁷ to bad spirits (Lk. 11:13; Mt. 7:11; Mt. 12:45). Jesus himself is filled with the Holy Spirit (Lk. 4:1, 14, 16-21) in order to resist unclean and bad spirits and in order to banish them by baptizing and washing men in the holiness of his burning breath (Mt. 3:11; Jn. 1:33)⁴⁸ thanks to his death. It is certainly first of all in function of the mission of this divine Third One in the salvation of humanity, that Jesus chose to call him Holy Spirit in order to signify that he is to *sanctify* us by making us mortify the works of the flesh thus making us become *spiritual* (cf. Rom. 8:5-13; Gal. 5:16-26) thanks to his fruits. The mission of the Spirit consists in freeing carnal and sinful men from the slavery of unclean spirits and of sin in order to sanctify them by love (cf. Rom. 5:5).

   This primarily functional meaning of the denomination chosen by Jesus to serve as a name for the divine Third One did not escape St. Bonaventure. He suggests that the Gospel calls the Third Person "Holy Spirit" in opposition to the impurity of the many earthly loves: "The term 'spirit', if it is used in reference to spiration, is fitting only for the person whose procession is one of love. In spiritual realities to spirate pertains only to love. As love spirated in a lawful and ordered manner is pure or on the other hand, as it is impure if it is spirated in a guileful and impure manner, so the person who is love is not only called spirit but Holy Spirit."⁴⁹

   Thus we could say that the symbolic image of breath to designate the divine Third One serves a polemical function that is perfectly consonant with its Old Testament antecedents; the *Pneuma* of the Old Testament is wind and tempest, wind that is the breath of Yahweh represented as a man in anger: "A blast from your nostrils and the waters piled high; the waves

---

⁴⁶M.-J. Scheeben, *op. cit., ibid,* note 10.
⁴⁷Cf. Ps. 143:10.
⁴⁸Cf. J. Isaac, *op. cit.,* ch. X, pp. 155-172.
⁴⁹St. Bonaventure, *In I sent. Exp.,* dist. X, part. I, quaest. III, conclusio: *Opera omnia.* Paris, 1868, v. I, p. 196. The pure love that is the Holy Spirit divinizes human love by purifying it.

stood upright like a dyke.... One breath of yours you blew, and the sea closed over them" (Ex. 15:8-10).

If we wish to be faithful to Biblical thought, instead of considering man or God in the light of natural and cosmic phenomena, we must instead consider these latter in the light of man so as to rise from him to God. This holds true for the wind, the breath of human respiration and the Spirit of God.

In the Bible the wind is normally associated with God as a divine power. Nevertheless, in contrast to the sea, which is the usual symbol of forces hostile to God, and of a formidable, savage and diabolical revolt, the wind, in its capacity of breaking all resistance, is the docile instrument of Yahweh (Job 26:10-13; Is. 51:9-10; Ps. 148:8; 104:4).[50] In the New Testament the wind remains the instrument of God and becomes the symbol of the Third Divine Person (Acts 2:2-3; Jn. 3:5-8). We can think of this Breath of Pentecost as also symbolizing the victory of the Risen One who breathes it forth upon his enemies in order to transform and convert them.

Moreover, the visible mission of the holy Breath for the salvation of men, and the anthropological meaning of its designation, so strongly highlighted by the breathing action of the Risen One, are already grounded germinally and remotely in the association the Old Testament establishes between breath, word and face of Yahweh. Thus Ps. 33:6 ("by his word the heavens were made, by the breath of his mouth their whole array") shows us "the breath that God emits at the same time that he puts forth his word";[51] "where could I flee from your face, where could I go to escape your spirit" (Ps. 139:7); "do not banish me from your face, do not deprive me of your holy spirit" (Ps. 51:11).[52]

Thus it appears that the Spirit of the Father and the Son wished to link his revelation to the disclosure of the human countenance in the breath of an ardent conversation or of a just anger. The face of the triune God reveals itself through the one and multifaceted face of man. The countenance of man becomes the symbol of the mystery of God.

Unlike the breath of the nostrils that always signifies wrath, the breath of the mouth is ordinarily (but not always[53]) a beneficent breath from which emanates life in the world. As long as man lives, there is in him an element that does not come from the earth and will not be absorbed by it at death: the breath, the respiration in which is found the principle of life in the view of the Hebrews (cf. Gn. 6:3; 6:17; 7:22 and especially 2:7). In this

[50]Cf. J. Guillet, *op. cit.*, pp. 211-212.
[51]M.-E. Boismard, O.P., "La révélation de l'Esprit-Saint" *RB* 55 (1955), 20.
[52]Cf. J. Guillet, *op. cit.*, p. 251: "the fear of being rejected from the face of God, deprived of his spirit, comes...from the naive idea that man insofar as he is alive remains animated by the breath that the face of God breathes into him"; and note 221.
[53]Cf. Is. 11:4; 30:27-28; cf. J. Guillet, *op. cit.*, p. 218, note 57.

sense breath is opposed to flesh which designates the living being as destined to death, being as fundamentally corruptible.

J. Guillet is thus correct in writing:

> The Hebrew conception of the living being conforms to its representation of the exterior world.
>
> In nature, to the properly terrestrial elements of earth and water—heavy and inert masses born out of chaos by a triumphant intervention of God—is opposed the wind with its quasi divine traits, subtlety, rapidity, power and docility. Likewise in the living being, to the feebleness and passivity of the flesh, destined to corrupt as a corpse, is opposed a force more mysterious even than the wind, but of an analogous nature: an imperceptible breath, apparently fragile and wavering but, nevertheless alone capable of rousing the body and of infusing it with the energies of life.
>
> Like the wind, but with somewhat stronger conviction and in more decisive terms, the Hebrew called this breath a breath of God, the *ruah* of Yahweh.[54]

From this angle there unfolds another aspect of the symbolic meaning of the breathing action of the risen Christ on his apostles, in order to give them together with the Spirit the power to remit sins. The Risen One who has regained his breath under the action of the holy Breath, thus manifests his power to resurrect the spiritually dead in the likeness of the resurrection of his own incorrupt corpse. This is the symbolic action of the new creation, of the second creation performed by the second Adam. At the time of the first creation God "breathed into the nostrils of man a breath of life and thus man became a living being" (Gn. 2:7). St. Paul thus makes the connection, "the first man, Adam, became a living soul; the last Adam has become a life-giving spirit" (1 Cor. 15:45). Filled with the Spirit of the One who raised him from the dead[55], Jesus gives life by giving his Spirit, by breathing him in. The second creation, like the first that it comes to complete, is accomplished by insufflation.

It is clear then, that in order to have life in all its fullness (which is the object of the Good Shepherd's coming: Jn. 10:10), man needs not only the created breath, a breath of life that gives him a living soul, but also and especially the uncreated breath of the Holy Spirit, the remission of his sins[56]

---

[54]*Ibid.*, p. 221.
[55]Cf. Rom. 8:11.
[56]Cf. Jn. 20:22-23: it is on the basis of this text that a liturgical prayer of the Latin rite refers to the Holy Spirit as "remission of sins"; the comparison that we make here and a little earlier between Jn. 20:22-23 and Gn. 2:7 is traditional, suggested by the Greek text (Septuagint) of Gn. 2:7 which already used the word to which John intentionally resorts: *enephusen,* and which St. Cyril of Alexandria underlined with an important nuance (*De Trin.*, dial. 4, *MG* 75, 907): for

which is transmitted to him by the risen breath of the Word of God made human word and even human breath.

In the New as in the Old Testament the breath issuing from God designates both the transcendence of God's power with respect to the weakness of all flesh (Jer. 17:5; Ps. 56:5; Mk. 14:38; Jn. 1:14; 3:6; 6:63) and the spirit proper to man, indeed his consciousness (Job 7:11; Gn. 26:35; 41:8; Jn. 11:33; 13:21).[57] It is not always easy to distinguish these two senses, especially since the second is intimately bound up with and dependent on the first. It is the divine and all-powerful breath that animates man and gives him consciousness.

Some[58] ask whether this force that comes from God and is destined to return to him (Gn. 6:3) can be anything other than a borrowed good in man, and whether it could be man himself? The New Testament answers this question clearly enough: for St. John (1 Jn. 4:1-3 Gr.) explicitly distinguishes between the created spirit that comes from God (*pneuma ek tou theou*) and the Spirit of God (*pneuma tou theou*). It is clear moreover that if the meaning of Jn. 19:30 is deliberately double—as we have already said—Lk. 23:46 alludes only to the created soul of Jesus. In spite of Hans Urs von Balthasar,[59] it would make no sense to say that Jesus commits to his Father his uncreated Spirit, but one could say very understandably that he commits his created spirit, his soul, in an act of unifying separation.

For the New Testament distinguishes not in order to separate, but rather in order to unite. St. Irenaeus grasped this very well: "(Jesus) has recapitulated (these things) in himself uniting man to the Spirit and placing the Spirit within man. He himself has come as head of the Spirit."[60] We could imagine no better commentary on Jn. 20:22-23.

The reflections that we have just outlined on the vivifying Spirit incline us to believe that Jesus also had in mind this all-powerful function of the Third Person in the work of salvation when he chose the name "Holy Spirit" to designate him.

One could then say that on the lips of Jesus and in his human mind, the word "Holy Spirit" already had the meaning to which St. Paul will allude in speaking of the Spirit of God and the Spirit of Christ: "The law of the Spirit which gives life in Christ Jesus has freed you from the law of sin and death.... If you live according to the flesh, you will die. But if by the Spirit you put to death the deeds of the body you will live" (Rom. 8:2-13).

---

the Alexandrine Doctor, the breath of life received by the first Adam is already the Spirit of the Son (cf. MG 74, 278) and not the natural life, the immortal soul. Or at least, not merely the latter.

[57]Cf. J. Guillet, *op. cit.*, pp. 220-225.
[58]*Ibid.*, pp. 226-227.
[59]Hans Urs von Balthasar, *Cordulla ou l'épreuve décisive*. Paris, 1968, pp. 25-26.
[60]St. Irenaeus, *Adv. Haereses*, V, 20.2.

In speaking of the Holy Spirit Jesus was proclaiming the spiritualizing and sanctifying mission of the Third Person and was inviting his disciples to submit themselves to this action of the Third Person.

He consciously took up an expression already present in the historically later parts of the Old Testament (Ps. 51:9-14; 143:10). These texts attribute to his holy Breath, as to a cause, the humility of man—and his submission to the good pleasure of Yahweh. The book of Wisdom speaks several times of the Holy Spirit in whom it sees the origin of human knowledge of the divine will (9:17) and also of a Breath of the divine power that penetrates all spirits (7:22-25). On the contrary the rebels bind themselves in alliances which Yahweh "does not *inspire*" and add sin to sin (Is. 30:1).

Although these texts do not explicitly affirm a plurality of persons in God, it would be too simplistic to call this Holy Spirit "impersonal," for he is presented as divine and in this respect as personal. Since the God of the Old Testament is not impersonal,[61] the Spirit who is identified with him could not be impersonal either. On the contrary these texts bespeak a frequent personification[62] of the Spirit, or better, his "hypostatization." They present him as God and simultaneously as a personal Being not yet really but verbally distinct from Yahweh (cf. Wis. 9:17). They thus prepare the revelation by Christ of the Person, of the distinct Hypostasis of the Holy Spirit.

This Spirit, the Spirit of Truth, often comes up again in the literature of Qumran, in the same style of "hypostatization" without a clearly distinct hypostasis.[63] A new preparation for the revelation of the Holy Spirit, willed by the Providence of the Word who enlightens every man.

Everything then leads us to think that Jesus, in choosing among so many other possible names that of "Holy Spirit" to designate the Third Person whom he came to reveal to the world, intended to teach that this Spirit already known to his disciples, thanks to the Old Testament and to the literature of the Essenian milieu, was not only a divine attribute but also a person distinct from his Father and from himself.

We could go further still: for Jesus there was no way to announce himself completely without announcing the Holy Spirit, the Spirit of Yahweh. The Old Testament presented this Spirit as bound up with the Messiah on whom he rested (Is. 11:1; 42:1ff.) and at the same time it announced an

---

[61]Cf. notes 7 and 8 of this chapter.

[62]According to *Petit Larousse* (1967) to personify signifies: "to attribute to an inanimate thing or to an abstract being the figure, the sentiments, the language of a person." It is clear that the Holy Spirit is not a thing nor an abstract being. In this sense, it is preferable to speak of "hypostatization" and not of "personification" of the Spirit in the Old Testament.

[63]On the relations between the literature of Qumran and the Gospel of John, see R. E. Brown, S.S., *The Gospel according to John* I-XIII. NY, 1966, p. LXII; on the precise point of the Holy Spirit, *ibid.*, and F. M. Braun, O.P., *RB* 55 (1955), pp. 18, 22 and 23 especially.

abundant outpouring of this Spirit (Is. 32:15-17; 44:2-3). Did not the discourse at the Last Supper mean to affirm that the Spirit who rested on Christ, the Anointed One (cf. Is. 61:1-2; Lk. 4:18) was at the same time a Person distinct from him and from the Father, but coming from him and from the Father?[64]

We will not now insist on this last point of view, which will come up again a little later, but we rather point out that Jesus, by a conscious and free choice of the word "Holy Spirit" to designate the Third Divine One, wished to bring to light the continuity and at the same time the originality of the New Covenant with respect to the Old.

We have then specified the reasons for which, in our view, Jesus named the divine Third One "holy Breath," by considering them from the angle of the effects of his visible mission; now guided by St. Cyril of Alexandria and by Scheeben, we shall attempt to grasp how Jesus also meant to signify by this designation the nature of his procession in the divinity.

b) *Jesus names the divine Third One holy Breath in order to make known the nature of his invisible procession*

We must show now, though not without partially anticipating later developments, the import of the symbolism of breath in the bosom of the Trinity. Cyril has launched us into this study by a profound remark: "You will call Holy Spirit him whom the Father sends forth essentially through the Son and who manifests to us his proper existence in the breath sent forth by the mouth as in an image."[65] The fact that the flesh of the Son instrumentally communicates the Spirit of the Father to men signifies that eternally the Spirit proceeds from the Father through the Son.[66]

A little earlier than the Doctor of Alexandria, St. Epiphanius had investigated the same problem in a different but complementary direction that would be taken up again by St. Augustine and followed by the Latin tradition: "the Holy Spirit derives from both (Father and Son) as spirit from spirit, for God is Spirit (Jn. 4:24)."[67] In other words, the Father is Spirit, the Son is Spirit; so it is not this that distinguishes them. How then can the Holy Spirit, who is also Spirit, be distinguished from them?

Augustine, with a profound subtlety that goes to the root of the difficulty

---

[64]Cf. Jn. 15:26; 16:7.
[65]St. Cyril of Alexandria, *De Trin.*, dial. 2, MG 75, 722-723.
[66]Cf. *ibid.*, dial. 2, MG 75, 907; the same thought is found in St. Bernard, sermo VIII, 2 in cantica cant., ML 183, 811: "indivisibilis Spiritus propterea in illo dominico flatu datus est, ut per hoc intelligeretur et ab ipso pariter tamquam a Patre procedere, tamquam vere osculum, quod osculanti osculatoque commune est."
[67]St. Epiphanius, *Haeres.*, III, 74.7.

and leads to an authentic doctrinal advance bound up with his whole Trinitarian theology, replies:

> Perhaps the Holy Spirit bears this name precisely because the Father and the Son can accommodate themselves to it. For in effect we give to him by special title the name we give to them by common title, since the Father is Spirit and the Son is Spirit, the Father is holy and the Son is holy. For thus in order to represent their mutual communion, there is need of a name that is applicable to both of them.[68]

Augustine's ingenious intuition about the Holy Spirit as communion, bond and reciprocal love of the Father and the Son (to which we shall return) allows him to grasp the most profound reason why the Man Jesus, whose language could not be the fruit of chance, chose to name the Third Divine One "Holy Breath": it was in order to symbolize thereby the secret of his procession.

The name of "Spirit" then is not only an absolute name that designates the divine essence common to the three Persons; it is also a relative name that designates the Third Person as relation to and between the other two. Scheeben offers a very good comment on this point: "The Third Person is the very expression and seal of the spiritual unity which the Father and the Son have in each other as one spirit—the absolute spirituality of the other persons is most distinctly expressed in Him and culminates in Him as in its summit."[69] Can we not say, as well, that in God as in man, intersubjectivity and interpersonality pertain to the very essence of spirituality? In signifying affectivity and love, breath symbolizes interpersonal reciprocity.

For St. Paul, the Spirit is at once the Breath of the Father and of the Son (Rom. 8:9), in conformity to the doctrine of Jesus in the discourse at the Last Supper (Jn. 15:26; 16:7). If it is true, as St. Fulgentius says that "the Breath always belongs to one who breathes, and is therefore relation to the Father and to the Son,"[70] "breathed" by the Father and by the Son, we can see in the light of the Pauline expressions just cited and of St. Augustine's fundamental intuition, that He is Breath of the Father toward the Son and

---

[68]St. Augustine, *De Trinitate*, V, XI, 12. There the saint writes further:"Since the Father, the Son and the Holy Spirit are but one God and since God is holy and is Spirit, one can call the Trinity Holy Spirit. Nevertheless, this Holy Spirit who is not the Trinity but whom one finds within the Trinity, by reason of the proper sense of the expression 'Holy Spirit,' has a relative name, since he relates both to the Father and to the Son, since the Holy Spirit is the Spirit of the Father and the Son." As we shall say later in citing St. Fulgentius, the simple name of breath presupposes a principle who breathes and, under this aspect, the name holy Breath is a relative name and not only absolute. See note 70.

[69]M.-J. Scheeben, *op. cit.*, p. 97.

[70]St. Fulgentius, *de Trin.*, c. 6: "Spiritus alicujus aspirantis est, ergo ad Patrem Filiumque refertur" (cited by Scheeben, *op. cit.*, p. 98); cf. St. Fulgentius, ML 65, 400.

of the Son toward the Father, and, to use a bold expression, the Breath which courses between them like a Kiss, the "Kiss of the Father and of the Son, the sweetest and most intimate Kiss,"[71] or more forcefully the "interbreath" at the heart of the Divinity.

A little later, in the twelfth century, Richard of St. Victor was to give us a still more profound vision of some of the anthropological presuppositions of the name chosen by Jesus to designate the Third Person:

> If there already exists a resemblance to the divine property in this breath of the material order that proceeds from the human organism, how much more real would this resemblance be in the breath that proceeds from the human spirit and is spiritual? What then is this breath of the human heart, lighter in some, stronger in others, more tepid in these, more fiery in those, if not an intimate affection of the soul, an impulse of flaming love?
>
> That is why we say that those are of one mind and act in one spirit, who have the same goal and the same purpose, who have the same loves, the same sentiments, the same desires. And, when this breath, spiritual in nature, is animated by piety and moves according to truth, it is then that it is truly holy, it is then that one can truly qualify it as holy. Without such a spirit, no spirit is holy, neither the spirit of man nor the spirit of an angel. It is clear that the spirit of man begins to be holy when he loves that which is holy, when he detests and abhors what is unholy. And it is indeed this sentiment of piety, it is truly the breath of this same spirit which makes of a multitude of hearts, one heart and one soul.
>
> It is thus in line with the image of this spirit which proceeds and is exhaled from many hearts that we name "Holy Spirit" the One who in the Trinity proceeds from the first two persons.

This magnificent page is extracted from the *Treatise on the Trinity*, book VI (devoted entirely to the names of the divine Persons), § 10.

The collective spirit of a human community serves as a starting point for Richard's understanding of the mystery of the Spirit's procession *a Patre Filioque*. He is right: the same St. Paul who, as we have already said, sees in the Holy Spirit the breath of the Father and of the Son, asks the Corinthians in reference to himself and Titus: "did we not act in the same spirit (*pneuma*)" (2 Cor. 12:18). The word designates a union of higher affectivities, the union of hearts, to use the expression employed, among others, in Acts 4:32 (the text to which Richard alludes).

The Holy Spirit produces the unity of spirit, the ecclesial communion (cf. 2 Cor. 13:13) symbolized by the kiss of peace (2 Cor. 13:12): "Greet one

---

[71]St. Bernard, *loc. cit.*, sermo VIII, I: "Illa itaque mutua gignentis genitique cognitio pariter et dilectio, quid nisi osculum est suavissimum sed secretissimum?"

another with a holy kiss.... The fellowship of the Holy Spirit be with you." St. Thomas Aquinas shows very well how the holy kiss of peace signifies the unity, the spiritual fellowship of Christians, and he suggests too that this kiss is in the image of the Spirit, of the divine Breath of the Father and the Son, thus offering a New Testament foundation for the doctrine of St. Bernard already cited. In his commentary on 2 Cor. 13:13, the "Common Doctor" expresses himself in this way: "The kiss is the sign of peace; for by the mouth that kisses a man breathes. When men exchange a kiss, this signifies that they unite their spirits (*uniunt spiritum*, the breath) in view of peace."

If the faithful kiss one another as a sign of charity and mutual union, as St. Thomas goes on to say, is this not meant to signify in the last analysis, through the mutual charity symbolized and sustained by this kiss, the Holy Spirit who achieves fellowship among them inasmuch as he is the fellowship, the kiss, the imperturbable peace between the Father and the Son? Is not this the best interpretation of Paul's thinking in the light of Augustine and Bernard as well as of Richard of St. Victor?

In his *Summa contra Gentiles* St. Thomas Aquinas has very well summed up some of the ideas presented here about the meaning and origin of the word "Holy Spirit." "The name of spirit," he tells us, "appears to be borrowed from animal breathing where air is inhaled and exhaled. Later this name comes to designate every impulse and movement of any body. Thus the wind is called breath (or spirit). As the air is invisible, the name of breath (or spirit) has been further transferred to all invisible and dynamic (*motiva:* literally, moving) substances and forces. For this reason the sensitive soul, the angels and God are called spirits; and God proceeding by love is rightly called spirit because love suggests a certain dynamic (motive) force"[72].

In the *Summa Theologica,* the Saint clarifies:

> The expression "Holy Spirit," understood in the sense of the two words taken separately, is an attribute common to the whole Trinity. In fact this term Spirit signifies the immateriality of the divine substance: since the corporeal spirit or breath is invisible and tenuous matter, we attribute this name to all immaterial and invisible substances. As to the word "holy," it signifies the purity of the divine Goodness. But if we take the expression "Holy Spirit" as a single word, then it is the name reserved by Church usage to designate that one of the three persons who proceeds by way of love.... In the corporeal world, the term "spirit" appears to evoke a kind of impulse and motion: in fact, we give this name "spirit" to

---

[72]St. Thomas Aquinas, *Summa contra Gentiles,* IV, 23, 1 (§3592 of the Marietti ed. Rome, 1961). The word *spiritus* has first of all a human meaning (breath) and only thereafter a cosmic signification (wind).

breath and to the wind. But the characteristic of love is to move and impel the will of the lover toward the beloved. As for sanctity, we attribute it to things that are consecrated to God. Since then there is a divine person who proceeds by way of love, the love by which God loves Himself, it is proper to call him Holy Spirit.[73]

What St. Thomas helps us to perceive but without saying it very explicitly, is that properly human breath and not only animal breath, the breath of man who is both matter and spirit, is the natural symbol of an immaterial and invisible love, is its sensible sign. This is most especially true in the case of the human breath of the Risen One when he breathes forth the Spirit with a view to the remission of sins. This human breath symbolized the human love of the Risen One for sinners and at the same time the Person of the Spirit of Love by whom he would remit their sins. Human love, expressed by a re-creating breath, sustains uncreated and divine Love.

Be that as it may, Suarez has well grasped and presented the sense of the expression "Holy Spirit" as signifying the procession of the Third Person, both in the teaching of St. Thomas and in that of the Fathers, in their effort to probe a "supremely appropriate name imposed by Christ himself"[74] well beyond the "usage of the Church" to which the Angelic Doctor alluded:

> The Third Person is, with good reason, called Spirit because he proceeds by way of love and impulsion and in addition, because he is a substantial love, supremely incorporeal and immaterial. Since this love is exceedingly pure and chaste, the word Holy is added, which declares the excellence of this procession and suggests also that this person is holy by essence, since he proceeds from the supreme love of the supreme Spirit.[75]

---

[73]St. Thomas Aquinas, *Summa Theologica,* I, 36. I. I and corpus.

[74]F. Suarez, S.J., *Opera Omnia.* Paris, 1866, v. I; *de Trinitate,* XI, I, 2: "vocatur Spiritus Sanctus, estque nomen ejus maxime proprium. Videturque ab ipso Christo impositum" (p. 774). Of course, this name in no way pretends to define the Third Person (cf. Jerusalem Bible, note g. on Ex. 3:16) and it in no way suppresses the transcendence of the ineffable mystery of the Holy Spirit with regard to human language; on the contrary, it helps to put it in relief, by reminding us that even the most appropriate name gives us only an analogical, not false but very limited knowledge of this mystery. See the treatise on the divine names in the *Summa Theologica,* of St. Thomas Aquinas, I, 13, especially article 3.

[75]Suarez, *loc., cit.,* p. 774: "tertia persona a Deo procedens spiritus merito appellatur, quia per modum amoris et impulsus procedit simulque illa voce significatum est, esse amorem substantialem, summeque incorpoream et immaterialem. Quoniam vero ille amor purissimus et mundissimus est, ideo addita est vox Sanctus, quae excellentiam illius processionis declarat simulque indicat personam esse sanctam per essentiam, quia ex dilectione summa summi Spiritus procedit." One cannot help admiring the beauty of the Latin expression. The link between animal breath and affective and loving impulse is not without foundation in the New Testament: cf. 1 Cor. 4:21; 6:17; 2 Cor. 12:18; Eph. 4:3; Ph. 1:27 (we are grateful to B. Kipper, S.J., who brought this to our attention).

From Yahweh to God the Father

Then, in the light of the Angelic Doctor, Suarez adds that if each of the words which make up the composite expression "Holy Spirit" is, as well as this expression itself, common to the Father and to the Son, the composite expression itself taken as a simple unity is proper to the Third Person.[76]

We can then say with Scheeben: "Breath or Spirit of the Father and the Son" is at once the richest, the most vivid, and the most concrete name that we can find or even may desire for the Third Person in God. The terms "Breath" and "Spirit" are here identical; in fact Greek and Latin have only the one word. In general we prefer the name "Spirit" because the oneness of life in God, which is exhibited in the Third Person is wholly spiritual and immaterial, and because in any case the word "spirit" is in common use to designate the possessor of spiritual life, although for that very reason its relative significance which must be retained, is not emphasized so much.[77]

This brief inquiry we have made into the history of theology permits us to verify the validity of Scheeben's intuition that we initially pointed out: the Risen Christ's breathing action was, in his human intention, a sensible sign of the mission and of the procession of the Third Person and in consequence it explains why he had already called him Holy Spirit or Breath. A post-Easter gesture of Jesus has specified and confirmed the meaning of his pre-Easter language.

We will terminate this inquiry by citing two Latin Fathers who, perhaps unwittingly, have admirably developed the Cyrillian understanding of this action of insufflation: Saints Fulgentius and Bernard. Their two harmoniously complementary interpretations illustrate the two aspects of the words which, on the lips of Jesus, expound his breathing action: "Receive the Holy Spirit. For those whose sins you forgive, they are forgiven; for those whose sins you retain, they are retained" (Jn. 20:22-23).

Fulgentius presents the Holy Spirit as the sword that proceeds from the mouth of Christ: "The apostle says: 'The Lord will slay the lawless one with the breath of his mouth' (2 Thess. 2:8). The only Son of God wishing to signify also that this Spirit is the breath of his mouth, says while breathing

---

[76]Suarez, *op. cit., ibid.*, p. 774, §3: Suarez' expression is particularly subtle; alluding to the text of St. Thomas to which our note 73 refers, Suarez writes: "adnotavit divus Thomas nomina *Spiritus* et *sanctus* et vocem complexam ex illis essentialia esse et communia Patri et Filio: nomen autem *Spiritus Sanctus* sumptum in vi unius vocis incomplexae esse proprium tertiae personae." Suarez cites St. Augustine in this sense: "Spiritus Patris et Filii, Spiritus Sanctus propria quadam notione hujus nominis in sacris litteris nuncupatur." (*De Civitate Dei*, XI, 1; ML 41, 325; the context shows evidently that St. Augustine sees in the name "Holy Spirit" a relative name and not only an absolute one; an important pastoral conclusion flows from this: we ought to explain in our preaching or catechesis that the Holy Spirit is the proper name of the Third Person inasmuch as he is the Breath of the Father and the Son). The Spirit, in proceeding from the Father and from the Son and because he proceeds from them, is related to them, is "toward them."

[77]Scheeben, *op. cit.*, p. 101.

on his disciples after the resurrection: Receive the Holy Spirit. It is, in fact, from the mouth of the same Lord Jesus that a two-edged sword issued, according to St. John in his Apocalypse (1:16). The breath of his mouth is thus the sword that proceeds from his mouth."[78]

While intent on showing that the Holy Spirit proceeds from the Son as well as from the Father, Fulgentius helps us to perceive a hidden dimension of the Johannine text: in pardoning sins by his apostles and by his Spirit, the Risen One destroys the wickedness of the lawless one by the Breath of his mouth; but this Breath is also a sword which retains them, that is, which punishes them.[79]

In this same insufflation St. Bernard also sees the kiss, the Spirit which the Risen One gives to the primitive Church.

> The kiss is not the corporeal breath, but the indivisible Spirit given in this breath so that we might understand that he proceeds equally from the Lord and from the Father as a kiss common to the one who embraces and to the one who is embraced.... The Father embraces, the Son is embraced, the Spirit is the Kiss as imperturbable peace and indivisible unity of the Father and the Son.[80]

St. Bernard develops this admirable image at length: he exploits all its contours. The Spirit is the eternal, secret kiss which no one can approach, the kiss which the Father and the Son give each other by their reciprocal immanence (Jn. 10:30). This kiss, at which no one can assist except the Holy Spirit himself inasmuch as he is the awareness of mutual love, the Bride Church asks of her Spouse (cf. Cant. 1:2) so that the Father and Son may thus be revealed to her (cf. 1 Cor. 2:10).[81] The Spirit is revelation of Father and Son inseparably, the one who reveals them and is revealed by the Son,[82] as well as the one who is the remission of sins. He is the "very sweet kiss, the *osculum suavissimum* with which God seals his convenant of love with the creature."[83]

It must be further noted that the image of the kiss is very much in line with that of the breath: for there is no kiss without breathing. In breathing

---

[78]St. Fulgentius, *De fide ad Petrum*, cap. XI, §52: ML 65, 696. Cf. Eph. 6:17 (the sword of the Spirit is the word: it is by and in the Spirit that the Risen One speaks to us) and also the texts cited in note 56 of this chapter.

[79]Cf. DS 1692 and 1715 (DB 905 and 925) where the Church affirms that it is by the imposition of sacramental penance that there is always realized, in every celebration of the sacrament of penance, the retention of sins (Jn. 20:23).

[80]St. Bernard, *sermones in Cant.*, VIII. 2, ML 183, 811: imperturbabilis pax, indivisibilis unitas.

[81]*Ibid.*, VIII. 5, col. 812: "at vero (Filius) dans Spiritum per quem revelat, etiam ipsum revelat; dando revelat, et revelando dat"; and col. 813.

[82]*Ibid.*, col. 814; and the text cited in the preceding note.

[83]Scheeben, *op. cit.*, pp. 110, 58, 59.

man inhales the universe, makes it his own, assimilates and integrates it in himself in order to give himself afterwards, thus enriched, to human persons in the exhalation of his breath of human love. So God in knowing himself as lovable, unites himself to himself by a loving breath which is his Spirit, the kiss by which the Father and the Son embrace the world in their embrace of one another.

In an age so preoccupied with the "language of faith" and its renewal, it would not be without value to show through a reflective process at once rational and affective (and therefore fully human) that Jesus in calling the Third Person Breath and Holy Spirit, not only chose an expression intelligible to all men of good will of all future times but even may have selected the most intelligible expression of all. In fact, this expression is not indissolubly tied to a definite cultural context. Instead it pertains inseparably to a symbolic link between two universally human phenomena: breathing and intersubjective love.

We could say with Dieringer and Scheeben:

> The speculation of the Church should start with the conviction that the language of Revelation is analogically the most correct in this matter and what it attests is objectively much more perfect than the words in question can express.[84]

And Scheeben adds, not without reason:

> For although they are only analogous, their analogy [of the names that the Church applies to the divine persons] is so suggestive, so cogent, and so striking, that an understanding of them conveys to us a clear and most resplendent notion of the sublime mystery. Truly we must marvel at the infinite wisdom of those persons who willed to reveal themselves to us through the medium of such terms.[85]

This last thought is particularly remarkable: if the Man Jesus chose the name Holy Spirit to designate the Third Person, his human intelligence and will thus perceived, saw and embraced a plan not only of the Word who assumed them, but also of the Father and of their Spirit. The Man Jesus in

---

[84]F.-X. Dieringer, *Lehrbuch der Katholischen Dogmatik*. Mainz, 1865, p. 192. For Dieringer, the fact that these imaged expressions do not equal their object is surely correct, but this in no way authorizes us to put in their place other still more feeble expressions. Scheeben cites him partially (*op cit.,* p. 114). Cf. DS 3882, 3886.

[85]Scheeben, *op. cit.*, p. 114. Cf. DS 3016 (DB 1796). On the whole question of the name of the Holy Spirit, one can also consult Petau (*Dogmata Theologica,* v. III, *de Trinitate,* VII, XII, 7. Paris, 1865, p. 359—where by an analysis of Greek semantics, the author shows the affective connotations of the term *pneuma*—and *passim*); St. Basil, *Traité du Saint Esprit, SC* 17. Paris, 1947, §109 *b, c* (the Spirit spiritualizes the soul); and our work *Christ for the World*. Chicago, 1976, ch. XV: the Eucharistic Heart of Jesus: giver of the other Paraclete, the Spirit of Truth.

virtue of his infused knowledge and of his knowledge drawn from the beatific vision, knew better than anyone else the expressions and the terminology that would be the most adequate vehicle of his Revelation for all centuries to come; but this very knowledge and the decision that accompanied it were precisely "infused" in him, a salvific gift of the Father and of the Spirit as well as of the Word to his holy humanity.

We think that Scheeben's original reflection helps us recognize an undeniable fact: the divine persons in revealing themselves to us in and by means of human language, have chosen those human names by means of which they wish to be known by us. These names are not a matter of indifference to them and so cannot be received and treated by us with indifference. The Spirit wants us to scrutinize the meaning of the name which he gives himself and invites us to give him, through the Man Jesus.

In the light of these observations we should now proceed to study the other title given to the Third Person by Jesus: Paraclete.

2. *The Third Person is named "another Paraclete," "the Spirit of Truth" (Jn. 14:16, 17)*

Today we recognize more and more that the expression Paraclete, so exclusively Johannine[86] in the New Testament, does not principally signify "Consoler." But what does it mean?

Defender, according to the meaning generally admitted by modern exegetes? At first glance it is far from obvious why a defender would have "to teach all," to "recall" what another has said, to "announce" things to come, and to glorify someone.... We note the curiously aggressive complexion that the activity of "defender"[87] takes in Jn. 16:8-11.

Several recent studies help us better understand the meaning of this mysterious Johannine term, in connection with the problematics proper to the Qumran[88] milieus and especially in the context of the pneumatology of the Acts of the Apostles and of the Synoptic Gospels.[89]

It seems that Jesus himself[90] and then St. John utilized a pre-Christian title while giving it a partially new meaning, in order to designate the mission of the Son and that of the Spirit.

---

[86]Jn. 14:16, 26; 15:26; 16:7-13; 1 Jn. 2:1.

[87]Cf. H.-M. Dion, O.P., "L'origine du titre de Paraclet," *Sc. Eccl.* 17 (1965), 143.

[88]Cf. O. Betz, *Der Paraklet*. Leiden-Köln, Brill, 1963; R. E. Brown, S.S., "The Paraclete in the Fourth Gospel," *NTS* 13 (1967) 113-132; F. M. Braun, O.P., *Jean le Théologien,* v. III/2, ch. IV. Paris, 1972.

[89]M. Miguéns, O.F.M., *El Paràclito,* Jerusalem, 1963; T. Preiss, *La justification dans la pensée johannique,* Hommage et reconnaissance (mélanges Barth). Delachaux et Niestlé, Neuchâtel, 1946, pp. 100-118.

[90]We share the opinion of several exegetes: "the very term *Parakletos* could go back to Jesus, it is connected to the Jewish notion of advocate," writes Spicq (*Agape.* Paris, 1959, v. III, p. 185) citing H. Behm, *parakletos,* Kittel, *Theol. Wörteb.,* V, 812 and different rabbinic texts which go

From Yahweh to God the Father

The Qumran circle had elaborated a doctrine of intercessors. Israel from time immemorial was characterized by the imagery and experience of the trial procedure. (Ethiopian) Henoch and the book of Jubilees place high value on the pleading of superhuman defenders and accusers before the throne of God (witnesses both for prosecution and for defense). Long before this Zec. 3:1ff. presented the scene of Joshua and Satan before the Angel of Yahweh. But the literature proper to the Qumran sect offers us a more systematic dualism: all humanity falls under the sway either of Michael or of Belial; they act on men by their spirits, whether of truth, i.e., fidelity to the divine law, or of error. The spirit of truth is identified with the spirit of holiness. The center of interest is moved from the heavenly tribunal toward the proceedings conducted on earth by the Master of Justice and his community against the people of Belial in giving, against them, witness to divine truth.[91]

A similar ethical dualism may be found in the "Johannine corpus," especially in the first epistle but also in the gospel. Juridical imagery also plays an important role there. This Gospel shows us Jesus conducting on earth a great trial procedure in behalf of the truth against the world (3:19; 5:22ff; 18:37b); when he is glorified he becomes our heavenly intercessor, our Paraclete (1 Jn. 2:1); by mounting the cross and ascending to heaven he has cast down the Accuser (*kategoros*, Apoc. 12:10; cf. Jn. 12:31) who day and night accused our brethren before God; thence comes the supreme assault launched here below by the prince of this world who now continues his function of *kategoros* only on earth. But thanks to the Spirit of Truth, to the earthly Paraclete placed in them by their heavenly Paraclete, the disciples valiantly continue the contest formerly engaged in by Him and "convince the world of justice" by "witnessing" to the divine Truth brought by Jesus (Jn. 15:26ff; 16:8-11). The schema of opposition between "paraclete" and "accuser" is thus an essential aspect of the Johannine theology of the Paraclete and of his ethical dualism.

back at least to the second century (Pirqé Abot). H.-M. Dion (*op. cit.*, p. 149) appears to think that we are dealing with an initiative of St. John. If this is in fact the case, John would then be synthesizing by means of this title the teaching of Jesus about the Holy Spirit, or at least several of its aspects. The choice of this title would still be divinely inspired, and this would be a divinely chosen name. The Paraclete would in any event have inspired the choice of the name that synthesizes the very diverse aspects of his mission, just as he inspired the Johannine choice of the name *Logos*.

[91]Dion, *op. cit.*, 144-145 (citing the instruction on the two spirits, *1QS* III-13 to IV-26). On the Spirit of Truth, see Brown, *op. cit.*, 123, where the author sums up the elements of the Johannine image of the Paraclete which were already visible in late, inter-testamentary Judaism. It is notably the doctrine of the personal angelic spirits guiding the elect faced with the forces of evil and teaching and leading men on toward the truth. But he also emphasizes that the influence of the Qumran literature on John does not seem to have been direct. For Brown, John's conception of the Paraclete starts from Jesus. He suggests that John could have availed himself of Jewish angelology to elaborate his pneumatology, just as the Christology of

This dualist theme, common to Qumran and to Johannine theology, thanks to an identification of the spirit of truth with the Holy Spirit, permitted an integration in one and the same great vision, of the Christian beliefs in the eviction of Satan by Christ, in the heavenly intercession of Christ, in the assistance given by the Holy Spirit to the witnesses of the faith before the tribunals of earth (Mt. 10:19-20 and parall.; Acts 4:8, 31; 5:32 etc.) and finally in the sending of the Holy Spirit by Christ (Lk. 24:49; Acts 2:33).[92]

In presenting the Holy Spirit as another Paraclete, Jesus shows him to us as the one who, with and through his disciples, renders witness to him on earth before the tribunals (Jn. 15:26-27); this Paraclete is the Spirit of Truth in a triple sense: he arouses fidelity,[93] true witness on behalf of Jesus (in opposition to false witnesses: Dt. 19:18; Prov. 14:5; Mk. 14:55-59; etc.) and finally he is the holy Breath sent by the Truth that is Jesus.[94] By this Paraclete, by this Spirit of Truth (Jn. 14:16-18) the first Paraclete, Jesus himself, our heavenly advocate (1 Jn. 2:1) will in some way return to earth as a consoler who does not leave his own orphans (Jn. 14:16-18).[95]

The second Paraclete through this testimony "will convince the world, confound it in the matter of sin and justice and judgment" (Jn. 16:8-11), that is, by his reproaches and his accusations he will reduce it to silence without argument against Christ and without means of escape. The inspired author of the book of Wisdom had already shown us how "the Omnipotent confounds the foolish" (1:3-8; 2:11; 4:20). The effect of this action of the

Heb. and Col. incorporated some prerogatives that Judaism attributed to the angels. Brown and Dion (*op. cit.*, 147-149) refute the affirmations or tendencies of Betz who identifies the Spirit with an angel, namely Michael. And here we are back to the problems that St. Basil and St. Ambrose confronted in the age of the *pneumatomachoi* (adversaries of the Spirit) and of semi-Arianism!

[92]Cf. Dion, *op. cit.*, 145 and 148. We think however that over against men and on earth, the devil has not been deprived of his functions of accuser (cf. Apoc. 12:12-13). The great synthetic vision appears to be, even before being St. John's, that of Jesus himself. It is, it seems to us, from Jesus that John received it. In this vision, the continuity of the accusing functions of the devil, apparently denied by Dion (*op. cit.*, 145: "hereafter deprived of his functions of *kategor*"), had nonetheless been well grasped by St. Irenaeus: "...in omnem terram mittens de coelis Paracletum, ubi et diabolum, tanquam fulgur, projectum ait Dominus. Quapropter necessarius nobis est ros Dei, ut non comburamus, neque infructuosi efficiamur, et *ubi accusatorem habemus, illic habeamus et Paracletum*" (*Adv. Haer.* III, 17. 3; MG 7, 930).

[93]Cf. the note of the Jerusalem Bible on 1 Jn. 3:19: "in the Old Testament, truth designated rectitude of moral life, in accord with the divine will (faithfulness to God). This sense is taken up again in St. John."

[94]Cf. R. E. Brown, *art. cit.*, p. 127. On the Spirit of Truth, see also our book on *Christ for the World*, ch. XV; note 23 of this ch. XV; and the work of Dom Diepen, O.S.B., in the collective work *Cor Jesu*, v. I, pp. 185-186. Rome, 1959: the visible mission of the Spirit carries a nuance of doctrinal charity.

[95]Cf. R. E. Brown, *art. cit.*, pp. 118, 131 (note 4) and 128. In spite of what Dion, among others, says (*op. cit.*, 143) the meaning "consoler," although secondary, is not inexact.

Paraclete is not necessarily an interior conviction of the accused but the fact that they remain without response and without excuse (Jn. 15:22), incapable of resisting and of contradicting (Lk. 21:15; Acts 4:13; 5:33; 6:10). Far from being able to convict Christ of sin (Jn. 8:46), it is these whom the Paraclete will convict of the sin of unbelief (Jn. 16:9).[96] Just like Jesus, during his ministry (Jn. 7:7), the Paraclete bears witness against the hatred of the world and shows that the world was wrong[97] in its trial against Jesus (its prince is already condemned) and thus "justifies" Christ (cf. 1 Tm. 3:16). In this trial the Spirit Paraclete is the earthly witness of Jesus, who is his own heavenly witness.[98] The bond between the two aspects of the trial appears with perfect clarity in the account of the death of Stephen: at the very moment that Stephen is condemned by the leaders of Israel, he sees the Son of Man, the judge of the end of time, standing at the right hand of God. He does not see him seated, in the attitude of the sovereign who judges and rules, but standing in the posture of a witness who intercedes before God in behalf of his witness and justifies him at the same moment that he is condemned by the "justice" of men: faith in Christ the Paraclete and in the Spirit Paraclete underlies the account (Acts 7:51-57).[99]

The activity of the Paraclete operating through the apostles of Christ, aimed at convicting and confounding the world in respect to sin and justice and judgment, not only results in leaving those who continue to resist him without reply and without excuse, but also is efficacious in converting a number of enemies of Christ into disciples. This twofold datum is supported by an attentive study of the first seven chapters of the Acts of the Apostles, compared with Jn. 16:8-11; and especially by an examination of the two discourses of Peter to the Jewish people (Acts 2:36-38; 3:12-19). Peter accuses his hearers of having crucified Christ, and, pierced to the heart, about three thousand of them submit themselves to Baptism (Acts 2:41; cf. 4:4) while the members of the Sanhedrin continue to resist the Spirit (Acts 7:51). It is not then to those who are already disciples that the Paraclete is sent to convince them, but first and foremost, to the non-Christians so that they may become disciples of Christ (Jn. 16:8-11).[100]

After these historical preambles and these clarifications of the Johannine use of the word Paraclete, we can now attempt to determine its meaning in the present state of theological and exegetical research.

---

[96]Such is the sense of the verb *elegchein* of Jn. 16:8—and this is well analyzed by Miguéns, *op. cit.*, pp. 176ff.

[97]Cf. Brown, *art. cit.*, p. 127.

[98]Here we are utilizing T. Preiss (a Protestant): "Le temoignage intérieur du Saint-Esprit," *cahier théologique de l'actualité protestante,* n. 13. Neuchâtel, 1946, ch. 2 and 3.

[99]Ibid.

[100]Against Berrouard, Brown, *art. cit.*, p. 132, note 1, and I. de La Potterie, *La vie selon l'Esprit.* Paris, 1965, pp. 101-105.

The word is Greek. In Greek it designates a person, not a thing: an advocate, more precisely the counsel for the prosecution, the one who initiates and conducts the proceedings (cf. Jn. 16:8-11). The word comes from *parakaleo*: to call before oneself (as advocate comes from *advocare*: to call to oneself).[101]

Hebrew had no special term to designate a lawyer, for this institution did not exist in Jewish legal process.[102] The defending witness partly fulfilled the role of advocate. But the Old Testament often shows us Yahweh acting in the tribunals on behalf of innocent people unjustly accused, sometimes as witness, sometimes as judge, sometimes as protector, comforter, avenger; it portrays him (in the position of defending witness) on the right of the accused in order to save him from his judges (Ps. 35; 109; Sir. 51:7; Ps. 9-10; cf. 2 Tm. 4:16-17).[103] Thus the Old Testament contains precedent for the concept of a divine paraclete, both God and intercessor, as is the case with the two Paracletes that the Johannine literature offers us.

In this "corpus" the Paraclete promised by Jesus and given by him is at the same time the witness for the defense in the trial of Jesus by the world, his spokesman and advocate; as well as the consoler, master, guide and supporting defendant of his disciples.[104] The Paraclete (masculine) is explicitly identified by Jesus with the Breath of the Truth (neuter) in Jn. 14:16.

The diverse aspects of the Mission of the Paraclete do not at first sight appear to be unified, as we already remarked.[105] Their real unity becomes clear when we recall that the Paraclete is sent by Jesus to his disciples for the sake of the evangelization of the world. It is then no longer surprising that this Witness teaches, guides and consoles by revealing the success that is to come in the work of evangelization.[106]

One might still object that not one of the texts of St. John's gospel relating to the Spirit Paraclete presents him as an intercessor for sinners

---

[101]Cf. J. Isaac, *op. cit.*, pp. 186-187; *Th WB* (Kittel), v. V (1954) pp. 798-812, art. "Parakletos" by Behm.

[102]R. de Vaux, O.P., *Les institutions de l'Ancien Testament*. Paris, 1958, v. I, p. 240; Miguéns, *op. cit.*, 242ff.

[103]*Ibid.*, 245-258.

[104]Cf. R. E. Brown, *art. cit.*, p. 118: "the concept of the Paraclete, like love, is a many-splendoured thing"...

[105]Cf. note 87 of this chapter.

[106]Cf. Jn. 16:13; Miguéns (*op. cit.*, 206-212) sees here in the light of the Apocalypse (17-19) the fall of the Roman Empire which follows the fall of Judaism (teaching of the Synoptics). It is difficult to believe that these events are here in view, at least the first (cf. Jn. 16:12; 6:60). Doubtless there is here an integration of a datum of angelology and of Jewish apocalyptic: often, in the apocalypses, angels reveal the meaning of a vision and guide toward the truth; the same verb is used for this purpose in the apocalypses and here (Jn. 16:13-14) by the Gospel: *anangellein*. Cf. I. de La Potterie, S.J., *La vie selon l'Esprit*. Paris, 1965, pp. 95-96.

the way the first epistle shows us Jesus Christ the Just as the advocate-paraclete for sinners before the Father (1 Jn. 2:1). This is undeniably true. But nothing in the Johannine presentation of the Spirit Paraclete opposes such an interpretation. And at the time St. John was editing his gospel, he found this paraclete concept already present under another form in St. Paul's Epistle to the Romans (8:26-27) with all the reality of the Paraclete except the name: "we do not know how to pray as we ought; but the Spirit himself intercedes for us with sighs too deep for words, and He who searches the hearts of men knows what is the desire of the Spirit and that his intercession for the saints is according to the mind of God" (cf. Rom. 8:26-27).

We should note in passing that the doctrine of the intercession of the two Paracletes, Jesus and the Spirit, supposes the doctrine of angelic paracletes as the historical condition of its appearance.[107] Pre-Christian Judaism, we may repeat, prepared by its Angelology, the New Testament Revelation of the Spirit, creator of the angels and intercessor for men in whom he inspires the desire to pray. This is the grain of truth in the error of the "Macedonians" (to whom we will return in ch. II), an error that is apparently being renewed today in certain sectors of Protestantism. In revealing the distinct personality of the Paraclete in the discourse at the Last Supper, Jesus did not only reveal that he was distinct from the Father and from himself. The first Paraclete also revealed that the second Paraclete, endowed with universal knowledge and capable of teaching everything and of leading toward the truth in its entirety (Jn. 14:26; 16:13), was and is a person, not created and angelic but divine and uncreated. More than once Jesus spoke of the angels (e.g. Jn. 1:15 and Mt. 18:10) but he never attributed to them a mission and powers like those he gave to the Spirit Paraclete (Jn. 16:13-14). It would be an error of exegesis to interpret these

---

[107]This is the element of truth contained in the opinion of Betz analyzed by Dion and Brown, *art. cit.*, pp. 125-126. If Brown is right (cf. note 91 of this chapter) in thinking that the Christology of the New Testament has incorporated some data of Jewish angelology, and that John's Christology conditions his doctrine of the Paraclete, then we can conclude that the pneumatology of the Paraclete is conditioned by the post-exilic development of an intercessory angelology that was itself anterior to the exile (cf. Brown, *art. cit.*, p. 121: "we may trace to early pre-exilic times the concept of the angels or 'sons of God' [demoted pagan gods] as participants in the heavenly court which decided the fate of the world"). We could then think that St. Gregory of Nyssa had been much more on target than he himself suspected when he said that polytheism prepared for the Trinitarian revelation in the plan of Providence. In fact polytheism prepared for the revelation of the Angels, which in its turn prepared for the revelation of the Spirit as distinct from them, in fact, their Creator—and also distinct from the other divine Persons. To condition historically and to prepare is not the same as to cause efficaciously: one cannot reduce the Third Person, the Holy Spirit, to the "gods" and to the angels through whom he has prepared his revelation.

clear texts in the light of those that are more obscure.[108] We should follow the inverse procedure and explain obscure texts in the light of those that are clear.

We can thus say that Jesus, during the discourse at the Last Supper, in revealing the other Paraclete, the Spirit of Truth, the Holy Spirit, had a twofold end in view: to reveal him as an "I" distinct from his own "I," and to reveal him as a spirit distinct from angelic spirits, as a divine Third One along with his Father and with himself. He revealed him in the framework of an ecclesiological discourse,[109] as being indissolubly his Witness and Advocate of the Church which would always be persecuted on earth by Satan who had fallen as lightning from heaven (Lk. 10:18) and cast upon the earth (Apoc. 12:9), where he trembles with rage since he knows that his days are numbered (Apoc. 12:12). Thus Jesus made the Church understand that the eloquence and wisdom (Lk. 21:15), the Spirit of the Father (Mt. 10:20) whom he had promised her for the time of persecution, was distinct from every created gift, from every created person and from the Father himself.

Faced with the richness and complexity of the title given by Jesus to this Spirit of *our* Father (Mt. 10:20), we should imitate the example given by Philo, by the Tannaim[110] in the second century, by St. Jerome and first of all by Jesus[111] himself: instead of trying to translate *parakletos* by another word, it is better to transliterate it: Paraclete, and explain it. This transliteration is still the least harmful solution: it preserves the unique character of the title without unduly emphasizing some aspects of its meaning to the detriment of others.[112]

---

[108]Thus for example the comparison of Acts 8:26 with verses 29 and 39 of the same chapter does not permit us to attempt a reduction of the Holy Spirit to the angelic category: see the note of the Jerusalem Bible on Gn. 16:7. Even if we admit that "the angel of the Lord" was a creature, we can still understand the account in Acts in this way: the divine Spirit made use of an angel to manifest himself initially to Philip.

[109]See Miguéns, *op. cit.*, ch. II, pp. 45-104.

[110]Philo uses the word "paraclete" as an adjective (*De mundi opif.* 23; *De Josepho*, 234; *In Flaccum*, 13); on the use of the word in the Tannaim, see Betz, *op. cit.*, pp. 36-116 and Dion, *art. cit.*, 145.

[111]See on this point note 90 of the present chapter. It is not at all unthinkable or impossible that long before the Tannaim Jesus had used a Hebrew transliteration of the Greek word *parakletos*: especially since there are reasons for believing that Jesus was bilingual, as were the apostles (cf. L. Cerfaux, *La voix vivante de l'Evangile*. Paris, 1956, p. 27). In this regard it is interesting to note that Franz Delitzsch, in his famous Hebrew New Testament, himself resorted to transliteration for retranslating into Hebrew the Greek word *parakletos*, while he rendered the "paraclete" of 1 Jn. 2:1 by "melitz," a Hebrew term used in Job 33:23 (cf. Brown, *art. cit.*, p. 116, note 1). But this book of Job (16:19; 19:25-27), precisely describes a heavenly defender and witness of Job the just man, who constitutes an antecedent for the role of the Spirit Paraclete with regard to Jesus: cf. Brown, *art. cit.*, p. 122.

[112]Cf. R. E. Brown, *art. cit.*, p. 119.

From Yahweh to God the Father

Appendix I: *The Kerygmatic proclamation of the Three, constitutive of the primitive community of Jerusalem*

Some authors, notably in contemporary Protestantism, give us the impression that the Trinitarian dogma is a Johannine creation quite posterior to the primitive kerygma.

This view lacks objectivity.

On the one hand, the Anglican exegete Swete[113] has shown that for Paul the Spirit is truly personal and distinct from the Father and from the Son. Swete's demonstration was reargued by C. Duquoq, O.P.[114]

On the other hand it is by no means proven that Mt. 28:18-20 does not give us the *ipsissima verba Jesu*. Surely, without denying a revealed datum, it is possible to see here simply (cf. however DS 3567 and 3999) an interpretation inspired by the Holy Spirit and thus infallible, of the intention of Jesus given by the leaders of the primitive community. But the formula "make disciples of all nations, baptizing them in the name of the Father and of the Son and of the Holy Spirit" offers no more than a vigorous synthesis of different teachings of the pre-Easter Jesus, as reported by the Synoptics, about his intention to establish a universal Church, his institution of Baptism and his revelation of himself, the Father and the Spirit. We do not find a single argument that would compel us to believe that this formula is not from Jesus himself. If some of the Eleven were still doubting (Mt. 28:17) a short while before hearing from the mouth of Jesus the command of universal evangelization and baptism, nothing can prevent our thinking that they could momentarily have forgotten or simply failed to consider a desire of Christ which came as a shock to their mentality. For the Holy Spirit had not yet descended on them and they still were dreaming of a temporal restoration of the Davidic kingdom (Acts 1:6). There was still need for a post-pentecostal action of the Spirit of Jesus to recall to the disciples all that Jesus had said to them not only before but even after his Pasch (Jn. 14:26; cf. 2:22: it is probable that only after Pentecost did the disciples recall the pre-Paschal saying of Jesus about the temple of his body, and not immediately after the Resurrection; cf. Acts 1:6). In Acts 10:47 we see the Spirit recalling to Peter the substance of Mt. 28:19.

Finally, if the book of Acts in general is the Gospel of the Holy Spirit distinct from the Father and the Son, this holds true particularly for its first section, which reports the faith and worship of the Jerusalem community: 1-12. Although the personal character of the Holy Spirit is not stressed very much in the first discourse of St. Peter to the Jewish people,

---

[113]*The Holy Spirit in the N.T.* London, 1910, pp. 283-294.

[114]"Le dessein salvifique et la révélation de la Trinité en saint Paul" (*Lumière et Vie*, 29, 1956, pp. 67-94).

nevertheless his distinction from the Father and the Son is already clear. Jesus is presented as being at the same time the receiver, the transmitter and the donor of the Holy Spirit (Acts 2:33 Gr. compared with 2:17 Gr.: Jesus is the Lord who gives the Spirit who is received from the Father and thus is distinct from both). Again Baptism in the name of Jesus (cf. Acts 2:38 and the note of the Jerusalem Bible; 19:2-5) is at once reception of the Spirit, of the gift of the Spirit and consecration to the Spirit, (cf. Mt. 28:19: *eis to onoma* and not *en to onomati*[115]), to a Spirit distinct from Jesus and at the same time his own.

What is more, the kerygma could not but have been Trinitarian, since it was essentially ordered to a Trinitarian baptism. But this Trinitarian character could have been relatively discreet at the outset of the kerygmatic heralding at the heart of a monotheistic Jewish world, and even to some degree more implicit than explicit. It was in proclaiming Christ crucified and risen that the Apostles proclaimed God, the Father of Jesus and the Spirit, the Breath poured out by the Risen One: the Trinitarian proclamation is made in the heart of a Paschal proclamation (a fact that should have "paradigmatic" and suggestive bearing on our own kerygmatic proclamation of the Trinity.)

Further, the kerygma is not a catechesis: the initial proclamation of the Trinitarian mystery did not claim to constitute a complete exposition of it and one that would suffice for leading an integrally Christian life, but only one sufficient to lead to the inauguration of this life in baptism.

The baptismal polarization of the Trinitarian kerygma helps us understand the presentation of the Holy Spirit as a gift of Christ (Acts 2:33; 10:45). For the first Christians, to be baptized is precisely to receive the Holy Spirit who is the Spirit-of-the-risen-Christ and it is also to receive him from Jesus. But it is to receive him from Christ after this same Spirit has led the neophyte to Christ. The Spirit leads to Christ, it is he who sends the Apostles to the non-Christians in order, afterwards, to give himself to them by Christ acting through his envoys. For the author of Acts there is a veritable Trinitarian-ecclesial cycle (which corresponds perfectly to Pauline thought; Paul was the teacher of Luke): a cycle that runs from the Spirit of the Father and the Lord Jesus to the Spirit himself by way of the Lord Jesus and his envoys.

It is precisely this cycle that the post-baptismal and post-kerygmatic catechesis will set out to study more deeply. We should not be surprised not to find this catechesis in Acts, since the aim of Luke, the author of Acts, was not to give us the content of what the Apostles taught already baptized Christians about the Father, the Son and the Spirit (cf. Acts 2:42); it was

---

[115]*A Catholic Commentary of the Holy Scriptures*. London, 1953, p. 904.

simply to give us the kerygma directed to the non-baptized who were in process of being conducted toward Baptism.

In contrast Paul, and especially John, give us their Trinitarian catecheses. Their example shows us well enough that it is still possible, when attempting to give a more profound Trinitarian teaching to already initiated Christians, to begin from the Paschal mystery: we need only think of the discourse at the Last Supper, of Romans 8, of 1 Corinthians 2.

But even such catecheses still do not lead in the New Testament to "prayers addressed to the Holy Spirit as to the Father and to the Son," a fact stressed and analyzed by J. Lebreton.[116] However such a prayer is logically postulated by the belief in the distinct personality of the Spirit already professed by the Church of Jerusalem, though only in an inchoative fashion. The kerygma already contains the cult of the Spirit in germ.

The reason for this is simple: the kerygma of the primitive Church, as O. Cullmann has observed, is substantially identical with the kerygma of Jesus or, to be more precise, this kerygma takes into account the catecheses of Jesus after the Supper, when, as we have seen, he revealed more clearly the distinct personality of the Spirit.

Would Cullmann admit this last point? We are not entirely sure. Although he retains Trinitarian dogma at least theoretically, he believes that the confession of Trinitarian structure is posterior to the confession of Christological structure and results from an evolution which has somewhat betrayed the sense of the primitive faith.

This certainly is not meant to imply that belief in the Father and in the Spirit was not as ancient as faith in Christ. But for the very first Christians faith in the former would have been in function of this latter faith: they believed in the Father and in the Spirit because of the Son and in relation to him, in the Father as the one who raised up Christ, in the Spirit as the Gift that Christ bestows at Baptism. To relegate Christ to second place in a Trinitarian confession would represent a displacement from the center of gravity in the object of faith, who is Christ. For Cullmann, to place the Father before Christ would be "to radically misconstrue the essence of Christianity."[117] And he adds, "Because he believes in Christ Kurios, the believer of the first century believes in God and in the Holy Spirit" (*Ibid.*, p. 42).

Yes, we would reply with Camelot, in the sense that it is in Christ that the mystery of God is revealed to the first Christians. But their faith in Christ rests on the witness of the Father (Mt. 3:17; 17:5; Jn. 5:31ff.) and is inseparable from their faith in the Father. These first Christians believed in the God of Abraham, Isaac and Jacob, who is also the God of Jesus before

---

[116]J. Lebreton, *Origines du dogme de la Trinité.* Paris, 1919, v. I, p. 351.
[117]O. Cullmann, *Les Premières confessions de foi chrétiennes.* Paris, 1943, p. 41.

believing in Jesus. They were Jewish converts. P. Benoît, from whom we have drawn in summarizing the ideas of O. Cullmann, replies, "We should rather say just the opposite: it is because he believes in the Father who raised Jesus...that the Christian believes in Jesus Kurios."[118]

We wonder whether there is not an excessive Christocentrism of Lutheran inspiration that partially keeps O. Cullmann from seeing more clearly that Christ, eternal Son, *eternally* receives his Divine Nature from the Father, and whether there is not some connection between his belittling of the confession of Trinitarian faith and of the Trinitarian kerygma of the first Christians (Acts 2:33), and a certain modalist tendency in his Christology, a functional Christology that lacks a healthy balance. In our opinion Cullmann has partially transposed into modern terms some unfortunate aspects of Luther's Trinitarian problematics, which we will examine later. That Christ is the center and Mediator does not prevent, but even somehow requires, that the Father be first in a universal way, at the very heart of the deity of which he is *fons et origo*, and the Word is himself *ad Patrem*.

Schillebeeckx rightly remarks, "In the apostolic kerygma, the mystery of Christ is seen fundamentally as arising from the mystery of God who embraces all things.... The primitive apostolic theme is this: on the basis of the resurrection, the Father gives the plenitude of the Spirit to Christ, who in turn sends the Spirit to the whole Church" (an allusion to Acts 2:33). We understand then how Schillebeeckx concludes by saying, "Christ reveals the Trinity as God-of-salvation."[119] He thus rejects (*ibid.*, 182) Cullmann's thesis according to which the transition of Christological symbols to Trinitarian symbols amounts to a distortion of authentic Christianity. Camelot says still more clearly, "to leave the Trinitarian formulas in the background is to risk profound distortion in construing the essence of Christianity" (*Op. cit.*, 333).

V. THE DIVINE AND REDEMPTIVE THREE: FATHER, SON AND SPIRIT IN THE NEW TESTAMENT

We can sum up the evolution of the New Testament in what concerns the revelation of the divine Trinity in this way: Jesus, initially presented as the Son of Man, then as Son of God, is finally called the Son. The one who sends him is first called God, then God the Father, then the Father. The Holy Spirit who initially descends on Jesus, is then shown as given and sent by Jesus, and as distinct from both the Father and the Son. We thus come to the

---

[118]P. Benoît, *Exégèse et Théologie*. Paris, 1961, v. II, pp. 207-209; Camelot, *Rech. Sc. Rel.*, 39, 1952, 333.

[119]E. Schillebeeckx, O.P., *Révélation et Théologie*. Brussels, 1965, p. 183.

formula of Mt. 28:19: "make disciples of all nations, baptizing them in the name of the Father and of the Son and of the Holy Spirit."[120]

This text is a perfect example, and even the example par excellence, of the presentation of the Father, the Son and the Spirit as a divine plurality. The emergence of the Son and of the Spirit as heavenly figures within the divine sphere, in the very heart of the God of the Old Testament, means that we have now reached a new conception of Yahweh, who is henceforth viewed in relation to his Son and his Spirit.

The effort of the New Testament writers consists especially in this: to associate the Son and the Spirit with God the Father in a transcendent relationship which maintains their distinction from him and at the same time from the created universe, the world of angels and men. What is evident in the New Testament is not primarily the multiple and splendid data about the Son and the Spirit considered individually but, far more prominently, their association with the Father in the numerous texts we call Trinitarian.

In passing it should be noted that this adjective (Trinitarian) is already an anticipation: only from the end of the second century are the Father and Son and Spirit numbered, and not till the third century does the Trinity become a theme that is considered in itself.

We must then acknowledge that there exists a difference of mentality between the New Testament and us. From our very infancy we think of the Three who are God, we think of the Trinity. But for the authors of the New Testament, though this assertion should be nuanced a bit (cf. 1 Jn. 5:20), the word God evokes not the Three, but the Father.

Yet it is these very authors who are at the origin of this difference of mentality between them and us.

It is then in their writings that we must first seek the presence of the divine plurality and then of our salvific relation with it. For the New Testament presents the living God as a Savior God; hence the Divine Three will be a redemptive Three.

1. *The New Testament reveals to us the Divine Plurality of Father, Son and Spirit*

It is not always easy to determine with certainty whether a text is Trinitarian or not. And if it is Trinitarian, it is not always clear that it is a "divine Trinitarian" text.

Thus Acts 2:33, at the beginning of the evolution, is Trinitarian. But does it affirm a divine Trinity and a pre-existence of the Son? "Now raised to the heights by God's right hand (or to the right hand, according to another

---

[120] On the evolution of the New Testament vocabulary concerning the Father, the Son and the Spirit, see B. Lonergan, S.J., *De Verbo Incarnato*. Rome, 1964, pp. 28-29 and 49-50. In Matthew we rarely read "the Son" without qualification (11:27), but on the contrary this is very frequent in John.

translation) he has received from the Father the Holy Spirit, who was promised and has poured him out."

If we read this text in isolation from the immediate context (2:17 Gr.) and from other statements of the same book (Acts 2:21; 4:12)[121], there would doubtless be room for pause. But viewed in the total context of Acts, the text is Trinitarian and divinely Trinitarian. Even Mt. 28:19 does not explicitly affirm the perfect equality of the Three, although it strongly suggests it.

It will then be useful to conduct an inquiry[122] aimed at discovering the texts—numerous indeed—that reveal a tendency to associate the Father, the Son and the Spirit, or which speak of the Father as executing his salvific plan through the Son and the Spirit. Gradually one will be struck by a fundamental operational pattern among the writers of the New Testament: their spontaneous inclination to think of the Three when they turn toward God.

a) Paul: 1 Cor. 12: 4-6:

"There is a variety of gifts but always the same Spirit: there are all sorts of services to be done, but always to the same Lord; working in all sorts of different ways in different people, it is the same God who is working in all of them." Here we have a Trinitarian formula: the Spirit is the Holy Spirit, the Lord is Jesus, God is the Father (as almost always in Paul).

The whole of chapter eight of the epistle to the Romans is a veritable Pauline treatise on the Spirit, on Christ, and on God. If it is true that Trinitarian formulas do not abound here, it is the whole structure of the chapter that is so. We shall shortly return to other passages of Paul.

One could object to these observations that the prologues of the Pauline epistles reflect a "binitarian" rather than a "trinitarian" structure. All of them (except Colossians) contain an initial phrase which despite some insignificant variations remains identical: "grace and peace from God our Father and the Lord Jesus Christ" (Phlm. 3). The Holy Spirit is absent, it would seem.

Nevertheless we cannot disregard the response St. Augustine already made to this difficulty: grace and peace signify the Holy Spirit, without whom there is neither grace that frees from sins nor peace that reconciles with God.[123] A reply whose validity is supported by the letter to Titus that begins in the same way and then goes on to present the outpouring of the

---

[121]Cf. A. Feuillet, *Introduction à la Bible*. Tournai, 1959, v. II, pp. 823-824ff.

[122]On the pastoral level, similar inquiries conducted within Bible groups would be an excellent occasion for in-depth study of the Trinitarian mystery.

[123]St. Augustine, *Epistol. ad Romanos inch. expositio*, ML 35, 2095-2097. This commentary as O. du Roy (*L'intelligence de la foi en la Trinité selon saint Augustin*. Paris, 1966, p. 378) stresses, dates from 394-395; thus it could come from St. Ambrose (*De Spir. Sancto*, I, 12, 126) and through him

Spirit as a gift of God through Christ our Savior: "And this Spirit He poured out upon us richly through Jesus Christ our Savior" (Ti. 3:6). In the whole New Testament the Spirit is the gift of God the Father and that of Christ. We see from this that the desire for the grace and peace given by God our Father and Jesus Christ is equivalent to a desire for the outpouring of the Spirit.

b) The Synoptics clearly present us with a Trinity in connection with the Baptism and Transfiguration of Christ, as an inauguration of his public life and then as an inauguration of his Passion. Comparing Luke 9:34-35 with Luke 1:35 we see that the presence of the Spirit is suggested at the Transfiguration. Unlike the Matthean redaction (Mt. 11:25-27), the Lukan redaction of the hymn of jubilation (Lk 10:21ff.) has the same clearly Trinitarian import.

c) At first glance St. John offers us few Trinitarian groupings comparable to 2 Cor. 13:13 and Mt. 28:19. Nevertheless, the structure of his gospel considered in its ensemble is Trinitarian. In presenting the Word turned toward the Father, the prologue implicitly shows us the Holy Spirit, as Serge Boulgakof[124] has rightly observed. The whole first part of the Gospel up to chapter twelve inclusive, shows us at length the relations between Father and Son. And finally the discourse at the Last Supper gives us a very rich doctrine of the Paraclete. In particular, the rhythm of chapter fourteen is Trinitarian: Christ (vv. 1-7) goes to the Father (vv. 8-14) in order that the Spirit be given us (vv. 15-17). The same rhythm is again repeated in the same chapter: vv. 18-21, 22-24, 25-26.

In his epistle St. John several times offers us the Trinitarian ensemble: 1 Jn. 4:2; 5:6-9.

2. *The New Testament reveals this Trinity as redemptive*

Here we wish to analyze the different roles of the Three in the structuring and execution of the plan of our salvation, according to the authors of the New Testament.

from Didymus the Blind, *De Sp. Sancto*, 16 (MG 39, 1048). Didymus writes: "Spiritus sanctus dictus est gratia...Qui participans est gratiae Jesu Christi eamdem gratiam habet datam a Patre per Spiritum Sanctum...Cum qui Spiritus Sancti acceperit gratiam, habebit eam datam a Deo Patre et a Jesu Christo domino nostro" (ibid., col. 1049-1050). Nothing forbids us to think that already in St. Paul the word grace applies not only to a created gift but also and even especially to the uncreated Gift; and precisely in Rom. 5:5 the Holy Spirit is presented as a gift of God (cf. 1 Jn. 4:10). The exegesis then that St. Augustine gives of the prologues of the Pauline epistles involves nothing improbable. It is rooted in the commentaries of a Greek author, Didymus, whose Biblical knowledge of the New Testament is well known. See also A. Pujol, *Verbum Domini* 12 (1932), 38-40; 76-82.

[124]S. Boulgakof, *Le Paraclet*. Paris, 1946, p. 155: S. B. sees in the preposition *pros*, "toward," the hypostatic relation between the Father and the Son which is the Holy Spirit. His commentary on the presence of the H. Sp. in the prologue is very suggestive.

The first Christians thought of the Three in relation to their own salvation and in function of it, and not at first in order to ponder the intimate relations of the Father, the Son and the Holy Spirit among themselves. What initially interested them is what we today call the "economic and functional Trinity" as opposed to the "immanent and ontological Trinity," to use terminology that is, however, questionable.[125]

We think that already the New Testament writers would never separate these two points of view and that for them the ontological Trinity was already immanent in the functional Trinity. The Father, the Son and the Spirit can only act if they are. The New Testament amply shows us, as we will come to see better still, that they exist only in mutual immanence, reciprocity and "circuminsession," and that they are a "We" where the "I" exists only in relation to the "Thou" and vice versa. But it also shows us that in some sense we are immanent to this mutual immanence of the Father, the Son and the Spirit and that our human "we" is thus immanent in the transcendent "We."

We can see this in a particularly striking way in three Pauline texts, all three of which present the threefold plurality as a saving one:

a) Gal. 4:4-6:

> When the appointed time came, God sent his Son, born of a woman, born a subject of the Law, to redeem the subjects of the Law, and to enable us to be adopted as sons. The proof that you are sons is that God has sent the Spirit of his Son into our hearts: the Spirit that cries: 'Abba, Father.'

Paul does not consider first and foremost the intimate relations between the Three independently of us; but rather their action in our regard: the Father adopts, the Son redeems, the Spirit cries and prays in making us pray.

Likewise, as the twice employed Greek word *exapesteilen* (to send) shows, the Son and the Spirit could not be sent if they did not exist with the Father "before" any earthly mission, or better, if they did not exist eternally and independently of this historical activity. Even before our hearts receive him and thanks to him cry out "Abba Father," the Spirit is eternally the Spirit of the Son: the text already hints at and necessitates the *Filioque*[126] doctrine.

In short, the salvific mission of the Son and of the Spirit in respect to us presupposes their eternal relations with the Father and the eternal relation

---

[125]Cf. K. Rahner, S.J., MS v. II (1967), pp. 327-336. And F. Bourassa, S.J., "Sur le traité de la Trinité," *Gregorianum* 47 (1966), 234-285.

[126]M.-J. Lagrange, O.P., *Aux Galates*. Paris, 1950, pp. 102-104; P.-F. Ceuppens, O.P., *Theologia Biblica*, v. II, *De S. Trinitate*. Rome, 1938, p. 119.

of the Spirit with the Son. The Trinity of the New Testament is inseparably immanent to us and immanent to itself, functional and ontological.

b) *The prologue of the Epistle to the Ephesians* (1, 3-14):
This text, too long to be quoted here in full, describes for us the role of the Father (vv. 3-11), of Christ (vv. 5-13) and of the Holy Spirit (vv. 13-14) in the dispensation of our redemption. The Father "blesses, predestines, chooses, reveals, adopts and recapitulates." Christ redeems or rather "in him" we find the redemption prepared by the Spirit who is the pledge of our inheritance. It is especially the Father who is presented as active in our redemption. We can understand why this imposing text was chosen by Vatican II and underlies its ecclesiological vision.[127] All the actions of the Father—and it is this that we are concerned to note here—are relative to us,[128] the sons of adoption. But at the same time Christ is presupposed to these relative actions and God is the Father of Our Lord Jesus Christ (Eph. 1:3). Otherwise we could not be his sons. The functional Trinity is inseparably the eternal Trinity.

c) *Lastly we cite 2 Cor. 13:13:*[129]
"The grace of the Lord Jesus Christ and the love of God and the fellowship of the Holy Spirit be with you." Here Paul presents grace as a gift of Christ, the love shown us by the Father, and he suggests that fellowship among Christians comes from the Holy Spirit inasmuch as he is himself the fellowship between the Father and the Son. True, the suggestion is remote, for directly he writes only of the union of minds and hearts produced by the Holy Spirit. But does he not produce this inasmuch as he is the common breath of the Father and the Son, as is quite clearly taught in Gal. 4:6? How could Paul say that "God sent into our hearts the Spirit of his Son" if this Spirit were not also the Spirit of God, that is of the Father? And if he is at once the breath of the Father and that of the Son, is he not thereby their communion, or fellowship? This is how St. Augustine[130] was to understand it. And this better explains how St. Paul in the text we are studying (2 Cor. 13:13) could see in the Spirit the origin of ecclesial fellowship.

Here too, though less evidently and perhaps more questionably, the functional Trinity is always the ontological Trinity, immanent to itself in its transcendence with regard to us.

Because we cannot here study all the Pauline affirmations[131] of the

[127]*LG* 2-4; cf. M. Philipon, O.P., in the collective work *A Igreja do Vaticano II*. Petrópolis, (Brazil), 1965, pp. 367-369.
[128]With a logical, not a real relation, of course.
[129]Ceuppens, *op. cit.,* p. 114.
[130]St. Augustine, *De Trinitate,* VI, V, 7.
[131]See on this subject Ceuppens, *op. cit.,* and J. Lebreton, S.J., *Origines du Dogme de la Trinité.* Paris, 1919, v. I, pp. 389-400.

economic Trinity, we will content ourselves with a general reflection. Is not the identity between the functionally redemptive Trinity and the ontological Trinity all the more sure for the authors of the New Testament inasmuch as the salvation of man, in their view, consists in the loving and collective contemplation of the eternal relations between the Father and the Son in their common Spirit?

Is not this in fact brilliantly evident in the sacerdotal Prayer of Jesus, reported by St. John (17:22-26): "that they may behold the glory which you have given me, because you have loved me before the creation of the world...that the love with which you have loved me may be in them"? And does not St. Paul insinuate clearly enough that we have received the Spirit of God in order to scrutinize the secrets of divine depths that are given us (1 Cor. 2:10-12)?

A personalist psychology and a personalist philosophy such as are prevalent today, will help us better perceive this identity between economic Trinity and ontological Trinity, transcendent and immanent to human persons. Who in fact pretends to know a human person without investigating the personal and familial relations that constitute his history? Can a friend really be uninterested in the spouse, the parents and children of his friend? Could he without falsifying the very meaning of friendship and reducing it to sterility be interested only in the benefits he receives from his friend, independently of the other persons who people his mental horizon? How much less could a Christian investigate the benefits received from the Father, Son and Spirit and his relations with each of the Three, without at the same time yearning to contemplate their relations among themselves? Especially when he knows that he is about to find himself intimately present to these reciprocal relations transcendent to and immanent in his own person?

In short, in the eyes of the New Testament authors, the divine triad that manifests itself as redeemer does not for all that cease to be a triad and a divine one. The salvation it offers to man and to men consists precisely in the revelation of its own inner life.[132] An exclusively functional theology is not faithful to the New Testament.

From another angle some might object that the diversity of functions attributed to the Three by the authors of the New Testament is more

---

[132]St. Augustine, with an ingenious simplicity, had already expressed this identity between functional Trinity and immanent Trinity when he insisted that the reason for the temporal missions of the divine Persons is none other than the revelation through them to created persons of their eternal processions: "For the Son, to be sent, is to be known in his origin from the Father. In the same way, for the Holy Spirit...to be sent, is to be known in his procession from the Father: mitti est Filio cognosci quod ab illo (sc. a Patre) sit...Spiritui Sancto mitti est cognosci quia ab illo (sc. Patre) procedat" (*De Trinitate*, IV, XX, 29).

apparent than real. Does not St. Paul (Rom. 5:5) show us that the Spirit pours into our hearts the love with which God loves us, God who is the Father? And as for the grace attributed to Christ (2 Cor. 13:13), is it not the identical and common effect of the action of the Three?

Certainly. For Paul there is no division of work among the Three. And yet their roles are not purely and simply interchangeable, either in his view or in that of St. John.

The Father is the one who conceives the divine plan of salvation, before the creation of the world. He sends his Son and their Spirit to realize this plan. The Holy Spirit is the Envoy given and poured out on us, the permanent Gift who dwells in us; he makes us pray and witness, assists the Church and its leaders in their decisions; he is the seal and the pledge of the final condition into which we will enter as heirs. This final state is characterized by a return to the Father by way of the Son (1 Cor. 15:24-28).[133]

These Three remain transcendent, unutterably superior to human thought. We are only adoptive sons, Jesus is the Son par excellence. The Spirit of God is in God as the spirit of man is in man. "The things that no eye has seen, and no ear has heard, things beyond the mind of man, all that God has prepared for those who love him. To us God has revealed them through his Spirit" (1 Cor. 2:9-10), said St. Paul, and he adds: it is this that we proclaim.

In proclaiming the mystery of the Three, the writers of the New Testament were conscious of proclaiming their own mystery immanent to this transcendent mystery: "God chose us in him (Christ) before the creation of the world" (Eph. 1:4); "I have loved them as you have loved me...before the creation of the world" (Jn. 17:23-24). In other words, the redeemed human plurality is already, "before" it even exists, present to the divine redeeming plurality. It is interior to the latter.

If men are the object of an eternal dialogue between the Three, is it surprising that the authors of the New Testament present human beatitude as the loving knowledge of the Trinity's inner life: "This is eternal life, that they may know thee, the only true God, and Jesus Christ whom thou has sent" (Jn. 17:3)? Why take offense at this reciprocity?[134]

We could even say that the most specific revelation of the New Testament is the revelation of this immanence of the redeemed human

---

[133]Thus everything leads us to believe that for St. Paul it is by the Spirit that the Father and the Son give themselves to man and it is once again by this same Spirit that man returns to the Son and to the Father. It is necessary to turn to the Holy Spirit in order to adhere to the Son (cf. 2 Cor. 3:17).

[134]What is implied in this declaration of Jesus as reported by John is that we can know him truly only if we know him as sent by the Father and, consequently, only if we know the bond of eternal filiation that binds him to the Father.

plurality in the divine, transcendent and redeeming plurality; and it is by the mysterious exercise of human relationships that man prepares himself for the face-to-face vision of the intra-divine relations (Mt. 25:31-46), which constitute the substance of the "Kingdom prepared from the foundation of the world" for the blessed of the Father of the King, and in which human relationships are in fact once again recovered.

The uncreated divine plurality wishes to have the human and created plurality enter into its own sphere, and it reveals itself to the latter in a disclosure of its intimate life that in no way diminishes its transcendence: "no one knows the Father except the Son and anyone to whom the Son wishes to reveal him." The Son has no need of the revelation which the sons must have in order to know the Father. But what answer will the sons give to the revelation of the Father through the Son?

VI. THE FATHER, THE SON AND THE SPIRIT IN THE CULT OF THE NEW TESTAMENT

As the work of salvation was begun by the Father who sent his Son to redeem us and to sanctify us by their Spirit, so the Church of the New Testament responds through its worship to the Father through the Son in the Spirit. But this Church of the New Testament also begins to associate the Son with the Father in the worship it directs to him. It does not yet however reach the point of rendering an explicit cult to the Spirit in any evident or universal way. This develops only in the course of the post-apostolic period.

a) *The Son associated with the Father as object of cult*

The evolutionary pattern of New Testament doxologies is simple: first they are oriented to the Father who alone is mentioned. In a second stage they are mediated through the Son and in a final stage they terminate in this Only Son as their direct and immediate object.

For the Hebrews to render glory to God is almost second nature. The New Testament and in particular the Pauline epistles reflect this attitude (Rom. 11:36; 1 Tm. 1:17; 6:13-16).

1. Gal. 1:3-5 *marks the beginning of this evolution:*

Grace to you and peace from God the Father and our Lord Jesus Christ who gave himself for our sins to deliver us from the present evil age, according to the will of our God and Father, to whom be glory for ever and ever! Amen.

Christ (and not only the Father) gives grace but the doxology strictly speaking does not express reciprocity for it terminates in a glorification of God our Father without explicit mention of Jesus Christ.

2. *Doxologies mediated by Christ:*
In a second logical stage, though one perhaps chronologically simultaneous, glory is rendered to the Father through Jesus Christ. This is the case in the whole of the two epistles to the Corinthians and in the epistles to the Galatians and Romans (dating from 57-58) 2 Cor. 1:20 ("it is through him—Christ—that we say 'amen' to the glory of God") and Rom. 16:25-27 ("to God who alone is wise, through Jesus Christ be glory for evermore"). This stands out still more clearly in Col. 3:17 ("whatever you do, in word or deed, do everything in the name of the Lord Jesus, giving thanks to God the Father through Him"), for here we see clearly that the injunction to honor God should be carried out through Jesus Christ and in his name.

3. *Doxologies addressed to Jesus Christ:*
God the Father has glorified his Son who is the Lord of glory (1 Cor. 2:8). Jesus himself had asked of the Father his own glorification: "Father, the hour is come, glorify thy Son that the Son may glorify thee" (Jn. 17:1). The Church had to imitate the attitude of the Father in realizing this prayer of Jesus Christ. Some texts (2 Tm. 4:18) remain ambiguous, for we do not know with all the desired clarity whether they intend to glorify the Father or the Son. But this very ambiguity is probably an element of the transition process. Other texts are perfectly clear: Heb. 13:21 ("...Jesus Christ, to whom be glory forever and ever"), 2 Pt. 3:18 ("grow in the grace and knowledge of our Lord and Savior Jesus Christ, to him be glory both now and to the day of eternity!"); and especially Apocalypse (1:5-6; 5:13) which associates the glorification of the Lamb with that of God (the Father) in the new canticle of redeemed creation[135]: "To him who sits upon the throne and to the Lamb be blessing and honor and glory and might for ever and ever!" (5:13).

To render immediate glory to the Son corresponds moreover to the explicit injunction of the pre-Paschal Christ, reported in Jn. 5:23: "That all may honor the Son, even as they honor the Father."[136] The perfect adorer of the Father, in revealing his equality with him, reclaims for himself the same adoration that he demands for his Father and which he is the first to render him (Jn. 8:49;[137] 4:23-24).

Doxology does not cover the whole of cult; it expands into acts of

[135]Cf. A. Hamman, O.F.M., *La Prière*, v. I. Tournai, 1959, p. 355, note 4; pp. 364ff.

[136]*Ibid.*, pp. 405-406. To this commandment corresponds the promise made by Jesus in Jn. 14:13-14, to grant the prayer made in his name, that is "relying on the mediation of Christ and on his role as intercessor" (cf. A. Hamman, *op. cit.*, 407).

[137]"I honor my Father and you seek to dishonor me." John here uses the same Greek word *timân* already utilized in 5:23 to say: "that all may honor the Son as they honor the Father." Hamman (*op cit.*, 405) comments: "The parallelism with the Father proves that the verb *timân* wishes to convey that we are here concerned with divine cult." This is an important affirmation: according to John, the pre-paschal Jesus already claimed for himself a cult of adoration.

thanksgiving. Here also there is an analogous pattern of evolution but one that is less accentuated. During his mortal life Jesus gave thanks to the Father (Mt. 11:25; Jn. 11:41). Paul thanks God the Father in the prologues of his epistles. In Rom. 1:8 Paul thanks the Father through Jesus Christ. In Col. 3:17 the Apostle moves on to an imperative: it is always in the name of the Lord Jesus and by him that thanks must be rendered to the Father. But explicit thanksgiving to Christ is reached only in 1 Tm. 1:12 (without the technical word *eucharisto* but with its equivalent *charin ago*): "I thank him who has given me strength, Christ Jesus our Lord, who judged me faithful enough to call me into his service."

We could however wonder whether the story of Lk. 17:16 (describing the adoring thanks of the Samaritan leper directed to the pre-Paschal Jesus) did not have a special significance for the post-Paschal community. In this text the evangelist seems to have intended to bring out the divinity of Jesus: "one of them when he saw that he had been healed, turned back, praising God with a loud voice and fell on his face at Jesus' feet, giving him thanks (the technical word *eucharisto* is used here). Now he was a Samaritan." Would not this text, in the context of the Christian community listening to the proclamation, amount to an invitation to worship Jesus and to direct their acts of thanksgiving to Him?

In any case, it is clear that at least the primitive community of the Jerusalem Church was acquainted with an immediate invocation of Jesus and did not limit itself to praying in his name.

This community would entreat the Father through the name of his "holy servant," Jesus: "they lifted their voices together to God...and now, Lord, look upon their threats, and grant to thy servants to speak thy word with all boldness, while thou stretchest out thy hand to heal...through the name of thy holy servant Jesus" (Acts 4:26; 29-30).

The formula "through the name of Jesus" prepares us for the next stage of cultic evolution: prayer to Christ. It comes quickly: in 36 or 37, Stephen would go to death making "this invocation: Lord Jesus, receive my spirit. And he knelt down and cried with a loud voice: Lord, do not hold this sin against them" (Acts 7:59-60). This is, of course, only a private invocation.

Besides this though, the Palestinian community used to repeat in its liturgical prayer: "*Marana tha:* Come Lord" (cf. 1 Cor. 16:22; Apoc. 22:20).[138]

---

[138]"This Aramaean formula can be translated in two ways: Our Lord has come (*Maran atha*, perfect), or: Come, Lord (*Marana tha*, imperative).... The origin of this form is to be sought in the Palestinian community.... It is perhaps the most ancient liturgical prayer addressed to Christ.... The preservation of the formula in Aramaean is perhaps explained by its phonetic ambivalence which allows it to express at the same time that the Lord is present invisibly in the midst of his disciples and that he kindles in their hearts the desire for the *parousia*, by this cry of expectation," says Hamman, (*op. cit.*, 275-276).

Even if it is not certain[139] that 2 Cor. 12:8 is reporting a private prayer of St. Paul directed to Christ himself, nevertheless this seems likely. And especially the usage of the Gospels in the liturgical life of all the first century communities leads us to believe that prayer to Christ was universally practiced and that the Gospel reading itself encouraged it. How else can we explain in fully satisfactory fashion the insistence with which the Gospels report to us the invocations to Christ by the sick[140] who beg to be healed: "a leper came to him, beseeching him and falling on his knees said to him: if you wish, you can heal me" (Mk. 1:40). Were not these pre-Paschal requests presented by the Evangelists to the community precisely in order to suggest a model for Christians in their post-Paschal prayer?

Observe too that the invocations or prayers to Christ cited here are not viewing him as mediator or intercessor before the Father, but are rather directed to him as to the final term of the petition.

From all we have said so far we can conclude that the primitive Church progressed from worship rendered to God and Father to worship of the Father through the Son and finally to worship rendered to the Son as to the Father. If the chronology of these different stages cannot be established with precision, the *terminus a quo* and the *terminus ad quem* are sufficiently clear.

b) *The Holy Spirit in the cult of the New Testament*

Unlike the Son, the New Testament does not offer us the Holy Spirit as an object of cult in an explicit manner[141] (unless perhaps apropos of Baptism in Mt. 28:19), but it regularly shows him associated with the act of cult. He appears neither as an adorer who renders worship nor (except in the baptismal formula) as the adored God, to whom cult is explicitly rendered. But the Spirit is present as One who pertains to the sphere of the divine into which we enter by worship. He is "at home" in the cult where he is present as the One who can assist us in this obligation, teach us to pray and render us capable of invoking God our Father and Jesus as Lord (Rom. 8:26-27 as explained by 8:15; Gal. 4:6; 1 Cor. 12:3). Apart from the baptismal consecration,[142] explicit worship of the Holy Spirit goes beyond New Testament practice and pertains to the Patristic age.

[139]Hamman (*op. cit.*, 270) contests it; but wrongly, we think. For the conversion of Paul is itself the fruit of the prayer addressed to Jesus by Stephen when he was dying; Paul was not unaware of this; Paul's request in 2 Cor. 12:8 far from expressing "confident friendship rather than prayer" (Hamman), expresses instead the one in the framework of the other.

[140]Cf. Mt. 8:27ff.

[141]Cf. S. Lyonnet, S.J., *Biblica* 32 (1951), p. 31: "Paul does not consider the Holy Spirit as a Person... whom one can invoke but as one by whom the Father forms us to the image of his Son."

[142]Cf. D. Buzy, *La Sainte Bible*. Pirot-Clamer, Paris, 1935, v. IX, p. 386: "the preposition with the accusative seems to suggest a movement toward the Trinity," says the author apropos of

Nevertheless, this explicit cult is rooted in the New Testament which prepares the ground for it. Does not Jesus say: "true adorers will adore the Father in Spirit and in Truth" (Jn. 4:23)? Thus he makes the Spirit appear as the principle of a new cult, of *the* new cult; the principle would one day be, and already was, in the human soul of Jesus, the term of this cult.

St. Paul writes to the Thessalonians (2 2:13): "God chose you from the beginning to be saved by the sanctifying Spirit and by faith in the truth." The Spirit sanctifies, that is, consecrates.[143] The day will come when those consecrated will explicitly adore their Consecrator. The Spirit of the Promise, the Holy Spirit marks the baptized with a seal (Eph. 1:13) for the day of Redemption (*ibid.*, 4:30).

The decisive point of Pauline doctrine on the cultic role of the Spirit of the Father and the Son is established through the Apostle's teaching on the relation between the Spirit and our prayer. He teaches us to pray, he makes us pray and cry out, like Jesus in his agony, "Abba, Father."

> When the Spirit cries: Abba, Father, the one who is praying is the first one to hear Him, he is the witness of the prayer the Spirit addresses to the Father.... The community of the faithful—and each one of its members—first hears the Spirit invoke and confess the name of the Father. This forms an introduction into the mystery, after which the faithful in turn translate it in prayer to God and confession before the world.... The prayer of the Spirit confesses and his confession prays. His prayer is a confession in and before the community.[144]

But what does the Spirit say, what does he cry out? Abba, Father. "The Aramaean term *abba* is an address that can signify at the same time My Father and Our Father.[145] ... The Messianic community has preserved the very expression of Christ doubtless in order to preserve the original polyvalence: My Father, Our Father."[146]

In Paul's view then, the Spirit's intervention in the cult appears intimately bound up with the consciousness (aroused by this intervention) of the fundamental truth of the New Testament: in the language of

---

Mt. 28:19 Gr., which we could translate: "Baptize them into the name of the Father, of the Son and of the Holy Spirit," that is consecrate them to the Three.

[143]Cf. Jn. 17:17: in both cases, the New Testament uses words related to *hagios*.

[144]Hamman, *op. cit.*, 293-294; the expression of Hamman, that sees in the pray-er the "first hearer" and the "witness" of the Spirit's prayer is more suggestive than precise, for the pray-er is not necessarily aware that it is the Spirit who inspires his prayer; it further appears to suppose that the divine person of the Spirit can really pray to the Father, whereas Rom. 8:15 shows the real sense of Rom. 8:26-27: the Spirit makes us pray, but he does not pray in the manner in which those pray whom he makes to pray.

[145]Cf. in the present chapter, §3, d.

[146]A. Hamman, *op. cit.*, 268.

Matthew and John, Father signifies simultaneously the intra-divine paternity of the Person-source with respect to an only Son, and the adoptive paternity of this Person-source with respect to the "brothers" of this only Son. For Paul the expression Abba, Father, had the advantage of recalling and recapitulating the prayer of the Pater, the prayer taught by Jesus, while at the same time recalling the overwhelming newness of the (supernatural) filiation of Christians. It thus allowed Paul to express his experience of the Church.[147] In the Spirit Paul sees the author both of this reality of filial life and of its prayer consciousness (cf. Rom. 8:14-15: "all who are led by the Spirit of God are sons of God...you have received the Spirit of adoptive sonship which makes us cry out: Abba Father!"). For Paul the Spirit prays only because he makes us pray; he makes us pray as sons in the Son. So we understand that for the Apostle the Spirit comes across as principle of prayer and not as its term. But this very discovery of the Spirit as the source of all prayer, this very recognition, will ultimately lead the temples of the Spirit to adore and invoke him in themselves (cf. 1 Cor. 3:16; 6:19; Eph. 2:21-22). In the fourth century, St. Basil will rightly underline the perfect continuity between the doxology "Glory to the Father and to the Son and to the Holy Spirit" and the New Testament: for such a doxology was already postulated and demanded by the Trinitarian baptismal consecration of which the risen Christ is both the past inaugurator and the present author (Mt. 28:19).

By way of terminating this chapter and this section on Trinitarian cult in the New Testament, we might emphasize the fact that in the Our Father and in the sacerdotal Prayer, Christ Jesus sets himself up as the model of the Christian's Trinitarian prayer.

In the Lukan redaction of the Pater the petition for the Kingdom is replaced (at least in some manuscripts) by another petition: "that your Holy Spirit come upon us and purify us" (Lk. 11:2). Then, shortly after having taught his disciples to pray, according to the same evangelist, Jesus says to them: "If you then, who are evil, know how to give good gifts to your children, how much more will the heavenly Father give the Holy Spirit to those who ask him" (Lk. 11:13; cf. St. Gregory of Nyssa, A. Palmieri, *D.T.C.*, art. "E. Saint," vol. V [1913], col. 733).

The orientation of the whole of Luke as well as Acts 2:33 authorizes us to think that Jesus asked for himself the outpouring of the Spirit which he received at the time of the Resurrection. We can say then with M. Sabbe:[148] "Luke is not so intent on giving us the ancient and precise formula of the Pater with its dramatic tension and its eschatological expectation, but

---

[147]*Ibid.*

[148]M. Sabbe, "Le Baptême de Jesus," a contribution to the collective book directed by I. de La Potterie, S.J., *De Jesus aux Evangiles*. Paris, 1967, pp. 207-209.

wishes rather, above all, to instruct Christians on the object of their petitions.... The redaction of Lk. 11:1 could have a very concrete meaning: if John taught his disciples how to pray, the Lord in turn, with his own prayer has taught us to ask the Father for his Holy Spirit. The contrast with John and his disciples concerns the petition for the Spirit as the divine gift that characterizes the life and saving work of the Christian Church." We would only add: by inculcating this "pneumatic" petition in his disciples, Jesus was introducing them into the secret of his personal pre-Paschal prayer in which post-Paschal Christians can thus participate, especially if (as Jn. 14:13; 15:16 suggests) they are careful to ask of the Father the gift of the Spirit in the name of his only Son. Thus understood, the Pater would moreover perfectly coincide with the prayer of the heavenly Christ: "I will pray the Father, and he will give you another Paraclete to be with you forever" (Jn. 14:16). As we will see later, it is especially by the gift of the spiritualized flesh of his Son in the Eucharist that the Father hears such a prayer, inasmuch as this flesh is the pledge of the glorious resurrection of the Christian and of his full spiritualization by the Spirit of the Risen One.

Thus also the sacerdotal Prayer of Jesus will be perfectly heard: "Father, the hour has come; glorify thy Son that the Son may glorify thee" (Jn. 17:1), that is: give him your Spirit in plenitude by raising him from the dead so that he will be able in turn to bestow him bountifully to your glory (cf. Acts 2:33). Some interpreters also think that the "We" of Jn. 17:21-22 designates the Holy Spirit,[149] as well as the love with which the Father has loved his only Son and which Jesus asks might be in his disciples (17:26). One can further see the Spirit in the glory that the Son had with the Father before the world was and with which he asks to now be glorified (Jn. 17:5; cf. 17:1). This is what St. Gregory of Nyssa saw here (Hom. 15 in Cant., *MG* 44, 1116 C-1117 B).

---

[149]Cf. H. Mühlen, *Der Heilige Geist als Person*. Münster, 1967, § 4.19-4.26, pp. 95-99ff.

II
Toward the Clear Affirmation of the Equality and of the Consubstantiality of the Father, the Son and the Holy Spirit

The New Testament culminates in the affirmation of the necessary insertion of human society, the one human family made up of so many diverse nations, into the bosom of the divine society of the Father, the Son and the Holy Spirit: "make disciples of all nations baptizing them in the name of the Father and of the Son and of the Holy Spirit" (Mt. 28:19).

This formula marks a high point in the Trinitarian revelation of the New Testament and at the same time postulates and demands the entire doctrinal development that follows it: after the New Testament has clearly shown that the Son and the Spirit pertain to the sphere of Yahweh, to the divine sphere, several more centuries will have to elapse before we come to an explicit recognition of the equality and the consubstantiality of the Father, the Son and the Holy Spirit in the possession of one and the same divine nature: "in the name of the Father, and of the Son and of the Holy Spirit."

In this formula are already contained in germ the Symbol of the Apostles and the dogmatic definitions of Nicaea and of Constantinople. Let us now analyze the successive stages of this doctrinal and cultic pilgrimage of the Church, the people called together by the Three, and directed toward its Trinitarian source.

I. IS THE SYMBOL OF THE APOSTLES CHRISTOLOGICAL OR TRINITARIAN?

Is the Symbol of the Apostles which we all recite and which binds together Christians of so many different confessions, originally based on the mystery of Christ or on the Trinitarian mystery? After recalling the history of its evolution, we shall attempt to unravel its theological and pastoral significance.

1. *The evolution and the Trinitarian structure of the Symbol*
We could sum up as follows the conclusions of contemporary historical

works:[1] the Symbol as it appears between the years 175 and 190, both Trinitarian and Christological, is the product of two symbols—one Trinitarian, the other Christological—of which it is difficult to say which is the more primitive.

The Trinitarian symbol was more brief and did not include the profession of Christological faith presently found in the second part and developed within it. This Trinitarian symbol was itself a part of the baptismal liturgy, first as a triple response to a triple interrogation at the core of the sacramental rite, then under the form of a symbol recited by the catechumen before baptism. Today, under the weight of additions to each of the three articles relative to each of the Three Divine Persons, the primitive Trinitarian structure appears largely obscured and we must turn to a very ancient Ethiopian recension in order to recover it in its purity.[2]

A Christological profession of faith, liturgical in origin, resulting in the last analysis from a crystallization of the kerygma, was integrated into the Trinitarian profession of faith between 175 and 190. Directed initially against the Gnostics and the Docetists, it appeared already in the *Demonstration of the Apostolic Preaching* of St. Irenaeus.[3] First inserted at the end of the third article on the Holy Spirit, it was later annexed to the second.

The two professions of faith that make up the Symbol are both, as P. Benoît has shown very well,[4] rooted in the apostolic kerygma.

The Symbol is then essentially a liturgical formula, which expresses the profession of faith of the catechumens and depends on the "form" itself of baptism.[5] This liturgical formula was developed under the pressure of heresies. Thus the profession of faith tends to become a rule of faith. This declarative Symbol pertains to the pre-baptismal catechesis. It is followed by the triple baptismal interrogation based on the profession of Trinitarian faith.

Today the Symbol itself appears as a summary exposition of the faith, transmitted to the Christian and even to the catechumen, in view of the profession of Trinitarian faith realized in the very act of baptism (a profession which this Symbol already contains but which has become less

---

[1] We could especially cite: J. de Ghellinck, S.J., *Patristique et Moyen Age*. Paris, 1946, v. I, esp. pp. 221-231; P.-T. Camelot, O.P., "Recherches récents sur le symbole des Apôtres et leur protée théologique," *Rech. Sc. Rel.*, 39 (1952), 323-337; J. Lebreton, S.J., *Histoire du dogme de la Trinité*. Paris, 1928, v. II, 141-173.

[2] *DS* 1: "in Patrem dominatorem universe, et in Jesum Christum, et in Sanctum Spiritum." Cf. also *DS* 4 and 5.

[3] St. Irenaeus, *The Demonstration of the Apostolic Teaching*, ch. 3, 6; cf. *Adversus Haereses*, I, 10, 1 (*MG* 7, 549).

[4] P. Benoît, O.P., *Exégèse et Théologie*. Paris, 1961, v. II, pp. 208-209.

[5] Important observations for pastoral work: as profession of faith, the symbol is an act of cult and a response to Revelation; the renewal of this profession of faith revives, in the Christian who is in the state of grace, the sacramental grace of Baptism.

apparent). Since the beginning of the present liturgical reform this profession is renewed with the baptismal promises during the Paschal Vigil.

Correctly situated against its historical background, the Symbol ceases to be the highly schematic artificial construction in twelve articles that we are perhaps accustomed to think of, and becomes once again what it has never ceased to be: an integral part of a liturgical rite instituted by Christ—baptism—and also the expression of faith in the Father, Son and Holy Spirit which the Three confer at the time of, and by means of, Baptism.

The linking of this Symbol with the Baptism instituted by the incarnate Son, helps us understand moreover that the addition of a Christological profession of faith to the Trinitarian profession is perfectly in order: for it is through Christ that we received the revelation of this Trinity to which we are united by the Baptism of which Christ is the author and the principal minister.

Simply from a historical point of view we can already say with Camelot: "The study of the prehistory of the Symbol leads us to the problems posed by the necessity, for salvation, of faith in the Trinity, and the relation of this faith with the equally necessary faith in Christ: in this the whole equilibrium of Christian dogma is involved."[6]

To these questions the Symbol replies: faith in the Trinity is necessary for salvation, faith in Christ is not possible without faith in the Trinity, for Christ is the only Son of the Father and the giver of the Spirit.

2. Theological-pastoral significance of this evolution

The genesis of the Symbol in the pre-Nicene Church attests at once the authenticity of the Trinitarian faith in the Church and the inchoative understanding of the mystery which the Church already possessed.

From the apostolic preaching and kerygma, the Church received not only a Christological formula of baptismal faith (Acts 8:36-38; 16:30-32), but also a Trinitarian formula of this faith that owes its origin to Christ himself: Mt. 28:19. This Trinitarian formula also came to the Church under a liturgical form.

The spontaneous conjunction by the Church of these two formulas into one shows on the one hand that the Church receives the two mysteries of the Trinity and of the Redemptive Incarnation with one and the same faith, and on the other hand manifests an already profound, though still incipient understanding of the mystery, but one that is moreover the criterion of a living faith.

Through the Paschal event of Jesus Christ, the human person is introduced into the intimacy of the Trinitarian life, into the unity of the Father and the Son which is their common spiritual Breath.

---

[6]Camelot, *op. cit.*, p. 337.

Such a conjunction of these two professions of faith into a single Symbol shows us very well what is the essential object of our faith and in what the mystery of our salvation consists. It already insinuates the identity, rightly stressed by K. Rahner, between the immanent Trinity and the functional Trinity—despite the reservations we have already had occasion to make about these equivocal expressions. It permits us to say with M.-M. Philipon, O.P.: "If we know how to bind together the diverse mysteries of the divine Revelation, we can affirm that there is at bottom, in the universe, only one integral mystery: the Trinity overflowing into the Church, the life of the Father communicated by the Son in the Spirit to the whole mystical body."[7]

It is precisely through Baptism that the Trinity flows initially into the Church, thus forming with it "a single integral mystery." In this single mystery, the Trinity occupies the center, for the articles or truths of our faith are structured by the Church around what St. Irenaeus calls "the three articles of our faith"[8]: the triple affirmation of the Father, the Son and the Holy Spirit. These three articles, or better, these three Persons constitute as Irenaeus again says, "the base of the edifice, the foundation of our salvation,"[9] that is to say, the base of the edifice of the Church, the Sacrament of our salvation.[10] The one Trinity which overflows through the waters of Baptism into the one Church, saves men by gathering together their diversity into its indivisible unity: *de unitate Patris et Filii et Spiritus Sancti plebs adunata,* said St. Cyprian less than a century after the definitive crystallization of the Symbol.[11]

At the same time that this joining of the two professions of faith into one symbol manifests the salvific will of the redemptive Trinity, it also signifies in a symbolic manner that Christ stirs up in the baptized a salutary curiosity about his relations with the Father and the Spirit and about their intimate communion, a curiosity already very evidently present in a Christian author who was a contemporary of the fusion—Athenagoras. Here is what he wrote around the year 175:

> Here below we are captivated by the sole desire to know the only true God and his Word, to know what is the unity of the Son with the Father, the community of the Father with the Son, what is the Spirit, what is the union and the distinction between the Spirit, the Son and the Father.[12]

---

[7]M.-M. Philipon, O.P., *Seminarium,* 1967, p. 226.
[8]St. Irenaeus, *Demonstration,* ch. 6.
[9]*Ibid.*
[10]*LG,* 1, 9, 48.
[11]St. Cyprian, *De Orat. Dominica,* 23; ML 4, 553; cited by LG 4.
[12]Athenagoras, *Apology,* 12; cf. Lebreton, *op. cit.,* v. II, pp. 492-505. It is to be noted that ch. 12 of the Apology is situated in a context of preparation for death and martyrdom, explicit enough in the very text of the chapter. In modern terms, it could be said that the personal

Such precisely is the fruit of the Paschal Mystery: to make us "pass" from a legitimately anthropocentric theology which considers principally the gift that the divine Persons make of themselves in the Paschal Mystery of Christ,[13] to a fully theocentric theology, which devotes itself to reflection on the reciprocal gift of the divine Persons, a gift inherent in the gift they make of themselves to human persons.

It could even be said that the Apostolic Symbol shows us, by its structure, the Three Persons in the very order in which Christ proclaimed them:[14] God the Father (Mt. 5-7), Jesus himself as the only Son (Mt. 11:27; 14:33; 16:16; Jn. 10:30 and *passim*) and the Holy Spirit, his glorifier (Jn. 14-16; Mt. 28:19).

The Christian religion, worshipping in Spirit and in Truth God the Father and Creator, distinguishes itself from polytheistic paganism. Christ is its center, Christ as Word and manifestation of the Father; and thus Christianity distinguishes itself from Judaism. Finally, this Christian religion lives from the life of the divine Spirit poured out by the Son, from the Father, to sanctify and unify the Church: "I believe in the Holy Spirit, in the holy catholic Church."[15]

Thus, the Christian religion distinguishes itself from Indian or African polytheism as well as from Brazilian syncretism[16] by faith in God the Father Creator of the universe, from Judaism by faith in the incarnate Son, and from heretical sects which falsely lay claim to the name of Christ, by faith in the Holy Spirit, soul of the Church (cf. Eph. 4:4-6).

The first Christians understood well the Ecclesial meaning of the equally Christological and Trinitarian Symbol: the baptismal Symbol became the sign of their union and of their convergence, the instrument through which they became more and more conscious of the identity of the faith which

Trinity personalizes to a supreme degree the human person by rousing in this person real relations with itself.

[13]Cf. Jn. 13:1; 16:28: if the Pasch of the Lord is his passing from this world to his Father, we can see why the Christian's participation in this passing demands that he pass from the consideration of the real relations he has with each of the divine Persons in order to unite himself (by participation) to the real relations They have among themselves, and which remain inherent in the real relations of the Christian with each of the Three, provided he is in the state of grace. I cannot believe in the Son without the eternal generation of the Son being present in me, for I participate in it by my act of faith, nor can I love the Spirit unless the eternal spiration of the Spirit inheres in my temporal charity which participates in it.

[14]The Good News which Christ announces, is that he achieves with his Father and their Spirit the salvation of man which consists precisely in the definitive self-donation of the Three to the saved person. The Trinity is the eternal Good News announced by Christ; to evangelize, is for him to reveal the Trinity as being the salvation of man.

[15]Cf. Camelot, O.P., *op. cit.*, p. 327, citing Nautin, and adding a note according to which Nautin's thesis is confirmed by a recently examined papyrus. Jungmann understands the third article of the Symbol in the same way.

[16]We are alluding to the religions called "Afro-Brazilian."

united them. The Symbol proclaims, says St. Jerome, "the confession of the Trinity and the unity of the Church," *confessionem Trinitatis et unitatem Ecclesiae.*[17]

Although about the year 160, according to St. Irenaeus' testimony, a Gnostic sect separated from the great Church, had borrowed (and deformed) the baptismal formulas (the sect baptized, he says, "in the name of the unknown Father of the universe, of the Truth that is mother of all beings, and of Him who descended on Jesus"[18]), Tertullian was to write some decades later: "Since the witness of faith and the guarantee of salvation have as security the Three Persons, we add mention of the Church, because where the Three are, the Father, the Son and the Holy Spirit, there is also found the Church, which is the body of the Three."[19]

The fusion of the two symbols, Christological and Trinitarian, answered then a profound and not merely time-conditioned need. Every Trinitarian formula must be Christological and vice versa. We do not believe merely in God, we also believe something about God: that he has come to us through his Son and their common Spirit in order to save us. About the Son we believe that once he was risen he sent us his Spirit. The Trinity of the Symbol is economic and functional while being, at the same time, ontological and immanent. It is the foundation of our salvation, for we are saved by the Father, by the Son and by the Holy Spirit. But in what does our salvation, effected by the Three, consist, if not in the unitive participation in their reciprocal relations?

Let us conclude this section by citing some perceptive lines from Schillebeeckx:

> It is in the history of salvation, inaugurated by creation and culminating in the man-Jesus, that the Trinity reveals itself both in its own intimate life and as being our salvation.... The Christological professions of faith are incomprehensible outside the Trinitarian framework.[20]

It is moreover for this reason that the first Christological professions of faith were developed and explicitated in a Trinitarian symbol, if the latter

---

[17]St. Jerome, ML 21, 830; the symbol was, for the Christians of the first centuries, the *contesseratio hospitalitatis* (Tertullian), by which the fraternity of a passing stranger was recognized, it was a seal indicating agreement in the manner of a contract. J. de Ghellinck, from whom we borrowed these notations (*op. cit.*, p. 225) adds: "around 366, a little peasant of the region of the lower Danube did not hesitate to reproach his bishop, Germinius of Sirmium, who had passed over to pneumatomachic Arianism, with having abandoned the faith of his baptismal Symbol, of which he himself remained proud by invoking the three divine persons, the Father, the Son and the Holy Spirit" (*Ibid.*, pp. 225-226).

[18]St. Irenaeus, *Adversus Haereses*, I, 21, 3.

[19]Tertullian, *De Baptismo*, VI, 1-2.

[20]E. Schillebeeckx, O.P., *Révélation et Théologie*. Brussels, 1965, p. 183.

was not actually the original. It is certain that the kerygma was clearly Trinitarian from the beginning (Acts 2:33 in the total context of the book), but this does not preclude the possibility that the first professions of New Testament faith were Christological or "binitarian" (ex.: Mt. 16:16; and, earlier in the order of the publication of the texts, Acts 8:37 Western version); and it is possible that the passage from the "implicitly Trinitarian" to the "explicitly Trinitarian" expression in the symbol (in 175-190) and in the Apology of Athenagoras was favored by the necessity of reaction against heterodox Judaeo-Christianity and the Gnosis, a reaction exemplified, par excellence, by St. Irenaeus. Such a hypothesis is by no means proven however, but it appears very likely, at least in the case of the commentaries, included in the symbol, on what St. Irenaeus called its "three fundamental articles."

II. TRINITARIAN DOCTRINES OF JUDAEO-CHRISTIANITY AND OF GNOSTICISM: THE REACTION OF IRENAEUS

It is somehow a law of human thought that a culture which receives Christianity tends spontaneously to reinterpret the revealed truths within its own categories. Heresies arise from the abuse of this inclination, as orthodox theology springs from the legitimate exercise of this law. This is verified from as early as the second century, especially in the heart of Jewish thought.

1. *Judaeo-Christianity confronted with the Trinity*

Christians of Jewish origin attempted to express the mystery in the categories of Jewish thought: not only of the Old Testament, but of a Judaism that is distinct from it. More precisely, the Word and the Spirit are represented as Angels, that is to say, following the etymological meaning of "Malak Yahweh," as envoys of God (the Father). A legitimate attempt. Like the term spirit, so the term Angel does not necessarily signify an illegitimate assimilation to the created universe.[21] But in point of fact, as J. Daniélou has noted "angelomorphic Judaeo-Christian theology will have an unfortunate effect on the theology of Origen and of the Arians."[22]

In the Judaeo-Christian writings, Michael at times appears identified with the Word, and Gabriel either with the Holy Spirit or the Word,[23] or at

---

[21] J. Daniélou, S.J., *Théologie du judéo-christianisme*. Tournai, 1958, pp. 168-169, observes: "The word angel has an essentially concrete value. It designates a supernatural being which manifests itself. However, the nature of this supernatural being is not determined by the expression, but by the context. The word represents the Semitic form of the designation of the Word and of the Spirit as spiritual substance, as persons.... Angel is their archaic equivalent."
[22] *Ibid.*, p. 179.
[23] *Ibid.*, pp. 171-182.

least the Word manifests himself under the form of an angel. The glorious Angel of Hermas designates the Word himself.[24]

The ambiguity to which this language was exposed is evident: either we are dealing with the promotion of the category of angel henceforth capable of designating a divine person, or instead, with the attempt to reduce the Word and the Spirit to the level of created spirits, of "angels" in the usual sense of the word. Daniélou observes: "It is sometimes impossible to discern whether they are talking about divine persons or about angels. A certain subordinationist tendency[25] is implied in many cases by this terminology. Finally, among some heterodox writers, the Word and the Spirit are frankly assimilated to angels in the proper sense of the term.... All these reasons were to bring about the very rapid decline of this first form of Trinitarian theology."[26]

There is also, we think, another reason. This "angelomorphic theology" could, in spite of the dangers of subordinationism, somewhat suitably express the missions of the Word and of the Spirit, both sent by the Father; but the concept of envoy or of angel was not, by definition, applicable to the Father. It is then incontestable that the concept (if one can so speak) of person lends itself better than that of angel-envoy to the elaboration of a truly Trinitarian theology.

2. *Gnosticism*

The phenomenon of Gnosticism is vast and complex. Its study has been renewed by the discovery of a Gnostic library at Nag Hammadi (Egypt) in 1947. Gnosticism in general must be distinguished from Christian gnosis.

The Gnostic movement taken in its totality[27] aims at seeing man achieve by himself an awareness of his own divine nature, an awareness that would be his salvation. For Gnosticism, salvation is then the act of becoming aware of man's divinity (a view that closely resembles some contemporary views). Man has fallen from his original condition and his shipwreck has led to his carnal and material existence; he must then seek to escape from this existence, not so much by the loving exercise of his freedom in charity, but rather by knowledge. Redemption becomes part of the necessary evolution of the world and depends very little on the freedom of man or on the love of

---

[24]Hermas, *The Shepherd*, Eighth Similitude, VIII, 1, 1-2; cf. Daniélou, *op. cit.*, p. 171: "it seems certain that the glorious angel of Hermas designates the Word himself."

[25]In the sense of false subordinationism, which denies the equality of the Word with the Father and of the Spirit with both; for there is a true subordinationism which recognizes the inferiority of the Word, as incarnate, with respect to the Father, and which Jesus himself professed in Jn. 14:28.

[26]Daniélou, *op. cit.*, p. 169.

[27]See the bibliography.

God. Such is, in bare outline, the movement that St. Irenaeus described at great length, especially in its Christian version.[28]

According to J. Daniélou,[29] Christian Gnosis had its origin in the rebellion against Yahweh of certain Jewish circles, after the catastrophe of the year 70 and the fall of Jerusalem. A revolt against God the creator of the world and of history. Yahweh is considered to be an inferior demiurge, author of a world that has run aground. The Gnosis is the revelation of the true God: it offers the possibility of returning to Him by way of a rupture with the world and with the Law. A radical dualism, a heresy at the heart of Judaism which had its prolongation in an heretical movement within Christianity.

Whatever one may think of this hypothesis, it is certain that Christian Gnosis attempted a reinterpretation of Christianity and in particular of the Trinitarian mystery, in Gnostic categories.

For it, the Father is a transcendent super-principle, without interior distinction, incomprehensible to himself, and ordinarily designated by means of negative terms. In him suddenly appears Thought (which manifests itself by successive emanations among which figure the Logos and Spirit-Pneuma). The Father contemplates himself in the pure light of his essence and there thus appears to him his virginal thought: "Ennoia."

The divinity is conceived as a plenitude or a *pleroma* of potentialities. The "I" of Gnosticism is nothing but an ultimate emanation from this Pure Light, which comes to an awareness of itself and discovers in itself the divinity of which it is but a fragment and to which it returns in a way that is both physical and infallible. Somewhat parallel to the way the transcendent super-principle, the Father became aware of himself in his Thought, his "Ennoia."[30]

Consciousness, knowledge, gnosis, salvation. We think all at once of spiritism (contempt of the flesh); of psychoanalysis, which can abusively be conceived as salvation by achieving self-awareness; and of the trinitarian and idealist Pantheism of Hegelian philosophy.[31] In these movements, just as in the Gnostic movement, not everything is false; and it has even been shown how the New Testament itself furnishes elements of a Christian gnosis.[32]

---

[28]Cf. K. Rahner, S.J., *LTK*, v. IV, 1960, art. "Gnosis," col. 1020: the author identifies Gnostic salvation with a "selbstbewusstsein" which would exclude by its very nature, every attitude of obedience to the Word. Affirmations that are too absolute in the view of E. Cornelis, O.P. (*DSAM*, v. VI, 1965, col. 533: art. "Gnosticisme").

[29]J. Daniélou, *Etudes,* v. 327 (1967), p. 604.

[30]We draw here on F.-M.-M. Sagnard, O.P., *Catholicisme.* Paris, 1962, v. V, art. "Gnosticisme," col. 72-73.

[31]A comparison very clearly suggested by Cornelis, *op. cit.,* col. 538.

[32]P.-T. Camelot, O.P., *DSAM,* v. VI. Paris, 1965, art. "Gnose chrétienne," col. 509-510.

It still holds nonetheless—at least this is J. Lebreton's interpretation[33]—that the essential characteristic of the non-orthodox Gnostic system is the conditioning of the relations between man and God by a long chain of intermediaries, of degradations and successive emanations of the divinity. The Trinity of the heterodox Gnostics evaporates in the *pleroma*, in the successive production by way of emanation, of very destitute divinities. The Father, likewise, is not recognized as Creator. The denial of the eternal Trinity is bound up with a revolt of the human person against his temporal, historical and suffering condition.

Under this aspect the study of the relations between orthodox and heterodox Christian gnoses, and, in consequence, the study of the work of St. Irenaeus, reassumes special importance today for the dialogue between Buddhists and Christians; it is to E. Cornelis' credit that he perceived and stressed this.[34]

The understanding of the Trinitarian doctrine of heterodox Christian gnosis has been renewed by the erudition and reflective analysis of A. Orbe.

For him, neither Irenaeus nor modern authors have grasped the depth of this first Trinitarian theology: they have stopped at a "mythology" which tended to hide from them the true and very logical Valentinian thought pattern. According to Orbe, the Valentinian Trinitarian theology presented some unacceptable aspects but it was not the dualist theology that Irenaeus imagined.

For Orbe, the heart of the Valentinian thought is an attempt to "explain conjointly the two great mysteries: the one, Trinitarian, that of the generation of the Word, the other, cosmological, that of the effusion of matter, by treating in one and the same overall perspective two other subsidiary questions, one Trinitarian, that of the procession of the Spirit, the other soteriological, that of the effusion of the spiritual Church in the world" (A. Orbe, S.J., *La teologia del E. Santo*, Rome, 1966, p. 588).

The fundamental idea of the Valentinians is the link that they establish between the procession of the Holy Spirit and the creation of matter. Their thinking is dominated by a certain analogy between the Holy Spirit and matter, the Logos and form. The origin of this view lies in the feminine character of the Spirit (the biblical *ruah*, a feminine substantive). Like Irenaeus they identify the Spirit with Wisdom, *hokma*. The Spirit-Wisdom is the mother of the Word. It expresses the divine essence on all levels of existence; starting from this substrate, the Father proceeds to form his Image; the Spirit can then be called the womb of the Father. Analogically, it is from the womb of unformed matter that God forms the world.

For Orbe, the multiplicity of aeons which constitute the Valentinian

---

[33] J. Lebreton, S.J., *op. cit.*, v. II, pp. 109-110 and 544, *passim*.
[34] E. Cornelis, O.P., *DSAM*, v. VI, art. "Gnosticisme," col. 523-541, *passim*. Paris, 1965.

pleroma, is a "mythic" (in the sense of "imaged") representation that signifies the diverse stages of the Trinitarian economy; in fact, we are confronted with only three principles and their unfolding. The *pleroma* is then a mythical way of setting forth a dynamic Trinitarian theology which is not very different from that of Tertullian and of Origen.

The process develops in three moments, which we will encounter again on the lower plane of the *kenoma* (cosmology): existence, formation, divinization.

The Father, by his will, gives rise from his substance, which is the Spirit, to the impersonal Monogenes identical with the *pleroma,* a sort of world of ideas, the archetype of creation, which already implies a certain determination.

In a second stage the Monogenes acquires a personal subsistence, he becomes the Logos. Stage of the "image," of the formation *kat'ousian.*

The Spirit-Wisdom manifests itself at this moment under the form of life, of *dynamis*: here we have the syzygy *Logos-Zoe* of Ptolemy (cf. J. Lebreton, *Histoire du dogme de la Trinité,* Paris, 1928, v. II, pp. 107-108: extracts from Hippolytus describing this syzygy or reunion).

Finally there comes the last stage, that of divinization, of the *morphosis kata gnosin.* Only this last stage establishes the Logos as fully God and divinizing by the action of the sanctifying Spirit. The Logos then becomes Christ, thanks to his anointing by the Spirit. This last stage is only completed through restoration in the *pleroma.*

For the Valentinians, as for some other theologians of the times, this Trinitarian development is ordered to the creation of the world.

For the Gnostics, the Spirit-Wisdom becomes a person only at the time of creation, thanks to the *kenoma;* then and thereafter it also becomes the sanctifying principle of the world.

While recognizing that A. Orbe has explored in depth the "impressive logic of the Valentinian system" as "no one had done before him," Daniélou is inclined to see in this system a "theogony and a cosmogony" rather than a "theology of the Trinity" (*Rech. de Sc. Rel.,* 56, 1968, pp. 121-125, in a remarkably lucid review of A. Orbe's packed book on which we have drawn). But note that Daniélou says nothing about the Gnostic theology of the procession of the Holy Spirit from the Word which Orbe especially stressed, and to which we shall return later when we study the genesis of the doctrine of the *Filioque.*

In any case, Daniélou does not concede that Orbe has proven his thesis: that, for the Gnostics, God the Father is the Creator of the world, and that Gnostic theology is not dualist. He continues to believe that it is a theogony, and that it is by no means evident that Irenaeus misunderstood it. Does it not anticipate the trinitarian-cosmic-ecclesial immanentism of Hegel and Schleiermacher, at least in some of its traits?

Whatever may be the aberrations of Gnostic theology denounced by Irenaeus, it must nonetheless be recognized that Harnack probably was partly right in his insistence that the Gnostics were the first Christian theologians; for they were the ones who first utilized in theology the psychological analogy and the notions of consubstantiality (*homoousios*: cf. Irenaeus, 1. 8.5.; *MG* 7, pp. 531-535) and of procession;[35] we cannot even exclude the possibility that their erroneous theories indirectly occasioned the ingenious Augustinian intuition that saw in the Spirit the communion of Father and Son.[36]

B. Lonergan gives us a good explanation of such a conditioning: as astrology preceded astronomy, so theogony preceded theology. Speculation develops first in a non scientific way and only afterwards in a logical, methodical, scientific manner.[37] In this development, St. Irenaeus' response to the Gnostics is still a matter of special interest even though it caused little advance in Trinitarian theology.

3. *Grandeur and limits of the Trinitarian witness of St. Irenaeus*

Irenaeus, as we already noted in passing, begins his exposition of the mystery from the three fundamental articles of the baptismal symbol, namely: the Father, the Son and the Holy Spirit. Let us cite some fundamental passages:

> Error has deviated strangely from the truth about the three principal articles of our baptism. The Gnostics, in fact, either despised the Father, or else failed to receive the Son by speaking against the economy of his Incarnation, or else failed to accept the Holy Spirit because they scorned prophecy. We must defy all these unbelievers and flee their society, if we truly will to be pleasing to God and reach salvation through him.[38]
>
> Here is the rule of our faith, the foundation of the edifice, and that which gives support to our conduct:
>
> God the Father, uncreated, uncontained, invisible, one God, the creator of the universe: this is the very first article of our faith.
>
> The second article: The Word of God, the Son of God, Christ Jesus our

---

[35] Cf. Harnack, *Dogmengeschichte*, v. I, pp. 250-292; for an opposite view, Lebreton, *op. cit.*, pp. 109 and especially 117-118 (from v. II); more favorable to the Harnack line: Leo Scheffezyk (*MS*, v. II, pp. 162-163); E. Cornelis, *art. cit., passim*.

[36] Cf. Cornelis, *art. cit.*: "The *Ecclesia* is precisely constituted by this kiss, which is *pneuma*, exchanged between the Father and the Son" (col. 534). Neo-Platonism, Plotinus and St. Epiphanius could have been other occasioning factors, as we shall see later. There does not exist any comprehensive work on the influence of heterodox Gnostic theology on the Catholic theology of the Great Church, from the Catholic point of view.

[37] B. Lonergan, S.J., *De Deo trino*. Rome, 1964, v. I, p. 40.

[38] St. Irenaeus, *The Demonstration of the Apostolic Teaching*, § 100. SPCK, London, 1920.

Lord, who appeared to the prophets according to the manner of their prophecy and the stage of the Father's plans; by whom everything has been made; who moreover at the end of time was made man among men, visible and palpable in order to recapitulate everything, to destroy death, to render life visible and to accomplish a communion of God and man.

And for the third article:

The Holy Spirit, through whom the prophets have prophesied, and the Fathers have learned the things concerning God and the just, have been guided in the way of justice, and who in these last days has been poured out in a new way upon our humanity in order to renew man all over the earth in the sight of God.[39]

As Lebreton has rightly remarked, "in order to judge the heresies (Irenaeus) brings them back to this fundamental rule and establishes their opposition to the three articles of the symbol: the Father, the Son and the Holy Spirit."[40]

In passing let us say: do we not find here a lesson for our pastoral conduct today? Why not confront atheistic Marxism, Freudian pansexualism and Gnosticizing spiritism with the three fundamental articles of the Apostolic Symbol, with the Three Persons who are the origin and end of our Baptism? Are not these doctrines in opposition to these articles: the first two to the Father, creator of work, of economic activity and of the sexual instinct of the human person, to the Son their Savior, and to the Spirit their sanctifier, while spiritism is opposed to the definitive Incarnation of the Son and moreover denies the Trinity altogether?

The Trinity was viewed by Irenaeus in relation to our salvation, to that which was later called the "economy." This salvific economy was seen as manifesting another disposition, internal this time, another economy signified by a certain order in our relations with the divine Persons. On this point Irenaeus offers us a very rich doctrine, a two-fold schema—descending and ascending—of the relation between man and God the Father, Son and Holy Spirit:

This is why at our new birth, Baptism takes place through these three articles, the Baptism that grants us the grace of new birth in God the Father by means of the Son in the Holy Spirit. For those who bear the Spirit of God are led to the Word, that is to say to the Son; but the Son presents them to the Father and the Father procures for them incorruptibility. Therefore, without the Spirit it is impossible to see the Son of God, and without the Son no one can approach the Father, for the Son is the

---

[39]St. Irenaeus, *Demonstration*, § 6.
[40]Lebreton, *op. cit.*, v. II, p. 542.

knowledge of the Father, and the knowledge of the Son of God is had by means of the Holy Spirit; as for the Spirit, it is according to the Father's good pleasure that the Son as minister dispenses him to whom the Father wills and as he wills.[41]

In the first schema, the descending one, the gift of the divine life comes from the Father, passes through the Son and the Spirit. In his return (ascending schema), the baptized man, thanks to the Spirit, knows the Son and in him the Father. The cycle is complete. It is thus that Irenaeus situates all the revealed truths, as also all errors opposed to them, with respect to the Trinitarian mystery, but not without stressing in his own way that the Father is the origin of the divine life: the Son dispenses the Spirit according as it pleases the Father and to whom the Father wills.

However, faced with the Gnostic extravagances, Irenaeus remained very timid with respect to the exploration of the ontological depths of the Trinitarian mystery and of the relations between the Three. For him, the generation of the Son by the Father is "ineffable," and he adds: "no one knows it: neither Valentinus nor Marcion nor Saturninus nor Basilides... but only the Father who has generated and the Son who is born."[42] Irenaeus then ridicules the first attempts, within Gnosticism, to use the psychological analogy in the explanation of the Trinitarian mystery: "That the (human) word is emitted by the thought and the mind, assuredly all men know. Those then who have invented the emanations have made no great discovery and they have revealed no great mystery in transferring to the Word, the only Son of God, what is known by everybody; they say that he is ineffable and unnameable and yet they recount his birth as if they had attended it as midwives, when they describe emanation and generation likening them to the uttered human word."[43]

Lebreton himself concedes that "there is perhaps some excess in the holy doctor's severity."[44] As a matter of fact, the analogy of the human word, at least insinuated by St. John (prologue), had already been exploited by the Apologists before Irenaeus, and will later be employed by Augustine and Thomas Aquinas; but in the essentially dialectical process, that of analogy, the Gnostics only followed the way of affirmation, without resorting to the ways of negation and eminence.[45] Without purifying concepts and language, they transposed into the Uncreated the created realities according to the created mode. Without saying so, that is really what

---

[41]St. Irenaeus, *Demonstration,* § 7. The Son "minister" could favor subordinationism.
[42]St. Irenaeus, *Adversus Haereses,* II, 28. 4-6; cf. Lebreton, *op. cit.,* v. II, pp. 551-552.
[43]*Ibid.,* toward the end.
[44]Lebreton, *op. cit.,* v. II, p. 552.
[45]*EF,* v. I, art."Analogie" by G. Söhngen (Paris, 1965); St. Thomas Aquinas, *Summa Theologica,* I, 13.

Irenaeus is reproaching them for; he is aware of the syncretist and pagan threats that heterodox Gnosticism presents; for him, as Lebreton rightly points out, "all these rash intrusions that aim to break open the divine secrets only lead to impious fantasies or to a sterile rationalism."[46]

However justified Irenaeus' reaction may have been, it must be recognized that no more than the Gnostics themselves did he have a grasp of an authentic theological analogy regarding the intimate mystery of the Trinity. He never discovered how to profit from the Gnostic errors so as to elaborate the psychological analogy starting from the two-fold datum of revelation and reason. Why did he not do then what Augustine would do two centuries later? The essential reason seems to be this: despite his genius, Irenaeus was not a philosopher, he did not have Neo-Platonism at his disposal, and was unable to make use of it, since Plotinus came after him. Philosophical and theological advances are tributary to time and through it to the partial temporality and historicity of human intelligence.[47]

Irenaeus' reserve in the consideration of the intimate mystery of the divinity, quite understandable in light of the excesses and imaginative frenzy of the Gnostics, does however lead to certain internal contradictions left unresolved which are perhaps even now less than perfectly perceived.

On the one hand Irenaeus initially gives a negative answer to a question that is closely connected with the analysis of this deep mystery:

> If it is asked, what did God do before making the world? we say the answer belongs to God. Scripture tells us that this world is a perfect work of God and that it began in time; but no text of Scripture tells us what God did previously. So the answer belongs to God and there is no need to try to imagine insane, reckless, blasphemous emanations....[48]

A little later, however, Irenaeus seems to think that Scripture does teach us what God was doing before he created the world:

---

[46]Lebreton, *op. cit.*, v. II, p. 537.

[47]Cf. St. Thomas Aquinas, *Summa Theologica*, I, 10, 5, c, ad 1m: "creaturae spirituales, quantum ad affectiones et intelligentias, in quibus est successio, mensurantur tempore.... Quantum vero ad eorum esse naturale, mensurantur aevo. Sed quantum ad visionem gloriae, participant aeternitatem." In the body of the article the Angelic Doctor clarifies the meaning of the word *aevum:* "non habet in se prius et posterius, sed ei conjungi possunt." The Angels and souls are then measured by *aevum* "quia esse eorum nec in transmutatione consistit, nec est subjectum transmutationis": this is only another way of affirming the immortality of the angelic spirit or of the human (soul) and at the same time denying the absolute character of its historicity which is bound up with it (more profoundly, in the case of man) only in view of making him arrive at the participated eternity of the glorious vision. Under penalty of denying the soul's immortality, one cannot fail to recognize that its essence escapes historicity. The complete man is a synthesis of eternity, of aeviternity and of history.

[48]St. Irenaeus, *Adversus Haereses*, II, 28, 3; cf. Lebreton, *op. cit.*, v. II, p. 554.

Not only before Adam but before all creation, the Word was glorifying the Father, dwelling in him, and was himself being glorified by the Father.[49]

Here Irenaeus seems to be recalling the Prologue of St. John and he cites the sacerdotal prayer of Jesus (Jn. 17:5, 24). In opposition to the unconscious Father of the Gnostics Irenaeus clearly affirms the mutual eternal glorification of the Father and the Son. This alone clearly explains other texts of Irenaeus.[50] We see thus that it is Scripture itself that obliges Irenaeus to view the mystery of the relations between the Father and the Son, independent of and "anterior" to creation, and to consider the Trinity in its inner life and not only in its relations with the world.

St. Irenaeus has preserved in a brilliant and profound way the deposit of Trinitarian Revelation. Even if he did not advance reflection on the Trinitarian mystery in its relation with the natural realities of man's intelligence and freedom, whose activity reflects the divine processions, he did examine this mystery in its connection with other truths of the faith and with the ultimate end of man.[51] This progress though only partial is itself a precious lesson for all Christian generations: when we cannot make truth advance by explicit integration in it of that element of truth which error conceals, we can and must preserve and transmit in its integrity the deposit of Trinitarian Revelation of which Christ is the plenitude. "O Timothy, guard what has been entrusted to you. Avoid the godless chatter and contradictions of what is falsely called knowledge (gnosis). For by professing it some have missed the mark as regards the Faith.... Guard the truth that has been entrusted to you by the Holy Spirit who dwells within us" (1 Tm. 6:20-21; 2 Tm. 1:14). Irenaeus understood that these words of Paul to Timothy were addressed also to him. We all then are deeply indebted to him.

III. THE TRINITARIAN HERESIES OF THE THIRD CENTURY: MODALISM AND SUBORDINATIONISM

These two heresies, opposed to one another, were summed up by Novatian in this way: "some identify Christ with the Father, others make of him a mere man." Both, by denying the Trinity, disfigure Christ by taking

---

[49]St. Irenaeus, *Adversus Haereses*, IV, 4, 1; Lebreton, *op. cit.*, v. II, p. 555 (Lebreton does not seem to notice the contradiction).

[50]For example, St. Irenaeus, *Adversus Haereses*, IV, 6, 7 (Lebreton, v. II, p. 591). See also, for an apparently different understanding, J. Ochagavia, S.J., *Visibile Patris Filius*, A Study of Irenaeus' Teaching on Revelation and Tradition, Or. Chr. Analecta 171. Rome, 1964, reviewed by J. Daniélou, Rech. Sc. Relig. 54 (1966), 308; we doubt however that future interpreters will retain J. Ochagavia's interpretation, which does not appear to admit Irenaeus' belief in a true eternity of the Son.

[51]Cf. DS 3016 at the beginning (DB 1796).

away from him his distinct divine personality. The two of them claim to be grounded on one and the same principle: there is only one God; from this undeniable principle they wish to conclude, by false reasonings, that there is only one person in God or that Christ could not be equal to the Father.

The result, Novatian concludes, is that the Lord was crucified between two thieves....

About these errors as about others we shall say here in general only what is essential, what is necessary either for grasping the later evolution of the dogma, or for showing their contemporary relevance, or for validating the doctrine of the Church.

1. *The Modalism of Sabellius*

Sabellius, perhaps identical in this respect with Praxeas (against whom Tertullian defended the Trinitarian dogma), represented the God of the New Testament thus: an only God, Father and Legislator in the Old Testament, who became flesh and Son in the New and sanctified the Church as Holy Spirit after Pentecost. In contemporary terms we would say that Sabellius yielded to a certain mono-personalist reading of the New Testament.

For Sabellianism God was one originally and eternally but he became trinity in time: Father at creation, Son at the time of the Incarnation and Sanctifier at the time of Pentecost, i.e. Holy Spirit. Thus the Three Persons were conceived as modes or functions of one really single Person, just as the same human person could be successively priest, doctor and magistrate.[52]

In our personalist era Sabellian modalism appears very outmoded. Nevertheless we would deceive ourselves greatly if we thought that the study of Modalism is without relevance for the doctrinal aspect of pastoral work today.

G.-P. Widmert, a Calvinist theologian and professor at Geneva, wrote in 1963:

> The preacher and the catechist unconsciously risk renewing the errors of Sabellianism or of Modalism which consider the titles of Father, Son and Spirit as mere labels, and the persons as successive masks put on by God. Trinitarian confusionism has a grave incidence on the conception of salvation; it threatens to make the individuality of the believer to founder on an anonymous redemption.... Modalism, on the level of popular piety, dissolves into gross pantheism.[53]

Does this danger threaten only the preacher or the catechist, and not the professional theologian? Must our reply not be negative, in the light of the

---

[52] J. P. Arendzen, *Holy Trinity*. London, 1939, p. 66.
[53] G.-P. Widmert, *Gloire au Père, au Fils, au Saint-Esprit*. Neuchâtel, 1963, p. 30.

present influence of an exclusively functional theology that inevitably glides toward Modalism? Such an influence now is felt in all the confessions.

What is more, modernist liberalism continues to orient numerous Protestants in a Modalist direction. Let us cite, with G.-P. Widmert, a characteristic example:

> Christian theology must conclude to the moral divinity of Jesus on earth, to the present divinity of Christ, while discarding the prehistoric divinity of Jesus and the eternal divinity of the Spirit. Thus it does not lead to a real trinity but to the unity of God, to the paternity of one God, to a sonship of Jesus that is not metaphysical but moral, to a communion of Jesus with his Father on earth, to the duality of God and of Christ in heavenly power, to the action of God or of Christ under the form of the Spirit.[54]

A significant declaration of 1912, which would certainly be counter-signed by many of today's Protestants. But of course an excessive fear of Modalism would constitute an opposite danger in the direction of tritheism, a danger that came to light at Nicaea, when some backed away from the term "consubstantial" for this reason.

Contemporary Modalists, moreover, would doubtless reply in the same way as Sabellius to those who might offer them the objection: how can you claim despite all this to still maintain the Trinity?

Sabellius retorted: the one God, who successively becomes Father by creation, Son by Incarnation and Spirit on the day of Pentecost, is not the same when he appears as Son as when he appears as Father. There is, not a real Trinity, but a trinity of the manifestation of God. In reality, God is Father-Son, *huiopator*.

Such a reply invites us to stress what we have already said: to truly overcome Modalism, it is necessary to show that the Trinity we venerate is not merely economic and functional but also ontological and immanent.

2. *Subordinationism and its cultic consequences*

The essence of Subordinationism consists in the affirmation that the Son, and *a fortiori* the Spirit are inferior and unequal to the Father. A perpetual temptation and one which should not surprise us. Would it not be much more astounding for a community of men who had known Jesus living among men and in their midst, who had seen him eat and drink, sleep and rise, walk and talk, subject to the sufferings and sadnesses of other men, to immediately start talking and writing about the consubstantiality of the Son with the Father, and this from the very beginning of that community's adherence by faith to the Paschal mystery?

---

[54]G. Fulliquet, *Précis de Dogmatique*. Geneva, 1912, p. 221 (cited by Widmert, p. 56).

Peter says that Jesus had been made Lord and Christ (Acts 2:36) and Paul writes (Rom. 1:4) that "Christ Jesus has been constituted Son of God with power...by his resurrection from the dead." These are difficult texts,[55] invoked by Subordinationists of all times. But their favorite text is 1 Cor. 15:28.[56] Yet these Apostolic statements present no difficulty if we remember four facts:

a) *the authors of the New Testament knew Jesus as man before believing in his divinity;*
b) *they did not distinguish with the precision of logicians between the human and the divine in Jesus Christ;*
c) *above all Jesus Christ did not cease to be man and as such subject to the Father, even though he was God and the Son of God;*
d) *only after Easter did Jesus come to exercise fully the omnipotence that he possessed since the Incarnation.*

In the light of all these statements put together we can understand how the pre-Nicene Fathers without exception left us expressions that could be interpreted in a subordinationist sense, but which do not always need to be understood in this way. A correct exegesis of their writings is often difficult, the more so because the subject is debated even among Catholic authors, though these agree that there was at most an error of theologians but not of the Church; Protestant (liberal and modernist) authors often give interpretations that are clearly modalist and subordinationist.

A decisive point emerges, however: for us to encounter in them not only equivocal expressions but also a doctrine that is clearly subordinationist, the pre-Nicene theologians would have to have had a clear and distinct idea of the subordination of Christ to the Father. But such a concept did not exist, just as there did not exist a clear and distinct idea of the consubstantiality or the equality between Son and Father.

Thus the case of Origen, for example, is controverted, even among his admirers and specialists.[57] We understand this much better when we encounter in him contradictory texts on the cult to be rendered to Christ. Here he tells us that we must invoke the Father alone but through the mediation of the Son, sovereign Priest;[58] there, he assures us on the

---

[55]About these texts, consult F.-X. Durrwell, C.SS.R., *La Résurrection de Jésus, mystère de salut.* Lyons, 1961, pp. 136 and 121ff.; and Lagrange, *Romains.*

[56]About this text, see Durrwell, *op. cit.,* 406-408; Lk. 2:51; 10:17; Rom. 13:1 (same Greek verb).

[57]See, e.g., J. Daniélou, *Origène.* Paris, 1948, pp. 249-258; I. Ortiz de Urbina, S.J., *El simbolo niceno.* Madrid, 1947, pp. 160-165; P. Nemeshegyi, S.J., *La paternité de Dieu chez Origène.* Tournai, 1960, pp. 85-100. This last author differs from the two before in affirming that Origen is not a subordinationist. We doubt however that he is fully convincing.

[58]Origen, *De Oratione,* 15. 1; Origen gives as reason that "God alone (that is to say, the Father) is good" (Mk. 10:18).

contrary that Christ, like God (the Father), should be invoked and petitioned and that we must offer him thanks, so as to do what he himself wished: "That all may honor the Son as they honor the Father" (Jn. 5:23).[59] Origen even gives a very orthodox exegesis of 1 Cor. 15:28: "The text 'the Son will subject himself,' does not mean to say that he is inferior. How could we treat as inferior the Son who is all that the Father is: 'Father, all that is yours is mine' (Jn. 17:10)."[60]

The examples just cited show the spiritual and cultic consequences of doctrinal errors about the relations and the equality between the Father and the Son. This point is always relevant, as some recent declarations of the ecclesiastical magisterium show: three of Pope Pius XII and one of the Second Vatican Council.

In 1943 Pius XII thus expressed himself in his encyclical *Mystici Corporis:*

> Some say that our supplications ought not to be directed to the person of Jesus Christ, but rather to God or to the eternal Father through Christ, since our Savior, as head of his mystical Body, must only be considered as Mediator between God and men. This is not only contrary to the spirit of the Church and the custom of Christians, but also an offense against truth. Christ in fact... is head of the whole Church according to each of his two natures; besides he himself has solemnly declared, "If you ask anything of *me* in my name, I will do it" (Jn. 14:14).[61] And although especially in the Eucharistic sacrifice—in which Christ as priest and victim fulfills in a special way the function of conciliator—prayers are often addressed to the eternal Father through his only Son, nonetheless it is not rare that they also are addressed to the divine Redeemer Himself.[62]

In 1947 the same Pontiff spoke to Christians of the soul of Jesus, adorer of the divine Person of the Word, as center of their Eucharistic thanksgiving: "let us plunge into the saintly soul of Christ and unite ourselves to him so as to participate in the acts of adoration by which he offers to the holy Trinity[63] a supremely acceptable and pleasing homage."[64] If Jesus as

---

[59]Origen, *In Epist. ad Romanos*, 8, 5; MG 14, 1166.

[60]*Ibid.*, 7. 5; MG 14, 1115. See other texts in I. Ortiz de Urbina, S.J., *El simbolo niceno*. Madrid, 1947, pp. 160-165. The subordinationist climate of O. is quite clear there.

[61]Cf. A. Hamman, O.F.M., *La prière*, v. I, *Le Nouveau Testament*. Tournai, 1959, p. 407: "verse 14 (of Jn. 14) is very much contested by the critics but without convincing reasons. It is not a repetition if you retain the 'me' on which, with *ego*, rests the accent of the phrase and which scans the progression. The verse affirms most clearly that the prayer in the name of Jesus reaches Christ himself and is addressed to the glorified Lord. And the prayer of the faithful for the intentions of the Church will always be granted: Christ in glory having assured his followers of his efficacious assistance."

[62]DS 3820.

[63]Note the presuppositions, at first sight so astonishing, of the affirmation: the Word offers himself; in fact, it is the divine Person of the Word to whom we must attribute the acts posited

man adores his own divine person of Word, the Christian cannot do less if he wishes to unite himself to Christ.

In 1956 Pius XII, speaking to a liturgical congress, said still more clearly:

> We wish to treat of the *infinita et divina majestas* of Christ, which the words *Christus Deus* translate.... The humanity of Christ has the right also to the cult of *latria* because of its hypostatic union with the Word, but his divinity is the reason and the source of this cult. So the divinity of Christ cannot remain somehow at the periphery of liturgical thought. It is normal for us to go *ad Patrem per Christum*, since Christ is the Mediator between God and men. But he is not only Mediator; he is also, in the Trinity, equal to the Father and to the Holy Spirit. Let it suffice to recall the majestic prologue of the Gospel of St. John: "The Word was God.... All things were made through him. And without him was not anything made that was made" (Jn. 1:1-3). Christ is the first and the last, the Alpha and the Omega. At the end of the world, when all enemies will have been vanquished and last of all death, Christ, that is to say the Word subsisting in the human Nature, will hand over the kingdom to God his Father, and the Son himself will subject himself to him who put all things under him, that God may be all in all. Meditation on the *infinita, summa, divina Majestas* of Christ can certainly contribute to a deepening of the liturgical sense.[65]

It will be noted how these texts offer us in the composite person of Jesus Christ, the perfect adorer, a synthesis of the God who has a right to our adorations, and of him who is the adorer par excellence. These texts certainly aim to fight against the practical and theoretical effects of a liturgical subordinationism.

Vatican II, conscious of the doctrinal presuppositions of liturgical life, has briefly synthesized all these teachings: "The Church, well-beloved spouse of Christ, invokes its Lord and passes through him to render its worship to the eternal Father."[66] These three words: *Dominum suum invocat*, suffice to repeat the imperishable truth: Christ is not only the mediator but also the term of the cult of the Church. We can add that in adoring the Son of God, the Church recognizes that he receives the divine nature from the Father, and that in consequence it adores Christ not only as God but also as Son of God and thus the Father remains the absolutely ultimate term of its cult. An analogous observation could be made with regard to the cult rendered

---

by the human nature, including therefore the act of adoration. If the incarnate Word can adore his Father and the Spirit, we do not see why he could not, as incarnate—that is the whole point—adore himself.

[64]Pius XII, *Mediator Dei*, AAS 39 (1947) 568.

[65]Pius XII, discourse to the 1st international congress of pastoral liturgy, AAS 48 (1956), 711-725; our translation is drawn from *Maison-Dieu*, 1956, p. 343.

[66]Vatican II, const. *Sacrosanctum Concilium*, § 7.

to the Holy Spirit, adored as Spirit of the Father and of the Son, a cult to which we will return.

IV. TERTULLIAN, "CREATOR" OF THE TRINITARIAN LANGUAGE OF THE CHURCH

Tertullian's thought is exceptionally interesting for those who wish to gain an awareness of the problems posed by the evolution of Trinitarian dogma. Although his greatest Trinitarian work, *Adversus Praxean*,[67] was written after he had abandoned the Catholic Church in favor of Montanism, his teaching about the Trinity is orthodox on the whole[68] and it had remarkably great influence inside the Church. It marks an important stage in the passage from a certain "cosmological" outlook on the Trinity toward a consideration of its inner life, by way of the doctrine of the missions of the Word and of the Spirit. Today it offers us a way toward a new synthesis between two inseparable poles of the mystery: the economic pole and the immanent pole. Its study consequently is still useful to help us to extract the treatise on the Trinity (rather than the mystery) from the "splendid isolation," in which, according to K. Rahner and others, it had been set off.

1. *The cosmological representation of the mystery in Tertullian*

It is as an African enlivened by the sun, thirsty for water and nourished by the fruits of his soil that Tertullian pictures the Trinitarian processions in the context of creation and sanctification. In this way he wishes to fight against the depersonalizing Modalism of Praxeas:

> God, as the Paraclete teaches, has produced his Word as the root produces the stalk, the source the river, the sun its ray. For these realities (*species*) are the projections (*probolai* is a term utilized by the Gnostics) of the substances from which they come. I would not fear then to compare the Son to the stalk that comes from the root, to the river that comes from the source, to the ray that shoots forth from the sun. In fact, if everything that is origin is engendering, and if everything that is originated is an offshoot of that from which it proceeds, with much greater reason is this true of the Word of God who has received as his name that of Son. And since neither the stalk is separated from its root, nor the river from its source, nor the ray from the sun, no more is the Word from God. That is why, relying on these examples, I affirm that God and his Word, the Father and his Son are two. For the root and the stalk are two individualities, but united; the source and the river are two

---

[67]Treatise written between 213 and 218.

[68]This is at least the opinion of J. Moingt and especially of B. Piault, cf. the texts cited in notes 69 and 76, Moingt is more nuanced.

realities but indivisible; the sun and its ray are two aspects of the same thing but inseparable.

But if what proceeds from another is necessarily second with respect to the one from which it proceeds, it is not, for all that, separated from it. Where there is a second, they are inevitably two, (*secundus ubi est, duo sunt*) and where there is a third, they are necessarily three. But the Spirit is the third after God and the Son, just as the fruit produced by the stalk but which comes from the root is the third; third as the rivulet that derives from the river but comes from the source; third as the tip of the ray relative to the ray and to the sun. Nevertheless, none of these would be alien to the original matrix from which each receives its properties.

So the Trinity, which derives from the Father in strictly arranged degrees, does not in any way contradict the monarchy and protects the nature of the economy.[69]

As has been rightly emphasized,[70] images abound, sing and live. The savory fruit of the Holy Spirit is plucked from the branch of the Son which is nourished by the root, the Father, origin of all life. The Holy Spirit comes from the Father through the Son.[71] The Father is also the source, the Son is the river originating in the paternal source, but the irrigation canals are the marvelous symbol of the Spirit given to souls. Water comes, but without the sun it would be more detrimental than useful. The Father here is the sun. The ray that he emits, the Son. But the ray, though emitted, is vivifying for us only if its fine point touches and warms us: so the Spirit is the vehicle of warmth and life.

---

[69] Tertullian, *Adversus Praxean,* ch. VIII, 5-7; *RJ* 375 (partial text); we utilized the translation of B. Piault, in his article, "Tertullian a-t-il été subordinatien?" *RSPT,* 47 (1963), 181-204; the translation is found on pp. 201-202. We have modified some details of the translation in the interest of greater fidelity to the original, which is found in the Latin patrology of Migne, v. 2, col. 153-196.

[70] B. Piault, *Le mystère du Dieu vivant.* Paris, 1956, pp. 76-77.

[71] We admit that we do not agree with the exegesis of this text regarding the procession of the Holy Spirit, which has been proposed by the celebrated patrologist P.-T. Camelot, O.P., in a note on "Spiritus a Deo et Filio" (*RSPT* 33, 1949, 32-34); if it is true that the preposition *ab* carries in Latin a different sense from that of the preposition *ex*, it is no less true that Tertullian says: "Spiritus a Deo et Filio sicut tertium a radice fructus ex fructice,...ex flumine...ex radio"; but we remember that "frutex, flumen, radius" represent the Son; and especially that the whole paragraph treats of the *probolai,* the *prolationes* of the Son and of the Spirit, and that Tertullian explicitly maintains that "omnis origo parens est et omne quod ex origine profertur progenies est.... Omne quod prodit ex aliquo, secundum sit ejus necesse est de quo prodit." It is not a question then of merely noting the order but just as much of noting through the order the origin and then the procession. We can then legitimately see here an allusion to the procession of the Holy Spirit *a Patre Filioque;* the unity of the spirating principle is even insinuated by the words "radix et frutex duae res sunt, sed conjunctae," and the words which follow. Above all the sentence that immediately follows the one analyzed by P. Camelot clearly

Tertullian thus gives us three groups of images strongly linked with one another, to signify the mystery both in its inner order and in its sanctifying effusion:[72] root-branch-fruit, source-river-rivulet, sun-ray-tip. It seems that Tertullian was the first to elaborate such a systematic, though inevitably deficient, cosmological representation of the mystery. If we are tempted today to smile at it all or to find it useless, is there not a hidden naiveness in this? For the psychological analogy, though assuredly less imperfect, still cannot pretend to represent the mystery adequately either, and the family and ecclesial images offer many difficulties as we shall see, should we wish to use them to picture the inner order of the mystery. Tertullian in reality was anticipating one aspect of Augustine's procedure which has gained relatively little attention: one that seeks not an image but some vestiges of the Trinity in the corporeal world. With our greater awareness today of the intimate bond between spirit and matter, we are able, better than the Neoplatonic philosophers, to grasp the realism of Tertullian's language. Does not this realism have the added advantage of being able to familiarize with the Trinitarian mystery the immense majority of men, who are doubtless less sensitive to an intrasubjective analogy and more familiar with cosmic realities? And are not these material representations rooted moreover in Scripture,[73] even though not as clearly as the family analogy?

To grasp in Tertullian the sense of the words "monarchy" and "economy" in the last phrase of the text cited above, we must remember that the Modalists were accusing the orthodox Christians of tritheism and in opposition to them boasted of rendering worship to one only God whose "monarchy" they prided themselves on maintaining. Tertullian replied that the monarchy (e.g. in the Roman Empire) did not prevent the monarch from associating his son in the exercise of his power.[74] Thus, it can be noted in passing, one encounters the political connotations of the Trinitarian controversies, connotations which will be still more visible at the time of Arianism.

As regards the "economy," this in no way signifies, as it does for the Fathers of the fourth century and for us today, the redemptive Incarnation

---

signifies that the Spirit "a matrice proprietates suas duxit," that is to say, from the Father. It seems impossible then to doubt the sense meant by Tertullian: it is relative not only to the order but to the origin of the Spirit regarding his mission and consequently regarding his eternal procession. This last point is otherwise confirmed by the famous phrase of *Adversus Praxean* IV, 1: "Spiritum non aliunde puto quam a Patre per Filium," cited by *RJ* 372 (*ML* 2, 159). For a different interpretation see J. Moingt, *Theol. trinit. de Tertullien*. Paris, 1966, c. III, p. 1067.

[72] To our knowledge there is, in St. Irenaeus, no integration of Trinitarian images relative to the inner mystery of the divinity.

[73] Cf. Wis. 7:26; Jn. 7:38-39.

[74] Cf. G. L. Prestige, *God in Patristic Thought*. London, 1964, pp. 98-99.

as distinct from the Trinity, but rather it signifies for Tertullian "the enumeration of the divine persons in the scriptural argumentation: it is the manifestation of the divine 'processions' in history by the ordered plurality of lordly and salvific activities."[75]

2. *"Prolations" and missions in Tertullian*

This is my faith: the Father, the Son and the Spirit are inseparable one from the other. One is the Father, another the Son, another the Spirit.... While they (the modalist Monarchians) affirm the identity of the Father, the Son and the Spirit and thus favor the monarchy over the economy, urged by necessity I say that the Son is another than the Father, not by diversity but by their distribution; another not because they are divided but because they are distinct, because the Father and the Son are not identical but numerically different one from the other. In fact, the Father is the whole substance, the Son is the derivation and a portion of this whole, as he himself attests: the Father is greater than I (Jn. 14:28).... The Father is another than the Son since he is greater than the Son: for he who generates is one, he who is generated is another; he who sends is one, he who is sent another; he who acts is one, he by whom he acts is another. It is then quite right that the Lord himself used this language with regard to the person of the Paraclete, not to signify their division but their rank: I will ask, he says (Jn. 14:16) the Father and he will send you another advocate, the Spirit of Truth. Thus the Lord affirms that the Paraclete is another than himself, just as we affirm that the Son is another than the Father, and he does this to signify that the Paraclete holds the third place, just as we have shown that the Son holds the second, with regard to the economy of the Trinity.[76]

In this passage, Tertullian wished to stress the distinction of the Persons at the heart of their indivisible unity. The masculine *alium* in opposition to the neuter *aliud*, recognizes that the Father, the Son and the Spirit are distinct subjects. Still better, distinct persons: Tertullian speaks of the person of the Paraclete (*in persona Paracleti*).

There is however a more embarrassing formula which recurs in two other texts of Tertullian[77] wherein the Son is qualified as "derivation and portion of the whole of the Father," *derivatio totius et portio*. Does such an expression permit us to uphold Tertullian's Trinitarian orthodoxy, to deny his subordinationism, and to recognize in him an affirmation of the equality of the divine Persons? Is the Son only a "portion" of the Father?

---

[75] J. Moingt, S.J., "Théologie trinitaire de Tertullien," *Rech. Sc. Relig.* 54 (1966), 358-359.
[76] Tertullian, *Adv. Praxean*, ch. IX, ML 2, 164; RJ 376. We have used Piault's translation (*op. cit.*, RSPT, pp. 191-192), while modifying it slightly (concerning the French text, Ed.'s note).
[77] Tertullian, *Adv. Praxean*, ch. XXVI.

To resolve the difficulty, we must view these expressions in relation to the Johannine text that they explain: "the Father is greater than I" (Jn. 14:28). It must be evident to us that the relation of the Son to the Father is a relation of dependence even in God, since the Son being generated, receives all from the Father, while the relation Father-Son is that of the one generating who actively communicates to the one generated the full divine substance, is that of the Father who has given his Son a mission and sends him into this world: *alius qui generat, alius qui generatur; alius qui mittit, alius qui mittitur.* There is no question here of an inequality of nature but of a dependence of Jesus in regard to his Father in his origin and in his mission. He who generates is greater, not by nature but according to his personal property of Father, than the one who is generated. Such is the explanation of Piault.[78]

Although incomplete the exegesis of Tertullian is partially correct while the "interpretation that understands *Pater major me est* of Christ considered merely in his human nature opens the way to the error of Nestorius: by making the human nature of Christ a personal subject who says 'I' on his own account"[79]: so Piault sees it, justly complemented by Lagrange.[80]

St. Hilary too adopts the same exegesis, and St. Thomas himself tells us with his own finishing touches:

> According to Hilary the Father is, even according to the divinity, greater than the Son and yet the Son is not inferior to him but equal. The Father is greater than the Son, not in power, greatness, eternity, but by the authority of the principle who gives. For the Father receives nothing from another, but the Son receives, so to speak, his nature from the Father by way of eternal generation. The Father is then greater because he gives, but the Son is not less but equal, because he receives all that the Father has.[81]

The precision of the exegesis given by Tertullian saves the orthodoxy of his *thought,* but not as much can be said for his *language* in the passage under consideration: this is the way the best living specialist on Tertullian puts it, "the Father is the whole, and not a portion of the whole. . . . He (Tertullian)

---

[78]Piault, *art. cit., RSPT* 194. But where does Tertullian say that the Son receives *all* from the Father? Piault gives us an exegesis of St. John rather than of Tertullian.

[79]*Ibid.*

[80]M.-J. Lagrange, O.P., *Evangile selon saint Jean.* Paris, 1946, p. 395 (commentary on Jn. 14:28): "The Christ of John never speaks simply as man but as being the Son of God incarnate. A God is compared to a God because he is man at the same time. It is not a man who speaks, it is the incarnate God, because of his human nature, not at all because of his personal relations with the Father." It seems to us that this is also what St. Augustine had in mind.

[81]St. Thomas Aquinas, *in Jo* 14:28; cf. *Summa Theologica,* III, 20. I, 2; *DS* 536.

fails to show that the Father, the Son and the Spirit are identical in substance...as the actual concept of consubstantiality demands.... He tends toward a metaphysical tritheism and an ontological subordinationism." J. Moingt adds, however, "Tertullian denies systematically that the three persons are three substances...he did not positively think that the Son is inferior to the Father in his being."[82] He tends toward this but resists the temptation.

How shall we explain the fact that Tertullian's language is not equal to his thought? On the one hand—but is this his fault?—his philosophical concepts are not sufficiently elaborated, in particular that of substance. On the other hand he lets himself be involved in Praxeas' problematics. "Praxeas sees in the divine plurality above all an offense against the monarchical power of the Creator.... Praxeas is not preoccupied with the 'disposition' of God before the beginning of the world; on the contrary he denounces as a division of substance the fact that the Son comes from the Father at the beginning. This would lead Tertullian to speak of the 'prolations' in the same perspective of time and exteriority, and not to investigate at all the eternal origins of the Son and of the Spirit as such. But his silence is not negation, nor even lack of recognition."[83]

For Tertullian God always has in him his *Ratio*, his Thought which becomes Word, *Sermo*, at the time of Creation. By the term *Sermo* Tertullian designates the emission of the Word as creative utterance. It is not divinity that the *Ratio-Sermo* receives by his generation (from God) at the time of creation, but his appellation of Son of God. The *Ratio* is eternal.

Here we meet again both the problematics of the Apologists (Justin, Tatian, Athenagoras), and in part that which is stimulating Cullmann's disciples today: the *Logos endiathetikos*, the Word latent in the bosom of God, which becomes the *Logos prophorikos*, the Word uttered and externalized in and on the occasion of creation (though Tertullian prefers to speak of *Sermo*, not of Word or *verbum*). The *Ratio-Sermo* is called Son only in his relation to Creation and Incarnation. Then God becomes Father.[84]

This doctrine which recurs in numerous texts of Tertullian,[85] is assuredly subtle. It would be interesting to compare it systematically with the contemporary functional theology of Cullmann. But in spite of Tertullian's obscurities, conceptual and verbal limits and the errors to which his doctrine is exposed, we can retain from it especially what is already found in the prologue of the Gospel of St. John: "Tertullian affirms equivalently that the Word of God is at the same time in the Father and in

---

[82]Moingt, *art. cit.*, pp. 360-362.
[83]*Ibid.*, 363.
[84]Cf. Piault, *art. cit.*, pp. 195-200; A. d'Alès, S.J., *La théologie de Tertullien*. Paris, 1905, p. 86.
[85]*Ibid.*, pp. 84-96. A. d'Alès has grouped and "organized" the texts.

this world."⁸⁶ While stressing more clearly than Tertullian did, if he has not rather denied it, that the Word is eternally Son independently of all creation, we cannot but share the fundamental thought of the apostate apologist provided we modify it: the "generation (of the Son) is at the same time a procession and a mission, in virtue of which the *Sermo* which is the Son, brings into this world the activity and life of God."⁸⁷ We are in the presence of a movement, wrote A. d'Alès, which starts from the divinity in order to arrive at creation, and this movement has a double aspect⁸⁸: the generation of the Word and the creation of the world destined for salvation.

While Tertullian's attention, faced with the Monarchians, concentrated on and aimed to demonstrate that the "projection" (*probole, prolatio*) of the Word into the world neither separated nor divided him from God-the-Father, wouldn't his value for the present generation lie in helping us better understand that the eternal generation of the Son by the Father cannot be separated from the creation of the world, from which however it must be carefully distinguished? and that the eternally uttered Word is the Word of a universe⁸⁹ that is eternally created⁹⁰ although temporal in itself? If it is not true that the Father is a real relation to the universe while he is a real relation to his Son (a point we will take up again), and if it is also not true that the Father generated his Son in view of creating the universe (as some texts of Tertullian would have us believe⁹¹) because the world is not a final cause of an uncreated activity, yet it is true that this world is present to the Father as he generates his Son. It is in eternally and presently generating his Son that with him and through him the Father creates the universe. Under pain of heresy we must affirm not only that the Father *with* his Son and their Spirit has created all things, but also that he presently creates all things *through* them,⁹² in that he gives unceasingly to the Son and to the Spirit the divine nature that is the sole principle of the creation of the universe. The Son is *Creator genitus*, according to St. Thomas' phrase.⁹³ The notion of begotten Creator allows us, by retaining the best in Tertullian's

---

⁸⁶Piault, *art. cit., RSPT,* 200; cf. Jn. 1:1, 10.

⁸⁷*Ibid.*, p. 193: one ought to say: the generation of the Son is a procession which prolongs itself in a mission.

⁸⁸A. d'Alès, *op. cit.,* p. 89.

⁸⁹St. Thomas Aquinas, *Summa contra Gentiles,* IV, 13. 5.

⁹⁰Cf. L. Malevez, S.J., "Nouveau Testament et théologie fonctionnelle," *Rech. Sc. Rel.* 48 (1960), 267-268: "the Son does not exist without placing (freely) the eternal divine act of creation in time." Cf. St. Thomas Aquinas, *Summa contra Gentiles,* II, 35.

⁹¹Tertullian, *Adversus Praxean,* VII (*generatus ad effectum*), ML 2, 161; RJ 373; adv. Hermogenem (200-206), XVIII. Cf. A. d'Alès, *op. cit.,* pp. 90-96.

⁹²Cf. DS 171 (DB 77): "si quis non dixerit, omnia per Filium et Spiritum Sanctum Patrem fecisse, id est visibilia et invisibilia, haereticus sit." To better grasp its import this condemnation must be compared with that which immediately precedes it there (DS 170; DB 76).

⁹³St. Thomas Aquinas, *Summa Theologica,* I, 34.3.1; cf. 45.6.2; see also the text to which note 89

writings, not to separate the cosmic action of God from his immanent activity. As he keenly perceived, it is in the notion of mission, that their perfect synthesis is realized.[94] Through it the begotten Creator is sent to his creation in order to sanctify it, that is to unite it to him and his Father.

Let us close this brief parenthesis that was intended to show the contemporary relevance of Tertullian's Trinitarian doctrine. "A word sums up his contribution to the Trinitarian dogma and describes the measure of his intellectual initiative: Tertullian created a new theological language... the rational language of the Trinitarian faith."[95] To him we owe "these well known formulas: *Trinitas*,[96] *tres personae, una substantia*, which he forged and which have become commonplace in Trinitarian dogma, as also have the more imaginative expressions: *Deum de Deo, lumen de lumine*, by which we still profess our faith."[97]

Could not the study of the genesis of this "new theological language"[98] that has now become ancient, stimulate our efforts for the renewal of the "rational language of the Trinitarian faith" in today's world?

V. A REMARKABLE DECLARATION OF POPE SAINT DIONYSIUS OF ROME IN 262

The anti-Sabellian reaction led St. Dionysius of Alexandria to an excess in the direction of tritheism.[99] The Pope of Rome, his namesake, judged it necessary to intervene in the debate by a document of magnificent balance. Let us read this very rich witness of faith, on which Tertullian's influence is perhaps not absent:

> I must address myself to those who suppress, separate, divide the most venerable dogma of the Church of God, the monarchy, into three powers or separated hypostases and into three divinities.... There are among you those who introduce these opinions, diametrically opposed, so to speak, to the thought of Sabellius.

---

of this chapter alluded: "Verbum in Deo conceptum ex eo quod seipsum intelligit...verbum unum et idem omnium rerum" (*Summa contra Gentiles*, IV, 13.5).

[94]St. Thomas Aquinas, *Summa Theologica*, I, 43.2.3: "missio includit processionem aeternam et aliquid addit, scilicet temporalem effectum."

[95]Moingt, *art. cit.*, pp. 367, 369.

[96]In truth, the first author to speak to us of a *Trinity* in God seems to have been St. Theophilus of Antioch, toward 182: *ad Autolicum*, 2, 15; RJ 180; MG 6, 1077; cf. Lebreton, *op. cit.*, v. II, pp. 505-513.

[97]Piault, *art. cit.*, p. 204. He alludes to *Adv. Praxean* II, 4: ML 2, 156 (RJ 371).

[98]Such is precisely the object of the exhaustive study published by J. Moingt on the "théologie trinitaire de Tertullien" (Paris, 1967, 4 vol.) where he studies in 1000 pages the ten short chapters (60 pp.) of the *Adv. Praxean* in the light of the whole of Tertullian's work. There he analyzes in particular the indirect influence of heterodox Gnostic theology on Tertullian.

[99]Cf. G. Bardy, DTC, art., "Trinité," v. XV, 2 (1950), col. 1646: "the whole of Arianism is contained, and more than germinally, in the formulas of the bishop of Alexandria"; RJ 609-610.

His blasphemy is to say that the Son is the Father and vice versa; but these preach in some way three gods by dividing the holy unity into three distinct hypostases that are entirely separated.

For it is necessary that the divine Word be united to the God of the universe and that the Holy Spirit have in God his abode and his habitation. And it is absolutely necessary that the Holy Trinity be recapitulated and gathered into one as in its vertex, I mean the omnipotent God of the universe. We must believe in God the Father almighty and in Jesus Christ his Son and in the Holy Spirit.... It is thus that we maintain the divine Trinity and at the same time the holy preaching of the monarchy.[100]

Several points of this strong text should be underlined. On the one hand the Pope rejects, not purely and simply but in a tritheist context, the affirmation of a Trinity of *hypostases*; we can thus understand why the Second Council of Constantinople will be able to speak of three hypostases in God without contradicting Dionysius of Rome, for these three hypostases will be presented not as separated but as three persons, united yet remaining distinct.

On the other hand, the original "point" of the document consists in presenting (in a very Pauline style[101]) the Father as the inner recapitulator of the Trinitarian mystery. For the almighty God of which it treats is evidently, following Pauline language, the Father to whom the divine Word is united and in whom the Holy Spirit has his abode and habitation. We are thus in the presence of a theological vision which recognizes in the Father the mediating link between the Word and the Spirit, a point which will be accentuated through a large current of Greek patristic tradition, and which in no way excludes the Word from being considered as mediator between the Father and the Spirit, or the Spirit from being considered as bond and mediator between the Father and the Son, affirmations that we meet again and again in the two patristic traditions, Latin and Greek.[102] We see thus that there are three ways, equally true and equally founded on Revelation, of considering the unification of three "dyads" in the heart of the Trinity.[103]

Finally, in refusing to "cut the monarchy into three principles," which

---

[100]We borrow this translation from G. Bardy, *ibid.,* col. 1647; the text is cited by St. Athanasius, *MG* 25, 461-465 and by *DS* 112-115 (*DB* 48-51).

[101]Cf. Eph. 1:10: it is *the Father* who recapitulates all under one single head, his Son Jesus Christ.

[102]As we will see later St. Epiphanius offers us, before St. Augustine, the Spirit as the bond of the Trinity. As regards the Word as mediator between the Father and the Spirit, this is a notion that is inherent in the doctrine of the Spirit proceeding from the Father through the Son: *a Patre per Filium*, a doctrine that is current among the Greek Fathers.

[103]Cf. J. de Baciocchi, S.M., *Nouv. Rev. Théol.* 77 (1955), 1036-1049; S. Boulgakof, *Le Paraclet.* Paris, 1946, 171-174.

would be a "diabolical doctrine," Pope St. Dionysius, by his document, placed a new link in the doctrinal chain that will lead to the Nicene term "consubstantial."[104]

VI. ARIUS, CONSCIOUS DENIER OF THE EQUALITY BETWEEN SON AND FATHER

It can be said that Cerinthus,[105] against whom St. John wrote his Gospel, was in part a remote precursor of Arius. To better grasp the import of the Arian error, it would be useful to recall briefly Cerinthus' teaching. He propagated a Gnosticism ahead of its time. Denying that Jesus was God, he distinguished between Jesus and Christ.

For Cerinthus, Jesus was a mere man, son not only of Mary but also of Joseph, superior to other men only in prudence, justice, and wisdom. After his Baptism, the supreme God, not the creator, sent him the Spirit, called Christ, in the form of a dove. Then Jesus began to announce this unknown God and to work miracles. Before his death, the Spirit Christ abandoned Jesus, who died as a mere man: cf. 1 Jn. 5:5 and Jn. 1:29-34. (These Johannine texts become much more clear, as also does Jn. 19:34-37, when we know the doctrine of Cerinthus against which St. John is fighting.) Cerinthus recognized a witness of the Spirit in the water at the time of the Baptism, but he denied the witness by blood. St. John on the contrary attests that the Spirit renders witness to Jesus as the true Christ, Son of God, even after his death (Jn. 19:31-37).

Cerinthus thus attacked the foundations of the Christian religion: according to him we are not redeemed by the blood of Christ, but have received a revelation of the unknown God, Father but not creator. At the same time Cerinthus denied the creative divinity and the redemptive work of Jesus. We see, therefore, why St. John fled his company in the public baths of Asia Minor[106] (cf. 2 Jn. 10-11). Above all he wrote his Gospel to show against Cerinthus that Jesus is the Son of God.

Cerinthus' attempt was the first effort to hellenize Christian dogma. Arianism repeated this, though in a different way.

Arius, who was born in 256 and died in 336, was ordained priest at Alexandria in 310 and proposed his system in 323, a system that drew inspiration from Greek philosophy, from Judaism in that he denied the

---

[104]Unfortunately we cannot here study the astonishing link that is constituted by the *Expositio fidei* of St. Gregory Thaumaturgus, where in a few brief lines that must be read, the Trinitarian dogma is admirably presented: *RJ* 611, *MG* 10, 984; cf. L. Froidevaux, *Le symbole de S. G. le Thaumaturge*, *RSR* 19 (1929), 191ff.; Jouassard (*Maria*, v. I, pp. 83-84, n. 22) and Laurentin (*Court Traité*. Paris, 1953, p. 161) doubt its authenticity.

[105]See G. Bareille, *DTC* v. II (1905), col. 2151-2155: art. "Cérinthe"; Irenaeus, *Adv. Haereses*, III, 11. 1 (*MG* 7, 880). G. Bardy, *DHGE*, 12 (1953), 169-170.

[106]We know St. John's remark as reported by Eusebius (*H.E.* III, 28; *MG* 20, 276): "Let us flee, lest the presence of such an enemy of the truth cause the walls to fall down."

divinity of Jesus, and from paganism in that he seemed to affirm secondary and intermediary divinities (Jesus and the Spirit) between the supreme God and the world. He was resuming the Gnostic attempt under a more rationalized form. We have here essentially a syncretism.

Let us sum up, in the very limited measure in which it is possible to do so in the present state of historical knowledge,[107] the essential aspects of Arius' system in what concerns the Trinity and especially the Word.

The Word was made, created from nothing, freely, by God. He is the instrument by which God created the world, the intermediary between God and the world, neither true God nor part of the world, neither eternal nor temporal. A very perfect creature, the adoptive but not natural son of the Father, he did not really know the incomprehensible Father, for the finite cannot know the infinite. He is foreign to and altogether unlike the personality and substance of the Father. For Arius the Word is only one of the many created powers of which God avails himself, like the locust and the grasshopper, as agents of the divine will. Before being engendered, there was a moment but not a time when the Word was not, since he was created before all time. He is not then coeternal with God the Father.[108]

What motivated Arius to adopt these positions? In the light of the few writings of Arius that we have, we can offer at least two fundamental reasons: on the one hand the Word was created precisely because God willed to create us and so that he could create us through him;[109] on the other hand, he understands generation as division of substance, transposes this concept into God without purifying it and then finds the operation impossible, since it would make God, who is a spirit, a body.[110]

We are reminded, it can be said in passing, of the objections that the Moslems still make today against the very notion of generation in God (just

---

[107]Except for his last profession of faith, we know Arius' texts especially through the writings of St. Athanasius; no complete work of Arius has come down to us; the documents of Arius have been assembled by G. Bardy, *Recherches sur saint Lucien d'Antioche et son école*. Paris, 1936, pp. 217-278; RJ has included some extracts; it would be extremely interesting to make a detailed study comparing Arius' final profession of faith (Bardy, *op. cit.*, p. 275) with his two pre-Nicene letters (*ibid.*, pp. 226-228, 235-237), and with the documents cited by Athanasius (RJ 648-651). We would probably succeed in demonstrating that, in spite of its orthodox tone, the final profession of faith does not in any way contradict the previous texts of Arius. See further J. N. D. Kelly, *Early Christian Doctrines*. London, 1968, pp. 226-231; for the Arians the Word is a peccable creature; and E. Boularand, S.J., *L'hérésie d'Arius et la foi de Nicée*. Paris, 1972, 2 vol.

[108]Cf. the letter of Arius to Eusebius (Bardy, *op. cit.*, pp. 226-228): "we suffer persecution because we say that (the Son) comes from nothing"; St. Athanasius, *contra Arianos*, I, 5-6 cited by G. Bardy, DTC v. XV, 2 (1950), col. 1652-1653 (art. "Trinité"); and by RJ 648-649.

[109]Cited by St. Athanasius, *Or. I adv. Arianos*, MG 26, 21; RJ 648.

[110]Letter of Arius to Alexander, cited by Bardy, *St. Lucien d'Antioche*, p. 237.

as the division that Cerinthus made between Jesus and Christ brings to mind the Moslem interpretation of the death of Jesus on the cross; we know moreover the Jewish origins of Islam.) We will see later the decisive and luminous replies that St. Hilary makes to this second difficulty, which pretends to reject the Trinity in the name of the divine spirituality and immateriality. We note further that it is in this context of an exclusively material and non-analogical understanding of the term *homoousios* that Arius, already before the Council of Nicaea, rejected it as unable to signify the unity of the Word and his Father; for him, to admit this would have meant that we were considering the Word to be a part of the Father.[111]

Before presenting the reply that the Council of Nicaea gave to Arius, we should briefly mention the political connotations of this doctrinal conflict, connotations destined to inflame it later. The gravity of the Arian crisis, in the course of which, some thirty years after Nicaea, about half of the bishops abandoned the orthodox doctrine, becomes more comprehensible when we perceive that the divine unicity (divine unipersonalism) appeared to offer a better justification for the existence of the monarchical Roman Empire. The eternal monarchy of God was the supreme exemplar of the Empire, a projection of the eternal in time. Such a mentality encouraged the official theologians of the Empire to exaggerate the divine unity, to see in the Trinity of persons a threat to the earthly monarchy, and thus inclined them toward the side of Arianism or Semi-Arianism. So they came to affirm that the Father is God in the proper and strict sense, while the Son is only a divine being of a category inferior and subordinate to the Father, somewhat the way the gods of the remote provinces had been subjected to the Emperor-God in the days of paganism.[112] Is it then just by chance that the Arian conflict exploded only after the conversion of the Empire to Christianity? Was not such a conversion, in a sense, a condition of the possibility of the conflict?

Cerinthus, Gnosticism, the ambiguities of Origen and Tertullian, even the conversion of Constantine, all these converged toward Arius' very clear and distinct affirmation in 323 of the "inequality" of the "supra-temporal"[113] and "created" Son with the eternal and uncreated Father. So without knowing it Arius rejoined the Pharisees, who only accused Jesus of "*making himself* equal to God" (Jn. 5:18; cf. 10:33), because they obstinately refused to recognize in Jesus the Son equal to the Father, the One who being "from on high" had deigned "to come down below" (Jn. 3:31; 8:23).

---

[111] Ortiz de Urbina, *op. cit.*, pp. 198-201.

[112] Cf. M. Schmaus, *Teologia dogmatica,* v. I, § 48.5, 6 (pp. 389-390), Madrid, 1960.

[113] In reality, for Arius, the Word is neither eternal nor temporal, he was created before all times and the times were created by his mediation. Cf. the text of Arius cited by *RJ* 651.

VII. THE REPLY OF NICAEA AND THE CLEAR AFFIRMATION OF THE EQUALITY BETWEEN THE SON AND THE FATHER

The council, the first ecumenical council, came together in 325 and quickly condemned Arius. It did not stop there: it wished to express positively the faith of the Church. It had a difficult task: with both humor and gravity St. Athanasius has described for us the tendency of the Arians to give a heterodox meaning to the proposed formulas. Let us cite him.

Initially, the council had wanted to limit itself "to proscribing the impious words of the Arians and to adopting those words which it was agreed are found in Scripture: that he (the Word) is not of the number of things drawn from nothing but is *from God*, really generated by the Father. The Eusebians (Arians), carried away by their inveterate error, pretended that the words *from God* also applied to us and that in this there was nothing special about the Word of God, since it is written: 'one only God the Father from whom comes everything' (1 Cor. 8:4)."

Then the Fathers, Athanasius continues, "seeing their malice and the artifice of the error, were obliged to express more clearly the words *from God* and to write that the Son was of the substance of God: thus no one could think that the words *from God* applied commonly and equally to the Son and to creatures; we must believe that everything else is created while the Word alone is from the Father."[114]

In the face of other analogous difficulties, St. Athanasius quickly comes to the essential statement: it is not enough to adopt the words of Scripture, for these are susceptible to being diverted from their meaning by the malice of men, as Scripture itself would have us understand ("in the heart of the impious, cunning devises evil"); so the bishops were "obliged to infer their doctrine from Scripture,"[115] that is, they had to unfold explicitly what was implicit in it.

Here is a truly important affirmation: a theology that aims at being purely biblical would be impotent to defend Scripture as well as impossible and useless. God wills that we put at the service of his Word, and notably of his Trinitarian revelation, human reason of which he is the author, and the language of men.

But let us continue to read St. Athanasius' development:

> They were then obliged to infer their doctrine from Scripture, to express more clearly what they had already said, and to write that the Son is *consubstantial* with the Father. They thus signified that the Son is, with regard to the Father, not only something similar but identical in its

---

[114]St. Athanasius, *De decretis Nicaen. Synodi*, 19-20 (*MG* 25, 449ff.: the pagination contains some errors, so you must follow the numeration of the paragraphs of St. Athanasius' work), Bardy, *DTC*, art. cit., col. 1654-1655; we use this translation.

[115]*Ibid.*

likeness; that the likeness and the immutability of the Son is altogether different from that which is attributed to us and which we acquire by virtue in keeping the commandments. Similar bodies can part company and exist apart from one another, as sons in relation to the men who are their fathers.... But the generation of the Son by the Father being by nature other than that of men, because he is not only like but also indivisible from the substance of the Father, because he and the Father are one, because the Word is always in the Father and the Father in the Word...the council had good reason to write this word "consubstantial" in order to confound heretical perversity and to show that the Word differs from creatures.[116]

In other words, in declaring the Word "consubstantial" or *homoousios* with the Father, the council wished to proclaim inseparably the dogma of the perfect divine unity and of the divinity of the Word, equal to the Father. It chose for this purpose a term of whose disadvantages it was not unaware: on the one hand the way the Gnostics had formerly misused it did not recommend it; on the other hand, were it not for the context and the manifest intention of the council, the term could be interpreted in a Modalist sense, as if the Son were identical with the Father to the extent of being numerically indistinguishable from him; later on we will encounter a problem regarding the council's intentions relative to the numerical or specific unity of the divine nature.[117]

Not allowing itself to be influenced by the possible abuses of the term, the council canonized it. Unlike Arius, it understood this term in the context of an analogical language. It must then be stated that in order to fight efficaciously against a rebirth of pagan syncretism, the council judged it indispensable to use a term that came to it through Clement of Alexandria from the syncretist literature of the Gnostics.[118] We shall shortly elaborate the significance of this fact.

After having thus partially reformulated the Symbol in function of the anti-Arian struggle, the council of Nicaea terminated its work by anathematizing those who would maintain any of the following four propositions:

—"there was a time when he (the Son) was not";

—"before being generated he was not";

—"he was made from that which was not or from another *hypostasis* or *ousia*";

—"the Son of God is created, changeable, mutable."[119]

---

[116]*Ibid.*
[117]Bardy, *DTC*, art. cit., col. 1656-1657.
[118]Ortiz de Urbina, *op. cit.*, pp. 192, 201.
[119]*DS* 125 (*DB* 54); Bardy's translation, art. cit., col. 1656.

These four anathemas assure our understanding of the non-Modalist sense of the Nicene "consubstantial." In other words (since the contradictory of an anathema is true), the council was teaching the uncreated pre-existence, the eternity and immutability of the Son of God by rejecting any idea of an alteration in the divine substance. The Son is spiritual and eternal.

VIII. CONFRONTATION OF MARXISM AND PSYCHOANALYSIS WITH THE DOGMATIC AND CRITICAL REALISM OF NICAEA

The doctrinal evolution which led to the decisive clarification of Nicaea raises two problems for our contemporaries, or more exactly, for some of them. Some, under the inspiration of Marxism or of Freudianism, look for the cause and the psycho-social conditioning of this dogmatic evolution, and believe they discover them in psycho-social factors of the human mind, to which they attempt to reduce the dogma. Others see here an unwarranted hellenization of Christianity: we refer here particularly to liberal Protestants and Modernists.

1. Representative of the first tendency is Erich Fromm, author of *The Dogma of Christ*, published originally in Germany in 1930.[120]

For Fromm the first Christians were revolutionaries who rebelled against God the Father by affirming that Jesus, a mere man and previously considered such, was adopted by God as his Son. For Fromm we are dealing with a myth that signifies an unconscious revolt against the oppression of tyrants. But the Council of Nicaea modified things: as the Christians were becoming the dominant and oppressing class, they would transform the idea of a Jesus who was a man adopted by God, into that of a Jesus, the Son of God who became man, of a Jesus equal to the Father, to symbolize the passage from revolutionary hostility to submissive obedience.

Fromm thus joins the Spiritists, the Liberal Protestants and the Marxists for whom the Church invented the Trinity, in function of material or class interests.

It is easy to see that Fromm's very artificial construction rests on sand. Well before Nicaea, Jesus himself affirmed his divinity and his equality with the Father,[121] obviously without employing these abstract expressions. The first Christians and particularly the Apostles, proclaimed in their kerygma not an adoption of Jesus by the Father but (without using the word) the divinity of the Son.[122] They were not revolutionaries and they

---

[120]An English translation (*The Dogma of Christ*. NY, 1963) and a Brazilian (*O Dogma de Cristo*. Rio de Janeiro, 1965). See the latter, p. 61, and the parallel idea of E. Bloch, in the present book, chapter VII, n. 54.

[121]This is the whole theme of the Gospel of St. John, notably in ch. 5, 8, 10.

[122]Cf. note 114 of ch. 1; Bardy, *DTC, art. cit.*, on the Trinity, col. 1580-1583.

had no intention of overthrowing the Roman Empire, as the letters of Paul show.[123] Inversely not all Christians of the fourth century were pure conformists; St. John Chrysostom preached on the rights of slaves; the Church favored the access of slaves to the priesthood and to marriage.

Far from signifying or favoring tyrannical oppression, the Trinitarian dogma is, on the contrary, as we shall see, a leaven, model and term of social progress. It is possible, moreover, to admit that in the divine plan the dogmatic response of the Church to the Trinitarian Revelation was historically conditioned by such or such a social evolution. There would here be question of a simple hypothesis which does not at all appear to be proven. Thus, for example, if there had ever been matriarchal societies, would they have received the Trinitarian Revelation through the categories of "Father" and of "Son"? But what cannot be true in any case is that social evolution not only conditions but even causes Trinitarian Revelation since this is essentially supernatural.

2. The second tendency, which suggests a "de-hellenization of the dogma" was represented by Harnack in the last century and by L. Dewart today.[124] For him Greek philosophy furnished the principal elements of our centuries-old conceptualization of fundamental Christian beliefs in the Trinity and in the Incarnation. From this results a disguised tritheism.

If it is true that the Trinitarian doctrines of Tertullian and of Origen were influenced by Stoicism and by Middle Platonism respectively, it must be stated that their subordinationist tendencies were rejected by Nicaea. Nicaea signifies precisely the rejection of the hellenization of dogma in the sense of a syncretism between Christianity and Greek polytheism.

The term that indicates this rejection is the adjective "consubstantial," *homoousios*. Up to Nicaea this term had been understood to signify "of the same stuff" or matter; so much so that when it was applied to the divinity it involved a metaphor drawn from material objects. Because of this connotation Arius had rejected it. The Fathers of Nicaea, far from finding at their disposal a clearly defined and immutable concept, were forced to employ this adjective "consubstantial" in a metaphorical sense in order to put it at the service of the Christian message. That is what history teaches us, as Lonergan[125] and Prestige[126] remind us.

The meaning of the metaphor, as Lonergan demonstrates, was not determined by a Greek concept but rather by a Hellenic technique (we

---

[123]Cf. Rom. 13:1-7; 1 Tm. 2:1-2; Epistle to Philemon.
[124]L. Dewart, *The Future of Belief*. NY, 1966.
[125]B. Lonergan, *Theological Studies*, 28 (1967), 344.
[126]G. Prestige, *God in Patristic Thought*. London, 1964, pp. 209, 197.

would prefer to call it simply rational[127] and human). The meaning of the Nicene "consubstantial" was thus formulated by St. Athanasius: "we must say of the Son all that we say of the Father, except the name of Father."[128] Such a semantic determination presupposes a reflection on propositions that is not very familiar to Hebrews. It explains the adjective consubstantial by a complex ensemble of propositions (one principal and two subordinate propositions): the Son is consubstantial to the Father, if all that is true of the Father is also true of the Son, except only that the Father is Father.

This rational technique offers an open structure: it does not determine what attributes must be assigned to the Father and in consequence to the Son; it leaves the believer free to conceive the Father in Scriptural, Patristic, Medieval or modern terms, and our historically oriented contemporary consciousness will find itself at ease in these four registers.

Nevertheless, this technique, however open it may be, is not at the disposal of all. Piaget has shown that only at the age of twelve years can a boy ordinarily operate with propositions. As a result other means are needed to transmit the doctrine of Nicaea to less developed minds. They must be discovered. But the Nicene formulation will always be needed to preserve from error minds that have attained the age of reason[129] and to guarantee them the possession of truth as much as this is possible.

In the last analysis Nicaea signifies, as Lonergan has shown so well, the passage from a non-critical dogmatic realism to a dogmatic and critical realism. There was here a transition from the implicit to the explicit by means of a notion borrowed from Gnostic theology (consubstantial) and by means of a dialectical process (heresy). Thus what was implicitly Trinitarian in Revelation became explicitly Trinitarian.

We have then a transition from a mentality that considers in God only his relative attributes (creator, just, good, provident, etc.) to another that considers God in himself, in a scientific and ontological manner. The first seeks God *quoad nos* and is based on categories close to religious experience. The second speaks to us of the Son who is consubstantial with the Father, a judgment that goes beyond all religious experience and analogous categories.

The categories of religious experience are primitive and pre-rational, at

---

[127]The "Greek miracle" essentially signifies the passage of humanity from a pre-rational mentality to a rational mentality, which does not necessarily mean rationalist.

[128]"Eadem de Filio quae de Patre dicuntur excepto Patris nomine," St. Athanasius, *Oratio III contra Arianos*, 4, MG 26, 328C-329B; cf. B. Lonergan, *De Deo trino*, v. I. Rome, 1964, pp. 1, 82-87; the author there shows how Athanasius has not only specified the meaning of the Nicene "consubstantial," but also the distinction between create, make, generate, terms that are confused in Greek thought.

[129]We drew, in the preceding developments, on the remarkable article of B. Lonergan, S.J., "The Dehellenization of Dogma," *Theological Studies*, 28 (1967), 344-345.

least in certain respects; they signify a passionate interest in one's own subjectivity. The center of interest which polarizes them is not objective truth, external reality, but rather "how things are in my mind." Kantian idealism and Luther himself could be linked with such a mentality.

The Word of God affirms realities in an absolute way: *est, est, non, non*. Isaiah and Paul do not preach themselves (except secondarily) but rather they announce an objective message of God. The word of God is not bound in an exclusive way to the subjectivity of the prophet, but it announces an extrinsic reality.

At a first stage dogmatic realism receives this Word in faith when the subject has become conscious of such an obligation, but without further reflection on its content, its presuppositions or its consequences. This is non-critical dogmatic realism, the position of the Apostles and generally of the primitive Church, except for Paul and John, at least tendentially. For does not the Gospel of St. John already manifest a certain awareness in the well-beloved disciple of what Athanasius will affirm almost three centuries later: "all that one says of the Father must also be said of the Son, except the name of Father"?

Tertullian remains in a non-critical dogmatic realism. He rightly sees that the Father and his Son have one and the same substance, *unius substantiae*[130] (materially close to the Nicene consubstantial), but he does not perceive its presupposition (the spirituality of the divinity) nor its consequence (the son cannot be called a portion of the Father's substance, as Tertullian nevertheless calls him).

Nicaea explicitly kept itself in the sphere of non-critical realism but it implicitly rejected it in affirming the Word to be consubstantial with the Father. To the Platonic language of similitude (otherwise valid in itself) it preferred the language of being: not only is the Word like the Father, he is also not a creature and he is not temporal but immutable and consubstantial with the Father.

Nicaea brought about the transition from God the almighty creator, considered *quoad nos*, to the ontological consideration of the divine substance, of God *quoad se*. In this same act Nicaea also crossed over from a religious language adapted to a particular people, time and circumstances, to a language, to a divine word that must be affirmed before every people of every time in every circumstance. This passage is nothing else than a transition from the prophetic discourse of the Old Testament, from the Gospel as proclaimed in Galilee by Jesus or afterwards by the Apostles in Jerusalem, from the simple ecclesiastical tradition passed on by Irenaeus, to the perfectly universal language of Catholic dogma. In some sense biblical

---

[130]Tertullian, *Adv. Praxean*, ch. II, *ML* 2, 156; *RJ* 371 "per substantiae unitatem...tres non statu nec substantia...unius autem substantiae quia unus Deus."

language only achieves its full universality when it becomes dogmatic language.[131]

This is what Paul VI has so well emphasized in his encyclical *Mysterium Fidei*, and precisely with regard to the mystery of the holy Trinity and the dogmatic formulas that pertain to it:

> At the price of work carried on for many centuries and not without the assistance of the Holy Spirit, the Church has fixed a rule of language and confirmed it by the authority of the councils. This rule has often become the rallying cry and the standard of orthodox faith. It should be religiously respected. Let no one arrogate to himself the right to change it at his pleasure or under pretext of scientific novelty.
>
> Who could ever tolerate the opinion that dogmatic formulas which were applied by ecumenical councils to the mysteries of the holy Trinity and of the Incarnation, no longer are adapted to our modern mentality and should be rashly replaced by others? ... These formulas, like the others the Church adopts for enunciating dogmas of the faith, express concepts which are not tied to certain cultural forms, nor to a particular phase of scientific progress, nor to a particular theological school. They express what the human mind perceives of reality by universal and necessary experience, and what it manifests by suitable and fixed expressions coming from current or learned diction. That is why these formulas are adapted to men of all times and of all places.
>
> Assuredly one can give these formulas a more clear and open explanation, as has been done with happy results, but this always must be in the same sense according to which they were adopted. Thus, the immutable truth of the faith will remain intact, while the understanding of faith will advance. As the first Council of the Vatican teaches, in regard to sacred dogmas, "one must preserve always the sense that our Holy Mother the Church has declared once and for all. It is never permitted to deviate from this under the specious pretext of a more profound understanding."[132]

---

[131]Of course the New Testament is accessible to all, but precisely because it needs to be unfolded in rational discourse so as to be adequately—though not exhaustively—grasped by the one who has attained the use of reason, dogmatic language gives it its full universality.

[132]Paul VI, encyclical *Mysterium Fidei*, Sept. 3, 1965, § 24-25. A little further on, § 46, he says that "transubstantiation" supposes a "new, ontological reality." In § 47 Paul VI stresses that "the power that operates this prodigy is the power of the omnipotent God who created the universe from nothing at the beginning of time." He could have said just as well: transubstantiation supposes the omnipotence of the Word who is consubstantial with the Father, the omnipotence of the generated Creator. The Tridentine dogma was already implicit in the Nicene "consubstantial": the one divine substance that is possessed in common by the Father and the Son creates all substances and converts some (bread and wine) into others (body and blood of Christ).

All this holds very specially for the Nicene "consubstantial" (as also for the two natures in Christ defined at Chalcedon). We are then likewise invited to give, as best we can, a clearer explanation of this formula to the men of our time who have reached the age of reason[133] and are able to reflect on propositions. It depends on us to make this formula, which is intelligible not to infants but to men of all times and places, effectively intelligible to men of our times. It could be culpably uncomprehended, however, either in consequence of their indolence or of our own. Adherence to Revelation does not dispense from an effort of reflection on the language of the faith and at the heart of the faith. The will to persevere in the Trinitarian faith, received at baptism, requires reflection on the presuppositions and on the consequences of its verbal expression. In every man who has reached the age of reason and is capable of reflecting on propositions, the dogmatic realism of the faith must pass from the non-critical to the critical stage, from the logically implicit to its explication, but this does not take place (as history shows) without explanation.

From the "one substance" of Tertullian to the "consubstantial" of Nicaea and of Athanasius, a dialectical schema was enacted. Of this dialectic the material principle is an objective contradiction (here between the two affirmations of Tertullian: the Son is a portion of the substance of the Father and nonetheless they are one only substance), the formal principle is either the light of reason alone or this same natural light strengthened by the supernatural light of faith common to all the faithful. The course of this dialectic is the elimination of the contradiction, either when it has immediately become explicit, or in a more progressive way and through a successive series of authors who try different ways of eliminating it. The term of this dialectic is either heresy (if one proceeds with the sole light of natural reason), or the progress of theological doctrine if the natural light of reason allows itself to be illumined and strenghtened by the supernatural light of faith, as in St. Athanasius.[134]

[133] As regards children, it will be more pedagogical to initially explain the divinity of Christ in non-Nicene terms to those of them who have not attained the age of reason (12 years, in Piaget's sense); this in no way prevents us from adding afterwards the word consubstantial, with a fitting explanation. In fact, as Lonergan brings out, this word is drawn from a material metaphor that is accessible to all: two pieces of a divided piece of bread are consubstantial, two men possess in common the human substance, etc.; it is even necessary thus to prepare the ground so that children can later on better grasp the meaning of the adjective applied to God with the necessary purifications. It would even be altogether advantageous that they learn by heart, from the catechism given in primary school, that the Word is consubstantial with the Father; later on they will understand the formula. This was the case for the abstract formulas of the catechism, in general, with St. Anthony-Mary Claret, as he himself recounts in his *Autobiography* (ch. IV).

[134] In the preceding paragraphs we have drawn on B. Lonergan, S.J., *De Deo trino*. Rome, 1964, pp. 48-50 and 104-112 of the first volume.

The evolution that led to the Nicene "consubstantial" entirely verified J. R. Geiselmann's contention:

> The false ideas of the heresy will be rejected only if one also rejects the form that the error takes. It is then essential to the dialectic to express the thesis according to the form taken by the cloak under which the heretical antithesis was concealed. It is only in this way that it will be grasped by all the contemporaries. Formulas must be chosen which are apt to bring about immediate recognition of the truth when compared with error. These formulas are at the same time symbols, that is, signs of recognition to which all those who hold to the truth of the Church can rally.[135]

"Consubstantial," as sign of reciprocal recognition of the true disciples of Christ, also becomes the sign of their common recognition, in the bosom of the Church and, together with it, of the Word made Flesh, an act of cultic and adoring faith. From this point of view Bonhoeffer, whom few would suspect of "religious language," was certainly not shocked by the Nicene anathemas that accompanied the proclamation of the consubstantial Word, as is apparent in these lines extracted from his course on Christology in 1933:

> We have lost the concept of heresy because there is no longer any magisterium. This is a terrible catastrophe. The present ecumenical councils[136] are not quite councils because the name of heresy has been expunged from their vocabulary. But we cannot have a confession of faith without being able to say: in the light of Christ, this is true and that is false.... The concept of heresy arises from the brotherhood of the Church and not from a lack of love. A man acts fraternally with regard to another if he does not hide the truth from him. If I do not tell the truth to my neighbor, I treat him as a pagan. And if I tell the truth to someone who is of another opinion, I show him the love I owe him.[137]

---

[135] J. R. Geiselmann, *EF* v. I, p. 377, art. "Dogme."

[136] Bonhoeffer here alludes to the great assemblies of the ecumenical movement (Lausanne, Stockholm, etc.).

[137] D. Bonhoeffer, *Gesammelte Schriften*, v. III, p. 206 (München, 1960). The text given is based on the notes of students assembled by E. Betge, the friend of Bonhoeffer. One could object that in these conditions Bonhoeffer himself would have been disconcerted by the attitude of Vatican II, when it refused to hurl any new anathemas: "Magis quam damnando, suae doctrinae vim uberius explicando putat (Ecclesia) hodiernis necessitatibus esse consulendum," said John XXIII in inaugurating the council (*AAS* 54, 1962, 792). But that did not prevent the council from denouncing diverse errors (*GS* 47. 2; 58; *AA* 6. 4;7); from censoring discriminations practiced by reason of race, color, class or religion (*NA* 5); from condemning total war as a crime (*GS* 80.4); and from recalling in a general manner that the bishops must be careful to ward off the errors that threaten their flock (*LG* 25), while insisting at the same time on the necessity of charity towards those who are in error (*DH* 11; 14; *GS* 28. 2). There is a slight

It is precisely this that the Church did at Nicaea. In proclaiming the consubstantial Word it only repeated in other terms, in ontological terms, the confession of faith that Simon Peter made at Caesarea-Philippi: "You are the Christ, the Son of the living God." Such a declaration constitutes, like that of Simon Peter, both a point of arrival, a fixed point, and a point of departure[138] toward new rational explorations of the revealed Trinitarian datum within the bosom of the faith. It had to lead to the clear and frank affirmation of the consubstantiality of the Spirit with the Father and the Son. Far from being an unwarranted hellenization and particularization of the Christian mystery, it was on the contrary an important step in the affirmation of its universality in space and in time. The "us" of the men among whom the Word—who was in the beginning with the Father—was made flesh and came to dwell, is the "us" not only of Hebrew thought, but of the entire "world" (cf. Jn. 1:14; 1:1; 1:9-11). Henceforth the Church is reflexively conscious of the presuppositions and the consequences of its confession of faith: in saying, You are the Son of the living God, it says to Christ: "You are coeternal with your Father, you are the uncreated Creator, the begotten Creator." Like Mary Magdalen, the Church does not seek the Risen One in the tomb of mere creatures.

Is this to say that the dogmatic language of Nicaea has achieved perfect clarity? This is not sure and it is contested even by some Catholic authors of very high repute.

In fact, they affirm that the anathemas of Nicaea identify *ousia* and *hypostasis* (*DS* 126; *DB* 54 *sub fine*). Among these authors we note Ortiz de Urbina (*El simbolo niceno*, Madrid, 1947, p. 268). However he himself notes that St. Basil (ep. 125; *MG*, 32, 548A) does not admit that the council identified the meaning of these two words: the council (if we correctly understand St. Basil's text alluding to Gnosticism) would have wished to say: "those who say that the Son of God has come from another person (meaning: another than the Father) or from another essence, the Catholic Church anathematizes (them)."

Whatever could be said of this very subtle debate, it is generally acknowledged that it was only from about 360 that the distinction between *ousia* and *hypostasis* in the current sense of nature and person, was widely recognized; it was approved by the Council of Alexandria in 362 and by St. Athanasius (cf. G. Bardy, *DTC* XV, 2, 1950, col. 1666, art. "Trinité"). The Arians claimed that the Nicene *homoousios* had a Modalist sense and signified identity between the Father and the Son, not only as regards essence but also as regards person (cf. St. Basil, Letter 214; *MG* 32, 788B).

difference between denouncing an error and anathematizing it; to declare an error heretical is not yet to anathematize it; Bonhoeffer aimed at the former, not the latter, not unaware of Gal. 1:8, 9; 3:13.

[138]Cf. R. Marlé, S.J., "Le dogme dans la foi," *Etudes*, v. 326 (1967), 17.

Very diverse interpretations of the Council of Nicaea were thus opposing one another. But going beyond these verbal questions we must look at the doctrine that was held; this St. Athanasius did in this period of transition:

> Those who accept all the other documents of Nicaea (Athanasius is alluding to the anathemas that condemn all idea of a mutable and created Son) and only have doubts about the *homoousios*, should not be considered as enemies... we speak to them as brothers to brothers who have the same conception as we have but hesitate only about the name. In confessing that the Son is of the *ousia* of the Father and not of another *hypostasis*, in confessing that he is not a creature nor a work, but true and natural offspring, eternally with the Father as Logos and Wisdom, these are not far from also accepting the expression *homoousios*. (*Concerning the Synods*, 41; MG 26, 755 A; cited by B. Pruche in his introduction to *Traité sur le Saint-Esprit*, of St. Basil, Paris, 1947, pp. 16-17).

Notwithstanding certain hesitations (thus, in 369 Athanasius again identified *ousia* and *hypostasis* in spite of his earlier adherence to the Council of Alexandria of 362; cf. Bardy, *DTC* XV, 2, col. 1666-1667), the distinction between these two words was not long delayed in being definitively established at the same time that the *homoousios* was accepted in the sense that Athanasius had already explained. Nicaea, in canonizing the consubstantiality of the Son with the Father, was a decisive step on the road which led to the affirmation of three consubstantial persons in possession of the one divine nature; Nicaea I prepared such an affirmation but it did not yet contain it. As long as essence or *ousia* on the one hand and *hypostasis* and person on the other were not clearly distinguished, the *homoousios* itself was not sufficiently clear.

IX. MACEDONIUS, BASIL, CONSTANTINOPLE I AND THE CULT OF THE HOLY SPIRIT

1. *State of the question: conditions of the possibility of Semi-Arianism*

The conscious, explicit and reflexive recognition of the divinity of the Holy Spirit and of its affirmation by the New Testament is a relatively late development in the Church.

On the one hand, attention was concentrated on the problems relating to the divinity of the Son, which were only resolved in 325 by Nicaea I; on the other hand, certain expressions of the New Testament seemed vague and did not favor this recognition of the personal divinity of the Holy Spirit. It is easier to say about a baby sheltered in a grotto who afterwards grows, lives and dies, that this Man is a Person, and to think of Him in personal terms, than it is to see a Person in What appears to be water, wind, tongues of fire.... To be poured out and diffused from high heaven is customarily said of rain rather than of a Person!

For all these reasons it is not surprising that the teaching of many Fathers of the first three centuries should remain vague, in spite of the explicit affirmations of the New Testament about the personality of the Paraclete, who was presented by Jesus as a "He" and not as an "it."

However, the Ante-Nicene Fathers were not ignorant of the personality of the Holy Spirit: Irenaeus, Tertullian, Gregory Thaumaturgus are very clear in this regard, in the texts we cited above.[139] St. Irenaeus however, while quite willingly considering the intimate relations between the Father and the Son, prefers to characterize the Holy Spirit by his effects.[140]

2. *Against this background we can better grasp the variety of opinions* about the Holy Spirit that existed in the Church in the fourth century, after Nicaea. St. Gregory of Nazianzus sums them up as follows: "for some He is an energy, for others a creature, for still others God; some refuse to make any pronouncement out of respect, they say, for the Scriptures which do not express themselves clearly on this subject; thus they take a position that is obscure and in fact extremely dangerous. Among those who regard Him as God, some keep this pious belief to themselves; others have the courage to preach it. Others who wish to be still more prudent, moderate the divinity in some degree. They accept the Trinity as we do; but at the same time they claim that only the first person is infinite in substance and energy, that the second is infinite in energy but not in substance, that the third is infinite in neither of these ways."[141]

This last position transposes Arianism from the domain of the Son to that of the Spirit. It is the phenomenon of Semi-Arianism which Augustine thus describes: "The Macedonians are so named from Macedonius;[142] the Greeks also call them *Pneumatomachoi*, because they stir up disputes on the subject of the Holy Spirit. About the Father and the Son they think, in conformity with orthodoxy, that both are one and the same substance or essence; they do not want to believe this of the Holy Spirit, of whom they say that he is only a creature. It is these that are preferably called Semi-Arians, since in this question (of consubstantiality) they are partially with the Arians, partially with us."[143]

Some of the "Macedonians" teach that the Holy Spirit is a creature of the Son as the Son is a creature of the Father. The Spirit, they say, is great, the Son is greater, the Father is supremely great. For them the Holy Spirit, even

---

[139]Cf. in particular the text referred to in note 104 of this chapter.

[140]Cf. the texts referred to in notes 39 to 41.

[141]St. Gregory of Nazianzus, *Or. theol.*, V, 5; MG 36, 137 DC.

[142]Archbishop of Constantinople in 342; we no longer have his writings.

[143]St. Augustine, *De haeres.*, §52; ML 42, 39; cf. E. Amann, *DTC* XIV, 2 (1941), col. 1790ff.: art. "Semi-Arians"; G. Bardy, *DTC* IX, 2 (1927), col. 1464-1478: art. "Macédonius et les macédoniens"; B. Pruche, O.P., Introduction to *Traité du Saint-Esprit* by St. Basil, SC 17. Paris, 1947, pp. 23-25: this is without doubt the most penetrating treatment of the subject and it clarifies the two that precede it.

if he is not God, is not a creature like others. They have to recognize that he is counted with the other two persons of the Holy Trinity, and this embarrasses them. They conclude that the Holy Spirit occupies a position intermediate between God and creature, but that it is not possible to establish his position any more precisely than this. It should be noted that the distinct personality of the Holy Spirit, with respect to the Father and to the Son or with regard to the "other angels," is not put in doubt by the Semi-Arians.

By their refusal to understand that the divinity of the Holy Spirit was the indispensable complement of the divinity of Christ, the Macedonians came to an impasse. They did not know where to place the Holy Spirit. The more logical among them were thus led to deny even the consubstantiality of the Son, which was admitted by the whole party at the beginning. Faith in the Holy Spirit and faith in the Son cannot exist, one without the other.[144]

3. *The reaction of Athanasius, Basil and Gregory of Nazianzus*

While this Semi-Arian propaganda was being spread, beginning about 342, the Church continued to baptize in the name of the Father and of the Son and of the Holy Spirit, thus glorifying the Three. In this way it manifested a faith which the Providence of the Holy Spirit would take charge of enlightening at the opportune moment. "The Paraclete, the Holy Spirit will teach you everything" (Jn. 14:26) including Himself, inasmuch as He is the Spirit "whom I shall send you and who will glorify me" (Jn. 16:7, 14). His instruments will be St. Athanasius and the three great Cappadocians.

Athanasius, in his four letters to Serapion,[145] set forth the fundamental principle for the solution of the biblical difficulties: the relation of the Holy Spirit to the Son is analogous to that of the Son to the Father.[146] The bishop of Alexandria shows at length the application of this principle in the New Testament: the Holy Spirit will glorify the Son as the Son glorifies the Father, the Spirit of the Son receives from the Son as the Son from the Father, the Spirit hears the Son as the Son hears the Father.

Note that St. Athanasius never calls the Holy Spirit God: he says that the Paraclete is not a creature, that he cannot be put on the same level as the angels and even that he is consubstantial to the Father and to the Son, but he does not call him God.

St. Basil follows the same method. He is content to deny that the Holy Spirit is a creature. He believes personally in the divinity of the Holy Spirit, but he avoids proclaiming this before his people. This is what has been

---

[144]G. Bardy, *DTC* IX, 2 (1927), 1478.

[145]Between 356 and 362; cf. the edition of *SC* no. 15. Paris, 1947, with J. Lebon's introduction, on the pneumatology of St. Athanasius (pp. 56-77).

[146]St. Athanasius, *Letters to Serapion*, III, 1; *MG* 26, 625; *RJ* 783; *SC* 15, pp. 164-165.

called the "economy" of Basil. His essential motive is nothing but the desire to reduce the number of blasphemers of the Holy Spirit.[147]

But the most original point in St. Basil's attitude, and one which had a decisive influence on the doctrinal position of Constantinople I, was to transfer the debate to the level of worship (a level on which Basil was attacked by a colleague in the episcopate).

Basil himself explains that after a certain incident that took place on September 7, 374, he wrote in the course of the following year his *Treatise on the Holy Spirit*, a moment that was important in the providential preparation of Constantinople I: "Very recently, as I was praying with the people, glorifying God the Father in this double fashion: sometimes 'with' the Son, 'with' the Holy Spirit, sometimes 'through' the Son, 'in' the Holy Spirit, some of those present accused us of having used strange and even contradictory words." So he resolved to "give an objective exposition of the validity of these words,"[148] an exposition that has lost none of its interest today.

The first of these two doxologies was the coordinating doxology (*sun*, with), the second expressed a subordination (*en*, in). For Basil the affirmation of the divinity of the Holy Spirit is bound up with a right understanding of the New Testament use of these prepositions.[149] The language problem was not born today nor even yesterday.... Basil makes use of both doxologies. Not content to affirm that the Holy Spirit is not a creature—a negative affirmation—he insists on the importance of the coordinating doxology, which proclaims the right of the Spirit to receive the same glory, the same honor and the same cult as the Father and the Son. The Arians preferred the subordinating doxology, which they interpreted in the sense of a difference of nature between Father, Son and Holy Spirit, and of which they availed themselves not to glorify the Son and the Spirit but to depreciate and blaspheme them. Basil, however, understood this subordinating doxology in a perfectly orthodox manner, and showed this by joining it to the other.

The coordinating doxology is, moreover, very ancient, for it goes back to

---

[147]J. de Ghellinck, S.J., *Patristique et Moyen Age*, v. III, Etude VII: a case of conscience in the Trinitarian conflicts over the Holy Spirit, pp. 311-338. Paris, 1948; Pruche, *op. cit.*, pp. 19-23; Paul VI alluded to this silence of St. Basil in his discourse to the Patriarch of Constantinople, Athenagoras, in July 1967, DC 64 (1967), 1381-1382. Was he not thus insinuating that he himself, the Pope, was observing at this same moment the same "economy of silence" regarding his proper infallible primacy, and that this silence did not signify any doctrinal surrender?

[148]St. Basil, *Traité du Saint-Esprit*, SC 17, pp. 108-110; ch. 3 of the treatise; cf. B. Pruche's introduction, pp. 1-3.

[149]*Ibid.*, ch. 5-21 (pp. 117-144): St. Basil there demonstrates: "that the prepositions used in the Trinitarian doxology (through, in, and with) have the 'same honor' for they apply indifferently (in the NT) to the Three Persons," according to Pruche's summary (p. 29, note 1).

the letters of St. Ignatius of Antioch.[150] By his treatise and by his action, Basil let it be understood that the equality in the cult of the Father, the Son and the Holy Spirit, the *homotimos*, was the existential consequence for us of the equality of the Three in the possession of the same identical divine nature, *homoousios*. It is in part thanks to him that the Church continues and will always continue to glorify together the Father, the Son and the Spirit: *Gloria Patri et Filio et Spiritui Sancto*. To renounce this coordinating doxology would be to renounce glorifying the Trinity as such, the consubstantial and indivisible Trinity. To renounce the subordinating doxology would be to renounce exalting the mediation of the Man Jesus in the cult rendered to the Father; the Church cannot consent to this either. The harmonious association of the two doxologies is the vital and indispensable expression of the Christian mystery taken in all its amplitude. This is what St. Fulgentius will perceive in the sixth century and express magnificently against western Arianism.[151]

St. Gregory of Nazianzus, however, proclaimed more plainly than Basil his faith in the divinity of the Holy Spirit and in the consubstantiality of the Spirit with the Father and with the Son. He emphasized two important points relative to the cult of the Holy Spirit and to the dogmatic development concerning his Person.

To the Semi-Arians who said, "we do not invoke the Holy Spirit but we pray in Him," Gregory replied: "in reality, the adoration of one is identically adoration of the Three, because the Three are equally God."[152] From this it followed that the Spirit was already adored in the subordinating doxology.

On the other hand, Gregory of Nazianzus sketched a theory of the development of Trinitarian dogma in his effort to explain the sluggish nature of our recognition of the divinity of the Holy Spirit. We had first to recognize the divinity of the Father, he said, revealed by the Old Testament, then that of the Son, revealed in the New Testament; the divinity of the Spirit is unveiled more clearly at the present time, when this Spirit dwells among us.[153] Of course, Gregory does not intend to deny that the

---

[150]Cf. G. Bareille, *DTC* VII, 1 (1922), col. 703, art. on Ignatius of Antioch; Bareille there cites the three texts of Ignatius on the Trinity (Eph. IX, 1; Magn. XIII, 1 and 2), of which the first two at least, without being doxologies, are situated in the same coordinating line as that studied in depth by Basil.

[151]*ML* 65, 796-802: St. Fulgentius there proposes, in magnificent Latin, a theological synthesis that is both spiritual and pastoral, on the biblical roots of the Trinitarian cult of the Church and on this cult itself.

[152]St. Gregory of Nazianzus, *Or.* 31, 12; *MG* 36, 145; cf. Basil, *Treatise on the Holy Spirit* 12, 28: "To name Christ is to confess the whole, for it is to show God who has anointed, the Son who has been anointed, and the unction which is the Spirit" (*SC*, 17, p. 156).

[153]Here is the exact text of the holy Doctor: "The Old Testament announces the Father clearly and the Son obscurely. The New Testament has manifested the Son but it has only

divinity of the Holy Spirit had already been clearly affirmed by the New Testament: he was merely alluding to a later explication which is still more clear.

4. *The definitive solution: Constantinople I: the Holy Spirit co-glorified with the Father and the Son*

Gregory of Nazianzus was together with Gregory of Nyssa a very active participant in this second ecumenical council. Constantinople I has left us the symbol called: Symbol of Nicaea-Constantinople, and justly so named, in a broad sense. For the conciliar Fathers had the intention of deepening and promoting the faith of Nicaea I[154] in a form more adapted to the heresies of the time and notably to the heresy of the Macedonians. That is how the many modifications are explained: only thirty-three of the one hundred seventy-eight words of the Symbol of Constantinople I are found in that of Nicaea I. This fact is explained by a whole set of omissions and of additions.[155] It is, moreover, important to study this Symbol of Constantinople I on the ecumenical level, for it is the only one that is admitted today by all the Christian Churches.[156]

It is precisely as regards the Holy Spirit that the Symbol of Nicaea was most substantially expanded. Nicaea I simply affirmed the faith of the Church in the Holy Spirit; Constantinople I added: "Lord and Giver of life, who proceeds from the Father, who is co-adored and co-glorified with the Father and with the Son, who has spoken through the prophets."[157] It will be noted that we have here a whole series of New Testament citations linked together.[158]

The council takes up again under the moderating influence of St. Gregory

---

indicated the divinity of the Holy Spirit. At present, the Spirit is among us and shows himself in all his splendor. It would not have been prudent, before one recognized the divinity of the Father, to preach openly the divinity of the Son, and as long as that of the Son was not accepted, to impose the Holy Spirit, if I may dare to express myself thus" (*Orat.* 31, 26; *MG* 36, 101; *Carm.* 1, 3, vv. 25-35; *MG* 37, 410). See the commentary on this text in Palmieri's article on the Holy Spirit, *DTC* V (1913), col. 729.

[154]J. N. D. Kelly, *Early Christian Creeds.* London, 1960, ch. X, pp. 296-331.

[155]*Ibid.,* p. 304.

[156]In fact, this symbol is admitted even by the non-Chalcedonian Churches (Coptic, Armenian, etc.).

[157]*DS* 150 (*DB* 86).

[158]Cf. 2 Cor. 3:17-18, 6; Jn. 15:26; cf. B. Schneider, O.F.M., *Biblica* 44 (1963), 364; this author stresses the biblical and Pauline character of the conciliar declaration; we could also cite with S. Lyonnet (*Biblica,* 32, 1951, 25-31) the remarkable commentary given by St. Cyril of Alexandria on 2 Cor. 3:16-17: "He who has seen the Son has seen the Father; but the Son is seen in the consubstantial Spirit. For, it is written: The Lord is the Spirit. Where identity of essence is found, there also ought to be entirely the absolutely immutable.... But that which you suppose the Son to be, that the Spirit is also, except for being Son" (*MG* 76, 1088ff.).

of Nyssa,[159] certain aspects of St. Basil's "economy of silence": it did not say explicitly that the Holy Spirit is God, but it implicitly affirmed this in saying that he must be "co-adored" with the Father and the Son. The expression "co-adoration" stressed simultaneously the fact that those "co-adored" are distinct from each other, and that the motive of their adoration is one and the same.[160] The three Persons must be adored but all three with one single adoration, in one identical cult inspired by the same motives and directed uniformly toward the Three Divine Persons. The particle "co" indicates the distinction of the Persons adored and the unity of adoration. If then one adores either the Father or the Son or the Holy Spirit, one can adore them separately but not exclusively, that is one can adore the Father alone without mentioning the Son or the Holy Spirit, but this cult necessarily implies the cult of the other two divine Persons. The term toward which our religion and our cult is directed is the Person.[161]

In other words, the council made its own the doctrine that we already saw set forth by St. Gregory of Nazianzus. What is more, it proclaimed that the Holy Spirit proceeds from the Father, without in any way clarifying the Son's role in this procession, doubtless to avoid appearing to favor the Arian tendencies which see in the Spirit a creature of the Son.

Unfortunately however, it is not possible for us in the present state of historical science, to gain an adequate idea of the pneumatological doctrine of Constantinople I. In fact, besides adopting the pre-existent Symbol already mentioned, the council had elaborated a dogmatic "tome" which is lost today. We have, however, an idea of the very great importance of its content through the later letter (382) of the Oriental Fathers to Pope St. Damasus. Although this letter does not seem to have been the object of an explicit confirmation by the Holy See, and thus would not be a conciliar document in the strict sense, its doctrine is in fact identical to that of the Roman council of 382 to which we will refer later.

This letter appropriates the vocabulary already utilized by the local council of Alexandria in 362 and by the Cappadocians (language that will be

---

[159]Cf. J. Daniélou, *Rech. de Sc. Rel.*, 57 (1967), 105-113, notably 109.
[160]Cf. DS 259 (DB 120).
[161]We draw here on A. Chollet, *DTC* III (1908), col. 2414-2415, art. "Culte"; it must be noted that, if Constantinople I presents the co-adoration of the Spirit as a fact, it does not make of this an explicit duty; we understand why: if one affirms that the Spirit is co-adored each time the Father or the Son is adored, one does not immediately affirm a duty to adore explicitly and particularly the Holy Spirit; the Roman council of 382 will go further and declare him to be heretical who says nothing of the universal duty of adoring the Holy Spirit (DS 174; DB 80). In his turn, Pope Leo XIII, in the encyclical *Divinum Illud Munus* (May 9, 1897), written at the request of Blessed Thérèse Guerra, insisted on the duty of invoking the Spirit (toward the end of the encyclical); the most important passages of this document are to be found in DS 3325-3331.

solemnly consecrated by Constantinople II in 554): "we believe there is one substance (*ousia*) of the Father and of the Son and of the Holy Spirit in three most perfect *hypostases* or three perfect Persons (*prosopois*)."[162]

Thus the post-Nicene crisis is definitively overcome, the crisis that was born in part from the apparent identification, in the anathemas annexed to the Symbol of Nicaea I, between *ousia* and *hypostasis*, between substance or nature on the one hand and person on the other. Henceforth, and in spite of St. Jerome,[163] *hypostasis* will signify first and foremost the person and not the nature.[164]

The "tome" of Damasus, elaborated at the time of the Roman council of 382, puts forth the same doctrine: "Three true Persons,"[165] "one single divinity and substance."[166] It is true that here, as in the synodal letter of Constantinople I, the adjective *homoousios*, "consubstantial," is lacking, but the reality is indicated by the expression "one single substance." In its conclusion the "tome" brings out the fact that "we are baptized in the Father and the Son and the Holy Spirit and not in the names of archangels and angels, as are the heretics,[167] Jews and pagans," and that "faith in the Trinity, that is in the Father, in the Son and in the Holy Spirit, in (their) one divinity and substance, is the salvation of Christians."[168]

We see thus that the synodal letter of Constantinople and that of the Roman council of Damasus definitively abandon the "economy of silence" which was preached by St. Basil and which still triumphed, against Gregory of Nazianzus but thanks to Gregory of Nyssa, in the Symbol at Constantinople in 381; the tome of Damasus declares heritical not only those who say that the Holy Spirit is a creature,[169] but also those who do not say that he is God.[170] Note the formulation: it is not what is said, but what is not said that is condemned as a heresy.

Apparently we have arrived at opposite poles from the "economy of silence" which St. Basil undertook to defend, and this only one year after

---

[162]See the text in J. Alberigo, *Conciliorum oecumenicorum Decreta*. Rome: Herder, 1962, p. 24.

[163]Cf. G. Bardy, *DTC* XV, 2 (1950), col. 1667 (art. "Trinité"). The important document of the Council of Alexandria of 362 can be found in the preceding volume.

[164]Or, if one prefers, the relation and not the absolute; cf. St. Thomas Aquinas, *Summa Theologica*, I, 29.4; and also our chapter III.

[165]DS 173 (DB 79).

[166]DS 177 (DB 82 at the end).

[167]DS 176 (DB 82): a partly ironic affirmation and allusion to the baptism given by the Arians who, since they disbelieved in the divinity of the Spirit, baptized in the name of the "angels," that is, of the Word and the Spirit, because they wished to reduce these two divine persons to the category of creatures.

[168]DS 177 (DB 82 at the end). You will note the force of the affirmation: salvation is found only in faith in the Trinity, for it is the way to its vision.

[169]DS 170 (DB 76).

[170]DS 168 (DB 74).

the Symbol of Constantinople which avoided a declaration of the divinity of the Holy Spirit. It is not without interest to note that the declaration of the Roman council justly constituted, in fact, a response to an anguished appeal which Basil, in 377, shortly before his death, addressed to the bishops of the West urging them to take a position that would go into detail about the errors to be rejected.[171] We could call this position "an economy of the word." *Tempus tacendi, tempus loquendi*.... In the face of error, silence cannot long be maintained.

The Church thus came to say clearly that the Holy Spirit is God and must be adored as such. The Spirit who guides it toward the recognition of the plenitude of revealed truth that is Christ,[172] could not but manifest himself to the Church as worthy of adoration, after he had made her adore the divinity of the Word who sends him to her. The world cannot receive the Spirit of Truth because it does not see him and does not know him, but the Church knows him because he remains with her and is in her (cf. Jn. 15:17). The primitive Church received the effusion of the Spirit, the post-Nicene Church recognized him as worthy of adoration equally with the Father and his only Son who both sent him. The Church never did and never will finish discovering the inexhaustible mystery of the Holy Spirit who is in her and sends her to the world, while he is being sent to her by the Father and by the Son; Augustine, Constantinople II, Florence, Vatican II will later mark the stages of this progressive cognitive and adorative discovery, and of the appropriation of what the Spirit of Christ has revealed about himself once and for all to this Church of which he is the soul. It is not true that the Holy Spirit wishes to be, or even that he is, an unknown God, or that he plays hide-and-seek with the Church and with the world.

The dogmatic response of the Church to the self-revealing Spirit, or if you prefer, the dogmatization of the Spirit by the Church, arouses in the believer a new reflection. All is the object of theology and of rational reflection in the bosom of the faith; all, but in a more particular fashion, doctrinal development itself. Only if the continuity of its successive stages appears can one comprehend its totality. What for the apologist is matter for proof and for the ecumenist matter for dialogue, arouses for the dogmatic theologian a reflection aimed at grasping the meaning of this homogeneous historical evolution. If the Church ceaselessly deepens its doctrine of the Holy Spirit, must we not see here first of all a fruit of this incessant invisible mission of the Spirit of Truth to her and to each of her members, of this salvific mission by which the Father and the Son send the Spirit essentially to unveil the secret of his procession by making rational crea-

---

[171] St. Basil, letter 263; *MG* 32, 976-981; cf. P. Galtier, S.J., "Le tome de Damase: date et origine" *Rech. Sc. Rel.*, 26 (1936), 402-403.

[172] *DV* 8.3 and 20.2 in the light of *DV* 2.

tures participate in love? Is not the Spirit who is co-adored and co-glorified with the Father and the Son, likewise co-loved in the cult that the Church offers to him? Did not the Church, by progressing in this perfect love of the Spirit which is adoration, merit to discover him, through St. Augustine, as the consubstantial and loving communion between Father and Son?

This point we have still to investigate in closing this chapter, but not until we have come to recognize more clearly in Scripture, thanks to Constantinople I and to the Patristic tradition, the consubstantiality, with the Father and the Son, of their common Spirit. Scripture is the foundation of dogma; but dogmatic progress allows, retrospectively, a better grasp of the meaning of Scripture.

5. *The implicit affirmation of the consubstantiality of the Spirit with the Father and with the only Son in the New Testament*

We can say that the New Testament shows us the Holy Spirit as Someone, as a pre-existent Person, as Someone who is God, and who is God as the Father and the Son are.

Someone: the authors of the New Testament conceive the Holy Spirit like God the Father, as someone who acts in the course of an encounter with his people. The Spirit who speaks through the Prophets is together with the Apostles witness to Jesus (Acts 5:32); this Spirit governs the Church (Acts 10:19; 13:2-4; 20:28); the diverse manifestations of this proper and distinct personality of the Holy Spirit are collected and summarized, as it were, by St. John the Evangelist when he passes from the neuter name of the Spirit (*to pneuma hagion*) to the masculine demonstrative pronoun, "this one (he)," with regard to the Paraclete (Jn. 14:26; *ekeinos*).

A pre-existent Person: the Spirit descends from heaven on the day of Pentecost; consequently he pre-existed this descent. Another sign of this is supplied by what the Evangelists tell us of the activity of the Spirit in Jesus, during his public life: Lk. 3:22; 4:1-2; 10:21.

Someone pre-existent who is God: the Holy Spirit is perfectly "at home" in the depths of the divine nature (1 Cor. 2:10-12), while no one knows the intimate thoughts of God: Rom. 11:34. The Holy Spirit produces in us effects that only God can produce: prophetic inspiration (2 Pt. 1:21), divine Revelation (1 Cor. 2:10-12; Jn. 14:26), pardon of sins (Jn. 20:22), our rebirth from God to eternal life (Jn. 3:5; 1:13; Ti. 3:5; 1 Jn. 5:8).

This Someone is God as the Father and the Son are: he is associated with the Father and the Son in the history of salvation. The Spirit is the witness of the Son, who is revealer of the Father, the Spirit says that which he has heard from the Son who himself says these words which he receives from the Father (Jn. 7:13; 8:28; 16:13-15). With St. Cyril of Alexandria we should apply to the Holy Spirit the Athanasian rule that was declared with regard to the Father and the Son: "That which the Son is, the Spirit is also, except the fact of being Son."[173]

In the light of these reflections and of the patristic tradition of the fourth and fifth centuries, we perceive more clearly that there are different ways of approaching the pneumatology of the New Testament.

A first sufficiently critical survey discerns the texts, limited in number, that speak clearly of the Spirit as of a Person distinct from the Father and from the Son. This first survey uses an analytical method, disects text after text, considering them only in their immediate context.

On the basis of the conclusions thus obtained, a new examination, more global and more concerned with the unity of New Testament language and with the situation of each text in the total context, recognizes in many of the texts, whose allusions might have appeared doubtful in the exclusive light of the first survey, clear endorsement of the distinct person of the Holy Spirit.

When the Synoptic Evangelists wrote and published their Gospels, a long time after the Resurrection, the Spirit of whom they spoke is certainly the Holy Spirit, distinct from the Father and the Son and promised by both of them; those who read them cannot interpret what they say of him in any other way, unlike those who heard the pre-Paschal Jesus.[174]

The New Testament revelation of the Holy Spirit is thus much richer than would appear at a first, strictly critical, glance. The best way to grasp the literal sense of Scripture, the sense intended by the sacred writers, and the *sensus plenior* intended by the Holy Spirit, is still to read it in the Church and with the Church, thus availing ourselves of the benefit and the increase of light that come from the doctrinal development which this same Spirit effects in her.

X. THE DOCTRINE OF ST. AUGUSTINE ON THE HOLY SPIRIT AS COMMUNION AND SOURCE OF COMMUNION

We are unable here to study the whole of St. Augustine's Trinitarian theology, so we limit ourselves to presenting certain aspects of his pneumatology in conformity with the overall design outlined in the introduction.

Even though the great Bishop of Hippo did not actually discover it, yet he is the very first to systematically elaborate the theological doctrine that considers the Spirit as the bond of love between the Father and the Son.

The majority of the Greek Fathers considered the Father to be the principle of the unity in the Trinity,[175] or the Son who was considered as a link

---

[173]Cf. the text cited in note 158 of the present chapter.

[174]Cf. DS 3999; you can read, in a different sense, L. Hodgson, *The Doctrine of the Trinity*. London, 1964, pp. 80-83.

[175]Cf. St. Gregory of Nazianzus, *Or.* 42, 15; MG 36, 476.

between the Father and the Spirit: so it was with St. Cyril of Alexandria, who died a little later than Augustine.[176]

Already, however, certain isolated formulations were preparing the ground for the Augustinian doctrine: St. Epiphanius taught that the Spirit is the bond of the Trinity and that he is middle between the Father and the Son.[177] St. Gregory of Nyssa came still closer to Augustine's synthesis of theology and economy, in the following text:

> Knit together by the unity of the Spirit as by the bond of peace, all will be one body and one spirit. But it would be better to present the exact words of the holy Gospel: "that all may be one as you Father in me and I in you." The bond of this unity is the glory, and this glory is the Holy Spirit, as anyone who is familiar with Scripture will agree if he reflects on the word of the Lord: "The glory that you have given me, I have given to them." For in all truth he has given them this same glory when he said: "Receive the Holy Spirit."[178]

This very beautiful text, however, does not reach the precision that Augustine will manifest. It suggests more than it says.

How did Augustine come to elaborate a doctrine that is today a common good peacefully possessed by the whole Church and one whose value is recognized even outside its visible limits?[179]

It seems we must see a factor favoring this elaboration in Augustine's reading of Plotinus, of Porphyry (this implacable adversary of Christianity contributed unwittingly to a decisive advance in Christian theology), and of several Christian theologians whom Augustine does not name, but one of whom might have been Marius Victorinus.

From the year 393, in fact, we already encounter an essential point of the doctrine. St. Augustine was preaching a sermon before a local council and in it made a notable statement:

> Some have expressed the daring belief that the common element

---

[176] St. Cyril of Alexandria, *MG* 75, 576sd; cf. *DTC* III (1908), 2505-2506, art. "Cyrille," by J. Mahé.

[177] St. Epiphanius, *Ancoratus,* 7 and 8; *MG* 43, 28-29. See on this subject the edition of St. Augustine's *De Trinitate* by Mellet and Camelot, *Bibl. Augustinienne,* no. 15, Bruges, 1955, v. I, p. 587, note 40. It is clear that a greater insistence on the *Filioque* (and this was the case with St. Epiphanius) prepared the ground for the doctrine of the Spirit as communion of love between Father and Son, and conditioned it in some way though it did not cause it.

[178] St. Gregory of Nyssa, *In Cant.,* hom. 15; *MG* 44, 1116C-1117B.

[179] Cf. S. Boulgakov, *Le Paraclet.* Paris, 1946, p. 95: "a particular aspect of the doctrine of the third hypostasis...constitutes the true contribution of St. Augustine to pneumatology: this is a doctrine of the Holy Spirit as intra-Trinitarian love, as love between the Father and the Son." Barth also expresses himself on the importance of this doctrine in his *Dogmatik,* I, 1, §12, p. 492, Zurich, 1947.

effecting the union of the Father and of the Son, that is to say, if I may so speak, the deity that the Greeks name *theotes*, is the Holy Spirit. Since the Father is God and the Son is God, the deity that unites them... should be equal to him (the Father) by whom he (the Son) is generated. This deity, which they would also understand as the love and the charity that they mutually bear to one another would be called, according to them, the Holy Spirit.[180]

The expression "the deity that unites them would be the Holy Spirit," seems awkward to us today, for it is as Person and not by the simple possession of the common divine nature that the Spirit is the bond between the Father and the Son. Note also that St. Augustine does not yet make his own the affirmation of these "some," an affirmation which in a corrected form will become pivotal to his own thinking.

After this historical introduction we will proceed to show rapidly how Neo-Platonism and Marius Victorinus prepared for the two essential points that are to be examined: the Holy Spirit is communion between the Father and the Son and for this reason, principle of the communion of the members of the Church with one another and with the Father and the Son.

1. *The Neo-Platonic influence*

We think this unfolds in three stages which we present in the order of decreasing temporal proximity to St. Augustine, though it is difficult to say whether this order corresponds to the historical order of influences exerted on him.

First of all, Marius Victorinus[181] wrote, about twenty years before Augustine's conversion, his beautiful Trinitarian hymns where five texts present the Spirit as the bond between the Father and the Son:

---

[180]St. Augustine, *De fide et symbolo* IX, 19; ML 40, 191; cf. O. du Roy, *L'Intelligence de la foi en la Trinité selon saint Augustin*. Paris, 1966, pp. 486-487. Augustine will reveal to us later, in his *De haeresibus* (ch. 52; ML 42, 39) written in 428, that the "some" were Semi-Arians and Macedonians involved in what we would be tempted to call a pneumatological Modalism, by denying the proper personality of the Holy Spirit and reducing him to being only the deity common to the Father and to the Son. Their pneumatology then would have been very different from that which is habitually attributed to *Pneumatomachoi*: the reduction of the Holy Spirit to the level of a creature. But Augustine used their formula in a very different sense; and his vague assertion does not exclude Marius Victorinus from among these "some": cf. *Adversus Arium*, III, 14-17 (SC 68, 469-497); with regard to the preparation of this evolution among the earlier Latin Fathers, see J.-M. Garrigues, *Procession et Ekporèse du S. Esprit, Istina* 17 (1972), 345-363.

[181]Cf. Marius Victorinus, *Traités théologiques sur la Trinité*, notes of P. Hadot, SC 68 and 69. Paris, 1960; J. Vergara, S.J., *La teologia del Espiritu Santo en Mario Victorino, Ecclesiastica Xaveriana,* 1956, 35-125; the author does not seem to have thoroughly examined the hymns in connection with the subject that interests us.

Adesto, sancte spiritus, patris et filii copula.
...In unum qui cuncta nectis, tu es sanctus spiritus.[182]
Omnes ergo unum spiritu...
Hinc singulis vera, hinc tribus una substantia est,
Progressa a Patre Filio et regressa Spiritu.[183]
Unus, unitor omnium, virtus unius operans, unum ut fiant omnia.[184]
Haec duo unum sancto junxisti spiritu;[185]
Tu, Spiritus Sancte, conexio es; conexio autem est quidquid conectit duo;
   Ita ut conectas omnia primo conectis duo;
   Esque ipsa tertia complexio duorum atque ipsa complexio nihil distans uno, unum cum facis duo.[186]

These hymns were written by Marius Victorinus about 363.[187] One cannot help but be struck by the extent to which the author ties up economy with theology, and the unifying mission of the Spirit in the world with his "situation" at the heart of the Trinity.

It is through M. Victorinus that Augustine knew and read the *libri platonicorum* which Marius had translated: probably some treatises of Plotinus and the *De regressu animae* of Porphyry, and these readings aroused in him an "unbelieveable fire."[188]

In the *City of God* Augustine himself identifies the Holy Spirit with the

---

[182]Marius Victorinus, First hymn, vv. 3, 5, *Traités théologiques*, v. I, p. 620; in these two verses we already have the essential of the Augustinian intuition: evidently as it is in love that the Spirit binds all in one, we must conclude that it is also as love that the Spirit is *copula* between the Father and the Son, and not only on a logical and noetic plane dear to Marius Victorinus. Cf. P. Hadot, *SC* 69, p. 1059.

[183]*Ibid.*, vv. 74-76, *SC* 68, p. 626. Marius here alludes to Porphyry. The expression of a return of the divine substance to the Father is however unfortunate, for it is the Person of the Son who gives himself to the Father in the unity of a common nature, and the Father does not lose this nature in giving it to his Son. It will not then return to him. We will have occasion later to return to a certain primacy of the nature with regard to the divine Persons, even with regard to the Father, which we find in the Greek Fathers but not in St. Thomas, as Malet brings out in his book, *Personne et Amour*.

[184]Marius Victorinus, Third hymn, vv. 98-99, *op. cit.*, p. 640.

[185]*Ibid.*, v. 138, p. 642.

[186]*Ibid.*, vv. 241-246, p. 650. Note the use of the word *complexio* and not *complexus*. That word signifies more ordinarily a logical junction, a sense that is fully coherent with the understanding that Marius Victorinus has of the role of the Spirit in the Trinity: *intelligere*. We do not understand then why the translator has translated it *embrassement* (i.e., an embrace) (p. 651), which however is not false, if we believe P. Henry, S.J.; "Another Plotinian feature is the identity of will and knowledge. For Plotinus, all knowledge is essentially a longing for, a desire of, the object..." (*Journal of Theological Studies*, New Series, vol. I, 1950, p. 47, 6). See *Traités théologiques*, v. II, p. 1087: explicative note.

[187]Cf. *Ibid.*, v. I, Introduction, p. 59.

[188]St. Augustine, *Contra Academicos*, II, 2, 5.

intermediary principle that Porphyry recognized between the Father and his Intellect, but not without showing the difference between this *Patris et Filii medium* of Porphyry and the "soul of the world" of Plotinus,[189] whose disciple Porphyry was. O. du Roy is altogether right in "conjecturing that a reading of Porphyry gave Augustine the idea of seeking the *intellectus fidei* of the Spirit on the side of the will," even if it be true, as the same author adds, that there is "no reason for thinking that Augustine could have found in the *De regressu* a median hypostasis defined as the mutual love of the other two."[190]

But how could Porphyry encourage Augustine in a direction which he did not explicitly suggest to him? The very title of Porphyry's work suggests it: *De regressu animae*. According to Plotinus, whose disciple Porphyry was, the whole of a spirit's life consists in the return through reflection to its source and in union with it.[191] Thus, as Smulders remarks, the Son, born of the Father, lives in uniting himself to the Father by knowledge;[192] for Marius Victorinus, this return of the Son to the Father, this "conversion" of the Only-Begotten, is the person of the Holy Spirit; for Augustine this return is, more than in Marius Victorinus, the work of love and, in consequence, the Spirit is the bond of love. St. Augustine's proper and penetrating contribution is to have joined the use of the *epistrophe*—the conversion toward the principle that Neo-Platonism preached—of a loving *epistrophe*, to the analysis of the biblical data on the loving relations between the Father and the Son in order to disclose in the Spirit the communion of love between the Father and the Son—a Son who returns to his Father in love.

2. *The Spirit, communion of love between the Father and the Son*

St. Augustine affirms many times this fundamental intuition. Here we limit ourselves to citing three texts; their different nuances complement each other.

In the first, Augustine draws on but transforms a thought of St. Hilary: "the ineffable embrace (*complexus*[193]) of the Father and of the Image does not take place without delight, without charity, without joy. This love, this pleasure, this felicity, we could say, this bliss, if a human term could ever

---

[189]St. Augustine, *De Civitate Dei*, X, 23.8-21.

[190]O. du Roy, *op. cit.*, pp. 262-264 and p. 264 note 1 at the end. The same author says correctly again: "This understanding of the Spirit-Charity and source of our union with God is only grasped through the increasing importance of the cyclic schema of exitus-reditus" (*ibid.*, p. 262).

[191]Cf. R. Arnou, *Le désir de Dieu dans la philosophie de Plotin*. Paris, 1921, pp. 84-85. See the important article of the same author on the Platonism of the Fathers, *DTC* XII, 2 (1935).

[192]P. Smulders, S.J., *DSAM*, v. IV (1960), art. "E. Saint," col. 1276.

[193]Does not the transition from the *complexio* of Marius Victorinus to the *complexus* of Augustine symbolize a whole evolution that lead to the explicit declaration of the Spirit as reciprocal and loving gift of the Father to the Son and of the Son to the Father?

express it suitably, Hilary has concisely called 'fruition' and in the Trinity this is the Holy Spirit."[194]

A little earlier Augustine had developed his thought:

> Whether he be the unity of the Two, or their sanctity, or their love, whether he be their unity because he is their love and their love because he is their sanctity, it is clear that the Holy Spirit is not one of the Two since he conjoins them, since it is he in whom the one generated is loved by, and loves in return, the one who generates him; he in whom the Two preserve the unity of the spirit in the bond of peace (Eph. 4:3), not by participation but by their essence, not by the gift of some superior third party but by their own (reciprocal) gift.... The Holy Spirit is then something common to the Father and to the Son...(their) consubstantial and coeternal communion.... Consequently, there are no more than three: the one who loves him who draws his being from him, the other who loves him from whom he draws his being, and this love itself. And if this love is not God, how is God charity? (cf. 1 Jn. 4:8, 16).[195]

Finally, in the last book of *De Trinitate*, St. Augustine attempts to show that his doctrine has a scriptural foundation. Even if it is not indisputable, his reasoning is nevertheless impressive, inspiring, indeed almost convincing; it rests entirely on what springs to light by comparing 1 John 4:7-19; Romans 5:5; Acts 8:20; John 4:7-14. St. John tells us both that love is of God and that God is love (1 Jn. 4:7-8); and that we recognize that we dwell in God in love, thanks to the fact that he has given us of his Spirit (1 Jn. 4:13): from this St. Augustine concludes that this love which is and comes from the God-who-is-Love is the Spirit who makes us abide in charity and pours it into our hearts (Rom. 5:5).[196]

Doubtless this demonstration will not convince everyone, but might we not ask those who say they are dissatisfied, if they are so certain that St. Augustine is wrong? In particular, to one who would object that "the God who is mentioned in the first Johannine Epistle and is there called Love, is the Father," could one not answer that the same Epistle calls Jesus Christ *ho alethinos theos*, the true God (1 Jn. 5:20), and that therefore it does not reserve exclusively to the Father the designation *ho theos*, "the God"? Moreover, St. Augustine by no means maintains that Love designates in God exclusively the person of the Holy Spirit.[197] A statement of St. Augustine partially and,

---

[194]St. Augustine, *De Trinitate*, VI, X, 11: *ineffabilis quidam complexus Patris et Imaginis*, in Mellet-Camelot's translation, *op. cit.*, p. 499; the translators have rendered the *usus* of Hilary by *jouissance* (fruition); cf. St. Hilary, *De Trinitate*, II, 33-35; ML 10, 73-75.

[195]St. Augustine, *De Trinitate*, VI, 5.7 (trans. cited, pp. 483-487).

[196]Cf. St. Augustine, *De Trinitate*, XV, 17.31; 18.32; 19.37. It is necessary to read these texts carefully.

[197]Cf. *De Trinitate*, XV, 19.37; ML 42, 1086.

indeed, modestly summarizes both his doctrine and his scriptural argument: "According to the Sacred Scriptures, the Holy Spirit is neither of the Father alone nor of the Son alone, but of both of them: and thus he instills in us the common charity by which the Father and the Son reciprocally love one another."[198]

Thus St. Augustine has constantly remained faithful to the doctrine that he set forth in his sermon of 393 mentioned above, but without yet making it definitively his own. He has developed it, but the essential was already expressed in this sermon, where he justly stressed that previous theologians had not examined very thoroughly the Holy Spirit's personal role in the bosom of the Trinity[199] (doubtless because they were more preoccupied with establishing his divinity). It is this that Augustine wished to do. Yet this personal role did not interest him from 393 on only in view of a better understanding in faith of the Trinitarian mystery in its inner workings, but also because of the singular light it casts on the economy. On this point his thought will grow richer.[200]

3. *The Holy Spirit, bond and principle of intra-ecclesial communion and of the communion of Christians with the Father and with the Son*

It is this Augustinian vision, intimately bound up with the preceding one as we shall see, that unveils for us an unsurpassable summit and at the same time the most profound synthesis ever elaborated between the two perspectives of Trinitarian immanence and economy, the link between the two effusions, internal and external, of the divine life. It is fitting then that we present the principal texts of St. Augustine and bring out their significance.

In sermon seventy-one we find a luminous resumé of the whole Augustinian position:

---

[198]*Ibid.*, XV, 17.27; ML 42, 1080. The holy Doctor adds in the same place: "Non itaque dixit Scriptura, Spiritus Sanctus charitas est; quod si dixisset, non parvam partem quaestionis istius abstulisset: sed dixit, Deus charitas est (1 Jn. 4:16), ut incertum sit, et ideo requirendum, utrum Deus Pater sit charitas, an Deus Filius, an Deus Spiritus Sanctus, an Deus ipsa Trinitas." The gist of Augustine's scriptural argumentation is summarized thus a little further on: "Spiritus itaque Sanctus de quo dedit nobis (1 Jn. 4:13) facit nos in Deo manere et ipsum in nobis: hoc autem facit dilectio. Ipse est igitur Deus dilectio" (*ibid.*, §31, col. 1082). To grasp the force that this syllogism has in Augustine's eyes one should read all of § 31.

[199]St. Augustine, *De Fide et Symbolo*, IX, 19, ML 40, 191: "ejus (sc. Spiritus Sancti) proprium quo proprio fit ut eum neque Filium neque Patrem dicere possimus." The problematic of 393 will remain the same in the *De Trinitate*. St. Augustine does not distinguish clearly between the essential love and the personal love (which he in no way confuses), also a notional love. Did he ever perfectly surmount the difficulty that he experienced and set forth in 393? It is not certain. But what appears evident, is that he wrote the *De Trinitate* to help himself see it more clearly, and not without fruit.

[200]The decisive progress will be realized at the time of sermon 71: cf. notes 201 and 206 and the texts to which they refer.

The Father and the Son have willed that we enter into communion among ourselves and with them through That which is common to them, and to bind us into one by this Gift which the two possess together, that is by the Holy Spirit, God and gift of God. It is in him in fact, that we are reconciled with the Divinity and take our delight in it.[201]

According to P. Smulders' excellent commentary,[202] Augustine "recovers Cyprian's conception: the communion of the faithful in the Church flows from the Trinitarian communion," but with a notable progress: for he shows us in the Spirit the "substantial and consubstantial charity"[203] of the Father and of the Son, something Cyprian did not do. Smulders stresses still another aspect of this pneumatic ecclesiology of Augustine: "the ecclesiastical communion, organized and hierarchical, is the sacrament of the unity of the Spirit. This is why the word peace, heavily charged with canonical overtones, can designate the Holy Spirit. Not only is he the peace that reconciles us with the Father and the Son,[204] but also the peace of the unity that unites the Father and the Son.[205]

To the people of Hippo, the bishop did not hesitate to explain with precision and depth that the Spirit joins us together and with the Father and the Son only because he is, first of all, their bond:

> The society of the unity of the Church of God, outside of which there is no remission of sins, is as it were the proper work of the Holy Spirit, with whom the Father and the Son cooperate, because the Holy Spirit himself is in some manner their fellowship. For the Father is not possessed equally in the same way by the Son and by the Holy Spirit, because he is not the Father of both. And the Son is not possessed equally in the same way by the Father and the Holy Spirit because he is not the Son of both. The Holy Spirit is possessed in common by the Father and by the Son, because he is the one Spirit of both.[206]

[201]"Quod ergo commune est Patri et Filio, per hoc nos habere voluerunt communionem et inter nos et secum et per illud donum nos colligere in unum quod ambo habent unum, hoc est per Spiritum Sanctum Deum et donum Dei. In hoc enim reconciliamur divinitati, eaque delectamur," St. Augustine, *Sermo* 71.12.18; ML 38, 454.

[202]P. Smulders, S.J., *DSAM*, v. IV (1960), 1280-1282: art. "E. Saint."

[203]St. Augustine, *In Jo.* 105, 3; ML 35, 1904 d ("charitas substantialis et consubstantialis amborum").

[204]St. Augustine, ML 35, 2095.

[205]St. Augustine, *In Jo.* 14, 9; ML 35, 1508.

[206]St. Augustine, *Sermo* 71.20.33: ML 38, 463-464: "Societas unitatis Ecclesiae Dei, extra quam non fit remissio peccatorum, tamquam proprium est opus Spiritus Sancti, Patre sane et Filio cooperantibus, quia societas est quodammodo Patris et Filii ipse Spiritus Sanctus. Nam Pater non communiter habetur a Filio et Spiritu Sancto; quia non est Pater amborum. Et Filius non communiter habetur a Patre et Spiritu Sancto quia non est Filius amborum. Spiritus autem Sanctus communiter habetur a Patre et Filio quia Spiritus est unus amborum."

Note here the extreme propriety of the terms employed by St. Augustine. We will perceive their precision still better in the light of the following chapters. He does not say that the Church is the proper and exclusive work of the Holy Spirit, and he could not say this, under penalty of contradicting the doctrine that he himself[207] has drawn from Revelation: the exterior works of the Three are common to them. He says then: *tamquam proprium opus*. This appropriation offers in his eyes the advantage of stressing what is precisely the intra-Trinitarian property that he was one of the first to discover: the Spirit as fellowship and communion of love between Father and Son. We understand thus how Smulders could write: "The love by which the Father and the Son embrace and communicate with one another, overflows into us, makes us love God and communicate with our brothers in the Church. And this fraternal love, an outpouring in us of the Spirit-Love, reveals to us the personal property of the Spirit. For Augustine, the supernatural life is a veritable participation in the Trinitarian life."[208]

It is in and by the mystery of the Church that the Spirit, "gift eternally (Augustine means gift of the Father to the Son and of the Son to the Father) is given in time"[209] to the extent of becoming our own yet without ceasing to transcend us. As the Bishop of Hippo says very well: "The relation of that which is given extends both to the donor and to the beneficiaries; so the Holy Spirit is in our language not only the Spirit of the Father and of the Son who have given him to us, but also ours who have received him...the Spirit of God who gives him to us and ours, who receive him."[210]

The eternal Spirit of the Father and of the Son, their Communion and their reciprocal Gift,[211] becomes then the Spirit of the Church in time, the temporal Gift which the Father and the Son make to her. The Breath of divine Love becomes the Soul of the universal Church, the Body of Christ. The principle of communion among Christians is at once consubstantial Communion between the Father and the Son and principle of the communion between the Father and the sons in the Only Son.

A perfect example of this Augustinian synthesis is found in the different commentaries that the Saint gave of the action of insufflation of the Risen One and of the words that accompanied it: "Receive the Holy Spirit" (Jn.

---

[207]St. Augustine, *De Trinitate*, I, 4.7; ML 42, 824: "indivisa opera Trinitatis, sicut et indivisa est Trinitatis essentia...(Tres) inseparabiliter operantur." Cf. DS 3326.

[208]Smulders, *op cit., ibid.*

[209]St. Augustine, *De Trinitate*, V, XVI, 17.

[210]*Ibid.*, V, XIV, 15; cf. St. Thomas Aquinas, *Summa Theologica*, I, 38.2.3.

[211]*Ibid.*, V, XI, 12: "ut ergo ex nomine quod utrique convenit (sc. Spiritus) utriusque communio significetur, vocatur donum amborum Spiritus Sanctus." We find here again St. Augustine's theological reflection on the signification of the very name of Holy Spirit: cf. our ch. 1, §4. About the name "Gift of God," proper name of the Holy Spirit, see F. Bourassa, S.J., *Sc. Eccl.* 6 (1954), 73-82.

20:22). On the one hand Christ signified that the Spirit of the Son proceeds also from the Son.[212] Was he not, this Spirit, the Force, the "power," the Dynamism which burst forth from Christ and healed all the sick (cf. Lk. 6:19)?[213] On the other hand Christ, by joining the remission of sins to the gift of the Spirit, was announcing that "the charity of the Church, poured out in our hearts by the Holy Spirit, remits the sins of those who share in it but retains the sins of those who do not."[214] Thus Jesus was proclaiming, by means of a sign that was at once twofold and single, verbal and real, the mission of the Spirit as extension of his eternal procession, and proclaiming himself as the eternal Spirator and temporal Donator of the Spirit whom he breathed on these creatures of flesh, who became "spirits" in their rebirth by the Spirit and the water that flowed forth together with Him, from his pierced side (cf. Jn. 3:6; 6:63; 19:34).[215]

It should, moreover, be observed that this synthesis is not achieved at the price of any sacrifice of the transcendence of the Spirit-Creator over the created spirits to whom he is sent in mission. St. Augustine takes care to point out that "the Lord, who speaks so often of his unity with his Father or of our union with one another, never says: 'that they may be one with us' but 'that they may be one as we are one.' "[216]

The Augustinian pneumatology of fellowship is doubtless, as Boulgakov perceived, the most original contribution of the great African doctor to Trinitarian theology. Besides originality, it has the merit of being in harmony with Scripture, the liturgy and Trinitarian metaphysics. The study of this harmony would require developments that we cannot make here, but some lines of these developments we can sketch here in order to encourage further research.

First of all it is in accord with Scripture, as Augustine himself has attempted to show in a subtle and profound demonstration which needs to be taken up again. Developing certain insights of A. Feuillet,[217] we can even ask in the light of Cant. 2:14 and 5:2, if the assimilation of the Holy Spirit to

[212]St. Augustine, *In Jo.* 99, 7; *ML* 35, 1889.

[213]*Ibid.*, St. Augustine here also cites Lk. 8:46; we see then that Schierse (*MS* v. II, p. 98) has not discovered anything new in seeing the Holy Spirit in the force that went out of Jesus; the Fathers already knew this...

[214]St. Augustine, *ML* 35, 1858. On this text, see Z. Alszeghy, S.J., "Carità ecclesiale nella penitenzia cristiana," *Gregorianum,* 44 (1963), 5-32.

[215]One could correctly say that the spiration of the Spirit is at the same time eternal procession and temporal mission, in view of the unifying sanctification of the Church (cf. note 87 of this chapter); besides, the mission is temporal only by its term and this formula in no way wishes to "finalize" an eternal and immanent, intra-Trinitarian action by a temporal effect, but to affirm that the mission, on the part of the Father and the Son, is as eternal as the spiration.

[216]St. Augustine, *De Trinitate,* VI, 3.4: "nusquam dixit: ut nos et ipsi unum"...

[217]A. Feuillet, "Le symbolisme de la colombe dans les récits évangéliques du Baptême," *Rech. Sc. Rel.,* 46 (1958), 524-544.

a dove (an assimilation that is common to the four gospels: Jn. 1:32; Lk. 3:22, etc.) does not signify, in the mind of the sacred writers, that the Church, the true spouse of the Lamb prophesied by the Canticle under the image of the dove, becomes the corporeal manifestation of the incorporeal Spirit, associated with this Lamb in virtue of his baptism of blood. He descends into the waters so that the new and heavenly Jerusalem can descend from heaven (Apoc. 21:2), all filled with his Spirit. The mission of Jesus is to "make the dove appear, that is the new people of God animated by the divine Spirit."[218]

Further, this Augustinian pneumatology is magnificently summed up by the conclusion of the Latin orations: *in unitate Spiritus Sancti Deus*. The unity, as St. Fulgentius so well saw,[219] to which allusion is made, is that of the Spirit himself inasmuch as he is not only common to the Father and to the Son but also their consubstantial and coeternal communion[220] (cf. p. 345, n. 41).

This also brings to mind the appropriateness of this doctrine with respect to Trinitarian metaphysics. Since the year 393 when he presented it for the first time before a local council, Augustine had defended it[221] against one objection: does not the statement that the Spirit is the communion of love between the Father and the Son reduce him to being their accident and, from this viewpoint, make us fall back into the error of the Semi-Arians, the Macedonians? In response to this Augustine would recall that in God there is no accident, for He is substance. Later, in a text we cited above, Augustine will say that the Spirit is "substantial and consubstantial charity": that is, in scholastic terms, He is at the same time essential love—the divine nature—and personal Love inseparable from the Father and from the Son since they possess the same nature in common. Augustine even turned the objection around, in showing those who accused him (in 393) of Semi-Arianism that they were in reality victims of a secret complicity with Manichaeism: for by representing God in the likeness of a body, they could only conceive the Spirit as bond of the Father and of the Son in the manner of a third body uniting the first two.

By his doctrine of consubstantial charity identified with the Spirit, Augustine fully displayed the Nicene consubstantiality while avoiding in a consummate way all Modalism that the latter could occasion: in seeing in the Spirit personal and consubstantial love, he distinguished him by a personal property from the Word, personal Wisdom, and showed thus that

---

[218]*Ibid.*, p. 540; cf. p. 541. Cf. St. Augustine, *ML* 42, 1093, 35, 1425-1436. A.-M. Henry, O.P., *L'Esprit-Saint*. Paris, 1959, pp. 41-42.

[219]St. Fulgentius, *Epist*. XIV, 36-38; *ML* 65, 426-427.

[220]*Ibid.*, 427: "nec solum commune aliquid eorum, sed etiam communionem consubstantialem coaeternamque."

[221]St. Augustine, *De Fide et Symbolo*, IX; *ML* 40, 192-193.

consubstantiality does not mean confusion. We can see then in the Augustinian doctrine, become Catholic doctrine today, a step too seldom explicitly recognized as such, a step toward the clear affirmation of the equality and the consubstantiality of the Three made by the Athanasian Creed and Constantinople II. A step whose significance and value are definitive[222] and which we will meet again under different angles in the course of this study. Through Augustine's reflecting as a Neo-Platonist on the word of God,[223] the Spirit manifested himself to the Church as the one who unifies her in being the personal unity of the Father and the Son; the breath that animates the whole ecclesial body is the One in whom the Unbegotten and the Only-Begotten meet one another in an eternal embrace.

[222]We know that Pope Paul VI has explicitly included this point in his profession of faith, June 30, 1968.

[223]We could say that Neo-Platonism historically but not intrinsically conditioned the development of the doctrine of the Spirit as communion of reciprocal love, and that the *Filioque* was both a condition and a cause of this. It is not at all astonishing that the Church had to wait for the end of the fourth century to begin to suspect that this doctrine pertained to the deposit of Revelation: we could say as much about the Assumption, or more exactly, that the ecclesial consciousness of the Assumption came still later, except perhaps for the Judaeo-Christians. N.B.: I deepen the origins of Augustine's Pneumatology in my book: *Introduction à l'histoire de l'Exégèse,* v. III, St. Augustin. Paris, Cerf, 1983.

III
One Single Divine Nature in Three Distinct Persons

Constantinople II and Lateran IV

For the Church, achieving explicit recognition of the perfect equality of the Father, the Son and the Holy Spirit, meant truly the end of a long discussion, but also the upsurge of a whole series of further problems.

Today the doctrine of consubstantiality clearly proclaims the possession in common by three equal Persons of a nature numerically one; but was this equally as clear in the fourth and fifth centuries?

The doctrine of consubstantiality poses the problem of numeration in God. We cannot avoid taking numerical count of Father, Son and Holy Spirit as being three. But three what?

A difficult question when it was posed for the first time. And the answer was: not three gods, but three Persons in one only God.

As a result the unity of God is highlighted with new and mysterious clarity. And as this one divine nature contains all conceivable perfection, a new question arises: what distinguishes one Person from another?

We must then reply to the following questions that successively arise: is the unity of the divine nature specific or numerical? How did the concept of hypostasis evolve historically and what does a divine Person signify today? How and in what sense was the notion of relation introduced into Trinitarian theology?

I. NUMERICAL OR SPECIFIC UNITY OF THE DIVINE NATURE?

The apparent simplicity of the concept of unity concealed some subtle ambiguities that had to be eliminated before we could speak in a consistent and orthodox way of the Trinity.

What do we understand by the divine unity?

Can we say with the contemporary Anglican theologian, L. Hodgson, that it is a "dynamic unity actively unifying in one only divine life the lives of the three divine Persons," an "organic unity"?[1] Or with Evagrius of

---

[1] L. Hodgson, *op. cit.*, p. 102; this is even, according to the author, his "main thesis" (*ibid.*). The expression "organic unity" was forged by Prestige to sum up Tertullian's doctrine on the internal economy of the Trinity: cf. *God in Patristic Thought*. London, 1964, ch. V, pp. 97ff.

Pontus, a lector of St. Basil, that "we believe in one only God, one not in number but in nature"?[2]

Have the Cappadocian and Post-Nicene Fathers truly restored polytheism under the form of tritheism by affirming not only three persons but also three gods? Was Harnack right in interpreting them in this sense?

To understand how these Fathers did not explicitly affirm but yet did substantially hold a "numerical" unity of the divine nature (in a sense that must be made more precise), we must recall certain data of the ancient problem of the one and the many.

Evagrius of Pontus has summed up in a few formulas a philosophical doctrine whose elements are found among the Cappadocians:
—number is a function of quantity;
—quantity is linked to corporeal nature;
—number is thus found only in corporeal nature;
—in consequence everything that is numerically one is not truly one nor simple in nature.

These principles draw their inspiration from Aristotle for whom every plurality of individuals of the same species depends on a composition of the essence. Aristotle, however, concluded from this that the first mover is one in essence and number; Evagrius on the contrary concluded that God, since he did not contain the principle of number (that is to say composition, matter), escapes all numeration and that the divine essence is not numerically one, any more than the Father or the Son or the Spirit considered separately.

And Evagrius triumphantly concluded: "how henceforth will anyone dare reproach us with being tritheists, we who absolutely discard number from the blessed and spiritual nature of God?"[3]

For St. Basil likewise "the inaccessible is beyond number."[4]

As may be observed, the Cappadocian Fathers had an acute sense of the divine transcendence and spirituality. St. Augustine in more measured terms will reveal an analogous preoccupation: *nec quoniam Trinitas est, ideo triplex putandus est.*[5]

When all this is said must we conclude that the Cappadocians denied numerical unity in God? that this was outside their affirmations, their intention? To say this would be to misunderstand them and to attribute to them a logic which, in fact, was not theirs. Evagrius, we have said, professed

---

[2]A letter attributed to St. Basil, but in reality the work of Evagrius of Pontus: *Epist.* VII in *MG* 32, 248C.

[3]*Ibid.*, 32, 249, 2; cf. R. Arnou, S.J., "Unité numérique et unité de nature chez les Pères, après le concile de Nicée," *Gregorianum* 15 (1934), 242-254.

[4]St. Basil, *On the Holy Spirit*, ch. 18, no. 44; *MG* 32, 149A.

[5]St. Augustine, *De Trinitate*, 6.7.9; *RJ* 1667.

"one only God, one not in number but in nature."[6] This unity of nature is neither specific nor numerical, it designates the divine spirituality. And yet to designate this Evagrius speaks of unity of nature! Now we can understand the bewildered cry of St. Gregory of Nyssa over this failure in the attempt to come to a satisfactory language: "How can the same thing be numerable and yet escape all numeration?"[7] How can there be in God three persons and one essence,[8] and yet no number?

We should not ask of the Cappadocians a solution of the difficulty which their Platonic philosophy, which despised matter, could not allow them to reach; but let us not have the slightest doubt either about their strict numerical monotheism. Otherwise how could St. Basil have written: "According to the property of the persons, the Father and the Son are one and one; according to the nature which is common to them, they are both one single thing"?[9]

For them the Monad or the One (note the Neo-Platonic vocabulary) is the Divine Nature, simple and indivisible, which the Father, Son and Holy Spirit possess equally, but which remains identically the same in those who possess it.[10] This is so true that St. Basil was reproached for not wishing "to employ in the plural any of the names that pertain to God; we profess in reality that one is the goodness and the power and the divinity and that all such names must be put in the singular."[11] Could a tritheist have signed such a letter?

It is thus clear that what the Cappadocians call "unity of nature" in the Trinity is the absolute simplicity of the divine essence. Such a simplicity involves the impossibility of being multiplied or of being divided or compounded. The unity of nature therefore contains the unity that is called numerical and surpasses it. This rigorous conclusion of R. Arnou[12] justifies I. Ortiz de Urbina's affirmation regarding Nicaea, of whose exact meaning the Cappadocian Fathers were certainly not unaware: "the *homoousios* of Nicaea does not signify in a formal and direct way the numerical unity of essence common to the Father and to the Son.... But does this mean that Nicaea in no way affirms this numerical identity? I do not believe so; in my opinion, the Symbol clearly says what we understand by numerical identity, not formally and explicitly through the *homoousios*, but implicitly and virtually."

[6]Cf. note 2.
[7]St. Gregory of Nyssa, *Orat. Catech.*, c. III, MG 45, 17D.
[8]Cf. Gonzales S., *Mia ousia, Treis Hypostaseis en Greg. de Nisa*. Rome, 1939.
[9]St. Basil, *On the Holy Spirit*, ch. 18, no. 45 (SC 17, p. 194).
[10]It is thus that R. Arnou (*op. cit.*) sums up (p. 252) different texts of St. Basil.
[11]St. Basil, *Epist.* 189, 2-3; MG 32, 685-688B.
[12]R. Arnou, *art. cit.*, p. 254.

And the learned exegete of the first ecumenical council reconstructs for us its implicit reasoning: "One and indivisible is the divine essence possessed by the Father; the essence of the Son is likewise properly divine; consequently the essence of the Son is the same as that of the Father, one and indivisible, i.e., numerically the same."[13]

The affirmation of the numerical unity of the divine essence is thus implicit in that of its simplicity and of its indivisibility. Both the orthodox and the Arians admitted the major premise relative to the Father, while the Arians denied the minor relative to the Son. Nicaea replied by declaring the divinity of the Son *per reductionem,* by reducing it to the divinity of the Father (a reduction of numerical identity).[14] This is very precisely what the Cappadocian Fathers understood and what St. Basil, in spite of some incoherencies of language in other places, magnificently expressed: "One is the Holy Spirit, united through the Son who is one with the Father who is one, thus completing the glorious and blessed Trinity."[15] *One* signifies here the simple and indivisible divine nature, but variously possessed by the Father, the Son and the Holy Spirit, in contradiction to Evagrius (cf. pp. 123-124).

What then did the Cappadocians lack in order to arrive at a correct expression of the numerical identity of the divine essence?

They lacked an analogical notion of the multiple which St. Thomas Aquinas would, later on, make luminously clear. He will, in fact, elaborate the distinction of number into predicamental and transcendental number: the first is encountered only in material realities endowed with quantity, while the second is encountered only in immaterial realities. Quantitative number adds an accident to being, while transcendental multitude signifies multiple realities in their respective indivision, without any accident. The divine nature is one with this unity, a transcendental one that is convertible with being: *ens et unum convertuntur.*

Let us rather read the text itself of the Common Doctor:

> Number is affirmed in God under the proper *ratio* of number and not under its generic aspect of quantity.... When we say: "the Essence is one," *one* signifies the essence in its indivision; when we say, "the Person is one," this attribute signifies the Person in indivision; and when we say "the Persons are several," we signify the Persons, each of them in indivision; for by definition multitude is composed of unities.[16]

Transcendental multitude adds to the subjects of which it is predicated only the indivision of each one: this is the multitude one affirms in God.[17]

---

[13] I. Ortiz de Urbina, S.J., *El simbolo niceno.* Madrid, 1947, p. 208.
[14] *Ibid.*
[15] St. Basil, *On the Holy Spirit,* ch. 18, no. 45 (SC 17, p. 194); MG 32, 152A.
[16] St. Thomas Aquinas, *Summa Theologica,* I. 30.3.
[17] *Ibid.,* ad 2 m; we should also refer to *I Sent.,* dist. 24, q. 1; *De Pot.,* 9.7, and in a more general

Do we not have here a perfectly satisfying explanation of the beautiful Basilian formula cited above: "One is the Holy Spirit, united by the Son who is one with the Father who is one, thus completing the blessed and glorious Trinity"? Each of the Three is One inasmuch as he is indivisible, and yet they are Three, distinct among themselves in the common possession of their indivisible essence, distinct in the manner in which they possess it.

What their exaggerated Platonism prevented the Cappadocians from seeing is that "our numerical terms truly affirm something in God, namely the realities themselves—Essence, Persons—which they qualify by adding to them their negation: indivision or distinction. It kept them from seeing that these terms could evoke a notion of one or of many disengaged from the limited mode of quantity and thus capable of being thence transposed—analogically—to God. They could thus, beyond their negation, posit in God their formal aspect in its positive reality—elevated of course to the divine mode."[18]

The mystery of the Trinity thus makes us rise from the composite and quantitative unity that daily experience furnishes to the absolutely simple unity it does not offer us; and also from the multiplicity inherent in each of the essences of this world, a multiplicity that is experientially perceptible, to the transcendent multiplicity of God Father, Son and Spirit. The God who gives us an experience of the quantitative and unified multiplicity of the world which is a universe, a unity of the totality, this God is also he who reveals himself beyond experience, but through it as being transcendent,[19] immaterial and indivisible multiplicity. As St. Basil would put it: "the Inaccessible is beyond number," material number, because it is immaterial Number, the God who is One and Three.

II. FROM GOD THE FATHER, SON AND HOLY SPIRIT, TO GOD IN THREE DIVINE PERSONS OR HYPOSTASES

The authors of the N. T. often speak to us, we have seen, of the Father, the Son and the Holy Spirit, they offer us ternary schemas of thought, but they never speak to us of the Three as Three. Now we must study the transition "from the named three to the numbered three" (Lonergan) in the history of Theology. The fact of numbering in God and in relation to God becomes a theme considered in itself.

The first Eastern Father to speak to us of the Trinity seems to have been

---

manner to questions 11 (unity of God) and 13 (critique of the names we give to God) of the first part of the *Summa*.

[18]H.-F. Dondaine, O.P., commentary on the treatise of the Trinity in the *Summa Theologica* of St. Thomas Aquinas. Paris, 1962, v. I, p. 189, explicative note 61.

[19]Cf. L. Hodgson, *op. cit.*, p. 108; we drew on his theme, but we have not developed it in the same way he did.

Theophilus of Antioch,[20] followed rather closely by a first Latin, Tertullian.[21] Already in Tertullian the Trinity signifies more than any simple triad and designates the number and the group of the three divine Persons in the unity of the divine essence or substance. Since St. Augustine the expression is reserved to God alone and is never used to designate creatures. The Trinity is thus an abstract noun which designates the concrete reality of the Father, the Son and the Spirit.

How did we come to designate the Three as Persons? Before retracing briefly the principal elements of this history, it might be well to recall that a genius like St. Augustine was not at all indifferent to the disadvantages of this word nor to its limits:

> When then someone asks: what are these three (i.e. the Father, the Son and the Spirit)? three what? we are hard put to find a specific or a generic noun that will cover these three (*haec tria*) but none comes to mind, for the transcendence of the divinity exceeds the resources of our normal vocabulary. When dealing with God, thought is more accurate than discourse, and the reality is more accurate than thought.... Where there is no difference of essence there is need of a specific name common to the three, but we do not find one. Person is a generic term since it can also be applied to man, even though there is such a distance from man to God.[22]

It is interesting to note that for St. Augustine the difficulty consisted in finding a common name applicable to each of the Three and to the Three alone, to the exclusion of men. We are still far from an analogical concept of the value of the term (and of language in general) such as we will find in St. Thomas. For St. Thomas the fact that the word, person, can be also applied to man, far from constituting a disadvantage, becomes rather an advantage. However, St. Augustine concluded:

> Why three persons, although we do not speak of three gods nor of three essences? Is it not because we wish to have a word which expresses in what sense we must conceive the Trinity and not remain absolutely silent when someone asks us what these three are, since three they are by our own admission?[23]

It is then without great enthusiasm and with much reserve that Augustine adopts the word Person to designate the Three. It is true that at the time he was writing no solemn decision of the ecclesiastical magisterium

---

[20] St. Theophilus of Antioch, *Ad Autolycum*, 2, 15; MG 6, 1077; RJ 180.
[21] Tertullian, *Adversus Praxean* 2; ML 2, 156; RJ 371. See our chapter II.
[22] St. Augustine, *De Trinitate*, VII, IV, 7. The whole seventh book must be read (from IV, 7 to V, 10), about person.
[23] St. Augustine, *De Trinitate*, VII, VI, 11.

had yet made the use of this word obligatory: only in 554 was the word canonized by Constantinople II. Let us retrace the stages of the trajectory of the term *hypostasis* to which the term person was assimilated.

1. *Vocabulary*

Hypostasis is a Stoic term which signifies a thing or an action. As thing, *hypostasis* signifies the base or foundation, that which is under or below, second "substance" or *ousia*. As act, *hypostasis* signifies for the Stoics the act of remaining under, of supporting, of subsisting, almost of existing: it is first substance.

The philosophical meaning of the word *hypostasis* could have developed in two directions: either along the line of an identification with *ousia* and essence, or along that of identification with the concrete act of subsisting in a substance, and in consequence it could lead in Trinitarian language to the affirmation of three hypostases in God. In the course of the development of Christian language the term *hypostasis* will slowly pass from the side of substance to the side of subsistence and of person.[24]

2. *The History*

For Arius toward the year 320, the three, the Father, the Son and the Spirit, are three *ousiai* and even infinitely unlike in *ousia*, with which *hypostasis* appeared to be identified.[25] Nicaea, we have already seen, like Arius seems to have identified *ousia* and *hypostasis*: we have also noted, however, that St. Basil (perhaps through projecting his own distinctions into the recent past of fifty years earlier) would not admit this identification (cf. pp. 91, 99).

In any case it is with the Semi-Arians that the evolution begins. In their struggle against Modalism they clung to the *three hypostases*. If Nicaea had left the impression that it spoke of one single *hypostasis* while Arius spoke of three, to the Semi-Arians nonetheless the expression *three hypostases* seemed to be a complement that was indispensable for correcting a false, modalist interpretation of "consubstantial."

So in 362 we come to the synod of Alexandria and to the admission by Athanasius himself of a double Trinitarian language.[26] The old defender of Nicaea admits the formula proposed by the Semi-Arians: *three hypostases, one ousia*, after inquiring into the meaning they gave it.[27] However, Athanasius continued to prefer his older vocabulary: one single *ousia* and *hypostasis* (with an identity of meaning for the two words). But he does not seem to have sought "to define what constituted the property of the divine persons, nor

[24] Cf. A. Guggenberger, *EF*, v. IV, Paris, 1966, art. "Personne," notably p. 427.

[25] Arius, texts cited by *RJ* 649-650.

[26] St. Athanasius, *Tomus ad Antiochenos*, 5-6, *MG* 26, 800-801; French translation in G. Bardy, *DTC*, XV, 2 (1950), col. 1666.

[27] *Ibid.*: this formula synthesizes different thoughts of Origen: *Contra Celsum*, VIII, 12 and in Ps. 135:2.

how they are distinguished"[28] or at least to designate this property by a specific word. The two Trinitarian languages thus remained very diverse and an agreement that sanctioned such contradictory terminologies (one *hypostasis* for some, three for others) could only be provisional. Unanimity in faith and in missionary proclamation of the fundamental truth of Christianity had to be capable of being translated into a unanimous usage of the terms that expressed it.

This was the goal that St. Basil pursued. His problematic and his aim can be thus summed up: in order that the Semi-Arian churches might accept without reserve the Nicene "consubstantial," the Nicene churches must profess without reserve the formula "three perfect hypostases." The profession of the Nicene "consubstantial" guarantees that the three hypostases are not understood tritheistically as three ousiai. Conversely the affirmation of three hypostases guarantees the non-modalist sincerity of the profession of faith in the three *prosopa*.

To justify the Cappadocian formula, *treis hypostaseis en mia ousia*, Basil—and here there is question of a decisive moment in the history of thought—clarifies the concept of hypostasis by interpreting it as "concrete act of subsisting" or in other words, as "subsistence." We could say, doubtless with a degree of simplification, that he effected a transition of the term hypostasis from second substance to first substance, from essence to the act of existing. He defines *hypostasis* as: "existence proper and perfect in itself."[29]

Note in this definition the presence of incommunicability (proper) and of substantiality (perfect in itself). In speaking of three hypostases it is the reality of the Trinitarian mystery that St. Basil wishes to salvage; the term *hypostasis* is perfectly chosen and fit for this purpose, for it has retained both from its etymology and from its other philosophical meaning, the power of signifying the subsistence[30] of a substantial being. If one acknowledges the divine persons as *hypostases*, the danger of taking them as evanescent modalities of the substance and thus the danger of Modalism is definitively averted.

The Latin and Western Fathers such as Jerome[31] had great trouble in accepting this Cappadocian dissociation of *hypostasis* and *ousia*; three hypostases (taken in the original sense of this word) seemed to them to be a profession of tritheism; since Tertullian they would have preferred to speak of three persons. This word translated into Greek as *prosopon* had

---

[28]*DTC*, XV.2 (1950), col. 1667.
[29]St. Basil, *Epist*. 210.4; *MG* 32, 773.
[30]See on subsistence the *Enciclopedia Filosofica*. Rome, 1957, v. IV, col. 1053-1055: art. "Sussistenza" by G. Provea and A. Gazzana.
[31]St. Jerome, *Epist*. 15.4; *ML* 22, 356; French transl. Bardy, *DTC* XV, 2 (1950) col. 1667.

progressively taken on a signification more precise than its original sense of "role," "stage mask," "passing or transitory aspect."[32] St. Gregory of Nazianzus brought about the definitive identification of *hypostasis* and *prosopon* (valuable in its turn for the identification of hypostasis and person). The conjunction of these two terms (which henceforth became classic for expressing what is numerable in God, his numerical "makeup") confirms the term *hypostasis* as a designation for a subsistent (and not merely for substance) and the term *prosopon* as a designation for a very real subsistent, a substantial subsistent.

We can understand how St. Basil, confronted with those who would have preferred to be content with three *prosopa* without accepting three *hypostases*, could write to the inhabitants of Neo-Caesarea:

> Sabellianism is Judaism, and it is introduced among you under the appearance of Christianity in the evangelical preaching. But in fact, he who says the Father, the Son and the Holy Spirit are one single being in several persons, and who allows for the three one single hypostasis, what does he accomplish but a denial of the eternal pre-existence of the Son of God?... Take heed: just as he who does not admit the community of substance falls into polytheism, so he who does not concede the propriety of the hypostases is drawn into Judaism.... It is not enough to enumerate the differences of persons, it is further necessary to admit that each person exists in a true hypostasis. In fact Sabellius himself did not reject this fiction of persons without hypostasis.... It is an error that has long been extinct but is now renewed by the inventors of this heresy without name, by these men who spurn the hypostases and deny the name of the Son of God.[33]

St. Basil ends another letter with this adjuration: "Do not reject the hypostases. Do not deny the name of Christ." For Basil faith in Christ is at stake in the doctrine of the divine hypostases; a failure to admit it makes of the Trinity a "masquerade" and reduces Christ, a "substantial" Person and divine hypostasis to a mask which replaces another and is destined to be replaced by a third....

3. *The term of the evolution*

Constantinople II: three consubstantial subsistences in one single divinity or divine substance (553).

The Fifth Ecumenical Council held at Constantinople in 553, began its dogmatic endeavor with a double definition, speculative and biblical, of the Trinitarian mystery.

---

[32]Cf. Schmaus, *La Trinitad de Dios*. Madrid, 1960, § 39 and 40.
[33]St. Basil, *Epist.* 210, 3-5: MG 32, 771-778.

The speculative definition brought to maturity the work of Nicaea and of Constantinople I; it was thus enunciated:

> If anyone does not confess the one nature or essence, the one force and power of the Father, the Son and the Holy Spirit, the consubstantial Trinity and one divinity which must be adored in three hypostases or persons, let him be anathema.

The Latin translation rendered hypostases by "subsistences," *subsistentiae*.[34] The proposition is of defined faith. It recapitulates and fixes the vocabulary. It has its partial origin in the letter of the synod of Constantinople (382) to Pope St. Damasus. The Greek word *hypostasis* was translated by "subsistence." But in 382 it was not yet a question of dogmatic definition. Since the Trinity in its entirety is called consubstantial, the expression is reversible: it is no longer only the Son, as at Nicaea, who is consubstantial with the Father, but also the Father and the Spirit are consubstantial with the Son, although the Father does not proceed from the Son. The Three are qualified as consubstantial in that they subsist conjointly in the same numerically single nature. Hypostasis, subsistence, person and *prosopon* are identified.

To translate the word *hypostasis* the word subsistence was preferred to the word substance so as to avoid confusion between essence and person: "we say that a reality subsists which exists in itself and by itself and not in another," St. Thomas Aquinas will explain later.[35]

The biblical definition that immediately followed the speculative affirmation, was thus expressed:

> There is one only God and Father, from whom everything (comes), and one only Lord Jesus Christ, by whom everything (exists), and one only Holy Spirit, in whom everything (subsists) (cf. 1 Cor. 8:6; Rom. 11:36; Eph. 4:5-6).[36]

One will note the opposition between the Three and the totality of creatures. The Trinity is explicated starting from the unity of the Father, from whom proceed one only Son and one only Spirit, under the seal of unity. They possess in the Father and in indivision the one same divinity, and are like him one only God. Trinitarian monarchy.

The distance between the two definitions, speculative and biblical, allows

---

[34]It seems that the Latin word *subsistentia*, which unlike substance does not imply accidents, and which designates the concrete being, was employed for the first —?— time by Rufinus (*Hist. Eccl.* I, 29; ML 26).
[35]St. Thomas Aquinas, *Summa Theologica*, I, 29.2 and "ad secundum."
[36]DS 421 (DB 213).

us to measure the road traversed in order to conserve and propagate the revealed truth.

4. *The meaning of this evolution to the eyes of faith*

Faced with such a development, apparently so technical and so abstract, one could ask to what extent faith is really involved? In reality, faith could not have avoided in the long run a greater precision in Trinitarian vocabulary. The confusion of words in the middle of the fourth century, constituted a perilous situation which could not have been prolonged without mortal danger for the faith. The Churches had to give a uniform and unanimous response to disturbing questions. The contradictory pluralism in the Trinitarian terminology was not limited to harboring germs of schism or heresy, rather it already concealed tendencies contrary to the true faith. The Nicene "consubstantial" could become dangerous without a complement; conversely the plurality of hypostases without the backdrop of the "consubstantial" would also have been perilous. Basil, man of action in doctrinal matters, wished to salvage the essence of Christianity by preaching the formula which finally took over: one nature, three hypostases or persons.[37] The speculative formula canonised at Constantinople II had the same meaning as the biblical formula by which this council enunciated the same faith; it was recognized that the second was no longer sufficient but was of course still necessary to express the faith.

III. PERSONAL PROPERTIES OF THE THREE AND THEIR DISTINCTION BY RELATIONS

Investigation by man's discursive intelligence never ends. The clarification of one point raises new questions, unveils new problems. Once the consubstantiality of the Three (which is common to them) was established and clarified, the question quite naturally arose: what is it that distinguishes them? If the Three, just as each one of them, are the same plenitude, the same "sea of substance, the same infinite and unlimited ocean of being"[38] what is it that allows us to distinguish them?

St. Athanasius had written: "the same attributes are predicated of the Father and of the Son, except the name of the Father." Assuredly. But the name Father cannot be a pure name, a vocal sound, there must be some property that the Father has and not the Son: otherwise we fall into the purest Modalism. And yet what reality could there be that is not contained in the Ocean of divine Being? It seems, as we have seen, that Athanasius neither posed nor resolved this question. This would be the role of St. Basil.

---

[37]In these developments on Constantinople II we have drawn, at least partially, on the course of P. Sesboüé (Lyons-Fourvière, 1965).

[38]Cf. St. Thomas Aquinas, *Summa Theologica*, I, 13.11, citing St. John Damascene; cf. *RJ* 1669 (Augustine).

1. *The Personal Properties*
In 376 St. Basil formulated his doctrine in a remarkable manner:

There is the same difference between essence and hypostasis as between that which is common and that which is singular.... If we do not consider the defined properties of each one, that is paternity, filiation and sanctification, but simply God by the common notion of essence, it is impossible to render a sound account of the faith. It is necessary then that we confess the faith by joining that which is proper to that which is common (*idion, koinon*). Divinity is common, paternity is proper: joining them let us say: "I believe in God, the Father." And we must proceed in a like manner in the confession of the Son: "I believe in God, the Son" (*eis theon patera, eis theon huion*).[39]

For Basil the doctrine of the divine properties is then at bottom only a corollary of that of the hypostases; it alone saves the reality of Trinity. Without the properties just as without the hypostases, it is impossible to account for the faith, for the evangelical data, or to avoid modalism. The other two Cappadocians will only clarify his thought further; where Basil spoke of paternity, filiation and sanctification, Gregory of Nazianzus, employing more technical language, prefers to use the terms *agenesis*, "genesis" and "procession" when naming the properties of the Father, the Son and the Spirit. The choice was very biblical in inspiration: cf. Jn. 15:26 (procession, *ekporeusis*).

2. *Distinction through relations*
Let us recall first of all and summarily what a relation is in the human sphere.

Peter is John's friend: we have here a relation, a reference of one being to another. It supposes the ordering of a subject and a term to which the subject orders itself or is ordered. Such a reference of the subject to the opposite term constitutes the relation itself. John is a term opposed to Peter in the relation which unites them.

The relation may exist in objective reality: Peter is truly like John; or it may exist only in my mind: I am an individual of the human species.

Unlike other modalities or categories of being, relation can be logical or mental without being real. The relation evokes no positive reality in its subject, but only the ordering of this subject to another thing. He who says substance, alludes to subject; quantity, to the measure of the subject; quality, to its disposition. But he who says relation, indicates pure reference to the opposed term (*respectus ad alterum*).

It is not surprising then that, in the physical world, relation has the

---

[39]St. Basil, *Epist.* 236, 6; MG 32, 884; RJ 926.

weakest being among all the accidents. It is more remote from substance than all the others. Hence its "ecstatic" character.

But at the same time that relation cries out for the being it lacks, the predicamental relation of the physical world is the being that does most to structure intelligibility in the created world. As its formal content is free from the limits of materiality, this notion is easily transposed into the spiritual domain: knowledge and love are relations. The concept of relation links the parts to the whole, the inferior to the superior, men among themselves, what is participated to the Absolute.

We might foresee then that relation can be mysteriously verified in God and in him can even be identified with substance.

As a result of scientific progress—whether in philosophy, sociology or the human sciences—we are discovering that the living spiritual being, however genuinely constituted on the level of substance in the "inseity" of his soul and of his body, is nevertheless situated in the world as well, by a complex of accidental relations of dependences, of dynamisms and of subordinations which coordinate him with others.

Heidegger even says that being can be reduced to relation. It is certainly necessary to say that man is situated inside a web of relations but without being identified with it.[40]

To say that in God the Persons are formally distinguished not by the common essence but by their reciprocal relations means that we make use of the problems of man the better to understand the mystery of God.[41]

What the Cappadocians did not discover[42] but spread in a definitive way throughout the Church, was the doctrine of the distinction of the Persons by interpersonal relationships. The divinity common to the Three, the divine Absolute, the divine In-itself and For-itself, leaves intact the relative aspect of the "with-respect-to-others" by which the Three are distinguished. The Absolute of the Essence, the "relative" of the Hypostases or Persons. The introduction of the doctrine of relations into the heart of Trinitarian theology and even of the doctrine of the Church took place in three successive stages:

[40]Cf. St. Thomas Aquinas, *Summa Theologica*, I, 29.4.4, and the entire body of the article; *De Potentia*, 9.4, where the saint shows very well that person, if we take this word in its formal sense, is an individual substance of the rational nature, and, only in a "material" sense is it in God a subsistent relation. Man has relations with other men, but his being, his act of being, is not constituted by these relations, whereas he is constituted by a real relation with the Creator.

[41]Or, if you prefer, we make use of problems occasioned by the relations among men who are distinguished by their multiple concrete natures, the better to grasp in faith the intimacy of the divine mystery, of the one nature of God.

[42]Cf. R. Arnou, S.J., "Arius et la doctrine des relations trinitaires," *Gregorianum*, 14 (1933), 269-272. The Trinitarian use of relation goes back at least to 260.

a) *by way of allusion:* already around 264 St. Dionysius of Alexandria hinted at this doctrine when he said: "if there is a Father, there is a Son";⁴³ the simple naming of the Father is already an implicit allusion to the Son. Here we have the idea but not yet the explicit concept of relation.

It is paradoxical to affirm that this notion which was a decisive instrument in the struggle against Arianism, is met explicitly for the first time in a letter of Arius, to be rejected by him, we might add. It is moving to think that a correct reflection, on Arius' part concerning the concept of relation, joined to a clear distinction between creation and generation (the work of Athanasius), could have prevented, at least in great measure, the tragic divisions between "Christians" in the fourth century. But doubtless it is better to recognize that Arius was doing little more than applying a veneer of Christianity over a tri-figured pagan polytheism. His conviction about the radical inequality of the Three would scarcely have allowed him to perceive the light afforded by the notion of relation, though he in fact referred to it in its technical and Aristotelian form (*ta pros ti*).

Here is the text of which Arius was the principal redactor: "The Son does not, either, have being simultaneously with the Father, as some say of relative beings, thus introducing two uncreated principles; but God as monad and universal principle, is over all."⁴⁴

It thus appears that at the time when Arianism was getting started, recourse was being made to the doctrine of relations in order to explain how the Father and the Son exist simultaneously from all eternity. In virtue of the bond that unites them, the Father can no more exist without the Son than the Son without the Father. How then could the Father be prior to the Son? Such an explanation evidently ran counter to the Arian errors.⁴⁵

b) *as an anti-Arian theme, beginning with the Cappadocians,* and thus, in the case of Gregory of Nazianzus. The Arians were saying: "If the Father signifies the essence, and if the Son is not the Father, the Son is not God. And if Father signifies the action of forming a Son, then the Son is created."

What is the answer to these sophisms? Let us listen to Gregory:

> O men so subtle! The name of Father signifies neither essence nor action but it indicates a relation, that which the Father has towards his Son or the Son towards his Father.⁴⁶

St. Thomas Aquinas would have nuanced this reply a bit and said: "the

---

⁴³St. Athanasius, citing Dionysius, MG 25, 501; RJ 609.
⁴⁴St. Athanasius, *Epist. de Synodis,* c. 16; RJ 651.
⁴⁵R. Arnou, *op. cit.,* p. 271.
⁴⁶St. Gregory of Nazianzus, MG 36, 96; RJ 990.

name of Father signifies directly a relation and, obliquely, the essence with which it is identical."[47]

c) *in the light of eternity, for St. Augustine.* The ingenious African deepened still more the doctrine received from the Greeks. The Arians were arguing thus: "the Father is unbegotten as regards substance; the Son is begotten as regards substance; in consequence the substance of the Father is other than that of the Son." Their fundamental postulate was: all that is said of God is said according to the substance.

Augustine denied this. But he did not insinuate that one can attribute accidents to God. Why? Accident always presupposes movement—and God is immutable. Accidents can change or be lost. In creatures all is substance or accident. But in God nothing can be changed or lost. It is not possible to attribute to God an accident of any kind. And yet, all that is said of God does not always refer to substance. Does there then exist in God a middle term between substance and accident? A middle term which, precisely, does not exist in the created world? Here is the knotty point of the problem. One must look for a solution between two equally unassailable propositions: nothing is attributed to God as accident, not everything can be attributed to him under the title of substance.

Aristotle, by way of the Cappadocians, offers Augustine the required middle term: relation, a category that is neither accident nor substance. God is Father, God is Son; these judgments designate relations which are not accidents.

Why? Because these relations are not mutable but eternal. The relations of Father and of Son escape movement, evolution, change. The Father is always Father, the Son always Son. The birth of the Son never had a beginning nor will it ever have an end, it is a continuous present, it is eternal. The Son is not Son by accident (as we are who begin and cease to be sons). The relation of the Only-Begotten Son is not an accident, but a datum which transcends time and movement.

But why then cannot this relation be reduced and brought back to substance? Because there exists an irreducible opposition between substance and relation. Substance is *ad se*, relation is *ad alterum*. If the Father were such in respect to himself and the Son also, both would be called "substances." But as the Father is such only because he has a Son, and reciprocally, one does not call them substances. Neither of the two is expressed as an Absolute, *ad se*, but each is named in respect to another, as a relative. In consequence the terms of Father and Son do not refer to substance, any more than they fall into the category of accidents.[48]

[47]St. Thomas Aquinas, *Summa Theologica*, I, 29.4.
[48]St. Augustine, *De Trinitate*, V, IV, 5ff.; I. Chevalier, O.P., "La théorie augustinienne des relations trinitaires," *Divus Thomas*, 18 (1940), 317-384, in particular p. 329.

Father and Son express immutable and eternal relations. The theory of relation radically destroys the Arian syllogism and goes so far as to ruin Arianism. It is as relation that the Son is the Begotten.

Augustine replies again in similar fashion to another difficulty raised by the Arians. The Father is the Unbegotten. Consequently, they say, he is toward himself, *ad se*, absolute. Consequently Father and Son do not have the same substance. Augustine's reply: to say that the Father is unbegotten is not an affirmation but a negation. Begotten expresses a relation. By the expression "unbegotten," it is not a substance but a relation that is denied. "Unbegotten" signifies "not-son." Thus the expression intends to say that the Father has no Father, is not Son, but not that he has another substance than the Son. The non-identity of relative terms does not have as consequence the non-identity of absolute terms, the diversity of substances.[49]

St. Augustine's profound reflections on substance and relation in the divine mystery allowed him to deduce three principal rules of Trinitarian language: "in this supereminent and divine sublimity":

—every absolute term (*quidquid ad se dicitur*) designates the substance;
—every relative term concerns, not the substance, but a relation;
—every absolute term attributed to one of the Three will also be attributed to the Three taken together in the singular and not in the plural.[50]

Thus the Father is all-powerful, the Son also, the Spirit likewise; and yet there are not three omnipotents, but one only omnipotent God, by reason of the substantial identity of the Father, the Son and the Spirit. One can, however, speak of three "co-omnipotents" in God.[51]

3. *Relation and Revelation*

The category of relation thus allows us to safeguard the plurality of hypostases in God without in any way denying the perfect unity of essence. But does Revelation really authorize Basil, Augustine, Thomas Aquinas "to introduce this category in God"?

Revelation discloses to us the personality of the Father and of the Son by way of these very names which are precisely relative names. The category of relation, far from being "introduced from outside," merely amounts to a clarification of what was implicitly contained in Revelation, germinally in the discourse of the God who reveals himself. Without adding anything to the revealed data, it allows the human mind to know and to adore its God in a clearer manner. Like the Nicene "consubstantial" which it complements, the category of relation is an element of the critico-dogmatic realism

[49]Ibid., pp. 330-334; St. Augustine, *De Trinitate*, IV, 6.7.

[50]Rules presented by I. Chevalier (*art. cit.*, p. 335) starting from St. Augustine's text in *De Trinitate* V, 8.9; XV, 3; VIII proemium. See also on this subject St. Thomas Aquinas, *Summa Theologica*, I, 39.

[51]Compare *DS* 75 and 800.

(Lonergan) which develops the logical presuppositions and consequences of the language of the New Testament. Thanks to the concept of relation, we can think of the intimate mystery of God (*intimior intimo meo*) and of the eternal coexistence of the Father and the Son without priority or posteriority (the Father is *ad Filium*, the Son *ad Patrem*), with the aid of our human experience and in terms which are at the same time human, true—though imperfect—and our own.

Relation, when applied to the mystery of the intimate life of God to explain therein distinction within the unity, permits us also to defend vigorously the perfect equality of the divine Persons, and their distinction not by elimination but by opposition of names. Father and Son are categories which reciprocally imply one another whereas seeing and being blind exclude one another. There can be one who sees without there being one who is blind, but there cannot be a father without a son.

The Pauline expressions of Spirit of the Father and Spirit of the Son indicate also, though in a way that is less immediately evident, the utilization by Revelation of the category of relation.

When God reveals himself to men, in a human language, his power and his wisdom utilize the resources of this language of which he is the first cause. Far from introducing our categories *a posteriori*, into his discourse, we simply unfold all the virtualities of the divine message by placing at its service all of our logical categories.

4. *Lateran IV (1215): identity between relations on the one hand and essence on the other*

The doctrine of relations was brilliantly set forth by the eleventh council of Toledo in 675; since this was a local council which was never formally endorsed by the Holy See, we cannot see in these texts (*DS* 528-530; *DB* 278, 280) an expression of the doctrine of the universal Church.

But we can, on the contrary, see such an expression in the case of four important affirmations of the Fourth Council (a general council) of the Lateran (cf. p. 146).

The council elaborated these affirmations in response to Joachim of Flora, a Calabrian monk who wished to reduce the unity of the divine Trinity to the kind of unity which can be apparent in a human group, or to the unity of the many believers in the one Church. Lateran IV then proclaimed:

—the identity of the Persons (all three or each of them) with the divine essence;
—the real identity of the Divine essence with the Father inasmuch as he generates the Son, with the Son inasmuch as he is generated by the Father, and with the Holy Spirit inasmuch as he proceeds from both;

—the absolute character of this essence by denying that the essence generates or is generated or proceeds;
—that there is no "quaternity" in God, which would be the case if there were a real distinction between Persons and Essence (Joachim of Flora was accusing Peter Lombard and, through him, the traditional doctrine, of affirming such a quaternity).

The importance of these declarations of Lateran IV is very great. Against certain Fathers,[52] the council insists on the non-primacy of the divine essence over the persons (the essence does not generate: this is another way of saying that the Father is truly *fons et origo totius divinitatis*); one can say that the council has defined the unfathomable mystery of the identification of the Absolute with the three Relatives in God. The absolute essence is not really distinct from the Persons who are relative to and really distinct from one another.

Granted that the council itself does not speak either of absolute or of terms that are reciprocally relative, yet it does bring out the mystery: there is in God an Absolute and Relations, the Absolute is the Relation(s), the Relations are the Absolute, in the bosom of the perfect simplicity of the divine Being. The distinction between Person and Nature is not real but a distinction of reason, whereas the distinction between the two processions is real.[53]

The council thus gave a clear response to Joachim of Flora: he had set out to transform the unity of God into a moral union of three gods, as if the Father, the Son and the Holy Spirit were three individuals of the same genus "God"; he leaned toward tritheism. Lateran IV recalled that God is indivisible, one in three persons who are not three separate individuals, like us, but three persons reciprocally correlative intimately possessing one and the same divine nature.

5. In 1441-1442, the Council of Florence, in another context, will, without however defining it, introduce relation into the dogmatic language of the Church by canonising an axiom that goes back at least to St. Anselm of Canterbury *omnia sunt unum ubi non obviat relationis oppositio*—(in God) all is one where the opposition of relation is not manifested; although initially this text was not conceived as a definition of faith, it has tended to become

---

[52] St. Gregory of Nyssa (*MG* 45, 589-594) and St. Hilary speak of a "genesis of the essence" or of a "nature generating or generated" (cited by A. Malet, *Personne et Amour*. Paris, 1956, pp. 15-16; the text of St. Hilary is extracted from *De Syn.* 4; *ML* 10, 494). It is very exactly, it seems to us, the kind of formulation which Lateran IV wished to eliminate and which leads in the last analysis to making the person of the Father come forth from an impersonal divine essence! See further Malet, *op. cit.*, pp. 71-76.

[53] We are drawing here on the commentary on Lateran IV by Cardinal J.-B. Franzelin, S.J., *De Deo trino*. Rome, 1881, pp. 338-339.

as much by the usage of later generations (*DS* 1330; *DB* 703). The denial of the doctrine of Trinitarian relations would today not only be the absurd elimination of the best means of defending the dogma, as it has been viewed since the third century; it would itself be close to, if not already, heresy.

IV. COMPLEMENTARY REFLECTIONS ON THE NOTION OF PERSON IN GOD

The definitive introduction of the notions of Person and of Subsistence into the Trinitarian language of the Church has committed Catholic theology to a continuous effort to penetrate the meaning of these terms.

We will limit ourselves here to two presentations whose value appears to us to be permanent: that of St. Thomas Aquinas in the framework of the more ontologically orientated medieval thought, and that of J. Alfaro, at the juncture of this ontological viewpoint and the personalist philosophy characteristic of our own times.

St. Thomas Aquinas, in his *Summa Theologica*[54] and elsewhere[55] was able to accomplish a tour de force: to develop a notion of Person which can be applied analogically and really to men, to angels, and to God; which permits us in consequence to start from a datum of experience so as to reach in faith an understanding of the Trinitarian Revelation; and which retains from the realism of the Greek hypostasis a reference to the essence, to the nature. For him, Person is "an individual substance of a rational nature" or "a distinct subsistent in an intellectual nature." While the principle of distinction of the human person with regard to others lies in the fact that it is this body and this soul, in God there is no distinction except that arising from the relation of origin. A Divine Person signifies directly relation and indirectly essence, or vice versa. Directly the relation, if we name this relation by way of hypostasis; directly the essence, if we are considering the latter as essence identical with the hypostasis. In the first case, we will be speaking, for example, of a divine Father, and in the second of God the Father.[56]

In the general and analogical concept of person that St. Thomas developed, the relation-aspect, which today we tend to inflate, remains secondary and "material," extrinsic to the notion of person as such, though in fact identical with it in God.[57]

Schmaus has energetically summed up the Thomistic doctrine of Person: it is being-in-itself and for-itself.

Person is being-in-itself, that is autonomous being, self-disposing being; it is self-possession, self-belonging; an individual differing from other beings, incommunicable. It is not an accident, a being-in-another.

---

[54] St. Thomas Aquinas, *Summa Theologica*, I, 29.
[55] St. Thomas Aquinas, *De Potentia* 9.1-4.
[56] Cf. B. Lonergan, S.J., *De Deo trino*. Rome, 1964, v. II, pp. 168-169 (quaestio XVI).
[57] St. Thomas Aquinas, *De Potentia*, IX, 4. Cf. note 40 of this chapter.

The person, finally, is being-for-itself, being which is end (not necessarily ultimate) and not pure means at the service of an extrinsic end. Its end is, at least in one respect, immanent in itself, and it attains this end by means of its own activity. The person is self-finality. It is for another at the same time that it is for itself but it is never, except in God, pure and simple for-another. This would not, it seems, preclude our saying that even in God, inasmuch as it is identical with the essence, the person is a for-itself. However, it is preferable to avoid this equivocal[58] expression, at least ordinarily.

We will see later, in presenting the mystery of the circuminsession of the Three, that we can complement Schmaus'[59] expressions and apply them more closely to the mystery of the Trinity by stressing that the divine Person, being-in-itself and for-itself, is also in another (and even in two others) and for another in the sense of toward-Another.

This is the approach that Alfaro adopts: Person is, in God, a subsistent Relation to a divine "Thou" who is himself a subsistent relation. The inner mystery of God is constituted by the vital communion between three consubstantial "I's". The divine Person is subsistent and spiritual Relation to a consubstantial "Thou." It is spiritual, that is consciousness and self-possession. It is "otherness," complete relatedness to a consubstantial Other. It is subsistence, that is pure actuality and infinitude, and thus unlimited spirituality and "otherness."

By comparison the human person is capacity for relation to a transcendent and non-consubstantial "Thou"; it is spiritual and other, but not subsistence at every instant, for it is not necessarily actual consciousness but capacity for consciousness; it is not pure consciousness, but finite consciousness, torn between self-possession and orientation toward a transcendent Infinite. Revelation leads us to a more profound knowledge of the human person: a man is a Person since he can be elevated to an "I-Thou" relationship with the divine Persons, with three divine "Thou's" and it is only at the heart of this immediate personal relation that he finds his proper fulfillment. The created person is not however constituted by the exercise of this immediate relation with the divine "Thou's," who are—and they alone are—subsistent and interpersonal[60] Relations, pure and eternal[61] Relations.

---

[58]It seems to mask the altereity of the divine Person. See on this point B. Lonergan, S.J., *De Deo trino*. Rome, 1964, pp. 169 bottom-170 top.
[59]You will find Schmaus' development in his *Teologia Dogmatica*. Madrid, 1960, v. I, § 39.
[60]J. Alfaro, S.J., "Persona y Gracia," *Gregorianum* 41 (1960), 20-21.
[61]Cf. Dom Ch. Massabki, O.S.B., *Le Christ rencontre de deux amours*. Paris, 1962, pp. 123-136.

Conclusion

"Make disciples of all nations, baptizing them in the (one) name of the Father, and of the Son and of the Holy Spirit."

We are now ready to appreciate better the exact sense of the Trinitarian formula contained in the baptismal command of the glorious Christ.

What does the one name of the Father and of the Son and of the Holy Spirit signify? St. Augustine rightly emphasized the point in commenting on this text: *non in nominibus sed in nomine*. Was he wrong in adding: *ubi unum nomen audis, unus est Deus*?[62]

The one name thus signifies for Augustine the Divine Nature.

In an apparently contrary sense, St. Gregory of Nyssa wrote: "It is by the confession of the holy name*s*, that is: the Father and the Son and the Holy Spirit, that the mystery of the faith is sanctioned";[63] St. Basil in like fashion wrote: "The Apostle, when he makes mention of baptism, often omits *the* name of the Father and of the Holy Spirit; however it must not be believed that the invocation of the 'Names' has no importance."[64]

For the two Cappadocians, the Name signifies in reality the Names; the words of Jesus do not accentuate the nature but the Persons.

Is there a way of reconciling these two interpretations and thus of probing more deeply the mystery of our Trinitarian salvation?

By presenting them in an order of increasing proximity to the sources, we can distinguish three solutions to the apparent dilemma: patristic, Johannine, pre-Johannine.

The solution of several Fathers (Basil, and already prior to him, Irenaeus) saw in the name of Christ himself the synthesis of the "three names." "To name Christ, is to confess the whole, for it is to show God who anointed, the Son who was anointed, and the Anointing which is the Spirit," St. Basil wrote immediately after the passage already cited.[65] Without his realizing it, this position was in a way, a return to the most archaic solution, as we shall see. But this is not too surprising: was not Irenaeus, who had already held it[66] long before Basil, more or less in the mainstream of Judaeo-Christianity?

This first solution rests on Acts 10:38 and has a tendency to abstract (as much as possible) from an analysis of the interplay of nature and persons in Mt. 28:19.

A deeper understanding is reached, we think, by the light thrown on Mt. 28:19, by Jn. 17:11-12: "Father, keep them in thy name which thou hast

---

[62]St. Augustine, *In Jo. tract.* 6, 9; ML 35, 1429.
[63]St. Gregory of Nyssa, MG 45, 880B.
[64]St. Basil, *On the Holy Spirit*, I. 28; MG 32, 116; RJ 945; SC p. 156.
[65]*Ibid.*
[66]St. Irenaeus, *Adversus Haereses*, III, 18.3; MG 7, 934 ab.

given me, that they may be one even as we are one. While I was with them, I kept them in thy name, which thou hast given me." If this *lectio difficilior* of the Johannine manuscript is not yet unanimously accepted, it nevertheless has some very solid defenders.[67]

The name of the Father and that of the Son are one single name, for the Father has given his name to his Son. The mission of Jesus was to make known not only the name of the Father, but also that he had received it. "To make known the Father's name is not only to look upon the living God with a new gaze, but to know that there is in him a distinction of mysteriously united persons."[68]

In fact, in affirming that the name of the Son is the Father's gift and that of the Father's name, in no way amounts to identifying the two distinct persons of the Father and of the Son. "By giving even minimal attention to the fact that, according to the conception of the Hebrews, the name of a person expresses his personal being and all that characterizes him, one will easily comprehend that, if the Father is in the Son and the Son in the Father, the Name of the one and the Name of the other reciprocally include each other,"[69] according to the appropriate observation of F.-M. Braun, O.P.

St. Cyril of Alexandria who long before the best modern exegetes had already grasped the necessity of maintaining the *lectio difficilior* of Jn. 17:11-12,[70] without excluding the "personalist" interpretation of F.-M. Braun, saw nevertheless in the Name given "the glory of the Divinity, of the Divine Nature."[71] It is Thomas Aquinas who will make in his commentary on the same scriptural text the synthesis of the two interpretations: the one that stresses the nature and the one that stresses the persons:

> "I kept them in thy name which thou hast given me." In thy name: this name is common to the Father, to the Son and to the Holy Spirit. This is so because the Father and the Son are one only God but also because in the name of Father is implied that of the Son: the father is he who has a son.[72]

We can thus synthesize the results to which the second solution leads:

---

[67]Cf. H. Van den Bussche, *Le discours d'adieu de Jésus*. Tournai, 1959, p. 144; F.-M. Braun, O.P., (see the following note); and especially J.-H. Bernard, *The Gospel According to St. John*. Edinburgh, 1928, v. II, pp. 568-569, who shows the transcendence of Jn. 17:11-12 relative to Num. 6: 27; Ex. 23:21. Whereas Phil. 2:9 constitutes a parallel text.

[68]F.-M. Braun, O.P., *Jean le Théologien*, v. III, 1. Paris, 1966, p. 114. Cf. p. 115, critical discussion.

[69]*Ibid.*, p. 115.

[70]Cf. J. Bonsirven, S.J., *Rech. Sc. Rel.* 39 (1951), 177-181, in a remarkable article "pour une intelligence plus profonde de saint Jean," where the author presents the texts of Cyril.

[71]Bonsirven, *art. cit.*, p. 179; cf. St. Cyril of Alexandria, MG 74, 512ff.

[72]St. Thomas Aquinas, *In Ev. Jo. Expositio*, cap. 17, lectio III, 2.

the names of Father, Son and Spirit form only one name because the Three are only one and this name has its origin in the Father, source of the whole Divinity. The Father in giving his name to his Son gives him his nature but also his person of Father, in such a way however that the nature is common in the perfect reciprocal immanence of the persons. The Son receives eternally the name and the person of his Father by the very fact of being eternally begotten. Through the Son the Father also gives his name to the Holy Spirit. A person receives the name of another by receiving from him the nature which is common to them and the subsistence which is proper to him, and which justifies his being called by another name. The one divine name is possessed in common by the Three who, as three, wish us to call them by three different and reciprocally relative names. The one Name communicates and reveals itself exteriorly in three Names. Augustine, Gregory of Nyssa and Basil do not in the least contradict one another. The declarations of the Johannine and pre-Paschal Jesus permit us better to understand the post-Paschal command of the Matthean Christ.

The second solution of itself orientates us toward the third, which also stems from a more profound analysis of the New Testament by the Anglican exegete C. H. Dodd. Daniélou sums it up thus:

> Dodd has shown that in the Gospel of John we are in the presence of a theological elaboration in which the Name has come to designate Christ. Christ manifests the Name of the Father (Jn. 17:6), but this manifestation is his own person. Dodd can write: "If the Name of God is the symbol of his true nature, then the revelation of the Name which Christ gives is that unity of the Father and of the Son, to which he bears witness."[73] In consequence when the Father glorifies the Son, he glorifies his Name. We have, thus, two equivalent formulas: "Father, glorify your Name" (12:28) and: "Father, glorify me" (17:5). It is essentially the unity of nature between the Father and the Son which is here affirmed, but also the fact that the Person of the Son is the revelation, that is the Name of the Father. John however preferred the term *logos* (word) to *onoma* (name) since it was more accessible to the Greeks. The Name is, in his Gospel, an archaic vestige.[74]

The sense of this last solution is basically identical with that of the second, but with a nuance. It puts us on the way to a better understanding of the process that leads to Mt. 28:19: it is because the Son is the Revelation of the Father that he can be called his Name. Language tells! Thus Daniélou has even asked if John, in addressing himself first to the Jews, had not

---

[73]C. H. Dodd, *The Gospel of John*. London, 1955, p. 96.

[74]J. Daniélou, S.J., *Théologie du judéo-christianisme*. Tournai, 1958, pp. 201-202. Engl. Trans., *The Theology of Jewish Christianity*, pp. 149-150.

initially presented the Son to them, not as the Word, but as the Name, in a first redaction of the prologue.[75] A point however that is unverifiable.

Whatever the case may be, if the Son can be called the Name of the Father inasmuch as he reveals him, it follows also that the Holy Spirit can be called the "name" inasmuch as he reveals the Father and the Son. Would not the profound sense of John (chapters 14-16) and of the passages about the Paraclete, the Spirit of Truth, suggest that the Spirit himself has a right to the Name? In this respect are they not a direct preparation for the command: "Baptize the nations in the name (or into the name) of the Father and of the Son and of the Holy Spirit" (Mt. 28:19)?

After these clarifications we understand better St. Thomas Aquinas' commentary on Mt. 28:19: to him this text appeared to insinuate not only the indivisibility of the substance of the Trinity, but also that "the Father is truly the Father of the Son, the Son truly Son of the Father, and the Holy Spirit truly the Breath of the Father and of God the Son," that is the doctrine of relations.[76] St. Augustine was right then in preaching the Trinitarian relations to the people baptized in them:[77] would we be wrong to follow his example today, once we have understood that Christ himself invites us to do this?

Appendix II: *Reply to a difficulty*

It is objected that even the most elementary reasoning proclaims that two realities that are identical with one and the same third reality are necessarily identical with each other. As the Catholic dogma proclaims that each of the three Persons is God, one and the same God, there cannot be they think, a real distinction between them. Consequently the divine Persons can only be simple modalities, of the same Divinity, logically but not really diverse.

Reply: The principle invoked is undeniable but its application to Trinitarian dogma is improper. Two realities are necessarily identical to each other, if they are identical with the same third thing under all its aspects, if there is between them and this third reality no distinction of point of view (called a virtual distinction).

Now the Divine Persons are identical with one and the same Divine Nature, but there exists a virtual distinction between them and this nature. The Father, the Son and the Spirit possess the same divine nature, totally, but not in the same manner: the Father possesses it inasmuch as he begets

---

[75]*Ibid.*, p. 202, note 1: St. John would have written initially: "The Name has dwelt among us." Daniélou also comments in an interesting way and in the same sense on texts drawn from the Epistle of Clement and from the Didache.

[76]St. Thomas Aquinas, *Catena in Mt. Ev.,* in Mt. 28:19.

[77]Cf. St. Augustine, *in Jo.* 8:26-27: tract. 39, *ML* 35, 1681-1686; Chevalier, O.P., *art. cit.,* pp. 365-371.

the Son, the Son inasmuch as he is begotten, and the Spirit inasmuch as he is spirated by the Father and the Son.

This distinction of points of view between each of the divine Persons and the divine Nature suffices to make the distinction possible, between the Persons themselves, no longer virtual but real. Paternity and filiation are, as relations, really distinct from one another, although these same relations when considered in their absolute being are totally identical with the perfectly simple divine Nature.

The unfathomable mystery in no way contradicts the rules of human logic.

Appendix III: *Theological designation of Lateran IV (1215) and Lyons II (1274)*

Pope Paul VI, in a letter to Cardinal Willebrands, president of the secretariat for Christian Unity, dated October 5, 1974 (*Oss. Romano*, Oct. 20, 1974, pp. 1-2), on the occasion of a theological congress celebrating at Lyons the seventh centenary of the Council of Lyons, qualifies it twice as a "general council" (in Latin: *synodus generalis*) and observes that it was "the sixth of the general councils celebrated in the western world."

Nowhere in this letter does Paul VI qualify this council as ecumenical; but nowhere, either, does he deny the ecumenicity of the council or of the other general councils celebrated in the western world. It must be noted further that these councils were not qualified as ecumenical before the sixteenth century and yet Pope Innocent III had wanted Lateran IV to be an ecumenical council (cf. Congar, art. cit. below, p. 380, n. 99).

Today several Catholic authors (Bouyer, Congar) deny their ecumenicity, notably in consequence of the historical works of V. Peri (*I Concili e le Chiese*, Rome, 1965), at least in the sense of full ecumenicity. See on this subject the study of Y. Congar, O.P., "1274-1974: structures ecclésiales et conciles dans les relations entre Orient et Occident," *Rev. des Sc. Ph. et Th.*, 58 (1974), 378ff., with bibliography; this author further observes (*ibid.*, p. 378) that one of the three senses of the word *generalis* qualifying a synod is precisely that of "ecumenical." See also Appendix IV, p. 198.

IV
Relations of Origin
The "Processions" in God

The divine Persons, mutually relative, realize a vital exchange among themselves: one Person produces another or is produced by another, from whom he "proceeds." The "processions" are essentially the "intra-divine productions." But these productions differ fundamentally from creation, which is a procession *ad extra* from nothing. Arius purely and simply confused procession and creation. In reality "it is not necessary to understand procession in the sense in which we encounter it in the corporeal world, whether by local movement or by the action of a cause on its external effect."[1] Procession in God remains within the agent himself. It is immanent action, without movement. God is spiritual and eternal, the term of his immanent action remains immanent in him. The processions are also not a sort of gradual development of the divinity rising from the depths of some mysterious divine unconsciousness. God is the Immutable. The procession is the eternal production, without any succession, of one divine Person from another, in an immeasurable act of power and of interiority. As used here the word is only a resumption of a word from John's gospel relative to the mission of Christ (Jn. 8:42).

It would be wrong also to understand this procession or production as signifying a pure passivity on the part of the person produced, on the analogy of works produced by men. In God, a Person is produced in such manner that he affirms with supreme clarity his own production and receives it with absolute joy. The Three constitute a single Pure Act.[2]

In our preceding chapter we saw how the Church came to recognize that the Three are distinguished by their mutual relations and by nothing else; but what are these relations? The Spirit of the Father and of the Son was bound to lead the Church to a more explicit knowledge of the relations which are at the origin of the Son and of his own person.

We must then, in the chapter that is now underway, elaborate successively the theologies of the Father, of the Son and of their Spirit, then

---
[1]St. Thomas Aquinas, *Summa Theologica*, I, 27.1 c.
[2]M. Schmaus, *Teologia Dogmatica,* v. I, La Trinidad. Madrid, 1960, § 53.

present their mutual immanence, their relation—of what kind?—with Creation, and finally show how the properties of the Three are legitimately brought out by appropriating to each works that are common to the Three. We will thus find ourselves alluding to the created analogies of the Trinitarian mystery without however making a systematic study of them.

I. THEOLOGY OF GOD THE FATHER, PRINCIPLE OF THE DIVINITY

The New Testament has much to say about the Father. However we are not in possession of a theological and biblical reflection that adequately synthesizes the teaching of Revelation on the first person of the Trinity.[3] Christology and Pneumatology have attracted more attention. Let us outline here some succinct aspects of this theology of the Father, on the doctrinal plane and on the level of cult.

The Father is the foundation and principle of intra-divine unity. It is the Father, and not the divine essence considered abstractly, who is the principle of the Son and of the Spirit; and a principle without principle, for the Father himself does not spring from some mysterious impersonal essence (cf. *DS* 1330-1331; *DB* 703-704). The Council of Florence says formally: "All that the Father is, and all that he has, he does not derive from another, but from himself; he is the principle that has no principle" (*ibid.*). The Father is *ex se*, he cannot then be *ab alio*. Much earlier a local council of Toledo had proclaimed the Father "source and origin of the whole divinity," *fons et origo totius divinitatis* (*DS* 525). An incomprehensible abyss of affirmation, the Father is eternally plenitude as source, *fontalis plenitudo*, without receiving anything from anyone, not only uncreated but also unbegotten. He is the divine essence, and yet it is not the essence which engenders the Son, but rather the Father who engenders the Son by way of the nature's principle of action, and who with the Son spirates the Holy Spirit.

The Father gives to his Son and to their Spirit his substance or nature without losing it and in giving it, and in giving it totally, he gives himself. Thus he gives and he retains (*DS* 526, 804-805; *DB* 276, 432). He remains in the Son and in the Spirit to whom he is essentially relative, at the same time that he communicates to them his essence and gives himself personally to them.

The Father is the summit of the Holy Trinity, the principle of the divine monarchy, the recapitulator of this monarchy (*DS* 112-115). With the Son and with the Spirit as a single principle but also through them and by them, he did not make but created heaven and earth (*DS* 170-171; *DB* 77-78; *DS* 1331; *DB* 704).

[3]Let us point out however the biblical and spiritual essay of Mgr. E. Guerry, *Vers le Père*. Bruges, 1947 and that of P. Galot, S.J., *Le Coeur du Père*. Bruges, 1957. But neither the one nor the other meant to present a systematic theology of God the Father.

Almost all the statements we have just enunciated were drawn from declarations of the magisterium, and most often from the extraordinary magisterium of the Church. Developing them in depth, theology tells us that the Father is not the cause but the principle of the divinity.[4] The theologians add: the Father begets his Son not by will but with will.[5]

These two affirmations signify that the generation of the Son is not "optional" (or "at will") and correspondingly is not a creation.

The Word and the Spirit are consubstantial with the Father because they receive from him their substance. The unity of the substance is the *principium quo* of the intra-Trinitarian communication; the Father is its *principium quod*. The Father, according to the majority of theologians, is eternal and personal communication of his substance to the Son and to the Spirit, to the point of being pure and substantial relation of generation and spiration. It is not the unity of substance, but the person of the Father who is the ultimate foundation of the intra-Trinitarian unity inasmuch as the unity of origin of the Son and of the Spirit is the beginning without beginning, the principle without principle which this first Person is.

According to the dogmatic analogy so strongly sanctioned by Vatican I (DS 3016; DB 1796), we shall acquire a better understanding of the mystery of the Father's paternity if we examine under its light the mystery of Mary's virginal maternity. By the eternal generation and by the Incarnation, the Father becomes the Father of the Man-Jesus Christ. The intra-divine fecundity of the Father is the ultimate foundation which makes the Incarnation of the Son possible.

Moreover it is the Church's magisterium that advocates our understanding the one by means of the other, i.e., the eternal nativity and the temporal nativity of Jesus Christ, and also the paternity of the Father and the maternity of Mary (DS 2801).

Mary begets her Son *with* love like the Father, but unlike the Father, also *by way of* love. For God, as for man, who is a rational animal, generation is a natural work, the work of the person by means of the nature. For man, in order to be fully human and to be pure, generation ought to be accompanied by the awareness of a spiritual love. The absence of love would constitute a veritable impurity in the generative activity of the human person. In itself the generative activity involves nothing impure, but the absence of love makes it impure.[6]

---

[4]St. Thomas Aquinas, *Summa Theologica*, I, 33.1.1.

[5]*Ibid.*, I, 41.2.1, 5; cf. DS 526.

[6]Cf. M.-J. Nicolas, O.P., *Théotokos*. Tournai, 1965, p. 75: "Nothing is more illuminating for defining the proper role of consciousness and of will in human generative activity than to consider it first in the mystery of the generation of the only Son. The Father begets the Son with love. The love is concomitant, it is not the natural activity according to which divine

No man was ever conceived and begotten with as much love as the Son of Man. Nevertheless his earthly generation is but a pale reflection of his mysterious and eternal generation, but it is also its closest reflection. Patristic tradition considered the virginal birth as the only one befitting Him who is born spiritually of the Father in eternity. The more spiritual this birth of Jesus Christ according to the flesh will be, the more it will resemble the eternal birth of the Son of God. The divine maternity is the closest created participation of the Paternity of the heavenly Father with respect to Jesus Christ, while in addition their term is identical.

Every man, by the exercise of physical, intellectual or spiritual paternity, makes of his very activity a vestige—in the first two cases—or an image (in the last case) of the transcendent paternity of the Father with regard to his consubstantial Only-Begotten. He thus orients himself toward his last end, the triune God. But at the heart of this last end, the Father, origin and source of the whole divinity, also appears, to use a bold expression, as the supreme point of return of the Word and of the Spirit and of all creation offered by the Word to the Father in the Spirit.

"When all things are subjected to him, then the Son himself will also be subjected to him who put all things under him, that God may be everything to everyone" (1 Cor. 15:28). The Son in giving himself to the Father, the Son Incarnate in subjecting himself to the Father, loses nothing of that which was subjected to him, of that which he is eternally. The recapitulating oblation simply reveals that the absolutely last end of the immutable cycle of the divine life coincides completely with its first source. Thus it is not without profound dogmatic justification that Catholic cult ordinarily terminates (but not necessarily, nor always, and this too we have seen[7] has a dogmatic significance) in the First Person.

Already in the sixteenth century, Suarez very clearly enunciated this principle of liturgical Trinitarian theology: "The prayers of the Church are ordinarily directed to the Person of the Father as to the first principle and the source of the divinity."[8]

The supreme ultimate end can only be identified with the absolutely first principle of the cult of the Church. The Father seeks and wills, the Father raises up for himself "true adorers in spirit and in truth" (Jn. 4:23-24),

---

generation comes about. This allows us to understand that the absence of the spiritual accompaniment of love and thus of consciousness, will constitute the real 'impurity' of human generative activity. As natural activity, it involves nothing impure by itself. As human activity, it calls for and demands consciousness and love, the role of the spirit. By its nature the human generative act postulates the intervention of the will which may be wanting through moral failure. This privation is a real blemish, for the exigency of spirituality is a necessity of human nature as such."

[7] Cf. our chapter II, notes 62-65.

[8] F. Suarez, S.J., *De Oratione*, I, 9.14-15; *Opera omnia*. Paris, 1869, v. 14, pp. 34-35.

worshippers who adore him through the Son and through the Spirit inasmuch as the Son and the Spirit receive from the Father, eternally, the creative omnipotence thanks to which they also have a right to adoration.

Nevertheless, the Church has rejected many a time the idea of establishing a feast of the Father: Urban VIII in 1628, then Innocent XII and Leo XIII (DS 3225) were of the opinion that such a feast could, in practice, favor tritheism. Is this decision absolutely definitive? It is difficult to say. The danger of modalism is also perpetual. There is not however any present indication that the Church intends to reconsider the question. The long endurance of this decision seems to render it definitive.

It goes without saying that the Church in rejecting a special feast of the Father has by no means rejected the cult of the Father, which she practices in her liturgy, nor devotion to the Father to the practice of which Christians cannot be too strongly urged. Each divine person, as such, is worthy of receiving a distinct cult. If it is true that our prayer to the Father should never exclude the other persons, for everything comes to us from the entire Trinity, still it is permitted to address ourselves to a single person alone, to the Father, for example, by a proper and formal intention. The reason is psychological: since we know these really distinct persons only in a confused and abstract way, our attention is able to be fixed on one of them alone.

Suarez thinks that beyond these general reasons there is a special reason for praying to the Father: is he not the only one to send the Son?

In short, "God the Father can receive a special adoration: an adoration because he is God, a special adoration because he alone is Father."[9]

Would such a devotion to the Father suggest some resemblance to Arianism? The Arians claimed to adore only the person of the Father and considered him alone to be God. If they were wrong in claiming that the Father alone had the right to a cult of adoration, we are in no way obliged to fall into the opposite error and to deny the Christian's right to offer a special (but not exclusive) cult to the Father.[10]

[9] M. Caillat, "La dévotion à Dieu le Père: une discussion au XVII siècle," *RAM* 20 (1939), 138. The whole article is suggestive (*ibid.*, pp. 35-49; 136-157). We drew on it here, in the paragraphs preceding the cited phrase.

[10] St. Fulgentius said very well: "Neque enim praejudicium Filio vel Sancto Spiritui comparatur dum ad Patris personam precatio ab offerente dirigitur. Cujus consummatio, dum Filii et Spiritus Sancti complectitur nomen, ostendit nullum esse in Trinitate discrimen. Quia dum ad solius Patris personam honoris sermo dirigitur, bene credentis fide tota Trinitas honoratur: et cum ad Patrem litantis destinatur intentio, sacrificii munus omni Trinitati, uno eodemque offertur litantis officio" (*Ad Monimum*, II. 5; ML 65, 184; Fulgentius had just successfully compared the Mass offered to the whole Trinity with the baptism celebrated in the one name of the Father, the Son and the Holy Spirit; if we baptize in the name of the Three, it is logical that the sacrifice also be offered to the Three, even if the names of two of them are not pronounced at the beginning of most of the liturgical prayers).

St. Gregory of Nazianzus and St. Bonaventure sum up admirably for us the reasons we have for exalting the person of the Father and consequently for rendering him a special cult; let us first listen to the Cappadocian Doctor:

> The Father is more Father than all those we know as such. He is Father in a proper and singular but not corporeal fashion. *Singulari modo Pater.* Only He is Father without partnership. *Solus.* He is Father of a single Son, *solius*, the Only-begotten. Without ever having been son beforehand, he is Father only: *solum.* He is Father in all and totally, which cannot be said of us: *totius Pater.* He is Father from the beginning and without end.[11]

Nine centuries later, the "subtle Doctor" sees in the Father the ultimate center of our repose: *centrum ultimate quietativum.*[12] And St. Bonaventure is of the opinion that charity should be appropriated to the Father: "charity is gratuitous love, love which only gives and receives nothing and this love is in the person of the Father"[13] thus furnishing a speculative justification of the New Testament language (cf. 1 Jn. 4:8, 16: as we have already said, for the authors of the New Testament, God ordinarily signifies the Father).

We can see then why St. Bonaventure commented with a particular eloquence on the prayer of Philip to Christ: "Lord, show us the Father, and we shall be satisfied" (Jn. 14:8): "We do not ask anything else: that is all we desire of you, since He is all in all.... In the fruition of the loving Father we will be blessed."[14]

The cult of the Father into which the theology of the Father emerges, thus presents an eschatological accent and polarization. This cult antici-

---

[11]St. Gregory of Nazianzus, *Oratio theol.* 25, 16; MG 35, 1221; RJ 983. One could comment thus on this text: if we compare human paternity and intra-divine paternity, we observe that a man can wait long years before generating and can even never have sons; when he becomes father, paternity is for him a new quality, distinct from his human nature, and, if he loses his son, he remains integrally man. Neither the relation of paternity nor that of filiation, though both are very real, constitute part of the human essence, nor do they enter as constitutive elements into our individuality. If I lose my father, I do not cease to be the same person distinct from every other, and my "I" does not change radically. While in God, the Father is eternally Father, nothing but Father (and, consequently, Spirator), totally Father and not accidentally but essentially Father. Between men, relations are temporal and temporary; they bind the liberties, though they remain accidental and fortuitous. In God, the Relation is a Person who gives himself eternally, in a manner both necessary and free.

[12]Duns Scotus, *Ox.*, I, d. 1, Q. 5, n. 3.

[13]St. Bonaventure, *Sent.* I, V, of b. 9, resp.; cf. St. Thomas Aquinas, *De Potentia*, 10.4.8: "Nihil prohibet intelligi eumdem amorem esse gratuitum ut est Patris, debitum vero ut est Filii: idem enim est amor quo Pater et quo Filius amat; sed hunc amorem Filius a Patre habet, Pater vero a nullo."

[14]St. Bonaventure, commentaries on the Gospel of St. John, cited by Miguel Oltra, O.F.M., in his "Introducción General" to the *Obras de S. Buenaventura*, v. V, BAC. Madrid, 1948, p. 26.

pates in some way the vision to which it leads. It is moreover inseparable from the cult rendered to the Son and Mediator, so much so that Noulleau, a famous Oratorian of the seventeenth century, could say: "To pray is to talk of God to Jesus Christ and of Jesus Christ to God."

II. THEOLOGY OF THE ETERNAL SON: CONTEMPORARY EXEGESIS AND MYSTERY OF THE GENERATION OF THE ONLY-BEGOTTEN

The Symbol of Nicaea-Constantinople proclaims the Church's faith "in one only Lord Jesus Christ, Son of God, Only-Begotten, born of the Father before all ages" (DS 150; DB 86). The definition of the Council of Chalcedon (DS 301; DB 148) exalts the two births, eternal and temporal, of Christ.

Over the centuries Catholic exegesis has always presupposed that the expression "Son of God" alluded to the eternal generation of the Son, without seeing any special difficulty in this.

But modern functional exegesis—especially non-Catholic—believes there is question here of a temporal name and takes no further interest in the eternal condition of the Son.

In 1950 Paul Henry, S.J., in the course of an ecumenical meeting on the procession of the Holy Spirit, asked whether there is biblical foundation for the doctrine of the procession of the Son from the Father.

After recalling the exegetical data, we will sketch here in the light of St. Hilary, a theological reflection on the eternal generation of the Son, followed by a brief initial presentation of the analogy of the word.

1. *Does the New Testament teach the eternal generation of the Son?*

In giving an affirmative answer to this question, it was customary in the past to cite a series of Johannine texts in which the Son speaks of his coming into the world from the Father, and which the Evangelist expressed in Greek by means of the preposition *ek* (Jn. 7:28-29; 8:14; 8:23; 8:42; 13:3; 16:28). Let us recall the last one cited: "I came from the Father and have come into the world; again, I am leaving the world and going to the Father." This has often been taken as an affirmation of two processions: one, eternal ("I came from the Father"), the other, temporal ("I have come into the world").

But today some object: if this interpretation is correct, then "to leave the world" and "to return to the Father" should signify a double return, temporal and eternal, to the Father. And they ask: what would this eternal return to the Father signify? They go on: the Greek aorist used here is more suited to an historical action than to an eternal procession. The exclusively temporal interpretation thus appears to them to be legitimate.

It is possible, however, to answer these diverse objections which do not appear conclusive. The eternal return to the Father signifies very simply that the Son is eternally *ad Patrem*, toward the Father, as he is eternally *a*

Patre and *in Patre*. The aorist is the Greek tense most suited to an allusion to the eternal life in God, since it abstracts from all temporal determination (*aoristos*, undetermined). Finally, Dodd in studying various prepositions whose sense is very close (*para, apo, ek*), points out that *ek* manifests origin in a more profound and even ultimate sense. Would not St. John, recasting in Greek the Aramaean phrases of Jesus, have intended, without distinguishing explicitly between eternal and temporal procession, to extend the image of procession to its ultimate point of departure in the inner divine life?[15]

In any case, the numerous Johannine texts on the mission of the Son into the world presuppose the traditional doctrine of the eternal generation of the Son. In fact the Johannine Gospel affirms with great insistence the mission of the Son into the world, an event that logically presupposes the traditional doctrine of the eternal generation. What else could be signified by the seventeen uses of the word *apostello* and the twenty-four uses of the word *pempo*?

John says with sufficient clarity that the Son is God and that he is sent by the Father into the world. As God, the Son is eternal, and he could not be sent unless he were born eternally from the Father, unless he were eternally Son. There is thus perfect continuity between the doctrine of the eternal generation of the Son and the most fundamental and most frequently repeated affirmations of the Gospel of St. John about the mission of the Son.

Another and more complex reasoning brings us to the same conclusion. The real mission of the Son into the world implies a mutual relation between Father and Son. On the Father's side such a relation must be eternal: the Father has no created nature assumed as his own, that could found a temporal relation. On the Son's side it must also be eternal, because it is mutual and if it is eternal in the Father, it must also be so in the Son.

Now this eternal relation is in the Sender *ut a Quo*, in the one Sent *ut Qui ab*: a way of saying that the eternal relation implied by the temporal mission is a relation of origin, and thus that the Son is eternally generated by the Father.

As the Son has also a human nature, a single eternal relation between the Father and the Son founds a double procession, one eternal, the other temporal. The temporal procession is moreover ordered to the manifestation of the eternal procession of the person sent, in this case, the Son. Opening in summary form an "economic perspective" on the consequences of the Son's eternal generation, we will say that the Son of God, the eternal Son of the eternal God, has become Son of Man so that his brothers in humanity may be able to participate at once in his eternal generation and in

---

[15] C. H. Dodd, *The Interpretation of the Fourth Gospel*. London, 1953, 259-262.

his eternal return toward the Father, becoming by grace *filii in Filio, ex Patre et ad Patrem*, like him. This is what J. Huby has very well brought out:

> In the heart of the divine life, the Son of God is completely turned toward the Father, totally related to Him. When he becomes incarnate to save the human race, his mission as Savior participates in this same relation: the ultimate term of the salvation he brings to men is by drawing them away from sin, to transfer them to God, to involve them in the movement by which the Son is eternally related to the Father.[16]

In short, the Son knows not only where he came from but also where he is going (Jn. 8:14). The eternal return to the Father in the Spirit is inseparable from the eternal generation of the only Son.

These two data appear then to be logically implied in the pre-Paschal discourses of Jesus, notably in his Jerusalem polemics with the Pharisees. Does this mean that Jesus' hearers, whose hatred, which is often more perceptive than love, did not prevent them from recognizing the fact that he was affirming that he has divine status and equality with the Father, were also able to perceive the sense of his, at least, implicit proclamation of an eternal divine generation? The least we can say is that this is not evident. M.-J. Lagrange correctly observes:

> We do not see that Jesus taught the Jews that he was the eternal Son of God, identical with the Father in nature but dependent on him *ratione originis*.... The Jews would hardly have been able to grasp this language: they had to climb the first step before ascending higher. What Jesus is constantly asking of them is that they recognize him as the One sent by the Father, who truly has a right to the title of Son, without clarifying whether he became Son of God in becoming the pre-existent Messiah, who then came into the world, or whether he was Son of God from all eternity. This second point was indeed the principal one, and easy to deduce: but we insist in pointing out a nuance between the historical teaching of Jesus as it called for acceptance and the more explicit theological teaching of John.[17]

In short, Jesus revealed explicitly during his earthly life that he "was one with the Father...as his pre-existent Son,"[18] but only implicitly, it seems, that he was the eternal Son, eternally begotten as Son by the Father.

What Jesus had revealed only implicitly before Easter, John disclosed explicitly in his Gospel, under the inspiration of the Spirit, after the Son's Pasch and his Ascension, or return to the Father. I. de La Potterie has very

---

[16] J. Huby, S.J., *Mystique paulinienne et johannique*. Bruges, 1947, p. 152.
[17] M.-J. Lagrange, O.P., *Evangile selon saint Jean*. Paris, 1936, CLVIII.
[18] *Ibid.*, CLVII.

ably shown this with regard to Jn. 1:18: "The only Son, *who is turned toward the bosom of the Father*, he it is who has revealed him." After justifying his new translation (not: *in* the bosom of the Father, but *toward* it), he explains its import:

> The very image of bosom, especially here where it is closely linked to the mention of Father and Son, evokes altogether naturally and in the first place the idea of generation.... The only Son is turned toward the bosom of the Father, toward this bosom of which he is the begotten. The text, then, clearly has to do with eternal generation: (cf. *on*, in the present). John shows us this in concrete and imaged fashion...as though describing the Son, eternally conscious of receiving from this bosom his whole life, his whole being: Christ himself will say equivalently: "I live by the Father" (Jn. 6:57).... The constant orientation of the Son toward the bosom of the Father as toward his origin, as toward the source of his own life (*eis ton kolpon*) depicts him in the eternal act of receiving the divine life from the Father.[19]

In short, Jn. 1:18, by forming an "inclusion" with Jn. 1:2 ("The Word was turned toward God") and by recalling 1 Jn. 1:2 ("The eternal life which by its very nature was turned toward the Father"), synthesizes the two-fold inseparable movement to which we have already alluded: the Son, eternally begotten by the Father, is eternally turned toward him and abides in him. Many other texts of the Johannine Gospel are thus clarified. When he speaks of the incarnate Son, the Evangelist continues to set before us the eternal Son, and it becomes also impossible to separate what Jesus says as incarnate Word and what he says as eternal Son. The one and only "I" of Christ is a divine "I", the "I" of an Eternal Son. Even if Christ did not explicitly reveal himself to the Jews as eternal Son, later the Spirit did reveal this by way of John. The New Testament teaches the eternal generation of the Son. There is biblical foundation for the procession of the Son from the Father.

2. *St. Hilary, theologian of the eternal generation of the Son*

The Arians, the Moslems who to some extent repeat their argumentation, certain Rationalists and present-day Spiritists, deceive the masses by means of sophisms such as the following:

—To be born and to exist are completely contradictory terms, for to be born signifies: that which was not, has received being.

---

[19]I. de La Potterie, S.J., "L'emploi de 'eis' dans saint Jean et ses incidences théologiques," *Biblica*, 43 (1962), 385-386. Note, however, that R. E. Brown, S.S., seems to contest the interpretation proposed by I. de La Potterie regarding Jn. 1:18 (*The Gospel According to John*. NY, 1966, p. 17) which however appears compelling to us.

—This can be proven: birth implies beginning; but that which begins does not exist; consequently the Son who is born has not always existed.

—Thus, they conclude, the Catholic doctrine is absurd: the Son who exists eternally cannot be born, because one is born in order to exist.

St. Hilary undertakes to demolish these sophisms. With more confidence in divine Revelation than in the reasonings of human cleverness, he stresses that the Prologue of John teaches at the same time the birth of the Son and his eternity as Word. The Word was with the Father, he was made flesh: the contrast between the imperfect and the aorist underscores the eternity of the Word followed by his entering into history; the imperfect is one of duration, which symbolizes the eternal. Everything was made by the Word and everything owes its origin to him, including time itself. The Word is the creator of space-time, and consequently he transcends it.[20]

From this transcendence of the Son of God's generation there follows exactly the contrary of what the Arians were teaching: since it is not an imperfect man who is born of another imperfect man but a perfect Son who is generated by a perfect Father, the Son of God who is born must be eternal.

All human generations participate in the nothingness from which they were drawn. No human father has always existed, nor could a son who is only man have always existed. Every man is born weak and can only arrive at his proper perfection in progressive fashion. Before being able to communicate his own nature to a son, he must first have undergone an extended period of growth. A long interval separates the becoming-man from the becoming-father.

Nothing of all this applies to the generation of the Son of God. The sole reason of his birth is the very nature of the Father, immutable and permanent. The Father simply is. He does not proceed from anything, he cannot evolve or increase or become. If the Father is really Father, he cannot have become such but is so eternally. But if the Father is eternally Father, the Son must also be eternally Son. For the generative act of the Father and the birth of the Son are correlative. The birth of the Son is not only prior to time but above it. The immutable Father begets in an immutable manner an immutable Son. That the Son is born signifies that he comes not from himself but from another; that the Son is eternal signifies that this Other does not cease to be his Origin.

[20]Cf. P. Smulders, S.J., *La doctrine trinitaire de saint Hilaire de Poitiers.* Rome, 1944, pp. 172-178. Previously (pp. 164-172), Hilary had shown the transcendence of the spiritual generation of the Son of God with respect to all carnal generation, a point that the Arians failed to recognize; Smulders sums up his thought thus: "The Father who is entirely spirit has need of the aid of no other to beget a son, he uses no corporal organs, he is not divided nor separated from his Son by his act of begetting, he does not give birth to his offspring according to the succession and the pangs of conception and of childbirth" (p. 165).

Consequently to be born and to begin are distinct terms. To be born signifies to receive. When the origin is eternal and does not cease to be communicated, the fact of receiving is also eternal. There is no beginning but there is nativity.

Thus Hilary's reply to Arius is that to be born and to exist always are not contradictory terms. To be born is to receive a nature; since this reception is eternal, there is no "before" the birth of the Son. One cannot even say that "he who was" is born; to talk that way would be to yield to one's imagination, since there is no "before" the birth of the Son.

This eternal birth is an ineffable mystery: nothing on earth was born before time. Thus Hilary could write that "the conclusion of our faith, of our discourse and of our understanding is that the Lord Jesus is born and yet always is" (*Dominum Jesum et natum esse et semper esse*).[21] The one who is born, is not he who was but He who is.

One can truly admire the depth of St. Hilary's analysis which brings into play such a brilliant time-eternity dialectic. Further we must stress the eternal and contemporary relevance of this profound study of the mystery. Is not a reflection on time and eternity at the heart of the reflections of a Jean Guitton for example? Not to mention Heidegger.

Let us note, in addition, that the Arian problematic which confronted St. Hilary encouraged him to emphasize the transcendence of the eternal generation of the Son with respect to every earthly generation rather than their analogy. St. Thomas Aquinas will venture more resolutely into this second course by stressing that for living beings "generation signifies the origin derived by a living being from its conjoined living principle, in the likeness of a nature of the same species."[22]

Having shown the biblical foundation of the doctrine of the eternal generation of the Son and having defended it against the Arian sophisms (renewed again in our day, as we have said) we should now set forth clearly the doctrine of the Church and its theological explanation.

3. *Catholic doctrine concerning the eternal Son and the psychological analogy*

The name of Son is just as much the proper name of the second divine Person as the name of Word which is also fitting to him. This point which is already clear to the reader of the Gospel of St. John, was made explicit by Pope Pius VI against the Jansenist synod of Pistoia.[23] Each of these two

---

[21]St. Hilary, *De Trinitate*, XII, 32, ML 10, 452-453.

[22]St. Thomas Aquinas, *Summa Theologica*, I, 27.2. Note on this subject the following difference: the father according to the flesh and the father according to the spirit transmit, the first, human life, the second, spiritual life (by word and sacrament) within a diversity of substances, but the heavenly Father gives his only-begotten Son divine life in perfect unity of substance: they are consubstantial.

[23]*DS* 2687 (*DB* 1597).

names expresses the personal property of the Son-Word, that which distinguishes him from the Father and from the Spirit. The Council of Florence adds a clarification: all that the Son is or has, he has from the Father.[24]

Revelation thus teaches us that the second Person proceeds from the Father, from the substance of the Father, by way of generation. The Son is the only-begotten Son, and is thus generated (Jn. 1:18; 3:16). This generation could not be a passage from non-being to being, for it would then be a creation that would terminate outside the inner divine being.

One could say consequently that the generation of the only-begotten Son is an act by which the Father produces a second divine "I" and communicates to him his essence in such a manner that this Son possesses the same single essence which is that of his Father. It is a necessary act, not by a blind and fatal necessity, but one that is clear and luminous, perceived and affirmed. This necessary act is intrinsically distinct from the act of creation which is founded on a free and personal decision of the triune God.

The generation of the only-begotten Son by the Father has forever been an accomplished fact, since its result is present, but on the other hand it takes place eternally without beginning or end. According to the point of view one takes, one can say that the Father begets or has begotten his Son: the perfect tense perhaps indicates better the eternity of the generation, since it signifies an essential result already attained which continues to manifest itself in the present.

If the doctrine according to which the Father generates his only Son by way and by an act of understanding is not an article of faith, it is nonetheless, according to the teaching of the Fathers and the theologians, a sure theological conclusion firmly rooted in the Bible (by way of the Johannine doctrine of the Word), which cannot be denied without temerity.

In fact the Scriptures manifest to us the second Person as being not only the Son, but also the Word, the Image and the Wisdom of the Father, the Wisdom begotten by Him. All these concepts define a mode of generation that is purely spiritual and even specifically intellectual.[25] Already some Greek Fathers like St. Basil[26] and St. Gregory of Nazianzus[27] had insinuated this theological interpretation of the generation of the Son. But it was

---

[24]DS 1331 (DB 704); the ecumenical council of Lyons said more precisely on the subject of the eternal generation of the Son: "Credimus Filium Dei, Verbum Dei, aeternaliter natum de Patre...duas habentem nativitates, unam ex Patre nativitatem aeternam, alteram ex matre temporalem" (DS 852; DB 462). Paul VI, in his profession of faith of June 30, 1968, returned to this point, expressing it actively and passively: the Father eternally begets the Son, the Son is eternally begotten by the Father (AAS 60, 1968, 437, § 10).

[25]Cf. St. Thomas Aquinas, *Summa Theologica*, I, 34.2, 3; and the corresponding notes of H.-F. Dondaine in the edition of the *Summa* already cited, treatise on the Trinity.

[26]St. Basil, *Homily* 16, 3; MG 31, 476; RJ 969.

[27]St. Gregory of Nazianzus, Or. 30.20; MG 36, 128; RJ 994.

left to the genius of St. Augustine to examine in depth the processions of the Son and of the Spirit by utilizing the consideration of man's intellectual and volitive activity.

Man's intimate life, his immanent activity as intelligent and free, constitutes a pale resemblance, but in no way, a demonstration of the intimate life of the triune God. In the eyes of St. Augustine, however, this is the most perfect resemblance of that divine life in the natural order.

The human "I," duplicates itself in self-consciousness and, without destroying the identity of its substantial "I," it opposes a thought "I" to its thinking "I." The thinking "I" represents for us the heavenly Father expressing the eternal knowledge he has of himself by uttering the "I" whom he thinks, his Word, his only Son. And just as our intimate thought precedes our exterior word, so the Word is the intimate word of the Father, the single word in which he expresses himself totally (in contrast to the multiplicity of our thoughts), and in which he expresses and contemplates the transcendent model of all possible creation.

Here we have been able to present only a very rapid sketch of the analogy of the interior word of man with the eternal generation of the Son-Word, but we will examine this thoroughly in the speculative part of this work.

It is surely necessary to stress the limits of this analogy. Our thoughts and our words are fleeting, passing, numerous; the Idea-Word of God is one and eternal. However certain human words move a whole epoch and a whole society, thus creating history and showing themselves active long after they have been pronounced: these are words that create history. They are already a less imperfect (though still very imperfect) image of the eternal Word. Moreover, the content of our words in comparison with the richness of our knowledge is poor, whereas God expresses himself totally in his one Word. Finally, our word is not a person distinct from us, but an accident distinct from our substance. The one Word of the Father is consubstantial with him while being personally distinct.[28]

It remains true, however, that this analogy has a solid foundation in Revelation. St. John wished to present to us the only Son as the Word, the manifestation of the Father which remains with him and in him. In this respect, St. Augustine was merely unfolding the potentialities of the prologue.

III. THEOLOGY OF THE SPIRIT OF THE SON/THE "FILIOQUE" (LYONS AND FLORENCE)

Reserving for the more speculative part of this treatise a more profound study of pneumatology, we wish to present here the historical evolution of the doctrine of the procession of the Spirit between the Greek patristic

[28]Cf. C. Boyer, S.J., "L'image de la Trinité, synthèse de la pensée augustinienne," *Gregorianum* 27 (1946), 173-199; 333-352.

period and the Council of Florence, while highlighting the theological-pastoral sense of this evolution, the current import of the controversy as well as the possibilities of progress.

1. *Conditions of the possibility of the controversy; The diversity of theological schemas*
The Greeks and the Latins have constituted two different branches in the heart of the one great Christian tradition. Whoever analyzes their thought runs the risk in turn of exaggerating or of minimizing their differences. We think that in the past they have especially been exaggerated. Perhaps it has not been sufficiently noted that the Greek speculation represents a first stage of elaboration and evolution of the Trinitarian dogma, to which the Latin reflection succeeds as a later stage. Our own era is characterized by a search for a broad synthesis of these two stages.

Here we would like to mark out the difference and the complementarity of the two schemas, the Latin and the Greek, with regard to certain questions of vocabulary which govern the understanding of the crisis of the *Filioque*.

Before the Arian epoch, both for the Latins (Tertullian) and for the Greeks, *God* is, in conformity with the language of the New Testament as a whole, primarily the Father. But beginning with the period of anti-Arian reaction, God signifies more and more the nature common to the three Persons. Among the Latins God is no longer the Father but only the Trinity.[29] But Vatican II returned in large measure to the pre-Arian mode of expression, without however excluding the other mode. Both are justified.

Among the Greeks there is a tendency to consider the Father as the one *supreme principle* (or *arche*) both with regard to the other two persons and with regard to the totality of creatures. The *arche* is the ultimate source. Among the Latins the common nature of the Three is the one principle of creation, the Father and the Son together are the one principle of the Spirit. The Council of Florence will brilliantly synthesize these tendencies (DS 1331; DB 704). It must be noted, however, that *principium* is a more generic term than *arche* which alone designates a "*supreme* principle," something that Florence also took into account.[30]

The Latin term *processio* has a more generic signification than the Greek New Testament *ekporeuesthai*, of which it is a translation. The Latin term evokes origin but without specifying whether this origin is immediate or ultimate. It is used both with regard to the generation of the Son and with regard to the spiration of the Spirit. The Greek New Testament term

---

[29]Cf. St. Augustine, *De Trinitate*, VIII. Proemium I; ML 42, 946; RJ 1670.
[30]In qualifying the Father as *principium sine principio*, while the Son is *principium de principio* (DS 1331; DB 704).

(*ekporeuetai*), on the contrary, is not used with regard to the Son as coming from the Father but only with regard to the Holy Spirit who proceeds from the Father (Jn. 15:26). From this some Orthodox theologians wrongly conclude that it cannot be used to designate the relation of the Spirit to the Son, but Apoc. 22:1 (cf. 1:16; 19:15) undermines the validity of this interpretation.

Finally, in modern theological language the term "procession" in the singular, tends to be reserved to the Holy Spirit: to his mission, to his procession from the Father and from the Son, to the proper (volitive) mode of this procession which distinguishes it from the generation of the Son.

In strict correlation with the term "procession," the Latin preposition *ab* signifies generic origin or derivation whether immediate or mediate. But in Greek the preposition *ek* signifies more specifically ultimate derivation. For many of the Greeks, to say that the Holy Spirit proceeds *ek tou huiou (ex filio)* would have seemed to suggest that the Son was the ultimate unoriginated root of the Spirit, which according to Catholic faith and Revelation is the privilege and the property of the Father. We say: for many Greeks, for we must point out that neither St. Epiphanius nor St. Cyril of Alexandria allowed themselves to be restrained by these grammatical scruples: both of them affirmed explicitly the procession of the Holy Spirit *ek tou huiou*.[31]

Speaking more generally we must distrust certain more or less consecrated "clichés," and especially, in the train of T. de Régnon, with regard to these two traditions, Latin and Greek. If there is at times among the Greek Fathers a tendency to view the Trinity and the unity beginning from the Father, we also find in their writings, among the Cappadocians, affirmations that would make the Persons, the Father included, issue from the essence, as we have already seen.[32] Among the Latins, too, who ordinarily seem to take their point of departure not purely and simply from the nature but from the unity of the nature, this point of departure does not at the same time exclude, as we saw in St. Augustine, its being the unity of nature precisely as possessed by the Father, the source and principle of the divinity.[33]

The difference between the Latin and Greek theological schemas has then been considerably exaggerated and simplified, and the variety of currents and schools within these two worlds overlooked. The exaggeration is due partly to polemic or defensive demands.

---

[31]Cf. St. Epiphanius, *Ancoratus* 8; MG 43, 29; RJ 1082; St. Cyril of Alexandria, *Thesaurus de Trinitate*, 34; MG 75, 585; RJ 2079; cf. Palmieri, DTC, V (1913), col. 738-739; 788; 792-794 (article on the Holy Spirit). However, they do not use the word *ekporeuetai* of Jn. 15:26 in this context.

[32]Cf. ch. III, note 52.

[33]Cf. section 1 of this chapter IV.

The real distinctions between the two traditions, however, are situated on the three following levels:

—*linguistic;* there were no good dictionaries and the different meanings of words were not always perceived in a reflex way. St. Thomas Aquinas himself got carried away with some too hasty judgments in semantic matters;[34]

—the *division* of the Trinity, if we dare speak this way, was different: it came after the Father for the Greeks, after the Son for the Latins; we will meet this point again a little later; but even such a division was in no way universal between the two groups, as is shown by the examples of St. Epiphanius and St. Cyril already cited;

—finally, the two traditions are situated at *two different moments* in the history of Trinitarian theological evolution within the Church; the Greeks never reached the point of investigating the mystery with the aid of the psychological analogy; they stopped short of this. But this does not prevent their Trinitarian schema from having certain advantages which we shall see.

We are here in the presence of a particular case of differentiation of terminologies, languages and theological schools, which was very strongly underlined by Vatican II:

> In the effort to penetrate revealed truth, the methods and approaches in understanding and expressing divine things have been different in the East and in the West. It is hardly surprising then that certain aspects of a revealed mystery have sometimes been better grasped or more clearly expounded by one than by the other. As a result, these diverse theological formulas are often to be considered as complementary rather than conflicting. With regard to the authentic traditions of the Eastern Christians, we must recognize that they are admirably rooted in Sacred Scripture, fostered and given expression in liturgical life, and nourished by the living tradition of the apostles and by the writings of the Eastern Fathers and spiritual authors; they are directed toward a right ordering of life, indeed, toward a full contemplation of Christian truth.... The Council declares that this entire heritage of spirituality and liturgy, of discipline and theology, in its varied traditions, belongs to the full catholic and apostolic character of the Church.[35]

We should note that in question here are the authentic traditions of the East, not certain post-Patristic pseudo-traditions (such as the origin of the Holy Spirit *a Patre solo* affirmed by Photius, as we shall see).

---

[34]Cf. St. Thomas Aquinas, *Summa Theologica,* I, 36.2 at the end.
[35]*UR,* § 17.

We can graphically summarize the diversity of the theological schemas of East and West by placing opposite each other the "Trinitariograms" of St. Basil and St. Augustine on the one hand, and of Photius on the other.

Basil and the Greek Fathers

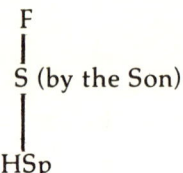

The Father is the sole principle of the divinity; from him proceeds the Spirit through the Son. From the Father, through the Son, to the Spirit the Divinity communicates itself.[36]

Photius altered this schema by denying that the Spirit proceeds from the Son and affirming that he proceeds from the Father alone:

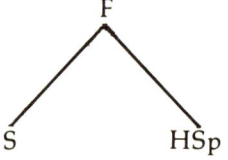

Such an idea was totally unknown to the Greek Fathers. Unlike them, Photius refused (like Theodoret) to acknowledge that the Son had any part whatever in the procession of the Spirit.

Augustine

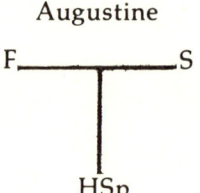

The Father is the sole principle of the divinity; from him proceeds the Son, and from their common love, as from a single principle, the Holy Spirit, *a Patre Filioque*. The Holy Spirit thus proceeds principally from the Father.[37]

In contrast Photius falsely attributed to the Latins a diagram explicitly repudiated by St. Augustine:

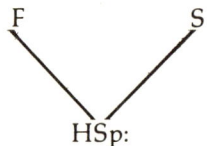

the Holy Spirit would proceed from the Father and from the Son as from two independent principles.

---

[36]Cf. B. Piault, *Le mystère du Dieu vivant*. Paris, 1956, p. 94: the third person is the "final term of the divine expansion," uncreated, and in some manner the principle of divine expansion in creation; cf. St. Basil, *On the Holy Spirit*, 18-47 (SC 17, pp. 197-199): "the essential goodness ...flows from the Father through the Son to the Spirit." But St. Augustine also knows this same schema: "Pater per Filium in Sancto Spiritu Trinitas est" (*Sermo* 126, ML 38, 703).

[37]St. Augustine, *De Trinitate*, 15.17.29; RJ 1678.

If these diagrams are helpful, it remains true that the Immense Trinity is quite beyond any limitation or spatial representation. But these visual aids at least prepare us to perceive better the historical evolution that will later occur.

2. *Brief historical sketch on the introduction of the "Filioque" into the Symbol, in the face of monopatrism*

We sing in the Creed that the Spirit proceeds from the Father and the Son, *a Patre Filioque*.[38] Originally, the Symbol of Nicaea-Constantinople said only that the Spirit proceeds from the Father (cf. Jn. 15:26). It quite simply took up the expression of Jesus in the Johannine Gospel. But little by little, beginning in Spain, the Filioque was introduced in opposition to Arianism and in order to affirm the equality of the Son with the Father. Thus we see that the Filioque originally was just as much a Christological as a pneumatological affirmation. It was later added to the pseudo-Athanasian symbol, the *Quicumque* (*DS* 75; *DB* 39), which originally dates from the second half of the fifth century. It also passed into the symbols of local councils, notably into the beautiful symbol of the eleventh local council of Toledo in 675 (*DS* 527; *DB* 277).

The doctrine of the Filioque, which was already that of the Greek Fathers Epiphanius and Cyril of Alexandria in the fourth and fifth centuries and that of the Roman Pontiffs Sts. Leo the Great, Hormisdas and Gregory the Great between the fifth and sixth centuries, is at the end of the eighth century that of the whole French Church, where the theologians of Charlemagne oppose it to the doctrine of a St. Tarasius,[39] a Greek who affirmed that the Spirit proceeds from the Father through the Son. But while Rome, though professing the doctrine of the Filioque, refused to include it in the Symbol, St. Paulinus the patriarch of Aquilaea, gave an ample treatment of the Filioque question at the local council of Cividale del Friuli or Frioul in 796. He declared that the addition of the Filioque was necessary because of the "heretics who murmur that the Holy Spirit proceeds from the Father alone," but without specifying which heretics he had in mind.[40] This declaration seems to show quite well that Photius did not purely and simply invent his doctrine of *a Patre solo*, unknown to the Greek Fathers: it was in

---

[38]The most accessible summary of the historical evolution of the *Filioque* is without doubt, for a beginning, that of E. Amann, *Histoire de l'Eglise*, v. VI; *L' époque carolingienne*. Paris, 1947, pp. 173-184 and 495-500. See also R. Slenczka, *Una Sancta* 13 (1981) 201-204.

[39]Pope Adrian I however defended the views of St. Tarasius against the theologians of Charlemagne, and the council of Florence showed, as we shall see, that the *per Filium* already tends toward the *Filioque*. On St. Tarasius and the theologians of Charlemagne, see A. Palmieri, *DTC* V (1913), col. 2313 (art. "Filioque").

[40]*DS* 617; Mansi, coll. Conc., v. 13 pp. 834-845 (Paris, 1902); here you will find the beautiful discourse of St. Paulinus: Palmieri, *DTC* V, 2314 (*art. cit.*).

existence before his time. Paulinus showed in depth how the consubstantiality of the Son with the Father demanded the Filioque.

If Rome was still defending the doctrine of the procession of the Spirit from the Father and the Son as one principle, it was also continuing (in the person of Leo III, 800) to oppose its insertion into the symbol, at least in the Eternal City itself; elsewhere however, in the Frankish empire, the insertion was already an accomplished fact.

It is in this context that we must understand Photius' treatise written toward 886 and entitled *Mystagogy of the Holy Spirit,*[41] in which the deposed and restored patriarch tries to show the heretical character of the Filioque while maintaining that this "heresy of the double procession is not held by the apostolic See," which shows that he simply was ignorant of the doctrine of Popes St. Leo the Great and Gregory as well as that of Leo III, and failed to distinguish the various aspects of the problem, both disciplinary and doctrinal, of the insertion of the two words into the symbol. For him the Son has no part in the procession of the Holy Spirit, who issues eternally *a Patre solo*. But we see that at least at this time[42] Photius does not urge against Rome the *a Patre solo* or monopatrism and was even hoping to draw Rome to his own views.

The mutual misunderstanding of positions would continue. In 1054, the bull of excommunication of Michael Cerularius (annulled in 1965) falsely accused this patriarch of having eliminated the Filioque from the symbol. Perhaps it would be possible to explain this text in the light of a new historical fact: the Holy See had allowed the inclusion of the Filioque in the symbol probably in 1014, on the occasion of the coronation of St. Henry II by Pope Benedict VIII (cf. Berno, *ML* 142, 1060-1061). In so doing it did not change its doctrine but only its discipline. The Greek East did not conform.

The procession of the Holy Spirit *ab utroque* was solemnly proclaimed by the general council of the Lateran in 1215 (*DS* 800; *DB* 428); it was further defined and clarified in the course of a first attempt at reconciliation with the East at the general council of re-union at Lyons in 1274 (*DS* 850 and 853; *DB* 460 and 463). We are dealing therefore with a revealed truth *de fide definita*, irreversibly professed by the Church. In a laudable effort at clarity and in order to refute a false interpretation of the Filioque Lyons went on to specify that the Holy Spirit "proceeds eternally from the Father and from

---

[41] Photius, *Mystagogia of the Holy Spirit, MG* 102, 280-391; S. Boulgakof (*Le Paraclet*. Paris, 1946, p. 102) remarks: "It is stupefying that the very learned patriarch, who knew the Greek Fathers much better than many of his predecessors and contemporaries, did not know that the patristic doctrine of the procession of the Holy Spirit...differed radically from his own." An interesting witness on the part of a theologian of the Orthodox confession.

[42] For it must be noted, that in his famous encyclical of 867, *Photius* accused the Roman Church of impious dogma and diabolical invention with regard to the introduction of the *Filioque* in the Symbol (*MG* 102, 725; Palmieri, *DTC* V, 2317-2318).

the Son, not as from two principles but as from one single principle, not by two spirations but by a single spiration." Thus the Photian interpretation of the Filioque was rejected. Emphasis was placed on the eternity of the procession of the Spirit in order to stress that it is not "temporally" posterior to the generation of the Son, with whom the Spirit is coeternal as with the Father. The patriarch of Constantinople, John Veccos, suffered exile (and died there) for having adhered to the dogma defined at Lyons and for having come to its defense.

In 1439 the ecumenical council of re-union at Florence made a new and threefold advance in the process of defining anew the doctrine already proclaimed at Lyons:

a) it "defines" that the interpretation constituted by the Filioque was added to the symbol in a licit and reasonable manner in order to declare the truth and because of an imminent necessity (probably an allusion to the heretical error of Photius: *a Patre solo*): DS 1302; DB 691;

b) it "defines" with greater precision the procession of the Spirit, who receives his essence (the divine nature) and his existence simultaneously from the Father and from the Son and proceeds eternally from both by a single spiration as from a single principle; the council states explicitly the reason for this: "everything that belongs to the Father, the Father has given to his Son by begetting him, except the fact of being Father; consequently, the Holy Spirit's proceeding from the Son, this the Son has eternally from the Father who eternally begets him" (DS 1300-1301; DB 691);

c) finally the council "declares": "the expressions of the holy Doctors and Fathers: 'the Holy Spirit proceeds from the Father *through* the Son' tends to signify (i.e., aims to make us understand) that the Son is also the cause (according to the Greeks) or the principle (according to the Latins) of the subsistence of the Holy Spirit, as is the Father"; *Ad hanc intelligentiam tendit ut per hoc significetur:* this complex expression does not mean to say that the Latin formula (*Filioque*) should be understood in the attenuated sense that certain Greeks gave to the *per Filium;* nor that the Greek and Latin formulas were simply interchangeable; but that the Greek formula (which, by the way, was also that of Tertullian)[43] suggests and prepares, in its orientation, the meaning that was explicated by the Latin formula. It shows in fact that the Son receives from the Father (the power) to be the cause or principle of the Spirit; the Greek Fathers held the essential of the Filioque when they said the Son is cause of the Spirit, while the Latins would satisfy the profound design of the Greeks when they affirmed with Augustine that the

---

[43]Cf. our ch. II, note 71; and ML 2, 159; RJ 372.

Holy Spirit proceeds principally from the Father, who is the principle of the whole divinity[44] (cf. DS 1301; DB 691).

Since Florence one cannot single out any new and important declaration or precision of the Church's Magisterium with regard to the procession of the Spirit, except the very recent profession of faith of Pope Paul VI (June 30, 1968) which proclaims, without however intending to define this point dogmatically, that the Spirit proceeds from the love of the Father and of the Son, a point already held by the ordinary magisterium for a long time but which now seems to be presented as an object of the faith of the Church, as a non-defined dogma (we know that the Church regards as non-defined dogmas revealed truths which its ordinary and universal magisterium explicitly recognizes as such).[45] We do not insist on this point which we shall take up later.

On the other hand we must now point out that in accepting the Filioque on the doctrinal level and in recognizing its legitimate and necessary insertion into the symbol, the Church does not intend to impose it on Eastern rite Catholics in the chanting of the symbol but only insists that they profess faith in it and recognize this legitimacy of its insertion.[46] Eastern rite Catholics then do not recite the Filioque in professing their Credo at Mass, except in the case of certain rites which have chosen to adopt it.

3. *The biblical foundation and the profound meaning of the "Filioque"*

A number of indications, which we must organize and synthesize, show us that the New Testament teaches at least implicitly the eternal procession of the Spirit not only from the Father but also from the Son.

We have already seen that St. Cyril of Alexandria, St. Augustine and in general a large current of Patristic tradition have thus understood the symbolic action of the risen Christ who breathed into his disciples by his human breath the uncreated Breath of the Spirit on the evening of his

---

[44]Cf. note 35 of this chapter; the text of St. Augustine which we cite there appears to be the basis of DS 1301 (DB 691); cf. J. Gill, S.J., *Concile de Florence*. Tournai, 1964, p. 226. It should moreover be noted that the Florentine definition had been prepared by the profession of faith of St. Tarasius, at the second council of Nicaea, which affirmed explicitly that the Holy Spirit proceeds from the Father through the Son: presented before the legates of the Pope, this was approved by the Council and afterwards defended by Adrian I against the theologians of Charlemagne, in a splendid document which amounts to a veritable summa of patristic thought on the subject (Mansi, concil., v. 13, col. 760-766; the profession of faith of St. Tarasius may be found in Mansi, v. 12, col. 1122).

[45]Paul VI, Profession of Faith of June 30, 1968, *AAS* 60 (1968), 437, § 10: "Credimus in Spiritum Sanctum, Personam increatam qui ex Patre Filioque ut sempiternus eorum Amor procedit." The affirmation harmoniously joins the *Filioque* with the procession of love. The two are placed on the level of faith: *credimus*.

[46]Cf. the bull *Etsi pastoralis* of Benedict XIV, in 1742: see A. Palmieri, *DTC* V (1913), 2341 (art. "Filioque"). The Greek-Albanian rite chants the "Filioque" in the symbol.

Relations of Origin 169

resurrection (Jn. 20:22). This text symbolically fulfills the precise words of the discourse after the Last Supper in Jn. 16:13-15 and 15:26.

Let us read once again these words which so aptly interpret the action described in Jn. 20:22:

> When the Spirit of Truth comes, he will lead you to the complete truth; since he will not be speaking as from himself but will say only what he has learnt; and he will tell you of the things to come. He will glorify me, since all he tells you will be taken from what is mine. Everything the Father has is mine. That is why I said: All he tells you will be taken from what is mine.... When the Advocate comes, whom I shall send to you from the Father, the Spirit of Truth who issues from the Father, he will be my witness (Jn. 16:13-15; 15:26).

A simplistic exegesis that lacks a theological background and is the work of exegetes who fail to reflect on the logical and metaphysical presuppositions of the scriptural texts, too often affirms that this text has in view only the mission of the Spirit and not his eternal procession. That the issue is first of all and immediately that of the temporal mission of the Spirit of Truth is beyond all shadow of doubt; but why should this fact exclude a reference to eternal procession as well? Once we understand that the mission itself presupposes and includes the eternal procession,[47] many of the otherwise insurmountable difficulties in understanding these texts simply cease to exist.

B. Lonergan in commenting on Jn. 16:13 rightly remarks:

> The Holy Spirit is said to depend on another.... A negative dependence: "he does not speak of himself" and a positive one: "all that he hears he will say." This reveals a dependence not only on the part of the disciples in what concerns the doctrine they must receive, but directly in the Spirit who teaches. So we can ask what is this real dependence of the Spirit with respect to the Father and the Son? We cannot say that the Holy Spirit hears because some accidental information comes to him. For the Holy Spirit, as God, is simple and immutable, there is in him no composition of substance and of accidents, nothing whatever comes to him that he had lacked previously. It follows then that the Holy Spirit hears because he receives his divinity itself from another; this reception is the eternal procession of the Spirit; not from the Father alone, but also from the Son.[48]

Let us clarify still further the meaning of the Johannine text: the Spirit

---

[47] Cf. St. Thomas Aquinas, *Summa Theologica*, I, 43.2.3.
[48] B. Lonergan, S.J., *De Deo trino*. Rome, 1964, v. I, pp. 230-233ff. These remarkable pages should be read.

who speaks to the Churches says what he hears from the Word, the one who glorifies the Father and who has received everything from the Father, and he takes from the Son the good which this one has received from the Father, the good of the omniscient divine nature; he thus proceeds eternally from the Father through the Son, or from the Father and the Son and consequently his mission in the Church and in the world is oriented to the glory of the Father and of the Son, to the glorification of the Father through that of the Son.

We can say further: the Spirit only takes from the Son what the latter has received from the Father and this is why in glorifying the Son it is the Father whom in the last analysis he glorifies. The mission of the Spirit reflects in time his eternal relation: he is not only *ex Patre Filioque* but also and by the same fact *ad Patrem et Filium, ad Patrem per Filium* (as he is *ex Patre per Filium*); eternal return to the Father and to the Son from whom he issues eternally. This is what his mission reveals in a palpable way. The Spirit speaks about the Word because he is first of all in his very being the eternal Listening to the one and only Word.

The importance of these Johannine verses (Jn. 16:14-15) for fathoming the revealed data about the procession of the Spirit received felicitous expression and emphasis by M.-J. Lagrange:[49] "These words are the most expressive that the New Testament contains on the unity of nature and the distinction of Persons in the Trinity, and especially on the procession of the Holy Spirit. However what is directly asserted is not the communication of the divine essence to the Holy Spirit but the communication of the truths to be revealed.... It is with good reason that Christian theology has founded on these two verses the doctrine of the procession which unites the Spirit to the Father and to the Son. It is clear that if the Mission in any way mirrors the relation of the Persons, the Holy Spirit proceeds from the Father and from the Son and not from the Father alone."

This point becomes still clearer when one looks more closely at Jn. 15:26 which the Photian school quoted in the contrary sense. In the same statement where Jesus says that the Spirit proceeds from the Father—or comes from him, if one prefers to translate it that way—he also says that he, the Son, will send him. Could he send him if he did not come from him—any more than he himself could be sent by the Father if he did not draw his origin from him? As the Son who is sent draws his origin from the Father who sends him, so the Spirit who is sent by the Son draws his origin from the Son who sends him. All that the Father has belongs to the Son, including the fact of being the Spirit's origin and of sending him. Jn. 16:15 and 15:26 reciprocally illumine one another.

---

[49] M.-J. Lagrange, O.P., *Evangile selon saint Jean.* Paris, 1936, p. 423.

And on these conditions we can better understand why Jn. 15:26 ends with the affirmation: "the Spirit of Truth will bear witness to me." Sent by the Son in time because he proceeds eternally from him, the Spirit of Truth renders to the Son the supreme witness precisely by revealing himself as the Spirit of the Son, the Spirit who proceeds from the Only Son. According to the luminous principle posited by St. Augustine ("for the Son, to be sent is to be known in his origin from the Father... for the Holy Spirit, to be sent, is to be known in his procession from the Father"[50]), we can deduce what he implies but does not say explicitly: "for the Holy Spirit, to be sent by the Son, is to be known in his procession from the Son." The Son then sends the Spirit in order that this Spirit may reveal himself as eternally his, the One who issues from him; and in a sense this is the supreme witness rendered by the Spirit to the Son, the perfect glorification of the Son by the Spirit (Jn. 16:14).

The Johannine texts we have cited finally acquire their full meaning and unveil the procession of the Spirit if we shed on them the additional light of Jn. 10:30, "The Father and I are one." They are also one, the Father and the Son, in the fact that the two of them as one send the Holy Spirit, and that he proceeds from both of them as from a single principle. It is in a perfect communion that Father and Son send him who is their Communion in his eternal procession.

"The Father and I are one": not separately then but together, precisely as one, do we promise you and send you the Spirit, and in consequence it is from us as one that he proceeds.[51]

The biblical analysis in which we have engaged has already led us into a study of the profound meaning of the *Filioque*. We could sum it up in a word: Christ being the fullness of Revelation, pneumatological truth is also Christological; or still more profoundly, the *Filioque* is an affirmation that is necessary so as to preserve faith in the Trinity as such and not reduce it to a "binity."

St. Thomas Aquinas explains this point very well:

> If the Holy Spirit did not proceed from the Son, he would in no way be distinguished from him.... The divine Persons are distinguished from one another solely by relations. But only inasmuch as they are opposed can these relations distinguish the Persons.[52] The proof of this is that the Father has two relations: by one he is related to the Son, by the other to

---

[50]St. Augustine, *De Trinitate*, IV, XX, 29: "mitti est Filio cognosci quod ab illo (sc. a Patre) sit," a point of view which is very exactly that of the Gospel of St. John: 16:27-28; 17:8.

[51]Jn. 10:30 and 16:13-15 constitute the biblical foundation of the "tamquam ab uno principio" of Florence.

[52]Cf. *DS* 1330 (*DB* 703) commented on in our ch. III, § III. 5.

the Spirit. However, as these relations are not opposed to one another, they do not constitute two Persons; they pertain only to a single Person, that of the Father. If then in the Son and in the Holy Spirit we could find only the two relations that relate each of them to the Father, these relations would not be opposed to one another, any more than the two relations that relate the Father to each of them. Therefore just as the Father is only one Person, it would likewise follow that the Son and the Holy Spirit would be only one Person possessing two relations opposed to the two relations of the Father. But this would be heresy, since we would hereby be destroying faith in the Trinity. It must be then that the Son and the Holy Spirit are related to one another by opposed relations. But in God there can be no other opposed relations than relations of origin, of principle as opposed to term emanating from this principle.[53]

St. Thomas Aquinas was only resuming with greater precision an insight St. Anselm had already expressed with some terseness: "it is in showing that the Spirit proceeds from the Son that we most successfully show why he is not the Son."[54] The Angelic Doctor continued: either the Son proceeds from the Spirit, which no one would hold (and he might have added: which has no scriptural basis whatever), or else the Spirit proceeds from the Son (which corresponds as we have seen to the sense presented by Scripture, understood in all its logical implications).

Conversely the Photian heresy, if we take the trouble to analyze its presuppositions and consequences, denies important truths concerning each of the three divine Persons:

—the immediate and direct unity of the Holy Spirit with the Son, which can only be a relation of origin;

—the perfect unity of the Father and of the Son who possess all in common, except paternity and filiation, but have in common the power to spirate;

—the indivisible unity of the person of the Father, since in the Photian view the property of Spirator would logically have to constitute another Person distinct from the Father (since it is independent of paternity). Or, if you prefer, the Photian position implies the attribution to the Father of a kind of double personality: *ad Filium* and *ad Spiritum Sanctum*.

Following M.-J. LeGuillou[55] we can thus sum up the theological import of the affirmation of the *Filioque*:

> To affirm the Filioque is to affirm definitively that the Spirit is not given to us independently of the Son.

[53] St. Thomas Aquinas, *Summa Theologica*, I, 36.2.
[54] St. Anselm, *De processione Spiritus Sancti*, cap. III.
[55] M.-J. Le Guillou, O.P., encyclopédie *Catholicisme*, art. "Filioque," v. IV. Paris, 1956, col. 1284.

To affirm the Filioque is to clarify the sense of the formula: the Spirit proceeds from the Father, since we take it for granted that the Father is never without the Son, since he is only Father in filiation. The procession of the Spirit has for its common origin the Father and the Son, immanent each in the other.

Reserving for the second part of our work a more profound explanation of the bond between the Father and the Son in the Spirit, of the procession of the Spirit and also a presentation of what concerns him in the psychological analogy, we prefer rather to cite here the clarification of the doctrine defined at Florence which the saintly bishop Josaphat Kuncievicz, martyred for Catholic unity in 1623, offers us in a catechism written for the Christian people: it summarizes the revealed truth clearly and profoundly:

Q. Do you believe in the Holy Spirit?
R. I believe that he is true God, the third Person of the Holy Trinity, proceeding from the Father through the Son.
Q. Does this mean that the Latins are inaccurate when they say that the Holy Spirit proceeds from the Father and from the Son?
R. No, the expression is correct. They have the same reality in view when they say that the Holy Spirit proceeds from the Son (*a Filio*) as we do when we say that he proceeds through the Son (*per Filium*).
Q. How can that be?
R. In the same way that Holy Scripture tells us of creation, that it is through the Son: "All things were made through him and without him nothing was made" (Jn. 1:3); "through whom also he (God) created the world" (Heb. 1:2). However, no one has ever reached such a point of impiety[56] as to refuse to believe that the creation of the world is the work of the Son (*a Filio*) as it is that of the Father; although Scripture does not say: *a Filio* but only *per Filium*.
Q. If it is true that the Holy Spirit proceeds from the Father and from the Son, then there are two principles of the Holy Spirit and not just one?
R. Not at all. Just as it does not follow from the fact that heaven and earth are created by the Father, by the Son and by the Spirit, that there are three trinities but only one; for the power through which the Three Persons create heaven and earth is one; likewise even as here also the conjoined and indivisible spirative power or virtue of the Father and of the Son is one, so through it the Father and the Son spirate (in the singular) not as two spirators[57] but as a single spirator. Thus Father and Son are (literally) one principle of the Holy Spirit.[58]

[56]The author here seems to forget that this impiety was precisely the error of certain Judaeo-Christians and of Photinus of whom Augustine was a one time victim.

[57]Cf. St. Thomas Aquinas, *Summa Theologica*, I, 36.4.1, 7: there are "duo spirantes" but "unus Spirator," as there is "unus Creator," "tres creantes." In the distinction of the persons of

In other words, the creation by the Three does not signify that there are three creators but only one; so also spiration by the Father and by the Son does not signify that there are two spirators but only one. The explanation of the martyr bishop is remarkably precise and at the same time as accessible as can be to the average Christian. Does this not also suggest that the Church can never give up explaining the most profound and the most difficult truths of Revelation when their serene possession is menaced by adverse circumstances? "I owe a duty to Greeks just as much as to barbarians, to the educated just as much as to the uneducated" (Rom. 1:14).

To the uneducated very particularly is the Church obligated to explain the heart of the mystery which they are destined eternally to contemplate by first living it.

4. *Present state of the controversy*

Influenced by their conversations with Old Catholics and Anglicans a number of Orthodox theologians for almost a century now have developed an attitude that distinguishes itself from rejection of the *Filioque*.

Today we are faced with two currents.

The first, resulting from the conversations just mentioned, recognizes that the *Filioque* was the formulation of ideas that are in fact found among the Fathers. Nevertheless it is not a dogma but only a "theologoumenon," that is a theological opinion. Sergius Boulgakov recognizes that the Greek formula "through the Son" has been interpreted as a participation of the Son in the procession of the Holy Spirit. An exegete such as Mgr. Cassien will recognize that Scripture leaves the way open on the question of the *Filioque*. As early as 1912 Archbishop Eulogius of Kholm, declared that in substance the two teachings (*Filioque, per Filium*) are identical. This first current thus approaches the solution adopted at Florence though it does not quite reach it.

A second current (Losski, Verkovski, Nissiotis, Evdokimoff, Clément) seeks to maintain at all cost and to justify the position of Photius, which it believes to be traditional. This current in fact is bound up with the Palamite doctrine of uncreated energies.[59] Thus Nikos Nissiotis charges "filioquism" with "christomonism," with "isolating the christological aspect and consid-

---

Father and Son, the spirative activity of both is one, signifying "in some way the nature with the property" (*Ibid.*, I, 36.4.1). See also I, 45.6.

[58] D. Nicola Contieri, *Vita di S. Giosafat*. Rome, 1867, Append. VII-IX; cited by Cardinal J. Slipyj, *De principio spirationis in SS. Trinitate*. Leopoli, 1926, pp. 17-18.

[59] It is M.-J. Le Guillou who thus presents us with the two currents existing in contemporary Orthodoxy: art. cit., col. 1284-1285. On the conversations between the Orthodox, Anglicans and Old Catholics, consult the article of A. Palmieri, "Filioque," *DTC* V (1913), toward the end, col. 2331-2336.

ering it superior to the pneumatological aspect;"[60] O. Clément writes that "filioquism..., by placing the Spirit even as to his hypostatic existence in dependence on the Son, has without doubt contributed to overvaluing the institutional and authoritative aspect of the Roman Church."[61]

A just reply has been given to these criticisms. "If there exists in Catholic ecclesiology a certain polarization toward the second person of the Trinity, it is the Incarnation that is the reason for this: this polarization or pre-eminence does not concern in God the second person as second person, or the Logos as Logos. And Catholicism rightly maintains the transcendence of the Spirit with regard to the incarnate Christ."[62] Above all it is historically very inaccurate to say with Losski that the *Filioque* is (on the dogmatic level) the sole reason for the separation. A number of Orthodox authors affirm the contrary.[63]

5. *The theological-pastoral sense of the doctrinal evolution which has led to the "Filioque" and prospects for the future*

The problem of the relation between the Holy Spirit and the Son which had already been perceived and investigated by Gnostic theology[64] under the figure of Eve (the Spirit) drawn from the side of Adam (the Word),[65] became unavoidable once the consubstantiality of the Son and the Spirit with the Father was defined. The Greek notion of the primacy of the Father as source of the whole divinity, or Tertullian's notion of monarchy, was biblical, elegant and useful for preaching and for piety but they did not touch the problem of the relation between the Son and the Spirit. The Greek formula (the Spirit proceeds from the Father through or by the Son), gave a response that was correct and had already been practically canonized if not defined by the Church at the Second Council of Nicaea in 787,[66] but it was not clear enough on the question posed.

Once the consubstantiality and the difference of the Persons, distin-

---

[60]Nikos Nissiotis, associate director of the ecumenical Institute of Bossey; cited in a note of *Lumière et Vie*, no. 67, on "Filioquism," p. 106.

[61]O. Clément, *L'Eglise orthodoxe*, P.U.F., 1961, p. 50; cited in *Lumière et Vie*, no. 67, p. 111.

[62]*Ibid.*, p. 113.

[63]See for example the citations of Kremos and of Mgr. Nectaire Kephales in A. Palmieri, *DTC* V (1913), 2321 (art., "Filioque").

[64]Cf. A. Orbe, S.J., *La teologia del E. Santo*. Rome, 1966, pp. 150-151; 530-531 (note that in Gnostic theology, as later for the Arians, the Spirit is inferior to the Son); cf. pp. 528-529.

[65]*Ibid.*, p. 549; cf. A. Orbe, S.J.,"La procession del E. Santo y el origen de Eva," *Gregorianum* 45 (1964), 103-118. The author establishes a veritable patristic dossier of this analogy, which he then pursues in the theologians.

[66]See notes 39-40. It should be noted that the defense of the profession of faith of St. Tarasius, before Nicaea II, by Pope Adrian I, in a letter to Charlemagne, is practically equivalent to canonical confirmation.

guished by their reciprocal relations, were established and with the help of the dynamism of the psychological analogy (love), all ambiguity as to the origin of the Holy Spirit from the Son had to be eliminated. The Magisterium had only to integrate the contribution of St. Augustine while elaborating what had already been the thought of Epiphanius and was also that of Cyril of Alexandria.

A number of Greeks, oblivious of these Fathers, have accused the Latins of innovation in the question of the *Filioque*. They have failed to notice that they were victims of a regressive attitude and unfaithful to the principles of Nicaea and of St. Athanasius. Fidelity to the past and especially to the current demands of presenting and deepening the revealed data renders necessary the introduction of new words: *ousia, homoousios, Filioque*. Uncritical dogmatic realism would deny the revealed reality if it set out to obstinately reject all critical reflection on the presuppositions, the significance and the consequences of the affirmation: the Spirit proceeds *a Patre*. The authentic Greek tradition, that of dogmatico-critical realism reveals itself in the *Filioque* inasmuch as this is a development of the *per Filium* and even of the *a Patre*.

A difficulty however comes spontaneously to mind. What is the ecumenical value of the councils of Lyons and Florence, in which so few Greek delegates participated and whose decisions were later rejected by the Churches which had in their favor a very rich doctrinal tradition and a past record of glorious services rendered to the faith (cf. p. 198)?

We must reply that formal ecumenicity is found where we encounter the principle of the visible unity of the Church, that is its foundation and its visible head, the Vicar of Christ, the Pope. As the Spirit is bound to Christ and dependent on him, so the *Filioque*, that is its dogmatic expression, is bound to the papacy: the two dogmas were defined at the same time at Lyons and Florence. If it is true that the *Filioque* in terms of its object is more important than the papacy, it is also true that its recognition has become in the eyes of the Roman Church which is mother and mistress of all the Churches (*DS* 850; *DB* 460) and of all the faithful, the sign and the manifestation of recognition of its own primacy. This is only normal, moreover, if we understand that this primacy is sacramental, sign and instrument of the absolute and universal primacy of Christ the Redeemer in and over his Church.[67] It is conjointly by the *Filioque* and by the recognition of the primacy of service and love of the Vicar of Christ that the Spirit wishes to glorify the Son from whom he proceeds and who is the Head of the Church of which he is the Soul.

Acknowledgment of the *Filioque* signifies and symbolizes, at the level of

---

[67]Cf. B. de Margerie, S.J., *Christ for the World*, ch. XIII.

critical-dogmatic realism, the full emergence of the infallible primacy of the Roman Pontiff as the dogmatically recognized guide in matters of dogmatic expression. Formerly, this primacy was already at work, but it had not yet become the object of dogmatic definition.

While waiting for this guide to be recognized by all, exchanges of ecumenical views[68] on the relation between the Spirit and the Son cannot but be very profitable; but they will never bear their full fruit unless the conversation takes as its point of departure the exact point where the schism was consummated and inaugurates reflection on the rules for elaborating the language of faith.

Is not this what St. Thomas Aquinas perceived at least obscurely when he stressed not only the extrinsic but also the intrinsic relation which binds the primacy of the Pope to the procession of the Holy Spirit from the Son? Here is how the Common Doctor expressed himself:

> The error of those who deny the primacy of the Vicar of Christ over the universal Church bears a resemblance to the denial of the procession of the Holy Spirit with regard to the Son. In fact it is Christ himself, the Son of God, who consecrates his Church and seals it by the Holy Spirit as by a character and a seal.... And similarly the Vicar of Christ, by his primacy and his solicitude as a faithful servant, keeps the universal Church subject to Christ.[69]

The Christ who governs his Church visibly through his Vicar, governs it invisibly through the Paraclete, the Spirit of Truth which he sends to her.[70] The strict parallel between ecclesiology and pneumatology so manifest in the *Filioque,* brings out the pneumatic and spiritual character of the divine institution of the papacy without exaggerating an external authority (as the Orthodox say) because it becomes interiorized by the Spirit of the Son, who promotes only the glory of the Father through submission to the Vicar of the Son.

The *Filioque* has then a signification that is not only Trinitarian but also ecclesiological and is perceived differently on one side and on the other. Their communion of faith in the Holy Spirit, the Spirit of the Father and of the Son, their common love for this single Spirit who binds them together,

---

[68]Like those which took place in France in 1950 and which were published by *Russie et chrétienté,* 1950, nos. 3 and 4 (on the "Filioque"); cf. also the dossier published by Istina 17 (1972) 257-467.

[69]St. Thomas Aquinas, *De erroribus Graecorum,* ch. 32: "Christus Dei Filius suam Ecclesiam consecrat et sibi consignat Spiritu Sancto quasi suo charactere et sigillo.... Et similiter Christi vicarius suo primatu et providentia universam Ecclesiam, tamquam fidelis minister, Christo subjectam conservat" (toward end of the ch.).

[70]Pius XII, *Mystici Corporis,* AAS 35 (1943) 227.

ought to help Catholics and Orthodox in a common deepening in their understanding of the relation between the Spirit and the Son of the Father. The Catholic Church could perfectly recognize and proclaim that the Holy Spirit proceeds *a Patre solo tamquam a principio primo et fontali, a principio sine principio et a Filio solo tamquam a principio de principio*. Such a formula,[71] synthesizing as it does diverse traditional data and certain expressions canonized by the Council of Florence (*DS* 1331; *DB* 704), would not be completely true however unless we were to add with the same council: *Pater et Filius non duo principia Spiritus Sancti, sed unum principium*. The Church could further appropriate and dogmatically define the formula of St. Augustine: the Holy Spirit proceeds principally from the Father.[72] We see then that the ecclesiastical magisterium has at its disposal diverse resources so as to acknowledge even more clearly than in the past the element of truth contained in the Photian error: the Holy Spirit proceeds *a Patre solo*. We need only complete it and the formula becomes true.

Florence has then clearly defined that the Spirit proceeds from the Father and from the Son, from the Father through the Son; the same council could have said, but did not say that the Spirit is eternally turned toward the Father and toward the Son; *ad Patrem et ad Filium, ad Patrem per Filium*, the reverse truth that would complement the former. However, the council did in some way suggest this point of view when it proclaimed, in the light of St. Fulgentius, the dogma of circuminsession which we must now study.

IV. CIRCUMINSESSION OR MUTUAL INDWELLING OR "INEXISTENCE" OF THE THREE

"Because of this unity (of nature) the Father is completely in the Son and completely in the Holy Spirit; the Son completely in the Father, completely in the Holy Spirit; the Holy Spirit completely in the Father, completely in

---

[71]We borrow the first part ("a Patre solo tamquam a principio primo et fontali") from M.-J. Le Guillou, O.P., *art cit.*, col. 1285.

[72]*Principaliter*: St. Augustine, *De Trinitate*, XV, 17.29; ML 42, 1081; RJ 1678; it will be noted that a theologian like K. Barth (*Kirchliche Dogmatik*, I, 1, pp. 503-504ff.) finds that Orthodoxy isolates without any right Jn. 15:26 from the affirmations on the Spirit of the Son, eternal spirator and not only "sender" of the Spirit in time. We think the Augustinian formula (the Spirit proceeds principally from the Father) renders faithfully the profound meaning of Jn. 15:26. It will further be noted that a renewed interest in the *Filioque* is current in the Protestant world: thus Don L. Berry, "Filioque and the Church," *Journal of Ecumenical Studies*, 5 (1968), 535-554; this author thinks that the profound meaning of the *Filioque* is that the Spirit glorifies Christ alone: "the work of the Holy Spirit revealing Christ alone" (p. 551); if we understand that an *ex Filio* has for corollary an *ad Filium* of the Spirit and that the mission of the Spirit to glorify the Son in time flows from his eternal orientation toward the Son from whom he comes forth, we will better grasp the foundation of this correct view. But perhaps certain sectors of the Protestant world, which minimize the importance of interior relations between the divine Persons, do not sufficiently see that the Spirit, in seeking to reveal Christ alone, the plenitude of Revelation (*DV* 2), seeks ultimately only the glory of the Father through the Son: the Father is *fons et origo totius divinitatis*, the Son is *ad Patrem*.

the Son." It was these formulas of St. Fulgentius, the Latin Basil, that the Council of Florence chose in order to express the doctrine of the "circuminsession" or *perichoresis* of the divine Persons within each other (*DS* 1331; *DB* 704). Note that the mutual immanence of the divine Persons is presented as a consequence of the unity of nature among them; the formulation of the Council of Florence suggests the "static" immutability of this mutual immanence by the use of the preposition *in* which however does not exclude what the doctrine of relations demands, namely that the divine Persons be each toward and with respect to the other: *ad* and not only *in*. The Council of Florence is not moreover the first text of the Magisterium to speak to us of this circuminsession: Pope St. Dionysius had done so as early as the third century (*DS* 112-115) in a text we have already studied,[73] which twice cited the question of Jesus to Philip, the New Testament basis of the dogma: "He who has seen me has seen the Father. How can you say: show us the Father? Do you not believe that I am in the Father and the Father in me?" (Jn. 14:9-10: the Greek preposition *en*, which is equivalent to the Latin *in* is used here and not the prepositions *pros* or *eis* as in Jn. 1:2; 1:18).

Having thus presented the Church's doctrine on the circuminsession of the divine Persons, it is appropriate to lay greater stress on its biblical foundation, its theological significance and its pastoral import.

In addition to the Johannine text already cited, this doctrine is again presented by the gospel of St. John in 10:38 and 17:21. The first of these two texts ("the Father is in me and I in the Father") has the distinct merit of establishing, in the view of St. John as well as in that of Jesus, the very explanation of the mode of unity of nature between the Father and the Son affirmed a little earlier in the same Gospel: "The Father and I are one" (Jn. 10:30). We see clearly that the Council of Florence simply continued in the same line as the Johannine Gospel in presenting the unity of nature as the foundation of circuminsession. It is because the Father and the Son are one in the common possession of the same and identical divine nature, because they thus perform the same works and pronounce the same words (Jn. 14:10-11; 10:32) which implies their perfect unity of nature, that they are mutually immanent the one in the other by a reciprocal immanence which conditions their common immanence in Christians and in the world, as well as the immanence of Christians and of the world, in the distinction of their natures, in the mutually immanent Father and Son: "You will know that I am in my Father and you in me, and I in you (Jn. 14:20); that they also may be one in us, as we are one: I in them and you in me, that all may be one as you Father are in me and I in you (Jn. 17:21-23: we have inverted the order of presentation); the Word was in the world (Jn. 1:10); in God we live, we move and we are (Acts 17:27-28)."

[73]Cf. our ch. II § V, pp. 85-87.

In revealing to us the circuminsession of the divine Persons, their mutual inexistence, the New Testament offers it to us as a term and a transcendent model (where there is perfect identity of nature) of the mutual inexistence, in the insurmountable diversity of natures, of Christians with one another, of Christians with the Father and the Son, and of God with the world. Christ invites us now to believe in the relations of mutual inexistence between the Father and him so that we may come later on to experience them in vision or at least in its mystical anticipation (compare Jn. 14:11 with 14:20), through the exercise of the mutual inexistence of unitive love among Christians, as well as between them on the one hand and the Father and the Son on the other (Jn. 17:21: that they may be one in us).

For the New Testament, the exercise of imperfect created inexistence and of intersubjectivity in love thus constitutes the condition for the full disclosure in vision of the perfect inexistence and uncreated intersubjectivity of the Father and the Son in the Spirit. Christians must break assunder the temporary and unnatural circuminsession that exists between Satan and the world (compare 1 Jn. 5:19: "the whole world is in the power of the Evil One"—*en to ponero*—with 1 Jn. 4:3-4: "the spirit of antichrist is already in the world.... He who is in you is greater than he who is in the world"), in order to release in all its brilliant splendor the original, permanent, definitive and final (improperly so-called) circuminsession, between the transcendent God and his created universe (Jn. 1:10; Acts 17:27-28) and through (but beyond) this, the perfect and eternal circuminsession between the Father, the Son and the Spirit.

It is precisely through the reciprocal inexistence of the Church and the world in the dialogue of salvation that the false and provisional circuminsession between Satan and the world is broken and there shines out anew the reciprocal inexistence between the Church and the three Coeternals, within which is disclosed their eternal reciprocal inexistence. Eternal life, toward which the paschal movement conducts Christians, does not consist only in knowing the Father and the one whom he sent, but also in knowing them one in the other and one by way of the other and in recognizing the imperfection of our unity in the light of their perfect unity and in its very heart: "that they may be one in us." Only the unity of the Father, Son and Holy Spirit is identity of nature. Circuminsession of likeness points toward circuminsession of identity in distinction (cf. *DS* 803; *DB* 431); the imperfect inexistence in the bosom of the Church and between it and the Trinity is polarized by the perfect Trinitarian inexistence.

This was precisely the merit of the Fathers of the Church, to unravel, against the background of the biblical data, the theological significance of circuminsession.[74]

[74]In our exposition we use the word "inexistence" not in the sense of a lack of existence but

St. Hilary uses the mutual relative immanence between an earthly father and son to help him portray the transcendence of the circuminsession in God between the coeternal Father and Son.

Hilary, though perhaps unaware of the expression, describes the reality of circuminsession thus:

> Since a son derives his nature from his father and since the latter communicates his proper nature to his son without any loss or division, by this unity of nature the father in some way remains in the son and the son is not entirely outside his father. This presence however is not perfect, for the father cannot communicate to his son the totality of his substance, nor does the son derive from his father everything that he is. In earthly generation in fact, the father surely transmits to his son certain beginnings and as it were germs of life, but he does not transmit to him all his living substance, nor is he in the son with his proper personality but only by way of his power as agent. As to the divine Father, who is all life and who communicates to his Son all his living substance, he is in his Son and he possesses his Son in himself in virtue of this perfect unity of nature.[75]

It is to be observed that for Hilary, the reciprocal immanence of the Father and the Son is bound up through the identity of their nature with the eternal generation of the Son by the Father. He has expressed this with incomparable and untranslatable splendor in his vigorous Latin: *alius in alio, quia non aliud in utroque; Pater in Filio, quia ex eo Filius; unigenitus in ingenito, quia ab ingenito unigenitus;*[76] *Deus in Deo quia ex Deo Deus est;*[77] *per Filium Pater...ex Patre Filius...unum sunt qui invicem sunt. Invicem autem sunt, cum unus ex uno est.*[78]

St. Fulgentius, who like St. Basil wrote with marvelous precision of

---

of existence in and toward another; on the other hand, we do not think that the reductive exegesis practiced by the Arians, who attempted to reduce the intra-divine circuminsession to a relation between Creator and creature, should prevent us from utilizing the Johannine texts in their most obvious sense: without denying the distinction of natures between Creator and creature, they show us in the reciprocal relation of immanence between Christ and Christians the image of the relation of reciprocal immanence between the Father and the Son. On the Arian exegesis one may consult St. Thomas Aquinas, *Commentaries on the Gospel according to St. John*, ch. 10, lectio 5; and *Summa contra Gentiles*, IV, 9.

[75] P. Smulders, S.J., *La doctrine trinitaire d'Hilaire de Poitiers*. Rome, 1944, p. 256; cf. pp. 255-262, where the author sets forth Hilary's doctrine on circuminsession; in the passage which we cite, he uses St. Hilary's *De Trinitate*, VII, 28; ML 10, 223-224. What Hilary does not bring out is that the earthly father does not possess numerically the same but only specifically the same nature as his son. We could add that the mutual immanence between the earthly father and son is often absent, e.g., if the father abdicates his role as educator or if there is a lack of friendship between the two.

[76] St. Hilary, *De Trinitate*, III, 4; ML 10, 77; RJ 862.
[77] St. Hilary, *De Trinitate*, IV, 40.
[78] St. Hilary, *De Trinitate*, VII, 31-32; ML 10, 226; RJ 867.

thought on the cult due to the three divine Persons, stresses the absolute inseparability of the divine Persons among themselves against the background of the relative inseparability of divinized human persons in relation to the Trinity: "If then the Trinity by infused charity makes our souls adhere inseparably to itself (cf. 1 Cor. 6:17), how could the persons of the same Trinity be separable?"[79] More profoundly he shows the inseparability of the Three as based on the inseparability of their reciprocally relative names: Father and Son, Holy Spirit who is Spirit of the Father and of the Son and thus relative to both.[80] And Fulgentius undertakes the explicit task of demonstrating the bond between this inseparable character of the Persons and circuminsession properly so called: "The Son testifies both that he is in the Father and that the Father is in him by the same inseparable unity of nature (Jn. 14:9ff.)."[81] We can see why the Council of Florence appealed to him for its presentation of the Church's thinking on circuminsession.

St. John Damascene is almost the first to have used,[82] to designate the reciprocal immanence of the Father and the Son, a term already accepted in Christology: *perichoresis*. *Perichoresis* evokes mutual compenetration and comprehension with an active nuance present in both, and lays the stress on the total character of this compenetration.[83] However the use that the Doctor from Damascus makes of it hinges on the mutual immanence of Father and Son, without special emphasis on this active compenetration.[84]

---

[79]St.Fulgentius, *Epist.* XIV, 14; ML 65, 405.

[80]St. Fulgentius, *Epist.* XIV, 9; ML 65, 400: "Hoc enim nomine (sc. Spiritu Sancto) non ad solum Patrem sicut Filius; nec ad solum Filium, sicut Pater; sed simul et ad Patrem et ad Filium refertur, quando et Patris et Filii Spiritus nuncupatur. Nam et cum ipse Spiritus sanctus dicitur donum, ad donatorem inseparabiliter refertur." Fundamentally the reasoning of St. Augustine himself.

[81]St. Fulgentius, *Epist.* XIV, 10; ML 65, 401.

[82]St. John Damascene, *De Fide orthodoxa*, I, 8; MG 94, 829A; cf. E. Chiettini, *Enc. Cattolica*. Rome, III (1949), 1709-1710.

[83]Cf. H.-F. Dondaine, O.P., *La Trinité*, v. II, p. 369, note 121, ed. of 1962.

[84]Cf. A. Deneffe, S.J.,"Perichoresis, Circumincessio, Circuminsessio," Z.K.T. 47 (1923), 507: "Bei der Trinitarischen Perichorese denkt der Damaszener nicht so sehr an ein dynamisches Eingehen der Einen Person in die andere, wie es in der innergottlichen Hervorbringungen und Ausgängen begründet ist, als vielmehr an ihr statisches, ruhendes Ineinandersein. Hierfür spricht der Umstand dass er an allen Stellen, so weit sie mir bekannt sind—aus De Fide orth. glaube ich alle Stellen angeführt zu haben—'en allélais' bezw. 'en allélois' sagt, während er bei der christologischen Perichorese bald 'en,' bald 'eis' und 'dia' gebraucht." One could say that this remark of Deneffe contributes definitively to liquidate the legend which still lingers on in so many manuals or books that do not verify the sources: the idea that the Greek Fathers had propagated a "dynamic trinitarian perichoresis" has no solid historical basis. For St. John Damascene perichoresis is explained by an *ekestai allēlōn*, a reciprocal possession of the divine persons (*loc. cit.*). Moreover, St. John Damascene is not the very first to have spoken of "perichoresis" in the bosom of the Trinity: earlier, pseudo-Cyril had already done this; neither the one nor the other, we must add, speaks of "perichoresis toward," the classical expression in

St. Bonaventure translates the *perichoresis* of Damascene by *circumincessio*.[85] St. Thomas Aquinas[86] prefers the spelling *circuminsessio* whose concept corresponds (as does the preceding one) to the Johannine data: one could say that "circuminsession" reminds us of Jn. 10:38; 14:9ff.; 17:21, while "circumincession" is in the line of Jn. 1:2 and 1:18. The Council of Florence opted for the spelling "circuminsessio."

For St. Thomas the foundation of circuminsession is not situated only in the unity of nature or in the reciprocity of relations, views that were already traditional earlier, as we have seen; in his commentaries on the Gospel of St. John,[87] the Angelic Doctor underlines that there is "a twofold unity in the Father and the Son, one of essence and one of love, and according to both of these the Father is in the Son and the Son in the Father"; this unity of personal love is the unity of origin of the Spirit, as appears from the parallel text of the *Summa Theologica*.[88] From this angle the saintly Dominican recaptures (though without using the term) the notion of "circumincession" as interpenetration or intra-divine subjectivity. Circuminsession is inseparably identified with circumincession: there is no *in* without an *ad* in the mutual relations between divine Persons.

We have explained the theological significance of circuminsession enough to disengage its pastoral import. We could sum it up this way: we are dealing with a key concept that could serve as a summary and synthetic refutation of almost all the Trinitarian heresies and one especially suited to a profound analysis of the mystery in harmony with a personalist philosophy of intersubjectivity.

Circuminsession, inasmuch as it is grounded on the unity of nature, the perfect numerical and transcendent unity of the divine nature, excludes tritheist Arianism as well as every other form of tritheism. St. Thomas Aquinas has very well expressed this first aspect: "The Father is in the Son since the Father is his essence which he communicates to the Son without the least change; the essence of the Father being in the Son, it clearly follows that the Father is in the Son. And since the Son is his essence, it likewise follows that the Son is in the Father where his proper essence is."[89]

Christology, but of "perichoresis in," which already foreshadows the Thomist "circuminsessio." See on this subject: G. L. Prestige, *God in Patristic Thought*. London, 1964, p. 298. In this respect, the council of Florence followed the Greek patristic tradition in adopting the spelling "circuminsessio."

[85] The Seraphic Doctor thus defines "circumincessio": "In solo Deo est circumincessio perfecta quia ratio circumincessionis est perfecta unitas essentiae cum distinctione personarum et quia hoc proprium est solius Dei," I Sent., dist. 19, 1.1.4 concl.

[86] Besides the texts cited further on, see *Summa contra Gentiles*, IV, 9.

[87] St. Thomas Aquinas, *in Jo.* cap. 17; lectio V: "duplex unitas essentia et amoris."

[88] St. Thomas Aquinas, *Summa Theologica*, I, 42.5.

[89] *Ibid.*

On the other hand, inasmuch as circuminsession signifies mutual inexistence, it presupposes real distinction between the divine Persons and in consequence excludes modalism. Pastoral teaching on circuminsession thus presents itself as the means par excellence for strengthening Christians against the constantly reviving temptations of modalism as well as of tritheism, with firm foundation in important texts of the Johannine Gospel.

In the polytheistic context of the Christians of India or Brazil (Afro-Brazilian polytheistic religions), circuminsession with its accent on the unity of the divine nature would also serve as a remedy.

We can sum up the services rendered to the defense of the other Trinitarian mysteries by presenting the mystery of the circuminsession revealed by Christ, in the light of these words of St. Fulgentius: "*inconfusa atque inseparabilis manet personarum distinctio.*"[90]

What is more, contemporary currents of personalist philosophy and of intersubjectivity encourage us to analyze more carefully the mystery of the "interpersonality" in God that is circuminsession. Is it not the mutual presence of the Father, the Son and the Spirit of the Father and the Son? The Protestant theologian Widmert writes very aptly:

> The divine monarchy, God in his unity and his simplicity, is the bond of this mutual presence of the Father, the Son and the Holy Spirit. Indissolubly complementary presences, they live in constant exchange of love. They render themselves present to the world in their common and perpetual, sovereign and merciful action. There is no confusion between them, no separation among them, they are neither confused with their creation nor separated from it.
>
> Presence is the act of the eternal present. It has pleased God to manifest his image in the man Jesus and to make his breathing heard in believers; this is the sign of his sovereign Presence.
>
> The communion of the divine presences at the heart of the one and simple monarchy is always renewed and never exhausted. Communion that realizes the establishment of the Kingdom of God (the reign of God), actually active in the life of believers, in the witness and liturgy of the Church, rendering them present to a world that is idolatrous or without God, this communion is all that, under a form still veiled, exercising its attraction on the world because it is eternally the communion of the presences of the Father, the Son and the Holy Spirit in their indefectible harmony. The Presences are perfections fully equal to one another.[91]

These lines constitute a remarkable effort to express the mystery of circuminsession in contemporary categories (presences and communion)

---

[90] St. Fulgentius, ML 65, 402.
[91] G.-P. Widmert, *Gloire au Père, au Fils et au Saint-Esprit.* Neuchâtel, 1963, pp. 64-65.

without neglecting what we believed could be called circuminsession, improperly so-called, between God and the universe or between Christ and Christians. Such an "imperfect *perichoresis*," which presupposes not unity of nature but diversity of natures,[92] is necessarily the point of departure for our reflection on the incomprehensible mystery of perfect circuminsession. The word *perichoresis* signifies etymologically "reciprocal containing" and it is by no means impossible but on the contrary quite probable that it issues from the centuries old technical usage in the Greek world of the verb *chorein* to signify the invasion of all things by God; God, the Spirit who penetrates everything, holds and fills everything, contains the universe.[93] It by no means follows from this, in spite of Suarez,[94] that the immensity of God the creator who fills space and overflows it, constitutes a good theological basis for thinking of the eternal circuminsession of the Three Divine Persons, which is a fact independently of all creation.

The text of Widmert just cited, insists on the mutual presence of the Three. Such a notion, though more accessible to us, does not correspond fully to the riches of circuminsession insofar as it is the mutual inexistence of distinct persons in identity of nature (of which Widmert is thinking when he speaks of the one and simple monarchy). St. Fulgentius had already stressed that the natural unity of three men (and *a fortiori* their reciprocal presence) is not in this sense an adequate image of the circuminsession of the Three Divine Persons; neither the soul nor the body of each of the three is one with those of the other two.[95] On the other hand, divine circuminsession is the mutual comprehension of Persons whose relations of origin are immanent in the one divine nature and who are really distinct, mutual comprehension due to the identification of each with the numerically one divine nature.

We are dealing with a comprehension in all senses of the word: reciprocal understanding that is exhaustive because infinite. If the Father is in the Son and the Son in the Father, it is because "the Father knows me and I know the Father" (Jn. 10:15) and because "the Father loves me" (Jn. 15:9) and "I love the Father" (Jn. 14:30). We rediscover here another ground for circuminsession, one which St. Thomas Aquinas already pointed out for us: no longer only the unity of the divine nature but the relations of origin: "It is clear that the intelligible Word in no way proceeds outwardly, but remains in the Intellect that pronounces it; in the same way the Object expressed by the Word is contained in this Word. And a parallel line of reasoning would

---

[92]See on this point Cardinal J.-B. Franzelin, S.J., *De Deo trino*. Rome, 1881, p. 235.
[93]Prestige, *op. cit.*, p. 289.
[94]Cf. A. Chollet, *DTC* II (1905), col. 2531: art. "Circuminsession."
[95]St. Fulgentius, *ML* 65, 396-397: "in tribus hominibus unitas naturalis, nullius tamen est cum duobus caro animave communis."

hold also for the Holy Spirit."⁹⁶ This aspect of circuminsession, viewed as reciprocal comprehension in understanding and love, was particularly and appropriately stressed by Scheeben.⁹⁷ We could summarize it, in the light of the personalist language of the Johannine Christ in the sacerdotal Prayer, by saying that the "I" of the Son is in the "You" of the Father and that together they constitute the *interpersonal* "We" which originates the *personal* "We," the Spirit, who in turn is immanent in the "I" of the Son as in the "You" of the Father.

The mystery of the reciprocal circuminsession of the Father, the Son and the Spirit in the depths of their single nature thus constitutes the synthesis of all the revealed mysteries regarding the Three who are one. Their total reciprocal immanence in knowledge and love, thanks to their perfect respective identity to the single divine nature, also helps us understand why the Three are, in it and by it, the one principle of creation and of the universe.

V. CREATION AND TRINITY

The Fourth Council of the Lateran in 1215 declared that the Trinity is the sole principle of the universe (*sola universorum principium: DS* 804; *DB* 432). Later the Council of Florence specified further that the Father, the Son and the Spirit are not three principles but a single principle of creation: *non tria principia creaturae, sed unum principium* (*DS* 1331; *DB* 704), just as, it went on to stress, the Father and the Son are not two but a single principle of the Spirit. These comparative formulas were moreover borrowed from St. Augustine.⁹⁸

What do these affirmations of the Church signify? That "the creative power of God is common to the whole Trinity, for it pertains to the unity of nature and prescinds from the distinction of Persons,"⁹⁹ as St. Thomas Aquinas put it. The external works of the Trinity are inseparable (cf. *DS* 535; *DB* 284). Creation as such does not reveal the inner heart of the divine mystery to one who does not yet know it through Revelation. Otherwise, the Trinity would be demonstrable by reason and Revelation would be useless or at least of secondary utility.

They further signify that the Son and the Spirit are, with the Father, co-creators of the universe; the Three constitute a single omnipotent Creator. And they are a logical consequence of the affirmation of the divinity of the Son and of the Spirit and of their strict equality with the Father.

⁹⁶St. Thomas Aquinas, *Summa Theologica*, I, 42.5.
⁹⁷M.-J. Scheeben, *Handbuch der Kath. Dogmatik*, v. II (1948), § 1036.
⁹⁸St. Augustine, *De Trinitate*, V, 14, 15; *ML* 42, 921; *RJ* 1662.
⁹⁹St. Thomas Aquinas, *Summa Theologica*, I. 32.1.

Finally these affirmations signify that the universe is (and we must say this in spite of the disadvantages of a strongly deficient spatial imagery) exterior, at least in certain respects, to the inner heart of the divine mystery; creation is not a generation; the universe is not God; the immanence of God in the universe does not impede his transcendence and their distinction. They imply the rejection of all the forms of Trinitarian pantheism of the idealist philosophy of the nineteenth century.

By insisting on what is common to the Divine Persons in the work of creation, do these affirmations of the Church signify that the distinction of the Persons is without importance for a correct appreciation of creation?

Not at all. We have already had occasion to note that as early as the Roman council of 382 the Church declares heretical anyone who denies that the Father created the visible and invisible universe through the Son and the Spirit (DS 171; DB 77).[100] St. Augustine too, from whom Florence borrowed the formula cited above, said the same: "If the Father, the Son and the Holy Spirit are one only God, then one only world was made by the Father, through the Son in the Spirit."[101]

But what do these formulas mean and how shall we reconcile them with the preceding ones?

If "the Father, the Son and the Holy Spirit are but one and the same principle with regard to the term produced *ad extra*, since, in the act of creating, relative opposition among them plays no part (cf. *omnia sunt unum ubi non obviat relationis oppositio*, DS 1330; DB 703), still it is the Three who create and in a definite order."[102] St. Thomas had already insisted on this idea: "Although common to the Three Persons, the divine nature belongs to them in a certain order: the Son derives it from the Father, the Holy Spirit derives it from the Father and the Son. Similarly, though the creative power is common to the Three, it does not belong to them without order: for the Son derives it from the Father and the Holy Spirit from both."[103]

We come thus to the delightful Thomistic expressions of *Creator genitus* and *Creator procedens*.[104] We have already had occasion to allude to the first of these with regard to Tertullian.[105]

For St. Thomas creation appears as a prolongation of Trinitarian action, an external prolongation which is even in some way present at the heart of the mystery while remaining exterior to it. The Angelic Doctor compares

---

[100]Cf. our ch. II, § IX. 4; note 92.
[101]St. Augustine, *in Jo.* 20:9; ML 35, 1561.
[102]Cf. E. Bailleux, *La création, oeuvre de la Trinité, selon saint Thomas, Revue thomiste*, 62 (1962), 31.
[103]St. Thomas Aquinas, *Summa Theologica*, I, 45.6.2.
[104]The expression "Creator genitus" is found in St. Thomas Aquinas, *Summa Theologica*, I, 34.3.
[105]Cf. our ch. II, note 93.

these two communications of being: the divine processions and creation. For him, as one commentator brings out,[106] the creative act is nothing else but the eternal action precisely as prolonging itself outward to attain a contingent term. But this eternal action is a Trinitarian action. On the side of God, the two acts are but one action identical to his being, but a distinction opposes them on the side of the terms: in the Trinitarian action we have Divine Persons who proceed actively as God from God and in God, while in creation we have beings drawn from nothing. A single and identical divine fecundity possesses the power to extend itself as act and in dependence on its primary term, to a secondary and contingent term, without being really limited by this term. "The power to generate (the Son) and the power to create is a single, identical power, if we consider the power in itself, but these powers differ according to their diverse relations to diverse acts."[107]

Still more profoundly, St. Thomas sees the imperfect communication of God "outwardly" in creation as totally dependent on the interior communication of God in God which is the only integral one: that of the generation of the Son and of the procession of the Spirit. "That which is first causes that which comes after and the perfect causes the imperfect. Now the procession of the Divine Persons is first with respect to the procession of creatures and it is more perfect, since the Divine Person proceeds from its principle in perfect likeness, while the creature on the contrary represents it only imperfectly. Thus the immanent divine processions cause the processions of things."[108] In other words, the generation of the Word and the procession of the Spirit are the exemplary cause of creation (a work common to the ungenerated Creator, to the generated Creator and to the proceeding or spirated Creator, who are only a single and unique Creator), and at the same time they are its final cause. It is not an impersonal God but only the Tripersonal God who creates the universe, a work of the divine nature that is common to the Three but diversely possessed by each of Them. The Son in creating does not cease to be Son and to receive his creative nature from the Father. It is in this sense that the generation of the Word is the exemplary cause of creation which nevertheless does not reveal it, at least directly.

The immanent processions of the Word and the Spirit are then exemplary causes of creation. St. Thomas expressed this as follows:

---

[106] E. Bailleux, *art. cit.*, p. 30.
[107] St. Thomas Aquinas, *De Potentia*, a. 2, a. 6.
[108] St. Thomas Aquinas, *Summa Theologica*, I, 45.6. obj. 1. The saint seems to accept this part of the objection.

Relations of Origin

According to the nature of their procession, the Divine Persons exercise a causality with regard to creation.... God is cause of things by his intelligence and by his will, just as the artisan with respect to the products of his art. The artisan operates in function of a concept of his intellect and the love of his will. So God the Father has performed the creation by his Word and by his Love which is the Holy Spirit. And in this way the processions of the Persons are patterns for the production of creatures, insofar as they include the essential attributes, which are knowledge and will.[109]

This last phrase is difficult to grasp at a first reading and needs some explanation. It could seem at first that the manifestation of the Divine Persons in creation (*post revelationem datam et acceptam*) is very imperfect, since it brings to light only the wisdom and the goodness of the First Cause. But on somewhat closer consideration it will become evident that through these attributes it is indeed the Divine Persons themselves who are in question and not simply God as such.

The wisdom and goodness of creatures in fact have their exemplary cause in wisdom and goodness as they are in God, that is in an ideal type whose eminence surpasses our concepts, an eminence that we cannot then define but of which we can say: this wisdom, in God, is such that by reason of it (*secundum quam*) is born a Divine Person, the Word; this goodness is such that by reason of it there proceeds another Person, the Holy Spirit.

Thus the exemplars of created wisdom and goodness are in a true sense the Wisdom of the Son and the Goodness of the Holy Spirit and in virtue of this exemplarity the Father has created everything by his Word and by his Love. The Thomistic formula is therefore justified: the eternal processions of the Divine Persons are the cause and the *raison d'être* of the whole (transitive) production of creatures.

Drawing our inspiration here from Dom Lucien Chambat,[110] we share his deep regrets that, due to inability to explain and justify it, this extremely savory and moving language of the Fathers: "the Father created all things by his Word and by his Spirit" has been abandoned, and that we have become accustomed to attribute the works *ad extra*, solely to the triune God without distinction of persons, rather than relating them to the Father, the

---

[109]*Ibid.*, I, 45.6 corpus; the saint had just explained how creation, being a production of the being of things, pertains to God according to his being, which is his essence, common to the Three persons. Then he adds the consideration we cited which allows him to nuance what he had said in I, 32.1 (see note 99).

[110]Dom Lucien Chambat, O.S.B., *Les missions des Personnes de la sainte Trinité selon saint Thomas.* Paris, 1943, pp. 183-184.

Son and the Spirit. The doctrine of St. Thomas, as we expounded it, can help us return to the way of the ancients. It allows us to admit in creation a real procession of the Son and of the Holy Spirit under the veil of the attributes according to which these two Persons proceed in God. We are not relying on any appropriated attributes but on the specific attributes according to which the Persons proceed in God, so that reason enlightened by faith can contemplate in creatures if not the Divine Persons immediately, at least a reality not perfectly intelligible without these Persons. The device of exemplarism will lead reason—not any reason, but reason enlightened by faith—to the Divine Persons and not only to the Divine Nature.

With St. Thomas Aquinas himself we could thus sum up the process of the Divine Persons' self-manifestation through creation to the mind of the believer: "God provides for everything according to the mode that befits it. Now the connatural way for man is to be led by the visible to the invisible. So God has in some way manifested to men both himself and the eternal processions of his Persons, through visible creatures according to certain clues (*seipsum Deus et processiones aeternas Personarum per creaturas visibiles secundum aliqua indicia quodammodo hominibus demonstravit*)."[111]

The cosmic order thus manifests the Trinity, not in the quasi-immediate manner of Tertullian, but through the mediation of man's intelligence and freedom as these unveil the Wisdom and the Goodness according to which the Word and the Spirit proceed in God. As is evident, such a manifestation of the Trinity is bound up with the validity of the psychological analogy which uses the human psychic model to help us better understand the unfathomable mystery of the divine processions.[112]

Exemplary cause they are indeed; the processions of the Divine Persons are also the final cause of creation and of its movement toward its end. This angle St. Thomas also stresses: "Just as it has been said that the procession of the persons is the reason for the production of creatures by their first principle, so is it also the reason of their return toward their end; for just as it is by the Son and by the Holy Spirit that we are created (*per Filium et Spiritum Sanctum sicut et conditi sumus*), so it is by them that we are reunited to the ultimate end (*fini ultimo conjungimur*)."[113]

If the processions of the Word and the Spirit from the Father are thus the exemplary and final causes of all creation, we can see that creation itself

---

[111] St. Thomas Aquinas, *Summa Theologica*, I, 43.7.

[112] In the view of St. Thomas as of St. Augustine, the evocative images of Tertullian, analyzed in our ch. II, offer us some vestiges of the Trinity in the cosmos, while it is only in the rational creature that we can discover an image properly so called of the Trinity; cf. St. Thomas Aquinas, *Summa Theologica*, I, 45.7. And the vestiges themselves make sense only for those who are images.... Cf. *In Decretalem I Expositio, Opusc. Omnia Theol.* Paris, 1927 (Ed. Mandonnet), v. IV, pp. 331-332.

[113] St. Thomas Aquinas, *I Sent.* dist. 14, q. 2, a. 2.

must be somehow mysteriously present in the very bosom of the uncreated mystery of the eternal processions of the Son and the Spirit. This is what the Angelic Doctor clearly affirms, recapturing thereby the best of the speculation of the pre-Nicene theologians:

> The name Word indicates reference to the creature.[114] ... In a single act God knows himself and all things; his one Word therefore expresses not only the Father but also creatures.... The Word of God is expression pure and simple of the mystery of the Father, but it is both expression and cause of creatures.... To name the Word is in effect to evoke the operative idea of the things that God makes.[115]

In other words, the Word is spoken by the Father eternally, not only as the expression of the knowledge he has of his own loveableness and goodness, but also as the uncreated expression of the knowledge he has of the loveableness of all creatures. "God knows and loves his essence, his truth and his goodness" even in their created reflections.[116] It is *also* according to this knowledge that the Word proceeds, but, as the knowledge of God "does not come to him from creatures—he knows them through his own essence—even though the Word expresses creatures it does not follow that he proceeds from them."[117] The Word is truly *Verbum omnium rerum* but without depending on them in the eternal utterance whereby he proceeds from the Father.

Likewise the Holy Spirit is the term of the love which the Father and the Son have in common, not only for their own uncreated goodness but also for the goodness of all creatures which reflect theirs:

> Just as the Father, by the Word that he generates, utters himself and every creature—since the Word generated by him suffices to represent the Father and every creature; so also he loves himself and every creature by the Holy Spirit, since the Holy Spirit proceeds as love of this first Goodness by reason of which the Father loves himself as well as every creature. By this we also see that in the proceeding Word and Love a reference to the creature is secondarily evoked: for the divine truth and goodness are the principle of the knowledge and love God has for the creature.[118]

[114] As opposed to the name of Son.
[115] St. Thomas Aquinas, *Summa Theologica,* I, 34.3.
[116] *Ibid.,* I, 27.5.2.
[117] *Ibid.,* I, 34.3.3.
[118] *Ibid.,* I, 37.2.3. Note in this context that St. Thomas at the same time that he introduces creation somehow into the heart of the Trinitarian mystery, also stresses the moral necessity of the Revelation of the Trinity for a correct comprehension of creation: "The knowledge of the divine persons was necessary to make us think rightly of creation. In fact, to affirm that God made everything by his Word is to reject the error according to which God has produced

In these last words we find again the same reasoning that allowed St. Thomas to establish that creation is caused by the divine processions: what has come into play is a focusing on the middle term of the attributes of divine knowledge and will according to which the Word and the Spirit proceed and in which he knows and loves every creature. The processions of the Word and of the Love-Spirit thus signify, though only secondarily, a (free) relation to the creature: here at last we have a correct, though no doubt incomplete, expression of what the pre-Nicene Fathers were trying to say. This secondary and free relation to the creature, we must add, is, for God triune in his real and interior relations, only a relation of reason.

Trinity and Creation: here all the difficulty of theological endeavor lies in fully harmonizing two lines of thought that are in dialectical tension but without contradiction, two affirmations St. Thomas maintains simultaneously. On the one hand, "the creative power of God is common to the whole Trinity for it pertains to the unity of nature without involving the distinction of persons," for the indivisible Trinity is the one principle of creation. On the other hand, because this one nature does not belong to the Three in confusion or indistinction but in a certain order, the Son receives the creative power from the Father and the Spirit from the Father and the Son. Further the eternal creative action is intelligent and voluntary and in this respect the intellectual generation of the Word and the loving spiration of the Spirit cause, exemplify and terminate the production of creatures. The Father creates through the Son in the Spirit as well as with his Son and their Spirit. We could perhaps say by way of synthesizing the Thomistic formulas, that the creative power, while immediately pertaining to the unity of the divine nature, mediately involves the distinction of the persons, whether under the formality of its intra-Trinitarian communication or under that of its intellectual and voluntary character.

There would thus doubtless emerge a justification at least in part of the daring reflection of Hans Urs von Balthasar: "The Father produced the creation in the Son and for the glory of the Son; but the Son created and saved it for the glory of the Father in order to offer it, once made perfect, to the Father (cf. 1 Cor. 15:24-28); finally the Spirit illumines it not in order to reveal himself[119] but to reveal the infinite love between the Father and the Son and to incorporate this love in creation."[120]

things by necessity of nature; and to posit in him the procession of Love is to show that if God has produced creatures, it is not because he needed them nor for any other cause exterior to him: it is through love of his goodness" (*Ibid.*, I, 32.2.3.).

[119]On the contrary, we believe with St. Augustine that the mission of the Spirit has for its end to reveal his procession from the Father and the Son: cf. the text cited in note 50 of the present chapter.

[120]Hans Urs von Balthasar, "L'Esprit, l'inconnu au-delà du Verbe," *Lumière et Vie,* 67 (1964), 122.

In short, if the Trinity creates and remains present to its creation, the latter is eternally and mysteriously implied, in a way that remains secondary and free, in the two divine actions which are its principle, its model and its term: the generation of the Son and the spiration of the Spirit, both of which are necessary.

VI. THE APPROPRIATION TO EACH OF THE THREE OF THEIR COMMON WORKS BRINGS OUT THEIR PERSONAL PROPERTIES

1. *Historical and pastoral introduction*

When St. Paul wrote to the Corinthians: "Now there are varieties of gifts, but the same Spirit; and there are varieties of ministries but the same Lord; and there are varieties of workings, but the same God who works all things in all" (1 Cor. 12:4-6), are we or are we not to understand him as intending to attribute, in a special manner and with a foundation in reality, miracles to the Father, ministries to the Son, charisms to the Spirit, or is this only a pious way of saying that miracles, ministries and charisms are in reality common works of the indivisible Trinity, without any distinction of persons, without a particular and personal relation of these activities with this or that Person?

Likewise, when the Symbol of the Apostles presents the Father as the omnipotent Creator, the Son as Savior and the Spirit as Sanctifier, is this just a convenient distribution that could be inverted without any disastrous consequences or is there in fact a "division of Trinitarian work," or, finally, do these expressions pertain to a more intricate line of thought?

Confronted with fourth century Arianism the Church energetically defended the unity of nature of the Three Divine Persons with its corollary: the unity of their operations (*agere sequitur esse*). The works *ad extra* are the common activity of the Three. The operation of the three inseparable Persons is indivisible. The same Cappadocian Fathers who have been so unjustly accused of tritheism as we have seen, vied with one another in stressing the indivisibility of the Trinitarian operations. We cite here but two of the Greek Fathers: Cyril of Jerusalem, first: "the gifts of the Father are not other than those of the Son and those of the Spirit; there is in fact only one single salvation, one single power, one single faith";[121] then, Gregory of Nyssa: "The Persons are not reciprocally divided by way of time, place, will, occupation, operation, or any of these affections visible among men."[122]

Two initial (and always reliable) rules of Trinitarian language have then been elaborated:

—the essential attributes (power, knowledge, love) are common to the

---

[121]St. Cyril of Jerusalem, *Cat.* 16, 24; MG 33, 952; RJ 834.
[122]St. Gregory of Nyssa, MG 45, 369; RJ 1039.

Three Persons because they are, precisely, attributes of their common essence;

—the properties (paternity, filiation, passive spiration) distinguish each person.

However true and necessary this way of speaking may be, can we really be content with it without allowing many Trinitarian attributions authentically revealed in the New Testament to entirely escape? The biblical writings, the liturgy, the Symbols, and finally, the Fathers attribute "as proper" to this or that Person predicates or functions that the dogmatic rule elaborated by the same Fathers on the basis of the same New Testament makes us declare common to the Three. How can we get out of these apparent dilemmas that oppose dogma and Bible, patristic text to patristic text, and texts of the New Testament to one another?[123]

The problem arose almost inevitably. It is surprising to realize that it did not arise in an explicit way during the patristic era but only did so in the West, in the Middle Ages.

Abelard, yielding to a temptation characteristic of neo-modalism, had identified the personal properties with the common attributes: the Father with Power, the Son with Wisdom, the Spirit with Goodness.

St. Bernard reacted vigorously. The Father also is Wisdom and the Son Power. What is common to the Three cannot be the property of one of them. The Church condemned Abelard (cf. DS 721-722, 734, 737; DB 368-370, 381, 384).

Some disciples of Abelard however, wishing to preserve the element of truth contained in the errors of their master, made some advance in the manner of posing the problem by saying: "It is legitimate to attribute in a special way to one Divine Person a common perfection but without denying it to the others; this was the procedure of the Fathers." From this they concluded that one could attribute in a particular fashion power to the Father, wisdom to the Son, goodness to the Holy Spirit. They thus brought about the decisive transition from the identification preached by Abelard to the appropriation which the Church was to retain. This is expressed with particular clarity in the encyclical of Leo XIII on the Holy Spirit, *Divinum Illud Munus* (1897; DS 3326) where we find a brief but substantial presentation of the doctrine of appropriation. Let us see now at closer range how this doctrine resolved the apparent dilemmas evoked above to the great benefit of Trinitarian spirituality and cult.

---

[123]It is interesting to observe how St. Ambrose for example shows that what is attributed by a text of the New Testament to one Person is also attributed by another text to another Person (*De Spiritu Sancto*, I, 12; ML 16, 734). A frequent patristic argument at the time of Arianism.

Relations of Origin

2. *Nature, foundation and importance of appropriations*

Appropriation is "a manifestation of the Persons by means of essential attributes," as St. Thomas Aquinas put it.[124] It is an effort to "illuminate the mystery of the Trinity by means of things more accessible to our reason than the properties of persons; for, beginning with creatures, the source of our knowledge, we can come to know with certitude the essential attributes of God,"[125] which, viewed in the light of the Revelation of the mystery of the Three, can help us better perceive the properties which distinguish them.

The Angelic Doctor specifies still further the nature of appropriation in these terms: "To appropriate is nothing else but to draw what is common toward what is proper (*commune trahere ad proprium*), not because that belongs more to one Person than to another, which would be opposed to their equality; but because what is common has a much greater likeness to the property of one Person than to that of another."[126]

Let us continue with St. Thomas, giving some examples:

> Power makes us think of principle: so it is appropriated to the Father who is the principle without principle; wisdom is appropriated to the Son who proceeds as Word; goodness to the Holy Spirit who proceeds as Love which has the good for its object. Thus it is the resemblance of the appropriated attribute to the property of the Person which founds on the side of the object the suitability of the appropriation, a suitability which exists independently of us.[127]

We thus perceive that the appropriations of the Symbol of the Apostles, in which we proclaim our faith in the omnipotent Father,[128] in Christ the Son and Savior, and in the Holy Spirit the Sanctifier, are full of meaning: the redemptive work manifests the Wisdom appropriated to the Word who proceeds by understanding, while the mission of the Spirit by which it is brought to completion, in sanctifying the Church, manifests the Goodness appropriated to the Third Person.

So we understand how St. Thomas Aquinas could further write: "The sole foundation of the appropriation is the resemblance to the property.[129]..." It is a real affinity "prior to the activity of our mind"[130] even

---

[124] St. Thomas Aquinas, *Summa Theologica*, I, 39.7.
[125] *Ibid.*
[126] St. Thomas Aquinas, *De Veritate*, 7.3.
[127] St. Thomas Aquinas, *I Sent.*, dist. 31, q. 1, a. 2.
[128] Cf. Bailleux, *art. cit.*, RT 62 (1962), 36-39.
[129] *Similitudo ad proprium*: St. Thomas Aquinas, *I Sent.*, d. 31, q. 2, a. I, ad I m.
[130] H.-F. Dondaine, O.P., *La Trinité*, v. II, p. 418 (Paris, 1962).

though it is evident that appropriation is essentially the activity of a rational creature in search of a better understanding of the Trinity.

But it is in noting that the essential attributes, thanks to this privileged likeness between perfection and person, "can reach by way of likeness the condition of *properties,* while remaining distinct from these in virtue of their character as *common,* thus justifying the name *ap-propriations*"[131] that the Common Doctor best reveals the acuteness of his theological genius.

Thus we have the rules of appropriations, which turn out to complete and nuance, but without weakening them in the least, the rules of Trinitarian language elaborated by patristic theology which we have already mentioned: one, a positive one, is that of affinity between personal property and perfection; the other, a negative one, is that of the non-exclusivity of the attribution of a perfection to a Person.

The difference between Power, Wisdom and Goodness of God on the one hand and Father, Son and Spirit on the other, consists precisely in this that paternity, filiation and spiration are incommunicable, while Power, Wisdom and Goodness are of themselves transmissible and in fact transmitted from one Person to another. Only the order of possession of these perfections and the modality they assume in each Person remain necessarily original.

It is true that a rigid insistence on the non-exclusivity and the common character of God's operations *ad extra* would tend to transform appropriation into far too clear and rational a device at the service of the unity of the essence but to the detriment and devaluation of the mystery.

It is doubtless preferable to insist on the affinity between a common attribute and a personal property. Thus to speak of appropriation is simply to respect the unity of the essence and the equality of the Persons within the context of heightening the awareness of the Mystery.

The appropriations presented by the Bible or by the Fathers take on their profound meaning only in the measure that other passages, biblical or patristic, spell out explicitly for us the distinctive characteristics of the Persons. The foundation of appropriation, a rational process within a Faith context, exceeds the scope of natural reason; appropriation is the work of reason enlightened by faith. Far from being a mere device or word-game that touches nothing of the real (Alain de Lille), it is a very fertile procedure for one who knows how to use it, a procedure that enriches our contemplation of the Father, of his Word and of their Spirit, in the properties that distinguish them.

---

[131]St. Thomas Aquinas, *I Sent.,* d. 31, q. I, a. 2, ad I m; St. Thomas there says very precisely: "Haec praepositio (sc. 'ad') quae venit ad compositionem vocabuli notat accessionem cum quadam distantia; quia hujusmodi attributa accedunt per similitudinem ad rationem propriorum et distant per communitatem, recte appropriata dicuntur."

Conclusion

Appropriation then places the entire creation, through the mediation of human reason, at the service of the contemplation of the revealed mystery of the personal properties and of their reciprocal relations.

Speculative theology culminates in humble and loving contemplation of its supreme object, a contemplation which is its indispensable complement and anticipates, by way of participation, the loving vision of the glory of the Three.

Bossuet put it magnificently:

> To love God is to love in unity the Father, the Son and the Holy Spirit; to love their equality and their order; to love and not to confound their operations, their eternal communications, their mutual relations and everything that makes them one while making them three.[132]

The Jew and the Moslem who, while remaining such, have accepted the grace of Christ, the grace of the Father, the Son and the Holy Spirit, without knowing it, yet in a very real way, love God as he is, Tripersonal. Not only can we rejoice with the Credo of the People of God professed by Paul VI in rendering thanks "to the divine Goodness because numerous believers are able to give witness with us before men to the Unity of God even though unaware of the mystery of the very holy Trinity," but we can also exult with joy in acknowledging this: that some who deny the Trinity as victims of an invincible and inculpable ignorance, in reality love this Trinity above all things and perhaps more than we do. They unconsciously love the Father, the Son and the Spirit in their order, their equality, their mutual relations, their eternal communications. And if these things have been revealed to us is it not so that we might reveal them to these others so that they too might love consciously and in the light the Reality which their conscience loves and, unconsciously, knows it must love?

Bossuet, in the text just cited, stresses that we love the order that exists between the Father, the Son and the Holy Spirit. This point deserves reflection so that we might better grasp all that is implicit in the command given by the glorious Christ: "Baptize them in the name of the Father, and of the Son and of the Holy Spirit." Let us listen to Bossuet again in a text which luminously synthesizes what we have been trying to say in the course of this fourth chapter:

> If the Son and the Holy Spirit proceed equally from the Father, without any relation between the two of them, one could just as well say: the Father, the Holy Spirit and the Son as: the Father, the Son and the Holy Spirit.
>
> But that is not the way Jesus Christ speaks.

[132] Bossuet, *Méditations sur l'Evangile*, The Last Supper, second part, XXVth day.

> The order of the persons is inviolable; because, if the Son is named after the Father because he comes from him; the Holy Spirit must come also from the Son, after whom he is named; and he is the Spirit of the Son as the Son is the Son of the Father.
>
> This order cannot be reversed: it is according to this order that we were baptized and the Holy Spirit can no more be named second than the Son could be named first.[133]

It is not without reason then that Christ chose and expressed a definite order in his way of speaking of the fundamental mystery that he came to reveal, just as it was not without reason that he chose for each of the Three names which would never pass away: "heaven and earth will pass away, but my words will not pass away." This order, like these names, expresses the relations of origin in God.

Appendix IV: *The doctrinal value of the Latin councils of the Middle Ages (Lateran IV and Lyons II)*

As a prolongation of what we said in Appendix III (p. 146), let us note the reflections this subject inspired in Louis Bouyer (*L'Eglise de Dieu, Corps du Christ et Temple de l'Esprit*, Paris, 1970, Excursus II, pp. 678-679) in connection with certain contemporary views of the non-ecumenicity of these councils:

> It does not follow that the dogmatic decisions of general councils posterior to the separation would not be of a very high authority. We have established in fact that the Church has always admitted that partial councils would in certain cases be able to express the *mens ecclesiae* in definitive fashion. This should be the case, up to a point, for all councils convoked by the Pope and confirmed by him, provided a considerable episcopal representation had been assembled.
>
> It is no less true that their decisions, even those that could be considered infallible and therefore irreformable, by reason of the fact that they were made in the absence of a considerable portion of the episcopate that might have represented a most venerable theological tradition, could still call for further complement any clarifications, which would not have been necessary in the case of an ecumenical council in the most ancient and truly full sense of the word.

One could also consult, somewhat in the same sense and on a related subject, B. de Margerie, S.J., "Dogmatic Development by Abridgement or by Concentration: Immaculate Conception and Assumption," *Marian Studies* 27 (1976) 64-98.

---

[133]*Ibid.* Which should not hinder Christians from being able to say with H. P. van Dusen: "I believe in the Holy Spirit and in Jesus Christ and in God the Father" (*Spirit, Son and Father*. London, 1960, p. 5). Cf. 2 Cor. 13:13; and the text of St. Irenaeus, cited on pp. 69-70.

V
Trinity, Ecumenism, Catholic Church

The Council of Florence almost[1] terminates the essential core of the Catholic Church's effort of Trinitarian dogmatization. This is not to say that the history of Trinitarian theology is at an end. And this not only because dogma and theology are two distinct approaches to the same mystery, but also because the rupture of Christianity in the sixteenth century led in different ways to a revival of the great Trinitarian quarrels of the first centuries. The ecumenical dialogue in our own twentieth century cannot but include a Trinitarian dialogue.

Since we are studying the Trinity in history, it is appropriate to consider rapidly some aspects of the Trinitarian theology of Luther, of Pentecostal pneumatology, the views of Barth and Rahner on Trinitarian language (persons or modes?) and finally the profession of faith of the World Council of Churches with regard to the Trinitarian mystery. We will thus be in a better position to grasp, in the following chapter, the Trinitarian doctrine of Vatican II, of the Dutch catechism and of Paul VI and to guess at some of the orientations of future Trinitarian theology.

In line with our particular objective here, one we explained in our Introduction, we will give special consideration to the person and the mission of the Holy Spirit in reviewing this inter-confessional and post-Florentine history of Trinitarian theology.

I. LUTHER: THE HOLY SPIRIT MEDIATOR OF THE REAL PRESENCE OF CHRIST IN FAITH

In order to understand some of the excesses of Luther's Trinitarian theology, we must first of all not neglect to consider the orientations that preceded it: those belonging to a sector of medieval theology which, particularly among Scotists, seemed to wish to deduce the persons from the divine essence. We have already had occasion to allude to the Greek patristic roots of such an error;[2] even if Duns Scotus did not really espouse this error, still he carried the consequences of his essentialist tendencies far enough to affirm the following paradox: "God, who freely manifests his essence to the

---

[1] We say "almost" because of the "Credo of the People of God," pronounced by Paul VI, June 30, 1968: see our ch. VI.
[2] Cf. our ch. III, § III. 4, note 52.

blessed, could stop right there their vision and love or he could stop it at a single Person with the Essence that it encompasses, without having them see and love another; for beatitude is defined by the infinity of the divine nature which is as it were its first object, while the persons are as it were a secondary object."[3]

Such an essentialist extreme, although counter-balanced in Blessed Duns Scotus by other, more balanced, formulas with regard to the Persons as object of beatitude,[4] explains in part Luther's reaction: a total denial of the "distinction between person and nature in God" seen as amounting to a "useless and frivolous philosophical invention."[5] In judging that this distinction[6] between the *esse ad se* of the nature and the *esse ad alium* of the Persons was "strictly speaking unthinkable," was Luther aware that he was imperiling the real distinction of the Persons among themselves, all three of whom are really identical with the one divine nature?[7] It certainly seems that he was not. Yet this was the logical and unavoidable consequence of his position, the refusal to speak of God sometimes as Essence, sometimes as Person. In the last analysis such a refusal implies a denial of a Trinity of really distinct Persons.

Paul Vignaux thus sums up Luther's thought: for him the Trinity is "a pure datum, in which our mind cannot discern any elements which it can later regroup while explaining some by others.... One should not speak of God sometimes as Essence, sometimes as Person. In naming him we name the essential unity of the Three Persons."[8] In other words, we can say that Luther prefers synthesis to distinctions, and a synthesis without distinction. But how can one elaborate a theology of the Trinity while in contempt of distinctions? Is not one thereby led logically to confuse the Persons?

As Vignaux again underscores,[9] Luther further rejects the metaphysical theories of the Trinity which posit in God the Aristotelian distinction of modes of production according to nature and according to will, in order to distinguish the two processions of the Son and the Spirit. "As early as

---

[3]D. Scotus, *Ox.* I, d. V, q. II, n. 6; cf. Vignaux, *Luther commentateur des Sentences.* Paris, 1935, p. 21, note 2.

[4]*Ibid.*, p. 23: "de facto erit una fruitio et una visio essentiae in tribus personis; de facto fruitio habitualis ordinata necessario simul est trium personarum, licet aliquando non actualis"; "personae terminant actum amandi ut quae amantur; persona in ratione sui includit essentiam; essentia est ratio formaliter terminandi actum amandi ut propter quam" (D. Scotus, *Ox.*, Prol., Q. IV, no. 32).

[5]"Distinctio nominis Deus personaliter et essentialiter est frivola et inutilis philosophiae confictio": Luther, W. IX, 31, 31ff. (I St. dist. II); cf. Vignaux, *op. cit.*, p. 25.

[6]*Ibid.*

[7]Cf. our ch. III, on Lateran IV (§III).

[8]Vignaux, *op. cit.*, p. 24.

[9]*Ibid.*, p. 27.

1511,"[10] Luther was sure that "we cannot truly distinguish the Persons"[11] Vignaux notes. Our thought remains outside the Trinity, its interior distinctions escape it.[12] Luther however does not reject a psychological theory of the soul as image of the Trinity: our resemblance to God constitutes a datum of faith. He even interprets the Trinity in dynamic terms.[13] In a sermon in 1514 he describes an eternal motion in God which does not change the nature of God; the Father is mobile being (*res mobilis*), the Son the movement of the being (*motus rei*), the Spirit its repose (*quies motus*).

It is not these considerations, however, on the intimate life of the Trinity that most captivate Luther or the interest of his reader: it is rather his vision of the mission of the Spirit. This is indeed a very paradoxical point: Luther has no doctrine on the procession of the Spirit, he rejects that offered him by the western tradition, and yet he gives us some very suggestive insights regarding the mission which is the prolongation of this eternal procession.

To the degree that we can trust the brilliant analysis of Lutheran pneumatology presented by the Danish Lutheran theologian, R. Prenter,[14] it seems that for Luther there is no real presence of Christ except in and through the work of the Spirit. The Holy Spirit is a real and divine sphere of revelation in which the risen Christ alone is present as redemptive reality. Outside of this sphere, Christ is no more than an idea. Luther knows no other Spirit than the Spirit of Christ. The Lutheran confession of the divinity of the Spirit is inseparable from a realistic understanding of the Christocentric work of the Spirit: the experience of his consoling and interceding action (cf. Rom. 8:26) which gains life for us in the death and darkness of our interior conflict by the inexpressible groanings of his intercession and which renders the living Christ so present that the activity of faith and of love flows directly from his presence, leaves room for no other view of the nature of the Spirit.

Luther often explains Romans 8:26 in the light of Zechariah 12:10: "But over the house of David and over the inhabitants of Jerusalem I will pour

---

[10]As early as 1511, therefore when Luther was still a Catholic. A refusal to distinguish the persons: is this not already fundamentally heterodox? Even if it is true, as the many allusions of Luther to the excessive distinctions of D. Scotus would lead us to believe, that this refusal is a reaction against the theology of the Subtle Doctor.

[11]Vignaux, *op. cit.*, p. 29, where the author cites a later text of Luther, dating from 1543-1544: "Audio unam essentiam et tres personae esse, Wie es zugehe, nescio, credam." The text is extracted from the works of Luther, W. XXXIX, 364A, 8-10. Luther goes back to a pre-Augustinian and even pre-Cappadocian theology of the Trinity.

[12]Vignaux, *ibid.*

[13]Luther, sermon of Christmas 1514, W. I, 20, 1ff.; cf. R. Prenter, *Spiritus Creator*. Philadelphia, 1953, p. 174.

[14]The work, indicated in the preceding note, was published at Copenhagen in 1946.

out a spirit of kindness and prayer. They will look on the One they have pierced." It is the Spirit of grace (*Spiritus gratiae*) that accompanies the word of the one who preaches on the grace and mercy of Christ the Redeemer, which wrests the hearers out of sin and death. But in order that this grace mediated by the Spirit of grace should be preserved against all the attacks of the demon, the Spirit of prayer (*Spiritus precum*) must come to intercede in us with unspeakable groanings (cf. Rom. 8:26) when we are in the darkness of interior conflicts. The Spirit of prayer draws us to Christ in faith, the Spirit of grace places us in the reality of Christ as his instruments in the works of love. The Spirit's means of action are the word and the sacraments of Christ.[15]

Although these views are in fact bound up with the specifically Lutheran doctrine of justification, they can be rightly separated from it. In the main they appear to us correct and indeed profound. They allow us a deeper view of the mission of the Spirit by making us more aware that we should understand the discourse at the Supper (the Spirit as witness and glorifier of Christ) in connection with Romans 8 (where the Spirit glorifies Christ in the Christian's experience of spiritual combat against the devil and against the flesh, a combat that should culminate in prayer).

Assuredly there are many other things that might be said about the Trinitarian theology of Luther. We are here content to stress what to us appears to be most original, whether in a negative or positive vein. It is evident that the rejection of all Trinitarian metaphysics, so consistent with the whole of Lutheranism, makes unavailable to it, in large part if not entirely, the benefit of twelve centuries of doctrinal progress made under the guidance of the Holy Spirit, and also endangers, objectively speaking, the benefit of this remarkably Christocentric presentation of the mission of this same Spirit. But it is nevertheless true that this latter represents an advance whose patristic and medieval antecedents deserve investigation. In emphasizing with Luther the truths he has preserved we testify to our union with the Lutherans in our confession of the Holy Trinity and in a willingness to let ourselves be invaded by the Christocentric action of the Spirit.

We should remember also that Vatican II moves partially in the same direction as Luther in stressing that the risen Christ acts in the hearts of men by the power of his Spirit (*GS* 38. 1) and that the Eucharistic flesh of Christ is vivified by his Spirit through whom he unceasingly exercises his sacerdotal function in our behalf (*PO* 5).

---

[15]Prenter, *op. cit.*, pp. 61, 89-90 (W. XLVI, 166, 10; 165, 2); 95; 190; 197; 245. The English translation has very much reduced the notes and source references of the original Danish; we must therefore simply take the author's word for many of his evaluations. He explains himself regarding this point in his preface dated December 18, 1952.

Let us cite in closing, the Lutheran commentary on the "Glory be to the Father, and to the Son and to the Holy Spirit," where, in the midst of a number of things that St. John of the Cross would have countersigned without difficulty, we note the specifically Lutheran emphasis:

> Let him who chants "Glory to the Father," offer at the same time his very vain glory, confessing his weakness and impotence; let him desire no strength and power save that which resides in God the Father.
>
> When he chants "Glory to the Son," let him abominate his own wisdom and offer his decision to immolate these beasts by confessing his madness and foolishness; let him not desire to be regarded as wise and prudent either in his own eyes or in those of men, except in God the Son.
>
> When he chants "Glory to the Holy Spirit," let him lay aside all confidence in his own justice and his own goodness after confessing his sins; let him desire of God the Holy Spirit to become just and good but only after putting to death the bestial opinion of his own justice. Thus it will come about that in abandoning all to God we leave nothing to ourselves but confusion and confession of our evils, our nothingness and our miseries. Thus are we justified, by rendering to everyone what belongs to him.[16]

It would certainly be very interesting to compare this commentary on the *Gloria Patri* with those of Basil and Fulgentius! We see little, if any at all, among the Fathers (Augustine excepted), of the dramatic dialectical tension here in evidence. In spite of the errors about the "bestial opinion of one's own justice" and about "the very vain glory" offered to God, it seems to us that Luther's text marks an advance indebted to the entire spiritual tradition of the Middle Ages, itself rooted in sentiments already so strongly cultivated in the patristic age: i.e., compunction, *penthos*.[17]

At the properly Trinitarian level however, the Lutheran commentary, while glorifying the divine Persons, does little to deepen a grasp of their interior relations. It is situated on an individual rather than on a collective level. We have here a Lutheran tendency which the history of Protestantism in some of its sectors will accentuate still further. But we cannot deny

---

[16]Luther, W. (1892) V, 198, 31ff.; IV, 206, 26ff. These texts, which date from 1513-1515, are cited by Prenter, p. 178; they are still of Luther's Catholic period. Prenter does not cite in his bibliography and does not seem to be aware of the remarkable analysis of Vignaux; thus he has failed to grasp the difference between the Lutheran theology of the Trinity and the patristic theology on the capital point of the distinction between nature and person. He believes that Luther here is carrying on the traditional line of thought.

[17]See Isidore of Seville, *Sententiae*, II, 12; ML 83, 613; Fulgentius, *Epist.* 4 ad Probam, ML 65, 339-344; Puyol, *Doctrine du livre de l'Imitation de Jésus-Christ*. Paris, 1898, p. 489; I. Hausherr, S.J., *Penthos*. Rome, 1944, pp. 209ff.

that for Luther the Church is the people of God created by the Holy Spirit.[18] There is then a centrality of the Holy Spirit in the Lutheran ecclesiology, which we are now going to see is still accentuated by the "Pentecostals."

II. PROTESTANT AND CATHOLIC PENTECOSTALISM AND THE MYSTERY OF PENTECOST

The prodigious success of the Pentecostal movement in certain countries of Latin America, such as Brazil where 73% of the Protestants are Pentecostals,[19] invites us to consider attentively the relation between Holy Spirit and Church as well as the substantial permanence and the significance of the charism of glossolalia.

The Pentecostal churches are communities built around the Holy Spirit. In their assemblies, the central position of the Holy Spirit is expressed in terms of structural liberty,[20] of power to convert and heal, and of personal sanctification. In the Pauline list of charisms (1 Cor. 12-14), they stress the gift of tongues and that of healing.

We are presently witnessing, particularly in the United States, the blossoming of a Pentecostal movement within the Catholic Church. The same charisms are here cultivated, as well as a prolonged and collective style of prayer.

For many non-Catholic Pentecostals the great sign of the baptism of the Holy Spirit is the gift of tongues, an ecstatic language from which expressions of praise, joy and thanksgiving burst forth.[21]

This leads us to say a few words about the meaning of the miracle of Pentecost, considered in the context of the four other pentecosts reported in the Book of Acts (2:2-4; 4:31; 8:14-17; 10:44-48; 19:5-6) and situated respectively at Jerusalem, Samaria, Caesarea and Ephesus.[22]

The miracle, according to many exegetes,[23] has a double signification: on the one hand it signifies the universal unity of the Church which "speaks all tongues, comprehends and embraces all tongues in its charity and thus triumphs over the dispersion of Babel" (*AG* 4); on the other hand it signifies

---

[18]Luther, W. A. XXX, I, 190, 4; Prenter, *op. cit.*, p. 242; on the meaning of these texts of Luther, see J.-L. Witte, S.J., "Le Saint-Esprit dans les églises séparées," *DSAM*, IV, 2 (1960), 1321-1323.

[19]See the collective volume *O Espirito Santo e o Movimento Pentecostal*, published in 1966 at Sao Paulo by the "Associação de seminários teológicos evangélicos" of Brazil.

[20]These churches are local churches, enjoying a triple autonomy, in financial matters, in government and in propagation of the faith.

[21]Cf. K. McDonnell, O.S.B., "The Ideology of Pentecostal Conversion," *Journal of Ecumenical Studies* 5 (1968), 110. See also, by the same author, an article in *America*, 118 (1968), 402-406.

[22]Cf. R. Spitz, O.P., *Et l'Esprit vint en eux*. Paris, 1968, pp. 82-85.

[23]Felten, Sickenberger, Jacquier, Allo, Médebielle, Renié, Lyonnet are among the Catholic exegetes who uphold the identification of the gift of tongues manifested on the day of Pentecost with the Corinthian glossolalia: see on this subject J. Leal, S.J., *N.T.*, v. II. Madrid, 1962, p. 30, ed. B.A.C.

an ecstatic and mystical prayer of divine praise, a "spiritual intoxication which makes the soul burst forth in a delirium of love, in songs, cries, tears and trances as used to happen to St. Mary Magdalen de Pazzi."[24]

For this exegetical current the Pentecost accounts of Acts should then be interpreted in the light of 1 Corinthians 14 where mention is made of "speaking in tongues."

But Dom J. Dupont, though initially favorable to this view, now thinks that this attractive interpretation is not really faithful to the sacred text which says that on the day of Pentecost: "all were filled with the Holy Spirit and began to speak in other tongues, as the Spirit gave them utterance" (Acts 2:4). According to him:

> If some aspects of it recall the gift of tongues (he means: the ecstatic prayer of praise in unintelligible tongues), we can attribute this to the fact that the author pictures the event of Pentecost to himself in terms of manifestations of the Spirit which are better known to him. The analogy with the gift of tongues however remains accessory, and it is more the difference than the resemblance that comes to the fore: the apostles spoke not in "tongues," but "in other tongues," in foreign tongues.[25]

The miracle's exclusive purpose is then to signify the universality of the Church and of its mission; it is unique and it is not accompanied by praise of God incomprehensible to the audience, (in contrast to what is described in 1 Cor. 14). Instead, the people say to one another: "we hear them telling in our own tongues the mighty works of God" (Acts 2:11).

Nevertheless the pentecosts of Caesarea and Ephesus (Acts 10:44-46; 19:6) are characterized by "speaking in tongues" in order to "magnify God" and by a "prophetic" speaking. "The irruption of the Spirit expresses itself here not only by the use of incomprehensible tongues, but also by inspired and perfectly intelligible speech belonging to the gift of prophecy."[26] While one who speaks and prays in tongues, to return to Pauline expressions, does not himself understand what he is saying, nor is he understood by others, unless he prays to have the gift of interpretation and obtains it (1 Cor. 14:2-5, 13, 28). In this way speaking in tongues is transformed into prophecy, to use the Pauline antithesis (v. 5).

Did not the day of Pentecost precisely see the transition from "speaking in tongues" to prophecy? and in the course of that very day? It is toward

---

[24]St. Alphonsus de Liguori, *Homo Apostolicus*, Appendix, I, 15. Cited by S. Lyonnet, S.J., "De glossolalia Pentecostes ejusque significatione," *Verbum Domini*, 24 (1944), 68.

[25]Dom J. Dupont, O.S.B., *Etudes sur les Actes des Apôtres*. Paris, 1967, 490-496; see the passage cited here, p. 496; cf. pp. 87-89; the same author had previously taken a different position in *Gnosis*. Paris, 1949, 204-210, where he shows in an interesting manner how the gift of tongues prolongs the descriptions of the Old Testament.

[26]Cf. Dupont, *Etudes*, p. 394.

this view that a number of Catholic exegetes are urging us when they stress the fundamental identity (despite some accidental differences) of the Corinthian glossolalia and the Jerusalem xenoglossy: thus, e.g., Le Camus:

> The identity of the gift becomes evident if one compares the identity of the expressions used to designate it. In the epistle to the Corinthians, Paul several times characterizes this phenomenon by the words "speaking in tongues" (1 Cor. 14:5, 6, 13, 23, 39). But the same formula is found not only in Acts 19:6 to express the charism conferred by the Holy Spirit on the disciples of Ephesus, but again in Acts 10:46 with regard to the converts of Caesarea. Yet Peter declares that what happened to Cornelius was an exact replica of what had happened at Pentecost (Acts 11:15). And in fact the phenomenon of Pentecost is determined by the same expressions: to speak in tongues (Acts 2:4).

And Le Camus adds a reflection that responds on point to Dom Dupont's objection: "We should not give too much weight to the presence of the word *heterais* by way of creating a difference, for this is also found in 1 Corinthians 14:21 and in 1 Corinthians 12:28; 14:5, 10, as to their sense."[27] In holding to the thesis of the substantial identity of the Corinthian events and those of Pentecost, we should not fail to stress a difference that is purely accidental: at Jerusalem, "Each one heard them speaking in his own tongue" (Acts 2:6), i.e., the 120 who "began to speak in other tongues, as the Spirit gave them utterance" (Acts 2:4), while at Corinth the New Testament does not explicitly specify that those who spoke in tongues were understood, although it does not exclude this.

What then is positively signified by the charism of "diversities of tongues" (1 Cor. 12:28) and that of "interpretation of tongues," charisms associated with the mysterious effusion of the Spirit of Christ?

Prat has given us a good resume:

> Glossolalia must be an articulated language; it must be intelligible, since it is a prayer, a psalm, a benediction, a thanksgiving (1 Cor. 14:16); it must have a coherent meaning since it expresses concepts (1 Cor. 14:19, cf. 14:9) and is susceptible to interpretation (1 Cor. 14:28, etc.); finally, it

---

[27]Mgr. Le Camus, *L'oeuvre des apôtres*. Paris, 1905, v. I, p. 20, note 1. P.-A. Lemonnyer, O.P., makes the thesis his own with a precise analysis of the difference between the glossolalia of Corinth and that of Jerusalem: "The principal difference lies in the fact that at Pentecost the hearers who ran up were Jews originally from the Diaspora but settled in the neighborhood, and these happened to know the strange languages that the 120 spoke, while in the case of Corinthian glossolalia we are dealing with pagans whose language was Greek like that of the Christians. A fact assuredly willed by God, but in itself and with regard to the nature of the charism, it remained accidental" (*DBS* I, 1928, col. 1240 art. "charismes"). But were there no strangers at Corinth?

must be a language comparable to barbarian languages (1 Cor. 14:21) and to the means that men and angels use to communicate their thoughts (1 Cor. 13:1).[28]

Still more precisely we can say with B. G. Haanappel:[29]

> The charism of glossolalia which we encounter in 1 Corinthians 14 can be thus defined: the gift of tongues consists in speaking in rational sequence languages never learned, in a state of ecstatic prayer. It does not consist in a mumbling of sounds: it is difficult to see why a supernatural operation of the Holy Spirit would be necessary to produce sounds that are inarticulate and without meaning "for the edification of the Church" (1 Cor. 14:5). We are dealing with logically connected expressions: "to pray, to sing a hymn, to bless, to give thanks" (1 Cor. 14:14-18) all are expressions that denote a free, unimpeded and complete use of a strange language as if it were one's own. In a state of ecstatic prayer: "my spirit prays, but my mind is unfruitful" (1 Cor. 14:14): the higher part of the soul, illumined by the Holy Spirit himself, rests in God while the natural intelligence does not understand the meaning of the words.
>
> The object of glossolalia is then not the preaching of the Gospel or the explanation of Christian truths; in no passage of the New Testament do we see a charismatic speaking in a strange language to men. On the contrary, the object of the charism is always prayer to God, praise of God (1 Cor. 14:2).

In short, we are not dealing with a miracle of hearing nor with a permanent gift of speaking in strange languages given to the Apostles for preaching the Gospel,[30] but rather with a "liturgy of the Holy Spirit" complementing the breaking of bread or "liturgy of Christ"[31] in the quiet evening gatherings and "suppers" at which the first Christians came together to commemorate the paschal mystery (cf. 1 Cor. 11).

---

[28]F. Prat, S.J., *Théologie de saint Paul*. Paris, 1920, v. I, p. 502. See in the same sense A. Lemonnyer: "Our charism is related to languages that were really spoken and thus intelligible in themselves, as 1 Cor. 14:11 confirms. But the speaker in tongues could himself have been ignorant of the meaning of the words he pronounced. In order to comprehend it he would have needed another gift, that of interpretation, of which some other person could also have been the beneficiary," cf. note 25, *op. cit., ibid.*

[29]B. G. Haanappel, C.SS.R., "A glossolalia no N.T.," *Revista Eclesiástica Brasileira*, 5 (1945), 54-58. This very well formulated definition may be compared to that of F. Prat: "a supernatural power of praying or praising God in a strange language with an enthusiasm bordering on exaltation" (*op. cit.,* v. I, p. 153). Haanappel speaks of "languages never learned," still unknown to the charismatic but already really existing.

[30]As St. Thomas Aquinas thinks, *Summa Theologica*, II, II, 176:1.

[31]Duchesne, *Histoire ancienne de l'Eglise*. Paris, 1907, v. I, p. 47: "the specifically Christian elements of this primitive cult were the Eucharist and the charisms, or extraordinary effusion

It remains for us to determine the function of this charism of the Holy Spirit in the economy of salvation both with regard to infidels and to the faithful (cf. 1 Cor. 14:22-25). With regard to the former, both Jews and Gentiles, and partly to catechumens, this charism is a sign whose purpose is, at least indirectly, to attract their attention and to arouse their admiring curiosity, a gift marvelously adapted to disposing non-believers to listen to the preaching of the Faith. With regard to the already baptized faithful, the gift of tongues is for them a sign that manifests the presence of the Spirit in the Church, a unifying presence which aims at undoing the confusion of tongues of Babel (Babylon). In both cases the charism is a manifestation of the Spirit given, in the last analysis, for the utility of the whole Body of Christ and for its "building up" by the addition of new members (cf. 1 Cor. 12:7; 12:20; Rm. 12:4-8; Eph. 4:12).[32]

Thus we could say that this charism would already have significance even

---

of the Spirit." An observation which admirably sums up 1 Cor. 10-14. Mgr. Duchesne's observation further draws our attention to an important fact: the effusion of the charisms of the Spirit took place in a special way, in the church of Corinth, during the celebration of the Eucharistic mystery. Glossolalia, a charism linked with baptism at Jerusalem, Caesarea and Ephesus, i.e., in the book of Acts (2:4ff.; 10:44-48; 19:5-6) appears for Paul to be bound up rather with the renewal of the mystery of the Last Supper. It is enough to note in this respect the identity of vocabulary of chs. 11 and 14 of 1 Cor.: in both chapters everything transpires in the assembly of the church (11:18, 22, 33; 14:4, 12, 19, 23, 28). All of this has a profound theological meaning: baptism is ordered to the Eucharist in which one drinks of the Spirit (1 Cor. 12:13) who prays in the one who communicates of the body of Christ with unspeakable groanings (Rom. 8:26), i.e., prayers in tongues, and who then inspires this communicant, out of charity for the other members of this Body, to ask for the gift of interpretation (1 Cor. 14:13). It is in the Eucharistic celebration that the Spirit makes us say: "Jesus is Lord" (1 Cor. 12:3). Through glossolalia and the charism of interpretation, the Spirit glorifies the Son and the Father, in the course of renewing the sacrifice of the Son to the glory of the Father. Speaking in tongues takes on the character of Eucharistic thanksgiving in a church where the faithful do not remain silent but all sing, teach, speak in tongues, interpret, reveal and prophesy, in order that everyone may be instructed and encouraged (1 Cor. 14:6, 26, 31). The Spirit breathes. He animates a living liturgy in which all participate actively. Notably all participate in the proclamation of the word. In 1 Cor. 14 we find a precious source of inspiration for the renewal of liturgical life.

[32]Cf. Haanappel, *art. cit.* At first sight it might seem that 1 Cor. 14:21-23 purely and simply contradicts this interpretation of an evangelizing finality of the charism of glossolalia. For its concrete effect can be, like that of the parables, to make one blind (cf. Mk. 4:11-12). Nonetheless it seems to us that, according to Paul, in the divine plan this charism is ordered to evangelization: the glossolalist, if he interprets his speaking in tongues, surpasses in utility the non-glossolalist prophet (1 Cor. 14:5). Paul desires all to speak in tongues and to prophesy (*ibid.*). Thus he recognizes that this charism can contribute at least in an indirect way to the conversion of infidels, thanks to the mediation of the charism of interpretation complemented by that of prophecy. See on this subject L. Fonck, S.J., *Quaestiones Paulinae*. Rome, 1910, § 59, p. 79. (The same author, we may remark in passing, affirms that the patristic tradition favors the identification of the charism of glossolalia of Jerusalem with that of Corinth; cf. *ibid.*, §61-62.

if it were not accompanied by its normal complementary charism of interpretation of tongues (1 Cor. 12:10, 30; 14 *passim*) and especially of prophecy. If the one who speaks in tongues speaks to God, this is meant, in God's design, to attract the attention of infidels so that they will later give their attention to the equally charismatic translator of this speech in foreign tongues and especially to the one who as prophet would exhort, console and edify them by announcing to them the message of salvation: "on the other hand, he who prophesies speaks to men" (1 Cor. 14:3). The interpreter translates the prayer made to God which the prophet then presents to men, with all the kerygmatic presuppositions that accompany this function.

Thus, especially on the day of Pentecost, it appeared that the "speakers in tongues"—120 of them that day—and the prophets—namely Peter—had complementary and successive missions. We are left with the impression that God first of all wishes to manifest his action through the ecstatic prayer which is addressed to him and which suggests to men the transcendence of his mystery, and afterwards to explain it through one of the ecstatic prayers. "One who speaks in a tongue speaks not to men but to God" (could we not say: in order to praise the marvels of God in the work of salvation of the world?), and "no one understands him, but he utters mysteries in the Spirit" (1 Cor. 14:2). These mysterious things, the great mystery of the unity of humanity in Christ brought about by the indivisible Trinity, are then explained by the interpreter and by the prophet: "On the other hand, he who prophesies speaks to men" (1 Cor. 14:3).

Through the glossolalists, the interpreters and the prophets, it is the same Spirit of Christ who glorifies the Christ who sends him. The Spirit speaks, interprets his word and explains it by prophesying. One and the same Spirit, through diverse instruments, speaks, interprets, prophesies, apportioning to each one individually as he wills (1 Cor. 12:10-11).

Just as we must distinguish this "authentic glossolalia inspired by the Holy Spirit, intelligible in itself, and whose use the Apostle regulates (in 1 Cor. 14) from a condemned pseudo-glossolalia which is not without analogy to the 'sacred frenzies' of ancient cults,"[33] we must also recognize in the

---

[33] C. Spicq, O.P., *Sainte Bible Pirot-Clamer*, v. XI, 2. Paris, 1948, p. 275 (commentary on 1 Cor. 14). Paul alludes to these "sacred frenzies" of the pagan cults in 1 Cor. 12:2. But in spite of certain appearances and some commentators, his appreciation of the charism of glossolalia remains fundamentally positive since it forms part of the "manifestations of the Spirit given in view of the common good" (cf. 1 Cor. 12:7). And this explains the duty of the glossolalist to pray for the gift of interpretation without which the ordering of glossolalia to the common good would be less clear. What is more, Paul's positive attitude is intimately bound up with his personal experience as a glossolalist (1 Cor. 14:8) who had himself obtained for the Christians of Ephesus (Acts 19:6) the charism of glossolalia not long before he commented on it in his letter to the Corinthians. Cf. R. Spitz, *Et l'Esprit vint en eux*. Paris, 1968, pp. 97-101, where the author shows the influence on Paul's thought of the Ephesus Pentecost of which he personally was a witness.

history of the Church the substantial permanence of this charism of glossolalia and of the two other charisms that accompany it: interpretation and prophecy.

Under what form does authentic glossolalia appear today and under what form has it appeared in the history of the Church? We think that the mystics to whom we already alluded and in a lesser degree all contemplatives, but especially those of the contemplative orders, do constitute, when they speak to God of the marvels of his grace in the Church and in the world, a permanent sign of the Holy Spirit offered to non-believers. Of them we can also say: "they speak not to men, but to God, and no one understands them... their spirit is in prayer, even though their mind draws no fruit from it" (1 Cor. 14:2, 14); their simple existence attracts attention and induces people to listen to the prophetic preaching of this Church which organizes contemplative life, the modern way of regulating the gift of tongues!

Just as at Corinth St. Paul long ago had to urge people to distinguish authentic and false glossolalias, so today and always the Church must discern authentic contemplative prayer, which is a service both of humanity and of God, from its counterfeits which are simply so many ways of escaping from the exigences of exercising the prophetic ministry of the new Covenant.

It is clear that in St. Paul's view, the glossolalia with which he himself was endowed (and even more than all the Corinthians, 1 Cor. 14:18) and which he desired for all his readers, is a charism inferior to that of prophecy which he even more earnestly desires for them (1 Cor. 14:5). St. Thomas Aquinas explains very well the reasons for this inferiority: the words which the glossolalist puts forth are mere signs of intelligible truth, like the phantasms of the imagination. That is why Augustine compares the gift of tongues to the vision of the imagination. The gift of prophecy, on the contrary, consists in the very illumination of the created mind by the Holy Spirit, in order that this created mind may become fit for understanding intelligible truth. Furthermore, the gift of prophecy is ordered to the knowledge of realities themselves, while the gift of tongues only produces a knowledge of words.[34]

In this connection it must be said that all the contemplatives who speak to God of the marvels of his grace, also enjoy the gift of prophecy in order to understand intellectually the praise that is offered; nevertheless, in their passive and infused prayer, their incapacity to translate in human terms their intimate experience of God (as was the case with Paul and the inef-

---

[34]Cf. St. Thomas Aquinas, *Summa Theologica*, II, II, 176.2; transl. by Spicq, *op. cit.*, p. 268. This text of St. Thomas does not take account of the mystical supra-rational aspect of ecstatic prayer inseparable from the gift of glossolalia.

fable words he heard in paradise: 2 Cor. 12:1-4; compare also with 1 Cor. 14:14), likens these contemplatives to glossolalists.

This, it seems, is the most permanent prolongation of the charism of glossolalia in the history of the Church, but it does not rule out transitory manifestations more immediately similar to the glossolalia of Corinth, Caesarea, Ephesus, Samaria and Jerusalem. We can reckon among these manifestations the ecstatic prayer and the prayer in tongues of certain non-Catholic Pentecostals. If these are validly baptized, they are in a "certain communion, albeit imperfect, with the Catholic Church" (UR 3). Their community constitutes a particular means of salvation not without connection with the general means which is the Catholic Church. The Spirit of Christ does not refuse to avail himself of this particular means of salvation whose strength derives from the plenitude of grace and truth entrusted to the Catholic Church (Ibid.).

One can and ought to say that in its permanent aspect the charism of glossolalia is one "of those elements or goods by which the whole Church is built up and vivified and which can and in fact do exist outside the visible limits of the Catholic Church"; which holds also for certain "visible elements" as Vatican II expressly brings out (UR 3). Must it not be said then that the charism of glossolalia evident in Pentecostal gatherings "comes from Christ, leads to him, pertains by right to the one Church of Christ" (Ibid.)?

We are then rightly inclined to see in these manifestations an element of the Church and a witness that the Spirit of Christ renders to himself. They retain their value of objectively orientating their audiences toward the one Church of Christ even though some use them abusively against her. In their own way they prolong the effect of the charisms of glossolalia, which could also exist in the same form within the Catholic Church among Catholic Pentecostals, or of those that exist effectively under the form of contemplative or ecstatic prayer of certain mystics or under more attenuated forms. As we mentioned earlier, we think that contemplative life in general should be ranked among the outstanding manifestations of these attenuated forms.

In this case, as in that of non-Catholic Pentecostals, the common point is that discourse addressed to God becomes the sign of a discourse God wants the world to hear. In speaking to God and in receiving from the Spirit this language addressed to the Father through the Son (cf. Acts 2:4: they were all filled with the Holy Spirit and began to speak in other tongues, as the Spirit gave them utterance), the prayers broadcast the fact that God does not cease to speak to the world. Far from being a dead God, he is a living God. If, despite the Pentecostals, the gift of speaking in foreign tongues is not the greatest sign of baptism in and by the Spirit, are they not right in thinking that contemplative ecstasy is the fruit of the presence of the Spirit given at baptism for one who places no obstacle to it? Would St. Bonaventure have expressed it otherwise?[35]

However this may be, and in spite of the reserves that are necessary in view of some orientations or manifestations of Pentecostalism,[36] it is clear that reflection on the mission of the Spirit "who speaks through the prophets" and through the whole prophetic people of the New Testament (Jl. 3:1-2; Nm.11:29; Acts 2:4; 1 Cor. 14:5), has everything to gain from ecumenical dialogue set up, if possible, between these Pentecostals and other Christians.

Could not the sacrament of Confirmation be seen as a permanent prolongation of the charism of interpretation of tongues revealed at Corinth? The Holy Spirit gives himself at Baptism in order to lead to ecstatic prayer and in Confirmation to help the Christian defend and propagate, and therefore translate the truths of faith perceived in the contemplative life. Likewise, it pertains to the charism proper to the sacrament of the anointing of the sick to effect periodically the healing of bodily ills, another preoccupation of the Pentecostals.

Though we intend to return to the charisms of the Spirit in our next chapter (apropos of Vatican II) we can now assert that dialogue with the Pentecostals would help us better reflect on the visible and invisible mission of the Paraclete. Does not one of the aspects of this mission consist in making us speak of the Father and of the Son? In stressing that the Spirit continues to make his prophets speak, the Pentecostals invite us to consider more closely how the Spirit wishes his prophets to speak of the Trinity in our times.

III. THE PROBLEM OF TRINITARIAN LANGUAGE IN THE MODERN AGE

Barth and Rahner draw our attention to the catechetical and kerygmatic consequences of the notion of personality current in our times. For many today, they think, "person" means essentially "self-consciousness."[37] Whatever possible efforts there may be to explain "person" in a less psychological and more ontological sense, these theologians think their impact will inevitably be limited and they will not prevent a tritheist understanding of

---

[35]Cf. E. Longpré, O.F.M., *DSAM*, v. I, 1936, col. 1828-1842: art. "Bonaventure." St. Bonaventure stresses the impossibility of explaining ecstatic prayer to others.

[36]Cf. F. Lepargneur, O.P., *op. cit.*, p. 54; Cardinal Agnelo Rossi, *Rev. Eclesiástica Brasileira*, 12 (1952), 767-792, notably p. 777 where the author stresses that in the view of Pentecostals the gift of tongues necessarily accompanies Baptism, which seems to contradict 1 Cor. 12:10, 30.

[37]Cf. A. Michel, *DTC* XV, 2 (1950), 1793: "Günther holds that all created beings are diverse manifestations of one and the same substance, nature. Unconscious in inferior beings, nature becomes conscious in man. This consciousness of self is for man the very principle of his personality. This definition of personality is directly descended from Descartes."

the Trinitarian mystery: for many, "three persons in God" will necessarily signify not three subjects reciprocally conscious by means of one divine consciousness,[38] but three consciousnesses. Why not then replace the word "person" by another word to designate the Three? And may we not add, these theologians observe, that the meaning of words and of the common language does not depend on the Church and on its Magisterium?

1. *Karl Barth (Dogmatik, 1932): let us not speak of Persons, but of Three Modes of the divine Being*

Hegel speaks of Person[39] but Schleiermacher prefers to avoid the word. Günther,[40] who is also cited by Barth, wanted to apply the modern concept of personality to the Three: person is self-consciousness; we have here the opposite solution. For Barth in 1932: "Roman Catholic theology still speaks of Persons in Trinitarian theology as if the modern concept of personality did not exist, as if the definition of Boethius ('individual substance of a rational nature') were still current and comprehensible by all: as if the meaning of this definition had been made so clear in the Middle Ages that thanks to it one could fruitfully speak of the Three Trinitarian persons (von den trinitarischen Drei)."[41]

Barth then proposes the elimination, pure and simple, of the concept of person in Trinitarian discussion and its replacement with the expression "modes of existence" that was already employed by the Cappadocian Fathers[42] and later approved by Catholic theologians such as Scheeben[43] and Bartmann.[44]

[38]Cf. B. Lonergan, *De Deo trino*. Rome, 1964, v. II, pp. 186-193.
[39]Cf. A. Chapelle, S.J., *Hegel et la Religion*, v. II: *La dialectique*. Paris, 1967, pp. 84-94.
[40]Cf. our chapter VII, §IV.
[41]K. Barth, *Dogmatik*, I, 1. Zurich, 1947, p. 378.
[42]The expression (in Greek *tropoi huparxeos*) is used notably by St. Amphilochius of Iconium, friend of St. Basil (fr. 15; MG 39, 112) and it signifies for him relation: *etoun scheseos*. Pseudo-Basil uses it with regard to the Father (PG 29, 681). On this point see J. N. D. Kelly, *Early Christian Doctrines*. London, 1968, p. 266 and especially G. L. Prestige, *God in Patristic Thought*. London, 1964, pp. 245-249. Prestige here brings out that the expression, at least in the case of the second and third persons, can contain a veiled allusion not only to their existence but also to their derivation from the paternal source, in short to their origin. St. John Damascene and St. Maximus the Confessor also use the expression; for Maximus, the holy Monad is a triad in its hypostases and modes of existence. Prestige clarifies: the expression *tropoi tes huparxeos* was applied as early as the end of the fourth century, to the properties that distinguish the divine Persons, to express the conviction that in these Persons or hypostases one and the same divine Being is present in expressions that are distinct, objective and permanent, although invariable in their content. We could thus summarize the Cappadocian doctrine: "God is one object in himself and three objects to himself" (p. 249).
[43]M.-J. Scheeben, *Handbuch der Kath. Dogmatik*, v. II. Freiburg, 1948, §910, p. 387: the divine Persons are "Relationen welche mit der Substanz Gottes identisch sind und dieselbe als *in einer gesonderten Weise* subsistierend oder sich selbst angehörig darstellen."
[44]B. Bartmann, *Dogmatik*, 1928, p. 169: "verschiedenen Besitzweise der Wesenheit."

Barth thus explains his choice:[45]

> In speaking of "modes of being" (*Seinsweise*) we mean the same thing that the name Person signifies, in a way that is not absolutely but relatively better, more clear and more simple.... The phrase "God is one in three modes of being, Father, Son and Holy Spirit" thus signifies: the one God and Lord is the one personal God, not in only one manner but according to the biblical revelation in the manner of Father, in the manner of Son and in the manner of Holy Spirit (*in der Weise des Vaters, in der Weise des Sohnes, in der Weise des Heiligen Geistes*: in the mode of Father, in the mode of Son and in the mode of Holy Spirit).

Barth goes on to say that the Father is Donor, the Son Receiver and Donor, the Holy Spirit only Receiver. Or: the Father speaks his Word which is the Son, the Holy Spirit is the Meaning of this Word. The Father is hidden, the Son is the Revealer, the Holy Spirit the Communication.

Lonergan criticizes[46] Barth's substitution proposal. He makes three objections to it, though none of the three appears decisive to us. He says that Barth's way of speaking would be "regressive," for after Lateran IV's definition which speaks of three persons—cf. DS 803-804; DB 431-432—the opinion of the Cappadocians could no longer be considered really traditional and moreover, a desire to return to their language would represent a regression. This criticism is hardly convincing: not only St. Bonaventure but also St. Thomas have explicitly called the persons "modes" of God;[47] St. Thomas identifies relation with a "determined mode of existence";[48] he defines person as a "mode of existing incommunicably"[49] when he is talking about human person as well as about divine person.[50] Are we to think that the two great medieval doctors, both later than the fourth council of the Lateran, adopted "regressive" ways of speaking?

A second criticism of Lonergan's is more understandable: he thinks that Barth denies the subsistence of each Person in God and only affirms that of

---

[45]Barth, *op. cit.*, p. 379.
[46]B. Lonergan, S.J., *De Deo trino*. Rome, 1964, v. II, pp. 193-195, q. XIX.
[47]St. Bonaventure designates the divine person as being a "modus essendi respectivus," "esse et sic esse sive modus essendi": *De Trinitate* III, 2 et ad 13 m (*Obras de S. Buenaventura*. Madrid, BAC, 1948, v. V). St. Thomas Aquinas writes in the *Compendium Theologiae* (I, 46): "In divinis *modus* ille quo Deus est in Deo ut intellectum in intelligente exprimitur per hoc quod dicimus Filium qui est Verbum Dei; ita *modum* quo Deus est in Deo sicut amatum in amante exprimimus per hoc quod ponimus ibi Spiritum, qui est amor Dei."
[48]St. Thomas Aquinas, *De Potentia* 2.5.4: "determinatus modus existendi sive determinata relatio."
[49]St. Thomas Aquinas, *Summa Theologica*, I, 30.4.2: "modus existendi incommunicabiliter."
[50]*Ibid.*, I. 30.4, corpus.

the triune God. Barth does indeed say this.⁵¹ But he contradicts himself immediately afterwards, a fact that Lonergan does not seem to have noted. After having cited a Catholic theologian, Diekamp,⁵² who, in clarifying the ideas of St. Thomas Aquinas, affirms the absolute subsistence of the divine personality and nature and within it three relative subsistences, Barth adds: "But precisely this relative *subsistere* of the Persons is a *subsistere* with a personal property (*aber eben dieses relative subsistere der Personen ist ein proprie subsistere*)."⁵³ Thus he does not really deny the subsistence of each person in God.

Finally, based on the preceding inexact interpretation of Barth, Lonergan concludes that in Barth's view one could say "Thou" only to this single subsistent and not to the Three. He easily shows that the New Testament encourages us to say "Thou" to each of the Three (cf. Jn. 17). But in reality Barth does not deny this point. If the Son says "Thou" to the Father, it follows that there is not just one to whom we in turn can say "Thou."

Lonergan however does correctly observe that it is not our habit to enter into dialogue with modes of being.⁵⁴ And it is this that suggests the valid criticism of the projected Barthian substitution: what appears both erroneous and unattainable is not the desire to speak of persons as modes of being in God but rather the desire to eliminate the term "persons" in speaking of the Three. The expression "modes" is correct but inadequate. This was already strongly brought out by Witasse in the seventeenth century:

---

⁵¹Barth, *Dogmatik,* I, I, p. 380: "was proprie subsistit, ist ja nicht die Person als solche, sondern Gott in den drei Personen, aber eben: Gott als dreifach proprie subsistens" (5th ed., 1947).

⁵²F. Diekamp, *Kath. Dogmatik.* Münster, 1921, v. I, p. 287: "Wenn es zulässig ist von einer absoluten Subsistenz Gottes zu sprechen, so folgt daraus nicht ohne weiteres dass man auch von einer absoluten Persönlichkeit Gottes in Umterschiede von den relativen Personen sprechen darf," for, as the author explains, when Thomas Aquinas wrote: "Exclusis per intellectum proprietatibus personalibus remanebit in consideratione nostra natura divina ut subsistens et ut persona" (*Summa Theologica*, III, 3.3.1), the word Person is used indeterminately prescinding from its communicability or incommunicability. Nonetheless one can speak thus of God as being one Person, prescinding from the Trinitarian mystery as St. Thomas does here. Diekamp further cites two other texts of the Angelic Doctor in the same sense: "In Deo sunt plures res subsistentes, si relationes considerentur; est autem una res subsistens, si consideretur essentia" (*Summa contra Gentiles,* IV, 14); "supposita divinae naturae non sunt principium subsistendi divinae essentiae; ipsa enim divina essentia est secundum se subsistens" (*De Potentia,* 9.5.13). As Diekamp brings out (p. 286), there is moreover real identity and only virtual distinction between the absolute Subsistence and the relative Subsistences of God.

⁵³Barth, *op. cit.,* p. 381. On the notion of subsistence, see our ch. III, notes 30, 34; to subsist signifies to exist by oneself. Cf. St. Thomas Aquinas, *Summa Theologica,* I, 29.2.

⁵⁴Lonergan, *De Deo trino.* Rome, 1964, v. II, p. 195: "non enim cum modis essendi colloqui solemus."

It no longer suffices to say that the Father, the Son and the Spirit differ by relations resembling modes, such as are positions, presences or absences. These kinds of relations attributed to the same substance will never amount to three distinct persons existing at the same time.... It must be said then that there are relations in the divine substance that distinguish the persons, since these persons could not be absolute substances. But we must also say that these relations, which must be substantial, are not sufficiently explained by simple modalities. It must further be said that the divine persons are not the same concrete thing under different denominations or relations, as would be a single man who is poet and orator, but three different concrete relatives in a single concrete absolute.[55]

We see that the discussion of the problem is older than it seemed to Barth. His rejection of the notion of person in Trinitarian discourse is doubtless bound up with his rejection of the analogy of being.[56] He has influenced Karl Rahner, whom we shall confront in this debate over vocabulary.

2. *Karl Rahner, (Mysterium Salutis, 1967[57]): let us not speak immediately or solely of Persons in God*

Rahner explicitly situates his reflection in the line of the reflections of Barth and Lonergan:

a) Rahner thinks that when we today affirm the Trinity of Divine Persons many people think of three spiritual centers of activity (*Aktzentren*), of three spiritual subjectivities, of three liberties. But nothing of the kind, Rahner observes, exists in God. There is in God only one consciousness and three subjects reciprocally conscious by means of this one consciousness diversely possessed by each. Consciousness is on the side of nature, it is a property of the Divine Being common to the Three Persons. For Rahner the representation of three spiritual centers of activity represents a lapse into tritheism.

[55]Remarks of Ch. Witasse, an Oratorian professor of the Sorbonne who died in 1716, on the book of an English anti-Trinitarian published in 1693-1694, Migne, *Theologiae cursus completus.* Paris, 1865, v. 8, col. 768-769.

[56]Cf. Y.-M.-J. Congar, O.P.: Barth has pushed "to its paroxysm the Protestant opposition to Catholicism which affirms a certain proportion between the finite and the infinite (*analogia entis*)...an idea that Barth criticizes as representing the denial of the quality of 'totally Other' which we must acknowledge in God" (*Catholicisme*, I, 1948, 1268). On the basis of this rejection of analogy, Barth really could not accept a transposition of the notion of person to God: person in God could only be "wholly other" with regard to the human person, and in consequence the concept of person is unusable for Barth in Trinitarian theology. In fact, Barth's thinking later evolved in a sense less unfavorable to analogy; but it does not seem that he drew from this evolution any new conclusion in Trinitarian matters.

[57]Karl Rahner, S.J., "Der dreifaltige Gott als transzendenter Urgrund der Heilsgeschichte," *Mysterium Salutis*, v. II. Köln, 1967, pp. 317-397.

b) Further, Rahner observes, the Church is not mistress of human language and has no control over the history of concepts. Despite the Magisterium's right in principle to establish a rule of ecclesiastical and community language, a word can assume an historical development which would render impossible its kerygmatic use without serious danger of tritheist understanding. Theology has the obligation to examine whether the word "Person" is irreplaceable or not.

c) But this word Person is there, sanctioned by the usage of fifteen centuries. There is no other expression that is really better,[58] more commonly intelligible and exposed to fewer false interpretations. Let us then continue to use it. But it is not necessary to use it from the very beginning of the treatise on the Trinity nor to use it alone.

d) The individual theologian cannot at his pleasure change by elimination of words the rule of theological language that is necessary in a Church which must confess its faith in cult and before the community at large. All that the theologian can do is to use the concept of person while explaining it in such a way as to preserve our contemporaries from false interpretations. If ecclesiastical authority forbids him to eliminate such concepts by his personal initiative, he nonetheless remains obliged to explain them. This is possible only by the use of other words. And such an explanation concretely implies the employment of other concepts. An explanatory concept does not mean the elimination of the explained concept but its development.

e) Rahner then introduces two concepts intended to clarify the concept of person: on the one hand that of three modes of self-communication of God; on the other, not that of three modes of existence of the Divine Being as does Barth but rather that of three distinct modes of subsistence in God.

Thus, Rahner thinks, one avoids the danger of a tritheist misunderstanding of the Trinity. The term "mode," like those of "person, procession, emanation," is a human category applied to God. Of course it is susceptible of being wrongly understood, as if it signified an accidental modality without which the Divine Being could exist.[59]

What is to be thought of these reflections of Rahner?

First of all it must be acknowledged that they constitute an outstanding effort to investigate in depth the problem of theological language in its twofold relation to the history of philosophical language and to the rule of language fixed by the ecclesiastical Magisterium. This effort proceeds, moreover, in a typically "Rahnerian" manner: first there is a criticism of the

---

[58]"Das Wort 'Person' est nun einmal da; ein wirklich besseres allgemein verständliches und weniger leicht Missverständnissen ausgesetztes Wort ist nicht da. So wird man wohl bei diesem Wort bleiben müssen..." (ibid., pp. 343-344).

[59]K. Rahner, op. cit., pp. 387, 343-344, 353-354, 389-392.

classical position, then a return to it. Rahner's own style encourages us to criticize his criticism.

Is it true that to affirm three centers of spiritual activity is tritheistic? We do not see why. This expression is not equivalent to the assertion of three consciousnesses in God which would amount to asserting three natures and so to tritheism, nor is it equivalent to asserting three liberties. It signifies rather three reciprocal "I's," three relations in the classical sense of the word. This is the way, moreover, it is utilized by a Nédoncelle[60] and by a Widmert[61] in our day. It in no way implies that the three centers have a diverse activity *ad extra;* they are the triple center of one and the same spiritual activity. But it recognizes that the Father and the Son are relational centers of activity, for how could one deny that the eternal generation of the Son is an act of the Father and that the active spiration of the Spirit is an act common to the Father and to the Son? How could one deny that in this respect the Father and the Son are centers of two distinct activities, the generation of the Son and the procession of the Spirit? We are dealing here with two intra-divine productions fittingly attributed to two distinct centers of distinct activities. In a more general way to affirm three centers of activity in God is to affirm three "I's" in God, of which each is the divine consciousness, since the divine Being is divine consciousness. A divine "I" can only be a conscious relation. The affirmation of three "I's," conscious in virtue of a single divine consciousness, has then nothing in common with tritheism.[62]

In the second place, the expressions proposed by Rahner not to replace the notion of person, but to clarify it (three modes of self-communication or

---

[60]M. Nédoncelle, *La Réciprocité des Consciences*. Paris, 1942, p. 81: "Christian theology proposes to us in the case of the Trinity the case of personal divine centers... what we would call the 'I' or the 'Thou' dogma calls person; what in our language was the 'we' will be in its language the nature of God in which the three Persons have one being simple and identical." We will see (ch. VIII, 1, 5, c) that a theologian like Mühlen prefers to see in the "We" of Jesus and the Father the single and active principle of the procession of the Spirit, without mentioning the divine nature as such. There is however no contradiction between these two views if we recall with St. Thomas Aquinas (*Summa Theologica*, I, 36.4.1) that: "the Holy Spirit proceeds from the Father and the Son inasmuch as they are one in spirative power, which in some way signifies the nature with the property."

[61]G.-P. Widmert, *Gloire au Père, au Fils, au Saint-Esprit*. Neuchâtel, 1963, p. 63: "The Church ...would be able to preserve the notions of person and hypostasis in specialized theological discourse and to substitute for them in popular enunciation of the doctrine expressions like 'center of revealing activity' or 'subsistent focus of divine activity' or 'subject of divine activity.'" We think these expressions could be useful for clarifying the notion of person but they could not replace it. We could make the same objections to them as to the expression "modes," at least in part: they are philosophical expressions without pastoral impact.

[62]We draw here on some reflections of E. Gutwenger, S.J., "Zur Trinitätslehre von Mysterium Salutis II," *Zeitschrift für Kath. Theologie*, 90 (1968), 325-328.

of subsistence in God) hardly appear suitable on the pastoral level. Since when does one invoke modes of being? One invokes subjects, "I's," persons. Here we meet again the argument from cult so dear to St. Basil with regard to the divinity of the Holy Spirit. We can also with E. P. Gutwenger deny that this terminology of Rahner's would be comprehensible even to the educated lay person. It could at most be employed in a philosophical circle.[63]

The same author offers a more radical objection to Rahner: three subsistential modes (*drei Subsistenz-weisen*)—does this not signify three modes of a single subsistence, an expression that savors of modalism? Surely this is not what Rahner means.[64] But it would appear that excessive fear of tritheism leads to a terminology that will be spontaneously understood by many in a modalist sense.

Further, mode is a determination of being. We are dealing with a common category but one that is much less common than the notion of person, a fact that Rahner, for that matter, brings out.

In the third place, if it is true that the Church is not in control of common language, if it is true that she must understand and speak the languages of this world,[65] it is also true that she, like every group and every society specifically distinct from others, must elaborate and improve her own proper language distinct from other technical languages just as she herself is distinct from humanity in general. Such an elaboration of a proper language is a sign of her self-identity. The Church, which by means of her Trinitarian discussions, has endowed modern society with the very notion of human person,[66] is fully justified in holding to the notion of divine Person and this for many reasons. Does it not appear even from linguistic usage that the notion of divine Person preserves that of human person? In a society that is mass oriented, depersonalized and of Marxist leaning, the very notion of human person disappears. Rahner does not seem to have perceived this factual link between divine Person and human person; he does not, however, deny it. He loses sight of analogy (which St. Thomas Aquinas perceived so well)[67] and for this reason maintains the notion of divine Person with less than enthusiasm and out of an obedience to the Church that is more sincere than it is convincing. But he is right in wishing to maintain and clarify the word.

Let us add to these critical reflections on Rahner a few complementary reflections on Barth's ideas. Even if we admit that Boethius' definition of person is not immediately intelligible to many of our contemporaries, who

[63] *Ibid.*, 328.
[64] *Ibid.*
[65] Cf. GS 44. 2; 62. 2.
[66] Cf. A. Guggenberger, *Encyclopédie de la Foi.* Paris, 1966, v. III, pp. 425-426, art. "Personne."
[67] Cf. St. Thomas Aquinas, *Summa Theologica*, I, 29.3.

habitually identify personality (more than person) with self-consciousness, is it not true nevertheless that it is understandable if clarified and explained? This definition remains necessary, intelligible, true. The ontological concept of person—*persona dicit aliquid distinctum subsistens in natura intellectuali*[68]—expresses what the human mind, the human person itself perceives of its own proper reality by immediate, universal and necessary experience[69]: it is adapted to men of all times and all places, to all human persons, always of course remaining susceptible to a more profound understanding. The psychological notion of personality is not the only modern notion of person; the ontological notion is just as modern. Precisely because it is for all times. Every man, in speaking, is making his way toward it.[70]

In brief, to replace the notion of Person is impossible; to express the Trinitarian dogma without it is also, today, unthinkable. But it is as indispensable to explain it as it is impossible to replace it. Theologians as a matter of fact have, for fifteen centuries, never ceased to explain it. Not new either in the reflections of Barth and Rahner is the endeavor to present other concepts to signify the same reality. Some statements of Ruysbroeck already moved in the same direction: "The divine nature is eternally active according to the mode of persons and eternally in repose and without mode according to the simplicity of its essence."[71] Note the expression: "the mode of persons," which associates and identifies the two concepts even more explicitly than did Bonaventure and Thomas Aquinas. This means that in its positive aspect the Barthian and Rahnerian attempt is in line not only with that of the Cappadocians but also with that of the great scholastic doctors. It is particularly striking that Barth and Rahner insist not only on the persons-modes but also on the notion of subsistence, so important in

---

[68]St. Thomas Aquinas, *I Sent.*, d. 23, q. 1, a. 3; cf. *De Potentia*, 9.4; cf. pp. 140-141 of this book.

[69]Adapting it to our subject, we draw here the reasoning of Pope Paul VI in the encyclical *Mysterium Fidei*, which we referred to and cited in our ch. II, § VIII, note 132. The experience of person is, par excellence, the universal and necessary experience; it is immediate as to the knowledge of one's proper substantiality, though not as to its acquisition for this is conditioned by sensible experience. Cf. p. 96.

[70]As Gagnebet, O.P., noted in a personal letter of April 10, 1969 to the author: "It is only by metaphysical concepts that one can express realities which are accessible only to metaphysical knowledge. These concepts are not foreign to men of today who use them a hundred times a day. They also form the framework of the nine parts of discourse according to which our grammars are divided. But in consequence of their scientific, technical or idealist formation people today never submit to personal reflection these notions which they use and which are also found correctly set forth in the dictionary of today's language, for example that of Robert.... It would be possible to get across to everybody notions like substance, essence, cause." We could add that a reflection on the personal pronouns would help everyone discover the ontological notion of person. For even when not conscious of self, the "I" is permanent. I do not cease to be an "I" when I go to sleep.

[71]Blessed Ruysbroeck, *Vérité* X, v. II, p. 215; cited by P. Henry, S.J., *Rech. Sc. Rel.* 41 (1953), 75.

Trinitarian theology. We thus encounter once again the permanent relevance and truth of the formula that issued from the Trinitarian conflicts of the fourth and fifth centuries: "three consubstantial subsistences in a single substance" (cf. p. 130).

If the problems of faith-language are of primary theological interest for many of our contemporaries, we can easily understand their affecting not only theologians individually but also the Churches as such. All of which the World Council of Churches has perceived and underscored.

IV. THE TRINITARIAN "BASIS" OF THE WORLD COUNCIL OF CHURCHES (1961)

On December 2, 1961 at New Delhi the World Council of Churches approved by a vote of 386 to 37, with seven abstentions, (426 votes expressed out of a total of 577 electors) the new formulation of its doctrinal basis:

> The ecumenical Council of Churches is a fraternal association of Churches which confess the Lord Jesus Christ as God and Savior according to the Scriptures and do their utmost to respond together to their common vocation for the glory of the only God Father, Son and Holy Spirit.[72]

What does this text mean? According to the explanation given by the central committee of the World Council of Churches, it signifies "less than a simple confession of faith and much more than a simple formula of agreement." This Basis is not presented as a Credo nor as a complete exposition of the Christian faith.

The formulation employed ("for the glory of the only God Father, Son and Holy Spirit") is rather a cultic formulation. It remains vague. Would it be acceptable, however, to anti-Trinitarian churches? We may doubt it. What is more, it was not adopted without quite a lively debate. The Baptists objected: "In the name of what word of Scripture can one impose this faith on the Churches?" The Russian Orthodox Metropolitan Nicodim replied: "The New Basis is linked with Baptism which makes us Christians: Go, teach all nations, baptize them in the name of the Father and of the Son and of the Holy Spirit."

In the same sense a Greek Orthodox theologian, Alivizatos, expressed the joy of the Orthodox in general, for whom the new Basis is the minimum of Christian faith. As early as 1948 the Church of Greece had suggested this extension, since faith in the Trinity is the specific work of Christian faith in conformity with Revelation and primitive tradition. There is no other Christian faith than faith in God Father, Son and Holy Spirit.

---

[72]This information and what follows is borrowed from A. Wenger, A.A., *Nouv. Rev. Théol.*, 84 (1962), 63-71.

It should be noted that the language of the cited formulation is exclusively biblical, with no allusion to the Nicene[73] "consubstantial" or to the intimate relations between the Persons of the Father, the Son and the Spirit. For anyone able to reflect on it, however, the formula employed (like that of Mt. 28:19) fully implies the doctrine of relations, as we showed in citing Augustine and St. Thomas Aquinas[74]: the only God referred to is Father of the Son, Son of the Father, Spirit of the Father and of the Son. Poor, in explicit content, this formula is rich in what is implied.

We can then understand the reaction of M. Fry, president of the Assembly of the World Council of Churches at New Delhi, at the conclusion of the debate: he asked all the delegates to join in a prayer of thanksgiving in gratitude to the Trinity for having brought the Churches to this step leading to the unity willed by Christ.

In order to further grasp the import of the formula, we should recall that many of the Protestant churches derive from the Trinitarian nihilism favored by the modernist liberalism of the beginning of the century. As opposed to these unitarian currents the formula of New Delhi marks an advance and a rectification; but it must be acknowledged that if we compare it with the "Credo of the people of God" pronounced by Paul VI on June 30, 1968, and with the Trinitarian section of this Credo (which we will examine in our next chapter), it appears very poor and vague. But does it not contain a promise of future development? It recalls the symbol of Nicaea-Constantinople whose presentation of the divinity of the Holy Spirit was also of a cultic character.

The formula of New Delhi is at least the occasion and even the cause for Christians of so many different Churches to praise Christ in common, as "only Mediator for the glory of the only God Father, Son and Holy Spirit" (UR 20). The more their communion with the Father, the Son and the Holy Spirit becomes stronger, the more will their mutual fraternity increase (UR 7).

---

[73]One can wonder if the World Council of Churches took into account the results of the experience of Nicaea, which correctly showed the impossibility of being content with a biblical style and the necessity of having recourse to the categories of reason in order to effectively defend the revealed truth and to protect the authentic sense of the biblical text.

[74]Cf. the text of St. Thomas Aquinas cited in our ch. III, § 5, note 76; and that of St. Augustine which will be cited in our ch. IX, 1, § 2, note 17: *De Trinitate* XV, 22.43; ML 42, 1090; see pp. 145, 331.

VI
The Trinitarian Doctrine of Vatican II

Vatican II consciously and deliberately situated its doctrinal message in the context of the ecumenical movement. This holds true also with regard to the Trinitarian mystery. Vatican II did not intend to present to us the fundamental mystery of Christianity in a systematic way, but rather to show us its omnipresence in the plan and in the economy of salvation. The work of the Redemption of the human race is the effusion of the mercy, or better the merciful self-effusion, of the Father through the Son in the Spirit. This could almost serve as a summary of the Trinitarian theology of Vatican II.

It is essentially "economic." In contrast to Nicaea I, to Constantinople I and II, to Lyons and to Florence, Vatican II gave hardly any direct or explicit attention (rare allusions excepted[1]), to the mystery of the processions and of the intra-divine relations, but rather embraced it in implicit fashion by way of investigating the mysterious sending of the Son and of the Spirit, which presupposes these processions and is the foundation for all renewed ecclesiology.

From this point of view nothing could be more instructive than a comparison of the Trinitarian texts of the eleventh local council of Toledo with those of the second ecumenical council of the Vatican. Toledo was abstract and didactic but in a charming way. Vatican II is a pastoral and missionary council. Like the Gospel, its primary concern is to proclaim in concrete terms the action of God who accomplishes his work of salvation among men, or rather, who reveals to them in the blood of the Lamb that he is their salvation. As this council is ecclesiological, and intends to show forth the true countenance of the Church and its mission of service to all humanity, it considers the action of each of the divine Persons in the heart of the Church but with no special concern to specify whether it is dealing with incommunicable personal properties or with appropriation. It simply uses the language of Scripture and leaves to the theologians the trouble of interpreting this teaching with scientific rigor.[2]

We could also add that Vatican II wished to give special importance to the

---

[1] Cf. *AG* 2: "the Father...from whom the Holy Spirit proceeds through the Son."
[2] Cf. M.-M. Philipon, O.P., "La Sainte Trinité et l'Eglise," in *L'Eglise de Vatican II*, a collective work directed by G. Baraùna, O.F.M., Brazilian ed., Petrópolis (Brazil), 1965, p. 363.

person and work of the Holy Spirit in the context also of the mystery of the Church.

We shall then examine here successively Vatican II's Trinitarian ecclesiology, then its pneumatology, and finally the post-conciliar Trinitarian doctrine of Paul VI in the context of the Dutch catechism.

I. TRINITARIAN ECCLESIOLOGY OF VATICAN II

The mystery of the Church is the realization in history of the design of the eternal Father, consummated by his Son and interiorized by their Spirit: this would sum up the two fundamental texts of Vatican II about Trinitarian ecclesiology (LG 2-4; AG 2-4). The Incarnation and Pentecost do not so much signify[3] the intra-historical irruption of two divine Strangers as the visible manifestations of the Word and of the Holy Spirit in the world created by them: "God decided to enter into human history in a new and definitive fashion by sending his Son in our flesh. Without the shadow of a doubt, the Holy Spirit was already at work before the glorification of Christ" (AG 3-4).[4] The Word and the Spirit were already present and active in the world before the Redemptive Incarnation, but now they are so in a new way.

The back drop of this Trinitarian ecclesiology is nothing else but what is found in the prologue of the Epistle to the Ephesians. There St. Paul presents each of the divine Persons at the source of the economy of salvation. First of all he stresses the initiative of the Father:

> Blessed be the God and Father of our Lord Jesus Christ, who has blessed us in Christ with every spiritual blessing in the heavenly places.
>
> Even as he chose us in him before the foundation of the world, that we should be holy and blameless before him. He destined us in love to be his sons through Jesus Christ, according to the purpose of his will, to the praise of his glorious grace, which he freely bestowed on us in the Beloved (Eph. 1:3-6).

Blessing, election, predestination and justification by grace are attributed to the Father, almost always moreover "in Christ." To the Son, in fact, a central role is ascribed:

> In him we have redemption through his blood, the forgiveness of our trespasses, according to the riches of his grace, which he (the Father)

---

[3] As the Word and the Spirit remain transcendent to the world in which they are by presence of immensity, we can say that their new coming at the time of the Incarnation and of Pentecost is an irruption. St. John of the Cross (*Spiritual Canticle*, XIV, 8) likens God to the "strange isles," because even for the angels the judgments of God on men are the object of a continually renewed discovery.

[4] Refer back to the note of the conciliar text.

lavished upon us: For he has made known to us in all wisdom and insight the mystery of his will, according to his purpose which he set forth in Christ as a plan for the fullness of time, to unite all things in him, things in heaven and things on earth (Eph. 1:7-10).

It is always the Father who graces and recapitulates in Christ. Finally the role of the Spirit is also underscored:

> In him you also, who have heard the word of truth, the gospel of your salvation, and have believed in him, were sealed with the promised Holy Spirit, which is the guarantee of our inheritance until we acquire possession of it, to the praise of his glory (Eph. 1:13-14).

The Spirit is here presented as the one who prepares the consummation of the redemption of the people of God.

We can understand why the chairman of the theological commission of Vatican II was able to see in the verses just cited the basic text which describes the respective role of the Three Divine Persons in the economy of salvation. Moreover, in the light of the conclusions elaborated in preceding chapters, we would more readily say that Paul describes the different roles that are appropriated to the Three (in function of their personal properties). For the work of salvation is indeed the common work of the Three, where each of the Three acts according to his personal manner of possessing the one divine nature.

Vatican II, however, did not introduce this text *in extenso* in either of its great Trinitarian and ecclesiological frescoes (LG 2-4; AG 2-4). But this in no way disqualifies this text from being the true keystone of the council's ecclesiology: for in reference to the constitution *Lumen Gentium* we can say with the same official chairman, Mgr. Charrue:

> After a brief introduction there follows a description of the eternal origin of the Church in the design of God the Father, who accomplished the work of redemption through his incarnate Son in the Holy Spirit, in such a way that the Church will appear as a "people that draws its unity from the unity of the Father, the Son, and the Holy Spirit."[5]

The Council further made its own that celebrated text of St. Cyprian[6] which to some extent seems to stress more the divine unity than the Trinity. But the prefatory declaration of the second "fresco" constitutes an explanation of its content which stresses rather the Trinity and the persons: "by her very nature the pilgrim Church is missionary for she takes her origin from the mission of the Son and the mission of the Holy Spirit

---

[5]Cf. Philipon, *op. cit.* (note 2), p. 369.
[6]St. Cyprian, *De Orat. dom.*, 23; ML 4, 553. Cited by LG 4 toward the end.

according to the design of God the Father" (*AG* 2)—a text that says a lot. If we recall that for all Catholic theologians the mission of the Son prolongs in history his eternal generation which it presupposes, and that the mission of the Spirit prolongs and manifests his eternal spiration, we can only conclude that the second council of the Vatican intended to show us the Church both as the prolongation of the divine processions of the Word and of the Spirit—which in some way renders these processions visible in history—and, we might even say, as the historical unfolding of the Trinitarian mystery itself.

Three observations must be made here:

—on the one hand, it seems that the decree *Ad Gentes* on the Missions intended to complete, on the Trinitarian level, the fresco of *Lumen Gentium*! A careful comparison of these two prologues would bring out many details which point in this direction; let us only note in passing a theology that is very conscious of the appropriation of creative action to the Father, the supreme principle in the universe as in the divinity: "This design (of God the Father) flows from the love-source (*ex fontali amore*) or charity of God the Father, who, being the Principle without Principle, from whom the Son is generated, from whom the Holy Spirit proceeds through the Son, has freely created us in his surpassingly great goodness and mercy" (*AG* 2);

—on the other hand, in line with the first observation, it would be difficult not to observe the harmony between the Trinitarian doctrine of creation, which we set forth in a previous chapter in the light of St. Thomas Aquinas, and the Trinitarian ecclesiology of Vatican II. The divine and eternal processions of the Son and of the Spirit appear as the conditions of possibility, the models and the eternal causes of a creation which is consummated in the Church and destined to be eternally integrated therein.

—Finally, the mystery of a Church sent by the Father, by the Son and by the Spirit, by revealing to us the mysterious sending of the Son and the Spirit by the Father, renders "visible" to us the incomprehensible salvific mystery of the Trinity which it bears within it; the Church is the sacrament of salvation only because it is the sacrament of the Trinity, the visible sign which bears in it the invisible and undivided Trinity so as to give it to the world. By receiving its unity from the unity of the Father, the Son and the Spirit, the Church is, so to speak, eternally generated with the Son and spirated with the Spirit who are sent to it and who, in it, proceed from the Father. The Church is the sacrament of salvation by being a mystery which carries within it the fundamental mystery, the mystery of the redemptive Trinity.[7]

A brief survey of some Trinitarian texts of Vatican II will help us better perceive how the Most Holy Trinity in the council's view is the source, the

[7]Cf. ch. IV, § 5.

model and the term or end of the one universal Church, its temple and its sacrament.

1. *The Trinitarian mystery is the origin and the cause of the Church*

Proceeding from the love of the eternal Father, the Church was founded by Christ in time and gathered into one by the Holy Spirit. It has a saving and eschatological purpose which can be fully attained only in the next life (*GS* 40.2).

The eschatological consummation of the Church is here appropriated to the Holy Spirit, term of the immutable movement of the divine life, bond between the Son and the love of the eternal Father, from whom the Church proceeds—note the use of this technical Trinitarian term—on the model of the divine Persons: the Word and the Spirit. To this Spirit, inasmuch as he is the personal bond of the Father and the Son, is attributed the gathering together of the Church in the pursuit of its ultimate end: thus in one and the same phrase we have a double appropriation (in the technical sense).

2. *The unity of the Trinity is the supreme model of the unity between Christians in the unity of the Church*

When the Lord Jesus prays to the Father that "all may be one...as we are one" (Jn. 17:21-22), he opens up new horizons closed to human reason by implying that there is a certain parallel between the union existing among the divine persons and the union of the sons of God in truth and love. It follows, then, that if man is the only creature on earth that God has wanted for its own sake, man can fully discover his true self only in a sincere giving of himself (*GS* 24, 2).

There is only a certain resemblance between the divine unity and the unity of the Church because the first unity transcends the second and because the dissimilarity of the two is still more striking.[8]

Nonetheless the first does not cease to be the "supreme model" of the second: "Of this mystery (the sacred mystery of the unity of the Church) the supreme model and source is the unity, in the Trinity of Persons, of one God Father and Son in the Holy Spirit" (*UR* 2 toward the end). Note that the conciliar text stresses not so much the unity of nature as the interpersonal unity of the Father and of the Son in the Spirit, their link and their bond: it is this unity which is the exemplar of the union of persons in the Church rather than the unity of nature which, however, is inseparable from it.

---

[8]The reader will find it interesting to compare in detail *GS* 24.2 with *DS* 803 (*DB* 431) and will get the impression that Vatican II intended to complete on a positive level the negative expression of Lateran IV; the comparison should also include *DS* 806 (*DB* 432 toward the end), which exalts at the same time the similarity and dissimilarity between Creator and creature.

3. *Finally, the vision of the Trinity is the end toward which the Church advances as it is in pilgrimage toward it (cf. LG 49 toward the beginning)*

The second council of the Vatican has thus presented the Most Holy Trinity as the efficient, exemplary and supreme final cause of the unity of the Church and of our union in the Church. The Church can logically terminate this presentation by an appeal addressed directly to the Religious who profess the evangelical counsels, and indirectly (by transposing a few terms) to all Christians destined to the perfection of charity:

> Let everyone who has been called to the profession of the counsels take earnest care to preserve and excel still more in the life in which God has called him, for the increase of the holiness of the Church, to the greater glory of the one and undivided Trinity which, in Christ and through Christ, is the source and origin of all holiness (*LG* 47).

The Church, which in giving herself to us gives us the Trinity, can demand of us that we give ourselves back to the Trinity so that she herself may more perfectly give herself to the mutual gift which the Father and the Son are to one another in the Spirit. Faced with an ambient secularism, Vatican II shows us that an increasing communion with the divine Persons is the condition for an ever greater fraternal life on the horizontal and ecclesial level:

> The faithful should remember that they promote union among Christians better, that indeed they live it better, when they try to live holier lives according to the Gospel. For the closer their union with the Father, the Word, and the Spirit, the more deeply and easily will they be able to grow in mutual brotherly love (*UR* 7 at the end).

In this text we recognize an allusion to 1 John 1:3-7, where a link is found between the two communions, the horizontal and the vertical, communion with the Father and Jesus Christ his Son, and communion between brothers. We could say (cf. 1 Jn. 1:6) that these two communions reciprocally condition one another and find their nourishment and their synthesis in the eucharistic communion (cf. *UR* 15), a point to which we will have occasion to return.

With M.-M. Philipon we could thus sum up the significance of the Trinitarian ecclesiology of Vatican II: the council has opted not for an ascending method that rises from observation of the deeds and actions of Christ up to his divinity, but for a descending method. Beginning with the love of the Father, it invites the Church to contemplate the mission of the Son who came through his Incarnation to found his Church and then after his return to the Father sent his Spirit to animate each of the members of his mystical body as well as all the ecclesial institutions. These two methods were equally possible: the first, the ascending method, would continue in the line of the Synoptics; the second, the descending method, in the line of St. John. In its point of departure the ecclesiology of Vatican II is not horizontal but vertical, precisely because it makes the Church to shine out in the light of the mystery of the Trinity[9] and particularly of the Holy Spirit.

II. THE ECCLESIOLOGICAL PNEUMATOLOGY OF VATICAN II

Vatican II offers us very rich doctrine on the mission of the Spirit in and to the Church on behalf of the world. We can distinguish two aspects of this mission: the link between the Spirit and the hierarchy, and the importance of the charisms by which the Spirit furthers the development of the Church. In this way Vatican II reacted vigorously both against the reduction of ecclesiology to a "hierarchology" and against the contempt for all structures, both divine and ecclesiastical, in all of which the Spirit acts as soul, as we shall see.

We cannot do better than to explain some conciliar texts chosen in the light of a pre-conciliar work of Y. Congar,[10] whose thought seems to have guided the council: *Esquisse du Mystère de l'Eglise.*

1. *The Holy Spirit fills and governs the whole Church, acting through a charismatic hierarchy*

The fundamental intuition of the second council of the Vatican is that the Lord Jesus constructs his Church both by his apostles and by his Spirit. It would not be false to say that the intention here was to react against a too exclusively Christological ecclesiology[11] that bound the Church to its past institution by Christ, without much attention being paid to its present animation by the Spirit of the risen Christ. Vatican II expressed its basic intuition thus:

> Before freely laying down his life for the world, the Lord Jesus organized the apostolic ministry and promised to send the Holy Spirit, in such a way that both would be always and everywhere associated in the fulfillment of the work of salvation. Throughout the ages the Holy Spirit makes the entire Church "one in communion and ministry; and provides her with different hierarchical and charismatic gifts," giving life to ecclesiastical structures, being, as it were, their soul, and inspiring in the hearts of the faithful that same spirit of mission which impelled Christ himself (*AG* 4).

[9]Cf. M.-M. Philipon, O.P., *Seminarium*, 1967, p. 225.
[10]Y.-M.-J. Congar, O.P., *Esquisses du Mystère de l'Eglise.* Paris, 1953, ch. IV: the Holy Spirit and the apostolic body, realizers of the work of Christ.
[11]*Ibid.*, pp. 176-179: under this aspect Congar analyzes the evolution of Möhler. He was an initiator of this reaction which was then continued, with greater balance, by Franzelin and by Pius XII (*Mystici Corporis*, 1943).

In other words, we cannot separate the institution of the Church by the pre-and-post paschal Man Jesus from the visible sending by the Risen One of his Spirit to his apostles.

The Spirit does the work of Christ throughout the whole period of the Church (cf. Jn. 14:16: I will pray the Father, and he will give you another Paraclete, to be with you *eis ton aiona,* for this eon, that is as Swete[12] understands it, for the time of the Church). In contrast to the apostles, the Spirit is not an instrument or a vicar of Christ, but the living water that flows from the source who is Christ to vivify the Church (cf. LG 4). Although the Holy Spirit transcends the apostles and their successors, the Holy Spirit and the apostles operate conjointly between the two comings of Christ.

What the episcopal college does visibly, the Holy Spirit does in the depths of the institution and of souls, by putting them in relation with Christ (cf. Jn. 16:13-14). It is together that the Lord Jesus and the Spirit utter the same identical message to the Churches (Apoc. 1:16; 2:1, 7). The external preaching of the apostles is intimately bound to the interior exhortation of the Holy Spirit (Acts 16:14) and this bond, of which the apostle is aware, constitutes his strength.

What is the nature of this very intimate union between the Holy Spirit and the episcopal college which succeeds the apostolic college, between the Paraclete and the ecclesial institution? Vatican II compares it to the Incarnation:

> Just as...the assumed nature inseparably united to the divine Word serves Him as a living instrument of salvation, so, in a similar way does the communal structure of the Church serve Christ's Spirit, who vivifies it by way of building up the body (Eph. 4:16).

So the dogmatic constitution *Lumen Gentium* (8.1) expresses it. The social organism of the Church, to which the Spirit of Christ is as indissolubly linked as is the Word to his human nature assumed once for all, is nothing but the sacramental and hierarchical structure of the Church, and, notably but not exclusively, the episcopal college presided over by the Sovereign Pontiff. This visible structure results from the juridical mission confided by Christ to his apostles, a body animated by the invisible mission given by him to the Holy Spirit, the soul of the Church (cf. Jn. 20:21; *DS* 3806 and other texts of Pius XII in his encyclical[13] on the Mystical Body).

---

[12]H. B. Swete, *The Last Discourse and Prayer of Our Lord.* London, 1914, p. 37, n. 1, cf. Congar, *op. cit.,* p. 142, note 3.

[13]Pius XII, *Mystici Corporis, AAS* 35 (1943), 218 and 224; in this last text Pius XII underlines in the light of Jn. 20:21-22 the association in the Johannine gospel of the visible mission of the Apostles with the visible and invisible mission of the Spirit.

Vatican II then intended to stress the inseparable link between the Spirit who animates the Church and its ecclesial body, between the Spirit and the divinely instituted structure of the people of God.

But how can we describe with greater precision the nature of this union above and beyond the metaphor of soul and body? This union, in contrast to that of the Incarnation, is not a personal, hypostatic union in virtue of which the Spirit and the Church would form a single substantial human-divine being, but a union of Covenant, linked to a promise of the living God that is infinitely stronger than any human commitment. It is not a union in being but in activity, which supposes a being-with[14] of the Spirit in relation to the Church. In this union, which is accidental and not substantial (like that of the Incarnation) and yet true, the Trinity efficaciously achieves contact between the Spirit and the Church, just as it is the efficient cause of the Incarnation of the Word: *tres uniunt, dum unus unitur.*

What is the foundation of this union between the Holy Spirit and the ecclesial institution? It is the union of operation that exists first of all between the Holy Spirit and Christ. But Y. Congar adds, "this union that is grounded in the mystery of the divine ontology, of the eternal relations, of the consubstantiality and circuminsession of the Divine Persons, was openly declared for Christ at the time of his baptism, and for the Church and the apostolate at Pentecost which was their baptism of the Holy Spirit (Acts 1:5)"[15]

Vatican II took up the same doctrine in almost the same terms:

> The "acts of the apostles" began with Pentecost, just as Christ was conceived in the Virgin Mary with the coming of the Holy Spirit and was moved to begin his ministry by the descent of the same Holy Spirit, who came down upon him while he was praying (*AG* 4).

In the last analysis then, we find that the foundation of the intimate union between the Spirit and the Church is the unity of will and operation of the divine Persons and their mutual inexistence, while never losing sight of the fact that the proper, personal character of each is presupposed in their common operation.

Thus we understand that this union between the Spirit and the Church, although only accidental, is yet profoundly real, so much so, that all other loving unions (between parents and children, husband and wife) are nothing by comparison. Sent by the Father and the Son, the Holy Spirit is

---

[14]Cf. Congar, *op. cit.,* p. 160 who thus compares and synthesizes (thanks to the concept of "being-with," suggestive of covenant and of an intersubjective ontology) Jn. 16:16; 16:17; 1 Cor. 3:16; 6:19. Congar opposes this intersubjective ontology to an ontic ontology of physical production.

[15]Congar, *op. cit.,* p. 157.

immanent in the Church as Love, as their Love. He is imprinted on it and in it as a seal (Eph. 1:13-14; 4:30). The Church becomes, in consequence, in the image of the Spirit of Truth who animates it, a society of light, of truth and love. By this intimate union the Spirit is poured out from Jesus Christ the Head and the Anointed One, perfumed since the Incarnation, by this divine Unction (cf. 1 Jn. 2:20, 27), onto the whole body of the Church, like an oil of joy and gladness that penetrates not only its surface but the totality of its being (cf. 2 Cor. 1:21-22)[16] for the final "day of Redemption" (Eph. 4:30).

The presence of the Holy Spirit in the Church is its interior supernatural foundation, the principle of its subsistence and of its unity. It is notably the foundation for the "operational infallibility" of the Church, to use an expression of Y. Congar: the infallibility of its magisterial or sacramental operations by means of which the visible Church is bound by the bond of apostolicity to the Lord's institution and tends toward his Return.

In the light of this definitive bond between the Spirit of Christ and the hierarchical institution of the Church, the thirteenth rule of orthodoxy of St. Ignatius appears to be fully justified:

> To attain truth in everything we ought always to be disposed to believe that what we see as white is black if the hierarchical Church so defines it, convinced that between Christ our Lord and the Church his Spouse there is but one and the same Spirit who governs us and directs us for the salvation of our souls, for it is by the same Spirit, the same Lord who gave the Ten Commandments, that our Holy Mother the Church is directed and governed.

But do the charisms of the Spirit reach only to the hierarchy? Vatican II is far from thinking so.

2. The Holy Spirit renews the whole Church by the simple and extraordinary charisms given to the laity

In 1953 Y. Congar could still write and not without some foundation:

> The charisms, a great number of them at least, do not come from the hierarchical operations. They are not without relation to the hierarchical ministry and ought to submit to it in order to be acceptable in the Church for the building up of the Body of Christ: however, they do not come from the apostolic ministry but from the Spirit. We have here an ensemble of facts which the life of the Church has not ceased and does not cease to recognize, to which nothing in its dogma is opposed, but which play hardly any role in current theology or ecclesiology.[17]

---

[16]Cf. S. Tromp, S.J., *De Spiritu Christi anima*. Rome, 1960, pp. 129-138.
[17]Congar, *op. cit.*, p. 166.

After Vatican II Congar could no longer write these lines, doubtless due in part to his own previous efforts. In describing with precision the charisms of the Spirit, he gave us to understand that there exists in the Church a free field in which the initiative belongs to this divine Spirit.

a) *The renovating charisms of the Spirit*

A wedding gift of Christ to his Church, the charisms are a permanent element of the divine structure of the Church and in this sense they are a part of the institution, for it is in part by means of them that the Holy Spirit is the soul of the Church. All this stands out clearly in the dogmatic constitution *Lumen Gentium*:

> It is not only through the sacraments and the ministrations of the Church that the Holy Spirit makes holy the People, leads them and enriches them with his virtues. Allotting his gifts according as he wills (cf. 1 Cor. 12:11), he also distributes special graces among the faithful of every rank. By these gifts he makes them fit and ready to undertake various tasks and offices for the renewal and building up of the Church, as it is written, "the manifestation of the spirit is given to everyone for profit" (1 Cor. 12:7).

Here (*LG* 12.2) Vatican II, recalling with St. Paul (1 Cor. 7:7) that "each one receives from God his proper charism," shows us the Spirit directing the Church not only by the hierarchy but also by his proper, immediate, charismatic intervention in all the faithful, recognizing however that it belongs to the hierarchy to judge of the authenticity and the exercise of the extraordinary charisms received by the faithful. The conciliar text cited above shows also the purpose of the charisms in the design of the Spirit of Christ: the good of the Church and its perpetual renewal until the consummation of its union with its Spouse (cf. *LG* 4 at the end).

It should come as no surprise that these charisms, by which each Christian becomes qualified to render useful services to the whole ecclesial body, should be specially attributed and appropriated to the activity of the Holy Spirit, while being a common gift of the Three: gratuitous gifts freely conferred for the benefit of another. They suggest him who preeminently is the Gift, the Holy Spirit, in whom the Father and the Son give themselves mutually one to the other, the Spirit who is the principle of all the gifts they together make to the world.[18] Is not the Holy Spirit himself grace, and preeminently so?

The distribution of these charisms freely given remains an unpredictable manifestation of the Spirit.

---

[18]Cf. St. Thomas Aquinas, *Summa Theologica*, I, 38; our formulation attempts to deepen and explicate on the intra-Trinitarian level the thought of the Common Doctor.

b) *The extraordinary charisms, the "free" field of the Spirit in the Church*

If the Spirit linked himself to the episcopal college, to the institution, and freely so, he remains at the same time sovereignly free and transcendent in it and with regard to it. And he manifests this by periodic irruptions: "sometimes he even visibly anticipates the apostolic action, while not ceasing to accompany and direct it in various ways" (*AG* 4: the council in a note refers to the many incidents mentioned by the Acts). Consequently we must stress with Y. Congar:

> ...the evident duality of ways by which the Holy Spirit operates, and by which the Church is also constructed:...the Institution and the Event. ... The body of Christ is built up by the regular, functional and hierarchical mediation of the instituted ministers, sacraments and other signs of the Church; it is also built up by the unforeseeable, occasional and fraternal mediation of the various encounters and unexpected signs which the Spirit of Jesus stirs up and which he offers to souls disposed to receive them.[19]

Let us cite some examples of these unpredictable lateral contributions to the building up of the Church: the effusion of the Spirit before baptism (Acts 10:44, 47), the addition of Paul to the apostolic college outside the normal channels—and yet today we call him the Apostle par excellence—Paul invited to take the road to Europe (Acts 16:6-7), the sending of Philip by the Spirit to the eunuch of the queen of Ethiopia (Acts 8), etc.

These examples are drawn from the New Testament, but naturally we could draw many more from the history of the Church. It will suffice to mention here the following historical gifts of the Spirit to the Church: Francis of Assisi, St. Ignatius of Loyola and his *Spiritual Exercises*, Blessed Helen Guerra inviting Leo XIII to write an encyclical on the Holy Spirit and effectively obtaining *Divinum Illud Munus* (1897), John XXIII convoking the second council of the Vatican.

All these "event" charisms were accepted by the Institution. Or, to put it better, they were integrated into it. Thenceforth they become part of the institution, so that in a sense one would not be able to reject them without tending to destroy it. This institutionalization of the charismatic gift flows logically from the law of growth of the institution itself under the action of the Spirit. Some charisms have a permanent and definitive value for the Institution. There are unique events from which all subsequent generations draw nourishment. These are charisms that do not pass away.

Because of these, and also because each member of the Church in every epoch will receive his charisms for the good of the whole Church of his time

---

[19]Congar, *op. cit.*, pp. 170-171.

and thus indirectly for the whole Church of all times, we can and ought to say that charisms are a permanent datum in the institution itself and one of its structures.

This must also be said for another reason: the ministry of the Spirit is itself the unfolding of the sacramental charisms (cf. 1 Tm. 4:14; 2 Tm. 1:6). The episcopal magisterium is linked to the effusion of the Spirit in the Sacrament of Orders (LG 21).

Let us also say with Congar that "the Holy Spirit does not cease to do inwardly what the hierarchical ministry performs visibly and outwardly, according to a covenantal bond. But he also intervenes directly, and first of all in the very activity of the apostles in order to direct as it were personally the increase of the Church and the building up of the mystical body."[20] Here we see the relevance of the Spirit as "event."

And it is quite right to appropriate to the Spirit these charisms given by the Three, inseparably, for the renewal and the rejuvenescence of the Church in the course of its pilgrimage toward Them: for is it not in him that the interior cycle of the Trinity is consummated? All the charisms, even those which at first glance seem divisive, are always oriented toward the consummation of the Church in its final inalienable unity; for this reason too they should be appropriated to the Spirit, who is the consubstantial and eternal communion between the Father and the Son.

Thus it is by way of the charismatic activity of Christians that the characteristic property of the Spirit in the bosom of the Trinity manifests itself in the Church. Through this activity we perceive better, in faith—and we are again borrowing this conclusion from Y. Congar—that "if the Church is always the work of the Holy Spirit who dwells in her, this is true not exclusively of the Spirit as bound to the institution and working in and by it. For the Holy Spirit retains a certain freedom of action—immediate, autonomous and personal. Thus there exists a kind of free field which constitutes one of the most revealing characteristics of the Church's life."[21]

Thus "the centrality" of the Holy Spirit shines out not only in contemporary Catholic theology but also in the official doctrine of the Church.

III. THE TRINITARIAN DOCTRINE OF PAUL VI AND THE DUTCH CATECHISM

In 1966 the Dutch catechism appeared, officially approved by the episcopate of the Low Countries. In regard to the Trinity and as well as on other questions, it compels us to investigate the problems, already encountered in the preceding chapter, concerning the language of faith in our times.

In truth Vatican II had already marked a stage in this area of the expres-

[20]Ibid., p. 169.
[21]Ibid., p. 171.

sion of the Trinitarian faith, one which we had no occasion to comment on in the developments immediately preceding.

In fact, Vatican II consciously and deliberately placed side by side with the post-Nicene Trinitarian language almost, if not altogether, exclusively employed by the ecclesiastical magisterium for centuries, a pre-Nicene biblical language. This remark applies especially with regard to the first person of the Holy Trinity.

In harmony with its biblical renewal and doubtless also with an ecumenical intention, Vatican II more than once speaks of God to signify not the Trinity but exclusively the person of the Father. This is clear, for example, in LG 17; we cite this text all the more willingly since it offers the advantage of synthesizing under an eschatological light the Trinitarian ecclesiology of Vatican II:

> The Church simultaneously prays and labors in order that the entire world may become the People of God, the Body of the Lord and the Temple of the Holy Spirit.

Nonetheless, post-Nicene language continues to be very much used; often there is question of the Triune God (UR 1, 2, 12, etc.). Most commonly, the first person is designated not by the expression "God" but by the terms "Father," "God the Father."

Moreover, as we have said, Vatican II did not intend to treat in depth the relations between the Father, his Son and their Spirit. The preceding councils had already done that; the task of Vatican II was something else.

Though the council by no means intended to expound on the totality of Christian doctrine and to present in its sixteen documents a kind of new catechism to the world, nevertheless the authors of the Dutch catechism for adults believed it sufficient, it seems, to speak of the Trinity with as little (or almost as little) systematic completeness as Vatican II. They preferred not to investigate in the light of Scripture the interior aspect of the mystery, the relations between the Persons, nor even to explain clearly the missions of the Son and of the Spirit (which after all presuppose the divine interiority). Were they influenced in this consciously or unconsciously by the functional theology in vogue today? We do not know.

In contrast to the method followed heretofore—and this difference represents a very legitimate option—the Dutch catechism presents the mystery of the Trinity only at the end of its teaching.[22]

Let us cite here the essentials of the Trinitarian presentation of the Dutch catechism, which takes up only a few lines in this book of 631 pages

---

[22]Cf. *Une introduction à la foi catholique, Le nouveau catéchisme pour adultes.* Paris, Ch. Ehlinger, 1968, pp. 628-630.

(very few lines indeed to devote to the fundamental mystery); they are, however, very rich:

> At the end of this book in which we have been speaking throughout of the Father, the Son and the Holy Spirit, a treatise of several pages would set this mystery too much apart. It would rather be necessary to repeat with all its nuances what we have said of Jesus of Nazareth, of his obedience to the will of the Father.... His destiny signifies and contains the eternal love between him and the Father. The Father and the Son send the Spirit over the world, the Spirit who is one with the Father (1 Cor. 2:10), one with the Son (2 Cor. 3:17), the Spirit who is himself the love between the Father and the Son, as is symbolized by the dove descending on Jesus while the voice resounds: "You are my beloved Son" (Mk. 1:10). The message of Scripture confronts us with the distinct persons of Father, Son and Holy Spirit and at the same time with their divine unity; all this with such force that we are allowed to confess one only God in three persons.[23]

Let us stop for a moment. The authors do not wish to speak too much of this Trinitarian mystery by itself but rather in connection with the divine Person and the human life of Jesus. This is another legitimate option. We continue our reading:

> All this becomes lived truth for us when we try to be with Christ. When the Spirit who proceeds from the Father and from the Son renders us capable of living with Jesus, we become aware that our existence, however poor and insignificant it may be, through Jesus finds its source in the Father and in Jesus flows toward the Father.... The Triune love can make us suspect in what direction to look for the answer to the question: why does the whole of creation exist? Because in God himself there is this "generating," there is this Spirit of Love toward the First-born, that is why the whole world was created.[24]

We note on the one hand the desire not to separate Trinity and creation, Trinity and human life; and on the other hand, in this context, the brief mention of the generation of the Son and the procession of the Spirit.

This is practically[25] all that the Dutch catechism in its 631 pages can find to say by way of systematic exposition about the initial and final mystery, about the Trinity. What it says is well formulated; but it is much too little, if we recall that we are dealing with a catechism destined for adults.

[23]*Ibid.*, p. 629.
[24]*Ibid.*, p. 630.
[25]We should add that there is a brief mention on p. 261 of the "mystery of one God in three persons, the Father who sends, the Son who is sent, the Spirit whom the two confer."

What is more, the theological commission designated by the commission of Cardinals to examine the Dutch catechism, remarked appropriately that this work rests solely on the biblical unfolding of Revelation, without taking account of the Church's professions of faith and teaching: notably, in speaking of Nicaea[26] the catechism finds a way (by a tour de force?) of avoiding use of the term "consubstantial."[27] The commission further expressed its fear that the Dutch catechism did not give a sufficiently central importance to this mystery of the Trinity, at least in its specific exposition of this subject.

In reality however, the attitude of the authors of this work is sufficiently explained in the framework of their overall position: namely, to speak everywhere of the Father, the Son and the Spirit in a diffused way but nowhere to treat the Three systematically, for this would be to set apart the mystery of the divine interiority: "we know that in order to know God we must not take leave of the place where his revelation has brought us, our everyday life, the world of men."[28]

Yet this position seems to contradict what the same authors explain very well with regard to the divine transcendence: "the biblical message proclaims that God himself is not part of this world."[29] This very correct principle the authors seem to have forgotten when they came to the Trinity, where they preferred not to stress the very transcendence that would precisely have obliged them to give the Trinity a treatment apart.

We can understand then the reaction of the commission of Cardinals appointed by the Holy See, when it adopted the opinion of its own theological commission:

> There should be a better presentation of the mystery of the three persons in God, which Christians appropriately contemplate with the eyes of faith and filialy love, not only in the economy of salvation where the Three adorable Persons manifest themselves, but also in the intimate life of the divinity, where they dwell eternally and whose vision we look forward to.[30]

We think this text was illumined in advance by the credo pronounced in the name of the people of God, on June 30, 1968, by Pope Paul VI: there we will see what would be the object or orientation of a "better presentation" of the mystery of the three divine Persons.

---

[26]*Ibid.*, pp. 112-116.

[27]Doubtless for the same reasons for which it avoids the expression "transubstantiation," whereas both expressions are utilized by the credo of Paul VI.

[28]*Ibid.*, p. 628.

[29]*Ibid.*, p. 617; if God is not part of this world, is it not normal to lift oneself above this world of men in order to know him? Cf. p. 439.

[30]Declaration of the commission of Cardinals, *AAS* 60 (1968), 690, § 9.

But before citing the text itself of the pontifical profession of faith, it is fitting to point out that instead of ending with a development on the Trinitarian mystery it begins with it. Is it not true that one may not easily (though this may be possible) end well where one has not begun?

We might further point out the extreme doctrinal importance of this text which, "without being a dogmatic definition," as the Pope specified, approximates this as much as possible.[31] Let us recall that besides defined dogmas there are non-defined dogmas, professed by the ordinary and universal magisterium of the Church (*DS* 3011; *DB* 1792).

The very first words of the Symbol of Paul VI are: "We believe in one only God, Father, Son and Holy Spirit." Then the credo extols with precision the God who is Creator and absolutely one. It then goes on:

> He is the One who is, which is what he revealed to Moses, and he is Love, as the Apostle John teaches us: in such a way that these two names, Being and Love, express ineffably the same divine reality of him who wished to make himself known to us, and who, "dwelling in light inaccessible," is in himself above every name, all things and every created intelligence.

Such is the preamble of the properly Trinitarian part of the credo, and it certainly differs notably, by its accent on transcendence, not from the general doctrine of the Dutch catechism but from the introduction to its Trinitarian chapter. If God the Revealer is above every created intelligence, it is indispensable for this intelligence to transcend mentally its everyday life so as to be able to approach this immense God whom the world of men cannot circumscribe. There is no entry into the Trinitarian mystery except by passing from time and spatio-temporal dispersion to eternal life, a fact that one hardly sees stressed in the Trinitarian chapter of the Dutch catechism but which in contrast shines out in the famous prayer of Sister Elizabeth of the Trinity: "O my God, Trinity, whom I adore, help me to forget myself entirely so as to be established in you, motionless and calm as if my soul were already in eternity."

This is certainly the disposition in which the credo of Paul VI would wish to establish us. Let us continue our reading:

> God alone can give us true and full knowledge [of this reality] in revealing himself as Father, Son and Holy Spirit, whose eternal life we are called to share by grace, here below in the obscurity of faith and beyond death in eternal light. The mutual bonds that eternally constitute

---

[31]Cf. J. A. de Aldama, S.J., "La profesión de fé de Pablo VI," *Estudios ecles.*, 43 (1968), 478-505; for this author the document is one of exceptional character which, by its structure and by the circumstances which surround it, has the same theological value as a dogmatic definition, even though the Pope was not intending to define: cf. p. 505.

the three persons, each one of whom is the same and only divine being, are the blessed and intimate life of the thrice holy God, infinitely beyond all that we can conceive by human standards.

We give thanks, however, to the divine Goodness for the fact that very many believers can give witness with us before men to the unity of God even though they do not know the mystery of the Most Holy Trinity.

We believe, then, in the Father who eternally generates the Son; in the Son, Word of God who is eternally generated; in the Holy Spirit, uncreated person who proceeds from the Father and from the Son as their eternal love.

Thus in the three Divine Persons, "coeternal" and "coequal" among themselves, are found in superabundant and consummated fashion, in the supreme excellence and glory proper to uncreated being, the life and the beatitude of the God who is perfectly one, and we must always venerate the unity in Trinity and the Trinity in unity.[32]

The characteristic traits of this profession of Trinitarian faith are, in addition to the above noted insistence on the transcendence of the mystery, the stress put on its eternity and on the beatitude of the divine Persons. It thus becomes clear that man, though called by grace to participate in these reciprocal relations of the divine Persons and in their happiness, is nonetheless not necessary for it. Even if this seems disconcerting to our feeble reason and still more to our narrow heart, we must have the courage to say that the happiness of man, which God wills and pursues even at the price of his suffering, is still not necessary for the existence of the infinite happiness from which it springs.

What Paul VI's profession of faith thus suggests, in contrast to the Dutch catechism, is that the essential beatitude of men consists not in their reciprocal relations (herein lies their accidental beatitude) but in the loving and participative contemplation of the reciprocal relations between the divine Persons and of the uncreated beatitude which is inseparable from them. Such is "the blessed and intimate life of God, infinitely beyond all that we can conceive by human standards"—therefore beyond the happiness that man left to his own resources could imagine or pursue—but which "we are called to share by grace." Already, "in the obscurity of faith" our initiated happiness and salvation consist precisely in the contemplative participation, forerunner of the eternal vision, in these "mutual bonds" of the divine Persons.

All this, which is strongly implied in the profession of faith, invites us to go beyond the opposition between the economy of salvation and the intimate life of the divinity that is still understandably present in the text of the

---

[32]Profession of Faith of Paul VI, AAS 60 (1968), 436-437, §9-10.

commission of Cardinals on the Dutch catechism cited above. The text strives with good reason to contrast terrestrial manifestation and eternal manifestation of the Trinitarian economy of salvation. The credo of Paul VI invites us to consider in faith here below the intimate relations between the divine Persons, relations which condition these Persons' salvific activity and are immanent to it; and to consider also that it is by participating in them that the theological virtues constitute our human salvific activity under the action of their grace. We thus find again a fundamental theme we have proposed several times already in this book, but this time guaranteed by the magisterium of the Church.

In this respect we could say that the vigorous affirmation of the credo of Paul VI results from the legitimate synthesis of three of its phrases (if we remove the allusion to the "Unitarians"): "the mutual bonds that eternally constitute the three persons are the blessed intimate life of the thrice holy God, in which we are called to participate by grace in the obscurity of faith. These mutual and eternal bonds are the eternal generation of the Son by the Father and the procession of the Holy Spirit from the Father and from the Son as their eternal Love."[33]

Here we touch on the point which appears to have escaped the authors of the Dutch catechism, and which nevertheless concerns the nature of the beatitude offered to man and thus constitutes an anthropological zenith: already in this life the salvation of man consists in the conscious participation in the intimate, inter-personal beatitude of God; the reciprocal relations of man and God are inseparable from the reciprocal relations between the divine Persons; in the sense of classical Greek patristic terminology, the economy of salvation consists in the unfolding of the theology, of the intimate mystery of the divinity.

But at the same time it should be acknowledged that no previous document of the magisterium, not even of the ordinary magisterium as far as we know, had stated explicitly that God's inner life of happiness consists in the mutual bonds which are the generation of the Son and the procession of the Spirit. Paul VI is here synthesizing elements proposed by Lateran IV (the identity between each of the Persons and the essence of God) and by Vatican I (the affirmation of the beatitude of God to which creatures add nothing).

We have here authentic doctrinal development on a vital point that

---

[33] We take advantage here of the "then" that begins the phrase "We believe then in the Father who eternally generates the Son..." and which, if we pass over the immediately preceding phrase (about non-Christians), necessarily points to the phrase before that, which identifies the persons with the relations and their beatitude with these relations, referred to by means of the word "bonds."

touches at once on the beatitude of God and man's own essential happiness. We could not pass over this in silence.

What is more, the affirmation: "We believe in the Holy Spirit, uncreated person who proceeds from the Father and from the Son *as their eternal love*," also constitutes a doctrinal development. An affirmation of the ordinary and universal magisterium is hereby recognized as such and recognized, in consequence, as non-defined dogma. It is no longer only the procession of the Holy Spirit *ab utroque (Patre et Filio) tamquam ab uno principio* which is proclaimed, now its mode is also proclaimed: a procession of love. Leo XIII and Pius XII had affirmed this in encyclicals, and it could probably be proven without difficulty that the bishops of the world had taught this thesis for a long time, one unanimously affirmed by all the theological schools within the Catholic Church, and that they even had taught it the way St. Augustine did: as divinely revealed. In saying of this procession of love, "we believe," the Pope is also presenting it as divinely revealed. The work of the magisterium during the council of Florence is thus opportunely brought to completion. What is more, the specific point we have just considered is especially important for ecumenical dialogue with the Christian Orient: it is even possible that the procession of the Spirit by way of the Father's love for the Son, a concept which Gregory Palamas admitted, though he rejected the *Filioque*,[34] may contribute to rendering the latter more intelligible for the Orthodox Churches.

The credo of Paul VI contains still other affirmations about the Holy Spirit but as they concern his mission we will consider them when we take up this point. They add nothing essential to Vatican II.

On the other hand, we should even now remark, in the context of the Dutch catechism, that this pontifical symbol expressly repeats that the Word is consubstantial to the Father. It is then the judgment of the magisterium that this expression is still relevant and useful, like that of "transubstantiation."

As we conclude these considerations on the Trinitarian doctrine of the modern magisterium it would be in order to answer an objection.

---

[34]Cf. Gregory Palamas, *MG* 150, 1144-1145: the Holy Spirit is "the ineffable love of the Father toward the ineffably generated Word, of which the Word and Son of the Father avails himself in turning toward the Father." On this subject see M. Jugie, A.A., *DTC* XI. 2 (1932), 1766, art. "Palamas"; the author does not seem to have sufficiently noted that Palamas, in order to avoid acknowledging the *Filioque,* avoids seeing in the Spirit the mutual love of the Father and of the Son, but sees there only the love of the Father for the Son, of which, once it exists eternally, the Son "avails" himself to love the Father. Thus the love of the Son for the Father does not appear coeternal with the love of the Father for the Son, i.e., identical with it, but rather posterior. There is here, it seems, an implicit negation of the eternity of this love. It is not clear under these conditions how one can safeguard the equality of the Spirit with the Son, since the Son avails himself of the Spirit.

When we describe man's beatitude in terms of contemplation of the Trinitarian God, as we have done in the light of ecclesial tradition and especially of Paul VI's profession of faith, are we not conceiving this beatitude according to a passive model that would tend to dishonor man and even urge him to betray his supreme duty: action? Does this not make God an object exterior to man—and so alienate him?

A difficulty like this betrays a lack of understanding of the doctrine proposed and of its true meaning. The beatifying vision of the transcendent God is an immanent activity, infused in man by the divine Persons who become in this way as fully immanent in him as the Creator can be to the creature. This is the supreme activity of man, bearing on its supreme "object," an object more intimate to his mind than his mind is to itself. It must even be said that it is in and by this vision of his archetype and of his own eternal and uncreated "superessence," as Ruysbroeck would say, that man, far from being alienated, becomes not only supremely active but also supremely identical to himself, being perfectly himself and perfectly man.

Man is created to the image of the triune God: by the loving vision of the Three, the human person participates in the eternal generation of the Son by the Father and in the eternal spiration of the Spirit by the Father and the Son. This vision is inseparably passive activity, in the sense that it is received and yet is an inamissible participation in the supreme Activity which is trinitarian.

By way of anticipative consequence, the earthly contemplation of the Trinity, that is of the eternal processions of the Word and of the Spirit present in him by the life of grace (cf. Jn. 14:21-23), is the supreme earthly activity of justified man. It is precisely in its very immanence that the Trinity discloses to him its inamissible transcendence, the ineffable incomprehensibility of the eternal generation of the Son and of the eternal spiration of the Spirit, an incomprehensibility which will only fully disclose itself as incomprehensible and as inamissible[35] in the depths of the beatific vision.

Conclusion

Vatican II had stressed the missions of the Son and of the Spirit in the history of salvation, but Paul VI in his profession of faith, who also accentuated the unifying and sanctifying mission of the Spirit, brought out more strongly than ever the eternal processions of these same divine Persons.

As we have remarked several times, the missions imply and prolong in

---

[35] We know that St. John of the Cross shows, in the *Spiritual Canticle*, that the mystery of the Trinity remains incomprehensible even and especially (because this soul is more conscious of it than any other created spirit) for the created soul of the incarnate Word, who sees the One and Triune God face to face.

history the eternal processions, and their goal is even to manifest these eternal processions and draw to them the attention of the historical beings that we are.

Paul VI has merely followed the movement so well traced by Augustine when he invites us to climb from the historical missions to the eternal processions, or better still, he has obeyed the very dynamism of the missions themselves.

Whatever may have been his intention on this particular point of his credo—an immensely important point—it is the Spirit of the Father and the Son, the Spirit who guides the magisterium, who through the conciliar and post-conciliar magisterium of the Church invites us in the face of contemporary atheism and existentialist despair to scrutinize, in that attitude of respectful adoration which is the act of faith, the unfathomable mystery of the eternal generation of the Son and of his own procession as eternal love.

The mission of the Spirit in the Church continues and will always continue: the Spirit who sends us Christ as man and who is sent to us by Christ as Only Son,[36] wills to lead us always closer to the plenitude of Revelation. This plenitude is Christ,[37] understood totally as the only Son who is eternally begotten as being eternally (together with the Father who begets him) the Spirator of the Holy Breath.

This Spirit is the Spirit of the Son, the Spirit of Christ, and Vatican II brings this out.[38] In the multiple use of these Pauline expressions by Vatican II we find in germ as it were a Christological concentration of the exposition of the Trinitarian dogma. It is true that this was not explicated, as was what we might call the ecclesiological concentration of the same mystery, by this council, whose peculiar mission was to investigate the mission of the Church; but it was suggested by such expressions as these and by others we have likewise cited.

Will it not be the task of the Church of the future, a task received from an invisible mission of the Spirit, to investigate further, over against atheism and in increasing communion with the other churches and in line with ecumenical aims, the mystery of the Trinity present in Christ?

Should we not apply to the Christian Churches also, as communities, what Vatican II proclaimed regarding the individuals who are their members: "the more perfect their communion with the Father, the Word

---

[36]Cf. Lk. 4:18; *AG* 3; *AG* 4; St. Thomas Aquinas, *Summa Theologica*, I, 43.8.

[37]*DV* 2 (Christ is the fullness of Revelation); 20 (the Paraclete Spirit was to lead the apostles into the fullness of the truth; cf. Jn. 16:13). It follows from the comparison of these two texts that the mission of the Paraclete consists in glorifying Christ by manifesting him fully in the course of the history of the Church.

[38]See for example *LG* 13; *AG* 11, etc.; cf. Gal. 4:6; Rom. 8:4, 10.

and the Holy Spirit, the more will they help to make our mutual brotherhood an interior and easy task"?

Let us add: the more will they discover themselves as Sister-Churches.

Does not the Spirit who speaks to the Churches, wish through them to glorify Christ as the only Son of the Father and as his own Spirator?[39]

---

[39]Apoc. 2:7; Jn. 16:14; 1:18; 3:16. Cf. M. Comeau, *Augustin exégète du IV évangile*. Paris, 1930, p. 289: "it is then supremely important for the Christian to know Christ for it is in Christ and by Christ that he can know and possess the entire Trinity."

Part II
Systematic Vision
Omnia Per Modum Unius

VII
False Trinitarian Systematizations, Their Presuppositions and Their Consequences

After a sufficiently detailed study of the history of Trinitarian dogma which has already involved grappling with many speculative problems, we must now undertake to present some of the great efforts to systematize the mystery. We will begin with those that appear false to us, either in their essential lines or in some of their roots or formulations, even where their general direction is, on the whole, more or less orthodox. Will not the truth stand out better against this background of error? And in every error is there not an element of truth that should be discovered and salvaged?

After having glanced rapidly at the Trinitarian mysticism of Eckhart and of Blessed Ruysbroeck, without overlooking St. John of the Cross, we will take up the Trinitarian and evolutionist pantheism of Hegel, the anti-Trinitarian evolutionism of the Spiritist movement, and finally the rationalist attempts of Günther. Thus we will have occasion to clarify the indemonstrable character of the mystery, and we will come to understand better the great difficulty of presenting this mystery in the context of a too exclusively psychological notion of person.

I. TRINITARIAN MYSTERY AND MEDIEVAL MYSTICISM

1. *Pantheist affinities of Eckhart*

In order to grasp these affinities it is first of all necessary to recall briefly Eckhart's philosophical vision, as Gilson has so brilliantly done: he showed very well the dependence of Eckhart's mysticism on his ontology.[1] While himself a Dominican, his philosophy was hardly Thomistic at base. Instead it was dominated by Neo-Platonism.

Without wishing to take sides among the divergent interpretations of Eckhartian specialists (notably Théry, Denifle, Oechslin, Walz), we might simply note with Duval,[2] the parallelism between Eckhart's Trinitarian theology and his rational psychology:

---

[1] E. Gilson, *La Philosophie au Moyen Age*. Paris, 1947, pp. 694-700.
[2] A. Duval, *Catholicisme*. Paris, 1952, v. III, col. 1260, art. "Eckhart."

Totally pure Unity is the center and summit of the very mystery of God, beyond the mystery of the Trinity. This unity of the divine essence is that of the Intellect, which is the Father, who generates Life or the Son, whence proceeds Being, who is the Holy Spirit. To this structure of the mystery of God, if this could be said, corresponds the structure of the soul. Just as there is a beyond in reference to the Three Persons, so there is a beyond in reference to the three faculties of the soul: memory, understanding, and will. This beyond is the "citadel" of the soul, its secret, a spark of the divine Intellect, and like it one and simple.

Reading these lines we think almost spontaneously of Porphyry and Plotinus, as well as the Platonic and Gnostic tendency to isolate the supreme God; Eckhart's speculation, however, leads to an inverse result: "in the soul there is something uncreated and uncreatable; if the whole soul were such, it would be uncreated and uncreatable, and that is the intellect" (DS 977; DB 527).

This proposition, condemned by the magisterium of the Church, shows very well that Eckhart is not a Pantheist pure and simple, but it shows also that he is partially so. Denifle, who exonerated him in part, is obliged to admit this: on the basis of the Latin writings of Eckhart it clearly appears that the "master," while recognizing the real distinction between essence and existence in creatures, nevertheless believes that the *esse* of God is the formal *esse* of all things.[3] M. de Wulf has also acknowledged this: "the identity of existence that envelops God and creature seems to compromise the distinction between finite and infinite: Eckhart here borders on Pantheism."[4]

Once the identity of existence between God and man is perceived, one is less surprised to read the propositions in which the Rhineland Dominican identifies himself either with Christ the Son of God in his eternal passive generation, or with God the Father inasmuch as he is creator and active generator of the eternal Word. The contradiction here involved does not seem to embarrass the "master," who nonetheless, despite his presuppositions about *esse*, never extends this double identification to every man but only to the justified:

Everything God the Father gave to his Only Son in the human nature, all this he has given to me. I exclude nothing, neither union nor sanctity. ...Everything that is proper to the divine nature is also proper to the just and divine man: consequently, this man does everything God does, and

---

[3]Denifle-Ehrlé, *Archiv für Litteratur-und Kirchen-Geschichte des Mittelalters*. Berlin, 1886, v. II, pp. 518-519.
[4]Cited by F. Vernet in his article: "Eckhart," DTC IV (1911), 2073.

with God he creates heaven and earth, and is begetter of the eternal Word, and without this man God could do nothing.... Everything God does is one: so he begets me as his son without any distinction (DS 961, 963, 972; DB 511, 513, 522).

These formulas, then, objectively speaking, signify a simple identification of the justified man with the Word, the Only Son of God or with the Father as the one who creates the universe and generates the eternal Word. We feel we must be dreaming. Is this really what Eckhart intended to say? Doubtless he intended this when he wrote these lines as well as at other moments, but this was not always the case. Before his death he made an act of full submission to the Apostolic See and of "revocation and reprobation of whatever in his teachings and writings could produce an heretical or erroneous understanding in the minds of the faithful" (DS 980; see the note). Moreover, these same writings contain many profound and correct views, albeit mixed with numerous errors. This explains his influence both on authentic mystics like Blessed Suso, and on Luther.

Besides this double identification between the *esse* of the creature and the divine *esse*, and between the just man on the one hand, and the Father creator and generator of his "Only" Son, on the other, we should also point out another effect of the Neo-Platonic influence on the "master": dislike for every form of distinction leads him to reject (at least in appearance) every transcendental number[5] in God, who is viewed as "outside of and above all number." Is it not the Trinity of persons itself that is rejected, at least implicitly, when he says, "There can be no distinction in God himself" (DS 973 and 974; DB 523 and 524)?

If it must be acknowledged that the anti-intellectualist horror of distinctions, so common in our twentieth century, leads logically to the denial of the Trinity and to pantheism, we must also admit on the other hand that Eckhart intended to deny a real distinction only in the essence and not between the persons; but he stressed the real identity between nature and person, without stressing with equal vigor, it seems, the real distinction between the persons (DS 974; DB 524 toward the end).

In the light of all that we have just said, we can allow that Eckhart was a distant and partial precursor of the Trinitarian theology of Hegel which we shall examine shortly.

In our opinion, a partial source of Eckhart's errors may possibly be seen in an unfortunate interpretation of some texts of St. Thomas Aquinas. It is likely enough that Eckhart believed he could find support in the Thomistic doctrine of the divine ideas in the Word, in which, considerably later,

---

[5]See our chapter III, with regard to this notion.

Harnack would see a "pantheism" of sorts. Let us cite one text among others[6] which is quite significant: one could here speak of a certain "panentheism":[7]

> From the fact that the likeness of the creature in the Word is productive and motive of the creature existing in its proper nature, it follows that in some way the creature itself moves and leads itself to being, inasmuch as it is produced in being and moved by its likeness existing in the Word.[8]

An astounding and daring text, to be sure, and yet one that firmly maintains the distinction between the ideal plane and the real plane. But did not Eckhart precisely confuse these? Against the background of other confusions and improper identifications already noted, we can see how he could arrive at this impossible and absurd identification of the justified man with the Word or the Father, of the created person with the uncreated Persons. At least at the time of these writings he was harboring not a pantheism pure and simple, but a pantheism of grace and existence (*esse*). Ruysbroeck, although partially situated in the same problematic, supplied a more orthodox though not perfectly satisfactory reply.

2. *Does Ruysbroeck sufficiently salvage the eternity of the Trinity?*

Like Eckhart, Ruysbroeck is a very difficult and synthetic author. Like him too he tried to find a greater unity between the immanent Trinity and the economic Trinity. He was certainly more successful in this: not only has the Church not condemned a single one of Ruysbroeck's propositions, she has even recognized him as Blessed, and a document of the Holy See expresses favorable sentiments toward his doctrine though in rather general terms.[9]

Let us first recall how Blessed Ruysbroeck develops a certain "Trinitarian panentheism" along the lines of St. Thomas and yet avoids the pitfalls of Eckhart's formulations:

> Before its creation the soul is present in the nature of God, according to the very modality, virtual or actual, that characterizes each of the divine Persons who are all identical with the one divine nature: in the nature as

---

[6]St. Thomas Aquinas, *Summa Theologica*, I, 18.4c, 2; *Summa contra Gentiles*, IV, 13.

[7]Cf. Lalande, *Vocabulaire de la Philosophie*. Paris, 1947, p. 713: art. "Panenthéisme": "everything is in God; a term created in 1828 and sometimes applied to other conceptions that were intended to be contrasted with pantheism." This term is notably utilized by Blondel.

[8]St. Thomas Aquinas, *De Veritate*, IV, 8.

[9]*AAS* I (1909), 165: the text of the Holy See, confirming the cult rendered to this Blessed, says: "scriptis Ecclesiae Christi doctrinam cum evangelicis consiliis docuit ac praedicavit"; but the text carefully refrains from saying that all the propositions of Ruysbroeck can be defended and are true!

identified with the Father the soul is, together with the Son, unengendered and not manifested; in the procession of the Son the created being proceeds in the likeness of the Father and lives in and by the life of the Son (Jn. 1:3-4); in the procession of the Spirit it is brought back to the unity of its nature and to the unity of the divine nature. The Trinitarian modalities of the soul in its eternal state, as uncreated ideal, of which the Word as perfect image of the Father is the source, these condition it likewise in its state as temporal creature, really distinct from the substance of God.[10]

We might dispute this or that expression[11] in which P. Henry thus summarizes Ruysbroeck's doctrine, nevertheless this text brings out very well the essential point: in the soul as also in God, there are, according to a Neo-Platonic schema, three "dialectic moments": the unity of departure or *mone* (the Father or the essence of the soul), the expression in act, the *proodos* (the Word which the soul resembles by Faith) and finally the return toward final perfection, the *epistrophe* or *teleiosis* (the Spirit, principle of return to the divine unity—as the Father was the principle of departure—and the charity that unifies the soul at the same time that it unites it to God).

Nevertheless in Ruysbroeck the Trinity of persons and the reality of their distinction and processions appear to be at least logically posterior to an ineffable beyond of the divine essence into which in another moment, logical if not real, these same persons then proceed to disappear. Let us rather read these obscure texts themselves:

> The unfathomable absence of mode in God is so dark and mysterious that it engulfs within itself all the divine modes...the properties of the persons in the rich embrace of the essential unity.... The persons and all that lives in God must yield before this unity.[12]

It is difficult to see, at first glance, how the real and eternal distinction of the divine Persons is compatible with such affirmations. We think at once of the *nirvana* of the Buddhists and of the unfortunate expressions of Joachim of Flora and of certain Greek or Latin Fathers according to whom the Persons come forth from an initially impersonal[13] essence. Here the Persons give the impression of being a dialectical moment between an initial impersonality and a final depersonalization of the divine essence. It is easy, too easy, to understand these texts in this way, but it is doubtful that such

---

[10] P. Henry, S.J., *Mystique trinitaire du Bx. J. Ruysbroeck*, Rech. Sc. Rel., 41 (1953), 52.

[11] The divine persons are always actually and never virtually identical with the divine nature, since they are coeternal.

[12] Ruysbroeck, *L'ornement des noces spirituelles*, final page. Cf. P. Henry, S.J., art. cit., R.S.R. 40 (1952), 367.

[13] Cf. our ch. III, §IV, d.

an interpretation corresponds to the "dialectical" thought of the author, as other texts reveal:

> The divine Persons lose and engulf themselves in the essential Love, that is to say in fruitful unity, and yet they always remain in the operations of the Trinity according to their personal properties. The divine nature is eternally active according to the mode of the Persons and eternally in repose and without mode according to the simplicity of its Essence.[14]
>
> There, in the unity of the essence, we find neither Father nor Son nor Holy Spirit nor any creature. There, the essence alone, that is the very substance of the divine persons.[15]

For P. Henry, "one can and ought to affirm with Ruysbroeck the ontological and dynamic simultaneity of the contrary and complementary dialectical moments."[16] We think it is unquestionable that Ruysbroeck believed in the eternity of the divine Persons who are always identical with the essence and never disappear; but with Bossuet we also think that his expressions, in their apparent negation of these revealed truths, are "strange" and "exorbitant"! It is also to be observed that the Church has not made her own the strange Trinitarian language of Ruysbroeck, whom she nevertheless beatified, while she did appropriate, in large measure, the Trinitarian language of Tertullian albeit he died outside her bosom. However interesting it may be, the Trinitarian doctrine of Ruysbroeck does not constitute a moment in the evolution of the Trinitarian language of the Church.

Ruysbroeck's merit, however, lies in offering us not only a rich and profound view of the procession of the Spirit, seen as a return of the Son to the Father,[17] but also an attempt to rethink, at the core of the Third Person and in line with Augustine's approach, the bond between "economy" and "theology." He expresses himself thus in commenting on John 17:21: "The Holy Spirit is the unfathomable love (of the persons) who holds them eternally embraced in love and fruition and all of us with Them: one life, one love, one fruition."[18] Elsewhere Ruysbroeck magnificently epitomized his thought on the bond between Trinity and paschal mystery:

> The contact of God draws us from within, effects unity at the most profound center of our being, exacting from us this joyous death which the Spirit produces when he makes man faint away in happiness, that is in

---

[14]Ruysbroeck, *Oeuvres*, v. II, 215; cited by T. Koehler, *R.A.M.* 40 (1964), 295-296.
[15]Ruysbroeck, *Degrés*, XIV end; v. I, p. 264; Henry, *art. cit.*, p. 349.
[16]*Ibid.*, p. 350.
[17]*Ibid.*, pp. 354-367: "the Father, initial unity, and the Spirit, terminal unity of the divine nature," P. Fransen, S.J., *Nouv. Rev. Théol.* 74 (1952) 183-185.
[18]Ruysbroeck, *Oeuvres*, v. I, p. 290.

eternal love, the embrace of the Father and the Son and the common joy of both. When with Jesus we mount toward the pinnacle of our spirit, on the mountain of nakedness without image...we feel the Fire of the Spirit which consumes us and dissolves us at the center of the divine unity.... The voice of the Father calls to us and says to us: Come back to me. To all his elect he says, according to his eternal words: "Behold my beloved Son in whom I am well pleased."

The Father and the Son have tasted in the future Incarnation, in the death of Jesus and in the return of the elect toward their eternal principle an eternal pleasure. If, through the Son, we are brought back to our origin, it is then that we hear the voice of the Father who says to us: Come back to me.[19]

In this very beautiful text we see how in the Paschal Mystery of the Only Son and in that of the Spirit's descent is found articulated the union of what Ruysbroeck calls the essential (in the soul) with the ideal and eternal "superessence" of the soul, the Triune God who dwells in it and who is eternally identical with the uncreated and creative Idea which he has of this soul.[20] Or, if you prefer, and to take up again the words of P. Henry cited above, the union of the created essence of the soul with its Trinitarian modalities in its eternal and uncreated state. And it is in the most intimate part of our soul that this real, and not ideal, uncreated Trinity dwells: it is within our very selves that we must return to the Father, thanks to the death of the Son, in the Fire of the Spirit, by way of the theological virtues which liken us to the Son (faith) and to the Spirit (charity).

An element of truth contained in the speculations of Ruysbroeck and Eckhart seems to us to have been retained by St. John of the Cross, who was undoubtedly influenced by the former. Speaking, as Maritain observes, as a mystic rather than as a speculative theologian[21] but, unlike Eckhart, conscious of this distinction, St. John of the Cross writes these astonishing lines: the Holy Spirit, by producing in the soul a "very delicate feeling and sentiment of love" elevates it to the point where it can "spirate in God the same spiration of love which the Father spirates in the Son and the Son in the Father, which is this same Holy Spirit whom they spirate within the soul during this transformation."[22] Commenting on John 17:24 ("I desire ...that they may see the glory which you have given me"), the mystical Doctor writes: "that is: that they perform in us by participation the same

---

[19]Ruysbroeck, *L'Anneau ou la Pierre brillante*. Brussels, 1920, ch. XII.
[20]The word "superessence" seems to be well chosen to synthesize the complex idea that Ruysbroeck has in mind; on this word, see A. Deblaere, S.J., *DSAM*, v. IV (1960), vol. 2, col. 1351ff.: art. "Essentiel et superessentiel."
[21]J. Maritain, *Les Degrés du Savoir*. Paris, 1946, pp. 750ff.
[22]St. John of the Cross, *Spiritual Canticle*, str. 38.

operation that I perform by nature, which is to spirate the Holy Spirit." The key word is spelled out: participation; St. John of the Cross means to say that by the virtue of charity, poured out in the soul by the Spirit (cf. Rom. 5:5), the soul participates in some manner in the procession of the Spirit in God. But there is no question here of entitative but rather of moral participation; for in the eyes of St. John of the Cross, it is clearly not the soul which produces the uncreated Spirit (whereas Eckhart, as we saw, thought that the justified soul engenders the Word and creates the world!), but rather the soul by faith and charity becomes a perfect image of the Father inasmuch as he produces his eternal Son, and of the Father and Son inasmuch as they spirate the Spirit. Thus St. John of the Cross writes (commenting on John 17:23): "one must not think that the Son intended to ask of the Father that the saints become one and the same thing by essence and by nature like the Father and the Son but that they may become so by union of love as the Father and Son are one in unity of love."[23] Even if his formulas are not perfectly clear (which is pardonable, given the extreme difficulty of the matter) yet they are less obscure than the equivocal assertion of Blessed Ruysbroeck: "All the spirits melt and fade into nothingness by the fruition of the Essence of God who is the Superessence of all essence,"[24] or his commentary (cited above) on a similar prayer of Jesus in John 17:21: "we all with them (the divine Persons) are one life, one love, one fruition." In all these cases the authors speak the language of mystical theology and not that of speculative theology. But St. John of the Cross seems more conscious of this through reservations the others do not exhibit, though it is true that it would perhaps have been preferable to avoid completely the expression "spirating the Spirit" when speaking of a creature.

What these authors are trying to say is that "the mystical experience tends from the beginning to the loving and fruitional knowledge of the Three divine Persons," according to J. Maritain's happy expression. Earlier the Angelic Doctor had already written: "The knowledge of the Trinity in unity is the fruit and end of our whole life."[25] And, as much as fifteen centuries ago, Augustine wrote: "The realities we have for enjoyment are the Father, the Son and the Holy Spirit."[26]

If the formulas of Ruysbroeck (unlike his thought) do not sufficiently preserve the transcendence of the eternal Trinity, and if those of Eckhart imply a "Trinitarian pantheism," which however he does not consistently teach, nevertheless they are both tributary to the doctrines of Augustine

---

[23] Ibid.
[24] Ruysbroeck, Le livre de la plus haute vérité, Oeuvres, v. II, pp. 220-221. Cited by T. Koehler, RAM 40 (1964), 302.
[25] St. Thomas Aquinas, I Sent., dist. 2, expos. textus.
[26] St. Augustine, De doctrina christiana, I, 5; ML, 34, 21.

False Systematizations 257

and of Thomas Aquinas, which is far from true in the case of "modern Trinitarian pantheism."

II. THE PANTHEIST SAVOR OF MODERN TRINITARIAN EVOLUTIONISM[27]

1. *Is Hegel a theologian of the Trinity?*
Several contemporary Catholic philosophers affirm this.[28] In contrast, theologians seem to deny it: H. Rondet does not even hesitate to speak of a "Trinitarian pseudo-theology" with regard to Hegel.[29]

Here is how he presents its essential lines, with the (inevitable) risk of simplifying them; but he is quite successful in giving us a genetic glimpse of Hegel's Trinitarian doctrine, which arises from his concerns as an historian and philosopher of history.

> Hegel is first of all an historian.
> The true God understands himself properly only in his relation with the universe he created—with the history of the universe and of humanity. It is in this temporal unfolding that God becomes conscious of himself.[30]
> This other that he posits outside himself in order to encounter himself again in it, is the visible and invisible universe, immense and alive, which has no other organic unity than that given it by the presence of the Idea, the Word, the Son of God.
> When man rises to participation in the very life of God, God is in man and man is in God, the finite and the infinite meet, God reveals himself to man and in man becomes conscious of himself.
> A man, in order to become conscious of his personality and to become what he is in potency, must express himself and give himself an objective history which will summarize his knowledge of the whole. So it is with God. God necessarily has a history. Universal History is that of Spirit attaining consciousness of itself. This history implies as it were three moments in the divine life: God before creation, God the creator, God who encounters himself again in creation and finally realizes that he has not gone out of himself.[31]

---

[27]We do not claim to be complete and so we do not treat here of the precursors of the "trinitarian pantheism" of Hegel: Spinoza, Fichte, Lessing.

[28]For example, A. Chapelle, S.J., although with some reservations: *Hegel et la religion*. Paris, 1967, v. II; *Dialectique*, 53-109; C. Bruaire, *Logique et religion chrétienne dans la Philosophie de Hegel*. Paris, 1964.

[29]H. Rondet, S.J., *Hégélianisme et christianisme*. Paris, 1965, p. 117, note 3.

[30]Note however that A. Chapelle protests against any idea of identifying God and man in Hegel (*op. cit.*, pp. 75-76).

[31]H. Rondet, S.J., "Divinisation du chrétien," *Nouv. Rev. Théol.* 71 (1949), 564-576.

Even if one could dispute the precision of one or another aspect of this suggestive presentation, it will suffice to read now a text of Hegel's own to see that it does not notably deviate from the substance of Hegelian thought:

> Christian theology makes of God, that is of the Truth, not an immobile being congealed in an empty unicity, but a Spirit, a being who enters into a process of differentiation with himself. This being posits outside himself an Other and comes to a consciousness of himself, not by abandoning this Other but by assuming it by way of a negation and a going beyond (*aufheben*). Theology expresses this process for purposes of representation by saying that God the Father (the Universal existing in himself) emerging from within his solitude creates a nature (something outside himself, external existence), generates a Son (his other self) and then by an infinite love sees himself in this Son and recognizes in him his own image and thus comes back to his unity. This unity is no longer abstract and immediate but concrete, resulting from a differentiation between Father and Son, and reaching its perfect realization and its verification in the Christian community by becoming Holy Spirit.

This text from the *Encyclopedia*[32] seems to us to sum up marvelously the Hegelian way of approaching the Trinitarian dogma. Note the negation of divine immutability, the apparent anteriority of creation with relation to the generation of the Son, as also the affirmation of a development of the divine unity which reaches its perfection only through the Church and through it becomes Holy Spirit. What is more, Hegel says explicitly that God "comes to the consciousness of himself,"[33] which only redoubles the denial of the divine eternity already implicit in the denial of immutability. Do we not have here a moving and global confirmation of the interpretation of H. Rondet given above? Other confirmations of it could be cited,[34] and especially the following lapidary assertion: "if I were not, God would not be,"[35] where once again we meet Eckhart.[36]

The Hegelian Trinity, a "childish representation"[37] when compared to the Concept, calls to mind in a surprising manner the Trinity which,

---

[32]Hegel, *Encyclopédie*, no. 381; cf. H. Rondet, S.J., *Hégélianisme et christianisme*. Paris, 1965, p. 104.

[33]This hardly supports the protest cited in note 30!

[34]For example: "Die Weltgeschichte ist die Darstellung der Göttlichen Prozesses, des Stufenganges, in dem der Geist sich selbst seine Wahrheit weiss und verwirklicht" (Hegel, *Die Vernunft in der Geschichte*, ed. Hoffmeister, p. 74).

[35]Hegel, *Der Begriff der Religion*, p. 257, ed. Lasson.

[36]From his earliest writings Hegel cites texts of Eckhart that were condemned by the Holy See; later, in 1814 it seems, he came to know these writings more precisely, thanks to Baader, and he was highly enthusiastic over them; cf. Chapelle, *op. cit.*, pp. 72-73; a little further on the same author analyzes the differences of perspective between Eckhart and Hegel (p. 74).

[37]An Hegelian text of 1824: *Die Absolute Religion*, cited by A. Chapelle, p. 67-68.

according to Orbe, the second century Gnostics extolled: in both cases the generation of the Word and the procession of the Spirit are considered inseparable from the creation of the world and its divinization in the Church. Could we not then say of this Hegelian Trinity what Daniélou said of the Trinitarian vision of the Gnostics: what we are dealing with here is more a theogony and cosmogony than a theology?

But let us not insist here on aspects that are but secondary relative to what we have already said: Hegel's rejection of number in God and also his depreciation of the notions and traditional terminology of "essence, nature, substance."[38] All these points, however important they may be, do not constitute the most original core of Hegel's thought on the Trinity. But they allow us at least to say with a Catholic admirer of Hegel: "The Hegelian texts on the Trinity can thus seem to be alien to the doctrine of the historical Church, especially when they bring forward the dogmatic terms as naive images to be subjected to rational comprehension."

Let it be clear that if Hegel did not make his own the Trinitarian language of the Catholic Church, the opposite is also true: not only has the Church not retained as valid the Hegelian "representation" of the Trinity but it has in no way sought to express its own doctrine in Hegelian categories and it has even many a time rejected attempts made in this direction, as we shall see in the case of Günther.

The motives for this are perhaps clear to the reader, but it is worth taking the trouble to review them with Rondet and Chapelle. Without dwelling on the dubious accusation of Sabellianism,[39] let us just say with Rondet that "the distinction between Missions and Processions seems to vanish"[40] since for Hegel "God would not be God without the world that he creates,"[41] which means primarily that God would not be God without Hegel (in conformity with the text cited above in which Hegel wrote: if I were not, God would not be!). Under these conditions, it is quite understandable why Rondet should pose the question: "did not Hegel end up constructing a species of Trinitarian pantheism along the lines of Lessing?"[42]

But in truth Hegel has formally rejected the accusation "otherwise the following misconstruction could arise...that the eternal Son of the Father and of the divinity which is Object for itself and objectified for itself, is the same thing as the physical and spiritual world and that by this Son one

---

[38]Chapelle, *op. cit.*, p. 97.
[39]Rondet is inclined to retain it (*Hégélianisme et christianisme*, p. 78); Chapelle rejects the accusation (*op. cit.*, p. 92).
[40]Rondet, *op. cit.*, p. 78.
[41]Hegel, *Der Begriff der Religion*, ed. Lasson, p. 148; cf. Rondet, *op. cit.*, p. 78.
[42]Rondet, *op. cit.*, p. 79.

ought only to understand this world."⁴³ A number of interpreters of Hegel (Niel, Hessen) protest then against the identification of Word and creation. Chapelle speaks of material error: "it is simply a material error to read in Hegel pure and simple identity of the divine Word and the created world."⁴⁴ But if there is not a "pure and simple identity," yet is there not an identity of some kind, *secundum quid*, as the scholastics would say? It is difficult to see how it is possible to deny this, in the light of a text like this: "understood as pure idea, this Other is the Son of God, but taken in its particularization it is the world, nature, finite spirit." And in this text which immediately before treated of the Trinity Hegel adds: "the finite spirit is thus posited as a moment of God. Man himself enters into the notion of God."⁴⁵ One isolated text could not prevail against the general sense of others.

It is not surprising then that many philosophers have interpreted Hegel thus: "among us men, there is an always perfectible reciprocity of knowledge and love, the veritable substance of historical becoming. The Father, the Son and the Spirit will be no more than logical moments, metaphysical aspects of the profound life of humanity and through that of the universe."⁴⁶ At most, the Trinity would be a cipher of man and of universal history.

But A. Chapelle helps us perceive an equally profound and distinct reason that explains the impossibility for the Church of adopting Hegel's Trinitarian speculation and a fortiori of expressing Trinitarian dogma in Hegelian categories:

> Hegelian thought unfolds on the contrary (i.e., contrary to Greek theology) starting from a principle of deficiency by means of which these two cancel each other: the primal Penury of the abstract universal and the native Poverty of the Difference determined in the final assent of the Spirit to its necessary rending and its free reconciliation. The principle of paternal generosity makes way for the negativity, the effacement of the Spirit.⁴⁷

---

⁴³An Hegelian text of 1824, extracted from *Die Absolute Religion*, cited by Chapelle, p. 101, note 285; Chapelle further cites other Hegelian texts which would point in the same direction but which he does not reproduce; the question could be asked whether Hegel did not adopt Fichte's distinction between the Word as virtual image of God, *natura naturans*, and the evolutive exterior Word, perfect image, become such through cosmic becoming, through creation: cf. J. Maréchal, S.J., *Le point de départ de la métaphysique*, cahier IV. Brussels, 1947, pp. 431-432. Here we are brought back to the pre-Nicene problematic of Tertullian! The evolutive Word is *natura naturata*.

⁴⁴Chapelle, *ibid.*, pp. 101-102.

⁴⁵Hegel, *Leçons sur la Philosophie de l'Histoire*, cited by Rondet, *op. cit.*, 117.

⁴⁶Rondet, "Divinisation du chrétien," *Nouv. Rev. Théol.* 71 (1949), 568.

⁴⁷Chapelle, *op. cit.*, p. 106.

This is truly the introduction of an evolution at the same time of God in the world and in God himself (the two are in fact inseparable), which constitutes a radical negation of the immutability and eternity of the Trinity, that is irreconcilable with the Catholic faith and with the definitions of the councils, and which explains the double rejection on the Church's part which we mentioned. The intimate life of God is not a passage from penury to plenitude; the Father is already *ex se*, not penury but plenitude of divinity. One could not aim to introduce "negativity" in a Catholic theological systematization of the intra-Trinitarian life. God, and particularly God the Father is infinite affirmation and positivity. The Father is not an abstract universal, the Trinitarian life cannot be degraded to the level of the psychological life of sinful man who is torn apart and reconciled.... That would be a veritable perversion of the psychological analogy!

In spite of some reaffirmations of the eternity of the Trinity or of the transcendence of the Word with respect to creation, it is the obvious contrary sense which is postulated by numerous Hegelian texts, with the attempt to introduce movement in the bosom of the Immutable and with the partial confusion between the intimate processions in God and evolution in creation; it is all this as well as its concern to preserve and transmit its own proper language (which is qualified as infantile by this idealist philosopher) that obliges the Church to reject the Hegelian version of the Trinitarian dogma.

Does this mean that nothing of the Hegelian speculation is to be retained? No. If he was wrong in depreciating the person of the Father, "poor" principle, in favor of the Spirit, term enriched by the "negativity" of the internal "movement" of the divine life, yet Hegel does stimulate us to elaborate a Trinitarian theology that will be more aware of the eschatological orientation of the temporal mission of the Spirit, the sanctifier and consummator of the Church. He does encourage us to value not only "protology" but also eschatology, the "salutary eschatology in which alone the Trinity effectively reveals itself in totality."[48]

Hegel, without being aware of it, does orientate himself in the same direction as St. Augustine (whom he does not seem to cite or know relative to the Trinity): in both there is the same insistence on the Spirit in the divine interiority and on the bond between the Spirit and the Church. Provided one is willing to dissociate carefully what is valuable in these inspirations from the enveloping matrix of errors, the best of the Hegelian aspirations lead us back therefore to the inspirations and intuitions of Augustine's genius, which we have already presented. In Augustine as in

[48]*Ibid.*, p. 60, note 47.

the Greek Fathers the primordial pole of Trinitarian contemplation is the Father, unfathomable source of all the divinity; but in Augustine the Spirit in whom the Son returns to the Father is also the final pole of this contemplation. Here is the truth toward which the Hegelian "representation" is pointing, according to which "the moments of the (Trinitarian) concept are organized with reference to their final unity in the Spirit."⁴⁹

It seems then at the end of these thoughts about Hegel that we can, or better, that we must answer the question we proposed initially: Hegel wished to be but was not effectively a theologian of the Trinity. And yet the influence of his thought, quite original in more than one point, has been great. And we can ask ourselves if without him we could have assisted at the vast attempt at "secularizing" and "laicizing" the Trinitarian mystery which Marxism represents, and which it undertook under the influence of Feuerbach.

2. *Feuerbach, the Trinitarian mystery and the unity of the human race*

For Feuerbach, the persons in humanity are entirely comparable to what the Christian doctrine teaches about the Persons in the Divinity. Feuerbach writes that the secret of the divine Trinity "is the secret of common and social life, the secret of the necessity of the thou for the I; and it consists in this truth: that no being (whether it be or be called man or God or spirit or I) is a true being, perfect and absolute, for itself alone, but that only the bond, the unity of beings of the same essence constitutes truth and perfection."⁵⁰

In brief, in Feuerbach's eyes the unreal divine Trinity signifies symbolically the true mystery of which it is the cipher: the mystery of the sociability of men. Plurality of men, unity of humanity.

In *The Essence of Christianity*, to which the beginning of this text refers back explicitly, Feuerbach makes his thought precise: "There are three persons, but they are not essentially distinct. *Tres personae aber una essentia*. One can arrive at this naturally. We can think of three and even a greater number which would be identical in their essence. If we men are distinct from each other it is due to individual, personal differences, but as regards the principal thing, the essence, humanity, we are one (*eins*)."⁵¹

This text suggests more than one reflection.

For the author the personality that distinguishes men appears to be accidental, while the unity of nature is presented as the substance to which the accident of person is referred. A point of view which will not astonish us in a precursor of Marxism. In the Christian mystery of the Trinity, on the contrary, the distinction and the opposition of persons are total.

---

⁴⁹*Ibid.*, p. 106, note 321.

⁵⁰Feuerbach, *Principes de la Philosophie de l'Avenir*, § 63.

⁵¹Feuerbach, *Das Wesen des Christentums*. Leipzig, Reclam, 1904, p. 342; trans. J. Roy, Paris, 1864, p. 276.

Further, Feuerbach appears to confuse the logical unity of the human race with the real numerical unity that the Christian doctrine recognizes in the indivisible essence of the Triune God. Men exist, but in concrete reality there does not exist one humanity: the word only designates a unity of order.

St. Thomas Aquinas, whom Feuerbach regarded as "one of the greatest Christian thinkers and theologians,"[52] wrote: "Socrates, Plato and Cicero are three men, while the Father, the Son and the Holy Spirit are not three gods, but only one God: in three supposits of human nature there are in fact three humanities, but in the three Persons there is only one divine essence."[53]

Here we meet again under a new slant a problem that we met before: that of the one and the many in God, but this time in comparison with the problem of the one and many in man. For Feuerbach and for Marx, the human essence is not found in any particular human "person," but only in the community, in humanity in its entirety; to say that man is a generic being, is to throw back on the logical abstraction, i.e., humanity, the dignity of the worker, of the concrete person.[54] Feuerbach and Marx are victims of the Hegelian idealism against which they believed they were reacting. They misunderstood the human person at the same time that they misunderstood the divine Persons, in favor of an unreal humanity which they divinized. In seeing in the Trinity a cipher of man, they make us inversely conclude that recognition of the divine Trinity is the concrete condition for the recognition of the individual personality of each man, created in the image of the Trinity.

On the contrary, the fathers of communism attribute to human nature the real unity (which it lacks) which they refuse to give to God: and so they come to replace the cult of the real Trinity by that of an abstract humanity.

Even from Feuerbach's admission it remains true that consideration of what Christianity teaches about the Trinity helps us to understand man. Here once again just as he already anticipated Hegel in what concerns the Spirit, Augustine, by developing the psychological analogy, has in an almost unsurpassable manner, allowed man to make a leap in the knowledge of

---

[52]*Op. cit.*, p. 238; French trans., p. 186, in a note where Feuerbach cites exactly the *Summa Theologica* I, 60.5 ad 1m; and I, II, 4.8c and ad 3m.

[53]St. Thomas Aquinas, *Summa Theologica*, I, 39.3.

[54]Cf. P.-D. Dognin, O.P., "Aux sources philosophiques du collectivisme marxiste," *RSPT* 48 (1964), 423; we owe it to this work that we discovered Feuerbach's interest in St. Thomas Aquinas and in the Trinity; see also on this subject S. Decloux, S.J., "Le mystère de l'Esprit d'Amour," *Nouv. Rev. Théol.* 91 (1969), 947-961. Note too, in this context, the Marxist reinterpretation of the Trinitarian dogma given by E. Bloch, *Das Prinzip Hoffnung*. Frankfurt, 1959: Christ is the perfect man, the eternal and immutable God and Father gives way to man, faith in Christ is the will to transform history, the Paraclete is the historical process.

himself. The Trinitarian revelation helps man to know better his human and natural essence.[55]

III. THE ANTI-TRINITARIAN EVOLUTIONISM OF SPIRITISM

Marxism is already an anti-Trinitarian evolutionism and in certain aspects a "materialist neo-unitarianism," if we dare risk such a comparison. As the "Unitarian" rejects all plurality of persons in God, so for the orthodox Marxist the only reality is polymorphous matter.

Spiritism represents another form of pantheism, a form which like Marxism has its remote origin in the idealist philosophical currents of the nineteenth century.

For a Leon Denis, "God is the universal soul of which every human soul is a spark, an irradiation. God is in the world as the soul in the body. God cannot be individualized, separated from the world, subsist apart from it."[56]

The Brazilian "Umbanda" goes still further, if that is possible: "God is the All and the I is a part of this All. God sleeps in the mineral, lies dormant in the vegetable, awakes in the animal, is conscious in man."[57]

In spite of the difference of language, does not this divinized evolutionism call to mind some aspects of that of Hegel? Let us read a bit further this citation from the program adopted by the first Congress of Brazilian "umbandism," in 1941: "Its philosophy consists in the recognition of the human being as a particle of the divinity, which emanates from it and is finally reintegrated into it at the end of a necessary evolutionary cycle."[58]

It is then not astonishing that Spiritism takes a position against the Christian doctrine of the Trinity: a God who evolves, who is at the same time *natura naturans* and *natura naturata* cannot be the immutable and eternal Trinity of the Christian Revelation.

Let us cite Leon Denis once again: "The strange conception of the divine Being that resolves itself in the mystery of the Trinity, is the result of the passions and material interests that entered into play in the Christian world after the death of Jesus."[59] Denis sees the origin of the Trinitarian dogma both in the Church's thirst for power, and in a Hindu legend that is the expression of a symbol; to establish its power, the Church needed to affirm the divinity of Jesus and thus it invented this dogma of which Jesus, John

---

[55]This point is well emphasized by the Italian philosopher M. Sciacca, "Trinité et unité de l'Esprit," *Augustinus Magister*. Paris, 1954, v. I, 595-602; and also by C. Boyer, S.J., "L'image de la Trinité, synthèse de la pensée augustinienne," *Gregorianum* 27 (1946) 173-199; 333-352.

[56]We cite according to B. Kloppenburg, O.F.M., *Ação pastoral perante o Espiritismo*. Petrópolis (Brazil), 1961, p. 219.

[57]Ibid.

[58]Ibid., text of 1941.

[59]Ibid., pp. 221-223.

and Paul had never thought! Nicaea marked the invention of the Trinitarian dogma![60]

This explanation brings back to mind liberal and modernist Protestantism. But it does not keep L. Denis from attempting another explanation along modalist lines that aims to absorb the mystery rather than attack it: the Trinity should be interpreted "as a concept representing the Divinity under three essential aspects: the living and immutable Law is the Father; eternal Reason or Wisdom is the Son; Love, creative and fecundative power, is the Holy Spirit"![61]

Depending on the case, we thus see evolutionism orientating itself in two opposite directions: it either presents evolution as an unfolding of the Trinity or it directly attacks the mystery. In both hypotheses its aim is to get rid of the mystery and its dogmatic expression.

While Hegelianism at its limit offers us a Trinitarian pantheism, Marxism and Spiritism give us an anti-Trinitarian pantheist evolutionism.

Thus Catholic theology of the nineteenth century was simultaneously confronted by these two pantheisms, Trinitarian and anti-Trinitarian or materialist-unitarian, both influenced by the Hegelian dialectic. How did it react? That is what we are going to see with respect to Günther and the criticisms leveled against him.

IV. THE TRITHEISTIC AND RATIONALISTIC TENDENCIES OF GÜNTHER

A. Günther wished to react against Hegel while partially employing his method. He started from a fundamental presupposition: person is defined by consciousness of self. On this base he constructed his a priori system of Trinitarian deduction which we can sum up thus.[62]

By his essence God has no consciousness of himself, else there would be in him only one self-consciousness, therefore only one person. If God knows himself, this can only be through the persons in him, by opposing himself to himself as subject to object and by affirming simultaneously the equality of this subject and this object. The self-conscious subject is the first person; the self-conscious object is the second person; the third person is the consciousness of the equality between subject and object, between Father and Son.

[60]Cf. B. Kloppenburg, O.F.M., *O Espiritismo no Brasil*. Petrópolis (Brazil), 1960, pp. 339-342. You will note the partial parallelism between the views of L. Denis on the Trinity and Nicaea and those of E. Fromm, presented in our ch. II. The objections we made to Fromm will then apply in part here. We could add further that the Christian Trinitarian doctrine differs from the pagan trinitarian doctrines which are polytheistic. The essential content of the Christian doctrine of the Trinity (one only God exists as Father, Son and Spirit who are really distinct among themselves by reciprocal relations) is found nowhere outside Christianity. What is more, the mythological preference for the numeral three can be a vestige of the real Trinity.

[61]Cf. B. Kloppenburg, *O Espiritismo no Brasil* (see preceding note), p. 341.

This necessary Trinity is connected to a necessary creation. In distinguishing itself from the other two each person denies that it is another person and precisely this negation of an absolute and infinite thing gives birth in God to the conception of the finite and the relative. The goodness of God demands that he give existence to these possible non-divine beings: thus a necessary creation appears as the consequence of a necessary Trinity.

Many Catholic theologians, among others the future Cardinal Franzelin, showed without difficulty the unacceptable character of this systematization, which attempted to accommodate the mystery to the fashion of the day without regard for either the magisterium or patristic tradition.

It has been observed that the triple consciousness in God by triplicating the persons (which Günther called the "theogonic process") leads to a veritable tritheism, something that theoretically speaking Günther certainly did not want,[63] but which corresponds nonetheless with his explicit affirmations: doesn't he teach that "the unity of the divine nature ought not to be understood in a numerically real sense, but only in a formal sense"?[64] For him there are as many absolute substances as persons.

One could object still further that the Son is not only object but also subject; that an object cannot be conscious of itself if it is not initially subject, person; that the patristic tradition never[65] presented the procession of the Holy Spirit as the fruit of an intellectual consciousness of equality between Father and Son.

So we understand why the magisterium of the Church in the person of Pius IX declared: "the works of A. Günther abound in grave errors against the Catholic faith and against a sincere explanation (of this faith) with respect to the unity of the divine substance in three distinct and eternal Persons" (DS 2828; DB 1655).

But it is fitting to criticize, if only briefly, the initial error of Günther which conditioned all the others: his identification of person with self-consciousness.

Consciousness or knowledge of self through oneself is an act which, in

---

[62]Cf. A. Michel, DTC XV, 2 (1950), 1795, art. "Trinité."

[63]Cf. H. Rondet, S.J., *Hégélianisme et christianisme*. Paris, 1965, pp. 121-135: appendix on the Hegelianism of Günther, whom Rondet wished to rehabilitate in part while still acknowledging the solid foundation of Pius IX's condemnation.

[64]Text cited by Cardinal Franzelin, *De Deo trino*, 1881, p. 294.

[65]According to P. Henry, such was nevertheless the idea of Blessed Ruysbroeck: "The Spirit is the unity of the Father and of the Son knowing each other as like each other and equals in the identity of the same nature and taking their delight in this same unity," *Rech. Sc. Rel.*, 40 (1952), 357-359. It must be noted, however, that in Ruysbroeck, here and especially elsewhere, the procession of the Spirit is formally a procession of love wherein the reciprocal knowledge of the Father and of the Son seems to be nothing but the prerequisite to notional love.

man, presupposes the previous existence of the being known by this act: *agere sequitur esse*. The "I" precedes the consciousness we have of it, otherwise this consciousness would create its object (as idealists think). The "I" would create itself, which is absurd. Among the moderns those who, since Descartes, identify person and consciousness of self, confuse the "I" with the perception of the "I" (phenomenalism). But in reality the phenomenological and psychological notion of personality presupposes the ontological, "substantialist" and metaphysical notion of person,[66] which we have already noted.[67]

In the second place, on the human and natural level, the theory of personality-consciousness leads logically to monstrous consequences: how can it be maintained without denying that sleepers, infants and insane persons possess the dignity of personality? Since they are not conscious of themselves how could they be persons? Günther's doctrine would lead us to identify infants, sleepers and the insane, purely and simply with irrational animals. We must on the contrary underscore that they possess a reason which can, with time or treatment, become conscious; they would not thereby receive their reason from the exterior.

Finally and especially, on the properly theological level, Günther's theory obliges us logically to deny both the unity of Christ and the unity of the divine nature. If there are as many persons as self-conscious substances, we could not admit that a person is numerically only one without admitting by that very fact that it is only one intelligence, only one will, only one consciousness of self. In brief, only one nature. Thus Christ would be divided into two persons, one divine, the other human. And at the same time the one God would be "tripled." By confusing persons and nature the Güntherian vision of person rejects the fundamental mysteries of Christianity.

But at least it has the merit of obliging us to underscore better the traditional teaching of the Church: that the Three "I's" of the holy Trinity are conscious by one sole act of self-consciousness; all three say "I" by a single and indistinct act.[68]

What is more, the identification that many moderns make of person and self-consciousness helps us underline the psychological and moral properties of the conscious and free person who is capable of rights and duties, worthy of chastisement and recompense, capable of attaining its end by its

---

[66]Cf. A. Michel, *DTC*, VII, I (1922), col. 1431-1436, art. "Hypostase."

[67]Cf. our ch. III toward the end.

[68]Cardinal J.-B. Franzelin, S.J., *De Verbo Incarnato*. Rome, 1881, 249-253; see also B. Lonergan, S.J., *De Deo trino*. Rome, 1964, v. II, pp. 186-196: "Assertum XII: Pater, Filius et Spiritus Sanctus per unam conscientiam realem sunt tria subjecta conscia tum sui tum cujusque alterius tum actus sui tam notionalis quam essentialis."

action. It must even be said that the absence of self-consciousness in a person does not result from his ontological personality and comes to limit the power of the person over the nature.

Faced with the grave consequences and significance of Günther's errors, errors shared by other Catholic theologians, the magisterium was understandably much perturbed: Vatican I had even prepared a dogmatic constitution on the Trinity, but it was not promulgated nor were the anathemas, which certainly were aimed at the doctrine of the Güntherians (whose leader, however, had died in the meantime in submission to the Church).[69]

We can also understand, for a correct proclamation of the mystery of the Trinity, the necessity of an ontological substantialist doctrine of person (*individua substantia naturae rationalis*, according to the famous definition of St. Thomas Aquinas[70]), a person which, as we have seen, is hypostasis and not merely a phenomenon.

V. THE TRINITY, WHOSE NON-IRRATIONALITY IS DEMONSTRABLE, IS A MYSTERY THAT IS INDEMONSTRABLE BY REASON: VATICAN I

That human reason by its own powers and even with the aid of actual graces cannot demonstrate the existence of the Trinity before or even after knowing the Revelation of the Three, is a truth that results from the teaching of Christ the Savior of this reason, and also from the teaching of St. Paul (cf. DS 3015-3016; DB 1795-1796).

Jesus manifested the transcendence of his relations with his Father, relations which could not be violated by the daring reason of man: "No one knows the Son except the Father, as no one knows the Father except the Son and one to whom the Son chooses to reveal him" (Mt. 11:27).

Against all the claims of the rationalism which constantly reappears out of man's partially corrupted reason, and against the pretensions of the semi-rationalism of Günther and his disciples, but without explicitly mentioning the Trinity, Vatican I insisted on the indemonstrable character of the "mysteries of Christianity," to use the title of Scheeben's celebrated book which sums up the best in nineteenth century Catholic theology on the subject (DS 3041; DB 1816).[71] Even in the heart of Revelation we can

---

[69]Cf. A. Michel, *DTC* XV, 2 (1950), col. 1797-1799.

[70]St. Thomas Aquinas, *Summa Theologica*, I, 29.1; the definition is borrowed from Boethius, *De duabus naturis*, ML 64, 1343.

[71]It is necessary however to clarify the texts of Vatican I cited here by the remark of Mgr. Charrue in his official report regarding the first chapter of the dogmatic constitution *Lumen Gentium:* "The word mystery does not refer only to something we cannot know or which is difficult to comprehend; it designates, as most recognize today, a divine and transcendent reality which is the bearer of salvation and which is rendered visible in some manner" (cited by

demonstrate rationally the impossibility of a rational demonstration of the Trinity: for human intelligence arrives at the knowledge of God through the created physical and spiritual universe, and even after Revelation it does not enjoy the intuitive vision of the Trinity. This created universe, however, is the common work of the Three Persons, as we already emphasized, and so through creation the property of each one of them is not immediately recognizable. Hence even after the Revelation of the Three, the world of the Three does not lead man's reason to a distinct and evident knowledge of the Three as such, even when it is illumined by faith.

Human reason can only demonstrate that God is not impersonal, that he is not deprived of the perfection of personality. It cannot demonstrate his tri-personality.

Reason can show the objective foundation of the distinction between nature and person, a distinction which implies an idea of perfection, of achievement and of incommunicability which are foreign to the concept of nature. It can show that it is not evident that one must conclude from the multiplication of persons to the multiplication of natures, in all domains.

Above all, our language on the subject of the transcendent God is necessarily analogical.[72] For nature and person are concepts borrowed from the world of creatures that are directly known, and thus in God they assume a transcendence that surpasses our reason without contradicting it. Before it knows Revelation, reason cannot know how this perfection of personality is realized in God. And after Revelation it cannot demonstrate that in God personality is not an absolute but a relative perfection which is attributed to three subsistent relations that are reciprocally opposed to one another and because of this distinct from one another.

With Scheeben it is necessary to observe that it is not impossible for reason to form a correct and true notion of the real God (who in fact is the Trinity) without conceiving him as a Trinity of persons. The Jews had an exact notion of God without knowing the Trinity. But it was a notion, we must note, that was inadequate and incomplete but not false. A notion so true that it prepared the full and integral notion of Christianity. An idea that was inexact only if one separated it from its development by denying the communication of divinity to several Persons. That is what Judaism and its adherents, but not all the Jews, did when faced with the plenitude of the Christian Revelation, and that is what the Arians of the fourth century did. Thus ... Church was led to condemn the notion of an incommunicable

---

M.-J. LeGuillou, C. ?., *Le visage du Ressuscité*. Paris, 1968, p. 153). Thus we can say that the mystery of the Trinity becomes visible in the Church while remaining nonetheless transcendent and incomprehensible. On the notion of mystery, see further K. Rahner, *EF*, v. III, art. "Mystère." Paris, 1966, pp. 161-167.

[72]Cf. St. Thomas Aquinas, *Summa Theologica*, I, 13.5 and the whole of Q. 13.

divine unity as contrary to the fecundity of divine life as known by Revelation.[73]

After its adhesion to Revelation reason cannot exercise its discursive reflection on any higher object than this Trinity and yet it always remains incapable of demonstrating it in a compelling manner. With Scheeben once again we observe that "the revelation and knowledge of the divine Trinity have a very great and lofty meaning for us, in spite of the fact, or rather because of the fact, that it is a supernatural and suprarational truth, a truth that is transcendental for nature and reason. By revealing this truth, which extends so far beyond nature and reason, God raises us above our nature and our reason."[74]

And so it appears that "as the divine nature regarded in its unity is the highest object, the crowning point of philosophy, so the divine Trinity is the highest and at the same time the most characteristic object, the center, and the very heart of theology."[75]

Theology, an essentially rational reflection, has then for supreme object the suprarational Trinity but without being at all able to demonstrate it. The discourse of reason is essentially movement while the Trinity is immutable. It is this immutability of the Trinity which precisely constituted the difficulty for a certain number of Christian thinkers especially since the nineteenth century. We must say a word about this.

VI. THE IMMUTABILITY OF THE DIVINE PROCESSIONS

In fact the dogma of the Trinity poses for many minds a special problem, distinct from that posed by the immutability of the divine nature as such. But the two problems are connected with one another.

Today many intellects see in the generation of the Word and in the spiration of the Spirit a double and "eternal" movement. For them there is no life without movement, without "dynamism." The Trinity would be a "dead God" if it had no movement.

Truth to say such a tendency is ancient. It could even be said that Marius Victorinus constructed his Trinitarian theology in great part by interpreting the mystery as the unfolding of a unique movement. In the Middle Ages St. Bonaventure admirably underlines the immutability of the generation of the Word and of the procession of the Spirit. St. Thomas presents a solution which synthesizes and outstrips earlier ones.

For Marius Victorinus the Father is a self-moving movement that thus generates his Son, who is movement that issues from the hidden paternal motion and becomes manifest. The Father and the Son are one sole move-

---

[73]Cf. M.-J. Scheeben, *The Mysteries of Christianity*. St. Louis, 1946, § 6, pp. 31-32.
[74]*Ibid.*, § 22, p. 131.
[75]*Ibid.*

ment, one sole substance, for the substance is movement. The single movement which proceeds from the Father has constituted the Son a person in such a manner that by receiving all the divinity from the Father by generation, this Son remains identified with the active single movement that gives the Holy Spirit his origin. The Spirit is himself movement which is divine, in its terminus, and movement which receives from the movement which is the Son (cf. Jn. 16:14-15).[76]

Here we had no intention of entering into the subtle meanderings of Marius Victorinus' thought but only to indicate its general orientation: it is a dynamic theology of the Trinity. Over against this dynamic theology the Trinitarian theology of immutability finds a remarkable and comparatively still more striking expounder in the person of St. Bonaventure.

The seraphic Doctor is clearly concerned with the objectors who view the processions as a movement and so prefer to say that the Trinity is not immutable. By close and successive reasonings St. Bonaventure rejects the doctrine of a mutable Trinity.

Thus God's supreme eternity does not admit movement and his supreme simplicity does not admit mutability. The Trinity is eternal and simple and so there is in it neither movement nor mutability.

This can be shown in this way: where there is eternity, there is no beginning, no succession, no deficiency. Every mutation, every change is a passing from non-being to being or from being to non-being or from being one thing to being another (*ab uno esse in aliud esse*); but there is no passing to being without beginning, or toward non-being without deficiency, or from one being to another without succession and variety. Thus the excellence of the eternal Trinity excludes all change.

This Trinity is supreme Act. Supreme actuality consists in a full return to oneself by intelligence and love (*plenam conversionem supra se intelligendo et amando*). Intelligence includes the word, and love the bond (*verbum...nexum*); just as it is not only not repugnant to his immutability for the first principle to know and love himself but even proper for him to do this, so too the generation of the Word and the spiration of Love are quite in harmony with

---

[76]We present synthetically the data elaborated at great length by J. Vergara, S.J., *Ecclesiastica Xaveriana* 6 (1956), 63-92; see especially the *Adversus Arium* of Marius Victorinus, ML 8, 1081; 1099; 1224; 1125; 1105; these texts are cited by Vergara, pp. 65, 67, 85, 81, 89. You will note the strange application of the doctrine of potency and act to the Trinitarian domain: "Quod vero de potentia actio, ideo de Patre Filius" (ML 8, 1099). In the eyes of P. Séjourné, Victorinus has not clearly distinguished the procession of the Spirit from that of the Son (DTC XV, 2, 1950, col. 2905-2926: art. Victorinus Afer, § V on the Trinity). Regarding Trinitarian doctrine and movement in Victorinus, see further P. Hadot, Introduction to *Traités théologiques sur la Trinité*, I, SC 68, Paris, 1960, pp. 79-81. What renders definitively unacceptable the dynamic aspect of Marius Victorinus' Trinitarian theology is his conception of the generation of the Word as a passing of the Father from potency to act. Cf. our ch. II, X, notes 181ff.

this immutability. For both pertain to him immutably and always in act. Consequently, if one understands immutability correctly, it not only does not exclude but does include the most blessed Trinity. And this because the supreme Immutable is necessarily a simple being that is eternal and actual according to a plenitude of perfect actuality and without any termination.

If it is true that among creatures generation signifies mutation, passage from potency to act, it is otherwise in God: in God generation is supreme act as regards principle and term and production, without any acquisition of new being; however it is reception of a true being that is actual and eternal; and thus, although it is a true production, it is not a true change.[77]

The beauty, that is the splendor of truth in these considerations of St. Bonaventure, does not suppress the interest that Marius Victorinus' theological effort offers us. For Scripture offers us the same tension between two opposed poles: "Wisdom is quicker to move than any movement" (Wis. 7:24); "I, Yahweh, do not change" (Mal. 3:6). However it is true that these texts deal with the divine nature and not with the Trinitarian mystery. But can we forget that this nature is really identical with the processions?

St. Thomas in explaining St. Augustine offers a synthesis-solution.

"Augustine," the Angelic Doctor states, "when he says 'The creator Spirit moves himself,'[78] speaks as Plato does, according to whom the first mover moves himself. Plato calls every operation movement. Thus intelligence, will and love are called movements. Because God understands and loves himself, some have said that God moves himself, but not in this sense that the movement is a mutation of one who exists in potency."[79]

Provided then that one excludes all evolution, all passage from potency to act in the divine nature, one can speak of movement and dynamism in God and so describe the divine processions as eternally gushing forth in the bosom of the God who does not change. This way of expressing it can help our contemporaries more than other expressions to understand that God is Life. But it has some disadvantages. For if it is admitted with regard to the divine processions that take place precisely according to intelligence and love, it will be more difficult not to extend it from the interpersonal domain to the domain of the divine nature.

It is then more exact, more profound, and very simply more true to say that the Father immutably generates his Son and the two immutably

---

[77]St. Bonaventure, *Quaestiones disputatae de mysterio Trinitatis*, VI, 2.

[78]The text of St. Augustine is found in *ML* 34, 388 (cf. 389), in a context where St. Augustine insists at length on the divine immutability; the precise meaning of the Augustinian text seems obscure, but it seems to have been well interpreted by St. Thomas Aquinas in the total context of St. Augustine's thought.

[79]St. Thomas Aquinas, *Summa Theologica*, I, 9.1.1.

spirate their Spirit. In the last analysis St. Bonaventure is more satisfying than Marius Victorinus.

That is what Scheeben perceived: "Life is an activity of the living being, an activity proceeding from within and remaining within that being. Since all visible activity becomes known through the movement it produces, and since a real transition from potency to act takes place in every created activity, or better, this activity is conceivable only in terms of such a transition, we generally describe every activity as a movement, and vital activity as an immanent movement. But in God no transition from potency to act is thinkable; nevertheless, or rather for this reason, He possesses the purest and most perfect activity; He is His own activity. Therefore He must possess the purest and most perfect life and must be Life itself, although no real movement can be predicated of His life. His immanent activity, His life, being the life of a pure spirit, consists in knowing and willing."[80]

Being eternal the generation of the Son is not a passage from a paternity in potency to a paternity in act,[81] just as the Son is not spirator in potency of the Spirit whose spiration would then actualize the potency. We must slough off images that are bound to our condition of temporal beings. Once again but under a new aspect we meet the problems that agitated the Arians, Augustine and St. Hilary. Theological reflection can and ought to be aided by the imagination but it must not be dominated by it under penalty of defeat.

Granting the real identity of nature and person in God, the following declaration of Vatican I therefore aims also at Trinitarian evolutionism (*DS* 3001; *DB* 1782): God is "unchangeable spiritual substance," and also "unexchangeable": so that on the one hand the Son and the Spirit do not result from an evolution of the Father or of the divine essence with which they are identical, and on the other hand nothing in the mutable and created universe can ever be given in exchange for the immutable and uncreated Trinity.

---

[80]M.-J. Scheeben, *The Mysteries of Christianity*. St. Louis, § 6, p. 32.
[81]Cf. the text of Marius Victorinus quoted in note 76.

VIII
Family, Church, Human Soul—
Imperfect, Complementary and Revealed
Analogies of the Divine Trinity

After running through some more or less erroneous attempts at systematizing the Trinitarian mystery with a view to a better understanding of the mystery, we are now going to examine those efforts that offer certain points of support in Revelation. In a book that is meant to be an introductory work, we must necessarily be brief. Without going back to the cosmic analogy that was manifest in Tertullian,[1] we will be content here to set forth the analogies which are more or less clearly insinuated by Revelation and which have a particular interest for contemporary understanding of the mystery. All three, we shall see, have been present to Christian thought at least for fifteen centuries, although in some cases in a somewhat veiled manner. And without doubt they will not cease to stimulate the intellectual acumen of theologians. These three are the family (insofar as it implies human friendship and intersubjectivity), the Church and the individual soul. We shall see how St. Thomas and B. Lonergan centuries apart have successively deepened St. Augustine's thought on this last analogy. We shall attempt to show the meaning, the importance and the limits of each of these analogies, as well as the complementarity of all three. The last analogy, that of the structure of the human soul, will help us perceive better the meaning of the Church's doctrine on the procession of the Holy Spirit and why there are only three persons in God.

I. FAMILY INTERSUBJECTIVITY AND FRIENDSHIP,
   THE FIRST REVEALED ANALOGY OF THE TRINITY

A. Orbe has convincingly shown that Gnostic theology elaborated the family image of the Trinitarian mystery in commenting on the account of the creation of Adam and Eve, and in the framework of a more ample system which we cannot set forth here.[2]

1. With him there is every reason to think that this image passed from Judeo-Christian theology to Gnostic theology and to St. Methodius of

---
[1] See our ch. II.
[2] Cf. A. Orbe, S.J., "La procesión del Espíritu Santo y el origen de Eva," *Gregorianum* 45 (1964), 103-118; notably 114-118 on the Gnostic vision of the problem.

Olympus who died toward 312, and thence to a whole series of Fathers, Syrian (Ephraem) and especially Greek. St. Gregory of Nazianzus—generally regarded as the only Father who put forth no heresy—made this image his own in the fifth and last of his great theological discourses.

Wishing to show that the Holy Spirit is God, consubstantial to the Father and to the Son and yet not Son, he introduced the image of Adam, Eve and Seth, in the context of an anti-Arian polemic.

"Show me," says the Arian, "how the one is son, the other is not son, and yet both are consubstantial, and I will admit that the one and the other are God." Gregory replies that it is not always necessary to find in sensible things a likeness of divine things. But nonetheless he cites the trinity Adam-Eve-Seth. "The work, the fragment and the product, do they not appear to be the same thing according to species?—Why not? Are they consubstantial or not? Why not? It is clear then that things which come into existence in different manners can have the same substance."[3]

Then the bishop of Nazianzus stresses that it is not a question of affirming a corporeal partition in the divinity, but of contemplating intelligible realities in a sensible image. The family image clinches the argument for him in favor of consubstantiality, but without establishing an explicit and precise parallel between each of the three divine Persons and each of the three human persons. However, if Adam appears likened to the Father, Eve would be likened to the Son rather than to the Holy Spirit, for one cannot say of the Son what Gregory says of Seth, that he was the product of the "work" (Adam) and of the "fragment" (Eve), while the Holy Spirit on the contrary is the "product" of the Father and of the Son as Gregory elsewhere implicitly recognized.[4] If the Holy Spirit is the stream which comes from the fountain of the Son and the light which comes from the filial ray emitted by the paternal sun, is it not he that is represented by Seth, "the product of the two," Adam and Eve?

If our interpretation of Gregory is exact, his analogy would be different from that of the other Fathers after St. Methodius and the Gnostics: for them Eve was the image of the Holy Spirit, Abel or Seth of the Son.

Whatever may be true of this detail, which has its importance (as we shall see), it still remains clear that Gregory was in no way shocked by this family image of the Trinitarian mystery, but rather the contrary. Brief as it is, his text and those of the other Fathers such as St. Methodius and St. Ephraem, do not permit us to say that the patristic tradition was against such an analogy. This is the least that can be said. No one had even partially rejected it before St. Augustine, it seems. And this despite the "Platonism of the

---

[3] St. Gregory of Nazianzus, *Orat.* XXXI (theol. V, § 11; *MG* 36, 144 Dff.).
[4] Cf. A. Palmieri, *DTC* V (1913), 787-788, art. "E. Saint."

Fathers" and the temptation to despise matter which is inherent in Platonism.

The aspect of the patristic tradition that we have seen thus puts us in the presence of two distinct family images of the Trinity: the first is explicit and assimilates Adam to the Father, Seth to the Son, Eve to the Spirit; the second is implicit in Gregory of Nazianzus and inverts the last two similitudes by seeing in Eve an image of the Son and in Seth that of the Spirit.

2. But it is the first family image that came down to St. Augustine and which he rejected,[5] not without good reason. For it seemed to him absurd to present the Holy Spirit as the mother of the son of God and spouse of the Father. And on the other hand St. Augustine thought that the human soul is the image of the whole Trinity, and not of only one Person.

These are the two essential reasons why Augustine rejected the family image. But again it must be noted that he neither knew nor explicitly rejected the family image as it was presented by St. Gregory of Nazianzus (with Eve assimilated to the Son, Seth to the Spirit). Nor did he exclude the world of sexuality from being among the corporeal "vestiges" of the Trinity, vestiges which are distinct from the spiritual image. And better still: in presenting the family image in the form in which he rejects it, he takes care to recall with St. Paul to Titus (1:15) that "all is pure for the pure."

There is still a third reason for Augustine's rejection of the family image, though in truth it is secondary to the two preceding ones. It consists in his interpretation of 1 Cor. 11:7: "For a man ought not to cover his head, since he is the image and glory of God, but woman is the glory of man." For thus woman considered as such (and not only under the aspect of her soul) is not the image but the vestige of God.[6]

What is to be thought of St. Augustine's reasoning?

We can understand why he was inclined to reject the assimilation of the woman to the Holy Spirit, for at first sight it appears to lead to an impasse in terms of the account of Genesis.

In the human family the woman does not issue from the son but gives him birth. Thus she would not symbolize the Spirit who proceeds from the Son but rather the Son from whom the Spirit proceeds, however paradoxical this may appear. We shall return to this point shortly.

Granted that St. Augustine has good reason to think that the human soul is the image of the whole Trinity, a matter we shall examine more thoroughly later. Yet this in no way prevents, we think, the relations

[5]St. Augustine, *De Trinitate*, XII, V-VII; ML 42, 1000-1005. St. Augustine there stresses that his rejection is motivated by the fear of tritheism and he also finds the family analogy contrary to Scripture (Gn. 1:26-27 in his estimate excludes the view that man is created to the image of one person only).

[6]St. Augustine, *De Trinitate*, XII, VII, 9; ML 42, 1003.

existing between three human persons from being able to constitute a functional analogy of the Trinitarian mystery. If the spiritual being of each person is an image of the Trinity, why should not the activity implied in each person's family relations, an activity both personal and interpersonal, *also* be a representation, deficient assuredly like the first, but still a representation of the relations between the divine Persons?

It is strange that St. Augustine, who developed so well and so profoundly the doctrine of the relations[7] within the God who is three and one, did not in our context perceive better (for he was not ignorant of it) the spiritual dimension of the family relations, for this would have kept him from relegating the family analogy solely to the side of matter. For it also has a spiritual aspect. For man is made to the image of God not only in his being and nature but also in his activity and relations. It seems to us then that St. Augustine—and we will have occasion to make this point more precise with regard to St. Thomas Aquinas who was a victim of the same limitation—was unfaithful to the revealed datum (Father-Son) in his appreciation of the family analogy and also to the dynamic of his own proper thought and to all that was implicit in the category of relation. For him the image of God is not *in* three men:[8] but why did he not perceive that it was *between* them in the relations which do not cease to be spiritual, however carnal they may be?

As to the interpretation of 1 Cor. 11:7, it is enough to note that St. Paul in no way denied that the woman is also created in the image of God, for this was something he read quite clearly in Gn. 1:27; but he added that she was also the glory of man. Independently of every other possible consideration of the literary genre whether of the text of Genesis or of that of St. Paul, their teaching certainly furnishes no basis for excluding but rather for accepting the family analogy in the only sense in which it appears fruitful to us: that analogically the woman represents the Son and the child the Holy Spirit. The immediate context of the cited passage (1 Cor. 11:7), clearly sets forth a parallelism between the relation of God-Christ and the relation of man-woman, and in consequence it insinuates the analogy between the relation of the woman with her husband and that of Christ with his Father: "the head of the woman is her husband, and the head of Christ is God" (that is, in Pauline language, the Father) (1 Cor. 11:3). If the man, Adam, is likened to God, to the Father, "from whom all paternity in heaven and on earth draws its name" (Eph. 3:15), how can we fail to conclude that the woman can legitimately be likened to Christ, that is to the Son?[9]

[7]See our ch. IV.
[8]St. Augustine, *De Trinitate,* XII, VII, 9: "In tribus hominibus."
[9]When we set forth the Augustinian conception of the Trinitarian image, we shall see the reason for this rejection of human relations as image of the divine relations. For St. Augustine no object exterior to the soul enters into its proper constitution and thus can be part of the

So we think that St. Augustine rejected one form of the family analogy of the Trinitarian mystery and that, in the measure in which he rejected it more completely in function of a too Platonic philosophy, he ought not to be followed. We further believe that in his *De Trinitate* he did not give the most real reasons for his rejection; these are insinuated in his commentaries on the Gospel of St. John. For in deepening the reasons why the Spirit is distinct from the Son and ought not to be called child of the Father, St. Augustine adds, and in evident allusion to the sex-oriented polytheistic cults among which the Christians were still living: "every son is a son of a father and a mother; let us put far from us the suspicion that there should be something like this between God the Father and God the Son."[10]

We can easily understand how the pagan "hierogamies" hindered the development of the family analogy of the Trinitarian mystery, however much this was insinuated (not to say more) by Revelation. The Gnostic origin of the theological elaboration of this analogy did not help to accredit it (as was the case with the word "consubstantial"). The favorable view taken of it by several Greek Fathers and especially by the theologian par excellence, Gregory of Nazianzus, was not enough to overcome the affective and speculative reasons of St. Augustine. We can wonder too whether the limitations of his marriage-theology, whose positive elements are undeniable, did not also work against the family analogy of the Trinity.[11]

3. The fact remains that St. Thomas Aquinas thought it good in this matter, unlike what he did in other matters, to take up the Augustinian position. But he only makes a brief allusion to our subject:

> The Holy Spirit proceeds immediately from the Father in that he has the being of the Father, and mediately in that he has it from the Son: there you have the sense in which one says that he proceeds from the Father through the Son. It is thus that Abel proceeded immediately from Adam, since Adam was his father; and mediately, since Eve was his mother and proceeded from Adam. But in truth, this example borrowed from a material origin seems to be a very poor choice to represent the immaterial procession of the divine Persons.[12]

However, the problematic of the analogy is different. Let us go back to the manner of Gregory of Nazianzus: here Eve no longer symbolizes the Holy Spirit, as in the version that was rejected by Augustine, but (implic-

---

veritable image of God. Here we take our inspiration from B. Schuler, *Die Lehre von der Dreipersönlichkeit Gottes*. Paderborn, 1961, § 25 and 29, pp. 105 and 115ff.

[10] St. Augustine, *In Jo.*, ML 35, 1890.

[11] Cf. J. C. Ford and G. Kelly, S.J., *Contemporary Moral Theology*, v. II, Marriage. Westminster, Maryland, 1964, pp. 380-382; A. Reuter, O.M.I., *Aug. doctrina de bonis matrimonii*. Rome, 1942.

[12] St. Thomas Aquinas, *Summa Theologica*, I, 36.3.1.

itly) the Son, since the Spirit is typified by Abel. Moreover, it is not the consubstantiality of the Spirit with the Father and the Son which interests Aquinas when he is expounding the analogy, but rather the procession of the Spirit *per Filium*. St. Thomas no longer wishes, as St. Gregory did, to use the family analogy to affirm the divinity of the Spirit, but rather to affirm against the Photian school the role of the Son in the procession of the Spirit.

It is fitting to note in passing how valuable the analogy is for expressing several points of the Trinitarian dogma; is not this fecundity (relatively speaking) a sign of truth? Whatever may be said of this, the negative conclusion of St. Thomas appears to us just as little convincing as that of Augustine.

For if this example "borrowed from a material origin" was truly such a "poor choice" to represent "the immaterial procession of the divine Persons," must we not say that the Revealer himself has deceived us in wishing to be called Father and Son? The material origin of a son with respect to his father is not different from that of the same son with respect to his two parents. Revelation itself leads us to this example which is not only material but also spiritual, for human sexual love in marriage is indissolubly both material or carnal and spiritual or immaterial. It is not only the love of two bodies, of two sensitivities, but more than this it is the love of two wills, of two souls (without which the bodies could not love one another, for human love in the proper sense of the word surpasses animal attraction).

The partly spiritual nature of human sexual love (whose dynamism strains toward an increasing spiritualization, especially due to the action of the sacramental graces of marriage) sufficiently enables us to say contrary to St. Thomas Aquinas that this example is quite well chosen to represent the immaterial procession of the divine Persons. Man is a being that is at the same time material and spiritual. There could not be a purely immaterial representation of the divine processions, since there is no human knowledge without images rooted in the materiality of the corporeal world. Since friendship is the human good par excellence[13] and conjugal friendship the most perfect form of human friendship[14] according to the same St. Thomas Aquinas, how can we fail to conclude that conjugal love and its fruit, the child, a fruit that is not merely material but eminently spiritual, is the most perfect, and, in the natural order, the most fully human representation of the mystery of the Most Holy Trinity?

It seems then that the very principles of the Angelic Doctor force the theologian to a conclusion contrary to that of the Angelic Doctor. Only the cultural context of the Middle Ages (which involved among other things a

[13] This thesis flows directly from the social nature of man.
[14] Cf. St. Thomas Aquinas, commentaries on the *Ethics* of Aristotle, book VIII, ch. 12: if man is "animal politicum" he is "multo magis animal conjugale."

certain depreciation of the role of woman and of which there are other traces in the work of the Common Doctor[15]) can explain the position he took against the family analogy. But to be more exact, must we not say that his position is only partially contrary to this analogy? For in fact in fidelity to Revelation he had no scruple about admitting this family analogy in what concerns the father-son relation;[16] it is only the extension of the analogy to women that caused him difficulty. And here we are touching a profound and mysterious point: Revelation itself has not explicated the conjugal aspect but only the paternity-filiation aspect of the family analogy of the Trinitarian mystery. We will have to ask why this is so and what are its consequences.

4. If it was the materiality of the analogy that always kept St. Thomas Aquinas from making it his own, this materiality did not prevent Scheeben from adopting it.[17] But instead of deepening the scheme which Gregory of Nazianzus and Thomas Aquinas offered us (father, mother, child corresponding respectively to Father, Son and Spirit), Scheeben preferred to let the analogy go back on the old track that was justly rejected by Augustine (the father-child-woman scheme). Therefore we do not insist on his contribution, which had the special merit of drawing attention to the importance of the subject.

5. This importance did not escape a certain number of contemporary theologians. Without doubt the most notable contribution is that of Heribert Mühlen in his work: *Der Heilige Geist als Person*. Here we are going to outline with broad strokes his presentation of the family intersubjectivity (I-Thou-We) as analogy of the Trinitarian mystery. Building on linguistic, phenomenological and exegetical analyses, he sees in the Holy Spirit the "We" of the Trinity and of the Church.

a) *Linguistic and phenomenological analysis: the conjugal "We"*
In all languages we encounter a fundamental structure. "I-Thou-We." All peoples understand by "I" not a simple individual but a subject who posits himself consciously before others. An "I" says "Thou" only to another

---

[15]St. Thomas wrote, following Aristotle, "naturaliter masculinum est melius et feminimum deterius" (*Polit.*, III, 1, 3) cf. G. Jacquemet, *Catholicisme*. Paris, 1956, v. IV, col. 1172: art. "Femme." Kristin M. Popik, "The Philosophy of Woman of Aquinas," *Faith and Reason* V, 1 (1979).

[16]St. Thomas Aquinas, *Summa Theologica*, I, 27.2; St. Thomas there shows the analogical character of the notion of generation and refutes (ad 1m) an objection based on the material aspect of generation in man. Ought he not have proceeded in the same manner regarding the father-mother-child image?

[17]Scheeben, *The Mysteries of Christianity*, appendix II. St. Louis, 1946, pp. 190-198. Doms is influenced by Scheeben (*Du sens et de la fin du mariage*. Paris, 1937, pp. 29ff.).

person, and then enters into dialogue with that person; while the "We" is said *to* another but *with* another.

In saying "Thou" a person has not yet entered into a reciprocal relation with another as long as this other has not treated him or her reciprocally as "Thou." And even when two persons treat each other reciprocally as "Thou," they have not yet adopted a common attitude before a third, something that happens in the "We."

The relation "I-Thou" is not only encounter but also union, covenant. A bond which is not exclusively mine or thine but ours. For example, for the two spouses the matrimonial covenant is not mine or thine but ours. The covenant is the expression or the sign of an intimate "We." Thus, the conjugal "We" is presupposed to the common act of the two spouses, the act of generation by which their two persons orient themselves in the direction of a third, the child. The conjugal act is a common act of the "I" and the "Thou," an "I-Thou" act in which the "I" and the "Thou" accept and give themselves reciprocally. In the context of a "relational" vision of person, Blessed Duns Scotus says that father and mother are two partial causes of the procreation of the child (Mühlen has studied Duns Scotus in depth).[18]

In short, the "Thou" and the "We" are two fundamental modes of the behavior of the "I."[19]

b) *Biblical analysis: "I-Thou-We" in the mouth of Jesus*

The "I am" of Jesus in the Gospel of St. John is self-revelation of Jesus as sent from the Father, or, more exactly, this "I am" signifies simultaneously Jesus and his Father, the Father as sending Jesus. It signifies the "I" of the Son inasmuch as he is in an absolute unity of action with the "I" of the Father. It does not then signify only the *Anihu* of the Father in the Old Testament, that is: "I am and no one is as I am,"[20] but also (cf. Jn. 8:16; 16:32) "I am not alone" and consequently "I and the Father." Thus the "I am" of Jesus has a dialogical sense. He does not come in his own name but in the name of the Father.

The relation between the two "I's" of the Father and of the Son is clarified in Jn. 17:21ff.: "That all may be one, even as thou, Father, art in me and I in thee." Here Jesus reveals to the disciples that he can say "Thou" to the Father in a unique manner, as no other person can. In the light of this text, one can see that it is not arbitrary to try to comprehend the Father-Son relation in the Trinity in the light of the analogy of the human "I-Thou."

---

[18] Blessed J. Duns Scotus, *Ord.*, I, d. 3, p. 3, q. 2, n. 496; III, n. 294; cited by H. Mühlen, *Der Heilige Geist als Person*. Paderborn, 1967, p. 78, § 3.50. Mühlen is also the author of a book on Duns Scotus: *Sein und Person nach Johannes Duns Scotus*. Werl, 1954.

[19] H. Mühlen, *Der Heilige Geist als Person*. Paderborn, 1967, pp. 61-73 (§ 3.30-3.44).

[20] In the sense that: no creature is as I am.

Perhaps, Mühlen seems to think, there is no better analogy than this one that was used by Jesus himself. (During his earthly life Jesus did not assimilate himself to the Word, but later this analogy of the Word is used by John.)

In speaking to the Father Jesus not only said "I" and "Thou" but also "We." Earlier he said "We" with the Apostles or with the Jews inasmuch as they were differentiated from the Samaritans (Jn. 11:11; 4:22). But Jesus never said (not even once) "we" with the Apostles with regard to the Father (cf. Jn. 20:17). He said: "my Father," "your Father" but not "Our Father"; and when he taught his disciples the "Our Father," he did not include himself in the "our."

And better still: in Jn. 14:23 and 17:21 Jesus says "We" with the Father thus distinguishing himself from the disciples, and on the side of the Father in opposition to men: "If anyone loves me...we will come to him and make our home with him." "That they may be one in us as we are one."

But in Jn. 14:23 Mühlen thinks the "We" is intimately bound up with the promise of another Paraclete (14:16, 26) who will abide with the disciples. This term "abide" recalls the abiding of the Father and of the Son in the soul of the faithful disciple. From this it follows, according to H. M., that the Paraclete is intimately included in the term "We" of verse 23.[21]

c) *The Holy Spirit, "We" in the Trinity*

Since Jesus spoke our human language and left to human words their permanent sense, and since there is a fundamental difference between the reciprocal "Thou" and the common "We," we can gather from Jesus' manner of speaking that his "We" is an allusion to the Holy Spirit.

Just as St. Thomas Aquinas speaks of the active spiration of the Spirit by the Father and the Son and also of the passive spiration which is the Holy Spirit and which he calls "subsisting operation,"[22] so we can say that the active spiration is an act of the "We" which the Father and the Son are and the passive spiration is the *subsistierende Wir-Akt,* the "We" in person, the intra-Trinitarian "subsistent We."

The Holy Spirit is the third "I" in the Holy Trinity and he is in a relation of "I-You" with the Father and the Son. St. Thomas Aquinas said: "two spirants but one sole spirator," *duo spirantes, sed unus spirator.*[23] In the Holy Spirit who is *ad Patrem et Filium* (DS 528; DB 278) the divine love of self returns to the Father and to the Son; the "We-Thou" produces an "I-You."

In the conjugal "We" we have an analogy of this Trinitarian "We." More precisely, the created "we" of the parents in the conjugal act evokes

---

[21]H. Mühlen, *op. cit.,* pp. 83-99 (§ 4.01-4.27).
[22]St. Thomas Aquinas, *I Sent.,* 32.1.2.4.
[23]St. Thomas Aquinas, *Summa Theologica,* I 36.4.7; cf. I, 36.4.1.

the procession of the Holy Spirit from the Father and from the Son as from one sole principle. Naturally the sexual differentiation and the biological aspects must be put aside. What is being considered here is the purely formal structure of this process, in which two persons as co-subjects of a common act produce a third. Through the analogy of the conjugal act (two persons, one sole principle), we can better understand the procession of the Holy Spirit *a Patre Filioque tamquam ab uno principio*. We are only applying the method advocated by Vatican I: "Reason illumined by faith, through a careful, pious and sober investigation, attains, thanks to the gift of God, to a very fruitful understanding of the mysteries, whether it starts from the analogy of natural knowledges, or from the linkage of the mysteries with one another and with the ultimate end of man" (*DS* 3016; *DB* 1796; *ex eorum quae naturaliter cognoscit analogia*).

In particular the analogy we are here considering permits us to grasp better and to illustrate the fact that the Son is not the instrument of the Father in the production of the Spirit. For the woman is not the instrument of her spouse in the procreation of the child, but a "partial cause."

It is fitting also to note the limits[24] of the analogy so as to throw into better relief the transcendence of the Holy Spirit's procession relative to the procreation of the child.

Thus while the child on the one hand is for his parents a "he" of whom they speak to one another, the Holy Spirit constitutes a "We" that is immanent to the "I" and to the "Thou" of the Father and the Son. The Holy Spirit is a bond that is immanent to the Father and the Son and the relation "We" is immanent to the relations "I" and "Thou," while the child remains a bond that is exterior to the parents.

On the other hand, the Holy Spirit has the same identical divine nature possessed by the Father and the Son but which he receives from them. The child, on the contrary, has a numerically different nature from those of each of his parents.

In the spiration of the Holy Spirit by the Father and the Son, the "We" in act manifests and constitutes the passage from the unity of essence or nature to the unity of interpersonal love.[25] The circuminsession of the "I-Thou" is achieved in the circuminsession of the "We" which is one person in two others and between two others. We could formulate Mühlen's thought in this way: the distinctive property of the Holy Spirit is to be a Person who is an Inter-Person.

---

[24]Mühlen, *op. cit.*, pp. 136-137; 76-81 (§ 5.57-59; 3.48-3.55.2.).

[25]Cf. St. Thomas Aquinas, in *Joannem* cap. XVII, lectio V, § 2214 ed. Marietti: "In Patre et Filio est duplex unitas sc. essentiae et amoris et secundum utramque Pater est in Filio et Filius in Patre."

d) *The Holy Spirit, as the "We" of the Father and the Son, is at the origin of the "We" of the Church*

In 1 Cor. 12:12-13 we see that the Holy Spirit gives the Church the ability to say "We" to the "You" of the world: "We have all been baptized in one Spirit to form one Body...we have all been made to drink of one Spirit." The Spirit is one and identical in us all, he is not exclusively mine or thine, but he is ours, as St. Augustine underlined it.[26] The identity of the Spirit of Christ in all the members of his Body, the Church, is the foundation and condition of the possibility of the ecclesial "We." The "We all" of 1 Cor. 12:13 is not a pure stylized formula but it has a profound ecclesial meaning: the same Spirit operates in all the members of the Church.[27] The Pauline "We" expresses the "corporate personality" of the Church and bears in itself the intra-Trinitarian "We" that is the Holy Spirit.

Mühlen further cites in this sense 1 Jn. 3:24: "And by this we know that He abides in us: by the Spirit which He has given us" (cf. 4:13). In a general way one can say that the "Johannine We" (an expression of E. Stauffer) is unthinkable outside the context of the salvific mission of the Spirit. For there is question here of the "we" of the first epistle of St. John.

Thus the prologue of this letter becomes clearer:

> That which we have seen and heard, we announce to you, so that you may have fellowship with us. As to our fellowship, it is with the Father and with his Son Jesus Christ (1 Jn. 1:3).... "We have fellowship with one another" (1 Jn. 1:7).

Our horizontal fellowship is conditioned by our vertical fellowship with the hierarchical Church, which is sign and token of fellowship with the divine Persons, and which is in itself in fellowship with the Father and the Son. There are then three distinct and convergent fellowships: between us, with the episcopal college, with the Father and the Son. These three fellowships presuppose the eternal and consubstantial fellowship of the Father and the Son in the Spirit.

The "We" of the Christians is thus intimately bound up with the Holy Spirit, the intra-Trinitarian "We," whom it makes visible to the eyes of faith and without whom the mystery of the ecclesial "We" would not be perceived. The Holy Spirit appears in the history of salvation through the "we" of Christians.

If the Son, as Son, has assumed into the unity of his personal property a human *nature*, the Holy Spirit on the contrary in virtue of his personal

---

[26]Cf. St. Augustine, *De Trinitate*, V.14.15; the "Spiritus noster," of which Augustine speaks regarding the Third Person, is an expression fully conformed to the New Testament (1 Jn. 3:24; 4:13; Rom. 8:15).

[27]Pius XII, *Mystici Corporis*, DS 3808 (DB 2288).

property binds many *persons* with Jesus Christ and with one another. The "We" of the Church, over against the "you" of the world, constitutes an analogy and a manifestation of the "We" which is the Holy Spirit, "We-in-Person" in the Church.[28]

e) *Critical reflections: the power and originality of the synthesis compel admiration. But they have not prevented some doubts.*

On the Trinitarian level we note that, according to A. Patfoort,[29] Mühlen's interpretation risks eliminating the doctrine of the magisterium on the Spirit as fruit of the mutual love of the Father and of the Son: "The We expresses a side by side position, while the mutual love is a face to face position realized in the I-Thou encounter...." However, Mühlen knows and cites this doctrine.[30]

On the level of the relation between the Spirit and the Church, one of the author's affirmations certainly must be nuanced. The Church is certainly a "We" which proclaims itself as such in saying "You" to the world; but in the Church there is also the "We" of the hierarchy which addresses itself to the "you" of the faithful (Acts 15:28) by putting itself in conformity with its proper mission on the side of the "We" of the Holy Spirit: "The Holy Spirit and we have decided not to impose other burdens than these." As we saw, St. John, in designating himself, uses a "we" that is all the more mysterious since he is the sole author of this first epistle! One could synthesize these two manners of speaking by saying that the "We" of the Church is concentrated in the "We" of the hierarchy which has the mission to express and form it, under the action and to the image of the Spirit, who is the "We" that is transcendent to and immanent in the "we" of the Church, and who forms this "we" of the Church through the "we" of the hierarchy.

It must be noted further that the attribution to the Holy Spirit of a unifying activity of the Church, not in virtue of a simple appropriation, but as consequence of a role of formal causality that is proper to the Third Person and corresponds to his personal property within the Trinitarian mystery, is a view that is certainly contested and perhaps contestable. But it is a view that should not be taxed a priori with heterodoxy and one that counts an increasing number of protagonists in the theological world inside the Catholic Church. And it appears to enjoy the support of the redactor of the encyclical *Mystici Corporis* (of Pope Pius XII), that is S. Tromp.[31]

With regard to Mühlen's fundamental thesis: that the "We" of Jesus, in

---

[28]Mühlen, *op. cit.*, 190-197; we have added the reflections on the three distinct and convergent fellowships.

[29]A. Patfoort, O.P., "La fonction personnelle du Saint-Esprit," *Angelicum* 45 (1968), 320-321.

[30]Mühlen, *op. cit.*, 5.66-5.68 (pp. 143-146).

[31]S. Tromp, S.J., edition of the encycl. *Mystici Corporis*, of Pope Pius XII. Rome, 1948, Univ. Gregoriana, Series Theologica, no. 26, p. 132; DS 3814 (DB 2890).

the discourse after the Supper, expresses both the active spiration of the Spirit by the Father and by the Son and his passive spiration or at least presupposes it, this appears to us to merit at least serious consideration. It poses the difficult problems that are bound up with the distinction between active and passive spiration of the Spirit; for the demonstration to be perfectly conclusive, it would still be necessary to establish that this "We" could not be interpreted as being only an allusion to the common activity of the Father and the Son in the works *ad extra*. For if that were the case, the "We" in question would no longer signify either the spirative property of the Father and of the Son (a non-hypostatic active property common to them) or the personal property of the Spirit. But it seems to us that H. Mühlen has not envisaged this hypothesis sufficiently, if at all.

6. It is now time to present some general conclusions and reflections about the conjugal and family analogy.

The family together with the person of each of its members is incontestably the natural reality par excellence from which one can by analogy rise notably, with the gifts of the Spirit, to a very fruitful though still very imperfect understanding of the Trinitarian mystery. Mühlen has perceived very well that the text of Vatican I, to which we alluded, not only permits but even demands such a reflection. And this will hold the attention of Trinitarian theologians still more in the future.

They ought to be inspired in this matter more by the example of St. Gregory of Nazianzus than by that of St. Augustine. There is need of an historical in-depth study on this subject, something that has barely been outlined so far: to determine what were the vicissitudes of the conjugal and family analogy in the course of the history of Trinitarian theology. It would particularly be necessary to examine not only the patristic and medieval tradition but also the reflections of Protestant and Orthodox theologians in this regard. We also think that a synthetic study of the treatment of this analogy in contemporary Catholic theology would be fruitful. Let it be enough to note here that it certainly enjoys the encouragement of a theologian as erudite as M. Schmaus.[32]

While awaiting studies of this type we can only make a few observations, limited indeed, but doubtless suggestive.

When the patristic and medieval tradition examined the problem it was content to present, and quite rapidly, a comparison between the trio "Adam-Abel (or Seth)-Eve" and the three divine Persons. The conjugal

---

[32]M. Schmaus, *Dogmatik*, I, 578: "es ankommt, die Hauchung des Geistes durch die Tat der Liebe und die Zeugung des Kindes durch die innigste Vereinigung von Mann und Frau als Siegel und Gewehr ihrer Liebe trotz der grossen und wesentlichen Unstimmigkeiten des Vergleichs deutlich sehen." Cited by Mühlen, *op. cit.*, § 3.48.1; pp. 76-77.

analogy, that is the partial resemblance between the structure of the conjugal act and that of the Trinitarian mystery, appears to be a modern discovery. The Fathers gave little thought to a resemblance between a family and the Trinity. However St. Augustine envisaged such an analogy,[33] but not between the conjugal act and the active spiration of the Spirit. The older Fathers appear never to have dreamed of it. Doubtless the abuses of Christian Gnostic theology and the dangers that would result from the presentation of such an analogy in the framework of a civilization still steeped in sensual polytheism, could only discourage this.

The family analogy of the Trinity can be broken up into two aspects: the paternity-filiation aspect and the conjugal aspect. It is clear that the first is suggested by Revelation and explicitly contained in it. It is permitted, nay even indispensable, to think that the second is at least insinuated. But up to recent times theological, logical and psychological or cultural reasons have not permitted the development and explication of this implicit content of Revelation.

First of all the theological reasons: such an explication supposes a solid acquisition of the doctrine of the procession of the Holy Spirit *a Patre Filioque tamquam ab unico principio unica spiratione*. Now if we leave aside the symbol *Quicumque* which is also called the Athanasian Creed (DS 75), since it is difficult to determine the precise date when this symbol was universally received in the Church, the first declaration...of the extraordinary magisterium of the Church on this subject is that of the general council of Lyons in 1274 (DS 850; DB 460).

Next the logical reasons: the natural tendency of the human mind inclined it to compare Seth, Abel or the child to the only-begotten Son, and not to the Holy Spirit. And at first glimpse this parallelism seemed more satisfying, since it underscored an analogical relation between earthly son and father and heavenly son and father. By a no less logical consequence one spontaneously inclined to partially liken the creation of Eve from the side of Adam to the procession of the Spirit, as for example St. John Damascene[34] did to symbolize the procession of the Spirit from the Father as far as it differs from the generation of the Son. But it never even came to mind for them to invert the logical order to reach a more dogmatically satisfying analogy, by likening Eve to the Word, the only Son. And yet, as we showed, this is the only road that permits us in this analogy to take account not only of the generation of the Son but also of the eternal procession of the Spirit in full conformity with the definitively elaborated Catholic dogma.

[33] St. Augustine, *De Trinitate*, XII, V, 5: "...trinitatem imaginis Dei...in conjugio masculi et feminae atque in eorum prole."
[34] St. John Damascene, *De fide orthodoxa*, MG 94, 816C-817A.

Lastly the psychological or cultural reasons: since it implies not only the father-son relation but also the role of woman, the family analogy cannot without danger be integrated into the didascalia and much less into the kerygma. This would favor a tritheist and sensual understanding of the Trinity, in other words a misunderstanding of it. Doubtless even today it would be inopportune to present it in this way in the context of Islam. We could even wonder to what extent it could be presented in its totality to Christian people, without danger of grave confusion in our hedonistic age.[35] However we think it might be the most expressive way of making someone begin to suspect the loving splendor of the procession of the Holy Spirit as *mutual* Love proceeding from the Father and the Son as from *one* principle by *one* spiration. For thus a child proceeds from the mutual love of the parents as from one principle by one act of two persons. And it would be easy to remove the dangers of confusion by recalling not only the material but also and especially the spiritual character of conjugal love, as well as the divine transcendence: "one cannot note a likeness between creature and Creator without having to note a still greater unlikeness" (DS 806; DB 432: *inter creatorem et creaturam non potest similitudo notari quin inter eos maior sit dissimilitudo notanda*).

It seems to us then that a great part of the difficulties that have for so long a time been urged against the explication of the conjugal dimension of the family analogy have disappeared today. We think the moment has come to deepen this analogy. Why not recognise the evocative character, not only on the pastoral level but also on the level of theological reflection, of the presentation of it that Canon Caffarel gives to young families:

> The child is the unimpeachable witness of the love of his father and his mother—in the eyes of men, but first of all in the eyes of his parents. The Holy Spirit is much more the witness of the love of the Father and the Son. He proclaims: the Father and the Son love one another, I am the living proof of this. Yes, the Holy Spirit is the proclamation, the acclamation of the love of the Father and the Son. Eternally in the bosom of the Trinity; within time in the bosom of the Church. And if it is true that on earth nothing is more admirable than the spectacle of two beings who love one another, what could we find more worthy of admiration in heaven and on earth than the spectacle of the mutual love of the two divine Persons shining out in the Holy Spirit? He is the feast of Love.
>
> We, the invited guests of the love of the Father and the Son, ought to be among men the witnesses of their mutual love. Or, more exactly, we ought to be wholly transparent to the Holy Spirit who dwells in us, the Spirit of whom I was just saying to you that he is the eternal witness of

[35]Cf. GS 47.2.

the love of the Father and the Son.... Each of us ought to be the witness of the love of the Father and the Son so that men, our brothers may understand that they also are the guests of the love of the Father and the Son and of their eternal joy. Such is indeed the highest conception of the Christian apostolate.[36]

In reading this text one can better perceive the great advantage of the conjugal analogy and how far it surpasses every other analogy of the Trinitarian mystery in its deep evocative value: It starts from the most ordinary and the most totally interpersonal human experience, the experience of conjugal dialogue into which that of paternity is inserted, an experience that is both profoundly human and at the same time divinized by the sacramental grace of marriage.

If in marriage human love has become sacrament of the divine grace of the New Covenant, sign of the union between Christ and the Church as St. Paul underscores it (Eph. 5:23); if already in the Old Covenant human love became the sign of the spiritual marriage between Israel and its God in the Canticle of Canticles, why would not the conjugal act in which St. Thomas saw an act meritorious of eternal life[37] and Dom Massabki saw a sacramental act at the moment of the consummation of sacramental marriage, why would this conjugal act not be the sign par excellence, in its very fecundity, of the intra-divine and eternal fecundity of the mutual love between Father and Son?

The inner logic of the New Testament does more than authorize such a conclusion. It demands it, if we wish to consider no longer only the natural love but this love as divinized by the sacrament of marriage to the point of becoming "efficacious sign and participating image of the union of Christ with the Church" (Massabki).[38] In fact according to the declaration made by Jesus in his discourse after the Last Supper, this union itself is the image of the Trinity (a point to which we shall return a little later): "As you, Father, are in me and I in you, may they also be in us... one as we are one: I in them and you in me, that they may be perfectly one" (Jn. 17:21-23). I in them: this is the union between Christ and the Church, of which marriage is the sign, according to St. Paul. One as we: this is the union of the Father and the Son in the Spirit, a union of love and not just a unity of nature.[39] Through the Church, Christian marriage thus symbolizes the unity of the Father and

---

[36]H. Caffarel, *Anneau d'Or*, 138 (1967), 440, 443-444 (extract from an article on "our God, the Holy Trinity").

[37]St. Thomas Aquinas, *Summa Theologica*, Supplement, 41.4: "si enim ad actum matrimonialem virtus inducat vel justitiae ut debitum reddat vel religionis ut proles ad cultum Dei procreetur, est meritorius."

[38]Charles Massabki, O.S.B., *Le Christ rencontre de deux amours*. Paris, 1962, p. 1256.

[39]See note 25.

of the Son in the Spirit. The conjugal act in the sacrament of marriage is divinized by the sacramental graces proper to marriage. Even when this act is no longer purely and simply sacramental, i.e., once the marriage is consummated, it is not merely an image and a vestige of the Holy Trinity (as in a non-sacramental marriage) but it is even a likeness of the Trinity, if we once again use medieval and always valid categories.

Far from being contrary to Scripture, as St. Augustine[40] thought, it appears that the conjugal analogy of the Trinitarian mystery flows logically from Scripture. In truth what Scripture offers us is a human and permanent relation of paternity and filiation or of marriage which evokes the intra-Trinitarian relations. Or more precisely the two aspects of the analogy mutually imply one another, for paternity and filiation are situated in the framework of a matrimonial relation. And if we admit with St. Paul the value of the universal paradigm of the Adam-Eve-Seth triad, then this matrimonial relation is an image of the mystery only in the measure that it is procreative.

It must be further recognized that according to Scripture the human couple is not directly and immediately an image of the Trinity, but only by the mediation of the pair Christ-Church.[41] While the relation between God and his Word is presented to us immediately through the categories of father and son, the child is nowhere presented as an analogue of the Spirit. But the spouse, as we saw, has a role parallel to that of Christ (cf. 1 Cor. 11). Only the father-son image of the Trinitarian mystery is truly detailed there.[42] So much so that an exegete declares, "to express the relations of the Father and the Son John gathers together the most delicate traits of human experience. Thus we are instructed very concretely: a Father loves, he gives, he tells secrets and gives commandments, he is honored and his honor overflows onto his own. The Son, the only Son, equal to his Father in everything and way above all others, receives everything from his Father, is

---

[40]St. Augustine, *De Trinitate*, XII, VI, 6: "respuimus istam sententiam...quia eam falsam divina Scriptura evidenter ostendit" (ML 42, 1001). The context clearly shows that St. Augustine rejects every form of family analogy (in the sense of image and not only of vestige) of the Trinitarian mystery in terms of his interpretation of Gn. 1:26-27 and in the context of his Trinitarian and anthropological doctrine: man can only be the image of the whole Trinity, so much so that he cannot at the same time in his interpersonal relations be a functional image of one Person in particular; a point of view by which Augustine unwittingly, Pauline as he was, contradicts Eph. 3:15 ("from the Father, from whom all paternity in heaven and on earth draws its name"). And thus he implicitly rejects the father-woman-child analogy we are presenting here.

[41]Cf. Orbe, *art. cit.*, pp. 114-118: Gnostic theology and also, it seems, the earliest orthodox exegetes of the Church, saw in the Genesis account of Adam and Eve the image both of the Trinitarian mystery and of the mystery of the Chruch.

[42]We mean to say: in Scripture.

never alone or intent on his own proper interests; he is of the Father, toward the Father, with the Father."[43]

So we must ask ourselves why the Revealing God has not wished to offer us in the same clear and immediately evident manner in the Scriptures a family analogy of the procession of the Spirit. One of the reasons for this, might it not be the limits of the conjugal aspects of the analogy, not only the extrinsic and common limits (the absolute transcendence and spirituality of the mystery), but also its intrinsic and specific limits: just as the Fathers vie with one another in stressing that the Spirit is not another Son of the Father and does not proceed by way of generation but by way of procession, and yet the conjugal analogy offers us the child and his procreation as the analogue of the Spirit and his procession. In other words, the analogy concerns itself rather with the formal structure of the processions of the child and of the Spirit (two persons constituting a single principle of the production of a third person, in a single act), while leaving aside what distinguishes these processions from the generation of the child or of the eternal Son. We are dealing with a complex analogy, that is less immediately understandable even when it is clearly set forth. So it is not astonishing that Revelation itself presents it in a more obscure manner.

As every analogy of the Trinitarian mystery remains deficient (cf. DS 806), it might be possible to show how the different forms of the family analogy of the Trinitarian mystery, including the one St. Augustine rejected, can express distinct and complementary aspects of the inexhaustible primordial mystery. This would be an interesting course to pursue with a view to a deepening of the family analogy we have been studying here.

We might say further that the family analogy essentially offers us a parallelism of loving relations without distinguishing between relation of knowledge and relation of love. And so it does not offer any special basis for differentiating the generation of the Son and the procession of the Spirit, on the level of mode, but only on the level of the number of persons intervening in the two cases. And here is precisely its force: while the *intra*-subjective analogy (the intellectual and volitive soul as image of the Trinity) offers no suggestion of the *tri*personal mystery in God, the family analogy by evoking the tripersonal, appears to concentrate in itself every possibility of *inter*subjective analogy by its *tri*personal aspect.

In this connection it is not without interest to note that, if Augustine rejected every form of family analogy, at the same time he set forth the bases for accepting the form we presented here, by recognizing that fraternal charity as such is the image of the Trinity which it bears in itself. In

---

[43]C. J. Pinto de Oliveira, O.P., "Rapports du Père et du Fils dans le IV Evangile," *RSPT* 49 (1965), 81-104.

other words, when Augustine admitted that every supernatural intersubjectivity was an image of the Trinity, by that very fact he admitted that the family built on the sacrament of marriage was also such an image, at least implicitly. "You see the Trinity, if you see charity": *vides Trinitatem si charitatem vides.*[44] A little further on Augustine explained it in this way: he who loves his neighbor spiritually, sees God—Charity itself—in an interior vision. We do not insist on this point now, but we shall take it up again when speaking of the ecclesial image of the Trinity.

II. ECCLESIAL INTERSUBJECTIVITY, SECOND REVEALED ANALOGY OF THE TRINITY

The eve of his Pasch the Lord Jesus Christ himself indicated and manifested that the reciprocal union of Christians would render his perfect unity with the Father credible. Thus Revelation offers us an image of the Trinitarian mystery which renders it more accessible once it has been revealed. The Revealer himself manifests the mystery of the Trinity and the mystery of the Church together, one in the other, one by the other, to make our faith in these two distinct and inseparable mysteries easier. The Church is the image, the body[45] and the temple of the Three. How is the Church the icon of the natural unity, the plurality, the processions and mutual indwelling of the three divine Persons? And what are the limits of this analogy?

1. *The universal Church, icon of the triune God*

In his sacerdotal prayer Jesus asks of his Father: "That all may be one. As you Father are in me and I in you, may they also be one in us, so that the world may believe that you have sent me. I have given them the glory that you have given me so that they may be one as we are one" (Jn. 17:21-22).

The unity of the Father and of the Son in the "We" of the Holy Spirit is the exemplary, efficient and final cause of the unity of Christians in the "We" of the Church.

The unity to which the Lord alludes here is at the same time unity of nature and unity of persons in the mutual love that is the Spirit of the Father and of the Son, as St. Augustine and St. Thomas recognized.[46] In the image of this double unity in God, there is a double unity among men, of which the second alone is proper to the Church; a unity of nature which is specific, but not numerical, and a "unity of charity which presupposes the unity of the Spirit (cf. Eph. 4:3). The latter is at the same time the commun-

---

[44]St. Augustine, *De Trinitate*, VIII, VIII, 12.

[45]Cf. Tertullian, *De Baptismo*, VI, 1: "Where the Father and Son and Holy Spirit are, there also is found the Church which is the body of the Three."

[46]Cf. St. Augustine, *De Trinitate*, XV, VI, 5-7; ML 42, 927-928; *in* Joan. Tr. 110-111, ML 35, 1920-1929; St. Thomas Aquinas, *in* Joan. c. 17, lectio III, § 1; V, § 2; VI, *in fine; Catena aurea in Joan.*, 17, § 3-5. See note 25 of this chapter.

ion of the Father and the Son and the source of the communion of the Church, in the unity of the Father and the Son."[47]

The Holy Spirit is the uncreated and only soul of the Church, the principle of its visible and invisible unity in charity. While always remaining the Church of the Spirit,[48] the Church which is inseparable from the Spirit Paraclete and filled by him and his gifts and his charisms, the Church maintains also the created bonds of its unity, bonds to which the fourth council of the Lateran, after St. Augustine, made reference, in a way that marked out the limits of the analogy. Reacting against a lost text of Joachim of Flora this council shows that the *analogatum princeps* is not the Church but the Trinity. Thus one should not attempt to reduce the unity of the Trinity to certain aspects of the unity of the Church, but on the contrary to clarify the Church's unity by that of the Trinity:

> When, therefore, the Truth prays for his faithful to the Father, he says: "I will that they should be one in us, as also we are one" (Jn. 17:22); this term "one" applied to the faithful means a union of charity in grace; applied to the Divine Persons, it indicates the unity of identity in nature ...for between Creator and creature no similarity can be found so great but that the dissimilarity is even greater (*DS* 806; *DB* 432).

In short, the unity of the Church does not signify numerical identity of nature in its members, but union of their wills; in God, on the contrary, there is only one Will of the three divine Persons. Can we not conclude that Jesus, in presenting his unity with the Father as model of the union among Christians, had in mind not just the unity of his divine nature but still more the unity of his interpersonal love in the Spirit? The Church is a communion of persons which is able to imitate the loving communion between the divine Persons and obligated thereto. Is it not this preferential aspect that Vatican II has correctly set forth in these words: "Of this mystery (of the unity of the Church) the supreme model is, in the Trinity of persons, the unity of the one God, Father and Son in the Holy Spirit (*unitas unius Dei Patris et Filii in Spiritu Sancto*)"?[49] Thus the one and universal Church appears in the eyes of the faith as the icon of the one Spirit of the Father and the Son.

2. *The universal Church, icon of the processions of the Word and the Spirit*

We can say that baptismal regeneration and the teaching of the magisterium of the Church on the one hand, and the communion among the

---

[47] F. Bourassa, S.J., "Communion du Père et du Fils," *Gregorianum* 48 (1967), 697, note 75 toward the end, of which we have modified the formulation.
[48] M.-H. Lavocat, O.P., *L'Esprit de Vérité et d'Amour*. Paris, 1968, v. II, ch. VII: "L'Eglise de l'Esprit" (pp. 271-287).
[49] *UR* § 2, toward the end.

faithful in sacrificial love on the other hand, are respectively the analogical images of the intellectual generation of the only Son of God and of the procession of love of his Spirit.

The hierarchy of the Church spiritually generates the laity by instructing it with a view to baptism or to perfect fidelity to the baptismal promises. As the Father generates his Son eternally by communicating to him his divine being, so does the Church regenerate men by communicating to them the divine and supernatural life of grace. The Church generates its children, not outside herself as do earthly mothers but by incorporating them in herself as the Father generates his Son by communicating to him his divine nature and abiding in him just as this only Son abides forever turned toward the bosom of the Father (cf. Jn. 1:18).[50] The Church, like the Father, begets only Christ, the total Christ: "My little children, with whom I am again in travail until Christ be formed in you!" (Gal. 4:19; cf. Phlm. 10).

In the measure that it communicates the truth, the Church resembles the Father who utters his one and eternal Word; in the measure that it is communion in the love and concurrence of all its members in the exercise of charity, the Church manifests to the eyes of faith the procession of the Spirit. Richard of St. Victor has said it very well:[51]

> What is then this breath of the human heart, lighter in some, stronger in others, in these more tepid, and in those more ardent, what is it if not an intimate affection of the soul, an impulse of blazing love? This is why we say that those have one spirit and act in one spirit, who have one design and the same resolve, who have the same affections, the same sentiments, the same desires.... It is then in the image of this spirit which proceeds and is exhaled from many hearts that we call the Holy Spirit the one who in the Trinity proceeds from two persons.

The breath of the reciprocal love of men, the "spirit" of the ecclesial community (if we take the word spirit in the most ordinary sense that it assumes today with regard to a human group), these then are the signs of the procession of love of the Holy Spirit, in the eyes of Richard of St. Victor. And so it is in a pneumatological sense that he interprets Acts 4:32: "The multitude of those who believed were of one heart and soul. No one said that any of the things which he possessed was his own, but they had everything in common." And Richard writes explicitly: "It is indeed this sentiment of piety, it is truly the breath of this same spirit which makes of a multitude of hearts, one heart and one soul."[52]

---

[50] Bossuet, sermon for the feast of the Holy Trinity, first point, at the end.
[51] Richard of St. Victor, *De Trinitate*, VI, 10 (SC 63, 399). We have already cited this text in our ch. I, in a different context.
[52] *Ibid.*

The text of Acts that we cited invites us to concretize the consequences of this pneumatological ecclesiology in the matter of common use of private property.

The Holy Spirit, who is given to us by the Father and by the Son, and who is their consubstantial and coeternal communion, pours out in our hearts fraternal love (cf. Rom. 5:5) and impels us thus to say to one another what the Son says eternally to the Father and what the Father of mercies (2 Cor. 1:3) repeats to the eldest Son (cf. Lk. 15:31): "all that is mine is yours and all that is your is mine; you are always with me" (cf. Jn. 17:10). By making, common as to use, according to our obligation of charity,[53] that which is our own as communicants in the same Eucharist and temples of the same Trinity, we become *one* among ourselves so that in the face of our fraternal, spiritual and temporal communion the world may believe (cf. Jn. 17:21) in the perfect and eternal communion between the Father and the Son in the immutable kiss of the Spirit. Each one ought to say to his Eucharistic fellow-communicant: "all that is mine is yours" so as to be able to hear in reply: "all that is mine is also yours: that is ours." And it is ours because the Spirit of the Father and the Son, manifested by our action, is also ours.

In the light of St. Augustine we can go a step further and observe that the Christian (or even the man unconsciously divinized) in loving his brother loves still more the love by which he loves him,[54] the love in which, we add, the Spirit of Love is present and the love which this Spirit gives and which represents him. But this fraternal love, if it is really supernatural, is always lived in function of the Church as communion of fraternal charity, and in the more or less proximate or remote radiance of his blazing light. To eyes illumined by faith, the exercise of fraternal charity thus constitutes each time a new revelation and manifestation both of the universal Church and of the eternal procession of the Holy Spirit, who is always sent to manifest his own procession in the gift of love.

3. *The reciprocal immanence of the Christians who are equal among themselves is the analogical image of the circuminsession of the divine Persons:*

The New Testament shows us not only the *cor unum* of the Christians, but also a "circuminsession of hearts" that are mutually present to one another in the bosom of the Church. St. Paul has expressed it eloquently:

---

[53]Cf. St. Thomas Aquinas, *Summa Theologica*, II, II, 66.2; John XXIII, encyclical *Mater et Magistra*, ed. Haubtmann, Paris, 1961, § 43: the Pope there underscores the priority of this natural right in the use of the goods of this world with regard to the right of private property, for the first is the reason for the existence of the second.

[54]St. Augustine, *De Trinitate*, VIII, VIII, 12: "Magis enim novit dilectionem qua diligit quam fratrem quem diligit. Ecce jam potest notiorem Deum habere quam fratrem: plane notiorem, quia praesentiorem; notiorem, quia interiorem; notiorem, quia certiorem."

Make place for us in your hearts.... You are in our hearts, to die together and to live together (2 Cor. 7:2-4). I hold you in my heart, you who are partakers of grace with me, both in my imprisonment and in the defense and confirmation of the gospel (Phil. 1:7).

It is love, and still more supernatural charity which produces this mutual indwelling of hearts in one another, this imperfect circuminsession in the diversity of the individual natures. While the understanding interiorizes, love exteriorizes and thrusts one toward and into the other. Like the divine Persons, the hearts which are mutually immanent, are fundamentally equal to one another; and love tends further to equalize some of the accidental inequalities that distinguish them. Thus we read in the book of Acts (2:44-45): "And all who believed were together and had all things in common; and they sold their possessions and goods and distributed them to all, as any had need."

In the mystery of the Church, inasmuch as the universal Church is present at each Eucharistic celebration and *in* each particular church (cf. LG 23), each particular church is in some way immanent in all the others. Since the universal Church is composed of particular churches (LG 23; *ex quibus*), its presence to one of them mysteriously but really entails the presence of all in each. There is thus a circuminsession of particular churches among themselves in the bosom of the universal Church, which also evokes the circuminsession of the divine Persons in the unity of the same indivisible divine nature.

This circuminsession of hearts and of particular churches in the unity of the universal Church is manifest at the time of the Eucharistic communion and of the prayer for the Church in the canon of the Mass. There it appears specially, notably in the case of concelebration between representatives of diverse particular churches (cf. UR 15. 1).

The preaching in the framework of the celebration of the sacred Mysteries is the supreme ecclesial manifestation of the eternal generation of the Word, just as the spiritual *and* sacramental communion (cf. DS 1648; DB 881), the partaking of the spiritualized body of the risen Lord, during the breaking of the one indivisible Bread, is the supreme ecclesial manifestation of the eternal spiration of the Spirit. In both cases, there are two invisible missions of the Word and the Spirit in some way rendered visible; and these missions, let us recall, are only their eternal processions prolonged in the bosom of history precisely to become manifest to the eyes of faith.

Communion in the hearing of the Word and in the breaking of the Bread produces and fashions the Church somewhat in the way the Father generates the Son, the Word of his Light, and the way both spirate their mutual love which is the Spirit.

So we can say that the mystery of the Church both as invisible and as visibly structured, as hierarchical as well as charismatic, as institution as well as community of salvation, offers us an organic and apparently complete analogy of the mystery of the Most Holy Trinity, an image both of the unity of nature and the plurality of divine Persons, of their processions and of their circuminsession.

Thus, without ever losing sight of the Transcendence of the Trinity relative to the Church to which it is more unlike than like (DS 806; DB 432), we can come through the analogy of these mysteries with one another (DS 3016; DB 1796), to relish a deeper awareness of the total and single mystery which is constituted by these two mysteries that are distinct but immanent one in the other: the mystery of the Trinity in the Church and the mystery of the Church, which is the body of the Three.

Of the three analogies we are here presenting (the other two being the family and the individual soul), it is the ecclesial analogy which is most explicitly contained in Revelation, and very particularly in the sacerdotal prayer of Jesus. But compared with the third (which we are now taking up) it has been relatively little studied. Here also, patristic investigations and monographs would be fruitful.

III. PERSONAL INTRASUBJECTIVITY, IMPLICITLY REVEALED ANALOGY OF THE TRINITY

In the course of the history of theological thought the last question that the analytical mind proposes is: why are there processions in God? How can we explain and justify the origin of the Son from the Father, and that of the Spirit from the Father and the Son? In our chapter IV we established the fact of these processions which Revelation offers us and on which the dogma rests as the confession of faith of the Church. But except for a few words on the intellectual mode of the Son's generation, we have not spoken, as much as human reason illumined by faith can speak, of the how and why of the two processions. Let us anticipate the answer we are going to examine successively in the light of St. Augustine, St. Thomas Aquinas and B. Lonergan: there is in God a Principle which from the plenitude of an infinite Intelligence utters an equally divine Word from which springs a personal Love.

1. *Trinity and unity of the human spirit in St. Augustine*[55]

Augustine's problem is this: since Revelation teaches that man was made to the image of God (Gn. 1:26), a God which it presents to us as one and three, we must admit a certain analogy between man and the divine Trinity. In each human person then there ought to be a trinity that evokes the divine Trinity. But for this intrasubjective trinity to be truly an image, it is

---

[55]We draw here on the remarkable pages of the Augustinian philosopher, M. Sciacca, "Trinité et unité de l'esprit," *Augustinus Magister*. Paris, 1954, v. I, pp. 521-533.

necessary that the second of its three terms be generated, and that the third proceed from the other two. In addition, the three terms must be consubstantial, distinct, equal and in such a way that the trinity does not exclude the unity.

If we succeed in discovering such an analogy in man, then the dogma manifests itself as corresponding to a structure of our being and in some way "incarnate" in us as the life of our life. In consequence, our love for the God who is one and three will be greater and more vitally inserted in us. Analysis and synthesis of the depths of the soul will facilitate our adhesion to God.

The problem posed by St. Augustine, or rather the problem that presented itself for him, is thus situated at the frontier between dogma and anthropology. To this problem he suggests two distinct answers[56] situated at two levels of thought:

a) *First trinity:* "*mens, notitia, amor*"

The spirit (*mens* or *animus*), which is the fine point of the soul (*anima*), is consciousness of self and volition of self. My spirit, the consciousness which I have of myself, the love I have for my spirit, and for my consciousness of myself, there you have three terms that are distinct by relative opposition, three terms that are mutually relative. These three terms are inseparable: the *mens*, which (according to St. Augustine) knows itself by essence, always generates knowledge of self, and from the two always proceeds self-volition.

What is more, these three terms are equal: perfect knowledge of oneself by oneself is equal to the knowing mind; and not inferior as when a body is known by the mind.

Still better: these three terms, the *mens*, its self-consciousness and its self-volition are not only equal to each other but also mutually immanent, not as three substances but by identity; not as wine, water and honey which are confusedly blended. The spirit, the self-consciousness and the self-volition are one single substance in which the three terms under consideration are distinguished as relative to one another, consubstantial and mutually immanent: the mind knows itself just as it loves itself, and it knows its love just as it loves its consciousness.[57]

This short exposition of the Augustinian doctrine is enough to make the image of the divine Trinity in the human spirit stand out. The *mens* is the imperfect image of the Father. The created mind is father because it gener-

[56] Among many others.
[57] Sciacca (*op cit.*, 528) goes so far as to say: "The spirit knows and loves itself entirely and knows all its love and loves all its knowledge." Thus he expresses his personal opinion, but this appears to us to be here below a manifest exaggeration which we are in no way obliged to attribute to St. Augustine. But it is true for the hereafter when image becomes likeness.

ates self-consciousness or the mental word. For Augustine, consciousness of self is produced by a true generation, without any exterior intervention. The mind knows itself by essence, without any passage from potency to act. The *mens*—"sola parens est notitiae suae."[58] The generation or genesis of self-consciousness is the essential intellectual act in the interiority of the spirit.

But the mind's desire to know itself cannot be satisfied by this act that generates self-consciousness: the *mens* does not stop there, but projects itself further in seeking union of the generated object with the subject; it is the act of love by which the will, loving the mind which knows itself, unites the two terms, mind and mental word of self-consciousness. The love of self proceeds from the mind and from the knowledge that the mind has of its own loveability. And so the Spirit proceeds from the Father and from the Word, and in the same way the man who loves himself, is, like God, a spirit who knows and loves himself.

St. Augustine has chosen this image of the Trinity (*mens-notitia-amor*) as a privileged image because it imitates in a better way the eternity of the Three Persons. In book XIV of the *De Trinitate*, Augustine declares that the true image of God ought to be as immortal as the soul and borrow nothing from the exterior world. Faith, contemplation of faith, will pass away. In consequence, the trinity that is realized in the soul by the virtue of faith (*in fidei retentione, contemplatione, dilectione*) is not the supreme image of the divine Trinity. "The true image, that which the creative Trinity has wished to realize in us, is consubstantial with us to such an extent that no man can exist without bearing it in himself and that nothing can ever entirely efface it."[59]

That is why St. Augustine expresses this supreme image of the Trinity (*mens-notitia-amor*) by another ternary formula: *mens meminit sui, intelligit se, diligit se*.[60] However man is not especially the image of God in that he remembers other things and knows and loves them (transitory activities which do not represent adequately the eternity of the divine Trinity), but rather in that he remembers himself, and knows and loves himself. In the

---

[58]St. Augustine, *De Trinitate*, IX, XII, 18.

[59]C. Boyer, S.J., "L'image de la Trinité, synthèse de la pensée augustinienne," *Gregorianum* 27 (1946), 177.

[60]St. Augustine, *De Trinitate*, XIV, 2.4. ("trinitas ista quae *nunc* in ejusdem fidei praesentis ac manentis memoria, contuitu, dilectione consistit, *tunc* transacta et praeterita reperietur esse, non permanens": an allusion to the beatific vision; the comparison bears less on the temporal image as opposed to the eternity of God than on the opposition of this image to its eschatological consummation, compared with which it cannot now be called image: "*nondum talis est trinitas ut Dei jam imago sit*," there is thus inherent in the vision a sublime loss of faith very different from what one ordinarily understands by loss of faith, because it implies not the sin of incredulity but perseverance in earthly faith to the end); 8, 11.

eyes of Augustine the perfect image is not intersubjective but intrasubjective. Love, however, is always at the source and at the term of the image, and so to the ternary formula centered on the self which we have just cited, there corresponds another formula: *amans et quod amatur et amor.*[61]

b) *Second trinity: "memoria Dei, intelligentia Dei, amor in Deum"*[62]

In the framework of St. Augustine's perspectives it is curious to note that this second trinity in which (to use scholastic language) the soul in theocentric *act* is the image of the triune God, is a trinity that is less representative of the eternal Trinity than the preceding trinity, since man can always lose charity for God. The atheist on the other hand, in the constitutive structure of his spirit, is an image of the Trinity,[63] and this, in an inamissible manner, and consequently, on this level, he is a more perfect image than is the believer or even the saint who, with a charity in act, is in a loving relation to God.[64] ...

Whatever is to be said of this paradox that we are going to try to explain, it is sure that Augustine also holds onto this second image. The believer through his faculties remembers the Trinity, contemplates it and delights in it.[65]

Our love of God unites memory and understanding; so does the Holy Spirit unite the Father and the Son; our love of God proceeds from the memory and the understanding as the Holy Spirit proceeds from the Father and from the Son; our love of God, even though as love it is affection and dilection, yet without understanding and memory it cannot exist, somewhat like the Holy Spirit who must be all that the Father is and all that the Son is, and yet simultaneously is properly their Charity, that is, proceeds by way of love.[66]

The act of love of God is really an image of the Trinity, even if it remains unconscious. In the memory is found the knowledge of God whence the interior word is born by which the soul thinks God and from their union charity is born. Just as from the knowledge of the Father the Son is generated and from their common love proceeds the Holy Spirit.[67]

While the first and supreme image of the Trinity was presented by Augustine in the formula already cited: *mens meminit sui, intelligit se, diligit se,*[68]

---

[61]St. Augustine, *De Trinitate*, VIII, X, 14.

[62]We are not sure that this formula is St. Augustine's but in any case it sums up his thought very well: cf. *De Trinitate*, XIV, 12.15.

[63]*Ibid.*, XV, 24.44: ML 42, 1091.

[64]See the texts to which note 59 refers.

[65]St. Augustine, *De Trinitate*, XV 20.39; ML 42, 1088.

[66]Cf. Boyer, *art. cit.* p. 341.

[67]*Ibid.*, p. 351.

[68]Cf. note 60.

the second image (which in no way suppresses but rather perfects the first), manifests the supremely decisive intervention of human liberty in the words in which it is presented to us: *Meminerim tui, intelligam te, diligam te.* Have we not here the supreme degree of the supreme image of the Trinity in this conclusive formula of the *De Trinitate*,[69] a formula that also symbolizes the entire life of St. Augustine?[70]

If St. Augustine rightly places some stress on the recognition of an image (of the Trinity) that is inamissible even in the unbeliever, the damned, the demon, the unconscious child,[71] his profound sense of the value of history and of grace in the realization of the vocation of created liberty on its way toward the Trinity does not permit him to be fully satisfied with his own declaration however undeniable it may be: that transient acts, even of the theological virtues, do not constitute the soul an inamissible image of the eternal Trinity. For he therefore says clearly that the *mens* which knows itself and loves itself is not itself formally an image of God because it remembers itself and knows itself and loves itself, but rather because it is capable of remembering God and of knowing and loving him. "If it acts thus, it becomes wise. If not, even if it remembers itself and knows itself and loves itself, it is foolish (*stulta*)."[72] And if it is foolish, how could it be the image of eternal Wisdom that is one and three?

The Doctor of Grace and Charity goes still further:

> He who knows that he loves himself, loves God; but of one who does not love God, even if he loves himself, something that is connatural to him, we can say without impropriety that he hates himself, because he persecutes himself as his own enemy.[73]

Briefly, one who does not remember God, nor know him nor love him, does not truly love himself; he does not know himself in what constitutes the supreme source of his loveability (God, sun of his spirit); he lives somehow in a perpetual oblivion of himself as image of the Trinity; in consequence he is not perfectly an image of the Trinity.

On the other hand here below, one who by hope remembers God in remembering himself, who by faith knows God in knowing himself, who loves God present in him in loving himself, such a one is not yet the perfect image of God whom he is ever able to forget, to misunderstand, or to hate. But he perfects this image in himself gradually and will become a perfect

---

[69]St. Augustine, *De Trinitate*, XV, 28.51.
[70]Cf. *Confessions* I, 1, 1: "Fecisti nos ad te, et inquietum est cor nostrum donec requiescat in te." This repose that appeases all our inquietudes, is it not the perfect knowledge, possession and love of the Trinity in the beatific vision?
[71]Cf. *De Trinitate*, XIV, V, 7, 8; X, V, 7.
[72]*Ibid.*, XIV, XII, 15.
[73]*Ibid.*, XIV, 14.18.

image when he will be fixed in the possession, the vision and the love of the triune God.

For St. Augustine the supreme image of the Trinity is inchoatively realized in the dynamism of the spirit, even that of an atheist, which is always (without knowing it) seeking God, but this supreme image will be perfectly such only in an eschatological manner. Man must become what he is. In between its already inchoatively real image and its still awaited eschatological perfection, the soul is ceaselessly becoming what it is by the exercise of hope, faith and love. It is only by acknowledging itself and willing itself such that the soul becomes fully the image of the triune God; self-consciousness and self-volition as such do not suffice. This fundamental datum of Augustinian thought remains masked if one is content to study book IX of the *De Trinitate*[74] in isolation, without clarifying it by the formal declaration of book XIV: *Haec igitur trinitas mentis non propterea Dei est imago quia sui meminit mens, et intelligit ac diligit se; sed quia potest etiam meminisse et intelligere et amare a quo facta est.*[75]

Such a possibility of remembering, knowing and loving God who is Trinity remains in the atheist, and for this reason in spite of his atheism he can be said to be an image of the Trinity, although very imperfectly.

Let us say more: in the light of book XIV the true sense of book IX of *De Trinitate* is disclosed; in deepening the memory he has of himself, man remembers the eternal God; in knowing himself, he recognizes God the author of his understanding; in loving himself, if he truly loves himself, that is truly wishes his proper Good, he loves God present in him. Thus the second trinity, memory-understanding-love of the Trinity, is implied by the dynamism of the first trinity, memory-understanding-love of self. Self-consciousness and self-volition, if they reach the goal of what they are and ought to be on the basis of self-memory, then become memory, understanding and love of God. The trinity and unity of the created spirit lead it to the Trinity and unity of the uncreated Spirit which it bears within itself, from which it springs, toward which it proceeds or even runs. *Memini mei, intelligo me, diligo me quatenus memini Tui, intelligo Te, amo Te; quamobrem meminerim Tui, intelligam Te, diligam Te.* We think this partial paraphrase restores the progression of Augustinian thought by understanding book IX in the light of book XIV of the *De Trinitate*.

c) *What is to be thought of this doctrine of St. Augustine? To what extent does it come from Revelation?*

An external criticism of Augustine's thought has been made, in addition to the self-criticism he had already elaborated.

---

[74]This J. Racette, S.J., has done very well: "Le livre neuvième du *De Trinitate* de Saint Augustin," *Sciences ecclésiastiques*, 8 (1956), 39-58.

[75]Cf. note 72 (same text).

The African Doctor has been accused of imprecision in his use of the terms *notitia* and *amor*, which now signify spirit, now its acts.[76] Other critics, like Schmaus[77] think they have discovered in Augustine a denial of all real distinction between the essence of the soul and its faculties, and even an affirmation of ontological consubstantiality between the soul's essence and its acts.

Essentially this aspect of external criticism is situated on the level of philosophical and rational reflection. Without yet entering into the domain of Revelation (unless perhaps indirectly, to the extent that a philosophical affirmation, by contradicting the sound use of reason, endangers the conservation and transmission of Revelation). But on the rational level it seems that St. Thomas Aquinas, as C. Boyer[78] has shown, has given us an interpretation of St. Augustine's thought that is profound, coherent and in harmony with the Augustinian text.

For St. Thomas[79] Augustine considers *mens* not abstractly but concretely and this "concrete" *mens* embraces at the same time the soul and its faculties. It is the soul manifesting itself in its higher powers, or if you prefer, in its higher activity. The *notitia* and the *amor* are not powers or faculties like intelligence and will but habits or acts. And the soul is present in its habits as in its acts (though not according to all its "virtue" or possibility). Thus one can say that the knowledge and love of the soul are consubstantial with and immanent to it.

If this exegesis is correct, and we see no convincing reason to deny it (the moderns however hardly seem to know it), some of the philosophical objections raised by the reading of *De Trinitate* disappear. What is more, such a reading would lead to a discovery of St. Augustine's self-critical effort: for he grasps perfectly that in us the *mens* with its acts, the soul in its higher activity, is that of one single person. On the contrary in God the generation of the Word and the procession of the Spirit constitute (with the Father who generates and spirates) three Persons. Nédoncelle has perfectly expressed the Augustinian option:

> In our experience there never is absolute unity between lovers, while in God the three Persons are one single substance. Thus the intersubjective love fails because it keeps us several persons; and the intrasubjective love fails because it keeps us alone. Plurality of the We, solitude of the I: apparently inverse evils which express the same defect of being, *in linea naturae*, then *in linea personae*.... Not that the two analogies

---

[76]Cf. Racette, *art. cit.*, pp. 53-57. The reproach is not devoid of foundation.
[77]M. Schmaus, *Die psychologische Trinitätslehre des Hl. Augustinus*. Münster, 1927, p. 272.
[78]C. Boyer, *art. cit.*, pp. 182ff.
[79]St. Thomas Aquinas, *De Veritate*, X, 1; *De spiritualibus creaturis*, II.I; *Summa Theologica* I, 87.1; *Quodl.* 7.4; *De Anima*, 12.5.

are incompatible. But Augustine has given his preference to the one that contains the idea of a more perfect substantial unity. The three faculties in us are only one substance. But when three friends meet, they remain three different men; friendship does not reduce their three substances. The comparison of the three faculties is wanting because it does not express the diversity of persons; the comparison of the three friends is wanting because it does not express the unity of substance. And in Augustine's opinion the second insufficiency is worse that the first.[80]

Augustine's option seems to us legitimate both for his day and even for our day, but in no way necessary. He had the merit of developing this option in a deeper fashion: why should we have the demerit of imitating him in that? For it seems more urgent to us today to show how man is the image of the tripersonal God rather than of the one God. Though intent on avoiding the perils of tritheism, which have been stressed for us with good reason by Barth and more recently by K. Rahner, we still think that Christian theology of all confessions has the task of deepening the mystery of man, personal and social, body and soul, as image of the Trinity. The body informed by the immaterial and immortal soul is not just any kind of material body whatever, for it already begins to be this spiritualized matter which it will become perfectly if it freely receives the sacraments of the glorified Christ. Hence under this respect it seems that we can say that it is more than a vestige and that in its way it participates in the quality that is proper to the image of the Trinity in the soul. Augustine's too Platonic philosophy did not permit him to develop the family image, in the way that he could have developed it on the basis of the Aristotelian doctrine of hylemorphic union. His rejection of every family image is an anachronism which we have no reason to retain today.

Ought we not at least to retain what some claim to have been his thought: that the psychological analogy is truly "revealed"?[81] It appears

[80]M. Nédoncelle, "L'intersubjectivité humaine est-elle pour saint Augustin une image de la Trinité?" *Augustinus Magister*. Paris, 1954, v. I, pp. 600-601.

[81]Cf. F. Bourassa, S.J., "Sur le traité de la Trinité," *Gregorianum*, 47 (1966), 270-271: "If the invisible perfections of God have been rendered visible by the things created, so much so that man is inexcusable if he does not recognize him in his works (cf. Rom. 1-2), then in the measure that even natural and philosophical introspection is capable of yielding man knowledge of what he is, this is already authentically a knowledge of God in his image. But Augustine was not content with these data of his philosophy... it is to the revealed analogy between man and God that St. Augustine appeals.... If man, made to the image of God, was made to know God by faith in his Word, he can and must necessarily know what it is to know God...what faith is, what charity is. In the love that is in him after the image of Him who has created him, he can recognize God who is charity.... It is in the framework of this revealed analogy that the Augustinian contemplation on the divine Trinity is developed." All of this appears to us substantially correct; however we would have preferred that the author had placed the adverb implicitly before the adjective "revealed."

difficult to us to answer this and establish apodictically that Revelation explicitly presents to us man's mental word or thought as the image of the eternal Word, and man's love as an image of the procession of the Spirit. But, and we believe this is what some have meant to say, it does seem correct to affirm that Revelation insinuates this doctrine and even contains it implicitly. It was precisely the merit of St. Augustine to make this implicit teaching explicit. On this point we shall refer the reader to what we have already said in other parts of this work.[82]

What is especially valid in St. Augustine's thought, because it is a definitive acquisition, is his fundamental intuition: there exists an indestructible structure of the *mens humana* that is constituted by a habitual knowledge and love of itself, before there is any intramundane contact or reflection whatsoever. Here we find the sanctuary where the immortal soul possessing itself forever, can discover itself as capable of God and image of the triune God. So it can more easily orientate itself toward this God, of whom it finds in itself an image that is indelible, although deformed, and in need of purification. "The image of God in us becomes more perfect in the measure that we penetrate its imperfection more thoroughly," C. Boyer says very rightly when commenting on St. Augustine.[83] Up to the day when the image will attain the perfect likeness of its transcendent model in the beatific vision: *in hac quippe imagine, tunc perfecta erit Dei similitudo quando Dei perfecta erit visio.*[84] To the medieval tradition St. Augustine will bequeath the distinction between vestige, image and likeness of the triune God, which sums up so well the ascensional dialectic of his thought and at the same time marks out its eschatological dynamism in a way that is faithful to Scripture: "What we will be has not yet been made manifest. We know that at the time of this manifestation we shall be like him, because we shall see him as he is" (1 Jn. 3:2).

2. *Thomist deepening and modifications of the Augustinian doctrine*

We cannot omit to point out in passing the admirable development St. Bonaventure gave to the doctrine of the soul as image of the Trinitarian God.[85] But here we prefer to analyze briefly the nuances and precisions this doctrine received in the thought of the Common Doctor.

a) *The soul, image of the Trinity*

The mind exists; the mind thinks itself by knowing itself and thus conceiving its word which is nothing else but its intelligible representation;

[82] Cf. ch. II, § X, 2; ch. IV, § II, see pp. 114-116, 158-160.
[83] Boyer, *art. cit.*, p. 342.
[84] St. Augustine, *De Trinitate,* XIV, 17.23.
[85] Cf. Olegario Gonzalez, *Misterio trinitario y existencia humana.* Madrid, 1966, pp. 564-603. The author gives a good bibliography on image.

the mind in and by its willing loves itself: here for St. Thomas lies the likeness of the divine Trinity that we can contemplate in the spirit of man.[86]

The Thomistic vision of the analogy is then more modest and more limited than the grandiose Augustinian presentation: the Angelic Doctor says explicitly that: "the mind in its physical (translate: ontological) existence, then the mind conceived in the thought, and finally the mind loved in the will, do not constitute one single nature (or reality): for the knowing of the mind is not its existing; and its willing is neither its existing nor its knowing."[87]

Thus Thomas clearly denies the consubstantiality among the three elements of the image, which Augustine was wont to affirm in fact with regard to other elements: for *mens* in Augustine, as we saw, is not purely and simply identical with the soul.

From this it follows that in St. Thomas the image of the human spirit is even much less than in Augustine (who also always exalted the divine transcendence) an adequate representation of the divine *nature*, and this was precisely the point of the Augustinian option, as we recognized with Nédoncelle. Aquinas stresses even better than his master Augustine the still more patent deficiency of the analogy on the *personal level*: "even in its existence, the mind (our soul) is not a person, it is not the subsistent whole, but only a part of this whole that is man."[88] But in God, Father, Son and Holy Spirit are each of them a "perfect person." Not only does the analogy not represent the Trinity of divine Persons by a trinity of human persons, but what is more it is not even one person who represents the Three Persons, just as it is not one single nature (but three numerically distinct natures) that represents the single divine nature.

For St. Thomas Aquinas, as for St. Augustine, it is not man then or woman who are images of God, nor consequently the human person, but

---

[86]St. Thomas Aquinas, *Summa contra Gentiles* IV, 26; cf. *Compendium Theologiae*, I, 50: "in homine tria quaedam considerari possunt, idest: homo in natura sua existens, et homo in intellectu existens, et homo in amore existens; et tamen hi tres non sunt unum quia intelligere ejus non est ejus esse, similiter et amare; et horum trium unus solus est res quaedam subsistens, sc. homo in natura sua existens. In Deo autem idem est esse, intelligere et amare. Deus ergo in suo esse naturali existens, et Deus existens in intellectu et Deus existens in amore suo unum sunt; unusquisque tamen eorum est subsistens." As Tillard interprets this very well (in his unpublished course on the Trinity, at Ottawa, p. 39): "we thus discover in the normal psychological life of the spirit, because of the very law and nature of the spirit, a triple presence: a triple presence whose result is the unity of the conscious life: I-existing (fundamental presence, radical and primary, presupposed by all the others), I-known-by-my-intelligence, I-loved-by-my-will (because I intuit myself as good). And *I in my plenitude as man*, here is the encounter of these three presences."

[87]St. Thomas Aquinas, *Summa contra Gentiles*, IV, 26; cf. H.-F. Dondaine, O.P., *La Trinité*. Paris, 1962, v. I, p. 231.

[88]*Ibid.*

only the immortal souls.[89] We have already indicated the difficulties inherent in this position.[90] We might add that under another aspect there could be doubt about his fidelity to the biblical datum: for Scripture does not present the breath into the nostrils of man as the exclusive likeness and image of God, but rather presents man and woman without any abstraction as the image of the Creator (cf. Gn. 2:7; 1:26-27; 5:1-3; 9:6).[91] To say that animals are not created to the image of God but that this is the privilege of man, in no way obliges us to reduce the image to the soul. Here we perceive an undue hellenization not of dogma, but of a theology. What is more, it must be recognized that Augustine and Thomas were not totally unaware of the problem raised here, though they did not know how to resolve it adequately. Thomas confines himself to saying that "the figure of the human body represents the image of God in the soul, by way of vestige."[92] In the framework of the Thomistic doctrine of hylemorphic union, he should have said more: namely that this figure participates in its way in the spirituality of the soul which it renders present by representing it. And thus one could say that man in his entirety is the image of God, while an animal is merely a vestige of God.

On the other hand, St. Thomas expands St. Augustine more precisely by underscoring that it is first and foremost by his intellectual and volitive activity and not by his "habitus" that man is the image of the Trinity. For this superior activity bears directly and immediately on the soul itself, indirectly and mediately on God. Man then is the image of the Trinity[93] not so much in that he knows himself as man in an absolute manner but rather in that he knows himself as capable of relating to God.

With less precision, perhaps, than St. Bonaventure[94] St. Thomas admits

[89]Cf. St. Thomas Aquinas, *Summa Theologica*, I, 93.6.2 and corpus. St. Thomas invokes a scriptural argument from the text of Col. 3:11 in which, with certain manuscripts and with Augustine and Ambrose before him, he reads: "The new man moves toward true knowledge by renewing himself to the image of his Creator. There is no longer question of Greek or Jew...of slave, of free man, *of man or of woman*" (cf. Gal. 3:28). Even supposing this to be the authentic Pauline text, something that for many contemporary exegetes is not certain (they do not retain the italicized words), one could still contest the interpretation given by St. Thomas: for St. Paul in 1 Cor. 11:7 clearly affirms that man as man distinct from woman is the image of God, without however denying that woman is also image.

[90]Cf. the developments of this chapter, I, 2 and 3.

[91]See the note of the Jerusalem Bible, on Gn. 1:26.

[92]Cf. St. Thomas Aquinas, *Summa Theologica*, I, 93.6.3; the Common Doctor cites St. Augustine, ML 40, 33, bringing out the fact that man is the only animal who lifts his head toward heaven and therefore: "corpus hominis...magis ad imaginem et similitudinem Dei quam caetera corpora animalium, factum jure videri potest."

[93]St. Thomas Aquinas, *Summa Theologica*, I, 93.7.8.

[94]St. Bonaventure, *I Sent.* d. 3 p. 2 a. 2 q. 1 in c: "proprie loquendo imago consistit in unitate essentiae et trinitate potentiarum, secundum quam anima nata est ab illa summa Trinitate

that if this intellectual and volitive activity in man is the image of God, then this same activity inasmuch as it is divinized is God's likeness. His positions on the single act of the beatific vision[95] logically should lead him to think that the perfect image of the Trinity will consist in this triple immutable and single activity, by which memory, intelligence and will in the predestined will possess the Father and the Son and their Holy Spirit in recognition, knowledge and love. But we have not encountered such an explication in him. Yet it is always in conformity with St. Thomas' doctrine to say that even in this life acts of memory, intelligence and will which are divinized by hope, faith and charity, are for the human soul the perfect and intimate mirror of the Father, the Son and the Spirit who inhabit its essence and through its faculties operate these acts. And it is precisely because the eternal Trinity is so totally transcendent that it can become not only profoundly immanent but even more interior to the soul than it is to itself.

Now however we must deal in greater detail with the Angelic Doctor's in-depth developments of the psychological analogy with regard to the word of intelligence and the breath of love.

b) *The mental word, image of the divine Word*

In man the concept, distinct from the act of thinking of which it is the term, is the fruit of the spirit in the act of knowing. It consists either in a definition or in an affirmative or negative proposition. It is a living likeness of the thing, intrinsic term of the thought and expression conceived by the spirit in the act of thinking. Such is the word or concept which emanates in created knowing.[96]

St. Thomas compares the mind which in the act of knowledge of the other is fecundated by it, to the mother fecundated by the seed of the father: the concept is their offspring. But this fruit remains joined to its principle, immanent to the mind which brings it in the world: for here, to be born and to be conceived is all one. The mind knows by expressing a word, and the emanation of the word is nothing else than the thought itself.[97]

Thus the Word of the Father is at the same time archetype of the created universe and term of the thought of the Father, but differently from our word he is not of another nature than he from whom he proceeds. Our

---

sigillari imagine similitudinis, quae consistit in gratia et tribus virtutibus theologicis." Thus the Seraphic Doctor distinguishes the image of likeness or of reformation from the mere image; cf. O. Gonzalez, *op. cit.*, pp. 598-603.

[95] A classical thesis of scholastic theology: if there were a succession of diverse acts in the intellectual vision of the divinity, then not one of them would satisfy the appetite of the intelligence or be truly beatifying.

[96] We draw here on H.-F. Dondaine, O.P., *La Trinité*. Paris, 1962, v. I, p. 219; cf. St. Thomas Aquinas, *De Potentia*, 8.1.

[97] Dondaine, *op. cit.*, v. I, p. 218.

concept is a quality, an accident of the spiritual substance, as is the thought that it completes. In the creature to be and to think are two things; in God they are not.

c) *The impulsive and non-representative presence of friendship, image of the Spirit*

St. Thomas gave himself over to a very profound analysis of human love from which he derived a better understanding of the procession of the Holy Spirit.

That which one loves, he says, does not exist only in the thought of the lover but also in his will though in a different manner. It is in the thought by a resemblance of itself; it is in the will of the lover in the way that the term of a movement exists in the corresponding motive principle, by reason of the harmony and proportion that it has with it.... The beloved is in the will as a pole of attraction and as somehow lifting the lover toward the beloved from within. But every intimate impetus in the living beings depends on the vital spirit or breath. It is fitting then to give to God who proceeds by way of love the name of Spirit, as proceeding by a kind of spiration. That is why the Apostle attributes to the Spirit and to Love an impetus as it were; all who are impelled by the Spirit are sons of God (Rom. 8:14).[98]

A new understanding of the very particular form of immanence of the beloved in the lover, and of the difference between this immanence and that of the object known in the knowing subject, these are the two interconnected elements which condition for the Angelic Doctor a better understanding of the distinction between the generation of the Son and the procession of the Spirit, a point on which St. Augustine hesitated to make a commitment.[99]

It is not a question of objectivity as in the case of the understanding, but of a presence, of activity and dynamism of the beloved in the lover. For the love which I have for a being is in me a grasp by that being, planted in the very heart of my life as Tillard[100] has so well said. This impetus does not come to me from the exterior or from a motivation that I would be obliged to impose on myself, but it comes from me. Thus in me this love is a mysterious preference of the one I love, a preference which makes this one "super-exist" in me in a way that is immaterial but none the less real and

---

[98]St. Thomas Aquinas *Summa contra Gentiles*, IV, 26.
[99]Cf. St. Augustine, *De Trinitate*, XV, 27.50 (ML 42, 1097); it must be recognized however that Augustine had prepared the ground (*In Jo tract.*, 26.2, 4, 7; ML 35, 1607-1608, 1610; RJ 1821-1823) where Augustine cites Virgil: "Trahit sua quemque voluptas."
[100]J.-M.-R. Tillard, O.P., unpublished course on the Trinity, p. 63.

active for all of that.[101] Instead of being "possession of another by me" (presence of knowledge), it is "possession of me by another," a presence of love, appeal, "suction"—as Tillard puts it in his picturesque fashion.[102]

As human knowledge, so human friendship is the lever of the Trinitarian theology of St. Thomas Aquinas, even in the analysis of the procession of the Spirit from the Father and from the Son:

> The presence of a being in the will, as presence of the beloved in the lover, depends on a double principle: on the conception that the mind makes of it—and on the very reality itself of which this conception is the expression or word. In fact, nothing is loved unless it is known under some formality; and one does not simply love the knowledge one has of a thing: but rather the thing itself is loved for the good in it. It follows then that the Love by reason of which God exists in his will as the beloved in the lover, proceeds at the same time from the Word of God and from God whose Word he is.[103]

Note well that St. Thomas does not claim in any way here or elsewhere, to demonstrate rationally the existence of a procession of love in God, even after having known this from Revelation. He is only concerned to manifest as much as possible a mystery that is inaccessible and impenetrable to human reason, since the real and positive mode of the divine thought is beyond its grasp. The argument then is a simple conjecture and yet very suggestive since it is drawn from the human procession of love.

We must recognize then that in his way of deepening the psychological analogy in Trinitarian theology St. Thomas is not lacking in daring.

For it is clear on the one hand that for him the analogy is indissolubly intra-and-inter-subjective in what concerns love: for it is very evident that the descriptions we have read or summarized apply before all not to the love each one has for himself but to the love which binds him to another. And thus St. Thomas without knowing or even willing it has prepared the ground for a better grasp of the family analogy, which however like St. Augustine he rejects.

On the other hand Aquinas frankly accepts as an instrument of a theology of the procession of the Spirit, an analysis of that which most completely resists all rational analysis: love. There is a natural mystery of human love which is more accessible to the intuition of the intellect than to rational discourse. From this comes the fascinating but difficult task of a

---

[101]H.-F. Dondaine, O.P., *op. cit.*, v. I, p. 228, note 1; cf. *Compendium Theologiae*, I, 45: the beloved moves the lover in his deepest interior and every mover must be in contact with him whom he moves.

[102]Tillard, *op. cit.*, p. 37.

[103]St. Thomas Aquinas, *Summa contra Gentiles*, IV, 26.

clear elaboration of pneumatology. We shall return to this point a little later.

While putting this off we must consider the most original effort aimed at a new presentation of the psychological analogy under the searchlight of Scripture and in an intersubjective dimension: that of B. Lonergan.

3. *The psycho-social analogy of B. Lonergan*

B. Lonergan, S.J., the Canadian philosopher and theologian, has attempted to systematize the cognitive and affective data of the presentation of the Trinitarian mystery in the New Testament, and especially in the gospel of John. He intends thus to furnish a more firm and more explicit biblical basis for the psychological analogy,[104] which so clearly becomes intersubjective.

a) *The hearing of the word of God*

The gospel of John explicitly considers the theme of the word of God, the Good News as object of preaching and hearing. He who does not hear this word is on the side of hatred, homicide, the world and the devil (cf. 8:31ff., notably 8:47). On the contrary he who hears the word so as to keep it, knows the truth, loves his neighbor and abides in intimate union with the Father, the Son and the Spirit: cf. Jn. 14:23-26.

In other words, hearing the word of God is for the authors of the New Testament an exercise of rationality and morality.

b) *The missions of the Son and of the Spirit in a context of dialogue*

There is more: St. John offers us, like Jesus himself, the missions of the Son and of the Holy Spirit under the form of discourse or locutions that are objects of a holy hearing: 8:26, 28; 14:10, 24. The Son and the Holy Spirit hear and speak: the Son hears the Father and speaks what he has heard (5:30: I judge according to what I hear...14:10: the words that I speak to you, I do not speak of myself), the Holy Spirit hears the Father and the Son and speaks what he hears (Jn. 16:13-15: all that he hears he will speak).

This twofold "hearing," holy and even divine, of the Son with respect to the Father and of the Spirit with respect to the Father and to the Son is opposed to the deafness of men who do not wish to hear the word of God because they prefer their darkness to its light: 6:60; 8:43-47. Many neither receive nor accept the witness of Christ (3:11, 32; 12:48), and the world cannot receive the Spirit of Truth (14:17). But on the contrary Christ receives from the Father, the disciples accept the witness of Christ (17:8) and the Holy Spirit receives in accepting what he hears from the Father and from the Son (16:13-15).

The acceptance we are dealing with is voluntary, real and personal.

[104]B. Lonergan, S.J., *De Deo trino*. Rome, 1964, v. I, pp. 276-298.

Voluntary, for those who accept and those who do not accept are contrasted; real, for they receive a word, a testimony; personal, for it is a person who is thus accepted or rejected.

c) *From missions to processions in a context of dialogue*

God the Father is called Light (1 Jn. 1:5) and Love in a psychological and ethical sense (cf. 1 Jn. 4:8; 2:9): the Light and the Truth, the Love and the Life are associated in him, and without any darkness or lie or blindness or hatred. As the word of Christ abides in his disciples (Jn. 15:7-8), as they abide in his word (8:31), so the Word of God, the only Son abides in his Father as the Word of Life, eternal Life, as immanent Word of him who is Love (cf. 1 Jn. 1:1-2). If the words of Christ can abide in the disciples in spite of the disappearance of their physical sound, how much more does God's eternal Word abide in God! It is the immanent, not transient Word of eternal Life.

But it is precisely this Word of the Father which is all that the Spirit of Truth (cf. Jn. 16:13-15) hears, speaks, announces, glorifies, takes and gives. He hears and receives the truth of the Father and of the Son in hearing and accepting the Word, the Word of the Father from whom he proceeds. He can only be sent by the Word (15:26; 16:7) to announce and glorify him as the only Son of the Father because he proceeds from him eternally, just as the Word can only be sent by the Father because he is his eternal Word and Thought.

Let us synthesize the data we summed up. The Word proceeds from the Father as a Son generated by the Father, who is Light and Love. (cf. Jn. 1:18), and entirely turned toward his bosom. The Spirit receives the Son and hears him as a Word born of the Light and Love.

The Word and the Spirit of Truth thus appear presented in the likeness of a true judgment of man and of an ethical act of the will proceeding from this authentic value-judgment. Or, more exactly, this judgment is the image of the eternal Word, and the ethical decision of the freedom which proceeds from it is the created image of the procession of the Spirit.

Thus what St. John tells us about the attitude of the disciples to the word of the Son and Word is the intersubjective analogy, both intellectual and volitive, of the intra-Trinitarian attitude of the Word and the Spirit, who hear sacredly with a view to speaking to men, because they are eternally Word and Hearing, Word of Goodness and Loving Hearing.

Thus the analogy that the New Testament Revelation offers us is more anthropological than purely psychological, more intersubjective than intrasubjective. Or, if you prefer, it is psycho-social. Its exact perception supposes not only a profound analysis of the purely interior processes of human knowledge and love, but also of knowledge and love between men, in the framework of language.

4. *Conclusion about the "psychological analogy" and the created analogies of the Trinity*

The doctrine which affirms that the Word has been generated by way of understanding and that the Spirit proceeds by way of love has not been the object of a dogmatic and solemn definition of the Church.

So it cannot be presented as a defined dogma.

But it appears to us to be taught by the ordinary and universal magisterium of the Church as a revealed truth, as a non-defined dogma (*DB* 1792; *DS* 3011). As a truth contained in Revelation at least implicitly. For how else can we explain its constant reaffirmation, by the catechism of the Council of Trent, and in what concerns the procession of the Spirit by way of love in the documents of Leo XIII (*DS* 3326 and 3330), of Pius XII (*Haurietis Aquas*) and of Paul VI (The Credo of the People of God in 1968)?[105] We may be permitted to refer the reader to what we already said on this subject.

B. Lonergan has the merit of showing by his profound biblical study that this analogy is much more in harmony with the scriptural data than some had suspected. In this light and that of the magisterial documents, this analogy is certainly more than a simple hypothesis, as Karl Rahner seems to say at times. But we think that his limited and partially negative appreciation can be explained by the too exclusively intrasubjective character that has been given to the Augustinian presentation of the psychological analogy in the past.

The road opened up by Lonergan orientates us toward a psychological analogy that is at the same time intra and intersubjective, toward an analogy that is psycho-social, psycho-familial and psycho-ecclesial. He does no more than expand with greater biblical rigor the more profound analysis of the love of friendship which St. Thomas Aquinas had already inaugurated.

The New Testament situates the Trinitarian Revelation in the framework of the family experience (father-son relations), of ecclesial-language experience (master-disciple relations, word given and accepted) and even of the mystery of the Church (groom-bride relation, symbolic of the relation Christ-Church which itself is symbolic of the Father-Son relation). It also presents us with the Church as the family of God: "you are no longer strangers nor sojourners, you are of the household of God" (Eph. 2:19).

All that we have said about the different analogies of the Trinitarian mystery therefore converges toward the declaration of a total analogy that is at the same time familial and ecclesial, but in its totality psychological and totally so in the sense that it embraces not only the individual spirit's interiority but also its social manifestation.

Thus it seems the ground has been prepared for a deepening of Trinitarian theology in this light, a deepening that is certainly more apt to make

[105] Cf. our ch. IV, § III note 45.

the whole people of God grow in the understanding, knowledge and wisdom of the fundamental mystery of its temporal and eternal beatitude, the mystery of the Father, the Son and their Holy Spirit (cf. DB 1796, 1800; DS 3016, 3020). The matrimonial family will help the Church, the family of God to set forth better the eternal Family of the Three. God is Spirit and what is born of the Spirit is spirit (Jn. 4:24; 3:6).

Do we not find in Roublev's admirable icon, representing the three divine Persons (by means of the representation of the three angels that appeared to Abraham) around a Eucharistic table, a beautiful symbol of this "total analogy" of the Sacred Trinity? And doesn't Christian art achieve the summit of its mission and its utility when it puts itself at the service of the contemplation of the Trinitarian mystery? If the Trinity manifested itself by images (the Ancient of days symbolizes the Father, the dove and the tongues of fire the Holy Spirit) why would it not be permitted to expand the psycho-social analogy in a series of artistic analogies of the most immaterial of the mysteries? The Church indeed has condemned by the voice of Popes Alexander VIII, Benedict XIV and Pius VI, the Jansenist rejection of every cult of the images of the Father and of the incomprehensible Trinity (DS 2325, 2668; DB 1315, 1569). The document of Benedict XIV even constitutes a profound treatise on this matter[106] of which some later commentaries do not perhaps take proper account.[107] It may be interesting to note that these representations of the incomprehensible Trinity

---

[106]You will find the integral text of it in Lambertini, *Bullarium*, v. 2, pp. 22-31. Benedict XIV there treats particularly of the representation of the Holy Spirit and of the image of the angels who appeared to Abraham.

[107]For example, V. Grumel, DTC VII, I (1922), col. 837-841: art. "Images." Speaking of images of the Trinity, the author writes: "These kinds of images, because they can easily lead into error, are not authentically proposed by the Church for the use and veneration of the faithful. The Church has no public cult for any of them, and although it is not forbidden to give them private veneration, it seems this would be contrary to its spirit. The Council of Trent also allows these images but with some reservation, thus intending to discourage their use, while ordaining that their true sense be explained to the people." Here the author alludes to Bossuet: "these pictures ought to be scarce according to the intention of the Council which leaves it to the discretion of the bishops to retain or suppress them, according to the usefulness or disadvantages that can derive from them" (*ibid.*, col. 812). This allusion to DS 1825 (DB 988: quod si aliquando...) recalls the necessity of teaching uneducated people the transcendence of God with regard to his representations: "non propterea divinitatem figurari, quasi corporeis oculis conspici, vel coloribus aut figuris exprimi possit." It would have been better to add an allusion to DS 1824 (DB 987) where the positive value of images is presented and where what is said applies also to the Trinity which is not excluded. But the most authorized commentary on the Tridentine decisions that speak explicitly of the images of Christ, the Virgin and saints but without alluding to those of the Trinity (DS 1823; DB 986), is without doubt the Brief, already mentioned, of Pope Benedict XIV, *Sollicitudini nostrae* of October 1, 1745. In reality this text by approving images of the Trinity instead of confining itself to tolerating them, implicitly rejects the points of view of St. Thomas Aquinas (*Summa Theologica*, III, 25.3.1; "ipsi autem Deo vero,

which are commonly approved by the Church, are in general images of the Redemptive Trinity: the dead Son is shown in the bosom of the Father to whom the dove, symbolizing the Spirit, unites him by a kiss. In spite of the dangers of tritheism to which some can be exposed by these images, they constitute a useful occasion and means of Trinitarian catechesis for those who would not at all be touched by the psychological analogy, and assuredly there are many such. They merely apply the Augustinian doctrine of Trinitarian vestiges in order not only to picture the creation of the universe by the Trinity, but also to invite creatures to return to this Trinity.

After this short digression on sensible and artistic expansions of the psychological analogy, we must now set forth in the light of this analogy the doctrine of the Church and of theologians on the Holy Spirit as bond of love between the Father and the Son, or better as their mutual Love and consequently the third and last person of the Trinity.

IV. THE SPIRIT OF THE FATHER AND OF THE SON, PERSONAL BOND OF THE MUTUAL LOVE BETWEEN THEM

Now we take up one of the most difficult and most profound problems of Trinitarian theology. Let us sum it up in a word: the Spirit proceeds, we have seen, by way of love, but does he proceed from the love that the Father and Son have in common for the divine essence or from their reciprocal love? After a brief historical resume of the problem, we shall indicate the solution that appears to us the most profound, and we shall attempt to show that to be the mutual love of the Father and Son is even the distinctive property of the Spirit. We shall see finally the conclusion which will result from this procession of love: the Spirit is the third and last person of the Trinity, and there can be no other person in God.

1. *Historical resume*

The problem originates from St. Augustine's Trinitarian theology, or rather it was the keenness of his mind that let him suspect it. For Augustine the Spirit, according to his distinctive property, is at the same time the Love which proceeds from the Word of divine Wisdom (nature aspect) and at the same time the mutual Love between the Father and the Son (personal aspect). We can say in consequence that St. Augustine constructed his Trinitarian synthesis according to a double schema: psychological (*mens-notitia-amor*) and personalist (the Father, the Son and their mutual love, the Spirit).

---

cum sit incorporeus, nulla imago corporalis poterat poni. Sed quia in NT Deus factus est homo, potest in sua imagine corporali adorari," and of St. John Damascene ("insipientiae summae est et impietatis figurare quod est divinum": *De fide orthodoxa* IV, 16; MG 94, 1172).

In the course of subsequent centuries the theologians and doctors of the Church split over these two lines of Augustinian orientation. Richard of St. Victor clearly opted for the personalist theology but with an original stress: for him perfect love is not love of self but love of another, the love of friendship and this perfect love between Father and Son requires that they communicate it to a third, to a *condilectus,* the Spirit, the common friend of both;[108] and it is just this notion of a common friend that St. Bonaventure will reject, although he will opt for the personalist line.

St. Anselm[109] on the contrary is the advocate of the "essentialist" line which takes up again the intrasubjective psychological schema of St. Augustine: the Holy Spirit is Love that proceeds from the Word as Love and by which God loves himself because of the infinite goodness of his essence. He proceeds from the Father and the Son inasmuch as they are one single principle, not from their mutual love. Abandoning St. Bonaventure's position, Blessed Duns Scotus made the Anselmian doctrine his own.

St. Thomas Aquinas achieved a synthesis of both doctrines of St. Augustine, the essentialist (or psychological) and the personalist. He was influenced by Richard of St. Victor but went beyond Richard's conflict between love of self and love of another. Today we find this conflict renewed in the Lutheran ambience[110] by the Swedish Lutheran theologian, Nygren (Eros and Agape); for Nygren love of self is imperfect, contradictory, impossible. On the contrary the Angelic Doctor had shown that charity is love of self and of neighbor, motivated by the supreme Good which is God.[111] The transcendence of the divine Goodness reconciles the love of self and the love of another: God is substantially love of the Good which is identical with his essence. He is perfect love of self and of his proper infinite amiability, without any admixture of egoism. Thus in St. Thomas' view the Spirit proceeds at the same time from the love which the Father and the Son have together for their proper amiability, and from the mutual love which links them: we will see shortly how the Thomist school attempted to synthesize these two views.

In simultaneously maintaining these two views that at first sight contradict one another, St. Thomas prepared and prefigured the work of the

---

[108]Richard of St. Victor, *La Trinité,* SC 63. Paris, 1959, V, VII.
[109]St. Anselm is the author of *De processione Sp. S. contra Graecos,* ML 158, 280-326.
[110]Luther did not admit a habit of charity distinct from the Holy Spirit. On this point see Vignaux, *Luther commentateur des Sentences.* Paris, 1935, p. 93. But Luther still admitted, when he was a Catholic, an act of love of man toward God. Later, according to the formula of Max Scheler, he considered "the interior act of love as one of the works useless for salvation" (Vignaux, *op. cit.,* p. 94).
[111]St. Thomas Aquinas, *Summa Theologica* II, II, 25; 26, 1-4.

Church's magisterium. The fourth Lateran Council had simply defined the procession of the Spirit *a Patre Filioque*, but without making it precise whether the Spirit was their mutual love or the common love they had together for their proper goodness. Neither of these two theses would be contrary to such a definition. Lyons and Florence, without rejecting the doctrine of mutual love, favored the other current to a certain extent by defining the procession of the Spirit from one single principle and by one single spiration: *tamquam ab uno principio et unica spiratione* (*DS* 850, 1300; *DB* 460, 961). Leo XIII presents the Holy Spirit as being at the same time the divine Goodness (divine essence) and "the reciprocal charity of the Father and the Son proceeding from their mutual love" (*DS* 3326, 3330). Pius XII made it still more precise: "the Paraclete Spirit is the personal love, that is of the Father for the Son and of the Son for the Father,"[112] and also the "mutual love."[113] Lastly Paul VI in 1968, in his Credo of the People of God, affirms, as we saw,[114] that the Holy Spirit is the eternal Love of the Father and the Son (*sempiternus Eorum amor*), a formula that seems to be closer to "mutual love" than to "common love" but without excluding this other explanation that is compatible with it.

Such are the declarations of the magisterium: on the one hand there is a dogmatic definition specifying that the Spirit proceeds from the Father and the Son as from one single principle and by one single spiration, a dogmatic definition that was formulated twice (at Lyons and Florence); on the other hand there is a constant and universal teaching of the ordinary magisterium which presents the Holy Spirit as the mutual and personal Love of the Father and the Son.

Immediately the problem presents itself: how are we to harmonize the more personal accent of mutual love with the more essentialist accent of one spiration? How can the Spirit issue from the Father and the Son as from one principle and simultaneously be their mutual Love? Doesn't this mutual love appear to be, unintentionally, a surreptitious return to the heresy of the two principles and two spirations of the Spirit that was so energetically condemned at Lyons (*DS* 850; *DB* 460)? And how can the mutual love that implies two persons, be identical with the one person of the Spirit?

2. *Toward a solution: Anselm, Thomas Aquinas, John of St. Thomas*

If for St. Anselm the friendship of the Father and the Son is not the proper principle that explains the second divine procession, it yet remains an aspect of the divine Love: "the Father loves himself, the Son loves

[112]Pius XII, *Haurietis Aquas, AAS* 48 (1956), 335.
[113]*Ibid.*, 310-311.
[114]Cf. our ch. VI, III.

himself and each loves the other"[115] because each one loves his essence as much in the other as in himself. The Holy Spirit is the Love by which God, the supreme Spirit, loves himself, the love which proceeds from the divine Memory (Father) and from his Thought (Word). Even in this doctrine in which the consideration of the essence is put in such strong relief, the mutual love of the Persons is not sacrificed, and in it we find in germ the solution we are going to admire in John of St. Thomas.

St. Thomas in the following luminous response has accurately set forth the data and insinuated the solution of the problem:

> If one considers the spirative power, the Holy Spirit proceeds from the Father and the Son inasmuch as they are one in this power, a power that in a certain manner signifies the nature together with the distinctive property (cf. I, 41.5). And there is no repugnance in a single property existing in two supposits when these have one single nature. But if one considers the supposits of the spiration, the Holy Spirit proceeds from the Father and the Son inasmuch as they are two: for he proceeds from them as the unitive love of both.[116]

In other words, the Holy Spirit proceeds from two persons inasmuch as they reciprocally love one another and inasmuch as by and in this reciprocal love they are one single Goodness which loves itself. The spirative power signifies at the same time the divine nature (essential love common to the Three) and the property of the Father and the Son (notional love).

St. Thomas is faithful to Anselmian Augustinianism in adopting the psychological theory as the basis of his Trinitarian theology, but he is equally faithful to Richard's Augustinianism in maintaining in a more personalist fashion than St. Anselm the thesis of mutual love. His originality lies in this that he reconciled these two theses by a theology of love which rises above the opposition between self-love and love of friendship. The synthesis that St. Thomas effects between the psychological or essentialist theory and the personalist theory of mutual love is conditioned by another thesis: that of love of self and love of friendship.[117]

Nonetheless, it seems to us that St. Thomas has not managed to explicate in a fully satisfactory manner the solution of the problem we are studying here. But thanks to the master, his disciple John of St. Thomas, a Portugese Dominican of the seventeenth century, will find the decisive formulas which M.-J. LeGuillou sums up for us thus:

---

[115]St. Anselm, *Monologion*, ch. 49-51.
[116]St. Thomas Aquinas, *Summa Theologica* I, 36.4.1.
[117]Cf. F. Bourassa, S.J., "Le Saint-Esprit unité d'amour du Père et du Fils," *Sciences eccl.*, 14 (1962), 381.

The love that is the Holy Spirit, proceeds from a love of friendship, the reciprocal love of the Father and the Son, the same love that accompanies the generation of the Word, and is common to the two persons inasmuch as it is operation of love with only one identical motive, the infinite Goodness that is common to them, but though common yet in that it pertains to the Father it bears on the Son and in that it pertains to the Son it bears on the Father.[118]

In the elaboration of this subtle and complex solution John of St. Thomas presupposes the doctrine of relations: the Father is always *ad Filium* and the Son *ad Patrem,* when the one and the other love the divine amiability that is common to them. In loving his Son the Father does not cease to love the divine amiability as and with this only Son with whom it is identified; in the same way the Son in loving the Father unites himself to him in the love of the same divine amiability. Thus in some manner their reciprocal love conditions and causes their common or notional love for the divine essence, from which issues the personal Love that is the Spirit. One can say then without contradiction that the Spirit has as origin the mutual love of the Father and the Son and that this mutual love is common inasmuch as it has for object and source the common nature qualified by their spirative property (cf. the text of St. Thomas cited above).

3. *The distinctive property of the Spirit is to be the personal bond of mutual love between the Father and the Son*[119]

This affirmation, which is not of Catholic faith but appears to be probable, signifies that the Spirit is distinguished from the Father and the Son only because he is their mutual love. As mutual love the Spirit is the reciprocal interpersonal love between the Father and the Son, the love by which each responds to the love of the other. The love of the Father does not regard solely the amiability of the Son, since as the divine essence it is common to both, but also the love which the only Son has for him.[120]

It may be interesting to note that the thesis presented here was explicitly examined and rejected by Luther, as Vignaux has shown in his book: *Luther, commentateur des Sentences* (Paris, 1935, pp. 31-36).

Luther knew St. Augustine's doctrine of the Spirit as communion of the Father and the Son, as their Love. He says explicitly that he does not affirm

---

[118]M.-J. LeGuillou, O.P., *Catholicisme*, v. IV (1956), col. 489, art. "E. Saint," citing John of St. Thomas, *Cursus Theologicus* q. 36, disp. XV, art. 4, no. 5, 6, 26; Vives, pp. 361-363, 374.

[119]We are here largely indebted to several works of F. Bourassa, notably his *Adnotationes ad Tractatum de S. Trinitate*, Pars systematica. Rome, 1966-1967.

[120] Cf. St. Thomas Aquinas, *I Sent.*, d. 10.1.3 c: "Spiritus Sanctus ut amor est unio Patris et Filii inquantum distinguntur in personis et sic uniuntur per consensionem amoris."

it: *haec tamen non assero sed occasionaliter recito*. He even considers this doctrine destructive of the whole teaching of the *Sentences* and St. Augustine's *De Trinitate*. For how can one make of the Spirit the bond of love of the two persons from whom he proceeds? Are not the Father and Son love by their common divinity, and have they not their bond in this unity of nature? Doesn't this doctrine affirm two different bonds between Father and Son: one the person of the Spirit, the other the divine nature that is common to the two? This reflection need not astonish us for we have already noted (ch. V, §1) the Lutheran rejection of the distinction between person and nature.

Having thus rejected the doctrine of the Spirit as communion of love between Father and Son, Luther is self-consistent in pushing all the way the consequences of his negation: and he does not hesitate to do this. To consider the Spirit as love of the Father and of the Son, would give one no hold (Luther thinks) on what constitutes the Spirit while distinguishing him from the other persons: how can what binds and unites be a principle of distinction? Thus Luther is totally unappreciative of the most ingenious aspect of the Augustinian intuition.

Luther goes still further and affirms that one cannot even appropriate charity to the Spirit in preference to the other persons: from the perfect identity of divinity with itself, one can see nothing emerge that calls for appropriation of love to one person. To him appropriation seems to be an empty play on words, without any foundation in reality: for he seems not to have grasped the relation of appropriation to the properties of the persons. And logically enough since as we saw he does not admit the distinction between person and nature, a failure that endangers the properties of the persons. On this point one can refer to the works of Luther (W., IX, 51, 23-32). We think also that F. Bourassa, without directly referring to Luther's problematics regarding the distinctive property of the Spirit, has in fact answered his objections in the passages we shall cite shortly.

It is no less striking to note the contrast that Karl Barth's thought offers us on the same subject. Inverting Luther he makes the thought of St. Augustine precisely and totally his own: thus the Spirit is the communion *Miteinander* of the Father and the Son, he is that which is common to them, not inasmuch as they are God, but inasmuch as they are the Father and the Son. He is their reciprocity (*Gegenseitigkeit*), their "one to the other" (*Zueinander*), the "one from the other" (*Auseinander*), and "the one with the other" (*Miteinander*). Thus Barth expresses himself, and does so very well in his *Dogmatik* (I, 1, § 12, p. 492, Zurich, 1947).

Let us close this short ecumenical digression so as to take up the study of the thesis on the property of the Spirit.

An objection to this thesis springs up spontaneously: how could the mutual love of two persons be a third person distinct from both of them? F. Bourassa has formulated it in this way:

> Mutual love, according to our way of conceiving this when we start from its created condition, is the reality of two acts of love, the lived experience by each of the lovers of their communion in the same good; it is also the consciousness of the reciprocity of their love, which constitutes their loving union. In created friends the acts of love as acts of the persons, as subjective acts are two but only one in their objective content, the loved good.[121]

He adds, however, that a more profound analysis of human love and of its ontological presuppositions shows that our experience only offers us on one hand difficulties against admitting this thesis, while on the other hand the elimination of the imperfections of human love makes it easier for us to admit the thesis when one considers uncreated love:

> The reason for this division in the bosom of love derives from its created condition, not from the very nature of love.... The reciprocity of spiritual love already tends to rise above the ontological division of acts of love, by the unity in the encounter. The second imperfection inherent in this unity comes from the fact that this reciprocity cannot reach substantial consistency equal to the Persons, by reason of the accidental character of love in the creature.
>
> Once these imperfections due to the created condition of love are eliminated, love appears in its transcendent condition identical with the good loved and willed by the persons, identical with the persons themselves as far as essential content but distinct from each of the loving persons in its relational condition, so as to be precisely the union of persons inasmuch as persons.[122]

In short, in created persons the reciprocity of friendship supposes two acts of love, both accidental with respect to the essence of each of the two friends. The bond between these two acts is the unity of the Good which causes their reciprocal friendship. The duality remains. In God on the contrary the Holy Spirit, personal Love, is one because he is identical with the essence by which the Father and Son mutually love one another, one as the Good they reciprocally desire, one because of the unity of the spirating principle since he proceeds as one from the Father and the Son who love one another and whom he unites in each one's singularity.[123]

---

[121] F. Bourassa, S.J., "L'Esprit-Saint unité d'amour du Père et du Fils," *Sc. Eccl.* 14 (1962), 412-413.

[122] *Ibid.*

[123] F. Bourassa, *Adnotationes;* cf. St. Thomas Aquinas, *Summa Theologica* I, 39.8: excluso Spiritu Sancto, qui est duorum nexus, non posset intelligi unitas connexionis inter Patrem et Filium.

We can also say that the biblical vision of the economic Trinity is in full harmony with the doctrine here proposed about the property of the Spirit in the "immanent" Trinity. Paul presents the Spirit to us as the bond of unity in that he is the cause of peace: "Apply yourself to maintain the unity of the Spirit by this bond that is peace. There is only one Body and only one Spirit" (Eph. 4:3-4). And this is said in the framework of a Trinitarian paragraph that aims to lay the foundation for the duty of unity among Christians. From this we can conclude that the Father and the Son, in whom the members of the Church are united by the bond of the Spirit in charity, ought also to be united among themselves by the same Spirit as by the Love in which they love one another reciprocally. Isn't this just the way that St. Augustine thought[124] precisely when he was commenting on the Epistle to the Ephesians?

Since the Spirit is the mutual love of the Father and of the Son, it is easy to understand that he is the third and last person of the Trinity, as F. Bourassa has shown:

> Personal love is primordially the loving love which involves the person as such. This personal and consequently interpersonal character of love is truly assured when one makes his subsistence and his transcendent unity consist in the object and not in the nature of love itself. But doesn't this final synthesis of the interpersonal unity in the unity of the essence result in detriment to the properly personal and interpersonal character of the friendship and in the risk of a quaternity that makes of the Spirit not only the Spirit of the Father and of the Son but the Holy Spirit of the God Trinity?[125]

V. REVELATION AFFIRMS THAT THERE ARE ONLY THREE PERSONS IN GOD

This affirmation (which is at least implicit in the New Testament: cf. Mt. 28:19) has been taught by the magisterium: "in God there is only a Trinity, not a quaternity" (*DB* 432; *DS* 804). In truth what the context excludes is that the three Persons form a quaternity with the divine essence which is not really distinct from any of the three; but in excluding every possible

---

[124]St. Augustine, *De Trinitate* V, 14.15; 11.12; VI, 5.7.

[125]F. Bourassa, "Communion du Père et du Fils," *Gregorianum* 48 (1967), 701. The author adds a little further on: "The Spirit as Love, cannot in his proper personality be distinguished from the Father and the Son so as to be their total reciprocity in love unless he proceeds from the one and the other toward one and the other, not as another loved being distinct from them in whom they encounter one another, for this would absolutize his property which is wholly relational; but as being their encounter itself, their relation of love of one toward the other" (*ibid.*, 703-705). This calls to mind a very beautiful formula of St. Thomas Aquinas: "Spiritus Sanctus et a Patre procedit in Filium et a Filio in Patrem non quidem sicut in recipientem sed sicut in objectum amoris" (*De Potentia* 10.4.10; cf. *Summa Theologica* I, 37.1.2).

quaternity, Lateran IV has also implicitly excluded the existence of a fourth divine person, and not only of a nature really distinct from the Persons.

In the light of the psychological analogy St. Thomas explains the reasons of fitness which illustrate this truth, a truth that is indemonstrable by human reason. He takes up this point in the two Summa's and elsewhere.[126]

On the one hand then we can conceive personal processions in God only according to actions that are immanent to the divine nature, that is the divine intelligence and will.

On the other hand "it is by a single and simple act that God knows all and wills all. So he cannot have in himself Word proceeding from Word or Love proceeding from Love; in him there is only one perfect Word and one perfect Love. In this his perfect fecundity is manifested."[127] In God there could not be two processions according to intelligence or two others according to love. God utters himself totally in one sole Word, and loves himself in one sole Love.

The procession of the Spirit exhausts the interior fecundity of God. It completes the interior cycle of divine life. The Spirit, who appears sterile in God, is fruitful as Creator. "Because the Spirit desires and loves what he has considered good, he sets to work outside to obtain it. Since then it is precisely goodness that one attributes to the Holy Spirit, one can thus grasp why the procession of the divine persons goes no further: what follows on it is the procession of creatures, or to put it differently, the procession of a term that is a stranger to the divine nature."[128]

Thus we are drawn to scrutinize more closely the action of the Father, the Son and their Spirit in the world of men.

Appendix V: *The anthropological analogy (Intellect-Word-Breath) of the Trinity in St. John Damascene*

For St. John Damascene the comparison *nous-logos-pneuma* constitutes a veritable introduction to Trinitarian theology. It is found in *An Exposition of the Orthodox Faith* and in his other treatises almost every time he speaks of the Trinity. The hypostases of the Son and the Spirit, though proceeding from the Father are yet inseparable from him just as our word engendered by our intellect is not separated from it but remains in it (*Dialogue against the Manichaeans*, MG, v. 94, col. 1512). They are only one God, just as in us intellect, word and breath form only one single man (*ibid.*, col. 1513). The Breath of God is not a current of air that vanishes (col. 1513). Without

---

[126]St. Thomas Aquinas, *Summa Theologica* I, 27.5; *Summa contra Gentiles*, IV, 24.11; IV, 26; *De Potentia*, 9.9.14, 15.
[127]St. Thomas Aquinas, *Summa Theologica,* I, 27.5.3.
[128]St. Thomas Aquinas, *De Potentia*, q. 9, a. 9 et diff. ad 14 m.

separating from the Father the Breath reveals the Word and the Word the Intellect.

It is permissible to see in this analogy a partial parallel to the Augustinian analogy of the trinity of the created spirit, but with this nuance that the Damascenian analogy rather seems to consider man in his psychosomatic totality and to be less oriented than the Augustinian analogy toward intrasubjectivity. This gives it a greater pedagogical value.

On this analogy see J. Grégoire, "La relation éternelle de l'Esprit au Fils d'après les écrits de Jean de Damas," *Revue d'histoire ecclésiastique,* 64 (1969), 731ff.

IX
The Active Presence of the Father, of the Son and Their Spirit in the World of Men

At the end of this study of the fundamental mystery of Christianity, it is appropriate to show how by their grace the divine Persons solicit the human society that they mercifully wish to encompass. The creative and omnipresent Trinity does not isolate itself but offers and gives itself. Between the invisible Father and the world, the missions of the Word and of the Spirit emerge, culminating in the Eucharistic sacrifice.

I. THE MISSIONS OF THE WORD AND OF THE SPIRIT, THE BOND BETWEEN THE FATHER AND THE WORLD

At one and the same time we have now reached the heart of the New Testament and the heart of the modern theological problem of the relations between God, Church and world.

At the heart of the New Testament, there are few facts more attested to than the missions of the Son (numberless texts of the Johannine Gospel can be cited for them) and of the Spirit (Jn. 14:16-26; 15:26; Lk. 24:49). We will content ourselves with transcribing this extract from St. Paul which is particularly remarkable because it synthesizes the two missions:

> But when the fullness of time had come, God sent his Son, born of a woman, born under the law, to redeem those who were under the law so as to confer on us the adoption of sons. And the proof that you are sons is that God sent into our hearts the Spirit of his Son crying, Abba, Father (Gal. 4:4-6).

All these texts show us that the missions of the divine Persons constitute a revealed fact, that the Father is not sent but comes to men (Jn. 14:23), while the Son and the Spirit come as sent by the Father.

This central datum of the New Testament cannot fail to illumine the problem of the relations between God and the world. Theological interest in the notion of mission lies precisely in this that it puts a very human and intra-mundane category that is heavy with intersubjectivity at the service of the data revealed by God[1] about his relation with the world as envisaged from the intra-Trinitarian point of view that starts from the Father.

Through the Missions we reach a divine History, the history of the personal communications between God and the world created by him.[2] The notion of mission which the Revealer God has "borrowed" from the world of relations between men he has created, helps us both to situate in the strictly divine horizon of the uncreated three Persons the secret of God's visits to his creatures and to consider the mutual deportment of the Three in their self-communication to creatures. The missions unveil for us the divine intersubjectivity against the background of human intersubjectivity in order to save it. The sendings of the Word and the Spirit bind history to its intra-divine origins.

The missions of the two Paracletes contain at the same time the secret of God, the secret of universal history and the secret of our salvation. The mission of the universal Church and the mission of each human person, which are ordered to the salvation of all men, draw their origin from the mission of the Son and the mission of the Holy Spirit, according to the plan of the Father whose invisible missionaries they are (cf. AG 2).

1. *Structure of the Mission of a divine Person*

A mission in the human sphere, for example an official mission, signifies a double relation: a relation on the one hand of subordination of the sent or mandated person relative to the person who sends or mandates, and on the other hand a relation of utility with respect to the persons to whom he is sent or among whom he must fill a new role if he is already present where he must be sent.

We can say then that mission essentially constitutes a mediation between the mandating principle and the beneficiaries of the sending of the one who is mandated. This mediation supposes an initial distance between them and a will to come together. The initial distance can be hostility and the will to come together can be a desire of peace (cf. Lk. 14:32). Mission manifests itself particularly in international relations. In this area missions aim to establish peace, to obtain reconciliation or to sign a treaty of alliance (*IM* 8, 17.20).

Thus when God, the transcendent God, offended by sin, wished to reconcile himself with the world, that is to reconcile it with him, he sent to it

---

[1] Note that the Greek verb *exapesteilen* used by Paul only in Gal. 4:4, 6 to signify the missions of the Spirit and of the Son, means "to detach away from oneself someone for a mission" (M.-J. Lagrange, *Epître aux Galates*. Paris, 1950, p. 102). On the Old Testament and Rabbinical context of this Pauline usage, you can read E.-M. Kredel, *EF*, Paris, 1967, v. I, p. 104, art. "Apôtres."

[2] Cf. H.-F. Dondaine, O.P., *La Trinité*. Paris, 1962, v. II, pp. 423-453: commentaries to clarify question 43 of the Pars prima of the *Summa Theologica* of St. Thomas Aquinas. We have drawn inspiration from this work more than once.

first his only Son and then their Spirit. In each case the mission of the sent Person consists in a double relation, with the One or Ones who send him and with those to whom he or they are sent. When there is question of God this second relation does not suppose an anterior absence—for God the Creator is always present to his creation—but a new mode of presence of the sent divine Person to certain beings, to rational creatures. And this new mode of presence constitutes a real relation in the creature but only a relation of reason in the sent divine Person.[3] This new mode of presence is nothing else than sanctifying grace. But in God the relation of the one mandated to the one who mandates is never a relation of subordination: since the one sent is equal to the one who sends.

In short, God is immense and so he is not absent from any place in the universe which he is ceaselessly creating. But each of the three divine Persons can give himself to intelligent and free beings as object of knowledge and love. The first Person can send the other two, the second can send the third on a mission to human persons that is at the same time divinizing and reconciling.

By a mission of a divine Person we understand more precisely the communication to beings or to some intelligent and free beings of one divine Person by another on the basis of the order of the Persons in God. The mission thus includes, as the Angelic Doctor[4] underscores, the eternal procession of one Person and adds to it a temporal effect. Thus it is the continuation of the intra-divine processions in the world created by God.

The mission of a divine Person then has four characteristics:

a) it involves no change in God or in the Person sent, because the three divine Persons are one and the same immutable God;

b) it involves a change, a mutation in the Person who benefits from the mission; this change is a new relation of this intelligent and free creature to one of the divine Persons or to the Three; or if you prefer, it is a new mode of presence of the uncreated Persons in the created persons, a temporal reality; the missions and donations of the divine Persons are realized in time, in the bosom of history (cf. Gal. 4:4: fullness of time);

c) this new relation is a created effect and caused by the whole Trinity because the works of God in the world are common to the three divine Persons. It must be said that under this aspect the whole Trinity gives itself by the missions of the Son and the Spirit; but the Son and the Spirit are sent because they will to be. The mission supposes neither command nor counsel from the Sender to the One sent;

---

[3] St. Thomas Aquinas, *Summa Theologica* I, 43.1.
[4] *Ibid.*, I, 43.2.3.

d) lastly this new real relation can be visible or invisible, but never solely visible. We shall return to this point later.

Immutability of the Sender and the One sent, change in the rational creature that is the beneficiary of the sending, change which is real and visible or invisible as the case may be, these are the structural data of the mission.

Scheeben[5] rightly emphasizes that the mission of a divine Person implies the synthesis of two elements, which are that Person's active gift of self and the (passive) gift of that Person by another. The mission in the passive sense (the most ordinary sense and the one that here implies the coming of a divine Person as a result of the action of another) is inseparable from the mission in the active sense (gift of self). For Scheeben "the term, the result of the mission's activity, that is, of the activity which carries out the mission,... is the introduction of the person concerned into the creature and His existence in the creature, an existence that is proper to the person sent, and is not common to Him along with the sending person": the Son sent is known by the one who receives him not only as God and as possessing the same divine nature as the Father but also as Son distinct from the Father.

An existence peculiar to the person sent: it is this, it seems to us, that St. Thomas Aquinas implies when he affirms with still more precision: "That the Son appears in the flesh, he has from the Father; that the Holy Spirit dwells in man through a new effect appropriated to him... this he has from the Father and the Son."[6] Or, in the words of H.-F. Dondaine: "for the Person sent, his divine origin is the common source both of his being and of his temporal presence."[7] But regarding the temporal presence we prefer to say that this divine origin is its ultimate source, since we must admit that the temporal presence is an effect common to the Three and among these the Father is the ultimate source while the Father and the Son together are the source of the Spirit.

From this structural analysis of the mission there flow two consequences: the first that in virtue of the mystery of the circuminsession of the three Persons, the mission of one implies the presence of the others; the second that contrary to human missions the divine mission does not suppose a local separation or a spiritual distance of one Person from another, of the one sent in relation to the sender. And on the other hand the creation and the conservation of the universe or the cooperation of God with his creatures are not a divine mission precisely because they do not

---

[5]M.-J. Scheeben, *The Mysteries of Christianity*. St. Louis, 1946, § 27, p. 152.
[6]St. Thomas Aquinas, *Summa contra Gentiles*, IV, 23.
[7]Dondaine, *op. cit.*, p. 428.

suppose a new mode of presence of God in creation, new with respect to another already existing mode of presence.

The mission then is half-way between the presence of God as Creator and his presence in the Incarnation.[8]

2. *Visible and invisible missions of the divine Persons*

In extricating the intellectual content of the Pauline text already cited (Gal. 4:4), Scholastic theology distinguished visible and invisible missions. The visible mission reveals the invisible[9] mission and is ordered to it. The effect of the visible mission is visible (the human nature of Christ, the dove or breath or tongue of fire symbolizing the Spirit of Christ). The effect of the invisible mission (the sanctification of the rational creature through the manifestation to it of a divine Person) is invisible. The visible mission of the Holy Spirit reveals his invisible mission in the heart of the Apostles after the Cross and the Cenacle, and in the soul of Christ after the Incarnation (cf. Lk. 5:1, 18).

The visible and invisible missions have some common traits: the visible mission is ordered to the manifestation of the divine Person who is sent, and the invisible mission is ordered to the self-donation of this uncreated Person to the created person. Both missions have for their end the sanctification of rational creatures, of created persons.

But they also admit some differences. The visible missions manifest to the world and in the world the Person sent, whether through a permanent effect united to this Person (the sacred humanity of Jesus Christ) or through a pure symbol[10] of the Person sent (dove, breath, tongues). The invisible missions manifest the Person sent not to the world but to the soul and they permit the soul to enjoy him (cf. Jn. 14:23; 14:21 in opposition to Jn. 7:4-5). Through the invisible mission the rational creature is elevated above the world by the Person sent and immersed in the Eternal,[11] since the

---

[8]Here we are thinking of the invisible mission; cf. St. Thomas Aquinas, *Summa Theologica* I, 43.2:"from all eternity, the Son proceeds so that he is God; in time he proceeds so that he is also man according to his visible mission or so that he is in man according to his invisible mission."

[9]*Ibid.*, I, 43.7.

[10]Theologians call the Incarnation a substantial divine mission and Pentecost a representative divine mission.

[11]Cf. St. Augustine, *De Trinitate*, IV, 20.28: "When in the course of time someone becomes conscious of his progress we speak of the mission of the Word but not of his mission in this world, for he does not, of course, appear in sensible fashion, i.e., he does not present himself under the senses of the body. Further in the measure that we can grasp something eternal we ourselves are not in this world; and the spirits of the just to the extent that they experience the divine are no longer in this world even though they still live in this body." It would be interesting to compare this text with that of the Dutch catechism, ch. VI, notes 23 and 27 of our work.

rational creature participates in the relation of the divine Person sent with his sender.

The visible mission is ordered to the invisible mission and is inconceivable without it, but the reciprocal is not true. Thus in the womb of Mary from the first instant of his human existence the eternal Word adorned his created soul with the gifts of his uncreated Spirit (an invisible mission of the Spirit) but the visible mission through which the Word sensibly represented this gift of the Spirit to his humanity only began at his Baptism thirty years later.[12]

Through the events of the visible missions (Incarnation, Pentecost) and through the advents of the invisible missions, there is accomplished both the return of intelligent and free creatures to God and the purpose of the whole history of the world: the manifestation of the inner glory of the three divine Persons to created spirits. By means of certain habits (infused theological virtues) and certain imperfect human acts, the missions of the Word and of the Spirit aim at and merit and produce the perfect and immutable act that is their *raison d'être*: the act of the beatific vision. In it, the history of man will be perfectly linked to its intra-divine origins.

The invisible missions on earth thus prepare those of the Kingdom consummated in glory. This earthly anticipation is constituted by the delectable exercise of the theological virtues of faith and charity. St. Thomas Aquinas has magnificently expressed how the image of the triune God which is the intelligent and free soul becomes the likeness of this God thanks to the missions of the Word and the Spirit:

> Grace renders the soul conformed to God. And when there is a mission of a divine Person to the soul through grace, the soul must be likened to this Person through some gift of grace. But the Holy Spirit is Love. It is then the gift of charity which likens the soul to the Holy Spirit and it is by reason of the gift of charity that we consider a mission of the Holy Spirit. The Son is the Word—and not just any word, but the Word that spirates Love.... There is then no mission of the Son for just any perfecting of the intellect. There is a mission of the Son only when the intellect is instructed in such a way that this comes to dissolve in an affection of love.... The terms St. Augustine uses are very significant: "The Son is sent when he is known and perceived": for the word perception in effect signifies a certain experimental knowledge. And this properly is wisdom or delectable knowledge.[13]

---

[12]St. Thomas Aquinas, *Summa Theologica* I, 43.7.6.
[13]*Ibid.*, I, 43.5.2: St. Thomas there cites St. Augustine, *De Trinitate*, IV, 20.28: "unicuique (Verbum) mittitur, cum a quoquam cognoscitur atque percipitur."

Thus the missions of the divine Persons have as their end experimental knowledge, first in grace, then in glory. God sends his Son and their Spirit to men to give them an intimate experience of his Trinitarian life, but first in the obscurity of faith. This experience is an earthly participation in the mystery of the divine processions: "the outpouring of divine, filial and supernatural love of charity in our hearts reproduces and prolongs the interior outpouring of the Father and Son in the Holy Spirit. We can say not only that love is given to us but even that the Holy Spirit himself is given to us in this love; or rather, as Scheeben[14] explains in an allusion to Rom. 5:5, it is because the Holy Spirit, the stream of divine love is poured out in our soul that the habit and act of charity that he produces enter into our heart. Through faith that is perfected by means of the gift of Wisdom, the justified man participates "experientially" in the generation of the Son by the Father and through charity in the spiration of the Spirit by the Father and the Son. Here we are touching the very essence of the missions of the Son and the Spirit insofar as these missions are prolongations in history of the eternal processions of these two divine Persons, making them the objects of the most sublime human experience: the "experience" of the Trinity.

The invisible missions of the Spirit and of the Son are realized in a certain order: by setting the heart on fire the Spirit leads us to the Son who enlightens the understanding, and he in turn leads us to the Father.[15] Bernard Lonergan[16] extends these thoughts of St. Thomas Aquinas and says that there will be a special relation of the Christian with the heavenly Father when this Christian reaches the beatific vision. For apropos of our return to the Father, Jn. 14:6 and Eph. 2:18 use the same preposition *pros* which designates the eternal relation of the Son with the Father (cf. Jn. 1:1; 13:1, 3; 17:11, 13). This is an interesting theological hypothesis, which harmonizes perfectly with other data of the mystery: the Father is specially present to the saints in glory (cf. 1 Cor. 15:20-28), the Son to all men as man and as brother, the Holy Spirit to the Church as its soul. However it must be noted that this special presence of one divine Person is nothing else than the delectable knowledge of his personal property, and that we cannot know the Spirit without knowing the Father and the Son of whom he is the breath and the bond; nor can we know the Father without knowing the Son nor the Son without the Father. For, to repeat an elliptical formula of St. Augustine: "there are three persons, the Father of the Son and the Son of the Father and the Spirit of the Father and of the Son."[17]

[14] M.-J. Scheeben, *The Mysteries of Christianity* § 29, pp. 150-163.
[15] Here we synthesize St. Thomas Aquinas' commentary on Jn. 14:26 and what he says of this in the *Summa Theologica*, I, 43.5.3.
[16] B. Lonergan, S.J., *De Deo trino*. Rome, 1964, v. II, p. 264.
[17] St. Augustine, *De Trinitate*, XV, 22.43; ML 42, 1090.

The primary characteristic we recognize in the invisible missions recalls that the spiritual creature is destined to be the theater of essential history: the history of the progress of the divine presence in the world.[18] In telling us of the missions of the Son and of the Spirit, the Revealer God helps us perceive this essential history beginning with its absolute center which is the Trinity under the aspect of the absolute and eternal events which are the processions of the Son and of the Spirit.

We could say that the visible missions, which as such and in the strict sense have ended, are somehow continued in the visible mission of the Church, which is the sacrament and visible sign of the invisible missions of the Son and the Spirit always at work.

The Father has sent his Son visibly and both have sent their Spirit, so that the Spirit by sending the universal Church to the world might lead all men to the Son and this Son might lead them invisibly, inchoatively now but later more fully and definitively to the Father. The visible and invisible missions form a cycle in which the union of creation with the Creator[19] is perfected and consummated.

Now let us re-read the text of St. Paul to the Galatians which gave us our starting point; we will better perceive its meaning and amplitude, since it joins so harmoniously the visible and invisible missions of the Son to the invisible mission of the Spirit of the Son:

> But when the fullness of time had come, God sent his Son, born of a woman, born under the law, to redeem those who were under the law, to confer on us the adoption of sons. And the proof that you are sons is that God sent into our hearts the Spirit of his Son crying, Abba, Father (Gal. 4:4-6).

"God sent his Son, born of a woman." The missions of the Son and of the Spirit bind the world to the Father by means of the mission confided to a Woman, Mary, in whom there takes place the synthesis between God and the World which we call the Incarnation. In agreeing to be the Mother of the Son Mary cooperated in a unique fashion in the mission of the Son, in his double mission—both visible and invisible. In praying with the Apostles after the Ascension, she cooperated in the visible mission of the Paraclete[20] and consequently in his invisible mission. Through the will and the grace of the Father she in some way mediated the visible and invisible missions of

---

[18]Cf. St. Thomas Aquinas, *Summa Theologica* I, 43.6.2.

[19]Cf. St. Thomas Aquinas, *I Sent.* d. 14, q. 2, a. 2.

[20]Mary "obtained by her very efficacious prayers that the Spirit of the divine Redeemer, already given at the Cross, was conferred on the day of Pentecost, together with prodigious gifts for the recently born Church": Pius XII, *Mystici Corporis*, AAS 35 (1943), 248.

the Son and of the Spirit, of which she was and remains the principal beneficiary. It is especially to the Heart of Mary that God the Father sends his Son and their Spirit, so that in this Immaculate Heart the society of human persons might be linked to the society of divine Persons.

3. *The mission of the Church, historical unfolding of the historical missions of the coeternal Word and Spirit*

We must hold, while seeking to understand their deep underlying harmony, two truths that are apparently opposed to one another: that the Father sends the Son and the Spirit to the Church, that the Son and the Spirit send the Church to the world.

The three divine Persons reside in the Church and they fill it with their divine and supernatural presence; the Spirit, who is the interpersonal unity of the Father and the Son, unifies the Church, the multitude of members of her who is the one and only dove of the Lord.

The indwelling of the Three in the Church is the fruit of the missions of the Son and the Spirit (cf. Jn. 14:21-23). This inhabitation is dynamic and progressive in the sense that the Three constantly come to it anew and give themselves to it in an always new and more profound manner, as is shown by its constant progress in faith, hope and charity (cf. *LG* 65). Ceaselessly the Father comes to the Church and gives his Son to it, and with and through his Son gives their Spirit. This constant renewal and intensification of the presence of the Father, the Son and the Spirit in the people of the triune God is the source of this people's constant fidelity to its duty of perpetual renewal.

Through this incessant renewal of the Church, the Son and the Spirit acquire an ever new way of existing in it *ad Patrem*. It is good to recall here that what characterizes an invisible mission is not only an increase of grace but especially an increase which effects the production of supernatural acts of a new species: for example an increase of charity that leads to the performance of miracles, or to the easy conquest of all temptations, or undertaking arduous tasks for the glory of God.[21] There are certain periods in the history of the Church in which the missions of the Word and the Spirit of Truth become more intense and marvelous: notably in times of apostasy when the Holy Spirit appears to wish to compensate for numerous losses by the intense fervor of some great saints and by the heroism of martyrs.[22] Are we forbidden to think that the post-conciliar period of the Church of the twentieth century is one of these times of more intense invisible missions of the only Son and of the Spirit of the Son?

---

[21]Cf. St. Thomas Aquinas, *Summa Theologica* I, 43.6.2.
[22]Cf. Cardinal Ch. Journet, *L'Eglise du Verbe incarné*. Bruges, 1951, v. II, pp. 462ff.

By these invisible missions which become partially visible thanks to their fruits, the Spirit "rejuvenates the Church and renews it perpetually, putting it on the way to perfect union with its Spouse" (*LG* 4). In the constitution on the Church and its Trinitarian prologue, Vatican II shows us the mission given by the Son to the Spirit on behalf of the Church. But it also shows us the Church sent to the world by the Son and by the Spirit. The Son who returned to the Father sends the Spirit to the Church to sanctify it incessantly (cf. *LG* 4). But he also with and by the Spirit sends the Church to the world to prolong his own proper mission: this is the fundamental point of view that we extricate from an attentive study (and comparison with *LG* 4) of the Trinitarian prologue of the missionary decree *Ad Gentes* (*AG* 4-5) in its pneumatological conclusion.

Let us re-read these texts:

> Christ has sent the Holy Spirit from the Father to accomplish his salvific work in the interior of souls and to impel the Church to expand... by insinuating in the hearts of the faithful the same missionary spirit which had impelled Christ himself (*AG* 4).
>
> The mission of the Church then is accomplished by that activity which makes her fully present to all men and nations. She undertakes this activity in obedience to Christ's command and in response to the grace and charity of the Holy Spirit.... In the course of history the Church's mission carries on and develops the mission of Christ himself who was sent to announce the Good News to the poor. By the same road that Christ himself walked the Church must walk under the impulse of the Spirit of Christ (*AG* 5).
>
> Constituted Lord by his Resurrection and given plenary power in heaven and on earth, Christ is now at work in the heart of men through the energy of his Spirit (*GS* 38, 1).

The invisible mission of the Son which he received from the Father and by virtue of which he sends his Spirit to his Church and to the world that he wishes to integrate into his Church, this mission is completed and prolonged by the sending of the Church to the world and it is carried out by the Son acting through the Spirit in a visible manner (cf. Jn. 20:21-23).

The sending of the Son and the Spirit by the Father is identical with the mystery of their eternal processions. The sending of the Spirit to the Church by the Son is identical with the mystery of his procession *a Filio*. In both cases temporal terms come to be associated with the eternal processions. But when the Son and Spirit send the Church to the world, the mystery of the eternal processions is presupposed but not immediately signified. What is signified first of all is the function or "juridical mission" given by the Son to the Apostolic College (Jn. 20:21), to use an expression of

Pius XII.[23] This juridical mission imitates and extends the generation and mission of the Son, but it is not identical with it. It becomes one with the sending of the Spirit to the Church by the Son, as the same Pope stresses: so that this mission properly speaking is to the juridical mission what the soul is to the body.[24]

Thus the Spirit is sent to the Church in a mission properly so called, a divine mission identical with his eternal procession *a Patre per Filium*. And the same Spirit that is given to the Church to unify and sanctify it sends the Church to the world by acting both in the heart of the baptized and in the heart of the non-baptized to whom he sends it. This Spirit impels the baptized to announce the Gospel and the non-baptized to embrace it. The Son sends the Church into the world visibly, the Spirit invisibly. The Son also acts invisibly through his Spirit thereby extending the effect of the mission that was visibly confided to the Church the night of the Resurrection.

This Spirit was at work before the glorification of Christ (*AG* 4). It is also at work in the souls of the non-baptized to give growth in them to the seeds of the Word[25] before he sends them the visible Church. Thus we perceive the close relationship between the invisible sending of the Spirit by the Father and the Son, and the souls which this Spirit justifies by the implicitly desired baptism, and the mission confided by this same Spirit to the Church and baptized souls on behalf of the world in order to incorporate it fully into Christ. Could we not say that the Father and the Son send the Spirit to the Church so that the Spirit may send the Church to the world? The mission that the Church receives from the Spirit of the Son, is it not to "unify under one Spirit all men of whatever nation, race or culture" (*GS* 92. 1)? The Spirit only sends the Church to the world in order to become the soul of this world incorporated into the Church. In sending it, the Spirit gives himself to the Church which he sends to the world in order to give himself through this Church to this world in a fuller fashion through Baptism and the Eucharist until he pours himself out most fully and openly at the *Parousia*.

In one single operation *ad extra* the Son and Spirit conjointly send the Church to the world and together water with the dew of their divine grace the good earth destined to receive the seed of the word of the Church (cf. *AG* 22).

What Paul VI said in his profession of faith in 1968 about the action of the

---

[23]Pius XII, *Mystici Corporis, AAS* 35 (1943), 224: "nulla oppositio inter invisibilem Spiritus Sancti *missionem* ac juridicum Pastorum Doctorumque a Christo acceptum *munus*." It must be noted however that John in 20:21-23 and elsewhere uses the same words (*apostello, pempo*) to designate the mission of the Spirit and that of the Apostles.
[24]Pius XII, *Ibid*.
[25]Cf. *AG* 11, 15.

Holy Spirit applies also to the non-baptized: "His action, which penetrates to the deepest interior of the soul, renders man capable of responding to the appeal of Jesus: Be ye perfect as your heavenly Father is perfect" (Mt. 5:48).

For it is the same Spirit that "penetrates to the deepest interior of the soul" of the non-baptized and "who protects and leads the Church" toward them by purifying "(its) members if they do not turn away from his grace."[26]

In stressing these aspects of the mission of the Spirit to the Church Paul VI shows that in harmony with the name of the One sent this mission has for its object the sanctification of the Church and indirectly that of the world. We can extend these insights by underscoring that the Spirit who is sent to the Church to sanctify it in turn sends the Church to sanctify the world.

Doubtless there are some who will object: since the invisible missions of the Spirit and the Word are essentially spiritual and take place in the interior of the soul they do not signify a contact between the divine Persons and the world. Sanctifying grace, which is their principal effect, is immaterial. Hence in the view of these critics the Church's visible mission is not really the extension of the missions of the Son and the Spirit.

We must make a triple response. In the first place man is a psychosomatic unity: hence what affects the human soul re-echos in the totality of the human person. It is to a human person as a whole and not only to the soul that a divine Person is sent. The essentially spiritual character of his action does not in any way suppress this fact.

In the second place the missions of the Son and of the Spirit are inseparably both visible and invisible: hence they signify that the Son and Spirit are sent in time, in history, to historical beings who are visible by their bodies and invisible in their souls. Sanctifying grace does not affect beings who cease to be spatio-temporal once they are touched by it. On the contrary, it divinizes their spatio-temporal condition.[27]

Finally and on a deeper level it must be pointed out that this divinization orients men toward what is proper to divine Persons: eternity. "In the visible mission, the Person comes into the world; by the invisible mission, the rational creature is elevated by the Person above the world into the eternal."[28]

The Father sends his Son and their Spirit to the Church in the course of time only to draw it, and through it the world, toward the eternity that is common to the Three. The missions effect participation in eternal life.

---

[26]Paul VI, Profession of Faith, June 30, 1968, *AAS* 60 (1968), p. 438, § 13.

[27]Cf. St. Thomas Aquinas, *Summa Theologica* I, 43.2: "Mission and gift bring to mind a temporal term: for why is one sent if not to be in some place?"

[28]H.-F. Dondaine, O.P., *La Trinité*. Paris, 1962, v. II, p. 424.

The mission of the Church then is to plunge the history of the human society into the eternity of the society of the divine Persons. To reach this goal it "is the function of the Church, led by the Holy Spirit who ceaselessly renews and purifies her, to make God the Father and his incarnate Son present and in a sense visible" (GS 21. 5). The Church, as the body of the Three according to Tertullian's expression,[29] makes visible and in a sense transparent the Trinity that is in it and to which it leads.

Isn't all this implied in the lapidary declaration of Vatican II that we cited?

The Church during her pilgrimage on earth is missionary by her very nature. For it is from the mission of the Son and the mission of the Holy Spirit that she takes her origin according to the design of God the Father (AG 2).

And isn't the Mass the unfolding par excellence of the salvific mission confided by the Father to his only Son and to their common Spirit?

II. THE TRINITY REDEEMING THE WORLD IN AND BY THE EUCHARIST

Vatican II has clearly insinuated that the Eucharist is the means par excellence of actual and always renewed union with the divine Persons:

Through the Eucharist the faithful united to the bishop gain access to God the Father, by his Son the Word made flesh who suffered and was glorified, in the outpouring of the Holy Spirit. And thus made "partakers of the divine nature" they enter into communion with the Most Holy Trinity (UR 15).

The Eucharist is the supreme manifestation of the Father, the Son and the Spirit. Nothing is clearer if we recall that the Son was made flesh and sent by his Father to reveal to us the mystery of his unity with the Father in the Spirit, and that it is by Communion that he extends his incarnation in each one of us. It is especially then that he manifests himself to us as the only Son, the Spirator and Giver of the Paraclete Spirit (cf. Jn. 14:21-26). He manifests himself to us as being the one who with his Father and their Spirit *effects* our salvation and who first of all *is* our salvation. And in what does the salvation consist which the Incarnate and Eucharistic Word effects in us, if not precisely in redeeming us from our culpable ignorance and scorn of the triune God by riveting us in loving contemplation of his Person as the One sent by the Father and as Sender of the Spirit?

Between the Trinity and the Eucharist there is the Paschal mystery. The Revelation of the Trinity is made within the Paschal mystery, is mediated to us in the double Trinitarian structure of the Eucharistic liturgy, and is

---

[29]Tertullian, *De Baptismo,* VI, 1; see SC 35, p. 75, note 3 for an interesting explanation by F. Refoulé, O.P., of this astonishing expression.

signified in the symbol of the Eucharistic Heart of Jesus. This is what we must now study in greater depth.

1. *Trinitarian revelation, Paschal revelation*

It is essentially in function of his return to the Father and in this perspective that Jesus has revealed his birth and his eternal origin. The nearer this return came, the more clear became the central revelation of Jesus: the God to whom he was returning was his origin but not his Creator, because he was his Father.

In the Johannine gospel "this return constitutes the most brilliant revelation of his origin and his innermost being." H. Van den Bussche, the Belgian exegete, has particularly highlighted this "theological vision which John considers fundamental."[30] Jesus says to all Christians what he said a little before his death: "I came from the Father and have come into the world; again I am leaving the world and going to my Father" (Jn. 16:28). Today and ever since the institution of the Eucharist "the true revelation consists in making the Father in Jesus known through his disciples. This is the first article of the faith of a Christian: Jesus is born of the Father (Jn. 8:42; 16:27-30; 17:8) and the Father has sent him (Jn. 3:34; 5:36-38; 6:29, 57; 7:29; 8:42; 10:36; 11:42; 17:3, 8, 21, 23, 25; 20:21)."[31] John saw this fundamental experience of return as the most decisive foundation of the faith in the divine origin of Jesus and in his divine filiation. And he expressed it according to a stereotyped schema that was content to join together the mention of his "coming from the Father" and his "return to the Father" (Jn. 8:14, 21, 23; 13:3, 36).

The Paschal return to his Father of the man Jesus is the sign of his eternal return as divine Person to the Father in the Spirit (the Spirit who was precisely revealed as a Person distinct from the Father and the Son in the course of the discourse after the Supper). No better moment could have been chosen, since the mission of the Spirit is the fruit and term of that of the Son.

It is in the Blood of the Lamb that the Trinity has wished to consummate the revelation of itself to the world. It is by the Mass (*ite, missa est*) that the mission of the Church, which sends Christians on mission to the world, is

---

[30]H. Van den Bussche, *Le discours d'adieu de Jésus*. Tournai, 1959, pp. 34-35. In the same sense see also Jn. 8:28-29 and L. Bouyer, *La Bible et l'Evangile*. Paris, 1951, p. 211: "To proclaim that Jesus is the Son of God...is to say that this living person must be considered as being God. But equally it is to say that this person has his divinity, however proper and essential it may be, from Another." "The divinity is present in Jesus only in a secondary fashion, for Jesus is God only in constant reference to the One who dwells always...in an inaccessible light" (*Ibid.*, p. 212).

[31]H. Van den Bussche, *op. cit., ibid.* The following sentence also draws its inspiration from this author.

realized ever better and better by manifesting the visible and invisible missions of the Son and the Spirit.

Is it not true that at each Mass "God sends his Son to renew the redemption" of men and to make us always more his adoptive sons in the only Son (cf. Gal. 4:4-5)? Is it not also true that at each Mass God sends again into our hearts the Spirit of his Son who cries Abba, Father, Our Father (cf. Gal. 4:6)?

These missions manifest not only the love of the Father for men but also the love of the Son for the Father (it is for love of him that he redeems men) and the love of the Spirit of the Son for the Father, the Spirit who makes the Father's adoptive sons invoke him.

The Trinity is present at the Mass inasmuch as it effects their salvation, that is inasmuch as this salvation turns them toward the Trinity and returns them to it as to a centripetal pole of attraction and not only as to the efficient cause of their existence. The action of the Trinity is merciful precisely in this that it orients the world toward itself.

Consequently, it is proper to analyze not only the structure of the gift that the Trinity makes of itself to the world in "descending" toward it, if we may dare to say this, but also the structure of the return of the world to it which it effects. Both structures are present in the Mass, and the second in a twofold manner, as we shall see.

As renewal of the sacrificial return of Christ to his Father and as anticipation of his return to men in the cloud of the Spirit, the Mass is the supreme manifestation of the love of the three divine Persons for sinful humanity, and at the same time the supreme glorification of the Trinity by this humanity incorporated into Christ and sanctified by him.

Is not its chief aim (if we may universalize a more particular suggestion of Vatican II apropos of the perseverance of religious) the "greatest glory of the Trinity which through and in Christ is the source and origin of all sanctity" (*LG* 47)? The Christ who is the mediator and plenitude of Trinitarian sanctification is the Christ of the altar and the tabernacle. It is especially due to the Mass that the Trinity is present to the world.

2. *Mass and Trinity: the twofold Trinitarian structure of the Mass*

In conformity with the two equally legitimate structures of Christian prayer, one pre-Arian and one post-Arian, the Mass can be viewed as a sacrifice offered to the Father by the Son in the Spirit or as a sacrifice offered to the Father, to the Son and to the Spirit.

In its ontological reality, a reality to which the expression of the Church's liturgy partially corresponds, the Mass is at the same time a "subordinative doxology" and a "coordinative doxology," to use categories that basically go back to St. Basil.

a) *The Mass, subordinative doxology*

As sacrifice of thanksgiving, the Mass is the offering of the Son to the Father in the Spirit. It is the prayer which Christ began on earth: "Father, I thank thee that thou hast heard me... thou hearest me always" (Jn. 11:41-42) and which he continues now in and by his Church. In celebrating the Mass the Church effectively realizes what Christ requested, for it entreats the Father (*Te igitur, clementissime Pater*) in the name of the Son (cf. Jn. 16:23-27). Better still, it is Christ himself who in the Mass intercedes with the Father on our behalf (Rom. 8:34; Heb. 7:25) in conformity with his own promise (Mt. 18:19-20: Christ is *also* present because the Christians are united in his name and through them he prays and is heard).

What is the fruit of this perpetual prayer of the well-beloved Son to the Father? Its prime, and in a sense even only object, as well as its principal fruit is the gift of the Spirit for the glory of the Father: cf. Jn. 14:13, 16; 15:8; Lk. 11:13.[32] In renewing the sacrifice of the new and eternal Covenant between his Father and his brethren, Jesus Christ the just one and our Paraclete with the Father (1 Jn. 2:1) begs him to give us another Paraclete and, in perfect unity with the Father, effectively gives him to us in the Eucharist. Is not the Eucharistic and risen body of Christ the Redeemer spiritualized by the vivifying Spirit? In receiving the Son we inseparably receive the Father who sends him, and the Spirit whom he himself sends with the Father: "he who receives anyone whom I send receives me; and he who receives me receives him who sent me" (Jn. 13:20; 15:26; 16:7; more than the disciples, the Paraclete Spirit is the one par excellence whom Jesus sends and whom the world cannot receive: 14:17).

The mystery of the Eucharist cannot be separated from the mysteries of the Missions and of the Circuminsession of the divine Persons: to receive the glorified Christ, to eat his flesh and drink his blood is at the same time to drink the Spirit (1 Cor. 12:13: "all were made to drink the one Spirit") who issues forth from his pierced side, and to receive the Father who is in the Son (Jn. 14:10). In the holy Communion, Father and Son give us and send us their Spirit, the interpersonal bond of their own unity, so that he might unite us with one another and with them. Thus is answered the ever-renewed and ever-answered prayer of the well-beloved and only Son of the Father: "as thou, Father, art in me, and I in thee, that they also may be in us... that the love with which thou hast loved me may be in them and I in them" (Jn. 17:21-26).

This prayer of the only Son of the Father (prayer for the outpouring of the Spirit) is clearly brought out in the new anaphoras of the Latin rite. They all show us the Church addressing itself to the Father, before the

---

[32]Cf. our ch. I, note 148.

consecration, through the sacerdotal intercession of Jesus Christ, and then after the consecration, commemorating his passage from this world to the Father in the anamnesis: *unde et memores*.

This request for the outpouring of the Spirit, made to the Father in the name and through the mediation of the Son, had almost entirely disappeared from the Latin rite before being reintegrated into it in the new anaphoras offered to the Church in 1968. These anaphoras correspond to the most ancient tendencies of the liturgy. Here it will be enough to recall the anaphora of Hippolytus, that was in use in Rome at the middle of the third century. In this anaphora the priest says to the Father immediately after the double consecration:

> We beseech you to send your Holy Spirit upon the oblation of Holy Church. And in bringing (them) together, grant to all those who partake of your holy (mysteries) (to partake of them) in order that they might be filled with the Holy Spirit (cf. Louis Bouyer, *Eucharist*, University of Notre Dame Press, 1968, p. 169).

An anaphora of Bishop Serapion of Thmuis, a friend and correspondent of St. Athanasius, in the middle of the fourth century, is more interesting still, for here the epiclesis or invocation of the Holy Spirit whose outpouring it asks of the Father, precedes instead of follows the double consecration:

> Give us the Spirit of light that we may know you, you the true one, and him whom you have sent, Jesus Christ. Give us the Holy Spirit, that we can tell and recount your unspeakable mysteries. Let the Lord Jesus, together with the Holy Spirit, speak in us (*ibid.*, p. 204).

Inspired doubtless by this double example and by dogmatic considerations on the transubstantiating efficacy of the words of Eucharistic institution, the redactors of the new canons have therein inserted a double epiclesis, one before and the other after the consecration. The first asks of the Father that the Holy Spirit sanctify the gifts of bread and wine (the formulas are almost identical in the three anaphoras) so that they may become the Body and the Blood of Our Lord Jesus Christ. It thus confirms what the Syrian Denis Bar Salibi had already insistently affirmed in the twelfth century: "the priest at the altar represents Christ: the repetition of the words of Jesus Christ shows that it is still Christ who consecrates at the altar, by the will of the Father and the operation of the Holy Spirit and by means of the sacerdotal ministry" (cf. S. Salaville, *Catholicisme*, Paris, 1956 v. IV, 307, art. "Epiclèse").

The second and post-consecratory epiclesis, expresses at one and the same time a conviction and a request: that the Eucharistic Communion fill the faithful with the Holy Spirit, who through the Eucharistic Communion unites them in one physical and in one mystical Body of Christ. It thus takes up a theme that St. Fulgentius had magnificently developed.[33] And like him it also recognizes in the unity of the Church the action of him who is the common Spirit of the Father and of the Son. Thus it completes on the ecclesial level the signification of the first epiclesis: Jesus the Sovereign Priest consecrates by his Spirit the bread and the wine, converting them into his Body and his Blood, both spiritualized. In these the Christians then communicate.

The fourth anaphora presents the first epiclesis after recalling the sanctifying mission confided by the Son to the Spirit whom he sends from the Father. It thus shows in the Eucharistic transubstantiation and communion the supreme acts of this sanctifying mission of the Spirit of the Son. "The epiclesis is a prolongation of Pentecost," Max Thurian rightly comments. This ante-consecratory epiclesis also signifies that in the measure that transubstantiation is a work *ad extra* of the Son, it is inseparably the work of the Father and of the Spirit (but which ought to be specially appropriated to the Spirit whose procession of love it evokes). This Denis Bar Salibi had already partly insinuated.

Max Thurian summed up very well the Trinitarian mystery of the Mass as a subordinative doxology:

> The Church addresses to the almighty Father the entire Eucharistic prayer *by* the mediation of the Son, the interceding high priest, *with* him really present in the memorial of his sacrifice, *in* him who gives himself to the members of his body by Communion; and in the unity of the Holy Spirit, who accomplishes the epiphany of the sacramental and of the ecclesial body of Christ. And the Eucharistic prayer is completed with a conclusion to the glory of God—the Trinity.[34]

Such a doxology thus expresses very well the truth of Christ as Priest and Mediator. But it does not express the truth of Christ as God. If the Son and Spirit are one God with the Father, must we not say also that the sacrifice of the Mass is offered not only to the Father but also to both his Son and Spirit? Now we must look more closely at this necessary consequence of rejecting subordinationism in the domain of divine cult. We already have had occasion to allude to it but without speaking explicitly of the Eucharistic Sacrifice.[35]

---

[33]St. Fulgentius of Ruspe, *Ad Monimum* II, 6-12; ML 65, 184-192; 788-791; 769; 812.

[34]M. Thurian,"La théologie des nouvelles prières eucharistiques," *Maison-Dieu*, no. 94, 1968, p. 94, cf. pp. 96-97, 100-101.

[35]See our ch. II, § III toward the end.

b) *The Mass, coordinative doxology, concerned for the equal glory of the Father, the Son and the Holy Spirit*

Here St. Fulgentius is the most eloquent witness of the Tradition and the clearest. With an incomparable verbal splendor he applies to this supreme doxology that is the Mass, the principles which St. Basil had applied to ordinary doxologies (at the end of the psalms, for example). The bishop of Ruspe explains that although the Church names only the person of the Father it is to the whole Trinity that it offers the Eucharistic sacrifice. Temple and sacrifice are bound together. Scripture tells us that we are temples of the Holy Spirit and so we immolate the sacrifice suppliantly not only to the Father and to the Son but also to the Spirit (cf. 1 Cor. 6:19).[36]

To deny this point would be to deny the Trinity, Fulgentius insists:

> Whoever denies to the Son and to the Spirit the sacrifice offered to the Father makes himself a stranger to the members of Christ. The Holy Church, which is the true Body of Christ, just as it is conscious of being one only temple and one only sacrifice offered to the Trinity, so it also is accustomed to offer one only sacrifice to the Father, to the Son and to the Spirit in the truth of faith, hope and charity.[37]

Here St. Fulgentius develops a subtle and profound thought: The Church is the sacrifice which she herself offers to the Trinity in offering Christ, since she is his Body.

Why then in the last analysis is the sacrifice really offered to the three divine Persons, when in the canon only the person of the Father is explicitly named as the term of the offering? Fulgentius gives us enough of an answer when he writes concerning thanksgiving: "Because one common grace is conferred on us by the Holy Trinity, one single thanksgiving is to be rendered in common (*communiter*) to the Father, to the Son and to the Holy Spirit."[38] And he adds: "in the truth of faith and in the simplicity of our heart." The single thanksgiving corresponds to the unity of operation *ad extra* and to the unity of nature of the Three.

---

[36]St. Fulgentius, *Contra Fabianum*, ML 65, 808-811: "Sancta enim Ecclesia Catholica non soli Patri, sed simul sanctae sacrificat Trinitati; et sicut ad solius Patris personam dirigens orationem, totam simul invocat Trinitatem." The author adds immediately: "ita quod Patri Deo immolat, simul Trinitati sacrificat." A little further on (811) Fulgentius emphasizes that Christ has made of his body a temple (Jn. 2:19) and offered it in sacrifice (Eph. 5:1-2); but the Church is the Body of Christ (Col. 1:18).

[37]St. Fulgentius, ML 65, 812.

[38]*Ibid.*, 814; cf. 812: "gratias agimus Patri per Filium quia aeternus atque immortalis Unigenitus Deus pro nobis temporaliter homo mortalis est factus; et gratias agimus Patri et Filio, quia idem Unigenitus Deus Patri Deo manet naturaliter coaeternus."

So we see the reason for this affirmation that at first glance is so astonishing: that the Church in naming only the Father yet offers its sacrifice just as much to the Son and to the Spirit. Why? Because the Son and the Spirit are not creatures but are, together with the Father, the one and only Creator; they are equal to and coeternal with the Father. To deny that the Eucharistic sacrifice is offered to them in reality even if not in words, would be simply to deny that the Father who is named is relation to the Son who is equal to him and always present in him and generated by him. Analogous reasoning would apply to the Holy Spirit. There is then no need to name the Son or the Spirit as terms of the sacrificial oblation in order that the sacrifice should be really offered to them as much as to the Father.

So fact corresponds to right. As the Son and Spirit with the Father create us, so they have a right to our adoration, and the form par excellence of this adoration is the sacrificial action. "Whether it be in prayer or in sacrifice the true faith makes no distinction of (personal) function: all that is offered to one person is necessarily offered to the Trinity."[39]

This thought of St. Fulgentius only applies to the particular and supreme case of the Eucharistic sacrifice—the general rule that was laid down by Constantinople I: that the Holy Spirit is co-adored and co-glorified with the Father and with the Son. In our comment on this declaration of the Creed of Nicaea-Constantinople, we already took occasion to bring out that it is licit to adore distinctly the Father or the Son or the Spirit without explicitly mentioning the other two Persons, but that it is not licit to mention one of the three exclusively, that is one of the three Persons to the exclusion of the other two.[40]

Yet someone might object that the four actual anaphoras of the Latin rite do not bring out this ontological structure of coordinative doxology. This observation would be very correct. For St. Fulgentius dealt with a canon that was structured like the first of our actual anaphoras. His argumentation, which we took over, was based not on an explicit oblation of the Eucharistic sacrifice to the Son or to the Spirit—such an oblation was lacking in the liturgy with which he was dealing—but on the implicit destination of the oblation that was made explicitly to the Father. This argumentation of his has since then lost none of its validity.

There is however a liturgical formula which constantly recurs in the Ordinary of the Mass (but not in the canon, except at the end), which marvelously symbolizes a harmonious synthesis of the two doxologies and the two structures of the Mass with regard to the Trinitarian mystery: we

[39]*Ibid.*, 808.
[40]Cf. our ch. II, § IX, 4, p. 106.

are alluding to the concluding formula of the prayers: "through Our Lord Jesus Christ your Son who lives and reigns with you in the unity of the Holy Spirit, God forever and ever."

This is a singularly compact and rich formula, which St. Fulgentius analyzes at length. In it he sees at the same time the affirmation of the Priesthood of Christ the Mediator due to his human nature (*per Dominum N.J.C.*), and therefore the affirmation both of the Redemptive Incarnation and of the one divine nature of the Son, the Father and the Spirit (*qui tecum vivit et regnat in unitate Spiritus Sancti*). Because Christ is truly man we say: "through Jesus Christ"; and because he is truly God we add: "who lives and reigns with you forever and ever." There is thus a rejection both of Arianism which denies the divinity of Christ and of Manicheism which denies his real humanity. And lastly Fulgentius shows us in the light of St. Augustine that the *in unitate Spiritus sancti* does not merely signify the community of divine nature between the Spirit, the Son and the Father, it also signifies the Spirit's personal property, which is to be an interpersonal relation between the Father and the Son and their consubstantial and coeternal communion: *ne solum commune aliquid eorum, sed etiam communionem consubstantialem coaeternamque*. In a more immediate allusion to the conclusion of our prayers, *in unitate Spiritus,* Fulgentius recalls that for Augustine the Spirit is between the Father and the Son the unity of both, *unitas amborum*. In this mention Fulgentius sees an intent to affirm that the Son and the Spirit do not reign with the Father as inferiors with a superior. Rather "the unity of the Holy Spirit, who is the communion of the Father and the Son, shows the unity of the divinity at the same time that it inculcates the one eternity, power, majesty and domination of the reign of the sovereign Trinity."[41]

Let us take up again the thought of St. Fulgentius. For him the conclusion of the prayers of the Mass highlights, over against the Father to whom it is addressed, first of all the human nature of Christ the Mediator who is inferior to the Father under this respect, then his equality with the Father in the possession of the one divine nature, and lastly the Spirit as being the communion and equality and unity between Father and Son.

It is true that St. Fulgentius does not comment on one of the very last words of the conclusion of the prayers: "Our Lord Jesus Christ, who lives and reigns with you in the unity of the Holy Spirit, *God,* forever and ever." The original Latin text makes it even clearer that it is concerned with the Son and not with the Holy Spirit, for it is the Son's divinity that it wishes to bring out. Probably this clause did not exist at the time of St. Fulgentius. Today its presence indirectly manifests the Trinitarian destination of the

---

[41]St. Fulgentius, *Epist.* XIV, 36-38; *ML* 65, 424-427. For a different interpretation see B. Botte, O.S.B., *Maison-Dieu* no. 23 (1950) 49-53: "in unitate Spiritus Sancti."

Eucharistic oblation of the Church, but directly shows that the Church in its liturgy is careful to render an equal glory to the Father and to the Son who is eternally equal to his Father.

We have thus studied the active presence of the Trinity in the world as it stirs up the sacrificial cult offered to it, the cult that is the supreme exercise of the virtue of religion by which the world re-unites itself to God. Under this aspect the Mass is already a sign of the Trinity to which it is offered. But this sacrifice is consummated in Communion and now we must make it clear in what sense the Eucharistic Communion is Trinitarian. We already made a short allusion to this, but now we are going to look into this theme more deeply, aided by the very rich symbolism that is bound up with the cult rendered to the Heart of Jesus.

3. *The Eucharistic Heart of Jesus, symbol of the redemptive Trinity*

Let us recall in the light of Karl Rahner the general meaning of symbol so as to show in what sense the Heart of Jesus symbolizes the Trinity and what is the Trinitarian symbolism proper to the Eucharistic Heart of Jesus.

For Rahner the symbol is the intimate center of the person insofar as it reveals itself in corporeity and expresses itself in it. The symbol is not exterior to what it symbolizes, but it is a part of the symbolized reality and constituted by it, an element of this reality which reveals and manifests it and is full of it.[42] It is not an image but an icon.

a) The Heart of Jesus can thus be considered as the symbol or sacrament par excellence of the New Covenant, as the commemorative, demonstrative and "prefigurative" sign of the economy of the Redeemer's grace. It is the symbol of the divine Person of Jesus inserted into the history of men.

The Heart of Jesus commemorates the past cause of his grace, it shows the present reign of this divinizing and redemptive grace, and it prefigures the future glory to which his gratuitous love as Savior destines the elect.

It thus appears as the sign of the "composite person" of Jesus Christ, of this theandric Person. More precisely it appears as the sign of this Person as loving and as present in this Heart of flesh. As sign of the Person of the Incarnate Word it is by that fact itself the sign, instrument and tabernacle of the Father and of the Spirit who are eternally immanent in the only Son. And so the Heart of Jesus appears as the sign par excellence of the creative, sanctifying and glorifying love of the Father, the Son and the Holy Spirit for the human race. The mystery of circuminsession makes of the Heart of Jesus a Trinitarian symbol.

As a direct sign of the love of the Word and consequently of the love of

---

[42] K. Rahner, "Zur Theologie des Symbols,"*Cor Jesu*, I, Rome, 1960, p. 504.

the Father and the Spirit for humanity, the Heart of Jesus symbolizes not only the divine Persons as loving but also the one nature possessed diversely by them, a nature that is loving and lovable.

It symbolizes then the love that is uncreated and creative, divine, eternal and essential, the love which the Word in common with the Father and the Spirit bears for the human race.[43] In consequence Christ's Heart of flesh symbolizes also the eternal love of the divine Persons for their own proper and single nature and its infinite lovability. It symbolizes as well the necessary love of the Father, the Son and the Spirit for the archetypal ideas of all possible and real creatures, as also their free and merciful love and their preferential predestinating love for many of the spiritual creatures.

As wounded, forever, by the lance of the Roman soldier and that of our sins, this Heart symbolizes the offended love of the Creator and the loving satisfaction of Christ the Redeemer.

As a commemorative sign of the past manifestations of theandric love, the Heart of Jesus is also a "demonstrative" sign of the actually sanctifying love of the Trinity: for it signifies the state of grace that is inseparable from the charity which is poured out in the souls justified by the Holy Spirit, the bond and mutual love of the Father and the Son (cf. Rom. 5:5). It is a sign not only of God's love for men but also of men's love for God and for other men.[44] It is thus the sign of the triumph of the charity of Christ over human egoism (cf. Rom. 8:35-58).

Finally the risen Heart of Christ is also a "prognostic"[45] or annunciative sign of the glorified love and inamissible charity that the Spirit of the Father and Son will grant the predestined. The promise of final perseverance made by the Lord to St. Margaret Mary in favor of those who communicate with his Heart, both keeps alive his gospel promises (cf. Jn. 6:54), and is also in reality the promise of his perfect and imperishable friendship. The Heart of Jesus thus becomes a sign of the "absolute future" of sinful man, to use an expression of Rahner's.[46]

In short, by being the symbol of his divine Person made man in a sinful humanity, the Heart of Jesus recapitulates his past passion, his present sanctifying action and his perfect gift of himself in the future. It is the icon

---

[43]Cf. St. Thomas Aquinas, *Summa Theologica* III, 15.4; 18.6; and Pius XII, *Haurietis Aquas, Nouv. Rev. Théol.* 78 (1956), 646, 648.

[44]*Ibid.*, p. 743: "the cult of the Sacred Heart is substantially both the cult of the love with which God has loved us through Jesus and the practice of the love we have for God and for our neighbor."

[45]On the notion of commemorative, demonstrative and prognostic sign, see St. Thomas Aquinas, *Summa Theologica* III, 60.3; here we have partly drawn on L. Ciappi, O.P., "La SS. Trinità e il Cuore di Gesu," *Cor Jesu*, Rome, 1960, v. I, 117-147.

[46]K. Rahner, S.J., *Est-il aujourd'hui possible de croire.* Mame, Paris, 1966, pp. 170-177.

of the eternity and historicity of the incarnate and composite Person of the humanized Word, Son and Spirator. It is the icon[47] of the Trinity.

b) *The Eucharistic Heart of Jesus, icon of Trinitarian divinization*

As we have established elsewhere,[48] we can now define the object of the cult rendered to the Eucharistic Heart of Jesus:

> The Church, in adoring the Eucharistic Heart of Jesus, loves the act of love, historically past, by which our Redeemer instituted the sacrifice and sacrament of the Eucharist, and the double act of love that is eternal and actual, uncreated and divine, but also created, voluntary and sensible, a love that incites him to immolate himself now and perpetually to the Father by the hands of his priests for our salvation, and to remain ceaselessly among us in our tabernacles and to unite himself physically to each human person in Communion, so as to love today in us and by us all men with a sacrificial love.

All this the Eucharistic species of bread and wine symbolize, in that they really contain the human Heart of the Incarnate Word. The Eucharistic Heart of Jesus is thus the symbol of the divinizing action of the Father, the Son and the Spirit in and through the sacramental sacrifice of the Eucharist.

First of all the Eucharistic Heart of Jesus is the icon of the Father's love for us in his Son. In receiving Christ in the sacrament we also receive the Father: "do you not believe that I am in the Father and that the Father is in me?" (Jn. 14:10). The Father is totally, loving tendency toward the Son, *ad Filium*; this is also true in the holy Eucharist. The Father who draws us, without whom no one can come to the Son or believe in him (Jn. 6:44), after giving us faith in his Eucharistic Son, loves us and manifests himself to us in setting up his dwelling in us by means of the Eucharist. He loves us with a love that comes to reward our faith in his Son and the love for him which as Father he pours out in us through his Spirit (Jn. 14:23; 16:27; Rom. 5:5).

This Father, present in us by grace and by the Eucharist, says to us: "Here is my well-beloved Son in whom I am well pleased: hear him." In receiving in our Communions the Father of mercies (2 Cor. 1:3) together with the well-beloved Son, we renew ourselves in fidelity to our vocation of adoptive

---

[47] By icon we understand here an image that participates in the reality that it represents; cf. K. Rahner, *Cor Jesu*, I, 495: according to him there is a double concept of image in tradition: a more Aristotelian concept according to which the image is the external symbol of a separated reality, and another, more Platonic concept according to which the image participates in the reality that it represents, by establishing a more or less real presence of the represented datum which "dwells" in it.

[48] Cf. B. de Margerie, S.J., *Christ for the World*, ch. XIV, A; the definition we propose includes and expands that of Leo XIII cited by Pius XII, *Haurietis Aquas*, Nouv. Rev. Théol., 78 (1956), 746.

sons in the only Son. The Eucharistic thanksgiving ought then normally to involve thanksgiving to the Father, thanksgiving from the prodigal son who returns to the paternal home (cf. Lk. 15:21). Should we not reply to the Father: "Father, I have sinned against heaven and against you, I am not worthy to be called your son; but here is your well-beloved Son, in whom you are well pleased, hear his supplication for the conversion of the world and for my conversion."

Then the Eucharistic Heart of Jesus is the icon of the adoring love of the only Son for the Father. The sole adorer, the perfect adorer, the divine adorer, the infinite adorer—to use Cardinal Berulle's beautiful expressions—comes in us by Communion to complete his mysterious adoration. And he adores the very love of the Father for us. The Eucharistic Christ is totally *ad Patrem, in nexu Spiritus Sancti*. The love of the Son for the Father is the Holy Spirit. And the love of the Son for men, for us sinners, is totally finalized by his single love for the only Father: *per nos ad Patrem*, "that the world may know that I love the Father" (Jn. 14:31). Men are only the immediate, not the ultimate end of the love of the Eucharistic Heart of Jesus for his Father: as "I live because of the Father, so he who eats me will live because of me" (Jn. 6:57). In us communicants Jesus Christ recognizes and loves the gift that the Father has given to him of our persons (cf. Jn. 17:9, 24).

Lastly the Eucharistic Heart of Jesus is the icon of the love of the Holy Spirit for us. In receiving Jesus and his Father, we receive the single Spirator of the "Breath of love" who is the Spirit of the Father and of the Son, and we receive therefore this holy Breath as present in the Father and in the Son from whom he proceeds eternally. It is in drinking the Blood of the Lamb that we "were made to drink of one sole Spirit" (1 Cor. 12:13). Christ comes in us to give us the Fire of his Spirit, Fire of the mutual love between the Father and himself (cf. Lk. 12:49) and to kindle it in us.

This Spirit who is the mutual love of the Father and the Son, proceeds from the Father and from the Son as from one single principle. He is uniquely and simultaneously *ad Patrem et ad Filium* (while the Son is only *ad Patrem* and the Father *ad Filium*). As such he makes us aspire to the perfect and pure love in the vision of his procession *a Patre Filioque*. Communion with this holy Breath transforms us (unless there is an obstacle on our part) into "tongues of fire" that announce the triune Love so as to conduct other men to its loving vision. The Spirit received in drinking the Blood of the Lamb impels us to render a cult to the very love which, in unity of nature with the Father and the Son, he ceaselessly manifests toward all mankind, and impels us also to draw others to it.[49]

---

[49]*Ibid.*, 641: "the cult owed to the love of the august Trinity toward all men."

Conclusion
The Redemptive Trinity, Salvation and Beatitude of Men

In the Eucharist we encounter and receive not only the Son but also his Father and their Spirit. Already present in us by grace (when this is the case), they give themselves *within* us more abundantly *to* us, thanks to the flesh of Christ. We can then say with St. Bernard: "Blessed, most blessed Trinity: it is to you that my trinity of misery[50] aspires miserably in the unhappy exile in which I drag myself along."

The blessed Trinity alas is the Trinity that is scorned by the immense majority of the "trinities of misery," of the memories, the profane and profaning intelligences and liberties of men. Our Eucharistic adoration of the Trinity then necessarily takes the form of a reparation united to the renewed expiation of Calvary. The blood of the only Son has not only expiated—and superabundantly—the culpable ignorance and scorn of the Father and the Spirit on the part of so many men, but also and especially the blasphematory denial of the primordial mystery. To deny the eternal generation of the Son, as well as the procession of the Spirit from the Son and the Father is, in a sense, a blasphemy that is worse than the denial of the creative and provident God, worse than atheism. Does not God the Father receive an infinitely greater glory from the uncreated Son (and the latter from the Holy Spirit) than from the created world?[51]

Voluntary ignorance of the Trinitarian mystery in which man was destined to participate eternally by contemplation, is indeed the ruin and unhappiness of man. Inculpable ignorance of the Trinity is certainly not his ruin but it is his greatest unhappiness. Unawareness of the Trinitarian indwelling is, in a rational being who has attained the age of reason, a hindrance, to say the least, to the full development of the missions of the Son and the Spirit. For they are not fully sent and given unless they are recognized for what they are by those destined to be recipients[52] of the

---

[50]This text of St. Bernard, in his homilies on the Canticle of Canticles, Sermon XI, § 5, alludes to the effects of original and actual sin on the human faculties.

[51]St. Thomas Aquinas, *Summa contra Gentiles*, III, 118; Monsabré, Carême de 1874, conférence 10, *Exposition du Dogme catholique*, II, 208-209, citing William of Paris, *De Fide*, III.

[52]Cf. note 13.

divine sending. Or better: they are fully sent only when, by the abundant outpouring of infused charity and the gift of wisdom,[53] the Word and the Spirit manifest in the obscure light of faith their mysterious and eternal processions, which are presupposed and included in their twofold sending.[54] In contrast to this quasi-experience[55] of the Trinitarian mystery there is a Trinitarian unawareness that constitutes in many who are baptized the height of spiritual immaturity.

By taking a more reflexive view of the essentially Trinitarian character of the redemptive work that is renewed in the Eucharistic sacrifice, theologians will help many of the baptized who are thus lacking in spiritual maturity in regard to the Trinity, who are very imperfect images of the triune Love, to become its perfect likenesses.[56] The liturgical reform inaugurated by Vatican II marks a great step forward in this direction. But the reform will not produce its fruit of Christian and Trinitarian development if liturgical prayer alone is fostered: personal Trinitarian prayer must be added.

To develop the Trinitarian prayer of Christians means then to put oneself at the service of the missions of the Son and the Spirit, as far as these missions are the self-unfolding of their eternal processions to men who, as objects of divine benevolence, are consequently filled with good will (cf. Lk. 2:14 Gr.).

Now these missions are salvific missions. "In our Redemption, the Father and the Holy Spirit are, together with the Son, the cause of our salvation. ... Doubtless only the Son becomes man, is born, suffers, dies and rises again. But he would do none of this if he were not sent by his Father and he would accomplish nothing if he did not together with the Father send the Holy Spirit.... Salvation then in the strict sense of the word is a Trinitar-

---

[53] Cf. St. Thomas Aquinas, I St. d. 15, q. 4, a. 1: "in receptione hujusmodi donorum habentur personae divinae novo modo quasi ductrices in finem vel conjungentes."

[54] Cf. St. Thomas Aquinas, Summa Theologica I, 43.2.3 clarifying St. Augustine, De Trinitate, IV, XX, 29: "for the Holy Spirit, to be sent is to be known in his procession from the Father," a text that St. Thomas repeats substantially in I, 43.5.2 (cf. note 13). He even explicates a point which St. Augustine had not touched explicitly: the mission implies not only the knowledge but also the love of the eternal procession by the rational creature. We however have preferred to write in our text: "lack of awareness of the Trinitarian indwelling hinders the *full* development of the missions of the Son and of the Spirit," so as to safeguard the invisible mission and its reality in infants in the state of grace before reaching the age of reason, as well as the possibility of sanctifying grace in those who invincibly and inculpably are unaware of the mystery of the Trinity. This point deserves more profound study. Cf. H.-F. Dondaine, O.P., La Trinité. Paris, 1962, v. II, pp. 451-452.

[55] St. Thomas Aquinas, Summa Theologica I, 43.5.2: "perceptio enim experimentalem quamdam notitiam significat."

[56] St. Bonaventure, Breviloquium, 5.1.3; "Dei similitudo quae est divinae imaginis perfectio deiformis," cf. Olegario Gonzalez, Misterio trinitario y existencia humana. Madrid, 1966, pp. 58-603.

ian work. The action of the three divine Persons is one identical salvation which each of them achieves by a personal gift," as F. Taymans d'Eypernon wrote.[57]

Salvation is the self-giving on the part of the Trinity, inaugurated at baptism. The plenitude of Redemption is the definitive consummation of this self-giving. Between this beginning and this consummation of our Trinitarian Redemption, we are always, to use Tertullian's phrase, more and more "debtors of the Three," of the Three "who vouch for our salvation" (*sponsores salutis*).[58] The Trinitarian grace of baptism is entirely polarized by the Trinitarian manifestation that is daily renewed in the reception of the Eucharist. The same "faith in the Trinity which brings us the grace of the remission of sins"[59] in Baptism, also brings it to us through the sacraments of Penance and the Eucharist. Just as, to use the words of St. Fulgentius, "the mystery of human Redemption is not at all accomplished if the name of the Son or the Spirit is omitted in Baptism,"[60] so it would be impossible to renew it with a view to its fuller[61] accomplishment if the Mass were not at least implicitly offered to the Son and to the Spirit. For the self-giving of the Trinity to man is at its fullest only within man's basic self-giving to the Trinity.

There is then in every human soul as ontologically triune (by memory, intelligence and freedom) a natural desire to see the Trinity which this vision alone can satisfy, as St. Bonaventure perceived so well: "nothing less than the Trinity can fill the soul that is capable of the entire Trinity.... Beatitude satisfies our appetite, yet nothing satisfies the thirst of the human soul but the Trinity."[62] The soul deprived of the Trinity does violence to itself. It is empty of Those without whom it cannot be fully itself but is rather alienated with the worst of alienations.

We can understand then why the Church declared incapable of absolution one who through culpable negligence would be ignorant of the mystery of the Trinity (cf. *DS* 2164; *DB* 1214), even if he had believed it before (*DS* 2165; *DB* 1215). And that holds true even in danger of death. The promise of a dying person still capable of hearing an explanation of the mystery, that he will take instruction about this mystery after his convalescence, is not enough: to be able to baptize him the missionary must explain the mystery to him (*DS* 2380; *DB* 1349a). This is what the Church specified

---

[57] F. Taymans d'Eypernon, S.J., *Sainte Trinité et Sacrements*. Bruges, 1949, p. 17.
[58] Tertullian, *De Oratione* 25; *De Baptismo*, 6.
[59] St. John Chrysostom, *Catéchèses baptismales*, 8th catechesis, 2.26, ed. Wenger. Paris, 1957.
[60] St. Fulgentius, *Epist*. 8.9; ML 65, 269.
[61] Cf. *LG* 17: "sacerdotis tamen est aedificationem Corporis sacrificio eucharistico perficere."
[62] St. Bonaventure, *I Sent*. d. 1, a. 3, q. 2, fund. 3; *IV Sent*. d. 49, p. 1, a. 1, q. 1, fund. 1; cf. O. Gonzalez, *op cit.*, p. 595.

in a decision of 1703 that was renewed in 1896. If he is at the point of death however, it is licit to baptize or absolve conditionally one who does not have an explicit faith in the mystery of the Trinity, if he is incapable of hearing an explanation of it.[63] Explicit faith in this mystery is thus necessary with a relative necessity of means; in case of impossibility implicit faith is enough.

The Church thus judges it must do all it can in order that the death of every man may be an act of union of his freedom with the Trinity, a "Trinitarian death," an ultimate profession of faith in the Father, the Son and the Spirit. Man's existence ought to correspond to—and develop to its ultimate limit—the Trinitarian structure of his essence; the miserable trinity ought to become perfectly happy by an ultimate adherence to the uncreated Trinitarian Beatitude.

The man who lives in the expectation of the perfect manifestation of the triune Love already anticipates here below his eternal Trinitarian life. His light is the Word, this word which the Father utters in eternity. But the Word is not a light enkindled outside his mind, it is an infinite light which shines interiorly in his soul. In this light he sees the Father in the dark clarity of faith, because this light is the splendor of the Father: "who sees me, sees my Father" (Jn. 14:9); in this light he also sees the Holy Spirit who proceeds from him. In this light he contemplates himself entirely illumined by it.[64]

Man who in his body is a vestige, and in his divinized soul an image of this Trinity that dwells within him, becomes always more and more its likeness. But only in the very heart of the vision will he fully achieve this likeness: "now we are children of God; and what we will be is not yet manifest. We know that at the time of this manifestation we shall be like him, because we will see him as he is" (1 Jn. 3:2).

With St. Gregory of Nazianzus the Christian knows that it is impious not to speak of the Trinity yet rash to speak too much of it. So he concludes his Trinitarian discourse in a prayer, in a doxology[65] to the redemptive Trinity:

> Glory to the Father who has delivered his Son for our redemption.
> Adoration to the Son who died on the Cross and who gives us life.
> Thanksgiving to the Spirit to whom we owe the initiative, the carrying out and the consummation of our redemption.
> May the Trinity that transcends all that is in the universe have mercy on us.

[63]Cf. A. Michel, *DTC* XV, 2 (1950), 1826-1827: art. "Trinté"; Prümmer, *Man. Theol. mor.*, v. I, § 499.

[64]Here we draw on Bossuet, "Sermon sur la sainte Trinité," 2nd point.

[65]A prayer read in the Aramaean language during the conciliar assembly of the 2nd Council of the Vatican, Sept. 25, 1964; see G. Baraúna, *A Igreja do Vaticano II*. Petrópolis, Brazil, 1965, p. 380.

INDEXES

I

Names of Authors*

Abbott, E. A., 16.
Abelard, 194.
Adnes, xviii n. 6.
Adrian I, Pope, 165, 168, 175.
Alacoque, M.-M., 347.
Alain de Lille, 196.
Alberigo, 107.
Albright, W. W. F., 13.
Aldama, J.-A. de (S.J.), 239.
Alès, A. d', 83, 84.
Alexander VIII, Pope, 314.
Alfaro, P., 140, 141.
Allo, 204.
Alphonsus de Liguori, St., 205.
Alszeghy, Z. (S.J.), 119.
Amann, E., 101, 165.
Ambrose, St., 34-44, 194, 307.
Amphilochius of Iconium, 213.
Anselm of Canterbury, St., 139, 172, 316-318.
Aquinas, Thomas, see Index IV.
Arendzen, J. P., 73.
Aristotle, 123, 135, 136, 279, 280.
Arius (Arians, Arianism), 62 n. 17, 63 80, 85, 87-91, 93, 99-104, 120, 125, 128, 129, 134-137, 147, 151, 156-158, 161, 165, 175, 181, 183, 193, 194, 269, 273, 275, 339, 345.
Arnou, R., 114, 123, 124, 134, 135.
Athanasius, St., 86, 88, 90, 94, 95, 97, 99, 100, 102, 109, 121, 128, 132, 135, 165, 176, 341.
Athenagoras, 60, 63, 83, 103.
Augustine, St., see Index V.
Bacciochi, J. de, 86.
Bailleux, E., 187, 188, 195.
Balthasar, Hans Urs von, 22, 192.
Barauna, 223, 353.
Bardy, G., 16, 85-88, 90-92, 99-102, 107, 128.
Bareille, G., 87, 104.
Barth, K., 111, 178, 199, 212-217, 219, 220, 320.
Bartmann, B., 213.
Basil, St., 31, 34, 55, 99-104, 106-108, 123-126, 128-130, 132, 133, 137, 142, 144, 159, 164, 181, 203, 213, 219, 339, 343.
Basilides, 70.
Baum, Gregory (O.S.B.), 10.
Behm, H., 32, 34, 36, 59, 63.
Benedict XIV, Pope, 168, 314.

---

*This index comprises a list of some of the more important authors mentioned in the text.

Benoît, P., 42, 58.
Bernard, St., 24, 26, 27, 29, 30, 194, 350.
Bernard, J.-H., 143.
Berrouard, 35.
Berry, L. Don, 178.
Berulle, Cardinal de, 349.
Betge, E., 98.
Betz, O., 32, 34, 37, 38.
Bloch, E., 92, 263.
Blondel, 252.
Boethius, 213, 219, 268.
Boismard, M.-E. (O.P.), 20.
Bonaventure, St., 19, 152, 183, 212, 214, 220, 270, 272, 273, 305, 307, 316, 351, 352.
Bonhoeffer, D., 98, 99.
Bonsirven, J. (S.J.), 143.
Bossuet, 197, 254, 294, 314, 353.
Boularand, E. (S.J.), 88.
Boulgakoff, S., 45, 86, 111, 119, 166, 174.
Bourassa, F. (S.J.), 46, 118, 293, 304, 318-322.
Bouyer, L., 146, 198, 341.
Boyer, C. (S.J.), 160, 264, 299, 300, 303, 305.
Braun, F. M. (O.P.), xx, 12, 23, 32, 143.
Brown, R. E. (S.S.), 23, 32-38, 156.
Bruaire, C., 257.
Bussche, H. Van den, 143, 338.
Buzy, D., 53.
Caffarel, H., 288, 289.
Caillat, M., 151.
Cajetan, St., 16.
Calmet, Dom, 10.
Camelot, P.-T. (O.P.), 41, 42, 58, 59, 65, 79, 111, 115.
Cappadocian (Fathers), 102, 106, 123-126, 129, 133, 134-136, 142, 152, 162, 193, 213, 214, 220.
Cassien, Mgr., 174.
Catherinet, Mgr. F.-M., 10, 11.
Cerfaux, L., 38.
Cerinthus, 87, 89.
Cerularius, Michael, 166.

Ceuppens, P. F. (O.P.), 46, 47.
Chaine, S., 11.
Chambat, Dom L. (O.S.B.), 189.
Chapelle, A. (S.J.), 213, 257-260.
Charrue, Mgr., 225, 268.
Chevalier, I., 136, 137, 145.
Chiettini, E., 182.
Chollet, A., 106, 185.
Chrysostom, St. John, 93, 352.
Ciappi, L. (O.P.), 347.
Claret, St. A.-M., 97.
Clement of Alexandria, 91.
Clement (Epistle), 145.
Clément, O., 174, 175.
Comeau, M., 245.
Confucius, xvii.
Congar, Y.-M. (O.P.), xviii, 146, 216, 229-235.
Constantine, 89.
Contieri, D. N., 174.
Cornelis, E. (O.P.), 65, 66, 68.
Crowe, F. E. (S.J.), xxi, xxii.
Cullmann, O., 13, 15, 16, 41, 42, 83.
Cyprian, St., 60, 117, 225.
Cyril of Alexandria, St., 18, 21, 24, 29, 105, 109, 111, 143, 162, 163, 165, 168, 176.
Cyril of Jerusalem, St., 193.
Damasus, St., 106, 107, 131.
Daniélou, J., xvii, 63-65, 67, 72, 75, 106, 144, 145, 259.
Deblaere, A. (S.J.), 255.
Decloux, S., 263.
Delitzch, F., 38.
Deneffe, A. (S.J.), 182.
Denifle-Ehrlé, 249, 250.
Denis, Leon, 264, 265.
Denis Bar Salibi, 341, 342.
Descartes, 212, 267.
Dewart, L., 93.
Didache, 145.
Didymus the Blind, 45.
Diekamp, F., 215.
Diepen, Dom (O.S.B.), 34.
Dieringer, F.-X., 31.
Dion, H.-M. (O.P.), 32, 33, 34, 37, 38.

Dionysius of Alexandria, 85, 135.
Dionysius of Rome, St., 85-87, 179.
Dodd, C. H., 144, 154.
Dognin, P.-D. (O.P.), 263.
Doms, 280.
Dondaine, H.-F. (O.P.), 126, 159, 182, 195, 300, 306, 308, 310, 326 328, 336, 351.
Duchesne, Mgr., 207, 208.
Duns Scotus (Scotism), 152, 199, 200, 201, 281, 316.
Dupont, Dom (O.S.B.), 205, 206.
Duquoq, P.-C. (O.P.), 39.
Durrwell, F.-X. (C.SS.R.), 75.
Dusen, H. P. Van, 198.
Duval, A., 249.
Eckhart, Master, 249-252, 255, 256, 258.
Ehlinger, Ch., 236.
Elizabeth of the Trinity, Sister, xvii.
Ephraem the Syrian, St., 275.
Epiphanius, St., 24, 68, 86, 111, 162, 163, 165, 176.
Eulogius, 174.
Eusebius, 87, 88.
Evagrius Ponticus, 122-125.
Evdokimov, 174.
Felten, 204.
Feret, H.-M. (O.P.), 16.
Feuerbach, 262, 263.
Feuillet, A. (S.S.), 17, 44, 119.
Fichte, 257.
Fonck, L. (S.J.), 208.
Ford, J. C., 278.
Francis of Assisi, St., 234.
Franks, R. S., 4, 13.
Fransen, P. (S.J.), 254.
Franzelin, J.-B. (S.J.), 139, 185, 229, 266, 267.
Froidevaux, L., 87.
Fromm, E., 92, 265.
Fulgentius, St., 25, 29, 30, 104, 120, 151, 178, 179, 181, 182, 184, 185, 203, 342-345, 352.
Fulliquet, G., 74.
Gagnebet, T. R. P. (O.P.), 220.

Galot, P. (S.J.), 148.
Galtier, P. (S.J.), 3, 108.
Garrigues, J.-M. (O.P.), 112.
Gay, Mgr., xxii.
Geiselmann, J. R., 98.
Germinius of Sirmium, 62.
Ghellinck, J. de, (S.J.), 58, 62, 103.
Gill, J. (S.J.), 168.
Gilson, E., 249.
Gonzalez, Olegario, 124, 305, 308, 351, 352.
Grégoire, J., 324.
Gregory the Great, St., 165, 166.
Gregory of Nazianzus, St., 3, 101, 102, 104-107, 110, 130, 133, 135, 152, 159, 275, 276, 278-280, 286, 353.
Gregory of Nyssa, St., xviii, 6, 37, 55, 56, 105-107, 111, 124, 139, 142, 144, 193.
Gregory Thaumaturgus, St., 87, 101.
Grumel, V., 314.
Guerra, Blessed Helen, 234.
Guerry, Mgr. E., 148.
Guggenberger, A., 128, 219.
Guillet, J. (S.J.), xx, 18, 20-22.
Guitton, J., 158.
Günther, A., 212, 213, 249, 259, 265-268.
Gutwenger, E. P. (S.J.), xx, 218, 219.
Haanappel, B. G., 207, 208.
Hadot, P., 112, 113, 271.
Hamman, A. (O.F.M.), 51-54, 76.
Harnack, A., 11, 68, 93, 123, 252.
Hausherr, I. (S.J.), 203.
Hegel, G. W. (Hegelian), 65, 67, 213, 249, 251, 257-266.
Heidegger, M., 134, 158.
Henoch (Ethiopian), 33.
Henry, A.-M. (O.P.), 120.
Henry, P. (S.J.), 113, 153, 220, 253-255, 266.
Hermas, 64.
Hessen, 260.
Hilary, St., 3, 12, 82, 89, 114, 115, 139, 153, 156-158, 181, 182, 273.
Hodgson, L., xvii, xx, 110, 122, 126.

Hormisdas, St., 165.
Huby, P. (S.J.), 155.
Hippolytus, 341.
Ignatius of Antioch, St., 104
Ignatius of Loyola, St., 4, 232, 234.
Imschoot, P. van, 5.
Innocent III, Pope, 146.
Innocent XII, Pope, 151.
Irenaeus, St., 1, 5, 22, 34, 58, 60, 62, 63, 65-72, 80, 87, 95, 101, 142, 198.
Isaac, J. (O.P.), 4, 8, 9, 16, 17, 19, 36.
Isidore of Seville, 203.
Jacquemet, G., 280.
Jacquier, 204.
Jeremias, J., 7.
Jerome, St., 38, 62, 107, 129.
Joachim of Flora, 138, 139, 253, 293.
John XXIII, Pope, 98, 234, 295.
John Damascene, St., 182, 183, 213, 287, 315, 323.
John of St. Thomas (O.P.), 317, 319.
John of the Cross, St., 203, 224, 243, 249, 255, 256.
Johnson, A. R., 4.
Journet, Ch., 333.
Joussard, 87.
Jugie, M. (A.A.), 242.
Jungmann, 61.
Justin, St., 83.
Kannengiesser, Ch. (S.J.), 13.
Kant, E., 95.
Kelly, J. N. D., 88, 105, 213, 278.
Kephales, Mgr. Nectaire, 175.
Kipper, P. B. (S.J.), xxi, 28.
Kloppenburg, B. (O.F.M.), 264, 265.
Koehler, T., 254, 256.
Kredel, E. M., 326.
Kremos, 175.
Kuncievicz, St. J., 173.
Lagrange, M.-J. (O.P.), 14, 46, 75, 82, 155, 170, 326.
Lalande, 252.
Lambertini (Benedict XIV), 314.
La Potterie, J. de (S.J.), 16, 35, 36, 55, 155, 156.
Laufer, F., xxi.

Laurentin, R., 87.
Lavocat, M.-H. (O.P.), 293.
Leal, J. (S.J.), 204.
Lebreton, J. (S.J.), 9, 41, 47, 58, 60, 66-72, 85.
Le Camus, Mgr., 206.
Lécuyer, J. (C.S.S.P.), 12
LeGuillou, M.-J. (O.P.), 12, 172, 174, 178, 269, 318, 319.
Lemonnyer, P.-A. (O.P.), 206-207.
Leo the Great, St., 165, 166.
Leo III, Pope, 166.
Leo XIII, Pope, 106, 151, 194, 234, 242, 313, 317, 348.
Lepargneur, F. (O.P.), 212.
Lesêtre, J., 7.
Lessing, 257, 259.
Lombard (Peter), 139.
Lonergan, B. (S.J.), xvii, xxi, 43, 68, 93, 94, 97, 126, 138, 140, 141, 169, 213-216, 267, 274, 297, 311, 313, 331.
Longpré, E. (O.F.M.), 212.
Losski, 174, 175.
Luther, M. (Lutherans), 95, 199-204, 251, 316, 319, 320.
Lyonnet, S. (S.J.), 53, 105, 204, 205.
Macédonius, 100, 101.
Malet, A., 113, 139.
Malevez, L. (S.J.), 15, 16, 84.
Marchel, W., 10.
Marcion, 70.
Maréchal, J. (S.J.), 260.
Margerie, B. de (S.J.), xviii, 5, 176, 198, 348.
Maritain, J., 255, 256.
Marlé, R., 99.
Marx, K., xvii, 69, 92, 262-265.
Massabki, Dom C. (O.S.B.), 141, 289.
Maximus the Confessor, 213.
McDonnell, K. (O.S.B.), 204.
Medebielle, 204.
Mellet, 111, 115.
Methodius of Olympus, 274, 275.
Michel, A., 212, 266-268, 353.
Miguens, M. (O.F.M.), 32, 35, 36, 38.
Mohammed, xvii.

Moingt, J. (S.J.), 78, 80, 81, 83, 85.
Monchanin, J., 6.
Monsabre, P., 350.
Mühlen, H., 56, 218, 280-286.
Nautin, 61.
Nédoncelle, M., 218, 303, 304, 306.
Nemeshegyi, P. (S.J.), 75.
Nestorius, 82.
Nicolas, M. J. (O.P.), 149.
Niel, 260.
Nissiotis, N., 174, 175.
Noulleau, 153.
Novatian, 72.
Nygren, 316.
Ochagavia, J. (S.J.), 72.
Oeschlin, 249.
Oltra, M., 152.
Orbe, P. (S.J.), 66, 67, 175, 259, 274, 290.
Origen, 63, 67, 75, 76, 89, 93, 128.
Ortiz de Urbina, I. (S.J.), 75, 76, 89, 91, 99, 124, 125.
Palamas, G., 242.
Palmieri, A. (S.J.), 55, 105, 162, 165, 166, 168, 175.
Patfoort, P., 285.
Paul, St., 22, 25, 26, 39, 46, 47, 49-55, 159, 168, 206-210, 220, 222, 224, 225, 233, 234, 265, 276, 277, 289, 290, 295, 307, 322, 325, 326, 332.
Paul VI, Pope, xx, 96, 103, 121, 146, 159, 168, 197, 199, 220, 224, 231, 235, 238-244, 313, 317, 335, 336.
Paulinus of Aquilaea, 165, 166.
Pazzi, St. M.-M. de, 205.
Petau, 31.
Philippon, (O.P.), 47, 60, 223, 225, 228, 229.
Philon, 13, 38.
Photius, 163-167, 170, 172.
Piaget, 94, 97.
Piault, B., 78, 79, 82-85, 164.
Pius VI, Pope, 158, 314.
Pius IX, Pope, 266.
Pius XII, Pope, 76, 77, 177, 229, 230, 242, 284, 285, 313, 317, 335, 347

Pinto de Oliveira, C. J. (O.P.), 291.
Plato (Platonism), 13, 15, 126, 263, 272, 275, 276.
Plotinus, 68, 71, 111, 113, 114, 250.
Porphyry, 111, 113, 114, 250.
Prat, F. (S.J.), 13, 206, 207.
Praxéas, 73, 78, 83.
Preiss, T., 35.
Prenter, R., 201, 202, 203.
Prestige, G.L., 80, 93, 122, 183, 185, 213.
Pruche, B. (O.P.), 100, 101, 103.
Prummer, 353.
Pujol, A., 45.
Puyol, 203.
Racette, J. (S.J.), 302, 303.
Rahner, K. (S.J.), xvii, 46, 60, 65, 78, 199, 212, 216-220, 269, 304, 313, 346-348.
Refoulé, F. (O.P.), 337.
Régnon, T. de (S.J.), 162.
Rénié, 204.
Reuter, A. (O.M.I.), 278.
Richard of St. Victor, 26, 27, 294, 316, 318.
Rondet, H. (S.J.), 257-260, 266.
Rossi, Cardinal A., 212.
Roy, O. du, 44, 112, 114.
Rufinus, 131.
Ruysbroeck, Blessed, 220, 243, 249, 252-256, 266.
Sabbe, M, 55.
Sabellius (Sabellianism), 73, 74, 85, 130, 259.
Sagnard, F.-M.-M. (O.P.), 65.
Salaville, S., 341.
Scheeben, M. J., 18, 19, 24, 25, 29-32, 186, 213, 268-270, 273, 280, 328, 331.
Scheffzyk, L., 68.
Scheler, M., 316.
Schillebeeckx, E. (O.P.), 42, 62.
Schleiermacher, F., 67, 213.
Schmaus, M., 14, 89, 130, 140, 141, 147, 286, 303.
Schneider, B. (O.F.M.), 105.

Schuler, B., 278.
Sciacca, M. F., 264, 297, 298.
Scott, E. P., 16.
Séjourne, P., 271.
Serapion of Thmuis, 102, 341.
Sesboue, B. (S.J.), 132.
Sickenberger, 204.
Slipyj, Cardinal J., 174.
Smulders, P. (S.J.), 114, 117, 118, 157, 181.
Spicq, C. (O.P.), 16, 32, 209, 210.
Spinoza, 257.
Spitz, R. (O.P.), 204, 209.
Starcky, J., 13.
Stauffer, E., 284.
Suarez, F. (S.J.), 28, 29, 150, 151, 185.
Suso, H. (O.P.), 251.
Swete, H. B., 39, 230.
Tarasius, St., 165, 168, 175.
Tatian, 83.
Taymans d'Epernon (S.J.), 352.
Tertullian, 6, 62, 67, 73, 78-85, 89, 93, 95, 97, 101, 122, 127, 129, 161, 175, 187, 190, 254, 260, 274, 292, 337, 352.

Theophilus of Antioch, 85, 127.
Théry, 249.
Thurian, M., 342.
Tillard, J.-M.-R. (O.P.), xxi, 306, 309, 310.
Tromp, S. (S.J.), 232, 285.
Urban VIII, Pope, 151.
Valentinus, 66, 67, 70.
Vaux, R. de (O.P.), 36.
Veccos, J., 167.
Vergara, J. (S.J.), 112, 271.
Verkovski, 174.
Vernet, F., 250.
Victorinus, Marius, 111-114, 270-273.
Vignaux, P., 200, 201, 203, 316, 319.
Walz (O.P.), 249.
Wenger, A. (A. A.), 221.
Widmert, G. P., 73, 74, 184, 185, 218.
William of Paris, 350.
Witasse, Ch., 215, 216.
Witte, J. L. (S.J.), 204.
Wolfson, H. A., 13.
Wulf, M. de, 250.

II

Biblical Citations

OLD TESTAMENT

Genesis

1	12
1:1	12
1:26	4, 297, 307
1:26-27	276, 290, 297, 307
1:27	277
2:7	20, 21
3:22	4
5:1-3	307
6:3	20, 22
6:17	20
7:22	20
9:6	307
11:6	4
11:7	4
16:7	38
26:35	22
41:8	22

Exodus

4:22-23	7
15:8-10	20
23:21	143

Numbers

6:27	143
11:29	212

Deuteronomy

19:18	34

2 Samuel

7	8

2 Kings

17:27-33	6

Job

7:11	22
16:19	38
19:25-27	38
26:10-13	20
33:23	38

Psalms

2	8
9:10	36
21:1	10
21:23	10
33:6	20
35	36
51:11	20
53:9-14	23
56:5	22
89	8
104:4	20
109	36
139:7	20
143:10	23
148:8	20

Proverbs

8	12
14:5	34

Canticle of Canticles

1:2	30
2:14	119
5:2	119

Wisdom

1:3-8	34
1:7	14
2:11	34
2:13-20	7
4:20	34
5:4-5	7
7	12
7:22-25	23
7:24	272
7:25-26	14
7:26	80
9	12
9:17	23
16:12-26	12
18:14-19	12

Ecclesiasticus (Sirach)

1	12
22:27	8
23:1-6	8
24	12
24:32-35	12
51:7	36

Isaiah

1:2-4	7
6:8	4
7:14	8
8:8-10	8
9:5	8
11:1	23
11:4	12, 20
30:1	23
30:27-28	20
32:15-17	24
42:1ff.	23
44:2-3	24
51:9-10	20
55:10	12
61:1-2	24

Jeremiah

3:19-22	7
17:5	22

Osee

11:1-4	7

Joel

3:1-2	212

Zechariah

3:1ff.	33
12:10	201

Malachi

2:10	7
3:6	272

NEW TESTAMENT

Matthew

3:11	19
3:17	41
3:28-30	19
5:7	61
5:43-48	8
5:48	336
7:11	19
7:21	9
8:27ff.	53
10:19-20	38
11:25	52
11:25-27	9, 45
11:27	61, 268
12:45	19
14:33	61
16:16	61
17:5	41
18:10	37
18:19-20	340
25:31-36	50
28:17	39
28:18-20	39
28:19	39, 43, 44, 45, 53-55, 57, 61, 142, 144, 145, 222, 322

Indexes

Mark

1:10	237
1:40	53
3:11	19
3:22	19
3:28-30	19
8:17	17
10:18	75
14:36	9
14:38	22
14:55-59	34

Luke

1:35	45
2:14	351
3:22	109, 120
4:1	19
4:1-2	109
4:18	24, 244
5:1	329
5:18	329
6:19	119
8:46	119
9:34-35	45
10:18	38
10:21ff.	45, 109
11:1	56
11:13	19, 55, 340
12:49	349
14:16-21	19
14:32	326
15:21	349
15:31	295
21:15	35, 38
23:46	18, 22
24:49	34, 325

John

1:1	1, 12, 99, 331
1:1-2	16
1:1-3	xx, 77
1:2	156, 179, 183
1:3	173
1:3-4	253
1:3-10	15
1:4	14
1:9	14
1:9-11	99
1:10	179, 180
1:12	11
1:13	109
1:14	22, 99
1:15	37
1:18	3, 11, 16, 156, 159, 179, 183, 245, 294, 312
1:29-34	87
1:32	120
1:33	19
2:16	10
2:19	343
2:22	18, 39
3:5	109
3:5-8	20
3:6	22, 119, 314
3:10	11
3:11	311
3:16	3, 159, 245
3:19	33
3:31	89
3:32	311
3:34	338
4:7-14	115
4:21	6
4:21-24	6
4:22	282
4:23	54
4:23-24	51, 150
4:24	24, 314
5	92
5:8	109
5:17	10
5:18	89
5:22ff.	33
5:23	51, 76
5:30	311
5:31ff.	41
5:36-38	338
6:29	338
6:32	10
6:44	348
6:54	347
6:57	156, 338, 347, 349

6:60	36, 311	13:1	61, 331
6:63	22, 119	13:3	153, 331, 338
7:4-5	329	13:20	340
7:7	35	13-21	22
7:13	109	13:36	338
7:28-29	153	14	18, 145
7:29	338	14:1-7	45
7:38-39	80	14:6	331
8	92	14:8	18, 152
8:14	45, 153, 155, 338	14:8-14	45
8:16	281	14:9	17, 353
8:21	338	14:9ff.	182, 183
8:23	89, 153, 338	14:9-10	179
8:26	311	14:10	311, 340, 348
8:26-27	145	14:10-11	179
8:28	109, 311	14:11	180
8:28-29	338	14:13	56, 340
8:31	33, 311, 312	14:13-14	51
8:34-37	11	14:14	76
8:41	10	14:15-17	45
8:42	10, 147, 153, 338	14:16	17, 18, 32, 36, 56, 61, 81, 145, 240, 282, 340
8:43-47	311		
8:46	35	14:16-17	32
8:47	311	14:16-18	34
8:49	51	14:16-26	325
8:58	17	14:17	311, 340
10	92	14:18-21	45
10:10	21	14:20	179, 180
10:15	185	14:21	329
10:18	18	14:21-23	243, 333
10:30	30, 61, 171, 179	14:21-26	337
10:32	179	14:22-24	45
10:33	89	14:23	282, 325, 329, 348
10:36	338	14:23-26	311
10:38	179, 183	14:24	311
11:11	282	14:25-26	45
11:33	22	14:26	17, 18, 32, 37, 39, 102, 109, 282, 337
11:41	52		
11:41-42	340	14:28	64, 81, 82
11:42	338	14:30	185
11:52	11	14:31	349
12:16	18	15:4-10	11
12:28	144	15:7-8	312, 340
12:31	33	15:9	185
12:47-49	12	15:16	56
12:48	311	15:17	45, 108

15:22	35	17:22	xx n. 12, 293
15:26	3, 24, 25, 32, 105, 133, 162, 165, 169, 170, 171, 178, 312, 325, 340	17:22-26	48
		17:23	256, 338
		17:23-24	49
15:26ff.	33	17:24	72, 255, 349
15:26-27	34	17:25	388
16	18, 145	17:26	56
16:7	3, 24, 25, 102, 312, 340	18:37	33
16:7-13	32	19:30	18, 22
16:8	35	19:31-37	87
16:8-11	32-36	19:34	119
16:9	35	19:34-37	87
16:12	17, 36	20:9	18
16:13	36, 37, 169, 244	20:17	10, 282
16:13-14	36, 37, 230	20:21	230, 334, 338
16:13-15	109, 169, 171, 311, 312	20:21-22	230
16:14	102, 171, 245	20:21-23	334, 335
16:14-15	170, 271	20:22	109, 119, 169
16:15	170	20:22-23	18, 21, 22, 29
16:16	230	20:23	30
16:17	230	20:31	14
16:23-27	340		
16:27	338, 348	*Acts*	
16:27-28	171	1:5	231
16:27-30	338	1:6	39
16:28	61, 153, 338	1:12	39
16:30	17	2:2-3	20
16:32	281	2:2-4	204
17	215	2:4	204-206, 208, 211, 212
17:1	51, 56	2:6	206
17:2	xx n. 12	2:11	205
17:3	xx n. 12, 49, 338	2:17	40, 44
17:5	56, 72, 144	2:21	44
17:6	144	2:33	34, 40, 42, 43, 55, 56, 63
17:8	171, 311, 338	2:36	75
17:9	349	2:36-38	35
17:10	76, 295	2:38	40
17:11	xx n. 12	2:41	35
17:11-12	142, 143	2:42	40
17:11-13	331	2:44-45	296
17:17	54	3:12-19	35
17:21	xx n. 12, 179, 180, 183, 254, 256, 281, 282, 295, 338	4:4	35
		4:8	34
17:21-22	56, 227, 292	4:12	44
17:21-23	179, 289	4:13	35
17:21-26	48, 340	4:26	52

4:29-30	52	8:5-13	19
4:31	34, 204	8:8-15	86
4:32	26, 294	8:9	25
5:32	34, 109	8:11	45
5:33	35	8:14-15	55
6:10	35	8:15	53, 54, 284
7:51	35	8:26	201, 202, 208
7:51-57	35	8:26-27	37, 53, 54
7:59-60	52	8:34	340
8	234	8:35-38	347
8:14-17	204	11:34	109
8:20	115	11:36	50, 131
8:36-38	59	12:4-8	208
8:37	63	13:1	75
10:19	109	13:1-7	93
10:38	142	16:25-27	51
10:44-46	205	*1 Corinthians*	
10:44-48	204, 208, 234	2	41
10:45	40	2:8	51
10:46	206	2:9-10	49
10:47	39, 234	2:10	xx, 30, 237
11:15	206	2:10-11	209
13:2-4	109	2:10-12	48, 109
15:28	285	3:16	55, 231
16:6-7	234	4:21	28
16:14	230	6:17	28, 182
16:30-32	59	6:19	55, 231, 343
17:22-34	5	7:7	233
17:26-27	6	8:4	6, 90
17:27-28	179, 180	8:5-6	6
19:2-5	40	8:6	131
19:5-6	204, 208	8:14	309
19:6	205, 206, 209	10:14	208
20:28	109	11	207, 208, 290
Romans		11:3	277
1:2	304	11:7	276, 277, 307
1:4	75	11:18	208
1:8	52	11:22	208
1:14	174	11:33	208
2:4	288	12	204
5:5	19, 45, 47, 115, 256, 295, 331, 347, 348	12:2	209
		12:3	53, 208
8	41, 44	12:4-6	44, 193
8:2-13	22	12:7	208, 209, 233
8:4-10	244	12:10	212

12:10-11	209	3:17-18	105
12:10-30	208	7:2-4	296
12:11	233	12:1-4	211
12:12-13	284, 340	12:8	53
12:13	208, 284, 349	12:18	26, 28
12:20	208	13:12	26
12:28	206	13:13	26, 27, 45, 47, 49, 198
12:30	212		
13:1	207	*Galatians*	
14	204, 205, 207-210	1:1	3
14:2	207, 209, 210	1:3-5	50
14:2-5	205	1:8-9	99
14:3	209	3:13	99
14:4	208	3:26	11
14:5-6	206-208, 210, 212	3:28	307
14:5-10	206	4:4	327, 329
14:8	209	4:4-5	339
14:9	206	4:4-6	46, 53, 325, 332
14:11	207	4:6	47, 244, 339
14:12	208	4:19	294
14:13	205, 206	5:16-26	19
14:14	207	*Ephesians*	
14:14-18	207	1:3	47
14:16	206	1:3-6	224
14:18	210	1:3-11	47
14:19	206, 208	1:3-14	47
14:21	206, 207	1:4	49
14:21-23	208	1:5-13	47
14:22-25	208	1:7-10	225
14:23	206	1:10	86
14:26	208	1:13	54, 232
14:28	205, 206, 208	1:13-14	47, 225
14:31	208	2:18	331
14:39	206	2:19	313
15:20-28	331	2:21-22	55
15:24-28	49, 192	3:15	277, 290
15:28	75, 76, 150	4:3	28, 115, 232, 292
15:45	21	4:3-4	322
16:22	52	4:4-6	61
2 Corinthians		4:5-6	131
1:3	295, 348	4:12	208
1:20	51	4:16	230
1:21-22	232	4:30	54, 232
3:16-17	105	5:1-2	343
3:17	49, 237	6:17	30

Philippians

1:7	296
1:27	28
2:9	143

Colossians

1:17	14
1:18	343
3:17	51, 52

2 Thessalonians

2:8	29
2:13	54

1 Timothy

1:12	52
1:17	50
2:1-2	93
3:16	35
4:14	235
6:13-16	50
6:20-21	72

2 Timothy

1:6	235
1:14	xx, 72
4:16	36
4:18	51

Philemon

3	44
10	294

Titus

1:15	276
3:5	109
3:6	45

Hebrews

1:2	173
1:3	14
2:12	10
7:25	340
13:21	51

2 Peter

1:21	109
3:18	51

1 John

1:1-2	16, 156, 312
1:1-6	228
1:2	156
1:3	284
1:3-7	228
1:4-10	74
1:5	312
1:7	284
2:1	32-34, 37, 340
2:9	312
2:18-23	14
2:20-27	232
3:1-2	11
3:2	305, 353
3:10	11
3:19	34
3:24	284
4:1-3	22
4:1-6	14
4:2	45
4:3-4	180
4:7-8	115
4:7-19	115
4:8	312
4:8-16	115, 152
4:10	45
4:13	115, 116, 284
4:16	116
5:2	11
5:5	87
5:6-9	45
5:8	109
5:19	180
5:20	43, 115

2 John

10-11	87

Apocalypse

1:5-6	51
1:16	30, 162, 230
2:1-7	230
2:7	245
2:11	xix
2:17	xix

2:29	xix	12:12	38
3:6	xix	12:12-13	34
3:13	xix	17:19	36
3:22	xix	19:15	162
5:13	51	21:2	120
12:9	38	22:1	162
12:10	33	22:20	52

III

Councils

1. LOCAL

Alexandria (362)	99, 100, 106, 128.
Frioul (796)	165.
Rome (382)	106, 107, 108, 187.
Toledo XI (675)	138, 148, 165, 223.

2. ECUMENICAL OR GENERAL (comprises the Pontifical councils of the Latin Middle Ages)

Chalcedon (451)	97, 153.
Constantinople I (381)	100, 103, 105ff., 131, 223, 305.
Constantinople II (553)	86, 107, 108, 128, 130ff., 223.
Florence (1439)	108, 139, 148, 159, 161ff., 167ff., 176-179, 182, 183 n. 84, 186, 187, 317, 242.
Lateran IV (1215)	138ff., 166, 186, 198, 200 n. 7, 227 n. 8, 241, 293, 317, 323.
Lyons II (1274)	146, 166, 167, 176, 198, 223, 287, 317.
Nicaea I (325)	89-97, 99, 105-107, 124, 125, 128, 153.
Nicaea II (787)	168 n. 44, 175, 175 n. 66.
Trent (1545-1563)	96 n. 132, 313, 314 n. 107.
Vatican I (1870)	96, 149, 241, 283, 286.
Vatican II (1962-1965)	
—in general:	76, 98 n. 137, 108, 161, 223, 225, 228, 236, 242, 243, 293, 353 n. 65.
—in particular:	
Decree *Ad Gentes* (*AG*) on the Missions:	
§2	5, 226, 229, 326, 337.
§2-4	224, 225.
§3-4	224, 225, 244 n. 36.
§4	229, 231, 234, 334, 335.
§5	334.
§11	244 n. 38, 335 n. 25.
§15	335 n. 25.
§22	335.

Constitution *Dei Verbum* (*DV*) on Revelation:

§ 2   178 n. 72, 244 n. 37.
§ 20   244 n.37.

Pastoral Constitution *Gaudium et Spes* (*GS*) on the Church in the Modern World:

§ 21   337.
§ 24   227.
§ 38   334.
§ 40   227.
§ 47   288 n. 35.
§ 92   335.

Dogmatic Constitution *Lumen Gentium* (*LG*) on the Church:

§ 2-4   224, 225.
§ 4   230, 233, 334.
§ 8   230.
§ 12   233.
§ 13   244 n. 38.
§ 17   236.
§ 21   235.
§ 23   296.
§ 47   228, 339.
§ 49   228.
§ 65   333.

Constitution *Sacrosanctum Concilium* on the Liturgy:

§ 7   77.

Decree *Unitatis Redintegratio* (*UR*) on Ecumenism:

§ 1   236.
§ 2   227, 236, 294 n. 49.
§ 7   228.
§ 12   236.
§ 15   228, 296, 337.
§ 17   163 n. 35.
§ 21   xix n. 8.

IV

Texts of St. Thomas Aquinas

Index Thomisticus, COMMENTARIES ON HOLY SCRIPTURE.

Catena aurea in Evangelia:
in Mt. 28, 19	145 n. 76
In Evangelium secundum Joannem Expositio:	
ch. 10, lectio 5	180 n. 74
14, 28	82 n. 81
17, 11-12	143 n. 72
17 lectio III	292 n. 46
17 lectio V	183 n. 87; 283 n. 25
In II ad Corinthios 13, 13	27

COMMENTARIES ON ARISTOTLE.

On the Nicomachean Ethics, VIII.12	279
On the Politics, III.1.3	280 n. 15

SCRIPTUM SUPER SENTENTIIS PETRI LOMBARDI, IN LIBRUM I.

D. 2 Exp.	256 n. 25
D. 10, 1, 3 c	319 n. 120
D. 14, 2, 2	190 n. 113; 332 n. 19
D. 15, 4, 1	351 n. 53
D. 23, 1, 3	220 n. 68
D. 24, 1	125 n. 17
D. 31, 1, 2	195 n. 127
D. 31, 1, 2, 1	196 n. 131
D. 31, 2, 1, 1	195 n. 129
D. 32, 1, 2, 4	282 n. 22

QUESTIONES DISPUTATAE

De Veritate

4, 8	252 n. 8
7, 3	195 n. 126
10, 1	303 n. 79

De Potentia

2, 5.4	214 n. 48
2, 6	188 n. 107
8, 1	308 n. 96
9, 1-4	140 n. 55; 140 n. 57; 220 n. 68
9, 5.13	215 n. 52
9, 7	125 n. 17
9, 9.14, 15	323 n. 126; 323 n. 128
10, 4.10	322 n. 125

THEOLOGICAL WORKS

Compendium Theologiae, I, 46	214 n. 47
I, 50	306 n. 86
Contra errores Graecorum, ch. 32	177 n. 69
In Decretalem I Expositio	190 n. 112
Summa contra Gentiles	
Liber II, 35	84 n. 90
Liber III, 118	350 n. 51
Liber IV:	
9	180 n. 74; 183 n. 86
13, 5	84 nn. 89, 93; 252
14	215 n. 52
23	328 n. 6
23.1	27 n. 72
24.11	323 n. 126
26	306 nn. 86, 87; 309 n. 98; 310 n. 103; 323 n. 126

SUMMA THEOLOGICA

Prima Pars

9.1.1	272
10.5 c ad 1 m	71 n. 47
11	125-126 n. 17
13.3	28 n. 74; 70 n. 45
13.11	132 n. 38; 125 n. 17; 269 n. 72
18.4	252 n. 6
27.1 c	147 n. 1
27.2	158 n. 22; 280 n. 16
27.5	323 n. 127

27.5.2	191 n. 116
27.5.3	323 n. 127
29.1	268 n. 70
29.2, c, 2	131 n. 35; 140 n. 54
29.3	219 n. 67
29.4, c, ad 4 m	134 n. 40; 135
30.3	125 n. 16
30.4, c	214 n. 50
30.4, 2	214 n. 49
32.1	186 n. 99
32.2.3	191 n. 118
33.1, 1	149 n. 4
34.3.1	84 n. 93; 159 n. 25; 187 n. 104; 191 n. 115
36.1.1	28 n. 73
36.2	163 n. 34; 172 n. 53
36.3.1	278
36.4.1, 7	173 n. 57; 218 n. 60; 282 n. 23; 318 n. 116
37.2, 3	191 n. 118
38	233 n. 18
38.2.3	118 n. 210
39	137 n. 50
39.3	263 n. 53
39.7	195 nn. 124, 125
39.8	321 n. 123
41.2.1, 5	149 n. 5
42.5	183 n. 88; 186 n. 96
43.1	327 n. 3
43.2	329 n. 8; 336 n. 27
43.2.3	85 n. 94; 169 n. 47; 327 n. 4; 351 n. 54
43.5.2	330 n. 13; 351 nn. 54, 55
43.5.3	331 n. 15
43.6.2	332 n. 18; 333 n. 21
43.7	190 n. 111; 329 n. 9; 330 n. 12
43.8	244 n. 36
45.6.1, 2	84 n. 93; 173 n. 57; 187 n. 103; 188 nn. 108, 109
45.7	190 n. 112
60.5.1	263 n. 52
87.1	303 n. 79
93.6.c, 2	307 n. 89
93.6.3	307 n. 92
93.7, 8	307 n. 93

Prima Secundae

4.8 c	263 n. 52

Secunda Secundae

25; 26.1-4	316 n. 111
66.2	295 n. 53
176.1	207 n. 30
176.2	210 n. 34

Tertia Pars

3.3.1	215 n. 52
15.4	347 n. 43
18.6	347 n. 43
20.1	82 n. 81
25.3.1	314 n. 107

Supplementum

41.4	289 n. 37

V
Texts of St. Augustine

Contra Academicos II, 2, 5		113 n. 188
De Civitate Dei		
X, 23.8-21		114 n. 189
XI, 1		29 n. 76
De Doctrina Christiana I.5		256 n. 26
De Fide et Symbolo IX, 18, 19		xix ; 112 n. 180; 116 n. 199; 120 n. 221
De Genesi ad Litteram VIII, 20		272 n. 78
De Haeresibus 52		101 n. 143; 112 n. 180
De Trinitate		
Liber I:	3.5	xxii
	4.7	118 n. 207
Liber IV:	6.7	137 n. 49
	20.28	329 n. 11; 330 n. 13
	20.29	xxi; 48 n. 132; 171 n. 50; 351 n. 54
Liber V:	4.5	136 n. 48
	8.9	137 n. 50
	11.12	25 n. 68; 118 n. 211; 322 n. 124
	14.15	118 n. 210; 186 n. 98; 284 n. 26; 322 n. 124
	16.17	118 n. 209
Liber VI:	3.4	119 n. 216
	5.7	47 n. 130; 115 n. 195; 322 n. 124
	7.9	123 n. 5
	10.11	115 n. 194
Liber VII:	4.7	127 n. 22
	6.11	127 n. 23
Liber VIII:	Proemium	137 n. 50; 161 n. 29
	8.12	292 n. 44; 295 n. 54
	10.14	300 n. 61
Liber IX:	in general	302
	12.18	299 n. 58
Liber X:	5.7	301 n. 71

Indexes

Liber XII:	5.5	287 n. 33
	5.7	276 n. 5
	6.6	290 n. 40
	7.9	276 n. 6; 277 n. 8
Liber XIV:	2.4	299 n. 60
	5.7-8	299; 301 n. 71; 302
	12.15	300 n. 62
	14.18	301 n. 73
	17.23	305 n. 84
Liber XV:	3	137 n. 50
	6.5-7	292 n. 46
	17.29	164 n. 37; 178 n. 72
	17.31	115 n. 196
	18.32	115 n. 196
	19.37	115 n. 196 and 197
	20.39	300 n. 65
	22.43	222 n. 74; 331 n. 17
	24.44	300 n. 63
	27.50	309 n. 99
	28.51	301 n. 69

In Johannis Evangelium Tractatus

6, 9	142 n. 62
14, 9	117 n. 205
20, 9	187 n. 101
26, 2.4.7	309 n. 99
39	145 n. 77
99, 7	119 n. 212
100, 9	278 n. 10
105, 3	117 n. 203
110-111	292 n. 46

Octoginta Trium Quaestionum Liber Q. 51   307 n. 92

Sermons

71, 12, 18	117 n. 201
71, 20, 33	117 n. 206
126	164 n. 36

References to St. Augustine in general: 25, 68, 70, 80, 82, 86, 108, 110ff., 127, 136, 144, 160, 164, 167-168, 176, 190, 192, 203, 210, 242, 245, 256, 261, 263, 272, 273, 274, 275, 277-278, 280, 287, 290-291, 295, 297ff., 307, 309, 313, 315ff., 318, 319-320, 345

VI

Analytical Index

Analogy, 70-72, 80, 88-89, 91, 125ff., 158ff., 219, 261, 269, 274-280, 283, 286-293, 295ff., 311-315, 323-324.
Angels, 37, 38, 63-64, 71 n. 47, 102, 107 n. 167, 314.
Arianism, 62 n. 17, 87ff., 125, 128, 135ff., 151, 156ff., 161, 181 n. 74, 183, 193-194, 275, 339, 345.
Baptism,
—formula of Mt. 28:19, 39-40, 68-70, 142ff., 197-198, 221-222.
—and Arianism, 62 n. 17.
—formula of Gnostic baptism: 62.
Beatitude, 240ff., 243, 299 n. 60, 308, 314, 330, 350ff.
Charisms, 204-212, 232-235.
Charity, fraternal, 295, 309-310, 330-331.
—revelation of the Holy Spirit, 118.
—of the Trinity, 291-292.
Church, xvii, xix, xx, 108-109, 116ff., 120, 176-178, 208ff., 217, 219, 223, 235, 284-285, 290, 292ff., 297, 333-337, 340-342, 351-353.
Consubstantial, Consubstantiality, 81-83, 90ff., 93-100, 109, 117ff., 129, 148-150, 166, 238, 242, 275, 298, 303, 306, 345.
Creation, Creature, 13-14, 186ff., 250-251, 255, 326-329.
Dutch catechism, 224, 235-241, 329.
Eternity (see Immutability).
Father,
—in general, 7ff., 50, 54-55.
—for the Gnostics, 65ff.
—relation, 135-137, 281ff., 331-332, 344.
—ultimate term of cult, 75-78, 150-153, 332, 343.
—recapitulator, 86, 148ff.
Heresy (according to Bonhoeffer), 98.
Holy Spirit,
—resume of the Holy Spirit in the NT, 109ff.
—wind, 20.
—collective spirit of the Holy Spirit, 26.
—names, 17ff., 24ff., 32ff.
—love, 26ff., 315-322, 349.
—kiss of peace, 26-27, 30-31.
—request for the gift of the Holy Spirit, 55ff., 340ff.
—makes us pray, 49, 202.
—cult of the Holy Spirit, 53-56, 100ff., 203.
—for the Gnostics, 66-68.
—for Luther, 201ff., 316, 319-320.
—eternal procession *a Patre Filioque*, 79-80, 112-121, 160ff., 278, 309, 315-322, 345, 350.
Image, xix, 274ff., 298, 314-315.
Immutability and Eternity, 91, 136ff., 157ff., 258, 264, 270ff., 328.
Inexistence, 180-181 n. 74, 178-186.
Language of the Faith, 31, 80, 82-85, 90ff., 127, 128-130, 138, 160-163, 176-178, 212-221, 261, 269.
Logos, 12-16.
Man, 64, 71 n. 47, 150, 302, 306 n. 86, 307, 312, 336.

Missions, 17ff., 81-85, 154, 169ff., 259, 325-337, 340, 351.
—of the Holy Spirit, 201, 207ff., 243-245; see also Holy Spirit.
Modalism, 73-74, 99, 112 n. 180, 120, 128-129, 133, 145, 151, 184, 194, 219, 265.
Names, 7, 9, 12, 17ff., 32ff., 142ff.
Number (one and many), 122ff., 145, 251, 262ff.
Old Testament, 3ff., 104 n. 153.
Panentheism, 252.
Pantheism, 14, 249-252, 256, 257ff., 264-265.
Paraclete, 17, 32-38.
Person, xvii, xx, xxi, xxii, 127-131, 134 n. 40, 140ff., 145-146, 199-201, 212ff., 263, 265-268, 281, 306, 320-323, 336.
Polytheism, 6, 61, 135, 264, 278, 287; see also Tritheism.
Prayer,
—of the Spirit, 37, 54 n. 144, 207-208 n. 31.
—to the Son, to the Spirit, 50ff., 152, 203.
Procession, 147ff., 161ff., 218, 243-244, 291, 296, 331-332.
Relations, xxi, 133ff., 152 n. 11, 218, 241, 277, 291, 319, 326, 344, 350.
Salvation, Trinitarian, 45ff., 62, 107 n. 168, 155, 240-241, 337, 351-352.
Son,
—adored in cult, 51-53, 74-78, 343-346.
—adorer, 76-77, 349.
—eternal, 153-160.
—action of insufflation of the Risen One, 18ff., 29, 118-119, 168.

—engendered Creator, 15, 84, 187-188.
—according to Arius, 88.
—manifests the name of the Father, 144.
—names the Holy Spirit, 19ff.
—name of relation, 135ff.
—distinct from the world, 251.
Substance, Subsistence, 128ff., 131 n. 34, 214ff., 221, 259.
Symbol (of Faith), 57ff., 99-100, 105, 195, 222, 239-243 (credo of Paul VI).
Trinity,
—origin, signification of the word, 126ff.
—foundation of reality, xvii.
—supreme act, 271-272.
—economic and immanent, 46-50, 59-62, 72, 74, 78, 80, 84-85, 118-119, 238, 240-241, 322, 326.
—synthetic presentations,
of Augustine, 164, 256.
of Irenaeus, 68ff.
of Basil, 103, 125, 130, 164.
of St. Thomas Aquinas, 145, 256, 323.
of Ruysbroeck, 252ff.
of Günther, 265ff.
of Block (Marxist), 263 n. 54.
Tritheism, 85-86, 87-89, 123, 139, 151, 183, 184, 193, 213ff., 216ff., 265ff., 276 n. 5, 288, 304, 315.
Unity, Divine, 122-126, 227, 240, 250, 263, 266, 270, 283, 292-293.
We (personal pronoun), 99, 186, 280ff., 292.
Word, 12ff., 158-160, 185, 260 n. 43, 287, 290, 308, 312, 323, 346, 353.

Bibliography

Alès, A. d', S.J. *Novatien*. Paris, 1924, ch. III, pp. 84-137.
— *Le dogme de Nicée*. Paris, 1926.
— *La théologie de Tertullien*. Paris, 1905.
Alfaro. *EF*, v. I, art. "Dieu," IV: Dieu-Père. Paris, 1967.
— *Gregorianum* 41 (1950), 1-25.
Amann, E. *L'Epoque carolingienne*. Paris, 1947, 173-184 and 455-500. (v. VI of *l'Histoire de l'Eglise* by Fliche-Martin); *DTC* XII, 2 (1935), 1542-1544 and 1602, art.: "Photius."
Ambrose, St. *De Spiritu Sancto, ML* 15.
Arendzen, J.-P. *The Holy Trinity*. London, 1939.
Arnou, S.J. "Arius et la doctrine des relations trinitaires," *Gregorianum* 14 (1933), 264-272.
— "Unité numerique et unité de nature chez les Pères après le Concile de Nicée," *Gregorianum* 15 (1934), 242-254.
"Associaçao de seminários teológicos évangelicos" of Sao Paulo, Brazil (a collective volume published in 1966) under the title: *O Espirito Santo, O Movimento Pentecostal*.
Athanasius, St. *Letters to Serapion, SC* 15 (Paris) 1947.
Audet, J.-P. *La Didaché*. Paris (1958), 358-367.
Augustine, St. *De Trinitate*, V (Bibl. Augustinienne, v. 15) and VII.
— *De Trinitate*, XII, V-VI.
Bailleux. "Personnalisme de saint Thomas en théologie trinitaire," *RT* 61 (1961), 25-42.
— "La création, oeuvre de la Trinité," *Rev. Thom.* 62 (1962), 27-50.
Balthasar, Hans Urs von. *Elisabeth de la Trinité et sa mission spirituelle*. Paris, 1960.
Bardy, G. *Recherches sur saint Lucien d'Antioche et son école*. Paris, 1936, 217-278.
— *DTC*, XV, 2 (1950), art. "Trinité."
— *Didyme l'Aveugle*. Paris (1910), ch. III.
Barré, H. *Trinité que j'adore*. Paris, 1965.
Barth, K. *Dogmatik* I, I, pp. 378ff.
Basil, St. *Treatise on the Holy Spirit, SC* 17, Paris, 1947.
Benoît, P., O.P. *Exégèse et Théologie*. Paris, 1961, v. II, pp. 193-211.
Bernadot, O.P. *De l'Eucharistie à la Trinité*. Paris, 1939.

Boismard. "Dans le sein du Père," *RB* 1952, 23-39.
— *Le Prologue de saint Jean.* Paris, 1953.
— "La révélation de l'Esprit-Saint," *RB* 55 (1955), 5-21.
Bonaventure, St. "Obras," *BAC*, v. V, pp. 22-29; 49-50, Madrid, 1948.
— *De mysterio Trinitatis*, VI, 2.
Boularand, E., S.J. *L'hérésie d'Arius et la foi de Nicée.* Paris, 1972, 2 vol.
Bourassa, F., S.J. *Sc. Eccl.* 7 (1955), 57-85; 151-172.
— "Le Saint-Esprit unité d'amour du Père et du Fils," *Sc. Eccl.* 14 (1962), 375-415; "Communion du Père et du Fils," *Gregorianum* 48 (1967), 657-705.
Boyer, C., S.J. "L'image de la Trinité, synthèse de la pensée augustinienne," *Gregorianum* 27 (1946), 173-199; 333-352.
Braun, F. *Jean le Théologien.* Paris, 1964, v. II.
Brown, R. E., S.S. *The Gospel According to John*, I-III. N.Y., 1966.
— "The Paraclete in the Fourth Gospel," *NTS* 15 (1967), 113-132.
Caffarel, H. *Anneau d'or* 138 (1967), 433-444, "Notre Dieu, la Sainte Trinité."
Caillat, M. "La dévotion à Dieu le Père: une discussion au XVIIe siècle," *RAM* 20 (1939), 35-49; 136-157.
Camelot, P.-T., O.P. *Rech. Sc. Relig.* 39 (1951), 323-338.
Camelot and Cornelis, O.P. *DSAM*, v. VI, Paris, 1965, art. "Gnose et gnosticisme."
Candal, M., S.J. *Encicl. Cattolica*, V, (1950), 1298-1299, Rome, art. "Filioque."
Carbone, V. *Il Vero Dio.* Florence, 1962, pp. 371-610.
Catherinet, F.-M. *Note sur un verset de L'Evangile de saint Jean, XX, 17, dans le mémorial Chaine.* Lyons, 1950, pp. 56-58.
Ceuppens, B. P., O.P. *Theologia Biblica*, v. II, *De S. Trinitate*, Rome, 1938, pp. 118-119 (Gal. 4:4-6), 166-169 (Apoc. 22:1), 234-243 (Jn. 14-16); pp. 55-66.
Chapelle, A., S.J. *Hegel et la religion*, II, 53-109, Paris, 1967.
Chevalier, I., O.P. "La théorie augustinienne des relations trinitaires," *Divus Thomas* 18 (1940), 317-384.
Clément, O. (Orthodox). *Transfigurer le Temps.* Neufchâtel, 1959, 131-133.
Congar, Y.-M.-J., O.P. *Le Mystère du Temple.* Paris, 1958, pp. 330-333.
Daniélou, J. *La Trinité et le mystère de l'existence.* Bruges, 1968.
— *Mythes païens, mystère chrétien.* Paris, 1966, ch. VII, pp. 87-105.
— *Théologie du judéo-christianisme.* Paris, 1958, ch. 5, pp. 169-196.
— *Origène.* Paris, 1948, pp. 243-258.
Deneffe, A., S.J. "Perichoresis, Circumincessio, Circuminsessio," *Z.K.T.* 47 (1923), 497-532.
Didyme l'Aveugle, *Traité du Saint-Esprit* (original Greek lost, Latin translation of St. Jerome), *MG* 39, 1031-1086; *ML* 33, 103-154.
Dion, H. M., O.P. "L'origine du titre de Paraclet," *Sc. Eccl.* 17 (1965), 143ff.
Dockx, O.P. *Fils de Dieu par grâce.* Paris, 1948, pp. 106-120.
Doms. *Du sens et de la fin du mariage.* Paris, 1937.
Dondaine, F., O.P. *La Trinité.* Paris, 1962, v. II, 405-425.
DTC, art. "Trinité," Scripture section.
Duchesne. *Histoire ancienne de l'Eglise*, v. I, Paris 1907.

Dupont, O.S.B. *Gnosis.* Paris, 1967, pp. 204-210: Etudes sur les Actes des Apôtres, Paris, 1967, 85-87, 461-501.
Dusen, H.P., Van, (Prot.). *Spirit, Son and Father.* London, 1950, ch. 2.
Duval, A. *Catholicisme,* III (1952), 1258-1263.
Folch Gomes, D. Cirilo, O.S.B. "Personalidade Psichologica e Misterio trinitario," *Liturgia e Vida,* 20 (1973) 2-28.
Fonck, L., S.J. *Questiones Paulinae.* Rome, 1910.
Fortman, Edmund J., S.J. *The Triune God.* London-Philadelphia, 1972.
Franks, R. S. (Anglican). *The Doctrine of the Trinity.* London, 1953, part I.
Fransen, P., S.J. *Nouv. Rev. Théol.,* 74 (1952), 183-185.
Franzelin, Cardinal, S.J. *De Deo trino.* Rome, 1881, ch. XIV, pp. 225-238.
Gachter, P., S.J. *Das Matthaüs Evangelium.* München, 1963, pp. 968-970.
Galot, J., S.J. *Le Coeur du Père.* Bruges, 1957.
Gardeil, *Structure de l'âme et expérience mystique.* Paris, 1927, v. I, 28-267.
Ghellinck, J. de, S.J. *Patristique et M. A.,* v. I, Brussels, 1948.
Gill, J., S.J. *Le Concile de Florence.* Tournai, 1964.
Gilson, E. *La Philosophie au Moyen Age.* Paris, 1947, 694-700.
— *Introduction à l'étude de saint Augustine.* Paris, 1943, 275-298.
Giuliani, S., O.P. "La famiglia e l'immagine della Trinità," *Angelicum* 38 (1961), 257-310.
Gonzalez, Olegario. *Misterio trinitario y existencia humana.* Madrid, 1965, 564-603.
Gordillo, M., S.J. *Compendium Theol. Orient.* Rome, 1950, ch. 1.
Guerry, E. *Vers le Père.* Bruges, 1947.
Guillet, J. Thèmes bibliques, Paris, 1951, *DSAM,* art. "Esprit-Saint."
Guillou, M.-J., Le, O.P. Art. "E. Saint" and "Filioque," *Catholicisme,* Paris, 1956, v. IV: *Russie et Chrétienté,* 1950, no. 3, 4.
Haanappel, B. G., C.SS.R. "A Glossolalia no N.T.," *Rev. Ecl. Brasileira,* 5 (1945), 54-58.
Hamman, A., O.P. *La Prière,* v. I, Tournai, 1959, 264-290, 405-407.
Henry, P., S.J. "La Mystique trinitaire du Bl. J. Ruysbroeck," *Rech. Sc. Rel.* 40 (1952), pp. 335-368; 41 (1953), pp. 51-75.
Henry, A.-M. *L'Essence de la Métaphysique.* Paris, PUF (1964), I, 385-418; II, 532-543.
Hodgson, Leonard. *The Doctrine of the Trinity.* London, 1964, pp. 219-225.
Holzmeister, *VD,* 20 (1940), 129-138.
Imschoot, P., van. *Théologie de l'A.T.* Tournai, 1954, v. I: *Dieu.*
Irenaeus, St. *Adv. Haereses, passim* and especially 1.21.3.
Isaac, J., O.P. *Initiation théologique.* Paris, 1953, v. II, pp. 143-206.
— *La Révélation progressive des Personnes divines.* Paris, 1960.
Jugie. *Théologie dogmatique orientale.* Paris, 1933, v. II, 296-536.
Kelly, J. N. D. *Early Christian Doctrines.* London, 1968, ch. V, IX, X.
Koehler, T. "La théologie mystique de la 'fruitio Dei,' " *RAM* 40 (1964), 289-310.
Leal, J., S.J. *N.T.B.A.C.,* Madrid, 1962, v. II, pp. 21, 29-31.
Lebreton, J., S.J. *Les Origines du dogme de la Trinité.* Paris, 1919, v. I, esp. pp. 323-408, 439-495; cit., v. I, note J, p. 590ff.; cit., v. I, note E, pp. 553-564; 314; 320-321.
— *Histoire du dogme de la Trinité.* Paris, 1935, v. II, pp. 141-173; Paris, 1928, v. II, pp. 81-121.

— *Rech. Sc. Rel.*, 34 (1947), 252-256.
Lemonnyer, A., O.P. *DBS*, v. I (1928), art. "Charismes."
Lonergan, B., S.J. *De Deo trino*. Rome, 1964, 2 vol., v. I, pp. 15-112.
Losski, V., *Mystichen Theologie der Morgenlaüdischen Kirche*, 1961, ch. 3, 8, 9. This author is Orthodox.
Lubac, H. De, S.J. *La Foi chrétienne*. Paris, 1969, ch. II and III.
Lumière et Vie, no. 67 (1964), 102-114: note on "filioquisme."
Lyonnet, S., S.J. "De glossolalia Pentecostes," *VD* 24 (1944), 63-75.
McDonnell, K., O.S.B. "The Ideology of Pentecostal Conversion," *Journal of Ecumenical Studies* (1968), 105-126.
— "Pentecostals and Drug Addiction," *America* 118 (1968), 402-406.
Malet, A. *Personne et Amour*. Paris, 1956 (cf. criticisms of this book made by Nicolas, *RT* 57, 1957, pp. 366-373; Dondaine, *RSPT* 43, 1939, p. 173; *Angelicum*, 1958, pp. 73-80).
Malevez, L., S.J. "N.T. et théologie fonctionnelle," *Rech Sc. Rel.* 48 (1960), 264-290.
Marchal. *Dieu Père*. Paris, 1966.
Maréchal, J. *Point de départ de la Métaphysique*, cahier IV (1947) on Fichte, 429-436.
Marius Victorinus. *Traités Théologiques sur la Trinité*, SC 68-69, Paris 1960.
Massabki, Dom C., O.S.B. *Le Christ, rencontre de deux amours*. Paris, 1962.
Michel, A. *DTC* VIII, 2 (1925), 2591-2601.
Miguens, M., O.F.M. *El Paráclito*. Jerusalem, 1963.
Moingt, J., S.J. "Théologie trinitaire de Tertullien," *Rech. Sc. Rel.* 54 (1960), 337-369.
Montes Moreira, A., O.F.M. *Potamius de Lisbonne et la controverse arienne*. Louvain, 1969.
Mühlen, H. *Der Heilige Geist als Person*. Paderborn, 1967. Cf. the judgment of A. Patfoort, O.P., *Angelicum* 45 (1968), 320-321.
Nemeshegyi, P., S.J. *La Paternité de Dieu chez Origène*. Tournai, 1960, pp. 85-100.
Nicolas, J.-M., O.P. "Le Don de l'Esprit," *RT* 66 (1966), 529-574.
Oechslin, H. L. *DSAM* IV, 2 (1960) 93-116; III (1957), 1432-1439; Eckhart: *Lumière et Vie* 30 (1956), 99-120.
Orbe, A., S.J. *Estudios Valentinianos*, v. IV, *La Teologia del E. S.*, Rome, 1966; cf. Daniélou, *Rech. Sc. Rel.* 56 (1960), 121-125.
— "La procession del Espiritu Santo y el Origen de Eva," *Gregorianum* 45 (1964), 103-118.
— *Adv. Hermog.* 17.18.45; *Greg.* 39 (1958), 706-748.
Ortiz de Urbina. *El simbolo niceno*. Madrid, 1947.
Palmieri, A. "Filioque," *DTC* V (1913).
Panikkar, R. *Journal of Ec. Studies* 5 (1968), 522-526: suggestive but utilizes an inadequate formulation.
Philipon, M.-M., O.P. *En présence de Dieu: Elisabeth de la Trinité*. Bruges, 1966.
Piault, B. "Tertullien a-t-il été subordinatien?" *RSPT* 47 (1963), 181-204.
Pinto de Oliveira, C. J., O.P. "Le verbe didonai comme expression des rapports du Père et du Fils dans le IV Evangile," *RSPT* 45 (1965), 81-104.
Potterie, I. de la, S.J. "Emploi dynamique de 'eis' dans Jo. et ses incidences théologiques," *Biblica* 43 (1962).
— *La vie selon l'Esprit*. Paris, 1965, pp. 65-100.
Prat, F., S.J. *Théologie de saint Paul*. Paris, 1920, v. I, pp. 152-155; 502-503.

Prenter, R. *Spiritus Creator*. Philadelphia, 1953. (English translation of original Danish).
Prestige, G. L. *God in Patristic Thought*. London, 1964, ch. XIV: coinherence.
Rabeneck, J. "Primera Persona Divina," *Est. Eccl.* 102 (1952), 353-363.
Racette, J., S.J. "Le livre neuvième du *De Trinitate* de saint-Augustin," *Sc. Eccl.* 8 (1956), 39-58.
Rahner, K., S.J. *Mysterium Salutis*, v. II, 317-397.
Renié, J. *La Sainte Bible*. Pirot-Clamer, XI, 520.
Reuter, A., O.M.I. *Augustini doctrina de bonis matrimonii*. Rome, 1942.
Rey, B., O.P. *A la découverte de Dieu*. Paris, 1972.
Rondet, H., S.J. *Hégélianisme et Christianisme*. Paris, 1965.
— "Divinisation du Chrétien," *Nouv. Rev. Theol.* 71 (1948), 564-567.
Roy, O. du, O.S.B. *Intelligence de la Foi en le Trinité selon Augustin*. Paris, 1966.
Sagnard, F.-M.-M., O.P. *Encyclopédie Catholicisme*, Paris, 1962, v. V, art. "Gnosticisme."
— *Introduction à SC* 34: Irenaeus, Adv. Haereses III.
— *La gnose valentinienne et le témoignage de saint Irénée*. Paris, 1948.
Scheeben, M.-J. *The Mysteries of Christianity*. St. Louis, 1946, esp. ch. 6 and 7.
Scheffczyk, L. *MS*, v. II, pp. 146-219.
Schlier, H. *EF*, v. II, Paris, 1965, art. "Gnose."
— *Essais sur le N.T.* Paris, 1968, pp. 115-132.
Schillebeeckx, E., O.P. *Révélation et Théologie*. Brussels, 1965, pp. 173-185.
Schmaus, M. *Téologia Dogmatica*, v. I: *La Trinidad*, Madrid, 1960.
Schuler, B. *Die Lehre von der Dreipersönlichkeit Gottes*. Paderborn, 1961.
Schulte, R. and Schierse, P.J. *Mysterium Salutis* II (1957), 47-131.
Sciacca, M. *Trinité et unité de l'Esprit*, Augustinus Magister, Paris, 1954, v. I, pp. 521-533.
Smulders, P. *DSAM* IV (1960): art. "E. Saint chez les PP. Latins"; *Doctrine trinitaire de saint Hilaire*, Rome, 1944.
Solano, J., S.J. *Est. Eccl.* 21 (1947), 5-34.
Starcky, J., *DBS* v. V, Paris, 1957, art. "Logos."
Thomas Aquinas, *Summa Theologica; De Pot.*, 9.
Tixeront, J. *Histoire des dogmes*, v. I, Paris, 1915, pp. 353-361; v. ii, 1912.
Tresmontant, C. *Métaphysique du christianisme*. Paris, 1941, ch. III, pp. 150-173.
— *Introduction à la Théologie chrétienne*. Paris, 1974.
Vatican II. "El misterio trinitario a la luz del Vaticano II," Salamanca.
Vergara, J., S.J. "Téologia del E. Santo en Mario Victorino," *Eccl.* 6 (1956), 74-94.
Vignaux, P. *Luther, commentateur des sentences*. Paris, 1935.
Wals, A., O.P. *Enciclopedia Cattolica* V (1950), 28-52.
Wenger, A., A.A. *Nouv. Rev. Théol.* 84 (1962), 63-71.

Bertrand de Margerie, S.J., is one of the most distinguished theologians of the Catholic Church today. He is well known for his scholarly books, such as *Christ for the World* and *Sacraments and Social Progress*. In addition, many of his articles have appeared in such periodicals as *Science et Esprit* (Montreal), *Esprit et Vie* (Langres), and *Word and Spirit* (Still River, MA).

A professor of theology, Father de Margerie has written with exceptional clarity this latest book which is the outcome of a course he gave in Brazil, Portugal, and the United States.

Other St. Bede's Titles

Word & Spirit, A Monastic Review—This yearly publication is an effort to promote a critical interest in the myriad aspects of our Christian heritage—its riches, difficulties, struggles and achievements—bringing together the work of scholars from around the world, each issue having a basic theme. Authors include such names as Hans Urs von Balthasar, Hubert van Zeller, Jean Gribomont, Jean Leclercq, Bertrand de Margerie, Jordan Aumann, Basil Pennington, Adalbert de Vogüé, Otilio Rodriguez, and many others.

> **Volume I**—Studies St. Basil the Great and the controversy surrounding the Holy Spirit, leading up to the First Council of Constantinople. Includes articles discussing the scholarship of Basil and others regarding the Holy Spirit.
>
> **Volume II**—On St. Benedict, his Rule, his way of life and his relevance today.
>
> **Volume III**—On the Holy Spirit and on Prayer. This issue studies prayer and the personal role of the Spirit in our lives.
>
> **Volume IV**—Dedicated to St. Teresa of Avila. Discusses various aspects of Teresa's life, Christology and prayer.

Standing orders for this annual review are available.

St. Basil the Great, *Archbishop Joseph Tawil, D.D.*

Basil was, from more than one point of view, a precursor whose prophetic views have lost nothing of their contemporary value. What made Basil so great was that he was able to join theory to practice, action to teaching and from particular situations to rise to the general laws which govern individuals, families and societies. A scholarly, yet very readable study of this extraordinary Father of the Church.

The Church, the Liturgy and the Soul of Man,
The *Mystagogia* of St. Maximus the Confessor.
First English translation, with commentary and notes by
Dom Julian Stead, O.S.B.

It is hoped that the rendering of this little book into English will bring it the recognition it deserves as a Christian classic among such other 'greats' as *The Cloud of Unknowing, The Life of St. Anthony,* and the *Confessions* of St. Augustine.

Centered on Christ,
An Introduction to Monastic Profession, *Augustine Roberts, O.C.S.O.*

This book evolved from Thomas Merton's mimeographed notes on the vows. Father Roberts revised them in the light of Vatican II and offers the later papal directives on the religious life. Besides chapters on each of the monastic vows, Roberts also discusses the meaning of monastic profession, spirituality of the religious, and the challenge of the vows. A definitive work on the subject.

Order From:

St. Bede's Publications
Box 132
Still River, Massachusetts 01467